NOTABLE POETS

NOTABLE POETS

Volume 3

Rainer Maria Rilke — Yevgeny Yevtushenko
953 – 1408
Indexes

from

THE EDITORS OF SALEM PRESS

SALEM PRESS, INC.
Pasadena, California   Englewood Cliffs, New Jersey

Essays originally appeared in *Critical Survey of Poetry: English Language Series, Revised Edition*, 1992, and *Critical Survey of Poetry: Foreign Language Series*, 1984, both edited by Frank N. Magill. Material from *Cyclopedia of World Authors, Third Revised Edition*, 1997, edited by Frank N. Magill, and new material have been added.

∞ The paper used in these volumes conforms to the American National Standard for Permanence of Paper for Printed Library Materials, Z39.48-1984.

Library of Congress Cataloging-in-Publication Data
Notable poets
        p.   cm. — (Magill's choice)
"From the editors of Salem Press."
Includes bibliographical references and index.
ISBN 0-89356-967-4 (set : alk. paper). — ISBN 0-89356-968-2 (v. 1 : alk. paper). — ISBN 0-89356-969-0 (v. 2 : alk. paper). — ISBN 0-89356-974-7 (v. 3 : alk. paper)
    1. Poetry—History and criticism—Dictionaries. 2. Poetry—Bio-bibliography—Dictionaries. 3. Poets—Biography—Dictionaries. I. Series.
PN1021.N68   1998
809.1'003—dc21
    [B]   98-26164
                                                  CIP

Third Printing

Contents – Volume 3

Rilke, Rainer Maria 953
Rimbaud, Arthur 964
Robinson, Edwin Arlington 976
Roethke, Theodore 988
Rukeyser, Muriel 1000

Sachs, Nelly 1009
Sandburg, Carl 1017
Sappho 1029
Schiller, Friedrich 1041
Scott, Sir Walter 1053
Sexton, Anne 1063
Shakespeare, William 1072
Shelley, Percy Bysshe 1085
Sidney, Sir Philip 1105
Snyder, Gary 1119
Spender, Stephen 1134
Spenser, Edmund 1146
Stevens, Wallace 1162

Tennyson, Alfred, Lord 1174
Thomas, Dylan 1188
Tu Fu 1200

Valéry, Paul 1207
Vallejo, César 1220

Vergil 1233
Verlaine, Paul 1247

Warren, Robert Penn 1257
Whitman, Walt 1268
Wilbur, Richard 1284
Williams, William Carlos 1296
Wordsworth, William 1310
Wyatt, Sir Thomas 1330

Yeats, William Butler 1342
Yevtushenko, Yevgeny 1374

Glossary 1384
Time Line 1407
Geographical Index 1411
Subject Index 1413

Complete List of Contents

Contents — Volume 1

Akhmatova, Anna, 1
Apollinaire, Guillaume, 9
Arnold, Matthew, 20
Auden, W. H., 31
Baudelaire, Charles, 44
Berryman, John, 55
Bishop, Elizabeth, 66
Blake, William, 77
Bly, Robert, 96
Breton, André, 106
Brooks, Gwendolyn, 114
Browning, Elizabeth
   Barrett, 125
Browning, Robert, 137
Burns, Robert, 153
Byron, George Gordon,
   Lord, 165
Celan, Paul, 183
Chaucer, Geoffrey, 191
Coleridge, Samuel Taylor,
   208
Crane, Hart, 224

Cruz, Sor Juana Inés de la,
   236
Cummings, E. E., 244
Dante, 255
Dickinson, Emily, 285
Donne, John, 299
Eliot, T. S., 318
Emerson, Ralph Waldo, 334
Ferlinghetti, Lawrence, 348
Forché, Carolyn, 356
Frost, Robert, 364
García Lorca, Federico, 376
Ginsberg, Allen, 386
Goethe, Johann Wolfgang
   von, 399
Graham, Jorie, 413
Graves, Robert, 421
H. D., 434
Heaney, Seamus, 445
Heine, Heinrich, 459
Herbert, George, 470

Contents — Volume 2

Hölderlin, Friedrich, 483
Homer, 494
Hopkins, Gerard Manley,
   507
Horace, 524
Hughes, Langston, 536
Hughes, Ted, 546
Keats, John, 559

Larkin, Philip, 578
Lawrence, D. H., 591
Levertov, Denise, 604
Li Po, 617
Longfellow, Henry
   Wadsworth, 627
Lowell, Amy, 639
Lowell, Robert, 650

Mallarmé, Stéphane, 670
Mandelstam, Osip, 679
Marvell, Andrew, 692
Matsuo Bashō, 705
Merrill, James, 713
Millay, Edna St. Vincent, 724
Miłosz, Czesław, 732
Milton, John, 746
Moore, Marianne, 760
Nemerov, Howard, 771
Neruda, Pablo, 780
Nerval, Gérard de, 793

Olds, Sharon, 803
Olson, Charles, 810
Ovid, 821
Paz, Octavio, 832
Petrarch, 841
Pindar, 852
Plath, Sylvia, 861
Poe, Edgar Allan, 874
Pope, Alexander, 886
Pound, Ezra, 903
Raleigh, Sir Walter, 918
Ransom, John Crowe, 929
Rich, Adrienne, 940

Contents — Volume 3

Rilke, Rainer Maria, 953
Rimbaud, Arthur, 964
Robinson, Edwin Arlington, 976
Roethke, Theodore, 988
Rukeyser, Muriel, 1000
Sachs, Nelly, 1009
Sandburg, Carl, 1017
Sappho, 1029
Schiller, Friedrich, 1041
Scott, Sir Walter, 1053
Sexton, Anne, 1063
Shakespeare, William, 1072
Shelley, Percy Bysshe, 1085
Sidney, Sir Philip, 1105
Snyder, Gary, 1119
Spender, Stephen, 1134
Spenser, Edmund, 1146

Stevens, Wallace, 1162
Tennyson, Alfred, Lord, 1174
Thomas, Dylan, 1188
Tu Fu, 1200
Valéry, Paul, 1207
Vallejo, César, 1220
Vergil, 1233
Verlaine, Paul, 1247
Warren, Robert Penn, 1257
Whitman, Walt, 1268
Wilbur, Richard, 1284
Williams, William Carlos, 1296
Wordsworth, William, 1310
Wyatt, Sir Thomas, 1330
Yeats, William Butler, 1342
Yevtushenko, Yevgeny, 1374

NOTABLE POETS

RAINER MARIA RILKE

Born: Prague, Austria; December 4, 1875
Died: Valmont, Switzerland; December 29, 1926

Poetry · *Leben und Lieder,* 1894 · *Larenopfer,* 1896 · *Wegwarten,* 1896 · *Traumgekrönt,* 1897 · *Advent,* 1898 · *Mir zur Feier,* 1899 · *Das Buch der Bilder,* 1902, 1906 · *Das Stundenbuch,* 1905 (*Poems from the Book of Hours,* 1941) · *Neue Gedichte,* 1907-1908 (2 volumes · *New Poems,* 1964) · *Requiem,* 1909 (*Requiem and Other Poems,* 1935) · *Die frühen Gedichte,* 1909 · *Das Marienleben,* 1913 (*The Life of the Virgin Mary,* 1951) · *Duineser Elegien,* 1923 (*Duinese Elegies,* 1930 · better known as *Duino Elegies*) · *Die Sonette an Orpheus,* 1923 (*Sonnets to Orpheus,* 1936) · *Vergers, suivi des Quatrains Valaisans,* 1926 · *Les Fenêtres,* 1927 · *Les Roses,* 1927 · *Gesammelte Werke,* 1927 · *Verse und Prosa aus dem Nachlass,* 1929 · *Späte Gedichte,* 1934 (*Late Poems,* 1938) · *Poèmes français,* 1935 · *Christus–Visionen,* 1950 (wr. 1896-1898) · *Aus dem Nachlass des Grafen C. W.: Ein Gedichtkreis,* 1950 · *Poems, 1906 to 1926,* 1957 · *Poems,* 1965 · *Uncollected Poems,* 1996

Achievements · Commonly ranked alongside Hugo von Hofmannsthal and Stefan George as a giant of modern German poetry, Rilke is perhaps the most controversial of the three regarding the critical and popular reception of his works. Although his substantial collections published soon after the beginning of the twentieth century, especially *The Book of Hours* and *New Poems,* were greeted with uniformly favorable recognition, there is wide disagreement among critics concerning the literary value of both his early poems and those of his final, major creative period. A significant key to the divided viewpoints is his boldly daring, uniquely creative use of language in strange new relationships, his peculiar departures from tradi-tional grammar and syntax, and his unusual forms of subjective and objective expression. The pure individuality of his poetic utterances often makes them difficult to understand and repels the reader who approaches Rilke's art with anything less than full and active concentration. As a result, the most problematic of Rilke's mature poems, especially the *Duino Elegies,* are regarded by some scholars as the most important German lyric crea-tions of the first half of the twentieth century, whereas others dismiss them as lacking substance. Regardless of these disagreements, Rilke's influence on the development of German verse is unrivaled by that of any other German language poet of his time.

Rilke's most lasting legacy and most important contribution to German poesy is the *Dinggedicht* (thing poem), an originally conceived interpretation of inner experience generated in response to encounters with external objects and phenomena that the poet transformed into symbols for the elements of human life. With *New Poems*, in which he perfected this particular form, Rilke made a breakthrough that was immeasurably far-reaching in its implications for the expansion of German poetry's expressive domain.

Biography · The life of René Karl Wilhelm Johann Josef Maria Rilke can be described in its entirety as a productive, if not always successful, search for fulfillment in reaction to an inhibiting, psychologically destructive childhood. Critical elements of Rilke's early experience contributed to his development as a hypersensitive individual unsuited to the demands of practical existence. They include the rapid failure of his parents' marriage; the rape of his personality by a mother who dressed him in feminine clothing and reared him for a time as a replacement for a lost daughter; a partial education in military academies and a school of commerce to which he could never adapt; and a brief exposure to the university world in Prague. The young Rilke responded to a continuing feeling of being out of place by trying diligently to become part of active cultural and artistic circles. While still a student, he published his first lyric anthology, composed Naturalistic plays, contributed literary reviews to newspapers and journals, and founded his own periodical. He also participated in cultural organizations, lecture presentations, readings of drama and poetry, and similar activities.

When Rilke left the university in 1896, he went to Munich. An incurable restlessness dictated his lifestyle from that time forward. His serious evolution as a writer began under the influence of significant figures whom he encountered in Munich; friendships with Jacob Wassermann and Wilhelm von Scholz were especially productive. Wassermann acquainted him with the writings of Jens Peter Jacobsen, which Rilke soon learned to treasure. Still more important was the relationship that he formed with Lou Andreas-Salomé, whom he met in 1897. It was she who persuaded him to change his name from René to Rainer. After she became his mistress, she exposed him to contemporary philosophical trends and the ideas of the Italian Renaissance. He quickly followed her to Berlin and later traveled with her and her husband twice to Russia, where he was introduced to Leo Tolstoy and other authors. The vast Russian landscape and the Russian people impressed him as examples of original, elemental nature. From them, he drew ideas and perceptions that informed his verse long afterward.

Rilke's only attempt to establish a permanent family situation ended in failure. In 1902, he dissolved his household in the Worpswede artists' colony, left his wife, the sculptor Clara Westhoff, and their daughter, and moved to Paris, where he intended to write a book about Auguste Rodin. His friendship with the famous sculptor was extremely significant for the direction of his poetic development in the years between 1902 and the beginning of World War I. Rodin provided Rilke with an example of strict artistic discipline that had profound impact upon his maturation as a poet. Even more critical to his literary growth during this time was Rilke's association with Paul Cézanne, whose painting technique contributed much to the evolving visual orientation of Rilke's verse. Not only special individuals but also Paris itself, the French people, and even the French language indelibly marked Rilke's subsequent creations, giving them substance and eventually, during his final years, their very medium of expression.

The atmosphere of two other locales gave peculiar flavor to Rilke's most powerful, most complex masterworks. The first was Duino Castle near Trieste; the second, the Château de Muzot in Valais. After visiting North Africa and Egypt in 1910 and 1911, he went to Duino Castle at the invitation of Princess Marie von Thurn und Taxis. There, he wrote the first two of the *Duino Elegies* before moving on to Spain and then back to Germany. The war years, which he spent primarily in Munich, constituted an unproductive interlude that was inwardly devastating to him. He found it exceedingly difficult to begin writing again when hostilities ceased. Only after moving to Switzerland and his secluded refuge at the Château de Muzot did he find inner peace sufficient to complete his finest lyric cycles. He spent most of the remainder of his life in the Rhône Valley, where he died of leukemia.

Analysis · During the course of his development as a poet, the creative task became for Rainer Maria Rilke a process of objectification and externalization of his own inner world. Couched in language that is notable for its musicality and its frequently playful moods are the peculiarities of a unique spiritual life that emerged from special responses to outside stimuli. The melody of lyrics rich in alliteration, assonance, consonance, and rhyme provides a naturally flowing framework for the presentation of the poet's feelings and reflections. Especially typical components of his verse are encounters with sorrow and pain, powerful absorption in specific objects, a strange blending of the experiences of death and love, and an overwhelming sense of isolation. The landscape of these revelations of self is transformed and varied in direct relationship to new outward contacts with people, things, and places. Russia, Paris, Duino, and Valais provide for different works, shaping influence and substance, timeless symbols and concrete reality, worldview and microcosmic conception. Taken in sequence, Rilke's cycles and poems document his endeavors to purify the portrayal of the scenes within him, to clarify obscurities and nail down uncertainties. By its very nature, this act of poetic refinement was deeply religious, reflecting a sincere humility in the face of creation's vast mysteries. Rilke's entire oeuvre proclaims a consciousness of an artistic calling that had its basis in an existential anxiety that was translated into joyful, almost rapturous affirmation of mortality.

Rilke's earliest published poems, which appeared in the collections *Leben und Lieder* (life and songs), *Larenopfer* (offering to the household gods), *Wegwarten* (watch posts), and *Traumgekrönt* (dream-crowned), are marked by a naïve simplicity and a degree of sentimentality that are absent from his more mature writings. Under the influence of Jens Peter Jacobsen, he created particularly sensitive lyrics centered on nature, as well as penetrating psychological portraits of people. Among his favorite subjects were women and children. Even in these youthful creations, there is already a strong emphasis on visual imagery, although the artistic focus of attention is frequently not the object that is described, but rather the spiritual stirrings that occur within the poet because of what he sees.

In *Mir zur Feier* (celebrating me), Rilke began to move away from the lyric forms and approaches of his student years, adopting in the transition techniques that he later perfected in his first broadly successful cycle, *The Book of Hours*. The poems of *Mir zur Feier* present in precise detail their creator's innermost personal concerns, describing in tones of religious fervor his yearnings, prayers, and self-perceptions. Framed in language that is rich in texture yet soft in tone, the poems glorify things that cannot be comprehended through human volition. These verse productions represent a calculated justification of the poet's art as a means of celebrating that which can be revealed in its essence and fullness in no other manner.

Similarly, the commemoration of self is a significant aspect of *The Book of Hours*, divided into three sections that were the product of diverse influences and experiences: Rilke's impressions of Russia and Paris, his love affair with Lou Andreas-Salomé, the dramatic writings of Maurice Maeterlinck and Henrik Ibsen, Friedrich Nietzsche's philosophical ideas, and the cultural legacy of the Italian Renaissance. The work as a whole portrays the author's movement toward an internalization of external phenomena in a poetic act of preservation and redemption. There is evident within the individual poems a new kind of friendly relationship between the poet and God's handiwork that surrounds him. Nevertheless, what is presented is definitely not a traditional Christian attitude toward life. These lyrics are the product of an aggressively demanding mind; in them, a strongly individual interpretation of the religious dimension of experience is advanced without equivocation. The thrust of *The Book of Hours* is to refine the notion that God is not static, a complete and perfect being, but rather a continually evolving artistic creation. Rilke insists that the reader accept this idea on faith, equating his poetic message with spiritual revelation. The result is a celebration of "this world" which the poet continued to elaborate and modify until his death.

Das Buch der Bilder (the book of pictures), another collection written at about the same time as *The Book of Hours*, is in some respects poetically stronger. Under the influence of Rodin, Rilke made the transition from a poetry informed by blurred feeling to precise, objective, carefully formed verse characterized by the complete sacrifice of the poet's immanence to an emphasis upon things in themselves. The creations of *Das Buch der Bilder* reveal the writer's progress toward the establishment of a literary integration of visual impressions with sight-oriented components of language. The artistic process becomes a perfecting of the act of seeing, in which the poet organizes the elements of the visual image through subjective cognition of his external world. Although these lyrics do not attain to the plastic monumentality of Rilke's later writings, they are forerunners of the *Dinggedicht* (thing poem) that are collectively the most important product of Rilke's years in Paris.

A reflection of Rilke's attention to impulses from Rodin's sculpture and Cézanne's paintings, the *Dinggedicht* is the product of disciplined and thorough scrutinization of its model. Outwardly, it seeks to offer the character and intrinsic constitution of an object that is described for its own sake in painstakingly refined language. On another level, however, it documents the acquisition of external things for the poet's inner domain, thereby transforming the physical phenomenon into a precise and specifically calculated symbol for a portion of his re-creation of the world for himself. Some of the poems analyze people, buildings, natural and artificial scenes, plants, animals, and even motifs from mythology and the Bible; others are lyric translations of statues and paintings. Each provides a segment of Rilke's new interpretation and clarification of existence. Unlike the earlier forms, the *Dinggedicht* renounces the commitment to melodic sound relationships and connected imagery chains. The exacting identification of the poem's external object and its reduction to its fundamental nature permitted the poet to place it into an absolute domain of pure symbol. Rilke achieved his most representative mastery of the *Dinggedicht* in *New Poems*, a collection in which heavy stress is placed on negative moods in the explication of the view that God is the direction and not the object of love.

An important consequence of Rilke's Paris experience was a reevaluation of his literary existence that led ultimately to a significant turning point in his career. The problem of an irreconcilable conflict between the demands of practicality and art was compounded by a philosophical crisis involving the tensions that he felt in his need to make a definitive break with Christianity and in his loathing of modern technology. Against this background, an encounter with Søren Kierkegaard's existential philosophy led eventually to Rilke's production of the mythologically exaggerated *Duino Elegies* and *Sonnets to Orpheus* as the peak of his literary endeavor. In these mature lyrics, the creative attitudes and symbolic devices of *New Poems* were refined and perfected. Rilke responded to many different stimuli—World War I, the works of Friedrich Gottlieb Klopstock, Johann Wolfgang von Goethe, and Heinrich von Kleist, Sigmund Freud's psychology, among others—in creating a culminating synthesis of his own poetic view of human life and destiny. Dactylic and iambic meters, free rhythms, questions, and exclamations provide the frame for bold images that pinpoint once again the fundamental directions of Rilke's work as a whole.

The verse written in French after *Duino Elegies* and *Sonnets to Orpheus* was anticlimactic for Rilke's career. It lacks the depth and profundity of earlier works, although individual poems achieve lightness and sparkle in their reflection of a new rejoicing in mortal existence. The three parts of *The Book of Hours* are discrete sets of deeply intimate confessions that arose out of special relationships and encounters that shaped Rilke's artistic outlook. "Das Buch vom mönchischen Leben" ("Of the Monastic Life"), written in 1899, reflects the strong influence of the poet's attachment to Lou Andreas-Salomé and the cultural, historical, and philosophical ideas to which she introduced him. His ecstatic love for Lou and their visits to Russia are the key elements that give "Das Buch von der Pilgerschaft" ("Of Pilgrimage") its specific flavor, while "Das Buch von der Armut und vom Tod" ("Of Poverty and Death") was a product of Rilke's impressions during his first year in Paris. The individual poems of the three cycles are experiments in which Rilke tested various symbols and metaphors, metric and rhythmic possibilities, and rhyme schemes in documenting a deep worship of life as a sacred motivating force.

"Of the Monastic Life" is a series of prayerful outpourings of the spirit in which a young monk addresses God. In this context, prayer is an elemental religious act with two goals: self-discovery in the process of establishing and expanding personal modes of expression, and the "creation" of God and the growth of a sense of brotherhood with Him in one's relationship to nature. The fictive prayer situations provide the setting for a portrayal of the innermost stirrings of the soul in an endless reaching outward to illuminate the divine. Melodic language and strength of visual image are brought together with rich imagination to reveal the lyricist's almost Franciscan sympathy with the world.

Specific items of the cycle "Of Pilgrimage" attain peaks of religious rapture in the glorification of the mystical union between man and woman, offered in newly intensified homage to Lou. Thematically, however, this portion of *The Book of Hours* focuses primarily on key aspects of the poet's Russian experience. It emphasizes especially the idea that the pious Russian people are the embodiment of humility and spirituality within a topographical frame that is the archetype of God's creation. Spatial relationships are particularly important as the vastness of the Russian countryside melts into the author's inner landscape. A few of the lyrics reveal an inclination toward things that need man, presenting them in impressionistic trappings that show a predilection for that which is most immediate and intricate.

"Of Poverty and Death," the final segment of *The Book of Hours*, anticipates the negative, sometimes melancholy tone of Rilke's later collections. Its substance is human misery presented in variations that expose in stark coloration the world of the homeless, the infirm, the abandoned, and the afraid. Christian motifs and themes are employed to accentuate Rilke's rejection of the Christian God, while rich images establish a substantial tie to "Of the Monastic Life" in the affirmation of God as an original poetic creation.

In their extreme subtlety and refinement of language, their worldly elegance, and their moral and emotional engagement, the most representative poems of Rilke's Paris period form the center of his work as a whole. The *Dinggedichte* of *New Poems* are a detailed reflection of his view that his poetic task was the interpretation and clarification of existence for the purpose of healing the world. By accepting, recognizing, and loving things for themselves, the poet places himself in a position to trace animals, plants, works of art, human figures, and other objects back to their true nature and substance. Precise seeing and artistic transformation enable him to project in symbols the content and meaning both of his surroundings and of that which is within him.

Divided into two loosely chronological parts, the *New Poems* examine in objectively plastic, precisely disciplined structures representative manifestations and individuals that belong to the world of nature and to humankind's most important cultural attainments, from the Bible to classical antiquity, from the Middle Ages to the Renaissance. Mystical inwardness is projected in carefully defined symbols that objectively externalize the events within the poet that are stimulated by the process of seeing. Gloom, absurdity, and disintegration are common moods in poems that question the possibility for everything, including man, to exist and thereby to become the subject of literature.

The symbolic portraits of *New Poems* focus on a broad variety of models. Among the most successful are those based on impressions from the Jardin des Plantes. "Der Panther" ("The Panther"), the earliest and most famous of the *Dinggedichte*, transforms its object into a symbol of heroic existence. By the very power of its seeing, the panther, like the poet, is able to create its own inner landscape, absorbing the visual impressions of external objects into itself, where it may modify, penetrate, or even destroy them. One of Rilke's most vivid depictions of rapport with an object, achieved in the act of intense observation, is given in "Archaischer Torso Apollos" ("Ancient Torso of Apollo"), the first work in the second volume of *New Poems*. The headless statue becomes a kind of spiritual mirror that directs the onlooker's gaze back into the self, enabling him to recognize the need for change in his own life.

Between 1912 and 1922, Rilke created the ten Duino elegies in monumental celebration of humankind as the final, most extreme possibility of existence. The ultimate refinement of the delineation of his own calling focuses no longer on the artist as interpreter and clarifier of his surroundings, but rather ordains the poet as a prophet and savior whose task is to preserve everything that has being. He thus becomes the protagonist and representative of humanity in a new religion of life that is an expression of unchecked aestheticism. By saving the world from a collapse that seems unavoidable, the poet engages in an act of self-purification and follows the only possible course of personal redemption.

Taken together, the elegies offer a mural of Rilke's inner landscape. Internalization of travel experiences, the lonely scenery at Duino Castle, the flight of birds, mythological constructs, and other phenomena create a background of timeless "inner space" against which the author projects his coming to grips with the existential polarities of life and death. Progressing from lament to profound affirmation of mortality, the poems glorify the fulfillment of humanity's promise to maintain all things of value through a process of transformation that rescues external nature by placing it in the protected realm of the spirit. The power by which this is accomplished is love, supremely manifested by lovers, people who die young, heroes, children, and animals. By bringing together earth and space, life and death, all dimensions of reality and time into a single inward hierarchical unity, Rilke sought to ensure the continuation of humanity's outward existence.

In the first elegy, the poet states his view of the human condition: imperfection, the questionable status of human beings, the experience of transience, the pain of love. Upon this basis he builds a new mythology of life. Its center is the non-Christian angel who appears in the second elegy as a symbol for the absolute and unattainable, the norm from which humankind in its limitations deviates. In a valid transformation of psychoanalysis into images, Rilke pinpoints the threat that exists within the self in the power of natural drives. Illumination of the brokenness, ambiguity, superficiality, and mechanical senselessness of human pursuits is followed in the sixth elegy by identification of the hero as a symbolic concept that contrasts with average life. The seventh poem of the cycle breaks away from the lament of human insufficiency, suddenly glorifying the here and now in hymnic language that moves to a confessional peak. Renewed expression of the idea that the difference between the human and the natural creature cannot be resolved is followed by an attempt to show that life must be accepted and made fruitful despite its limitations. The culminating elegy creates a balance between mourning and celebration that unites the antithetical problems in a grand, affirmative vision of pain and death as destiny and the only true evidence of existence.

Other literary forms · The rich symbolic content and specific themes that characterize Rainer Maria Rilke's famous lyrics also inform his narrative prose. Recollections of his boyhood and youth are given romantic, fairy-tale coloring in *Vom lieben Gott und Anderes* (1900; republished as *Geschichten vom lieben Gott,* 1904; *Stories of God,* 1931, 1963), a cycle of short tales that replace traditional Christian perceptions of God with depictions of a finically careful artist. *Die Weise von Liebe und Tod des Cornets Christoph Rilke* (1906; *The Tale of the Love and Death of Cornet Christoph Rilke,* 1932), a terse yet beautifully written story, is more like an epic poem than a prose work, especially in its emphasis on the power of the individual word and its intensely rhythmic language. The psychologically intricate novel *Die Aufzeichnungen des Malte Laurids Brigge* (1910; *The Notebooks of Malte Laurids Brigge,* 1930, 1958) is one of Rilke's most profound creations. Written from the point of view of a young Danish nobleman living in exile in Paris, it offers in random sketches a peculiar summation of the central concerns of the author's literary art.

In the decade between 1894 and 1904, Rilke wrote more than twenty plays, many of which were lost and never published. The most important of his remaining theatrical works are either pessimistically Naturalistic or intense dramas of the soul. *Jetzt und in der Stunde unseres Absterbens* (1896; *Now and in the Hour of Our Death*) and *Im Frühfrost* (1897; *Early Frost*) reflect the influence of Rudolf Christoph Jenny in their materialistic determinism, while later pieces such as *Höhenluft* (1897; *Air at High Altitude*) and *Ohne Gegenwart* (1898; *Not Present*) document a development in the direction of Symbolism, motivated especially by the dramatic theories of Maurice Maeterlinck. Rilke's best-remembered play is *Die weisse Fürstin* (1929; *The White Princess*), which in its lyric depth and power illustrates his view that drama and poetry have similar goals.

Apart from his writings in other genres, Rilke also produced a few works of nonfiction. Most notable among these are the biographical study *Auguste Rodin* (1903; English translation, 1919) and the descriptive lyric essays of *Worpswede* (1903). Much of his extensive correspondence has been collected and published. Especially important for what they reveal of his artistic personality and poetic process are volumes of letters exchanged with Lou Andreas-Salomé and Princess Marie von Thurn und Taxis.

Select works other than poetry

LONG FICTION: *Am Leben hin*, 1889; *Die Letzten*, 1902; *Die Weise von Liebe und Tod des Cornets Christoph Rilke*, 1906 (*The Tale of the Love and Death of Cornet Christopher Rilke*, 1932); *Die Aufzeichnungen des Malte Laurids Brigge*, 1910 (*The Notebooks of Malte Laurids Brigge*, 1930; 1958; also known as *The Journal of My Other Self*).

SHORT FICTION: *Zwei Prager Geschichten*, 1899; *Vom lieben Gott und Anderes*, 1900 (republished as *Geschichten vom lieben Gott*, 1904; *Stories of God*, 1931, 1963); *Erzählungen und Skizzen aus der Frühzeit*, 1928.

DRAMA: *Murillo*, pb. 1895 (English translation, 1979); *Jetzt und in der Stunde unseres Absterbens*, pr., pb. 1896 (*Now and in the Hour of Our Death*, 1979); *Höhenluft*, wr. 1897, pr. 1969 (*Air at High Altitude*, 1979); *Im Frühfrost*, pr., pb. 1897 (*Early Frost*, 1979); *Vigilien*, wr. 1897 (*Vigils*, 1979); *Ohne Gegenwart*, pb. 1898 (*Not Present*, 1979); *Waisenkinder*, pb. 1901 (*Orphans*, 1979); *Das tägliche Leben*, pr. 1901 (*Everyday Life*, 1979); *Die weisse Fürstin*, pb. 1929 (*The White Princess*, 1979); *Nine Plays*, pb. 1979.

NONFICTION: *Auguste Rodin*, 1903 (English translation, 1919); *Worpswede*, 1903.

Lowell A. Bangerter

Bibliography · An authoritative and thorough biography of Rilke is Donald Prater, *A Ringing Glass: The Life of Rainer Maria Rilke*, 1986; it features an extensive bibliography. A psychologically based critical biography is David Kleinbard, *The Beginning of Terror: A Psychological Study of Rainer Maria Rilke's Life and Work*, 1993. A third biography is Ralph

Freedman, *Life of a Poet: Rainer Maria Rilke*, 1996. E. M. Butler presents the approach and the judgment of the mid-twentieth century in *Rainer Maria Rilke*, 1941. A valuable attempt to assess Rilke's permanent position in literature appears in Timothy J. Casey, *Rainer Maria Rilke: A Centenary Essay*, 1976. Rilke's voluminous letters, in which he worked out his philosophical and theological positions, are represented in R. F. C. Hall, *Rilke: Selected Letters, 1902-1926*, 1946. The periodical *Modern Austrian Literature* collected several important essays in a special Rilke issue in 1982. A second useful compilation is Frank Baron, Ernst S. Dick, and Warren R. Maurer, eds., *Rilke: The Alchemy of Alienation*, 1980. Romano Guardini's analysis of the poetry in *Rilke's "Duino Elegies": An Interpretation*, 1961, remains illuminating.

ARTHUR RIMBAUD

Born: Charleville, France; October 20, 1854
Died: Marseilles, France; November 10, 1891

Poetry · *Une Saison en enfer*, 1873 (*A Season in Hell*, 1932) · *Les Illuminations*, 1886 (*Illuminations*, 1932)

Achievements · Arthur Rimbaud's meteoric career has forever earned for him a place as the brilliant *enfant terrible* of French verse. Since his death, he has attracted more critical attention than any French poet save Stéphane Mallarmé. A revolutionary both in his life and in his art, Rimbaud exerted a radical influence on the scope and direction of French poetry. He has been credited with introducing *vers libre* (free verse), which has come to dominate modern poetry, and his systematic cultivation of dreams, hallucinations, and madness anticipated modern interest in the irrational side of man. He became, for a time, the patron saint of André Breton and the Surrealists. Rimbaud's conception of the poetical "I" as "other" ("Je est un autre") has been acclaimed as an intuitive perception of the unconscious that predated its mapping by Sigmund Freud. Finally, Rimbaud was the first French literary figure to sound a distinctly feminist note in his writings, condemning the cultural repression of women and looking forward to a future day of liberation when they would assume their rightful place in society and art. Faithful to his own precept, "Il faut être absolument moderne" ("We must be absolutely modern"), he prefigured key trends in modern art and thought.

Biography · Jean-Nicolas-Arthur Rimbaud was born in the provincial town of Charleville on the Franco-Prussian border. His mother, Vitalie Cuif, was of peasant stock and a devout Jansenist; his father, Captain Frédéric Rimbaud, was an itinerant army officer who abandoned the family when Rimbaud was only six years old. A brilliant student, Rimbaud completed nine years of schooling in eight, earning numerous literary prizes in the course of his studies. His earliest attempts at verse were in Latin, followed by his first poem in French, "Les Étrennes des orphelins" ("The Orphans' New Year's Day Gifts"), published in January, 1870. Encouraged by his teacher, Georges Izambard, Rimbaud sent off three poems to the Parnassian poet Théodore de Banville, who, however, failed to express any interest.

Library of Congress

The outbreak of the Franco-Prussian War in July, 1870, put an end to Rimbaud's formal schooling. Alienated by the hypocrisy of provincial society, which he satirized in various poems composed in the early months of 1870, he ran away from home three times: first to Paris, then to Belgium, and again to Paris. He was back in Charleville when the Paris Commune was declared on March 18, 1871. Although much critical attention has been devoted to Rimbaud's possible ties with the Commune, there is no clear evidence that he ever left Charleville during the crucial period of the Paris uprising. On May 15, Rimbaud composed his celebrated "Lettre du voyant" ("Seer Letter"), addressed to a friend, Paul Demeny. Rimbaud's break with traditional poetry was by this time already complete, and on August 15, he again wrote to Banville, enclosing a new poem, "Ce qu'on dit au poète à propos de fleurs" ("What One Says to the Poet in Regard to Flowers"), a vitriolic attack on Parnassian poetics. Shortly thereafter, Rimbaud also sent off eight new poems, in two installments, to Paul Verlaine, who responded with the famous phrase "Venez, chère grande âme, on vous appelle, on vous attend" ("Come, dear great soul, we call to you, we await you").

Rimbaud arrived in the capital with a copy of his newly composed poem, "Le Bateau ivre" ("The Drunken Boat"), which brought him some notoriety among the Parisian literary crowd. The young poet's obnoxious behavior soon alienated him, however, from both Verlaine's family and his fellow artists, and March, 1872, found him back in Charleville. Rimbaud returned to Paris in May and there began a series of escapades with Verlaine which some have characterized as simply youthful exuberance and others as an unhappy love affair. The pair fled first to Brussels, then to London, where a quarrel erupted. Verlaine returned to Brussels, where he was soon followed by Rimbaud.

In Brussels, events soon took a tragic turn. In a moment of drunken rage, Verlaine fired on Rimbaud, wounding him slightly in the hand. The incident might have ended there, but Verlaine later accosted Rimbaud in the street, and the frightened youth sought help from a passing policeman. The authorities intervened, and Verlaine was sentenced to two years in prison. Rimbaud returned to his mother's family farm at Roche, where he completed *A Season in Hell*, begun in April. In late 1873, Rimbaud again visited Paris, where he made the acquaintance of the young poet Germain Nouveau, with whom he traveled to London in the early months of 1874. Almost nothing is known of this second friendship beyond the fact that it ended with Nouveau's abrupt return to Paris in June of that year.

In 1875, Rimbaud embarked on a new series of travels which led him to Stuttgart, across the Swiss Alps on foot into Italy, and back to Charleville via Paris. After visiting Vienna in April, 1876, he enlisted in the Dutch colonial army on May 19 and set sail for Java. He deserted ship in Batavia (modern Djakarta) and returned to Charleville. In May, 1877, Rimbaud was in Bremen, where he attempted (in vain) to enlist in the American Marines. Subsequent travels the same year took him to Stockholm, Copenhagen, Marseilles, Rome, and back to Charleville. In early 1878, he visited Hamburg, returning during the summer to work on the family farm at

Roche. In October, he again traversed Switzerland on foot, crossing the Alps into Italy. There he took the train to Genoa and embarked for Alexandria, later departing for Cyprus, where he worked as a foreman in a marble quarry. Stricken with typhoid, he returned to Charleville in May, 1879, once again spending the summer at Roche. In March, 1880, he was back in Cyprus, where he found work as a construction foreman. An intemperate climate and a salary dispute soon forced him to resign his position and to seek employment elsewhere.

Rimbaud spent the remaining eleven years of his life as the business agent of a French colonial trading company in the remote wilds of Abyssinia (modern-day Ethiopia) and Aden. At the end of this time, he had amassed, through agonizing labor and in the face of constant adversity, the modest sum of 150,000 francs (approximately thirty thousand dollars). In February, 1891, intense pain in his right knee forced him to return to France for medical treatment. Doctors in Marseilles diagnosed his illness as cancer and ordered the immediate amputation of the infected right leg. The cancer proved too widespread to check, however, and Rimbaud died in a state of delirium on November 10, 1891. According to a tradition spawned by his devout sister, Isabelle, who was with the poet in his final moments, Rimbaud returned to Catholicism on his deathbed. Since Isabelle is, however, known to have tampered with her brother's personal letters, critics have given little credence to her testimony.

Analysis · Arthur Rimbaud's early verse (of which he published only three short pieces in various academic bulletins) falls into two general categories. First, there is his satiric verse, exemplified by such poems as "Les Premières Communions" ("First Communions") and "Les Assis" ("The Seated Ones"), which attacks religious hypocrisy and the sterility of bourgeois society. Second, there is his erotic verse, typified by such poems as "Vénus anadyomène" ("Venus Emerging from the Waves") and "Le Coeur volé" ("The Stolen Heart"), which speaks of the trauma of sexual coming-of-age. A pastiche of traditional styles and forms, these initial works nevertheless evidence a brilliant gift for verbal expression and announce the theme of revolt which informs all of Rimbaud's writings.

On May 15, 1871, Rimbaud declared his emancipation from traditional poetics in his celebrated "Seer Letter," addressed to his friend Paul Demeny. This letter, Rimbaud's *ars poetica*, begins with a contemptuous denunciation of all previous poetry as nothing more than rhymed prose. Only Charles Baudelaire, "un vrai dieu" ("a true god"), is spared and, even then, only partially—he frequented a self-consciously artistic milieu, and he failed to find new forms of expression. Rimbaud then calls for a radically new conception of the poet's mission: "Car je est un autre" ("For I is an other"). It is the essential task of the poet to give voice to the repressed, unconscious "other" that lies concealed behind the mask of the rational, Cartesian "I"–the "other" which societal restrictions have condemned to silence. This can be accomplished only by "un long, immense et raisonné dérèglement de tous les sens" ("a long, immense and reasoned derangement of all the senses"). Unlike his Romantic predecessors and such Symbolist contemporaries as Mallarmé, who passively awaited the return of the muse, Rimbaud insists on the active role the poet must take: "Le Poète se fait voyant" ("The poet makes himself a seer"). The poet must actively cultivate dreams, hallucinations, and madness. In so doing, he becomes the great liberator of humanity, a Prometheus who steals fire from the gods, the spokesman for all of those whom society has ostracized: "Il devient entre tous le grand malade, le grand criminel, le grand maudit–et le grand Savant!" ("He becomes, more than anyone, the great sick one, the great criminal, the great accursed one–and the great Learned One!"). Such a poet will be "un multiplicateur de progrès" whose genius, unrestrained by societal taboos and the limitations of rational thought, will lead humankind into a new golden age.

Throughout the remaining months of 1871 and the following year, Rimbaud endeavored to give form to this poetic vision in a new series of songs and verse which are best exemplified by two poems which critics have universally acclaimed as masterpieces: "Le Bateau ivre" ("The Drunken Boat") and "Voyelles" ("Vowels").

Perhaps the best known of Rimbaud's works, "The Drunken Boat" was composed during the summer of 1871 and presented to Verlaine in September of that same year. Although the work borrows from a wide variety of sources (Victor Hugo, Baudelaire, Jules Verne, and Vicomte Chateaubriand, to name but a few), it remains a stunning and original tour de force–particularly for a young poet of sixteen. The poem, composed of twenty-five quatrains in classical Alexandrines and narrated in the first person, is a symbolic drama in three acts. In the first act (quatrains 1 through 4), set on a vast river in the New World, the boat recounts its escape from its haulers, who are massacred by screaming natives, and its subsequent descent toward the sea. There follows a brief, transitional interlude (quatrain 5) in which the boat passes through a ritual purification: Its wooden shell is permeated by the seawater which cleanses it of wine stains and vomit and bears off the boat's rudder and anchor. The second and central act (quatrains 6 through 22) tells of the boat's intoxicating maritime adventures and its fantastic, hallucinatory vision of a transcendental reality which ordinary mortals have only glimpsed in passing. Yet, the boat's long and frenetic voyage of discovery ultimately begins to turn sour. After braving whirlpools, hurricanes, raging seas, and Leviathans from the deep, the boat unexpectedly declares its nostalgia for the ancient parapets of Europe. In the third and final act (quatrains 23 through 25), the boat's delirious optimism turns to anguished despair. Its quest for the absolute has at length proved futile, and the boat now seeks dissolution in death. If it desires a return to European waters, it is to the cold, black puddle into which a sad, impoverished child releases a boat as frail as a May butterfly. At the same time, the boat realizes the impossibility of any turning back to its previous mode of existence. It can no longer follow in the wake of the merchant ships, nor bear the haughty pride of the military gunboats, nor swim beneath the horrible eyes of the prison ships that lie at anchor in the harbor.

"The Drunken Boat" reflects both Rimbaud's new conception of the poet as "seer" and the influence of the French Symbolists, such as Verlaine and Baudelaire, who sought to replace the effusive, personalized verse of the Romantics with a symbolic, impersonal mode of expression. Critics have generally equated the work's "protagonist," the boat, with the poet himself, reading the poem as a symbolic account of Rimbaud's own efforts to transcend reality through language. Most critics are also agreed that the poem's final two stanzas, while they suggest the advent of a new self-awareness, evince a disillusionment with the "seer" experiment and prefigure Rimbaud's later renunciation of poetry.

Rimbaud's celebrated sonnet "Vowels," written in decasyllabic verse, dates from the same period as "The Drunken Boat" and was similarly presented to Verlaine in September, 1871. Another of Rimbaud's "seer" poems, the work postulates a mystic correspondence between vowels and colors: "A noir, E blanc, I rouge, U vert, O bleu" ("A black, E white, I red, U green, O blue"). The poem has its literary source in Baudelaire's famous sonnet "Correspondences," which had asserted an underlying connection between sounds, perfumes, and colors and had popularized the concept of synesthesia. Another probable source for the work has been found in an illustrated alphabet primer which Rimbaud may have read as a child and which has served to elucidate some of the sonnet's enigmatic imagery. Perhaps the most ingenious interpretation of the poem is that of the critic Lucien Sausy, who argued that the work exploits correspondences not between sound and color (there are, in fact, few traces of such matching within the phonetic content of the poem) but rather between the visual form of the vowels themselves and the images to which the latter are linked: *A*, if inverted, thus suggests the delta-shaped body of a fly; *E* (written as a Greek epsilon in the manuscript), if turned on its side, suggests vapors, tents, and glaciers; and so on. (Sausy's interpretation, first advanced in *Les Nouvelles Littéraires*, September 2, 1933, is available in the notes to the Pléiade edition of Rimbaud's works.) As a counterbalance, however, one might mention Verlaine's explanation of the sonnet: "Rimbaud saw things that way and that's all there is to it."

By his own account, Rimbaud composed *A Season in Hell* during the period from April to August of 1873. The only book by Rimbaud, the publication of which was supervised by the poet himself, *A Season in Hell* was printed in Brussels in the fall of 1873 in an edition of five hundred copies. Rimbaud was, however, unable to pay the printing costs, and this first edition, save for six author's copies which circulated among his friends, remained in the attic of a Brussels publishing house until discovered in 1901 by a Belgian bibliophile, who did not make his discovery public until 1914. The text, which Rimbaud had originally intended to entitle "Livre païen" (pagan book) or "Livre nègre" (Negro book–the French adjective is pejorative), consists of nine prose poems and seven poems in verse, the latter all contained within the section "Délires II" ("Deliria II"). The work has been variously acclaimed by critics for its original and stunning verbal display, its fantastic, visionary imagery, and its prophetic pronouncements concerning Rimbaud's own future. As the title indicates, *A Season in Hell* is Rimbaud's poetic attempt to come to grips with his recent "dark night of the soul"–his unhappy adventure with Verlaine and his anguished experience as "seer." Viewed from the perspective of Rimbaud's own metaphysical dictum–"I is an other"–the work, narrated in the first person, recounts a confrontation between the rational, conscious "I" and the irrational, unconscious "other" which the poet had systematically worked to cultivate.

The text opens with a brief introductory section (untitled) in which the poet evokes with longing his lost state of childhood innocence. He recalls his frenzied flight from reason, his revolt against traditional concepts of beauty and morality, his pursuit of crime, and his cultivation of madness. He momentarily dreams of regaining his former state of innocence through a return to Christian charity but immediately rejects the latter as an empty illusion. Inescapably condemned to death and damnation, he dedicates his opus not to the traditional poetic Muse but rather to Satan. This introductory segment serves to announce the key themes which the body of the work will subsequently develop: the abandonment of the "seer" experiment, the nostalgia for the comfort afforded by traditional Christian values, and the attainment of a new self-awareness which, however, prevents any naïve return to the past.

In the following prose poem, "Mauvais Sang" ("Bad Blood"), the poet attributes his failure to transcend the vulgar world or reality to some inherited defect which now condemns him to a life of manual toil. Nor does he envision any hope in the progress promised by Cartesian rationalism and the advent of science. The world may yet be headed toward total destruction. Disillusioned with Western civilization, he seeks imaginative shelter in what he perceives as the savage freedom of black African society. His amoral utopia is, however, destroyed by the arrival of the white colonialists, who impose their debilitating Christian ethics by force of arms. Momentarily seduced by Christianity, the poet ultimately rejects it as an infringement on human freedom and refuses to embark on a honeymoon with Jesus Christ as father-in-law. Rather than remain enslaved, he hurls himself to his death beneath the horses of the conquering Europeans.

The conflict between Christianity and paganism is further developed in "Nuit de l'enfer" ("Night in Hell"). Here, the poet is engulfed in the fires of Hell, to which his parents have condemned him through baptism and catechism lessons. His suffering derives from his inability to choose between the absolute but terrible freedom offered by Satan and the serene but limited freedom promised by the Christian God. Hell, in short, is a state of eternal and lucid alienation.

"Délires I" ("Deliria I") introduces a "Vièrge folle" ("Foolish Virgin") who recounts her difficult life with "l'Époux infernal" ("The Infernal Spouse") who seduced her with the false promise of an amoral and transcendent Paradise. Numerous critics have found in this passage a mythic retelling of Verlaine's intellectual and erotic seduction by Rimbaud; other critics have preferred to read the passage as emblematic of the seduction of the poet's rational and moral self by his own irrational and amoral unconscious. In either case, the poem is a bitter indictment of Rimbaud's failed efforts to transform reality.

In "Délires II" ("Deliria II"), subtitled "L'Alchimie du verbe" ("Verbal Alchemy"), the poet looks back on what he now views as an act of folly: his attempt to transcend reality through the systematic cultivation of the irrational and the invention of a new language that would draw in all the human senses and give voice to everything in humanity that had previously been barred from expression. He gives as tangible examples of this enterprise six verse poems, the visionary imagery of which speaks symbolically of his hunger and thirst for the absolute, his frustration with past theology and future technology, and his fervent conviction that he has indeed found the mystic line of juncture between sea and sky, body and soul, the known and unknown. This metaphysical quest has ultimately failed, the poet says, for he has been damned by the rainbow—an ironic allusion to the rainbow sent by God to Noah as a sign of future redemption.

As his dream-filled night draws to a close, and morning approaches, the poet awakes to hear the strains of the hymn "Christus venit" (Christ has come) resounding through the somber cities of the world. His career as "seer" has ended with the bleak dawn of reality.

The four remaining prose poems, all of them brief, further expand upon major themes in the work. In "L'Impossible" ("The Impossible"), the poet tells of his futile efforts to reconcile Christianity and Eastern mysticism and his ultimate rejection of both. In "Éclair" ("Lightning"), the poet finds momentary comfort in the dignity of work but cannot avoid perceiving the vanity of all human efforts in the face of death and dissolution. "Matin" ("Morning") announces the end of the poet's night in Hell. In spite of the limitations imposed by the human condition, he chooses life over death. Although all men are slaves, they should not curse life. In the final passage, "Adieu" ("Farewell"), the poet renounces his unsuccessful career as "seer" in favor of a newfound divine clarity, the anguished self-knowledge which his experience has brought him. There will be no turning back to the past for solace, nor any attempt to seek oblivion in the love of a woman. "We must be absolutely modern," the poet declares; for himself, he is content to possess the truth that one is both body and soul.

Illuminations was published in 1886, without Rimbaud's knowledge. Some years earlier, he had left a manuscript of the work with Verlaine, whence it passed through several hands before it was published in the Symbolist periodical *La Vogue*, appearing in book form (edited and with a preface by Verlaine) later in the same year.

Although more than a century has passed since the first appearance of *Illuminations*, a number of fundamental questions concerning the collection remain to be resolved, and perhaps will never be definitely resolved. There is first the matter of the title. The manuscript itself is untitled, and the only evidence for the title by which the collection is known is the statement of Paul Verlaine, a notoriously unreliable witness. In a letter written in 1878 to his brother-in-law, Charles de Sivry, Verlaine says: "Have re-read *Illuminations* (painted plates). . . ." Later, in the preface to the first edition of *Illuminations*, he adds that "the word [that is, "illuminations"] is English and means *gravures coloriées*, colored plates," claiming that this was the subtitle which Rimbaud had chosen for the work.

The question of the title and subtitle may seem a mere scholarly quibble, but it is more than that, for at issue is the significance which Rimbaud himself attached to the title and, by extension, the spirit in which he intended the work to be read. Some critics, accepting Verlaine's testimony without qualification, suggest that by "painted plates" or "colored plates," Rimbaud meant the cheap colored prints which had recently become widely available. The tone of the title, then, would be highly ironic. Other critics suggest that Verlaine garbled Rimbaud's meaning— that Rimbaud had in mind the illuminated manuscripts of the Middle Ages. Still others reject Verlaine's testimony on this matter as another of his fabrications, arguing that by "illuminations" Rimbaud meant moments of spiritual insight; some readers have seen in the title a reference to the occult doctrines of Illuminism.

Another important ongoing debate concerns the date of composition. It was long believed that *Illuminations* preceded *A Season in Hell*, but in recent decades this assumption has been seriously challenged. Again, the question of dating may appear to be of interest only to specialists, but such is not the case. The conclusion to *A Season in Hell* has been widely regarded as Rimbaud's farewell to poetry. If, in fact, he wrote *Illuminations* after *A Season in Hell*, many existing critical interpretations are invalid or in need of substantial revision.

This argument for dating *Illuminations* after *A Season in Hell* is primarily based on the pioneering research of Henri de Bouillane de Lacoste. Bouillane de Lacoste's graphological analysis of the manuscript, in conjunction with other, more subjective, arguments, has persuaded many scholars to accept Verlaine's once-rejected assertion that the work was written during the period from 1873 to 1875 in the course of Rimbaud's European travels. On the other hand, there are a number of reputable Rimbaud scholars who find Bouillane de Lacoste's analysis inconclusive at best and who thus retain the old chronology. In any case, one cannot know with certainty the date of composition of the individual poems themselves, nor is there any clear indication of the final order in which Rimbaud intended them to appear. The reason for Rimbaud's prolongation of his poetic career beyond his abdication from poetry in *A Season in Hell* seems destined to remain a mystery.

Illuminations is regarded by many critics as Rimbaud's most original work and his consummate contribution to French poetry. While it represents a continuation of the "seer" experiment conducted in his earlier verse, it also marks a radical departure from the narrative, anecdotal, and descriptive modes of expression to be found in his previous poetry and in that of his contemporaries. The poems in *Illuminations* are strikingly modern in that each forms a self-contained, autoreferential unit which stands independent of the collection as a whole and remains detached from any clear point of reference in the world of reality. They do not purport to convey any didactic, moral, or philosophical message to the reader. Ephemeral and dreamlike, each emerges from the void as a spontaneous flow of images generated by free association. They are works in which the rational "I" allows the unconscious "other" to speak. As manifestations of the unconscious, they reveal an almost infinitely rich condensation of meaning which defies any linear attempts at interpretation. They thus elucidate Rimbaud's earlier remark in *A Season in Hell* that he "reserved all translation rights." They are, again in the poet's own words, "accessible to all meanings." If they are coherent, it is in the way dreams are coherent, and, like dreams, they speak from the hidden recesses of the mind. Hermetic in form, they lead down a different path from that charted by the Symbolist verse of Rimbaud's contemporary, Mallarmé: They reflect not an aesthetic obsession with the problematics of language but a perpetual striving to give voice to all that reason and social mores have condemned to silence.

Although *Illuminations* consists of a discontinuous series of pieces devoid of any central narrative plot, critics have drawn attention to a number of major recurring themes to be found within the text. Given the work's dreamlike qualities and its close affinity with the unconscious, it is not surprising that the theme most often cited by critics is that of childhood. Numerous passages in the work evoke the blissful innocence of childhood, Rimbaud's "paradise lost," irrevocably destroyed by the advent of civilization and Christianity. The theme is developed at particular length in the two prose poems "Enfance" ("Childhood") and "Après le déluge" ("After the Deluge"). In the first, the child-poet tells of his Satanic fall from a state of divine omniscience and absolute freedom into a subterranean prison where he is condemned to silence. In the second, which ironically alludes to the biblical story of the Flood and the promise of divine redemption, the poet sees the natural innocence of childhood as being progressively corrupted by the rise of civilization, and he ends by conjuring up new floods that will sweep away the repressive work of society.

A second and related major theme, exemplified by such prose poems as "Villes I" ("Cities I"), "Villes II" ("Cities II"), and "Métropolitain" ("Metropolitan"), is that of the city. Although modeled in part on the Paris and London of Rimbaud's own time, the cities in *Illuminations* are phantasmagoric, shimmering cities of the future which present a vision of technological wonder and bleak sterility. Promised utopias, they repeatedly and rapidly degenerate into vast urban wastelands which devour their pitiful human prey. In the end, they are bitterly renounced by their creator and verbally banished back to the void from which they emerged.

A third major theme is that of metamorphosis—a theme that is a logical outgrowth of Rimbaud's own assertion that "I is an other." For Rimbaud, as his "Seer Letter" makes clear, the seemingly stable Cartesian I is merely an illusion which masks the presence of a multiplicity of repressed others.

There is no central, defining human essence. In *Illuminations*, the poet thus undergoes a continual series of metamorphoses. In "Parade," he appears as a procession of itinerant comedians; in "Antique," as the son of the pagan god Pan, at once animal, man, and woman; in "Bottom," as the character in William Shakespeare's *A Midsummer Night's Dream* (1595-1596) who seeks to appropriate all the other characters' roles; and finally, in "Being Beauteous," as the incarnation of beauty itself. There are no limits to one's being, Rimbaud suggests, if one will only realize the vast potential within.

Select works other than poetry

MISCELLANEOUS: *Œuvres complètes*, 1948 (*Rimbaud: Complete Works, Selected Letters*, 1966).

James John Baran

Bibliography · An excellent book on Rimbaud is Enid Starkie, *Rimbaud*, 1947. Another good source is Wallace Fowlie, *Rimbaud*, 1965. A great deal of criticism and biography continues to be published about Rimbaud, including Cecil Arthur Hackett's *Rimbaud: A Critical Introduction*, 1981; Edward J. Ahearn's *Rimbaud: Visions and Habitations*, 1983, which explores the poet's surroundings in relationship to his poetry; and the unique 1992 book *Rimbaud's Theatre of the Self*, by James R. Lawler, which translates Rimbaud's work into a theatrical progression, explaining why the poet stopped writing to explore the dark side of his personality. A good volume to place Rimbaud in poetic context, from the Symbolists on, is Marjorie Perloff's definitive *The Poetics of Indeterminancy: Rimbaud to Cage*, 1981. Finally, for devotees of pop culture, Rimbaud expert Wallace Fowlie published in 1994 *Rimbaud and Jim Morrison: The Rebel as Poet*, a book that relates Rimbaud to the 1960's counterculture.

EDWIN ARLINGTON ROBINSON

Born: Head Tide, Maine; December 22, 1869
Died: New York, New York; April 6, 1935

Poetry · *The Torrent and the Night Before,* 1896 · *The Children of the Night,* 1897 · *Captain Craig,* 1902, 1915 · *The Town Down the River,* 1910 · *The Man Against the Sky,* 1916 · *Merlin,* 1917 · *Lancelot,* 1920 · *The Three Taverns,* 1920 · *Avon's Harvest,* 1921 · *Collected Poems,* 1921 · *Roman Bartholow,* 1923 · *The Man Who Died Twice,* 1924 · *Dionysus in Doubt,* 1925 · *Tristram,* 1927 · *Collected Poems,* 1927 · *Sonnets: 1889-1927,* 1928 · *Cavender's House,* 1929 · *Collected Poems,* 1929 · *The Glory of the Nightingales,* 1930 · *Matthias at the Door,* 1931 · *Nicodemus,* 1932 · *Talifer,* 1933 · *Amaranth,* 1934 · *King Jasper,* 1935 · *Collected Poems,* 1937

Achievements · For some twenty years before he gained acknowledgment as a poet of major proportions, Edwin Arlington Robinson had been publishing some excellent poems, particularly in the form of lyrics with a dramatic base. Indeed, his special genius has always been ascribed to the shorter poem, even though he has thirteen book-length narrative poems to his credit, eleven of which were published individually as books between 1917 and 1935 and two of which—*The Man Who Died Twice* and *Tristram*—were awarded Pulitzer Prizes in the 1920's. In 1921, the first edition of his *Collected Poems* earned for Robinson his first Pulitzer Prize.

In the 1920's, when T. S. Eliot and Robert Frost were acknowledged literary masters, Robinson was hailed by some discerning critics as America's foremost poet. In addition to the three Pulitzer Prizes, he was given honorary degrees by Yale University in 1922 and Bowdoin College in 1925. At the close of the decade, the National Institute of Arts and Letters presented Robinson with a gold medal in recognition of his outstanding accomplishments. Chosen by the Literary Guild of America as a monthly selection, *Tristram* sold over 50,000 copies. Not without good reason, *Tristram* and most of the long blank verse narratives are not read much today; they are dull and wordy. Some, however, contain passages of exceptional power, notably *Lancelot* and *The Man Who Died Twice*—the latter being the most impressive of the long poems.

In many of his shorter poems and in a few of his middle-length narratives, such as "Ben Jonson Entertains a Man from Stratford" and "Rembrandt to Rembrandt," Robinson's use of language is consistently superior and often brilliant. For example, he infuses his infrequently used but nonetheless striking images drawn from the natural world with metaphorical or symbolic meanings that contribute greatly to an understanding of his themes. Whether in the shorter or the longer pieces, Robinson is, above all, a poet of rational content, one who believes that what the poem says is of the utmost importance. His themes are both serious and significant.

Robinson may properly be classified as a traditional poet since he wrote regularly in blank verse, used meter, rhyme, and patterned stanzas, and was attracted to the English sonnet, a form in which his triumphs are many and which he expanded to include nontraditional subject matter, such as prostitution, suicide, and euthanasia. His most accomplished poems, among the best of their kind in English, are relatively brief yet intense and penetrating studies of the residents of Tilbury Town, the imaginary community that Robinson created based on Gardiner, Maine. His themes reflect a full awareness of the painful lives that many must endure. In these superior shorter poems, these compelling character studies, Robinson addresses the need to try to understand one's fellow man and to have compassion for him.

Biography · By the standards of the biographer's world, the life of Edwin Arlington Robinson provides little that is exciting. Born on December 22, 1869, in Head Tide, Maine, the third son of Edward and Mary Palmer Robinson, he led a life characterized by a very low profile, even after he was acknowledged by a number of critics and scholars in the 1920's as America's most distinguished poet. He shunned the public attention that was his for the asking, preferring instead to write in relative seclusion and to associate with only a very few close friends. Occasionally, he consented to an interview, but he never gave lectures or public readings of his poetry, or engaged in any activity in which he would have been the center of attention.

Ten months after his birth, the Robinson family moved to Gardiner, Maine, where his father, who had made his fortune in the timber business, became a civic figure and was elected to the state legislature. Although his father saw little need for his sons to receive college educations, he consented to sending Dean, his first born, to Bowdoin to begin the study of medicine. After Robinson took an extra year of high school and did odd jobs around Gardiner for a period, expressing all the while his disinclination for the world of business (the route taken by Herman, the second born), he was finally permitted to enroll in Harvard in 1891 as a "special student," where he remained for two years. Robinson treasured these years, and although he was never fully accepted by the student literati, he did publish five poems in *The Harvard Advocate*.

The decade following his years at Harvard was beset by family tragedies and discouragement; his resolve to be a writer elicited but few rewards. He paid for the publication of his first book of poetry, *The Torrent and the Night Before;* a friend paid the cost of printing *The Children of the Night*, the second; and *Captain Craig*, the third, was first rejected by five publishers and accepted only on the condition that its expense would be underwritten by friends. Although these volumes contain a number of excellent poems, they received little critical attention. Robinson's fortunes changed in 1905, when Theodore Roosevelt was sent a copy of *The Children of the Night* by his son Kermit. Roosevelt found a sinecure for the poet—who was living in New York in an impoverished state, discouraged, and given to drinking—with the United States Customs Service, a position he was to hold until the Taft administration. It gave him the opportunity to write free from financial worry, a condition which had plagued him since the Panic of 1893 took the family fortune.

He spent the summer of 1911 at the MacDowell Colony in Peterborough, New Hampshire, a retreat for artists to which the poet would return each summer for the rest of his life for three months of uninterrupted writing. The rest of the year he spent in New York, with occasional trips, mostly to Boston, to see friends. Then in 1916, *The Man Against the Sky*, his fifth volume of poetry, was favorably received, and Robinson was recognized as a significant American poet. Toward the end of his life, Robinson devoted nearly all his creative efforts to the long narrative poem, publishing eight book-length poems between 1927 and his death in 1935.

Analysis · In response to a 1931 letter from Bess Dworsky, who was preparing a thesis on Edwin Arlington Robinson's "philosophy," the poet wrote: "I am rather sorry to learn that you are writing about my 'philosophy'—which is mostly a statement of my inability to accept a mechanistic interpretation of the universe and of life." Critics have called Robinson an idealist, a Platonist, a transcendentalist, a pantheist, and many combinations thereof. While it is indeed possible to identify in his poetry some elements of all the above, he was not an advocate of any philosophical system. He was most assuredly aware of the scientific and philosophical concepts that pressed toward a "mechanistic interpretation of the universe and of life," which he rejected in favor of a personal idealism that nonetheless accepted the reality of matter. As Chard Powers Smith argues in *Where the Light Falls: A Portrait of Edwin Arlington Robinson* (1965), "He never denied the material world. What he did was to face it, defy it, and deny its capacity to destroy him." Against the forces of materialism he posited a life of the mind, and, as Smith suggests, "He respected the unique inner integrity of all individuals and he never judged anyone, in life or in fiction [poetry], for he did not know what pressures they had been under."

Several comments that Robinson made serve to illustrate his purpose in writing poetry and provide us with external evidence that, coupled with the internal evidence of the poems themselves, identifies his major thematic concerns. In a letter to Harry de Forest Smith, dated May 13, 1896, Robinson said what he hoped his poems would do:

> If printed lines are good for anything, they are bound to be picked up some time; and then, if some poor devil of a man or woman feels any better or any stronger for anything that I have said, I shall have no fault to find with the scheme or anything in it.

Writing to Smith again in February 3, 1897, Robinson reaffirmed his position: "I also make free to say that many of my verses [were] written with a conscious hope that they might make some despairing devil a little stronger and a little better satisfied with things—not as they are, but as they are to be." Sixteen years later, in reply to William Stanley Braithwaite's inquiry about his central "message," Robinson is reputed to have answered in terms remarkably consistent with his statements made years earlier:

> I suppose that a part of it might be described as a faint hope of making a few of us understand our fellow creatures a little better, and to realize what a small difference there is, after all, between ourselves, as we are, and ourselves, not only as we might have been but would have been if our physical and temperamental make-up and our environment had been a little different.

While this response may sound as if Robinson had embraced the philosophical determinism of the naturalistic writers, Robinson was quick to correct that impression: "If a reader doesn't get from my books an impression that life is very much worth while, even though it may not seem always to be profitable or desirable, I can only say that he doesn't see what I am driving at."

From *The Torrent and the Night Before* to *Dionysus in Doubt*, the last volume to contain significant shorter poems, the dual concept of understanding and compassion, Robinson's major thematic concern, is strongly evident in such outstanding poems as "Luke Havergal," "The Clerks," "The Growth of 'Lorraine,' " "The Whip," "How Annandale Went Out," "Flammonde," "The Gift of God," "Veteran Sirens," "The Poor Relation," "En Passant," and "Eros Turannos." Very closely aligned to the motif of understanding and compassion is the belief exemplified in many of his poems, and most convincingly so in "Eros Turannos," that no one person is ever able to fully understand another person. Although this may seem incompatible with Robinson's preoccupation with understanding and compassion, it is not, for the poet believed that the very act of trying to understand is of extreme value in itself.

In terms of technique—other than the conventions of rhyme and meter—Robinson works consistently in three areas worth noting: image patterns, irony, and the deliberate withholding of information. Robinson is not the New England poet who celebrates or even writes about snow, lilacs, or the like. In fact, he is lean in his use of imagery from the natural world; however, when he does draw upon the natural world, his images are functional, not decorative, and they are often framed in a metaphorical or symbolic context. Wherever his images come from—colors, a visionary light, water, leaves, to name a few sources—they often serve in patterns as ordering devices to provide unity and to enhance meaning. They contribute to the complex texture of some of his best poems, such as "Luke Havergal," "For a Dead Lady," and "Eros Turannos."

Irony is one of Robinson's most consistently employed tools, and he uses it variously to achieve various ends. In "How Annandale Went Out," for example, irony is situational and understated; the doctor-speaker feels that it is absurd in the first place that he is on trial for a justified mercy killing, and he pleads his case almost casually. In "The House on the Hill" and "Eros Turannos," Robinson is overtly caustic in his attitude toward people who feel compelled to speculate on the circumstances and personalities of others without much in the way of verification. In "The Man Against the Sky" the concept of a mechanistic universe is soundly indicted, while in "Cassandra," sarcasm is leveled, not very subtly, at American materialism. In "New England" the irony is so complex that readers first thought the sonnet was an attack on the rigidity of the Puritan afterglow in New England, when the poem actually denounces those who have wrongly interpreted this region.

While poets such as T. S. Eliot, Ezra Pound, and Wallace Stevens provide what amount to acceptable puzzles in their poetry, Robinson was, for a period, the object of some scorn for his obscurity. Since he was not given to the esoteric, readers perhaps came to him expecting to find neat, rational answers in technically sound poems. Because his language is relatively uncomplicated, descending probably from the Puritan "plain style," readers were confounded and even angered at not being able to determine what some of his poems meant. These interpretive problems derive from Robinson's technique of deliberately withholding information in the poem in order to make readers think, to reward them when they arrive at their own understanding.

The most accomplished of Robinson's shorter poems, "Eros Turannos" is the favorite of anthologists and the poem most representative of Robinson's major thematic concerns and techniques. Set in a village on the coast of Maine, it recounts the courtship of a man and woman, and then tries to explain what happened to the woman once the man died. The speaker of the poem takes deliberate pains to inform readers that they are really failing to understand her situation because they actually do not know what, in fact, she is experiencing.

The poem consists of six stanzas of eight lines each, with an ababcccb rhyme scheme and a metrical pattern of iambic tetrameter for all lines except those ending with the b rhyme. These are indented in the text and are in iambic trimeter with one extra unaccented syllable at the end of the line. The title is Greek for "Love, the Tyrant."

At the outset of this poem, which is narrated in the present tense to give its dramatic situation a sense of immediacy, the reader learns that the woman is afraid of the man despite his "engaging mask," that she has just cause for discounting him as a potential husband, but that she is willing to disregard her fears and uncertainties about him because she is more afraid of the "downward years," of growing old alone. Her insecurity is not merely a product of her relationship with the man; rather, it is a component of her personality: She is simply afraid of life.

As "Eros Turannos" progresses to the close of the third stanza, which marks the end of the first part of this little drama, the woman is depicted as being once capable of penetrating with her "blurred sagacity" beneath his mask to the "Judas that she found him"; however, she finally relinquishes all objections, at whatever cost to her, and agrees to the union. So far, the reader may feel that the woman deserves pity, and the man, scorn; but in typical Robinson fashion, the situation is not that simple, for just as the woman has deliberately deceived herself into believing that marrying a man she fears and cannot trust is a lesser evil than growing old alone, so too has he been deceived into marriage by the prospect of living rather comfortably with her in a setting replete with tradition that "Beguiles and reassures him." Robinson adopts the stance that there are inevitably two sides to every story, and he is most reluctant to pass judgments. There are some exceptions, of course, such as the despicable Aaron Stark in the sonnet of that name. By and large, however, if judgment is to be passed, the reader must do so from whatever understanding he or she comes to in the poems. Almost always, the reader learns to have compassion once he or she understands the situations confronting the characters, their personal inadequacies or hells—or understands at least to the best of his or her ability.

The first three stanzas thus establish and resolve, for a time, the problems facing the man and the woman by having them marry. The husband
is absent in the second part of the poem, the last three stanzas, and the wife
is living alone. From the way she is described in the first four lines of the
fourth stanza, it is evident that a considerable time has passed and that she
is either in or rapidly approaching old age. In addition, she is suffering
from a collapse of her mental faculties. The "pounding wave" repeats the
same song: her husband's dirge. The word "illusion" refers to the speaker's
conception of the manner in which the wife had viewed her husband who
now is dead. Her fears of living alone in the "downward years" have
materialized. Hiding from the world, she has become an object of curiosity
and idle speculation among the Tilbury Town folk.

At the beginning of the fifth stanza, the speaker, who, in Robinson's
characteristic manner, identifies himself as a townsman by the use of "we,"
comments ironically on the inability of people to know other people and
on the penchant "we" have for gossiping. Yet, just as the use of the words
"veil" and "visions" reinforces the illusory nature of the wife's assessment of her husband, so do the townspeople fall prey to illusions; they
are mistaken in their conception of the "home, where passion lived and
died," in their conjectures about the man and woman who enacted the
drama. The point that Robinson insists on making is a familiar one in his
poetry.

The opening lines of the final stanza state that whatever the townspeople
are saying can do the wife no harm, for she has striven with a "god" and
is oblivious to everything else. She made a lifelong commitment, not only
to her husband, but to "Love, the Tyrant," as well, and she is living
with—suffering—the consequences. Exactly "what the God has given" to her
is unknown, but in his effort to approximate what he thinks it might be,
the speaker formulates three similes. Since he is uncertain, he uses the
words "though" and "or" to qualify his perceptions. Although critics
uniformly admire the striking images that close the poem, they avoid
commentary on what the images mean, preferring instead vaguely to call
attention to their symbolic significance. Confusing as these images may be,
they represent to the speaker his conception of the woman's mental death,
which is what she finally received from the "god," "Love, the Tyrant," once
her husband died. When waves break (the first image), they are finished,
through, dead; the "changed familiar tree" (the second image) is a tree in
autumn, its leaves going or gone, and a symbolic representation of death
or impending death; and, lastly, the blind who are driven down "the
stairway to the sea" suggest the "downward years" of the first stanza and
serve as the concluding representation of death. Blindly driven by "Love,

the Tyrant," the wife is being driven to death, just as the blind would drown
were they forced into the sea. Words referring to vision and sight form a
basic image pattern that unifies the poem and underscores the thematic
concern: stanza (1) *mask;* (2) *blurred, sees, looks;* (3) *sees, dimmed;* (4) *illusion;*
(5) *veil, vision, seen;* (6) *blind.* While not explicitly related to the motif, a
second pattern of imagery also helps to unify the poem. Since the physical
setting is a harbor community, water and nautical imagery is found in the
infinitives "to sound" and "to secure," and in the mention of "foamless
weirs," "sense of ocean," "pounding wave," "waves breaking," and "like a
stairway to the sea." Finally, in keeping with the time of year in the second
part of the poem, Robinson refers to the autumnal images of a "falling leaf"
and "a changed familiar tree." Robinson is at his best in "Eros Turannos,"
a moving lyric unified through patterns of imagery, through the consistent
use of the present tense, and through a logically balanced structure dividing the poem into cause and effect. It is through the speaker's struggles to
understand the wife that the reader comes to an understanding of and
compassion for her.

In both "The Whip" and "How Annandale Went Out," as in "Eros
Turannos," Robinson withholds from the reader an easy understanding of
the central issues of the poems, thus forcing the reader to a scrupulous
reading. When the reader does become aware of the circumstances behind
the actions of the characters, he or she understands and feels compassion
for them. Both poems, but especially "The Whip," have been the subject
of considerable critical attention.

"The Whip," a forty-line poem in five stanzas of eight iambic trimeter
lines with an ababbcbc rhyme scheme, is narrated by a Tilbury Townsman
who has no obvious connection with the characters whose recent drama,
which led to a suicide, he is trying to fathom. The setting is apparently a
funeral home. The victim is in an open coffin and the speaker quizzically
addresses him.

In the first stanza the speaker reveals that the suicide victim had been
married to a woman who treated him tyranically and ruined him. During
their marriage he constantly doubted her fidelity and became a cynic. As
the poem progresses through the second and third stanzas, the speaker
comments that the wife indeed had taken a lover and left. As a result, the
husband chose death by drowning. Yet the speaker, recognizing that "the
gall we drink/ Is not the mead we cry for," feels that the husband's plight
did not justify his suicide. It was not "a thing to die for."

The specifics surrounding the suicide begin to take shape in the fourth
stanza as the speaker, still bewildered by the situation, notices a blue mark
"like a welt" on the husband's face; and in the final stanza the speaker and

the reader come to understanding at the same time. The "chase" referred to in the fifth stanza involved the husband on a horse pursuing the wife and her lover, who were either on one horse or on separate ones. As they were crossing a river, the wife struck her husband in the face with her riding crop; hence the title, "The Whip." He fell off his horse and chose to drown. Earlier in the poem, knowing only that the husband committed suicide, the speaker asks, "Then, shall I call you blind?" He ends the poem with "Still, shall I call you blind?"—a question rhetorically posed, for the speaker has come to the realization that the husband's suicide came at a moment of emotional and physical frenzy. This knowledge finally becoming clear to him, his attitude undergoes a change.

"The Whip" is a little masterpiece of mystery and subsequent revelation. It is a testimony to Robinson's skill that he manages to have both the speaker and the reader simultaneously come to the realization of what actually happened. One of many in his repertoire of shorter poems devoted to the subject of suicide (others include "Luke Havergal," "Richard Cory," "The Growth of 'Lorraine,' " and "The Mill"), its thematic concerns are typically Robinson's: the interdependence of understanding and compassion, and the difficulty of knowing another person. Robinson wants us to understand the factors that lead to suicide and to have compassion for the victims. It should be remembered that, in Robinson's time, suicide was looked upon much more harshly and with much less understanding of the causal factors than it is today.

"How Annandale Went Out" is an English sonnet in which Robinson once again deliberately withholds information in order to make the impact of the poem more powerfully felt. It is also one of his sonnets that expands the range of the form by dealing with euthanasia, hardly the stuff of which sonnets were made prior to the twentieth century.

The doctor-speaker of the sonnet, which is entirely enclosed in quotation marks, is presenting the court with his reasons, however obliquely stated, for committing euthanasia in the case of Annandale, a man whose illness or injury, never identified, had reduced him from a man to a thing. The doctor refers to him in the octet as "it," "apparatus," and "wreck," terms which initially misdirect the reader but which establish the doctor's frame of mind. The doctor calls himself "Liar, physician, hypocrite, and friend," and, in the sestet, asks the court to bear in mind that he knew Annandale before misfortune reduced him to a "ruin." In addition, he asks the court to remember the "worst you know of me" and to consider his position with "a slight kind of engine," which probably refers to a hypodermic needle, the instrument with which he committed the mercy killing. He closes by saying, "You wouldn't hang me? I thought not."

This poem works so well because of the doctor's view that the entire situation of the trial is nothing less than ironic. "It is absurd," he seems to be saying, "that, given the circumstances, I should do anything other than put an end to the terrible suffering of my friend. This trial mocks the very humanitarian impulse in man." The power of the poem resides in the doctor's method of presentation. His ironic indictments, coupled with the very serious nature of the situation, generate tension; by not identifying the source of Annandale's suffering, Robinson places the focus clearly on the doctor.

It is possible that Robinson's frustrations in not being able to write successful plays or fiction led him to expend the effort that he did on his long blank verse narrative poems. They may have satisfied his need to tell a story, to dramatize at length what he so nicely accomplished in his shorter poems. The longer works, like the shorter poems, are full of troubled characters from all walks of life. In detailed observation that often is tedious and conversations that are often lifeless, Robinson presents characters on the verge of or just after a trauma. Wallace L. Anderson observes in *Edwin Arlington Robinson: A Critical Introduction* (1967) that "most of the poem[s] [are] concerned with . . . efforts to find out why. . . . It is necessary, in other words, for the characters to understand each other and themselves. Robinson's concern in the long poems is essentially the same as in the short ones."

Since they are based, however loosely at times, on the myths that constitute the Arthurian legends, *Merlin, Lancelot,* and *Tristram* must necessarily deal with formed characters, events, and eventualities; yet the characters are troubled, they court and reach disaster, and they must gain understanding. Yvor Winters, in *Edwin Arlington Robinson* (1946), remarks of Lancelot in the poem of that name: "[He] is not free, because of the Light; that is, because he has acquired understanding which he before had lacked, and of understanding one cannot divest oneself." With some exceptions understandably made for the Arthurian poems, Robinson's characters, whether in the longer poems or in the superior shorter ones, are often the maimed, the outcast, and the forgotten of society. While many are able to endure their situations stoically, others cannot and, as a result, choose antisocial behavior. For all, the poet has compassion, and he asks that of his readers, too.

Other literary forms · Early in his literary career, well before he gained prominence as a poet, Edwin Arlington Robinson wrote a number of short stories that he planned to incorporate in a volume entitled *Scattered Lives.* The stories do not survive, nor does the novel he tried his hand at writing some years later, but the twenty-six pieces of extant prose were collected by Richard Cary in *Uncollected Poems and Prose of Edwin Arlington Robinson* (1975). Of interest primarily for what they reveal of the life of this most private man, these undistinguished prose pieces include essays, autobiographical sketches, introductions to books, and like matter.

It was in drama, particularly in the years 1906 to 1913, that Robinson hoped to make an impression as some of his New York friends had in their attempts to revitalize the theater. Robinson did not relinquish the hope that he could achieve moderate success with his plays until 1917, when he finally recognized that his very considerable skills as a poet were not compatible with those required for the theater. His two published plays—*Van Zorn* (1914) and *The Porcupine* (1915)—were ineffective. The former was produced, however, in February, 1917, by an amateur group that used the facilities of a Brooklyn YMCA. It had a run of seven days.

Robinson was a prolific letter writer. Some of his letters have been collected in three major editions: *Selected Letters of Edwin Arlington Robinson* (1940), compiled by Ridgely Torrence with the assistance of several of the poet's friends; *Untriangulated Stars: Letters of Edwin Arlington Robinson to Harry de Forest Smith, 1890-1905* (1947), edited by Denham Sutcliffe; and *Edwin Arlington Robinson's Letters to Edith Brower* (1968), edited by Richard Cary. The letters that interest the student of Robinson the most are those to Harry de Forest Smith, a close friend from Gardiner, Maine, to whom the poet, during a very difficult time in his life, expressed in an uncharacteristically open fashion his thoughts and feelings on a number of subjects, including his literary likes and dislikes, his own struggles as a writer, his years at Harvard, and his cultural growth.

Select works other than poetry

DRAMA: *Van Zorn*, pb. 1914; *The Porcupine*, pb. 1915.

NONFICTION: *Selected Letters of Edwin Arlington Robinson*, 1940; *Untriangulated Stars: Letters of Edwin Arlington Robinson to Harry de Forest Smith, 1890-1905*, 1947; *Edwin Arlington Robinson's Letters to Edith Brower*, 1968.

MISCELLANEOUS: *Uncollected Poems and Prose of Edwin Arlington Robinson*, 1975.

Ronald Moran

Bibliography · Many secondary sources attempt to put Robinson's poetry into some greater perspective. These include Hyatt H. Waggoner, *American Poets from Puritans to the Present*, 1984, which describes Robinson's works in relation to the totality of American literature, and Kenneth Pobo, "Edwin

Arlington Robinson: Atlantis D.O.A. in Maine," *Pleiades* 13 (1993), which discusses the relationship of Maine to Robinson's works. Steve Kerby, "Robinson's 'Hillcrest,' " *Explicator* 51 (1993), discusses this one work's poetic structure and relationship with Romanticism; Glorianna Locklear, "Robinson's 'The Mill,' " *Explicator* 51 (1993), presents Robinson's treatment of the imagination of his female characters; and Carol Cedar Amelincks, "Death, Darkness, Desolation: Native House-Imagery in the Poems of E. A. Robinson," *University of Mississippi Studies in English* 8 (1990), discusses the use of house imagery as Robinson's vehicle for addressing death and darkness. Two works which present good introductions to and descriptions of Robinson's renditions of the Arthurian tales are Rebecca Cochran, "Edwin Arlington Robinson's Morgan Le Fay: Victim or Victimizer?" *Platte Valley Review* 19 (1991), and Valerie Lagorio and Mildred Leake Day, eds., *King Arthur Through the Ages*, vol. 2, 1990.

THEODORE ROETHKE

Born: Saginaw, Michigan; May 25, 1908
Died: Seattle, Washington; August 1, 1963

Poetry · *Open House*, 1941 · *The Lost Son and Other Poems*, 1948 · *Praise to the End!*, 1951 · *The Waking: Poems 1933-1953*, 1953 · *Words for the Wind*, 1958 · *I Am! Says the Lamb*, 1961 · *Sequence, Sometimes Metaphysical*, 1963 · *The Far Field*, 1964 · *The Collected Poems of Theodore Roethke*, 1966

Achievements · A number of critics consider Theodore Roethke and Robert Lowell to be the most important poets of the postwar generation. Although Roethke's achievement with traditional forms, such as the difficult villanelle, is impressive, he will be remembered primarily for his longer poems, the series of "sequences" in which he broke new ground by forging a unique poetic voice that conveys the intensity and complexity of his emotional, psychological, and spiritual struggles. Roethke created a new style in which one finds a kind of "psychic short hand," to borrow the poet's phrase. With the telescoping and distortion of images, the striking juxtaposition of the commonplace and the bizarre, he evokes a variety of states of consciousness under great stress, including those of the child, the mentally ill, and the mystic. Influenced by William Wordsworth, Walt Whitman, and William Butler Yeats, he explores the depths of the psyche and captures the associative movement of the mind.

Roethke received many honors and awards throughout his career, including two Guggenheims (1945, 1950), the Tietjens Prize (1947), the *Poetry* Magazine Award (1951), the Levinson Prize (1951), and the American Academy of Arts and Letters Award (1952). Yet he did not receive widespread recognition until the publication of *The Waking: Poems 1933-1953*, which won the Pulitzer Prize for poetry in 1953. The last decade of the poet's life was a period in which he received his most prestigious awards and attracted the attention that he so much desired. *Words for the Wind*, new poems, together with a selection of poems from previous volumes, won the National Book Award and the Bollingen Prize in *Poetry* as well as five other awards. *The Far Field* brought him a second National Book Award. Roethke's reputation has been steadily increasing since 1953. His poems have been translated into many foreign languages and there have been a number of critical books and many articles published on his work.

Biography · Theodore Huebner Roethke was born in Saginaw, Michigan, on May 25, 1908, to Otto Roethke and Helen Huebner Roethke. With his brother Charles, Otto Roethke owned an enormous greenhouse consisting of several buildings enclosing 250 thousand square feet under glass. The young Roethke was fascinated by his father's gigantic plant kingdom, and the greenhouse world would later become a literary storehouse of poetic images for the adult poet. In his fifteenth year, however, his ordered life was shattered. After his father and Charles quarreled, the greenhouse was sold. Charles committed suicide several months later, and shortly after that, Otto died of cancer, suffering greatly before his death. Otto's strong influence on his son can be seen in the poetry.

The first member of his family to attend college, Roethke was graduated from the University of Michigan at Ann Arbor in 1929. He spent one term at the University of Michigan Law School and then in 1930 transferred to the graduate school, where he studied English for two terms. Then he did graduate work at Harvard and decided to abandon career possibilities in law and advertising in order to become a poet.

In 1931, *The New Republic* and *The Sewanee Review* published Roethke's poems. After teaching English at Lafayette College, Pennsylvania, from 1931 to 1935, he accepted a position at Michigan State College in East Lansing. During the 1935 fall term, he suffered his first attack of a manic-depressive disorder that was to haunt him for the rest of his life. These mental breakdowns typically lasted from one to six months.

When Michigan State College failed to renew his contract, he accepted a position at Pennsylvania State College from 1936 to 1943 and again for one year in 1948. In 1941, his first volume of poetry, *Open House*, received praise from the critics. Because of his mental illness, he was not drafted during World War II but taught from 1943 to 1946 at Bennington College, Vermont. In 1947 he accepted an associate professorship at the University of Washington in Seattle and was promoted to professor the next year. The University of Washington was to be his academic affiliation for the remainder of his life; here he wrote his best poetry, taught courses on "The Writing of Verse" and "Types of Contemporary Poetry," and attracted many fine students, a number of whom became poets themselves.

In 1953 Roethke married a former student, Beatrice Heath O'Connell, and published *The Waking: Poems 1933-1953*, which brought him the critical attention that he had been eagerly awaiting. During the next decade, he published several more volumes and his reputation grew. He died of a heart attack in 1963.

Analysis · Theodore Roethke can be best understood as a poet in the tradition of nineteenth century English and American Romanticism. His early poetry of the 1940's and 1950's has some significant similarities to that of the English Romantic poets, especially William Wordsworth and John Keats, while his later poetry, especially "North American Sequence," owes a large debt to Walt Whitman. In general, one can see a number of essential Romantic characteristics in his poetry. Although he often objectifies his feelings in concrete images, he also directly expresses emotion. Feeling over analytical reason, spontaneity over logic, exuberance over calculated thinking can be seen throughout his verse; dancing, singing, and jubilant exclaiming are ubiquitous.

Roethke's subject is that of the Romantics—the exploration of the mind or "imagination." While his voyage into the depths of his own mind is, at times, terrifying, it has positive consequences. The imagination's repeated attempts to affirm itself in the face of threatening reality is a constant ritual and a source of tension in Roethke's work. Often the imagination can transform the external world, at least momentarily, and the poet feels redeemed.

Nature functions in Roethke's poetry in a particularly Romantic fashion. He writes of nature not to achieve an objective perception of it or a lyrical description of its beauty, but as a way to attain a more profound awareness, a "vernal wisdom." Nature takes a variety of forms in his poetry; it mirrors the emotional vicissitudes of the poet. It may be vindictive or affirmative to the point that the poet merges momentarily with it. He does make clear, however, that dissolving one's identity and merging with nature is an uncommon experience, for humankind has a keen awareness of its separateness that is very difficult to ignore. In "Moss Gathering," the poet as a young boy sorrowfully realizes his separateness from the primordial order of nature when he digs up a loose carpet of green moss.

While Roethke is an affirmative poet who sees the process of becoming as ultimately joyful, there is a Keatsian ambivalence in his work. The beautiful and the grotesque, the joyful and the painful are inextricably related. Even "Dinky," one of his "Poems for Children," has a macabre quality fused with its lightheartedness.

Finally, not only Roethke's sensibility but also his style is Romantic. While his style displays a number of Romantic characteristics, such as spontaneity, direct expression of emotion, and intuitive perceptions, the most important characteristic is its meditative quality. As in the important works of Wordsworth and Keats, Roethke's poetry progresses associatively, according to the discursive movement of the mind, not according to the dictates of logic. In short, his best work mirrors the meanderings of the imagination, or to paraphrase him, the goal is to capture the movement of the mind itself.

Roethke has many attributes in common with Wordsworth, who wrote meditative poetry in which the interaction between the mind and the natural world is the central preoccupation. Both poets reveal an aspiring quality in their work; both use simple language; both rely on recollections of childhood as a source of their poetry and a key to their perception of the mystery of the human condition. In *The Prelude* (1850) Wordsworth similarly explains his strange experiences—"that calm delight/ Which, if I err not, surely must belong/ To those first born affinities that fit/ Our new existence to existing things" (see Book I, 11, lines 543-557). Sometimes both poets seem to be expressing animism: "Every flower/ Enjoys the air it breathes" (Wordsworth's "Lines Written in Early Spring," 11, lines 10-11). This Wordsworthian image of natural phenomenon "breathing" appears often in Roethke's poetry. In fact, he takes the idea to its logical conclusion—stones breathing. Yet it is unlikely that either poet really believed that nature and inanimate objects were endowed with sentient life. Both were realistic poets who depended heavily on precise observation. Significantly, Roethke seems to have borrowed Wordsworth's notion of the importance of the "eye close on the object," or as Wordsworth wrote in the Preface to *Lyrical Ballads* (1800), "I have at all times endeavored to look steadily at my subjects."

The mind enmeshed in nature can be seen in the poetry of Keats and Roethke, and both poets describe the mind in similar metaphoric fashion. Roethke writes of "The leafy mind, that long was tightly furled,/ Will turn its private substance into green,/ And young shoots spread upon our inner world" (*Collected Poems*, p. 11); Keats of "some untrodden region of my mind/ Where branchéd thoughts, new grown with pleasant pain . . ." ("Ode to Psyche," 11, lines 51-52). Keats's oxymoronic last phrase suggests the contraries of existence with which both Roethke and Keats wrestle throughout their work. Mutability is a painful reality that is finally accepted and affirmed. Life is viewed as process.

"The Visitant" (*Collected Poems*, p. 100) is Roethke's "La Belle Dame sans Merci," although here the awakened speaker is not so "alone and palely loitering" as Keats's knight; he is also more easily reconciled to his situation than Keats's knight, and the evanescent tone and the delicate evocation of the landscape is in direct contrast to the stark images of Keats's poem. Nevertheless, despite the difference in style in these two poems, there are significant stylistic affinities between the authors. Both use sensuous, suggestive imagery that conveys the complex vicissitudes of the emotions. In their works one sees subtle shifts of feeling and emotionally charged language that works toward a strong identification with external reality.

In Roethke's later poetry Whitman is a strong influence, and he acknowledges this fact in both his poetry and his letters. He borrows Whitman's techniques, especially his cataloging and his free-verse style, his "loose line," in Roethke's phrase. In his long poems, such as "North American Sequence," one finds Whitman's playfulness, irony, and comic relief; like Whitman, Roethke realized that these qualities are necessary in a long work in which it is impossible to maintain a single tone.

Roethke was also influenced by Whitman's mysticism. In "North American Sequence" there is the Whitmanesque desire to achieve a becoming that is not self-conscious—in which the poet tries to dissolve his self, to merge with the landscape. Both poets try to absorb and absolve the self and provide the necessary harmony that the world can never provide. There is the need in both poets to be free from the body by extending it throughout the landscape.

One must be careful, however, not to overstate Whitman's influence. While Whitman's catalogs are often mundane lists, Roethke's are not; rather, he seems to be borrowing nature's rhythm and applying it to the human realm. In general, Roethke does not have that tone of massive innocence that dominates Whitman's poetry. Roethke harmonizes the landscape, makes it part of him, but there is the feeling that it can be done for him alone.

Roethke's poetry developed from his early conventional verse with its regular meter and rhyme to the later innovative poetry with its associative, free-verse style. In his first collection, *Open House*, there are abstract, rhetorical poems as well as sensuous, pictorial ones. The poems of this volume are traditional in form and content, and Roethke does not speak with a unique voice, as he does in his subsequent work. "The Prayer" is a typical early poem with its closed couplets, regular rhythm, and slightly ribald humor. "The Premonition" has lucid images that take on symbolic power: "Hair on a narrow wrist bone" suggests a father's mortality. Minute observation of detail in "Interlude" also takes on symbolic significance. "Mid-Country Blow" shows the power of the imagination that can so dominate the senses that the poet still hears the "sound of the sea" even after his eye has proved his vision false. The poem is reminiscent of many of William Carlos Williams' poems, in which a banal scene is transformed into a vivid experience of near revelation. "The Bat" portrays a deliberate correspondence between the man and the animal realms; "When mice with wings can wear a human face" suggests a mysterious horror in which humankind participates. In contrast, D. H. Lawrence's poem by the same name emphasizes humankind's separateness from the demoniac bat's universe.

"Idyll" can be taken as the representative poem of the first volume. The gulf between complacency and minatory reality is evoked by the contrast of the sleeping town and the encroaching unnamed "terror." The poem is divided into three stanzas with a rhyme scheme that creates a sense of regularity broken only in the final line. The "we" of the poem is meant to draw the reader into the work, while the present tense emphasizes the immediacy of the poem's situation. The slow rhythm conveys the sense of the inexorable encroaching darkness.

The first stanza depicts a scene in which something is "amiss." A child's tricycle inexplicably "runs crazily," evoking a mood of innocence being menaced. The second line describes the representative man of the sleeping town. He is completely self-absorbed, a stumbling drunk who talks to himself. In stanza two the darkness envelops the "well-groomed suburban town." "Creeps" suggests a bestial presence that the town, "indifferent to dog howls" and "the nestling's last peep," refuses to acknowledge. Like a drunk of the first stanza, the people of the town exist in a self-satisfied state. The final stanza evokes a surrealistic scene—the world is dissolving in "the black revolving shadow" as a far-off train "blows its echoing whistle once." The "unmindful" people go to sleep in their houses precariously located at the "edge of a meadow." The failure of rhyme and the monosyllabic finality of "guns" in the last line emphasize the disconcerting contrast between the complacent town and threatening external reality.

The Lost Son and Other Poems breaks new ground with the "greenhouse poems" and the longer associative poems that form the last section of the volume. These longer associative poems become part of a sequence in the next volume, *Praise to the End!* The title of this later volume is taken from an obscure passage of Wordsworth's *The Prelude* (I, lines 340-350) and provides an important clue to Roethke's basic intention in his volumes of poetry of 1948 and 1951. Wordsworth suggests in this passage of *The Prelude* that the mind can order into a meaningful whole disparate, painful experiences of the past. Like Wordsworth, Roethke believes that the individual can create his identity only after he has plumbed the depths of his psyche, even though this interior journey might be terrifying and could at times lead one perilously close to madness. In this sequence, which focuses upon the psychological development of the child and the spiritual regeneration of the adult, Roethke uses a unique style similar to that of the shorter "greenhouse poems."

"Root Cellar" is a representative greenhouse poem and clearly reveals Roethke's method. The "poem" evokes the paradoxical situation in which the remarkable vitality of natural life seems threatening to the self. The fecund realm of this strange plant life is not a human one; no human could exist in this thriving subterranean world. The cellar represents both womb and tomb, fecundity and destruction. The alliteration in the first three lines stresses the contrary pulls of the life force (evoked by the vitality of the bulbs breaking out of their boxes) and the death wish (evoked by the darkness). The ambivalent nature of the scene is further emphasized by the description of the growing plants in sexual imagery that has negative connotations: "Hunting for chinks in the dark" and "lolling obscenely." As the poet closely observes the procreative forces of nature, he becomes keenly aware of the noxious odor that accompanies vital growth. The sixth line—"And what a congress of stinks!—" divides the poem. Next follows an accumulation of details, stressing the richness and rankness of the plants. Life is seen as an irreversible bursting forth; even the dirt appears to be breathing at the end.

In short, the self feels attracted to and threatened by this subterranean world. The "greenhouse poems" remind one of some of D. H. Lawrence's poems in which he is seeking his primeval self, his deepest being that remains submerged in the primitive regions of nature. The problem for both Roethke and Lawrence is that while humans want to recapture the primal mystery, they feel alienated from their spiritual and physical origins.

The Waking contains a selection from Roethke's previous volumes as well as new poems, some of which owe a large debt to Yeats, as Roethke himself admits. The title poem, however, does not reveal Yeats's influence; with its series of paradoxes and its Wordsworthian exuberance, it might be considered a metaphysical-romantic hybrid. This much-anthologized poem is not only one of the most difficult in Roethke's canon but also one of his best.

"The Waking" is a villanelle and thus is divided into five tercets and a concluding quatrain; it systematically repeats lines one and three of the first tercet throughout the work. The lines are end-stopped, and the intricate rhyme scheme links the stanzas together. The rhyme scheme and the steady, lofty rhythm create a sense of inexorable movement.

The structure and rhythm of the poem perfectly fit the content. The first four stanzas alternate two paradoxical truths that the work expresses: "I learn by going where I have to go" and "I wake to sleep, and take my waking slow." In the final stanza these two paradoxes are repeated in the last two lines. Though seemingly the opposites of each other, both suggest an acceptance of the inevitable—more specifically, they suggest an acceptance of mortality amid the flux of everyday existence.

Roethke suggests that underlying the chaos of existence is a fundamental unity. The series of oppositions, paradoxes, and seemingly unrelated statements in the poem are deliberately utilized by the poet to demonstrate an underlying unity. The interwoven rhythm and the repetition link the dissimilar elements together. The intricate form of the poem itself, with its wide-ranging content, suggests that there is coherence in the flux of existence—if one would only allow oneself to become aware of it.

In this poem the self has come to terms with the human condition. In addition to conveying the tone of jubilant resignation, the repetition in the work emphasizes the poet's intense awareness and acceptance of identity. "I wake," "I feel," "I learn," "I hear" are the beginnings of lines. In the middle line of each of the first five stanzas, the poet unfailingly expresses acceptance. Although he feels the presence of death, he can affirm his situation.

Stanza four, the most obscure section of the poem, takes this feeling of affirmation to a mystical point. "Light takes the Tree; but who can tell us how?" The evocation of transcendence is followed by doubts about whether a human can attain it, and the answer to the question is as enigmatic as the original question that prompted it: "The lowly worm climbs up the winding stair." This response is ambiguous, suggesting the procreative power as well as mutability, affirmation as well as negation. While the lowest creature ascends to the heights (a spiral tree is a common image of the transcendent in Roethke), humankind paradoxically becomes aware of its transitory nature.

At the end of the work, the poet exhorts his reader to "take the lively air." The concluding rhyme (slow/go) breaks the rhythm and creates a sense of finality. The poet has accepted the fact that he will die, yet he realizes that his awareness of his imminent death has made him alive to the possibilities of existence and allowed him a glimpse of the eternal. The final note is one of celebration.

Words for the Wind is Roethke's best single volume. The best parts of the work are the largest section entitled "Love Poems" and the final section, the sequence of five poems entitled "Meditations of an Old Woman." These two sections reveal a new development in Roethke's poetry. "Meditations of an Old Woman" represents the poet's most impressive achievement in capturing the labyrinthine movement of the mind, but the length and complexity of the sequence allows only a few brief comments here on Roethke's remarkable innovations in this mode. The powerful, tormented sensibility evident in the sequence is expressed in a vivid and complex style characterized by subtle tonal changes, comparisons of past and present, recurring symbols, patterns of imagery, and repetition of key words, to name only the most important. The compression of imagery and the intense lyrical quality of the work resemble Keats's odes, while the meditative sequence as a whole has the expansiveness of Wallace Stevens' "variations on a motif."

There are a number of different kinds of love poems in *Words for the Wind*, and they represent an achievement in style of nearly the magnitude of "Meditations of an Old Woman." "The Dream" presents an odd mixture of the sensual and the ethereal. In "Words for the Wind" the poet sings of his communion with his lover. In fact, this title poem evokes an evanescent sensual love similar to that in Denise Levertov's "Our Bodies," although Roethke is much more ethereal than Levertov. In "The Sententious Man" the attitude toward the self and the world is ambivalent. Spiritual emptiness is a formidable threat in these poems, and much of the time there is no separation of the "kiss" and the "abyss." Feeling alienated, the self strives for communion and love.

Roethke vividly expresses the awareness of existential nothingness in "The Renewal": "I paw the dark, the shifting midnight air." Yet the lost self may be found again, for there is the possibility of rebirth in the morning when the poet experiences a mystical identification with the inanimate world: "I touched the stones, and they had my own skin." The constriction of the self is being overcome. "The whole motion of the soul lay bare," the poet says, after he sees the "rubblestones begin to stretch."

In Roethke's final volume, *The Far Field*, he becomes very mystical. Total dissolution of the self is often the goal; it can be seen in the abstract poems of *Sequence, Sometimes Metaphysical*, in the love poems, in the "Mixed Sequence" poems, and in the "North American Sequence." In this latter volume Whitman's influence is particularly evident. Whitman sees death as rejuvenating, and sometimes he describes it erotically or maternally. Like Whitman, Roethke continually, almost ritualistically, discovers death and the beneficent quality inherent in nature. One loses one's identity to the point that he or she is consumed—death is the final culmination of all growth.

Despite its power, the "North American Sequence" does not break new ground, for it is very similar in technique to "Meditations of an Old Woman." *Sequence, Sometimes Metaphysical* is a more original work. First published in 1963 in a limited edition of 330 copies by the Stone Wall Press (Iowa City, Iowa), it came to form the concluding section of *The Far Field*, Roethke's final work. It is an appropriate culmination of the poet's career, examining in an innovative style the recurring themes in his canon—the relationship of the imagination to reality; the possibility of transcendence and the mystical annihilation of consciousness; and the search for identity.

"In a Dark Time," the most difficult and probably the best poem of the sequence, focuses upon these themes.

The poem bluntly asks Roethke's obsessive question: "Which I is *I*?" There is no simple answer. Stanza one suggests that the inner "eye" of the imagination paradoxically begins to see "in a dark time," as the despairing poet probes the primordial depths of the psyche. A series of metaphors of the poet's spiritual journey follows. He meets his "shadow," his other self, in the "deepening shade," the ever-darkening journey into the night regions of the soul. The poet exists in an in-between time—he exists between the extremes of the heron, a bird associated with the earth and the sea, and the wren, a bird of the air, as well as between the beasts of the hill and the serpents of the den.

Stanza two suggests that "madness" can be regarded as the spirit's visionary perception as well as the ultimate fragmentation of the psyche. The illogical events of an intrinsically meaningless world are at odds with the spirit's quest, and consequently the poet has known "the purity of pure despair." Here "pure" suggests completeness as well as visionary intensity. "Pinned against a sweating wall" stresses the acuteness of the poet's spiritual torment. Yet this torment, which is both visionary perception and disintegration of the imaginative mind, leaves the poet in confusion: Is he ascending to the ethereal heights or descending to the ignorant depths? He cannot be certain whether he is heading toward constriction in the depths or freedom on the heights, and thus he is left on the threshold.

In stanza three, Roethke states the method by which he works—"A steady storm of correspondences!" Connections between inner and outer worlds occur. "Storm," "A night flowing with birds, a ragged moon" suggest the difficult obstacles that the poet must overcome on his spiritual journey in which he hopes to create a new identity—it is a hope that can become a reality only by the eradication of the conscious ego. After the painful "Death of the self in a long tearless night," the supernatural emerges out of the everyday. The imagination has transformed mundane reality; in the light of the common day, midnight has come "again." Midnight is a magical time for Roethke, the brink of visionary transcendence; "again" suggests that this visionary state has occurred before—perhaps it refers to that time of spiritual unity in childhood when one does not feel estranged from nature.

In stanza four Roethke suggests that it is necessary to descend into the darkness to attain inner illumination. On the brink of transcendence as well as insanity, he cannot reach a transcendent realm and thus remains pondering his identity on the threshold, looking upward. Finally, the soul does complete its journey. Although the poet has fallen to the depths of despair, he now "climbs" out. The poet eradicates his excessively self-conscious ego and attains a heightened awareness in which his sense of estrangement from the external world is overcome.

In the poetry of Roethke, the Romantic problem of the relationship of the self to external reality becomes an obsessive concern. The attempt to overcome the age-old romantic dichotomy between the self and the world can be seen throughout his work, from the earliest poetry to the posthumous volume, *The Far Field.* Roethke searches for his true identity amid the chaos of modern life. The supposition behind this quest is that the mundane world is intrinsically meaningless, and therefore the poet must affirm reality by his imagination. The mind must endow the external world with meaning or the poet walks a never-ending tightrope over the abyss, always a step away from despair and madness.

For Roethke, the mind is the most efficacious defense against the cold multiplicity of the modern world because it can create order and because it fuses inner and outer worlds. When the mind achieves a complete identification with the external world, the tension between the self and the world dissipates. To achieve this identification is extremely difficult; but the heroic task of the modern poet, Roethke believed, is to make the attempt.

Other literary forms · Theodore Roethke devoted most of his energy to his poetry. Ralph J. Mills, however, has filled one small volume, *On the Poet and His Craft: Selected Prose of Theodore Roethke* (1965), with Roethke's essays and reviews. He has also edited *The Selected Letters of Theodore Roethke* (1968). In *Straw for the Fire: From the Notebooks of Theodore Roethke, 1943-1963* (1972), David Wagoner has selected and edited revealing passages from Roethke's 277 working notebooks and 8,306 loose sheets. All three of these books are very useful in understanding Roethke's difficult poetry, for the poet speaks about his own work as well as about poetry in general.

Select works other than poetry

NONFICTION: *On the Poet and His Craft: Selected Prose of Theodore Roethke,* 1965 (Ralph J. Mills, Jr., editor); *The Selected Letters of Theodore Roethke,* 1968 (Mills, editor); *Straw for the Fire: From the Notebooks of Theodore Roethke, 1943-1963,* 1972 (David Wagoner, editor).

Allan Chavkin

Bibliography · In the years following Roethke's death, many worthwhile biographical and critical resources on Roethke and his work have been published. The first full-length biography is Allan Seager's *The Glass House: The Life of Theodore Roethke*, 1968. Additional references include Edward Buell Hungerford, *Poets in Progress: Critical Prefaces to Ten Contemporary Americans*, 1962; Ralph J. Mills, *Theodore Roethke*, 1963; Richard Kostelanetz, ed., *On Contemporary Literature: An Anthology of Critical Essays*, 1964; Arnold Stein, ed., *Theodore Roethke: Essays on the Poetry*, 1966; William J. Martz, *The Achievement of Theodore Roethke: A Comprehensive Selection of His Poems with a Critical Introduction*, 1966; Karl Malkoff, *Theodore Roethke: An Introduction to the Poetry*, 1966; Ursula Genug Walker, *Notes on Theodore Roethke*, 1968; James Dickey, *Babel to Byzantium: Poets and Poetry Now*, 1968; Jerome Mazarro, ed., *Modern American Poetry: Essays in Criticism*, 1970; William Heyen, comp., *Profile of Theodore Roethke*, 1971; James R. McLeod, *Roethke: A Manuscript Checklist*, 1971; James R. McLeod, *Theodore Roethke: A Bibliography*, 1973; John Vernon, *The Garden and the Map: Schizophrenia in Twentieth Century Literature and Culture*, 1973; Richard Allen Blessing, *Theodore Roethke's Dynamic Vision*, 1974; Rosemary Sullivan, *Theodore Roethke: The Garden Master*, 1975; and Jenijoy LaBelle, *The Echoing Wood of Theodore Roethke*, 1976.

MURIEL RUKEYSER

Born: New York, New York; December 15, 1913
Died: New York, New York; February 12, 1980

Poetry · *Theory of Flight*, 1935 · *U. S. 1*, 1938 · *A Turning Wind: Poems*, 1939 · *Wake Island*, 1942 · *Beast in View*, 1944 · *The Green Wave*, 1948 · *Elegies*, 1949 · *Orpheus*, 1949 · *Selected Poems*, 1951 · *One Life*, 1957 · *Body of Waking*, 1958 · *Waterlily Fire: Poems, 1935-1962*, 1962 · *The Outer Banks*, 1967 · *The Speed of Darkness*, 1968 · *Twenty-nine Poems*, 1972 · *Breaking Open: New Poems*, 1973 · *The Gates*, 1976 · *The Collected Poems of Muriel Rukeyser*, 1978 · *Out of Silence: Selected Poems*, 1992.

POETRY TRANSLATIONS: *Selected Poems*, 1963 (of Octavio Paz); *Sun Stone*, 1963 (of Paz); *Selected Poems*, 1967 (of Gunnar Ekelöf; with Leif Sjoberg); *Early Poems, 1935-1955*, 1973 (of Paz); *Brecht's Uncle Eddie's Moustache*, 1974; *A Mölna Elegy*, 1984 (of Ekelöf)

Achievements · With the publication of *Theory of Flight* in the Yale Series of Younger Poets in 1935, Muriel Rukeyser began a long and productive career as a poet and author. Her work also earned for her the first Harriet Monroe Poetry Award (1941), a Guggenheim Fellowship (1943), the Copernicus Award and Shelley Memorial Award (1977), an honorary D.Litt. from Rutgers, and membership in the National Institute of Arts and Letters. She also won the Swedish Academy Translation Award (1967) and the Anglo-Swedish Literary Foundation Award (1978) for her translations.

While Rukeyser has been linked to W. H. Auden, Stephen Spender, and other political poets, her work more clearly evolves from that of Ralph Waldo Emerson, Herman Melville, and Walt Whitman. From Emerson and the Transcendental tradition, she developed her organic theory of poetry, from Melville, her poetry of outrage. From Whitman, however, she obtained perhaps her most distinguishing characteristics: her belief in possibility, her long, rhythmic lines, her need to embrace humanity, and her expression of the power and beauty of sexuality. Her feminist views link her also with Denise Levertov and Adrienne Rich, while her experimentation with the poetic line and the visual appearance of the poem on the page remind one at times of May Swenson.

Although Rukeyser's work has been relatively well regarded, she has received little critical attention. Yet the quality and quantity of her work and the integrity of her feminist and mythic vision suggest that she will come to be seen as a significant figure in modern American poetry.

Biography · Muriel Rukeyser was born on December 15, 1913, in New York City, the daughter of Lawrence B. Rukeyser, a cofounder of Colonial Sand and Stone, and Myra Lyons, a former bookkeeper. Her childhood was a quiet one, her protected, affluent life a source of her insistence on experience and communication in her poetry. In *The Life of Poetry* (1949), she tells of recognizing the sheltered nature of her life: "A teacher asks: 'How many of you know any other road in the city except the road between home and school?' I do not put up my hand. These are moments at which one begins to see."

Rukeyser's adult life was as eventful as her childhood was sheltered. In 1933, at age nineteen, she was arrested and caught typhoid fever while attending the Scottsboro trials in Alabama; three years later, she investigated at firsthand the mining tragedy at Gauley Bridge, West Virginia; and in 1936, she was sent by *Life and Letters Today* to cover the Anti-Fascist Olympics in Barcelona as the Spanish Civil War broke out around her. These crusades dramatize her intense conviction in the sanctity of human life and her desire to experience life actively, and they all served as inspiration for her poetry, fulfilling her declaration in "Poem out of Childhood" to "Breathe-in experience, breathe-out poetry."

Throughout the remainder of a life filled with traveling and speaking for causes in which she intensely believed, Rukeyser never stopped learning, teaching, and writing; she declared that she would never protest without making something in the process. The wide range of knowledge in her poetry and criticism and the large volume of poetry and prose she published testify to this fact. She attended the Ethical Culture School and Fieldston School, Vassar College, Columbia University, and the Roosevelt School of Aviation in New York City, and she learned film editing with Helen Van Dongen. Besides conducting poetry workshops at a number of different institutions, she taught at the California Labor School and Sarah Lawrence College and later served as a member of the board of directors of the Teachers-Writers Collaborative in New York.

Rukeyser made her home in New York City, except for the nine years she spent in California and the time she was traveling. She moved to California in 1945 and shortly afterward married painter Glynn Collins (although the marriage was soon annulled). Three years later, she had an illegitimate son and was disowned by her family, experiences which figure prominently in her poetry after this date. She moved back to New York in 1954 to teach at Sarah Lawrence College.

Rukeyser left Sarah Lawrence College in 1967. Although in failing health, she continued to write and protest. For the Committee for Solidarity, she flew to Hanoi in 1972 to demonstrate for peace, and later that year she was jailed in Washington, D.C., for protesting the Vietnam War on the steps of the Capitol. In 1974, as president of the American center for PEN, a society that supports the rights of writers throughout the world, she flew to Korea to plead for the life of imprisoned poet Kim Chi-Ha. Rukeyser died in New York City on February 12, 1980.

Analysis · "Look! Be : leap," Muriel Rukeyser writes in the preamble to the title poem of her first collection, *Theory of Flight*. These imperatives identify her emphasis on vision, her insistence on primary experience, and her belief in human potential. Focusing on this dictum, Rukeyser presents to her readers "the truths of outrage and the truths of possibility" in the world. To Rukeyser, poetry is a way to learn more about oneself and one's relations with others and to live more fully in an imperfect world.

The publication of *Theory of Flight* immediately marked Rukeyser as, in Stephen Vincent Benét's words, "a Left Winger and a revolutionary," an epithet she could never quite shake although the Marxists never fully accepted her for not becoming a Communist and for writing poems that tried to do more than simply support their cause. Indeed, Rukeyser did much more than write Marxist poems. She was a poet of liberty, recording "the truths of outrage" she saw around her, and a poet of love, writing "the truths of possibility" in intimate human relationships. With the conviction of Akiba (a Jewish teacher and martyr who fought to include the Song of Songs in the Bible and from whom, according to family tradition, Rukeyser's mother was descended), Rukeyser wrote with equal fervor about social and humane issues such as miners dying of silicosis, the rights of minorities, the lives of women and imprisoned poets, and about universals such as the need for love and communication among people and the sheer physical and emotional joy of loving.

Unlike many political poets, Rukeyser tried to do more than simply espouse: to protect, but also to build, to create. For Rukeyser, poetry's purpose is to sustain and heal, and the poet's responsibility is to recognize life as it is and encourage all people to their greatest potential through poetry.

Refusing to accept the negation of T. S. Eliot's *The Waste Land* (1922), Rukeyser uses images of technology and energy extensively in her early volumes to find, in a positive way, a place for the self in modern technological society, thus identifying herself with Hart Crane and with the poets of the Dynamo school. "Theory of Flight" centers on the airplane and the gyroscope. The dam and the power plant become the predominant symbols in "The Book of the Dead," in *U.S. 1*, her next collection.

U.S. 1 also contains a series of shorter, more lyrical poems entitled "Night-Music." While these poems are still strongly social in content, they are more personal and are based on what Rukeyser refers to as "unverifiable fact" (as opposed to the documentary evidence in "Theory of Flight" and "The Book of the Dead"). This change foreshadows the shifting emphasis throughout her career on the sources of power about which she writes—from machinery to poetry to the self. It is this change in conception that allowed Rukeyser to grow poetically, to use fewer of the abstractions for which many critics have faulted her, and to use instead more personal and concrete images on which to anchor her message.

This movement is evident in *A Turning Wind.* She begins to see the power and the accompanying fear of poetry, and her poetic voice becomes increasingly personal, increasingly founded in personal experience. Poetry becomes the means, the language, and the result of looking for connections or, in Jungian terms, a kind of collective unconscious. Rukeyser notices, however, that poetry is feared precisely because of its power: "They fear it. They turn away, hand up palm out/ fending off moment of proof, the straight look, poem." The fear of poetry is a fear of disclosure to oneself of what is inside, and this fear is "an indication that we are cut off from our own reality." Therefore, Rukeyser continually urges her readers to use poetry to look within themselves for a common ground on which they can stand as human beings.

The poetic sequence "Lives" (which extends through subsequent volumes as well) identifies another of Rukeyser's growing interests—"ways of getting past impossibilities by changing phase." Poetry thus becomes a meeting place of different ideas and disciplines. It is a place where the self meets the self, diving to confront unchallenged emotions in the search for truth, and a place where the self can face the world with newly discovered self-knowledge. Using the resources they discover both inside and outside themselves, people can grow to understand themselves and the world better. The subjects of the "Lives" exemplify values and traditions Rukeyser believes are important to the search.

Rukeyser's growth as a person and as a poet, then, has been a growth of the self, realizing her capabilities and her potential and, in turn, the capabilities and potential of those around her. She becomes increasingly open in her later poems, discussing her failed marriage, her illegitimate son and subsequent disinheritance, her son's exile in Canada during the Vietnam War, and her feelings about age and death. Yet while these poems may seem confessional, she is not a confessional poet such as Robert Lowell or W. D. Snodgrass. The details of her life, she tells the reader, are events she must consider from various angles as she dives within herself as Adrienne Rich goes "Diving into the Wreck," looking for the essence of being. "The universe of poetry is the universe of emotional truth," Rukeyser writes in her critical work *The Life of Poetry*, and it is the "breaking open" of her preconceived emotions to discover emotional truth that allows her to become closer to the humanity around her. "One writes in order to feel," she continues. "That is the fundamental mover."

In "Ajanta," Rukeyser makes perhaps her first statement of inner emotional truth, according to poet-critic Virginia R. Terris. In this mythic journey within the self, Rukeyser realizes that self-knowledge is the prerequisite for all other kinds of knowledge.

Yet behind her search for self-knowledge and expansion of the self into the world is her belief in the necessity of communication. The silence she experienced at home as a child had a profound effect on her, and in many early poems, such as "Effort at Speech Between Two People," communication is ultimately impossible. This same silence appears to be at the root of many of the world's problems, and Rukeyser's open outrage and inner searching are attempts to right the problem, to achieve communication. By the time she wrote "Ajanta," silence had become a positive force, allowing her the opportunity to concentrate on her journey within.

Rukeyser has at times been criticized for combining disparate images within the same poem, as in "Waterlily Fire," from her collection by the same name, but this seems unjust. Far from being unrelated elements, her images grow, change, and develop throughout a poem and throughout her poetic canon. She puts the responsibility of making connections on the reader; she gives clues but does not take all the work out of the poem: "Both artist and audience create, and both do work on themselves in creating." Rukeyser is not an easy poet, and one cannot read her poetry passively. Yet she is a rewarding poet for those who take the time to look at and listen to what she is doing.

Another distinguishing mark of Rukeyser's poetry is the numerous poetic sequences (such as "Lives") which are connected by a common situation, theme, or character. "Waterlily Fire," for example, is a group of five poems about the burning of Claude Monet's *Waterlilies* at the Museum of Modern Art in New York City. "Elegies" is a collection of ten poems extending over three volumes. "Poem out of Childhood" is a cluster of fifteen poems, of which one is also a cluster of three, centered on Rukeyser's childhood—what she learns from it and how she uses it poetically.

Rukeyser's interest in poetic sequences grew from her training as a film editor:

The work with film is a terribly good exercise for poetry . . . the concept of sequences, the cutting of sequences of varying length, the frame by frame composition, the use of a traveling image, traveling by the way the film is cut, shot, projected at a set speed, a sound track or a silent track, in conjunction with the visual track but can be brought into bad descriptive verbal things and brought into marvelous juxtapositions.

The sequence makes more apparent to readers the necessity of looking for connections among poems—recurring images, phrases, and sounds—than could separate poems.

In *The Speed of Darkness*, Rukeyser returns to her preoccupation with silence, expressing it both structurally in and as a subject. From her earliest poems, she used space within lines (often combined with a proliferation of colons) to act as a new type of punctuation—a metric rest—but in *The Speed of Darkness*, she places greater emphasis on the placement of the poem on the page to achieve this metric rest, for space on the page "can provide roughly for a relationship in emphasis through the eye's discernment of pattern."

Rukeyser's verse has often been characterized as half-poetry half-prose because of the long, sweeping, encompassing, Whitmanesque free-verse lines especially noticeable in her early poems. In *The Speed of Darkness* and later poems, however, she moves toward shorter lines and works with smaller units of meaning in order to compensate for breathing. At times, her arrangement of these poems ("The War Comes into My Room," "Mountain: One from Bryant," and "Rune," for example) approaches Swenson's iconographs in their experimentation with the visual and physical movement of the line.

Perhaps another reason for the new, shorter lines is that they are more suited for the introspective journeys of Rukeyser's later work than are the long, flowing, altruistic lines she used earlier. They also help her to control more effectively her penchant for verbosity and maintain the development of her images. Yet the length and conclusion of the later lines are not without precedent. Many of the most powerful passages in the early poems were journalistic or cinematic passages, not yet matured but still effective in their performance. "The Book of the Dead" is especially noteworthy in this respect, for it contains the seeds of the concrete image and colloquial diction fully realized later.

Rukeyser's diction also gives ample reason for labeling her poetry half-prose. Yet as startling as it may be to encounter words such as "eugenically," "silicosis," and "cantillations" in her poems, these words make the reader pay attention. She also employs words and even sounds as physical, musical, and thematic ties within and among poems in the same way other poets use rhyme and in the same way she uses image sequences.

With the variety of line length and placement evident in Rukeyser's work, it is not surprising that her canon is characterized by a rich variety of styles. Her experiments with language, line length, and rhythm easily lend themselves to experiments with different verse styles, including but extending beyond elegies, sonnets, odes, rounds, and rondels.

While she uses traditional as well as nontraditional verse patterns, she often treats even her most traditional subjects untraditionally. Because of her belief in the community of humankind, she has written many love poems, yet she approaches even the most personal subjects in an unexpected way. A notable example is "Letter, Unposted" from *Theory of Flight*, which is centered on the traditional theme of waiting for a lover. Yet it is distinguished from other such poems by the speaker's refusal to languish in love and to see nature languishing along with her. The letter remains unposted because the speaker cannot write all the traditional sentimental foolishness expected of her. Instead, as in even the bleakest situations about which Rukeyser writes, she sees the positive side: "But summer lives,/ and minds grow, and nerves are sensitized to power . . . and I receive them joyfully and live : but wait for you." The speaker rejoices in life rather than feeling sorry for herself.

Although a feminine consciousness is evident in every volume of Rukeyser's poetry, *The Speed of Darkness* also begins a new and more imperative feminist outlook. In the same way that she refused to be simply a Marxist poet, she is not simply a feminist poet. Rukeyser sees with a feminist point of view, but rather than rejecting the masculine, she retains valuable past information and revisualizes history and myth with female vitality. For example, in "Myth," one learns that Oedipus was not as smart as he thought he was; he did not answer the Sphinx's riddle correctly after all: " 'You didn't say anything about woman.'/ 'When you say Man,' said Oedipus, 'you include women / too. Everyone knows that.' She said, 'That's what / you think.' " "Ms. Lot" adds another perspective to the biblical story of Lot and his wife, and in "Painters" (from *The Gates*) she envisions a woman among the primitive cave painters.

Other poems written throughout her career on more contemporary issues reveal the strength of women while upholding their nurturing role. The mother in "Absalom" (from "The Book of the Dead") will "give a mouth to my son" who died of silicosis, and Kim Chi-Ha's mother in "The Gates" is portrayed as a pitchfork, one of Rukeyser's few uses of simile or metaphor. She also refuses to let women take the easy way out as some have been trained to do: "More of a Corpse than a Woman" and "Gradus Ad Parnassum," for example, display the vapidity of the stereotypical passive rich woman.

Yet while women are strong in Rukeyser's verse, they are still human. Sex is one of the driving forces in her work, and she frequently expresses the joys of love and sex, especially in *Breaking Open*. Significant examples are the powerful eroticism of "Looking at Each Other," the honesty of "In Her Burning" and "Rondel," and the power of sexual renewal in "Welcome from War." Giving birth is also a powerful image in many of the poems.

"The Gates," a fifteen-poem sequence organized around Rukeyser's trip to Korea to plead for the release of imprisoned poet Kim Chi-Ha, synthesizes her recurring images and messages in a final, powerful poetic statement. Like "Night-Music," this sequence is at once social commentary and personal discovery, but it takes a much stronger stance in demanding freedom of speech and assessing Rukeyser's own development as a poet in the light of Kim Chi-Ha's life.

"Breathe-in experience, breathe-out poetry" begins "Poem out of Childhood," the first poem in Rukeyser's first collection. Muriel Rukeyser wrote a poetry developing organically from personal experience and self-discovery, a poetry bringing the anguishes, miseries, and misfortunes of human beings around the world to her readers' attention, a poetry demonstrating her exhilaration with life and love. Readers cannot hide from reality in her poetry, nor can they hide from themselves. There is always the journey, but possibility always lies at its end: "the green tree perishes and green trees grow." Rukeyser's challenge to the world she left behind is found near the end of "Then" (in "The Gates"): "When I am dead, even then, / I will still love you, I will wait in these poems . . . I will still be making poems for you / out of silence." The silence and passivity against which she fought throughout her life will not triumph if her readers are alive to her words and to the world around them.

Other literary forms · In addition to her own poetry, Muriel Rukeyser published several volumes of translations (including work by the poets Octavio Paz and Gunnar Ekelöf), three biographies, two volumes of literary criticism, a number of book reviews, a novel, five juvenile books, and a play. She also worked on several documentary film scripts. The translations were exercises in writing during dry spells; the biographies, like her poetic sequence "Lives," combine her interests in the arts and sciences. The two volumes of literary criticism (along with her uncollected book reviews) are central for understanding her views concerning poetry and life.

Select works other than poetry

LONG FICTION: *The Orgy*, 1965.

DRAMA: *The Color of the Day: A Celebration for the Vassar Centennial, June 10, 1961*, pr. 1961.

NONFICTION: *Willard Gibbs*, 1942; *The Life of Poetry*, 1949; *Poetry and the Unverifiable Fact: The Clark Lectures*, 1968; *The Traces of Thomas Hariot*, 1971.

CHILDREN'S LITERATURE: *Come Back, Paul*, 1955; *I Go Out*, 1961; *Bubbles*, 1967; *Mayes*, 1970; *More Night*, 1981.

MISCELLANEOUS: *A Muriel Rukeyser Reader*, 1994.

Kenneth E. Gadomski

Bibliography · Louise Kertesz's *The Poetic Vision of Muriel Rukeyser*, 1980, provides in discursive narrative form a biography and detailed discussion of all the works, including a somewhat tendentious account of Rukeyser's reception throughout her long career as a writer. She is stronger on Rukeyser's "vision" than on her "art." Yet her discussion is full, providing a valuable bibliography of the critical reception of Rukeyser's works. Kate Daniels' well-selected edition of Rukeyser's poems, *Out of Silence*, 1992, has a useful preface. Biographical information may also be found in *Contemporary Authors*, New Revision Series, vol. 26.

NELLY SACHS

Born: Berlin, Germany; December 10, 1891
Died: Stockholm, Sweden; May 12, 1970

Poetry · *In den Wohnungen des Todes,* 1946 · *Sternverdunkelung,* 1949 · *Und niemand weiss weiter,* 1957 · *Flucht und Verwandlung,* 1959 · *Fahrt ins Staublose,* 1961 · *Noch feiert Tod das Leben,* 1961 · *Glühende Rätsel,* 1964 (parts 1 and 2 of the cycle), 1965 (part 3, in *Späte Gedichte*), 1966 (part 4 in the annual *Jahresring*) · *Späte Gedichte,* 1965 · *Die Suchende,* 1966 · *O the Chimneys,* 1967 · *The Seeker and Other Poems,* 1970 · *Teile dich Nacht,* 1971

Achievements · Sachs arrived at her characteristic poetic style late in life. She was heavily influenced by the German Romantic poets and did not consider her lyric poetry of the years prior to 1943 to be representative of her mature work, excluding those poems from the collection of 1961. Her first published book, a small volume of legends and tales published in 1921, was heavily indebted in style and content to the Swedish novelist Selma Lagerlöf. In the 1920's and 1930's, Sachs published lyric poetry in such respected newspapers and journals as the *Vossische Zeitung* of Berlin, the *Berliner Tageblatt,* and *Der Morgen,* the journal of the Jewish cultural federation.

Sachs's stylistic breakthrough came with the traumatic experience of her flight from Germany and exile in Sweden. The play *Eli* was written in 1943 but published privately in Sweden in 1951; it was first broadcast on Süddeutsche Rundfunk (South German Radio) in 1958, and had its theater premiere in 1962 in Dortmund. Acceptance of her poetry in West Germany was equally slow, partly because her main theme (Jewish suffering during World War II) stirred painful memories. In the late 1950's and 1960's, however, she was hailed as modern Germany's greatest woman poet and received numerous literary prizes. She was accepted for membership in several academies. In 1958, she received the poetry prize of the Swedish broadcasting system and in 1959, the Kulturpreis der Deutschen Industrie. The town of Meersburg in West Germany awarded her the Annette Droste Prize for women poets in 1960, and the city of Dortmund founded the Nelly Sachs Prize in 1961 and presented her with its first award. In the same year, friends and admirers published the first volume of a festschrift, followed by the second volume, *Nelly Sachs zu Ehren,* on the occasion of her seventy-fifth birthday in 1966. On October 17, 1965, she received the

Peace Prize of the German Book Trade Association, and on December 10, 1966, she was awarded the Nobel Prize for Literature. Berlin, the city where she was born and in which she had lived for nearly half a century, made her an honorary citizen in 1967. The city of Dortmund, Germany, and the Royal Library in Stockholm, Sweden, have valuable collections of her letters and transcriptions of her early poems in their Nelly Sachs Archive.

Biography · Leonie (Nelly) Sachs was born in Berlin on December 10, 1891, the only child of William Sachs, an inventor, technical engineer, and manufacturer, and his wife, Margarete (née Karger). The family lived in very comfortable financial circumstances, and Sachs was educated in accordance with the custom for daughters of the upper-middle class. Although both of her parents were of Jewish ancestry, Sachs's family had few ties with the Jewish community and did not practice their religion. Sachs attended public schools from 1897 to 1900, but for reasons of poor health was removed and received private instruction until 1903. She then attended a private secondary school for daughters of wealthy and titled families and finished her education in 1908 without any formal professional training. In the summer of that year, she fell in love with a man whose name she never revealed. That experience, which ended unhappily, escalated into a crisis, making Sachs consider suicide. The man was later killed in one of Germany's concentration camps.

For the next twenty-five years, even after the death of her father in 1930, Sachs led a sheltered and not particularly noteworthy existence. She produced some poetry, read extensively, and did watercolors, some of which have been preserved in the Nelly Sachs Ar-

The Nobel Foundation

chive in Stockholm. In 1906, Sachs received Lagerlöf's novel *Gösta Berling* (1891) as a birthday present. Her admiration for the writer resulted in a correspondence between the two, and Sachs sent Lagerlöf many of her own literary experiments. Through the intervention of Lagerlöf and the brother of the reigning Swedish king, Sachs and her mother received permission to emigrate to Sweden in 1939. Shortly after Lagerlöf's death in 1940, Sachs received orders from German authorities to appear for deportation to a work camp. Leaving all of their possessions behind, Sachs and her mother fled Germany, arriving in Stockholm on May 16, 1940. They took up residence in a small apartment in the industrial harbor area, where Sachs remained until her death in 1970.

The imagery in Sachs's later lyric poetry draws to a large extent on influences from her youth. Her father's extensive collection of rocks, gems, and fossils was a source of inspiration to her, and she continued his hobby with a collection of her own in Stockholm; not unexpectedly, the use of the stones as a cipher is very prevalent in her work "Chor der Steine" ("Chorus of the Stones"). From her father's library she was also familiar with the work of Maria Sibylla Merian, a seventeenth century entomologist and graphic artist who specialized in the study of butterflies. Sachs's poem "Schmetterling" ("Butterfly") exemplifies her metaphoric use of this and other insects in her work. In 1959, Sachs wrote that of all childhood influences upon her later works, her father's musical talent was paramount. When he played the piano during evenings after work, she frequently danced for hours to the strains of his music. In addition to her early lyric poems, which she characterized as "dance and music poems," the motif of the dance is also important in her later work.

In 1960, Sachs returned to Germany for the first time since her exile in order to receive the Annette Droste Prize. Not wishing to spend a night in Germany, she stayed instead in Zurich, traveling the short distance to Meersburg only in order to accept the honor. Hearing the German language spoken again proved to be so traumatic, however, that she experienced a "memory trip to hell." In Zurich, she met Paul Celan, another exiled poet, who invited her to his home in Paris. The meeting resulted in a continuing correspondence, but Celan was in the midst of a personal crisis as well and the relationship may have contributed to Sachs's difficulties. After her return to Stockholm, Sachs suffered a mental breakdown and was hospitalized with severe delusions of persecution. Although she worked feverishly during the next decade, she continued to suffer periodic attacks in which she imagined herself persecuted and threatened with death. Her cycle *Noch feiert Tod das Leben* (death still celebrates life) was written while she recovered in the hospital. Celan attempted to aid her recovery through an intensive, supportive correspondence which was also, however, an attempt at self-healing, inasmuch as he suffered from a similar ailment. Their poetry, beginning with Sachs's *Noch feiert Tod das Leben* and Celan's *Die Niemandsrose* (1963), shows their continuing "dialogue in poems." In the spring of 1970, Sachs became mortally ill and thus was not informed when Celan was reported missing early in April of that year. He was later found—an apparent suicide by drowning; his funeral services took place in the Cimetière Parisien near Orly, France, on the same day in May on which Sachs died in a Stockholm hospital.

Analysis · It is difficult to speak of development in Nelly Sachs's poetic works, inasmuch as she was well beyond fifty years old when she produced her first significant poems. It is true that she had published lyric poetry before the 1940's, but this early work has little in common with that of her mature years. Most of the poems from the 1920's and 1930's are thematically quite distinct from the later work, devoted to musicians such as Johann Sebastian Bach, Wolfgang Amadeus Mozart, Jean-Philippe Rameau, and Luigi Boccherini or dealing poetically with certain animals, such as deer, lambs, and nightingales. The Nelly Sachs archives in Dortmund and in Stockholm have copies of a substantial number of these early efforts.

In contrast, the work of Sachs's last twenty-five years concerns itself largely with existential problems, particularly with topics related to the Holocaust and rooted in personal experiences of flight, exile, and the death of friends. Her first collection of poems, *In den Wohnungen des Todes* (in the habitations of death), refers in its title to the Nazi death camps and is dedicated to those who perished there. It is a mistake, however, to perceive her work solely in the context of these historical events. Her topic is on a larger scale—the cycle of life itself: birth, death, rebirth—and Sachs develops various metaphors and ciphers to express the agony and the hope of this cycle.

While it is desirable to interpret Sachs's work separately from the context of specific historical events, it is almost impossible to analyze an individual poem without relying on information gained from a broader knowledge of her work. This difficulty is the result of her frequent use of ciphers, poetic images that can be "decoded" only by reference to other poems in which the same images occur. Such a cipher in Sachs's work is the stone. Its properties are chiefly those of inert matter: lack of emotion, or lifelessness. The cipher may depict human callousness, death, or desolation in different contexts, and it is related to similar poetic images such as sand and dust—decayed rock—which signify the mortal human condition.

The poem "Sinai" from the collection *Sternverdunkelung* (eclipse of the stars) contains entirely negative images of the stone. Sachs compares the ancient times of Moses, in which humanity was still in intimate contact with the divine and thus vibrantly alive, with the present state of lifelessness; there are only "petrified eyes of the lovers" with "their putrefied happiness." Recounting Moses' descent from Mount Sinai, Sachs asks: "Where is still a descendent/ from those who trembled? Oh, may he glow/ in the crowd of amnesiacs/ of the petrified!" The eyes of the lovers turned to stone signify the death both of sensibility and of sensuousness, and the inability to recreate or reproduce. It is ultimately a death of humankind. The call is for one perhaps still alive among the multitude of those dead in mind and body.

Scarcely less negative is the stone cipher in the poem "Wenn nicht dein Brunnen, Melusine" ("Melusine, If Your Well Had Not"), from *Und niemand weiss weiter:* If it were not for the possibility of transformation and escape, "we should long have passed away/ in the petrified resurrection/ of an Easter Island." Easter Island's petrified statues are merely reminders of an extinct civilization, not a resurrection from the dead. Still, the poem indicates that transformation is possible (the symbol for it is Melusine). In the poem "Chorus of the Stones," from *In den Wohnungen des Todes,* stones are, like the statues of Easter Island, venerable objects depicting the history of humankind. The stone is symbolic of all that has died, but it carries memories within it and thus is not entirely devoid of life. The last lines of the poem even offer the hope that the stone is only "sleeping," that it may come to life again: "Our conglomeration is transfused by breath./ It solidified in secret/ but may awaken at a kiss."

Three ideas in "Chorus of the Stones" suggest that death is not the final answer to life: The lifeless entity (the stone) contains memories; it is imbued with breath, a necessary element of life; and it may be awakened by an act of love. Transformation, resurrection, and transfiguration are therefore within the realm of possibility. Such a flight from lifelessness to a new beginning is nevertheless fraught with difficulties. In "Chassidische Schriften" ("Hasidic Scriptures," from *Sternverdunkelung*), Sachs writes: "And the heart of stones,/ filled with drifting sand,/ is the place where midnights are stored." "Drifting sand" is sand blown skyward by the wind; thus, while it is inert matter, it has lost this inertia momentarily on the wings of the wind. The dead has come to life. Midnight, on the other hand, represents the end of one day and the dawning of the next, a time of rebirth. Sachs contends that the stone, dead as it is, is imbued with the desire for rebirth and transubstantiation. Another possibility for the stone to attain a semblance of life is offered in "Golem Tod!" ("Golem Death!"

from *Sternverdunkelung*). There, "The stone sleeps itself green with moss." The suggestion that the stone is merely sleeping, not dead, and that it is capable of producing living matter (moss) is also an affirmation of the possibility of renewal of life after death. The most dramatic depiction of the rebirth of the dead is to be found in Sachs's poem "Halleluja" ("Hallelujah"), from the volume *Flucht und Verwandlung* (flight and metamorphosis). The poem describes a mountain rising from the sea by volcanic action. The rock is portrayed as a beloved child, the crowning glory of its mother, the ocean, as it thrusts forth from the womb to the light of day. While still embedded in the sea, the rock showed signs of sustaining life. As in "Golem Death!" with its stone covered with moss, this rock has been nurturing life. For the sea algae, birth of the rock means death, which the "winged longing" of the rock will bring about; although one form of life dies, another takes its place. These poems therefore encompass the cycle of life and death of living and inert matter on Earth.

In tracing the cipher of the stone, it is evident that the nihilism of the earlier cycles has given way to a guarded optimism in the later ones. A more traditional image of transfiguration is that of the butterfly. Its life cycle includes the apparent death of the homely caterpillar and its reemergence from the cocoon as a beautiful winged creature, and thus it is readily adaptable as a symbol of the soul's resurrection after physical death. Sachs uses the image of the butterfly within this tradition. The poem "In der Flucht" ("Fleeing," from the volume *Flucht und Verwandlung*) compares the flight of the Jews from their persecutors with the never-ending process of transformation, mutation, and metamorphosis. There is no rest and no end (no "Amen") for that which is considered mortal (sand, dust), for it experiences endless metamorphoses. The butterfly, itself a symbol of metamorphosis, will reenter the lifegiving element at its death and complete the cycle of life.

In "Butterfly," from *Sternverdunkelung*, the butterfly is depicted as a mortal creature (one made of "dust") which nevertheless mirrors the beauty of a world beyond: "What lovely hereafter/ is painted in your dust." The butterfly is a messenger of hope for those who are dying, because it is aware through its own metamorphosis that death is only sleep. The butterfly is the symbol of farewell, just as it was the symbol of the last greeting before sleep.

More obscure than the image of the butterfly are Sachs's ciphers of music and dance. The dancer appears to be able to defy gravity in graceful and effortless leaps and spins. A new image of man is created in the dance—that of emancipation from earthly limitations and acceptance into the sphere of the incorporeal. On this premise, Sachs bases her depiction of the dancer as a re-creator, savior, and emancipator from material limitations. In the poem "Sie tanzt" ("She Dances," from *Noch feiert Tod das Leben*), the dancer rescues her lover from the dead. This act of rescue is not meant to save him from physical death, for he is no longer alive; metamorphosis is her aim. This she achieves, paradoxically, by her own death: "Aber plötzlich/ am Genick/ Schlaf beünt Sie hinüber" ("But suddenly/ at the neck/ sleep bends her over"). In German, the word "over" (*hinüber*) signifies "to the other side" and thus clearly suggests death; this connotation is underscored by the image of her bending at the neck (hanging) and by the word "sleep," which Sachs frequently uses as a synonym for physical, but not spiritual, death. In the act of dancing, the dancer has liberated both the dead lover and herself. The metamorphosis has released her from life and has rescued him from death. They are united in the spiritual realm. In *Flucht und Verwandlung*, a somewhat different form of creation is discussed in the poem "Tänzerin" ("Dancer"). Here the dancer becomes the vessel for the hope of the future, and Sachs depicts with physiological clarity the birth canal for a messianic prophecy: "In the branches of your limbs/ the premonitions/ build their twittering nests." The dancer's body becomes the maternal, life-giving promise of the future.

In the poem "She Dances," the beginning and the end of life are shown to coincide at the point of metamorphosis, the dancer being the agent. The medium for transfiguration is music. The poem "O-A-O-A," in *Glühende Rätsel* (glowing enigmas), describes the rhythmic "sea of vowels" as the Alpha and Omega. Music is the means of metamorphosis: "Du aber die Tasten niederdrücktest/ in ihre Gräber aus Musik/ und Tanz die verlorene Sternschunuppe/ einen Flügel erfand für dein Leiden" ("But you pressed down the keys/ into their graves of music/ and dance the lost meteor/ invented a wing for your anguish"). The English word "keys" is ambiguous, but the German *Tasten* refers solely to the keys of a piano in this context. The graves are made of music, the transforming factor, and are being played like the keys of a piano, while dance provides the wings for the flight from the corporeal.

Finally, in the poem "In der blauen Ferne" ("In the Blue Distance," from *Und niemand weiss weiter*), the pregnant last lines combine the ciphers of stone, dust, dance, and music in the depiction of metamorphosis: "the stone transforms its dust/ dancing into music." The lifeless element needs no mediator here but performs the ritual of transubstantiation into music (release from corporeal existence) by "dancing" as "dust"—an action functionally identical to that of the drifting sand in the poem "Hasidic Scriptures."

It has frequently been assumed that Nelly Sachs is chiefly a chronicler of Jewish destiny during World War II, a recorder of death and despair.

This narrow view does not do justice to her work. Sachs's poetry has many aspects of faith, hope, and love, and need not be relegated to a specific historical event or ethnic orientation. Sachs writes about the concerns of every human being—birth, life, love, spiritual renewal, and the possibility of an existence beyond physical death. To diminish the scope of her appeal is to misunderstand her message and to misinterpret her work.

Other literary forms · Nelly Sachs published the short play, or "scenic poem," *Eli: Ein Mysterienspiel vom Leiden Israels* (1951; *Eli: A Mystery Play of the Sufferings of Israel*, 1967). Her prose works are collected in *Legenden und Erzählungen* (1921).

Select works other than poetry

SHORT FICTION: *Legenden und Erzählungen*, 1921.

DRAMA: *Eli: Ein Mysterienspiel vom Leiden Israels*, pb. 1951 (*Eli: A Mystery Play of the Sufferings of Israel*, 1967); *Zeichen im Sand: Die szenischen Dichtungen*, pb. 1962.

NONFICTION: *Paul Celan, Nelly Sachs: Correspondence*, 1995.

Helene M. Kastinger Riley

Bibliography · Lawrence L. Langer, *Versions of Survival: The Holocaust and the Human Spirit*, 1982, brilliantly illuminates the paradoxes in Sachs's verse. A. Alan Steinbach, "Nelly Sachs–Nobel Laureate," *Jewish Book Annual* 25 (1967), surveying Sachs' life and career, finds hope triumphant. Edward Alexander, *The Resonance of Dust: Essays on Holocaust Literature and Jewish Fate*, 1979, concludes that Sachs, yearning for transcendence, resists its consolations. Ehrhard Bahr, "Flight and Metamorphosis: Nelly Sachs as a Poet of Exile," in John M. Spalek and Robert F. Bell, eds., *Exile: The Writer's Experience*, 1982, argues that Sachs' meditations on exile develop a characteristic Jewish theme. Marie Syrkin, *The State of the Jews*, 1980, analyzes the distinctiveness of Sachs' artistic achievement. For in-depth discussion of her best-known play, see David Bronsen, "The Dead Among the Living: Nelly Sachs' *Eli*," *Judaism* 16 (Winter, 1967). Eli Wiesel, "Conversation with Nelly Sachs," *Jewish Heritage* 10 (Spring, 1968), offers an intimate look at the writer. See also Elisabeth Strenger, *Nelly Sachs and the Dance of Language*, 1994; Timothy Gahti and Marilyn Sibley Fries, eds., *Jewish Writers, German Literature: The Uneasy Examples of Nelly Sachs and Walter Benjamin*, 1995; and Robert Foot, *The Phenomenon of Speechlessness in the Poetry of Marie Luise Kaschnitz, Günter Eich, Nelly Sachs, and Paul Celan*, 1982.

CARL SANDBURG

Born: Galesburg, Illinois; January 6, 1878
Died: Flat Rock, North Carolina; July 22, 1967

Poetry · *Chicago Poems*, 1916 · *Cornhuskers*, 1918 · *Smoke and Steel*, 1920 · *Slabs of the Sunburnt West*, 1922 · *Selected Poems of Carl Sandburg*, 1926 · *Good Morning, America*, 1928 · *Early Moon*, 1930 · *The People, Yes*, 1936 · *Home Front Memo*, 1943 (verse and prose) · *Chicago Poems: Poems of the Midwest*, 1946 · *Complete Poems*, 1950 · *Wind Song*, 1960 · *Harvest Poems: 1910-1960*, 1960 · *Honey and Salt*, 1963 · *Breathing Tokens*, 1978 (Margaret Sandburg, editor) · *Ever the Winds of Chance*, 1983 (Margaret Sandburg and George Hendrick, editors)

Achievements · In "Notes for a Preface" to his *Complete Poems*, Carl Sandburg remarked,

> At fifty I had published a two-volume biography and *The American Songbag*, and there was puzzlement as to whether I was a poet, a biographer, a wandering troubadour with a guitar, a midwest Hans Christian Andersen, or a historian of current events whose newspaper reporting was gathered into a book *The Chicago Race Riots*.

That puzzlement has persisted since Sandburg's death in the critical reevaluations of his career. Sandburg was by turns journalist, poet, biographer, folklorist, and children's writer, and this is what makes it so difficult to assess his reputation. Was he a great poet, as Gay Wilson Allen has asked, or was he primarily a journalist and biographer? Somehow Sandburg's stature seems greater than the quality of his individual works. Certainly he was a great communicator—as writer, poet, folksinger, and entertainer—whose poetry reached out to millions of Americans, and certainly he was, like his hero, Abraham Lincoln, a great spokesman for the common man. Sandburg had a particular genius for reaching out to ordinary people and touching their lives through his poetry and song. In his public performances, one felt the power of a dynamic personality, which helped to establish the popularity of his poems.

During his lifetime, Sandburg published seven major volumes of poetry, and at his death he left enough uncollected verse for an additional posthumous volume, *Breathing Tokens*, which was edited by his daughter Margaret. Contained in these volumes are more than a thousand free-verse poems.

In *The People, Yes*, he compiled a record of American folk wisdom, humor, and truisms which Willard Thorpe called "one of the great American books." Besides his six-volume Lincoln biography, he completed biographies of his brother-in-law, the photographer Edward Steichen, and of Mary Todd Lincoln. His delightful children's books, the most popular of which remains *Rootabaga Stories* (1922), were read and admired by many adults, including the architect Frank Lloyd Wright. For many years Sandburg was a regular columnist for the *Chicago Daily News*. In 1928, he was named Harvard Phi Beta Kappa poet, and twice he won the Pulitzer Prize: in 1940, in history, for his *Abraham Lincoln: The War Years* (1939) and, in 1950, in poetry, for his *Complete Poems*. Yet for many Americans he is best recalled as the genial, white-haired folksinger and poet, the embodiment of folksy Americana.

Even though Sandburg was perhaps justly called "America's best loved poet" during his lifetime, his reputation has steadily declined since his death in 1967. Most of all he has suffered from critical neglect, and his poetry has been largely dismissed for its sameness and lack of development, its lack of poetic structure, and Sandburg's lack of control over his material. At least one critic has found merit in Sandburg's last volume, *Honey and Salt*, but the consensus now seems to be that his poetry has been overvalued. It may well be that he will be remembered most for his Lincoln biography, but that judgment waits upon a full assessment of Sandburg's poetic career.

Chronologically, Sandburg belongs with Vachel Lindsay and Edgar Lee Masters as one of the poets of the "Chicago Renaissance." Like these other writers, he was one of the "sons of Walt Whitman." Early in his career, he adopted a style of loose, rhapsodic free verse, massive detail, a line pattern of parallelism and coordination, and the idiom and cadences of ordinary American speech. At his best, he is a verse reporter—a lyrical poet of the marketplace and the factory. His *Chicago Poems* are *vers libre* sketches of the city and its inhabitants in their various moods, but his poetry is often little more than sociological description in the service of liberal ideology. More than the others of his generation, Sandburg was the poet of labor and the common man. Along with Whitman and Lincoln he held a mystical faith in "the American people." He shares Whitman's principle of inclusiveness and his "cosmic affirmations" but lacks Whitman's innate sense of organic form that gave shape to his effusions. Sandburg's Imagist techniques were noted by Amy Lowell, and some of his poems, notably "Fog," may owe something to haiku, but Sandburg never developed a consistent critical theory, and his occasional pronouncements about his work or about the nature of poetry (as in *Good Morning, America*) are for the most part unenlightening.

Sandburg was thirty-six before he enjoyed any prominence as a poet, and much of the credit for discovering and promoting his work must go to Harriet Monroe, the editor of *Poetry: A Magazine of Verse*, which she published out of Chicago beginning in 1912. Through her magazine, she promoted the poetic innovations of the Imagists and the free-verse experimentations of Ezra Pound, William Carlos Williams, Marianne Moore, and others. She recognized and encouraged the new American poetic talent of her generation, but she was especially partial to the poets of the "Chicago School." Sandburg must certainly be counted as her protégé, even though he soon found a wider audience.

Although he began as a poet, Sandburg lacked the discipline and control to master fully the art of verse. The prose poem was his natural medium, and the biography of Lincoln was a natural subject for a prairie poet reared in Illinois. Through his biography, Sandburg wished "to restore Lincoln to the common people to whom he belongs." In *Abraham Lincoln: The War Years*, his epic portrait of Lincoln virtually becomes a history of the entire Civil War era, a vast accretion of factual material which presents Lincoln the man in the context of his times. Sensitive to criticism that *Abraham Lincoln: The Prairie Years* (1926) had been too "mythic" and free in its interpretations, Sandburg was determined in *The War Years* to stick close to the historical record. Even Lincoln's major contemporaries—Ulysses S. Grant, Robert E. Lee, Jefferson Davis, and others—receive full biographical treatment. Allen Nevins praised Sandburg's historical biography for its "pictorial vividness" and "cumulative force."

Perhaps Sandburg's greatest poetry appears in the final chapters of volume four of *The War Years*, in which he describes the impact of Lincoln's death on the nation in passages of lyrical free verse that rival in their power and eloquence Whitman's great elegy, "When Lilacs Last in the Dooryard Bloom'd." With characteristic humor, Sandburg observed of his work, "Among the biographers I am a first-rate poet, and among poets a good biographer; among singers I'm a good collector of songs and among song-collectors a nice judge of pipes."

Biography · Carl Sandburg was born on January 6, 1878, in Galesburg, Illinois, the second of five children in the family of August and Clara Sandburg, Swedish immigrants of peasant stock. August Sandburg was a blacksmith's helper with the Chicago, Burlington and Quincy Railroad, and his wife kept house with the children and later took in boarders. The two had met in Illinois while Clara was working as a hotel chambermaid, and August had come to town as a section hand with the railroad. Carl had an older sister, Mary, a younger brother, Martin, and two younger sisters, Esther and Martha. Two other younger brothers died of diphtheria.

The Sandburgs were a thrifty, hardworking family, regular in their Lutheran Church attendance and conservative in politics. The elder Sandburg worked sixty hours a week at the railroad shops and spent his remaining time at home with his family. He had a reputation as a sober, dependable worker. Although both Carl's parents could read, they were not bookish and did not encourage their children's education. August Sandburg was scornful of books other than his Swedish Bible, and he never learned to read or speak English very well. His wife Clara had a better command of English and could sympathize with her son's interest in reading.

Sandburg's memories of Galesburg were of the close-knit, immigrant, working-class neighborhoods, the commemoration of the Lincoln-Douglas debate at Knox College, the pageant of General Grant's funeral procession, the excitement of the Blaine-Cleveland Presidential campaign, and the tension during the railroad strike of 1888. In his childhood autobiography, *Always the Young Strangers* (1953), Sandburg recalls playing baseball in cow pastures, walking along dusty roads to the county fair, carrying water for the elephants at the circus, and swimming in the forbidden brickyard pond. He enjoyed a typical if not always carefree Midwestern boyhood.

With seven children to be fed on his father's fourteen-cent hourly wage, Sandburg knew the pinch of childhood poverty, although his parents managed to provide the family with basic necessities. His elder sister Mary graduated from high school, but his family could not afford the same for Carl, so he left school at thirteen, after completing the eighth grade. From then on, his education came through practical experience. He would have continued in school but the extra income was needed at home. Sandburg wanted to learn a trade, but there were no openings for apprentices; as a teenager, he worked variously as a porter, newspaper boy, bootblack, bottlewasher, delivery boy, milkman, ice cutter, housepainter, and at other odd jobs. From these early job experiences came much of Sandburg's sympathy for labor and his identification with the common man. When he was nineteen, Sandburg spent a summer hoboing his way across the Midwest in boxcars, stopping in small farm towns to work for a meal or a place to sleep. He reached Denver before returning to Galesburg in the fall of 1897.

When the news of the sinking of the battleship *Maine* arrived on February 15, 1898, Sandburg enlisted as an infantryman in Company C of the Sixth Illinois Regiment of the State Militia. The men trained in Virginia and were on their way to Cuba when yellow fever broke out, and they were diverted to Puerto Rico. Along the way, Sandburg carried two books in his knapsack—an infantry drill regulation manual and a dictionary. From the army he sent back dispatches to the *Galesburg Evening Mail.* After his company had spent a month in Puerto Rico with intense heat, poor rations, and mosquitoes, Spain surrendered and the troops were mustered out in New York. By September, Sandburg was back in Galesburg with $122 in discharge pay. He decided to enroll in Lombard College as a special student.

Lombard was a small Universalist liberal arts college with a curriculum flexible enough that Sandburg could concentrate on humanities courses and avoid those he disliked, such as mathematics. Word came to him after his first year that he had been chosen for an appointment to West Point. Although Sandburg readily passed the physical examination, he failed in mathematics and grammar, so he continued at Lombard and became active in basketball, debating, drama, the college newspaper, and the yearbook. A professor there, Philip Green Wright, encouraged Sandburg's writing interests and later arranged privately to publish several of his early poetry volumes. Although he apparently enjoyed college life, Sandburg was never graduated from Lombard; in the spring of his senior year the call of the road proved irresistible, and he left school to wander again as a hobo. This time he worked his way across the country selling stereoscopic slides and absorbing the language and folklore of the people. The next four years found him restless and unwilling to settle down to any steady employment. Once, he was arrested for vagrancy in Pennsylvania and spent ten days in jail. After his release he continued west to Chicago, where he lectured and helped edit a lyceum paper.

In 1908, Sandburg met an organizer for the Social-Democratic Party in Wisconsin, who offered him a job in Milwaukee. At a party rally there, he met a young high school teacher, Lillian ("Paula") Steichen, who was home for the holidays. A shared ardent idealism and belief in socialism attracted them to each other, and by the spring of 1908, they were engaged. They married on June 15, 1908, and settled near Milwaukee. Sandburg continued to work as a party organizer and met Emil Seidel, Socialist candidate for mayor of Milwaukee. After his election, Seidel asked Sandburg to serve as his private secretary. This Sandburg did for two years before returning to newspaper work on the *Milwaukee Leader*. Meanwhile, his first daughter, Margaret, had been born in 1911, and his modest salary at the *Milwaukee Leader* no longer sufficed.

A Chicago newspaper strike in 1913 shut down the major dailies and temporarily expanded the readership of the small socialist tabloid, the *Chicago Daily World*. Sandburg was offered a job with a raise in salary and moved his family to Chicago, but when the strike ended, he lost his position. Several newspaper jobs later, he found a secure place with the *Chicago Daily News*, where he served as a special correspondent and columnist for the next fifteen years.

Meanwhile, Sandburg was writing verses at night and assembling notes for what was to become his monumental Lincoln biography. On a hunch, he submitted some of his "Chicago Poems" to *Poetry* magazine, where they were published in the March, 1914, issue and won the Levinson Poetry Prize that same year. *Poetry* editor Harriet Monroe was at first disconcerted by the boldness of the opening lines of "Chicago," but she recognized their strength and championed their free verse. At the age of thirty-six, recognition had finally come to Sandburg for his poetry. The money from the Levinson prize went to pay the hospital bills for the birth of Sandburg's second daughter, Janet, but he was still not earning enough from his poetry to support his family without his newspaper work. He remained active in the socialist movement and, along with Jack London, contributed much of the copy for the *International Socialist Review* in 1915; he became disillusioned with the socialist position on World War I, however, and eventually left the party, even though he remained liberal in his politics.

A publisher's representative for Holt, Alfred Harcourt, was so impressed with Sandburg's verse in *Poetry* that he asked to examine additional poems and persuaded his firm to publish them as the *Chicago Poems* in 1916. This began a long and cordial relationship between Sandburg and Harcourt, who later founded his own publishing firm. In 1918, Sandburg was sent to New York to cover a labor convention and while there discovered he had been chosen to travel to Sweden as a special war correspondent. His knowledge of Swedish served him well there, and he was glad of the opportunity to learn more about his cultural roots. He spent the remainder of the war in Stockholm, and while he was abroad, Holt brought out his second volume of poetry, *Cornhuskers*.

Sandburg returned to the United States a seasoned reporter and a poet with a growing reputation. In 1920, Cornell College in Iowa invited him to read from his poetry, and Sandburg made his first of many visits there, entertaining the audience with a public reading and then taking out his guitar to sing folk songs for the rest of the evening. This combination of poetry recitation and folk song fest came to be the standard Sandburg repertory on his tours and won for him many admirers. Also in 1920, his third daughter, Helga, was born, and a third poetry volume, *Smoke and Steel*, was published. *Slabs of the Sunburnt West*, another collection of verse, followed in 1922, along with *Rootabaga Stories*, a collection of children's stories that Sandburg had originally written for his daughters.

By 1923, Sandburg was deeply involved in a project that would occupy much of his time for almost the next twenty years—his multivolume Lincoln biography. The plans for the book originally grew from a conversation with Alfred Harcourt about a proposed children's biography of Lincoln, although Sandburg had been interested in Lincoln since childhood and had for some years been storing up anecdotes, stories, books, articles, and clippings about him. As the manuscript progressed, it rapidly outgrew its juvenile format and Sandburg continued it as a full-scale adult biography, written in clear, concise language. The two-volume *Abraham Lincoln: The Prairie Years* met with such immediate success that Sandburg was inspired to continue his biographical portrait in the four-volume *Abraham*

Lincoln: The War Years, which won for him the Pulitzer Prize for history in 1940. These same years had seen him publish a fifth volume of poetry, *Good Morning, America*, and *The People, Yes*, a compilation of American folk sayings, proverbs, clichés, and commonplaces.

More than anything else, Sandburg earned critical acclaim for his Lincoln biography, hailed as the "greatest biography by one American of another." Literary awards and honorary degrees were bestowed upon him, including Litt. D.'s from Yale and Harvard. In 1945, the Sandburgs moved from Michigan to "Connemara," a picturesque mountain farm in Flat Rock, North Carolina, where Mrs. Sandburg continued to raise her prize-winning goats. The 1950's saw Sandburg reap the harvest of his long and successful career. He was honored by the states of Illinois and North Carolina and asked to give a joint address before both houses of Congress on February 12, 1959, the 150th anniversary of Lincoln's birth. During the last few years of his life, Sandburg spent more and more of his time at "Connemara," surrounded by his family and his grandchildren, who called him "Buppong." He died at the age of eighty-nine on July 22, 1967, after a brief illness. After his death, tributes came from throughout the country, including a message from President Lyndon Johnson, who spoke for all Americans when he said that Sandburg ". . . gave us the truest and most enduring vision of our own greatness."

Analysis · In "The American Scholar," Ralph Waldo Emerson foresaw the conditions from which American poetry would emerge when he remarked that "I embrace the common, I explore and sit at the feet of the familiar, the low." The American poet would have to sing of "the shop, the plough, and the ledger." His subject matter would come from the world of trade and commerce and his language would be that of the common person. The democratic muse would be prosaic; there would be no sublime flights of poesy. Still, it would take a vigorous poetic imagination and a clear sense of poetic form to refine this ore to the pure metal of poetry. Otherwise the poet might well be overwhelmed by his material and slip imperceptibly from poetry to prose, from singing to talking. This is the problem with much of Carl Sandburg's verse, and it is intensified by his indifference to poetic craftsmanship and form.

Sandburg makes clear his distaste for formal poetry in his "Notes for a Preface" to his *Complete Poems*. Instead, he is interested in the raw material for poetry, in the unpolished utterances and colloquial speech of Midwest American life. In this same Preface, he lists eight poetic precursors—chants, psalms, gnomics, contemplations, proverbs, epitaphs, litanies, and incidents of intensely concentrated action or utterance which form a vital tradition in the history of poetry. This list closely resembles the folk material he selected and edited for *The People, Yes*, and it suggests in many ways the limitations of Sandburg's poetics. He is the poet of names and places, of trades and occupations—of unreflected experience and undifferentiated fact. Without the discipline of poetic form, however, Sandburg's material proves refractory even by the loose standards of *vers libre*. Robert Frost, a poetic rival, once remarked apropos of Sandburg that "writing free verse is like playing tennis with the net down." The amorphous character and mechanical reiterations in so much of Sandburg's verse point to precisely this lack of the shaping imagination that Frost believed to be essential to the poetic vision.

In *Chicago Poems*, for example, which many critics believe to be the best of his early volumes, the vigorous lines of the opening apostrophe to the city itself are followed by a casual assemblage of character sketches, place descriptions, fleeting impressions, and renderings of urban life. Occasionally the sheer emotional power of a poem will register, as with the grief of "Mag," the frustration of "Mamie," or the anger of "To a Contemporary Bunkshooter," but most of the verses never transcend their prosiness. "Poetry," Sandburg once said, "is the achievement of the synthesis of hyacinths and biscuits," but too often he presents only the latter—the prosaic and commonplace—rather than lyrical compression or poetic eloquence. Notable exceptions can be found in the sustained metaphor of "Fog" or the lyrical delicacy of "Nocturne in a Deserted Brickyard," but for the most part, Sandburg rejects the overrefinement of the genteel tradition by employing the coarse, vigorous language of the common people to present a frank, honest portrayal of his city in all its various moods. Poems such as "They Will Say" express a compassionate regard for the conditions of the working class, though other selections such as "Dynamiter" can be polemically one-sided. As Gay Wilson Allen, the most perceptive Sandburg critic, has observed, "A prominent theme in *Chicago Poems* is the longing of ordinary people for the beauty and happiness they have never known." The poem "Style" shows Sandburg aware of the stylistic deficiencies of his verse, but he insists that, for better or for worse, they are his own.

In *Cornhuskers* and *Smoke and Steel*, Sandburg continued to explore the poetry of the Midwest, rural and urban. *Cornhuskers* includes a wider range of material than his first volume, and many of the poems reveal a new lyricism. Some of the most memorable titles evoke seasonal moods of the prairie landscape—"Prairie," "Prairie Water by Night," "Laughing Corn," "Falltime," and "Autumn Movement." Perhaps the most accomplished poem, "Prairie," shows Sandburg experimenting with variable lines and sprung rhythm. "Fire-Logs" offers a romantic treatment of a Lincoln legend and "Southern Pacific" comments ironically on the fate of a railroad baron.

Smoke and Steel extends the material of the previous volume, but on a less optimistic note. The title poem celebrates America's industrial prowess, but other selections reveal Sandburg's awareness of the darker side of American life in the 1920's—in the cynicism of "The Lawyers Know Too Much" and "Liars" and the gangland violence of "Killers" and "Hoodlums." Even with the inclusion of poems to his wife and daughters, *Smoke and Steel* is a less affirmative volume than Sandburg's earlier work.

By the time *Slabs of the Sunburnt West* was published, Sandburg had reworked the same material too often. Too many of the poems in this short volume are frankly repetitive of his earlier efforts, or else derivative of Walt Whitman in their vague inclusiveness and generalized evocations of "the people."

With *Good Morning, America* and *The People, Yes*, Sandburg introduced a new direction in his work by reverting to the raw material of poetry in the slang and lingo of the people. Henceforth, as a poet of the people, he would take his material directly from them. In *Good Morning, America*, he offers something of an *ars poetica* in "Tentative (First Model) Definitions of Poetry," a collection of thirty-eight whimsical definitions of poetry. The problem with these definitions is that they seem to deny the role of poetic artistry by implying that poetry can be "found" virtually anywhere and that it consists of virtually anything that strikes the poet's fancy. At this point perhaps more folklorist than poet, Sandburg seems satisfied merely to collect and compile the words of the people rather than to exert artistic selection and control over his material. *The People, Yes* may have value as a collection of verbal portraits of the American people, but whether it is poetry in any traditional sense is debatable.

Two subsequent collections, *Complete Poems* and *Harvest Poems: 1910-1960*, each included new material and evinced a deepening of Sandburg's poetic talents. During the 1940's, he experimented with a new form of dramatized poetry or recitation—designed to be read publicly with musical accompaniment. Several of these occasional poems—"Mr. Longfellow and his Boy" and "The Long Shadow of Lincoln: A Litany"—are notable for the new note of somber dignity in his free verse. Sandburg read his Lincoln litany as the Phi Beta Kappa poem at the College of William and Mary in 1944 and used the occasion to draw an implicit parallel between Lincoln's struggle during the Civil War and the nation's efforts during World War II. This same patriotic note was struck in his moving elegy on Franklin Delano Roosevelt, "When Death Came April Twelve 1945."

Sandburg published one additional volume of poems during his lifetime, *Honey and Salt*, which appeared when he was eighty-five. This volume demonstrates the steady mastery and control of his craft that critics had sought for in his earlier work. The verses are less strident and ideological, more quiet and reflective in their wisdom. Several notable poems, including "Honey and Salt," "Foxgloves," and "Timesweep," indicate the range of his achievement in what may be his finest volume. Additional poems of merit appeared in the posthumous volume *Breathing Tokens*, which suggests that William Carlos Williams and others may have been too quick to dismiss Sandburg's poetic achievement on the basis of the *Complete Poems*. Perhaps that achievement must now be reassessed. His two fine collections of children's poems, *Early Moon* and *Wind Song*, also deserve critical attention.

A major objection among Sandburg's critics has been his lack of development. Detractors point to the formulaic nature of his poems and their lack of intellectual content or complexity. They comment on his neglect of prosody and his disdain for the traditional poetic devices that make poetry a "heightened and intensified use of language." They also comment that Sandburg did not master the major poetic forms—the elegy, the ballad, the sonnet, or the lyric. The neglect of form in favor of expression is certainly a trait common to much of modern poetry, and one must ask, finally, whether Sandburg is any more deficient in this respect than his contemporaries, or whether his neglect since his death has been more a matter of present standards of critical taste.

Other literary forms · Besides his poetry, Carl Sandburg wrote a multivolume biography of Abraham Lincoln, composed children's stories, collected American folk songs, and worked for many years as a journalist.

Select works other than poetry

LONG FICTION: *Remembrance Rock*, 1948.

NONFICTION: *The Chicago Race Riots*, 1919; *Abraham Lincoln: The Prairie Years*, 1926 (2 volumes); *Steichen the Photographer*, 1929; *Mary Lincoln: Wife and Widow*, 1932 (with Paul M. Angle); *A Lincoln and Whitman Miscellany*, 1938; *Abraham Lincoln: The War Years*, 1939 (4 volumes); *Storm over the Land: A Profile of the Civil War*, 1942; *The Photographs of Abraham Lincoln*, 1944; *Lincoln Collector: The Story of Oliver R. Barrett's Great Private Collection*, 1949; *Always the Young Strangers*, 1953; *Abraham Lincoln: The Prairie Years and the War Years*, 1954; *The Sandburg Range*, 1957; "Address Before a Joint Session of Congress, February 12, 1959," 1959; *The Letters of Carl Sandburg*, 1968 (Herbert Mitgang, editor).

CHILDREN'S LITERATURE: *Rootabaga Stories,* 1922; *Rootabaga Pigeons,* 1923; *Abe Lincoln Grows Up,* 1928; *Potato Face,* 1930; *Prairie-Town Boy,* 1955; *The Wedding Procession of the Rag Doll and the Broom Handle and Who Was in It,* 1967.

Andrew J. Angyal

Bibliography · Significant book-length studies of Sandburg include Hazel Durnell, *The America of Carl Sandburg,* 1965; Richard Crowder, *Carl Sandburg,* 1964; North Callahan, *Carl Sandburg: Lincoln of Our Literature,* 1970, and Jeffrey H. Hacker, *Carl Sandburg,* 1986. Harry Lewis Golden, *Carl Sandburg,* 1961, discusses Sandburg's musical as well as literary pursuits. Gay Wilson Allen's *Carl Sandburg,* 1972, is brief but informative. For articles on Sandburg and his writing, see Chris Beyers, "Carl Sandburg's Unnatural Relations," *Essays in Literature* 20 (Spring, 1995); C. K. Doreski, "From News to History: Robert Abbott and Carl Sandburg Read the 1919 Chicago Riot," *African American Review* 27 (Winter, 1992); Joseph Epstein, "The People's Poet," *Commentary* 93 (May, 1992).

SAPPHO

Born: Mytilene or Eresus, Lesbos, Asia Minor; c. 612 B.C.
Died: probably Mytilene, Lesbos, Asia Minor; c. 580 B.C.

Poetry · *Poetarum Lesbiorum Fragmenta*, 1955 · *Sappho: A New Translation*, 1958 · *Lyra Graeca*, volume 1, 1958 · *Sappho: Poems and Fragments*, 1965 · *The Poems of Sappho*, 1966

Achievements · One of the most admired poets of the ancient world, Sappho was widely popular not only during her lifetime but also for centuries after. Although she wrote nine books of poetry, very little of the corpus remains. Except for a very few phrases on vase paintings or papyri, Sappho's poetry has been preserved primarily in small bits that happened to be quoted by other writers. There are some 170 of these fragments extant, and although there may be among them one or two complete poems, most of the fragments consist of only a few lines or a few words. For Sappho's poem fragments, the numerical system of Edgar Lobel and Denys Page, *Poetarum Lesbiorum Fragmenta*, is used.

These fragments indicate that Sappho's poems were largely lyrical, intended to be sung and accompanied by music and perhaps dance. Although in form her poetry was thus traditional, in content it differed significantly from the larger body of Greek verse, which was written primarily by men. Whereas other Greek poets were mainly concerned with larger and more public issues and with such traditional masculine concerns as war and heroism, Sappho's poems are personal, concerned with the emotions and individual experiences of herself and her friends. In exploring and describing the world of passion, in particular, Sappho departed from conventional poetic themes. Perhaps that is one of the reasons that her poetry was so popular in the ancient world.

Sappho's work has continued to be popular, however, not only because of the timelessness of her subject matter, but also because of the exactness of her imagery and the intensity of her expression. Although her style is simple, direct, and conversational, her poems are powerful in creating an impression or evoking an emotion. Her world is therefore not the larger world of politics or warfare, but the smaller world of personal feeling; nevertheless, in depicting the outer limits of that world—the extremes of jealousy as well as tenderness, the depths of sorrow as well as the heights of ecstasy—Sappho's poetry sets a standard to which all later writers of lyrics must aspire.

In addition to being well-known for her subject matter, Sappho has come to be associated with a particular metrical form. Although she was probably not the inventor of Sapphic meter, it has been so named because of her frequent use of it. In Sapphic meter, the stanza consists of three lines, each of which contains five feet—two trochees, a dactyl, and two more trochees—with a concluding fourth line of one dactyl and one trochee. The first line of the "Ode to Aphrodite" in the original Greek illustrates this meter. This ode is thought to have been accompanied by music written in the Mixolydian mode, a musical mode with which Sappho is also associated. Plutarch, in fact, claims that this mode, which is said to arouse the passions more than any other, was invented by Sappho.

Sappho's enduring reputation is based, however, upon the fragments of her poetry that remain. Although those fragments themselves indicate her poetry's worth, there is in addition the testimony of other writers regarding the greatness of her accomplishment. She was praised and revered by a long line of ancients, including Solon, Plato, Aristotle, Horace, Catullus, Ovid, and Plutarch. Proving that imitation is the highest form of praise, some later poets actually incorporated her verse into their own compositions; Catullus' Poem 51, for example, is a slight reworking of a poem by Sappho. Plutarch, who, like Catullus, admired this particular ode, described it as being "mixed with fire," a metaphor which could accurately be applied to the entire body of Sappho's poetry which remains.

Biography · There are few details about Sappho's life which can be stated with certainty; the only evidence is what other writers said about her, and there is no way of knowing whether what they said is true. She is thought to have been of an aristocratic family of the island of Lesbos and to have had three brothers and a daughter named Cleis; dates of her birth and death, however, are not known. Athenaeus, writing around A.D. 200, claimed that Sappho was a contemporary of Alyattes, who reigned in Lydia from 610 to 560 B.C.; Eusebius, who was writing in the late third and early fourth centuries A.D., refers to Sappho in his chronicle for the year 604 B.C. Other writers indicate that Sappho lived at the time of another poet of Lesbos, Alcaeus, who seems to have been born around 620 B.C. It seems safe, therefore, to conclude that Sappho was born sometime during the last quarter of the seventh century and lived into the first half of the sixth century B.C.

Sometime between 604 and 592 B.C., Sappho seems to have been sent into exile in Sicily by Pittacus, who was then a democratic ruler of Mytilene on Lesbos; an inscription on the Parian marbles of the third century B.C. provides confirmation. Although it seems likely that such an exile would have been for political reasons, there are no clear references in any of the fragments of Sappho's poems to indicate that she was specifically concerned with political matters; in fact, based upon those fragments, her poetry appears to have been very much apolitical.

Whether Sappho was married is also uncertain; some say that she had a husband named Cercylas, but others believe this report to be a creation of the Greek comic poets. More suspect is the story that Sappho committed suicide by leaping from the Leucadian Cliff when rejected by a sailor named Phaon. To begin with, this story did not surface until more than two hundred years after her death, but more significant is the fact that Phaon has been found to be a vegetable deity associated with Aphrodite, and a god to whom Sappho wrote hymns. These hymns are thought to have provided the basis for this apocryphal account of her death.

There are, however, some assumptions which can be drawn from Sappho's own words. Her poetry indicates that she was the leader of a group of young women who appear to have studied music, poetry, and dance and who seem to have worshiped Aphrodite and the Muses. As the daughter of an aristocratic family, Sappho would probably not have conducted a formal school, but was more likely the informal leader of a circle of girls and young women. Scholars know from other references in her poetry that there were several such groups on Lesbos, with leaders who were rivals of Sappho.

Many of Sappho's poems also concern her romantic relationships with various women of her group, a fact which has evoked various responses throughout history, ranging from vilification to denial. Her reputation seems to have been first darkened in the fourth century B.C., long after her death, when she was the subject of a number of comic and burlesque plays; it is believed that many of the unsavory stories that came to be associated with Sappho were generated during this period. A serious and most unfortunate effect of this created and perhaps inaccurate reputation was that much of Sappho's work was later deliberately destroyed, particularly by Christians whose moral sensibilities were offended by some of the stories which circulated in the second, fourth, and eleventh centuries A.D. Sappho's reputation was also reworked by later scholars who admired her poetry but who were discomfited by her love for women; among their efforts to dissociate Sappho from her sexuality was the widely circulated story that there were in fact two Sapphos, one the licentious and immoral woman to whom all the unsavory tales applied, and the other a faultless and asexual woman who wrote sublime poetry. Most scholars today believe that there was only one Sappho, but they also believe that most of the stories told about her were untrue.

Thus, because of the legendary tales that have come to be associated with Sappho, and because of the lack of reliable historical evidence, there is little knowledge about her life which is certain. It seems reasonable to assume that she lived on Lesbos, that she was a poet, and that she valued personal relationships, about which she wrote. Both during her lifetime and after, she was much admired; statues were erected in her honor, coins were minted bearing her likeness, and she is said to have been given a heroine's funeral. Beyond these small pieces of information, scholars must turn to the fragments of her poetry for knowledge and understanding.

Analysis · Since Sappho's poetry is largely personal, it concerns her immediate world: her dedication to Aphrodite, her love of nature and art, and her relationships with lovers, friends, and family. Her poetry reflects her enjoyment of beauty in the natural world and the close connection that existed between that world and the lives of herself and her friends. Their worship of Aphrodite, their festive songs and dances, are all celebrated with flowers from the fields and with branches from the trees. Her poetry also reflects her love of art, whether in the form of poetry, the music of the lyre, or the graceful movement of a maiden in a dance. Since these interests are, however, always presented through the perspective of a personal response, a chief defining characteristic of Sappho's poetry is that it is highly emotional.

Most of the extant fragments of Sappho's poetry were quoted by later writers to illustrate some point of dialect, rhetoric, grammar, or poetic style, and those writers usually quoted only that portion of Sappho's poem which was pertinent to their point. It is fortunate, then, that Dionysius of Halicarnassus, a Greek writer of treatises who lived in Rome around 30 B.C., quoted in its entirety Sappho's "Ode to Aphrodite," to illustrate "the smooth mode of composition." This poem, the longest of several by

Sappho honoring Aphrodite, appears to be the most substantial complete work of Sappho which remains.

The ode contains the usual components of a celebration prayer to Aphrodite: the Invocation, the Sanction, and the Entreaty. The Invocation to the goddess consists of a series of epithets, "Dapple-throned Aphrodite,/ eternal daughter of God,/ snare-knitter"; the Sanction asks the goddess' generosity and assistance and reminds her of past favors she has granted; and the Entreaty urgently appeals to the goddess for aid in the present situation. Sappho employs this traditional form in a fresh way, however, not only by her use of vivid metaphors and lyrical language, but also by using the Sanction to reveal something of the goddess' character as well as something of Sappho's own psychology.

As Sappho employs it, the Sanction is a narrative passage within which both she and the goddess move back and forth in time. After describing a past occasion when the goddess came to Earth in a carriage pulled by sparrows, Sappho then recounts the goddess' questioning of her at that time. Using in her narrative the past tense and the indirect question, Sappho recalls the goddess' remarks: "You asked, What ailed me now that/ made me call you again?" Abruptly, then, Sappho places the goddess' gentle chiding within the present context; the poem shifts to direct discourse as the goddess questions Sappho directly: "Whom has/ Persuasion to bring round now/ to your love? Who, Sappho, is/ unfair to you?" This mix of the two temporal perspectives links and blends the present with the past, emphasizing not only Sappho's recurring states of anxiety over new love, but also illuminating the special and friendly relationship between the poet and the goddess: Aphrodite has obviously assisted Sappho before in similar matters of the heart. Continuing to reveal Sappho's character, the goddess reminds her that they are beginning a now-familiar pattern: A bemused Aphrodite recalls, "If she [the desired lover] won't accept gifts, she/ will one day give them; and if/ she won't love you—she soon will/ love." Sappho, manipulating the tradition of the Sanction for new purposes of self-mockery and character revelation, thus discloses her love for the courting period, as well as the shift in attitudes which will inevitably occur between her and her new lover. After the goddess' assurance that the sought-after lover will very shortly be seeking Sappho, the reader is then returned to the poem's outer frame, the prayer, as Sappho begs the goddess to help at once, to "Come now! Relieve this intolerable pain!"

Within the form of a traditional prayer honoring Aphrodite, the poem thus presents a delightful variety of tone. It discloses not only the intensity of Sappho's passion for the desired lover, but also her wry recognition that this intensity will be limited by time and by her own nature. The poem similarly indicates not only the immensity of the goddess' power but also her gentle amusement at the joys and woes of her followers; although Sappho's present sufferings in love will soon be in the past, a pattern underscored by the poem's movement between present and past time, there is every reason to believe that the goddess will assist Sappho once again in achieving the lover who will end her present suffering. In revealing not only something of the character of Aphrodite but also something of the character of Sappho, the poem thus transcends the limitations of its genre: it is a prayer, to be sure, and a narrative, but it is also a charmingly refreshing analysis of the poet's own psychology.

Although there are a few other fragments of poems honoring Aphrodite, the largest number of Sappho's fragments which remain are concerned with love, a subject which occupied much of Sappho's attention. One love poem which may, like the "Ode to Aphrodite," be nearly complete, is the large fragment sometimes called the "Ode to Anactoria," although the poem may have been written for Atthis or even for some other woman whom Sappho loved. An unknown writer who has been labeled "Longinus," in a Greek work believed to date from the first or second century A.D., quoted this fragment to illustrate Sappho's mastery in depicting physical sensations. Extraordinary in its exquisitely precise delineation of the extremes of passion, the poem is also notable for the contrast between the control of its first section and the revealed intensity of its latter section, with the resulting alternations in tone as the speaker sits in the presence of two people, the woman she loves and the man who is evidently enjoying that woman's attentions.

Concisely and with control, the poem beings:

> He is a god in my eyes—
> the man who is allowed
> to sit beside you—he
> who listens intimately
> to the sweet murmur of
> your voice, the enticing
> laughter that makes my own
> heart beat fast.

This calm and steady beginning establishes an outer mood of control, an atmosphere of containment and casual social interplay; the poem turns, however, upon the word "laughter," and the rest of the fragment describes, rapidly and with great intensity, the physical symptoms of the poet's great passion. All of her senses are affected: her "tongue is broken," and she sees nothing; she hears only her "own ears drumming" as she drips with sweat;

and, as "trembling shakes" her body, she turns "paler than dry grass." In one of Sappho's most superb lines, she declares that "a thin flame runs under/ my skin." Then, ending this rapid and graphic description of the physical results of intense emotion, the poet remarks, in a powerfully reserved manner, that "At such times/ death isn't far from me."

Scholars have long debated the cause of Sappho's passion, arguing whether it is love or jealousy or both; scholars have also quarreled over the identity of the woman and the relationship between the woman and the man who sits beside her. Such discussions are, however, ultimately irrelevant; the poet's salient point is her own overpowering feeling for the woman to whom she is listening, a feeling which prevents Sappho from exercising over her body any control; it is the physical manifestations of that feeling, the effects upon the body of great passion, which Sappho is recording. Within the poem, the effects of that passion are heightened by the contrast which turns upon the word "laughter"; just as the poem is divided between the controlled description of the outer situation and the blaze of feelings within the poet, so Sappho and the man are divided in their response to the woman's laughter; he "listens intimately," calmly, while Sappho experiences a whole cascade of violent physical and emotional reactions.

Sappho's description in this poem of the effects of passion has not been surpassed, although a number of later poets, including Catullus, have imitated, translated, or adopted her ideas. None, however, has been able to convey such intensity of feeling with the economy and precision of Sappho. It seems safe to say that there are few who would dispute Longinus' claim that this poem illustrates "the perfection of the Sublime in poetry."

In addition to considering the physical effects of love on the individual, Sappho also analyzes love's nature and power. One such poem, 16 L.-P., which refers directly to Anactoria, appears on a papyrus of the second century. The poem begins with a paratactic trope, a common device which presents the theme as the culmination of a series of comparisons:

> Some say a cavalry corps,
> some infantry, some, again,
> will maintain that the swift cars ´
> of our fleet are the finest
> sight on dark earth; but I say
> that whatever one loves, is.

More than illustrating normal differences of opinion, this means of introducing the theme establishes, as well, a decided difference between male and female values: Sappho seems clearly to imply that while men would see the ideal of beauty to be things having to do with war, she sees the ideal of beauty to be the thing beloved—in this case, the absent Anactoria.

Sappho then reinforces her contention that the beloved is the world's most beautiful sight by a reference to Helen, who had her pick of the world's men; in contrast to what one would expect, however, Helen was obliged, because of love, to choose "one who laid Troy's honor in ruin," one who "warped" her "to his will," one who caused her even to forget the "love due her own blood, her own/ child." Sappho uses the story of Helen to illustrate love's power to make insignificant all ordinary considerations and constraints. Yet Sappho clearly intends no judgment against Helen; the purpose of her allusion is simply to demonstrate the power of love and, by analogy, Sappho's love for her beloved.

Only then, after establishing by example and comparisons the supremacy and strength of love, does Sappho reveal in an apostrophe the name of her beloved. Addressing Anactoria and expressing her fear that Anactoria will forget her, Sappho confesses that the sound of her footstep, or the sight of her bright face, would be dearer "than glitter/ of Lydian horse or armoured/ tread of mainland infantry." In an intricate linking of end and beginning by means of metaphor and comparisons, the poem thus moves full circle, back to its starting place; the final sentence of the fragment reinforces the idea contained in the opening sentence as it simultaneously contrasts the tread of the infantry with the delightful sound of Anactoria's footstep, and the glitter of armor with the bright shine of Anactoria's face. In such ways Sappho clearly exposes the conflicting value systems which underlie her poems and those of her male contemporaries.

Several other fragments of varying size also treat the power of love, among them a particularly felicitous line quoted by Maximus of Tyre around A.D. 150: "As a whirlwind/ swoops on an oak/ Love shakes my heart." An overpowering natural phenomenon, love is presented here as an elemental force which completely overcomes the lover, both physically and emotionally. As the wind physically surrounds the oak, so does love overpower the lover physically as well as emotionally. Love, a force which cannot be denied, is thus depicted as a violent physical and emotional assault, to which one may well respond with mixed feelings.

Sappho explores the ambiguity of the lover's response to love's violent assault in another fragment, quoted by Hephaestion around A.D. 150: "Irresistible/ and bittersweet/ that loosener/ of limbs, Love/ reptile-like/ strikes me down." Again, love is depicted as an absolute power and as a violent force—in this instance as a reptile which, attacking a passive victim, creates in her a weakened state. That state is not, however, altogether unpleasant, as is indicated by the exquisite sensuality of the adjectival phrase describing love as "that loosener of limbs." Love's duality—its violence and its sweetness—and the lover's ambiguity of response—as the victim of assault and as reveler in love's sensuality—are further underscored by the oxymoronic adjective "bittersweet," an epithet for love which Sappho may have been the first to use.

In addition to analyzing the nature and effects of love, Sappho also writes of love's termination, of separation, loss, and grief. One such fragment, 94 L.-P., found in a seventh century manuscript in very poor condition, contains many lacunae and uncertain readings. Nevertheless, enough of the poem remains to prove that Sappho was defining the state of bereavement and the effectiveness of memory in alleviating that state. In the course of exploring these themes, however, the poem presents an enchanting account of the life led by Sappho and the members of her group as they worshiped Aphrodite, celebrated the beauty of nature, and gloried in one another.

Like the "Ode to Aphrodite," the poem uses a frame of present time to contain an account of past time; in this poem, however, the past time frames an even earlier period, so that there are three time periods represented. Beginning in her present situation, Sappho, alone, reveals her emotional state at the loss of her beloved: "Frankly I wish I were dead." Attempting then to console herself, Sappho recalls the occasion of their parting; at that time, in contrast to the present situation, Sappho controlled her grief in order to comfort her lover, who was overcome by weeping. On that occasion, Sappho urged her beloved to remember their former happiness and to comfort herself with the memory of their love. At this point in the past, the poem then removes to its third temporal setting, that idyllic period when the two were actually together. In a passage of great lyrical beauty, Sappho recalls the details of their life:

> think
> of our gifts of Aphrodite
> and all the loveliness that we shared
> all the violet tiaras
> braided rosebuds, dill and
> crocus twined around your young neck
> myrrh poured on your head
> and on soft mats girls with
> all that they most wished for beside them
> while no voices changed
> choruses without ours
> no woodlot bloomed in spring without song.

In re-creating, at the moment of their farewell, this earlier time of delight in love, nature, and each other, Sappho consoles her beloved by reminding her that the joys they shared are preserved in memories and that those memories can provide solace. At the same time, from her position in the outer frame of the poem—the present context—Sappho attempts to comfort herself by the same means.

Although the poem, on the one hand, asserts the consolation that memory can offer, it testifies as well to memory's limitations. Even though Sappho has shared the joyful events of which she reminds her beloved, the poem nevertheless indicates all too clearly that memory's ability to ease grief is restricted. As Sappho tersely and flatly demonstrates by her opening statement, in no way can memory truly compensate for the beloved's absence. Still, the enchantment of those memories remains, and even though they cannot totally eliminate the pain of parting, they can provide some surcease by powerfully evoking the time when the lovers' joy in nature and in their love created for them an existence truly idyllic.

In addition to these personal poems, private accounts of her own and her friends' feelings and activities, Sappho also wrote some poems of a more public nature. Notable among these "public" poems are a number of fragments from her epithalamiums, or wedding songs. Some of these are congratulatory pieces honoring bride or groom, some appear to have been part of good-humored songs of mockery or wedding jest, and some seem to have been serious considerations of what marriage meant, especially for a woman. Of the latter, particularly worthy of comment are two fragments thought by some to be part of a single poem concerning the loss of maidenhood. As is true of other poems by Sappho, opinion is divided as to the poem's ultimate meaning, some believing that it alludes to an ungentle lover who does not properly appreciate the maiden whose virginity he destroys, and others believing that the poem refers generally to the destruction of innocence and the loss of girlhood joys that marriage necessitates.

The fragments employ two similes, the first comparing the blushing girl to

> a quince-apple
> ripening on a top
> branch in a tree top
> not once noticed by
> harvesters or if
> not unnoticed, not reached.

The location of the apple high in the tree permits it to ripen without disturbance, perhaps as a girl's careful upbringing or superior social standing might shield her from importunate suitors. The second fragment compares the loss of the virginal state to

> a hyacinth in
> the mountains, trampled by shepherds until
> only a purple stain
> remains on the ground.

Through the powerful image of the delicate hyacinth roughly trod into the earth, the poem clearly delineates the destructive power of love and marriage.

That image is countered, however, in another fragment from an epithalamium, 112 L.-P., which rejoices in marriage and celebrates the groom's winning of the girl he desires. The bride is described as "charming to look at,/ with eyes as soft as/ honey, and a face/ that Love has lighted/ with his own beauty." Sappho, clearly indicating her own opinion as to which is the lucky partner in the marriage, reminds the groom, "Aphrodite has surely/ outdone herself in/ doing honor to you!" Such songs were thought to have been written for the weddings of Sappho's friends, and would have been accompanied by music and dance.

Sappho's legacy is meager in size, consisting of one or two poems which may be complete, together with a number of shorter fragments that tantalize by their incompleteness even as they enchant with what they do provide. These few pieces clearly manifest the enormous poetic talent that Sappho possessed: a genius for capturing a mood, for portraying an experience, and for depicting an emotion. While her poetry is personal in dealing with her own responses to life, it is, paradoxically, also universal; the feelings she describes, even though they are her own, are shared by all human beings who ever love, lose, or grieve, or who experience jealousy, anger, or regret. One of the first poets to explore the range and depth of the human heart, Sappho well deserves Plato's epithet for her, "the tenth muse."

Evelyn S. Newlyn

Bibliography · Sappho's language and the fragmentary nature of her poetry make the translation and interpretation of her work a formidable feat. *Greek Lyric,* vol. 1, 1982, gives all of her known works in the original Greek with careful translations and informative notes by David Campbell. This volume also contains translations of the ancient *testimonia* (biographical notices) concerning Sappho's life. Good general discussions of Sappho and her times may be found in David A. Campbell's chapter of P. E.

Easterling and B. M. W. Knox, eds., *The Cambridge History of Classical Literature*, vol. 1, 1985; Anthony J. Podlecki, *The Early Greek Poets and Their Times*, 1984; Denys Page, *Sappho and Alcaeus*, 1970 (which contains translations of and commentaries on twelve of Sappho's poems); and Jim Powell, "Afterwords: Special Section on Sappho," *TriQuarterly* 86 (Winter, 1993). Valuable articles (from highly disparate perspectives) addressed to Sappho's homoeroticism are Hector Williams, "Lesbos' Poet Laureate," *Archaeology* 47 (July/August, 1994); John J. Winkler, "Sappho and the Crack of Dawn (Fragment 58 L-P)," *Journal of Homosexuality* 20, nos. 3-4 (1990); and Nicole Albert, "Sappho Mythified, Sappho Mystified, or the Metamorphoses of Sappho in Fin de Siècle France," *Journal of Homosexuality* 25, no. 2 (1993).

FRIEDRICH SCHILLER

Born: Marbach, Germany; November 10, 1759
Died: Weimar, Germany; May 9, 1805

Poetry · *Anthologie auf das Jahr 1782*, 1782 · *Xenien*, 1796 (with Johann Wolfgang von Goethe) · *Gedichte*, 1800, 1803 · *The Poems of Schiller*, 1851 · *The Ballads and Shorter Poems of Fredrick v. Schiller*, 1901

Achievements · Although most of Schiller's verse was written for a highly intellectual audience, it also enjoyed popular success. His "thought poems" laid the groundwork for the ensuing development of the poetry of ideas and brought him rightful recognition as Germany's most important eighteenth century composer of philosophical lyrics. On the other hand, his didactic purpose and his capacity for evoking moods akin to those of folk literature, especially in his ballads, made Schiller also a poet of the common people.

Schiller's poems and other writings were quickly recognized for their quality by the German literary establishment and were published in the significant periodicals of the time. Supported by Christoph Martin Wieland and Johann Gottfried Herder, Schiller became an important force among the artistic giants in Weimar, even prior to his friendship with Johann Wolfgang von Goethe. During the decade of their poetic collaboration, Schiller joined Goethe in shaping literary attitudes, approaches, and forms that influenced German poets and determined the nature of German letters from that time onward.

Even in his own time, however, some of Schiller's poetic works were highly controversial. The "Epigram War" that he and Goethe waged against their critics was evidence that his works were not universally well received. During the years after his death, Schiller's reputation in critical circles waned in direct relationship to the increased advocacy of realism and, eventually, naturalism. Near the beginning of the twentieth century, however, a Schiller renaissance began on two levels. Writers such as Stefan George and Hugo von Hofmannsthal, who advocated a return to classical literary values, praised Schiller for his poetic models of idealism and beauty. In addition, a new awareness of his work grew among the public. Such poems as "Das Lied von der Glocke" ("The Song of the Bell") were memorized in school, exposing a new generation of German youth to Schiller's thought. Although he was overshadowed by Goethe in pure

poetic endowment, Schiller's impact on the whole of German literature is such that Thomas Mann called his works the "apotheosis of art."

Biography · The early life of Johann Christoph Friedrich von Schiller was shaped by two powerful influences: the Swabian Pietism of his origins and the "benevolent" despotism of Karl Eugen, Duke of Württemberg. After serving as a lieutenant in Bavarian, French, and Swabian regiments, Schiller's father was rewarded with an appointment as superintendent of the duke's gardens and plantations. While Schiller's parents had planned for him to enter the ministry, those intentions were frustrated when the duke insisted that he be enrolled in a military academy at Stuttgart in 1773. After a brief and inconclusive period of legal studies at the academy,

Schiller left the institution to become a medical officer in Karl Eugen's army. His dislike of the school's restrictions contributed substantially to the attacks on tyranny prevalent in his early writings.

Schiller's first poem was published in a Swabian literary magazine in 1776, and others appeared there and elsewhere during the remainder of his school years. Two months after his graduation, he rented a room from a widow, Luise Vischer, whom critics long regarded as the model for his Laura odes. While still in Stuttgart, Schiller wrote his first play, *The Robbers.* It premiered in Mannheim in January, 1782, and Schiller traveled, without the duke's permission, to attend the opening performance. Following Schiller's second secret theater visit to Mannheim, Karl Eugen placed him under two weeks' arrest and forbade him to write. The arrival of the Russian czar in Stuttgart took Karl Eugen's attention away from Schiller, and the latter fled to Mannheim.

Existence in Mannheim was a constant struggle for the young Schiller. His literary efforts brought him little monetary profit, and he survived only through the help of his friends. When the manager of the Mannheim theater refused to renew his contract as house dramatist, Schiller published a literary journal in an effort to straighten out his fiscal affairs. The emotional strain caused by his precarious economic condition and his unsuccessful encounters with women during those years is reflected in the poetry that he wrote after leaving Stuttgart. Not until he was rescued from financial disaster by Gottfried Körner and other admirers in 1784 did Schiller's personal life gain stability sufficient to foster the harmonious mastery of thought and form that typifies his more mature lyric creations. The friendship with Körner was a direct stimulus for the famous poem "An die Freude" ("Ode to Joy"), which Beethoven used for the choral movement of his Ninth Symphony.

A major turning point in Schiller's life came in 1787, after he had spent two relatively carefree years in Körner's household in Dresden. Disappointed by an unrewarding relationship with Henriette von Arnim, Schiller left Dresden for Weimar. There, he renewed an acquaintance with Charlotte von Kalb, the unhappy wife of an army major. Her friendship had created emotional problems for him in Mannheim, but she now introduced him into philosophical circles in Jena that influenced his life for years. In Weimar, he also made contact with Wieland and Herder, whose favor gave him access to the court.

In 1788, Schiller met Johann Wolfgang von Goethe for the first time. Although no close relationship developed at the time, Goethe soon recommended him for a professorship in history at the University of Jena. The stable situation provided by an annual income allowed Schiller to marry

Charlotte von Lengefeld in 1790. His professional involvement in the years that followed reduced his poetic activity but moved him to concern himself more extensively with the philosophy of Immanuel Kant. His philosophical studies ultimately had a major impact on his creative work. In Jena, during the winter of 1790-1791, Schiller experienced the first attacks of the tuberculosis that eventually caused his death.

The most artistically productive period of Schiller's life began in the summer of 1794 when Goethe agreed to collaborate with him in the editing of a new journal. The intimate friendship that arose between the two authors provided them with mutual stimulus and gave rise to timeless masterworks of poetry and drama. Friendly competition between them in 1797 and 1798 yielded some of the most famous ballads in German literature. Also in 1797, the last of Schiller's historical writings was completed, winning for him membership in the Swedish Academy of Sciences. During the final years of his life, Schiller was feverishly active, writing the best of his mature plays, adapting works by William Shakespeare, Louis Picard, Gotthold Lessing, and Goethe, traveling, and gathering new dramatic materials in defiance of the malady that slowly destroyed him. Newly completed lines for "Demetrius," an unfinished play that might have become his greatest masterpiece, were found lying on his desk on the day he died.

Analysis · In his essay "On Naïve and Sentimental Poetry," written soon after he began collaborating with Goethe, Friedrich Schiller outlined and clarified the characteristics of two kinds of poetic art, attempting to defend his own creative approach in the careful justification of "sentimental" literature. In contrast to the naïve poet, whose work is an expression of nature, Schiller's modern lyricist is a reflective creator who seeks to regain in his poetry a natural state that has been lost. The naïve poet moves the reader through an artistic presentation of sensual reality, while the sentimental poet achieves his effect in the successful development of ideas. Throughout Schiller's literary career, the conceptual tension between "naïve" and "sentimental," couched variously in the polarities of nature and culture, real and ideal, ancient and modern, and substance and form, remained the key to his poetic endeavor. Each new poem represented a concerted effort to create through art a harmonious resolution of the perpetual conflict between these fundamental aspects of man's existence.

The poetry of Schiller's youth is especially interesting for its clear illumination of the broad spectrum of eighteenth century literary forces that molded his attitudes. In the *Anthology for the Year 1782*, which was published to counteract what Schiller saw as the smarmy bent of other

Swabian collections of the time, there are poems that reflect such diverse influences as the pathos of Friedrich Klopstock's odes, the Anacreontic tendencies of the early Enlightenment, Gottfried August Bürger's massive realism, Albrecht von Haller's philosophical lyrics, the political tendentiousness of Christian Friedrich Daniel Schubart, Christoph Wieland's Rococo style, and the purposeful tastelessness of *Sturm und Drang*. Although personal encounters provided immediate stimuli for some of the works, the calculated refinement of perceptions through the process of reflection sets the philosophical tone of Schiller's verse from the outset.

The naïve/sentimental dichotomy is visible in two characteristic forms in Schiller's early poetry. "Der Eroberer" ("The Conqueror") exemplifies Schiller's juxtaposition of political and divine order in the concept of the "noble criminal," an almost mythical figure who goes beyond the limits of conventional morality. The conquering tyrant emerges as the adversary of God and the destroyer of moral order. In the Laura odes, however, which are central to the lyrics of Schiller's youth, the focus of poetic tension is the tortuous conflict between love's physical and spiritual dimensions. By 1780, in direct response to the writings of Adam Ferguson and under the mediated influence of Francis Hutcheson and the philosopher, Lord Shaftesbury, Schiller had developed a personal metaphysics in which love is the binding force that holds the world together. The Laura odes and poems such as "Der Triumph der Liebe" ("The Triumph of Love") constitute the major literary treatments of those ideas.

The years immediately following the publication of the *Anthology for the Year 1782* were a transitional period in Schiller's growth as a lyric poet. In the lines of "Der Kampf" ("The Struggle") and "Resignation," the poet broadened the basic themes of his earlier works. While exploring in depth the conflict between man's right to joy and the reality of a tear-filled existence, he questioned the validity of God's justice in forcing man to choose between earthly pleasure and spiritual peace. Some of the lyrics written between 1782 and 1788 examine the possibility of achieving a harmony between the polar forces that act upon man; other poems conclude with terrible finality that the only alternatives, pleasure in this world or hope of peace in the world to come, are mutually exclusive. Only the famous "Ode to Joy," which praises the harmony between God and a glorified world in a profound affirmation of earthly existence, forms a distinct anomaly in the otherwise troubled reflection that typifies the verse produced during this period of Schiller's life.

The major poetic works of Schiller's mature years, beginning with the first version of "Die Götter Griechenlands" ("The Gods of Greece"), written in 1788, and ending with "Das Siegesfest" ("The Victory Celebration"), composed in 1803, offer a more calmly ordered, evenly balanced, and formally perfected presentation of the fundamental Schillerian dichotomies than can be found in the emotionally charged poems of the early 1780's. With increasing emphasis on natural order as an answer to the problems of civilized society, Schiller attempts to resolve the tension between the ideal and the real. Instead of seeking to establish an internal harmony between the spiritual and physical elements of man's being, he tries in the later poems to move his reader to accept an external creation of the desired metaphysical unity in art. The appropriate models for the new synthesis were to be found in the artistic and literary legacy of the ancients. Schiller's most powerful philosophical poems present the search for a golden age of accord between rational man and nature and the need to regain that state through reflection.

It is important to understand that these writings are not simply versified philosophy. In Schiller's eyes, the poet differs from the philosopher in not being required to prove his assertions. Instead, the poet employs a variety of devices to convey his message on several levels of perception, at once teaching and moving the reader through his own personal enthusiasm. To achieve his purpose, Schiller masterfully cultivated a variety of poetic forms, ranging from the epigram to the ballad to the highly stylized "thought poem."

As a consciously developed form, the epigram is a special phenomenon of the collaboration between Schiller and Goethe. It is a particularly powerful genre for Schiller. His epigrams are basically of two kinds: satirical and purely philosophical. The sharply barbed satirical poems focus on poets, thinkers, and critics of his time, especially those who attacked Schiller and Goethe, as well as the literary movements and specific currents of thought that they represented. Epigrams in the other group, primarily the "Votivtafeln" ("Votive Inscriptions"), are more general in focus and didactic in purpose.

Schiller's ballads, which are also important documents of his friendship with Goethe, represent more clearly than the epigrams the general tendency of classical German poetry to seek and establish the harmony between the ideal and the real. In that regard, they are especially clear illustrations of Schiller's aesthetics. Many of them follow a pattern established in 1795 in "Das verschleierte Bild zu Sais" ("The Veiled Image at Sais") and are best described as lyrically narrated parables that resolve the poet's metaphysical conflicts by appealing to the natural nobility of the human soul. A second type of ballad, exemplified by "Die Kraniche des Ibykus" ("The Cranes of Ibycus"), addresses itself to art's ethical and moral purposes, employing the elements of legend to achieve its goals. The ballads are the most readable of Schiller's lyric works, simply because they benefit from his mastery of drama.

Among the poems of Schiller's final creative period are some of the most extraordinarily beautiful "thought poems" in German. While stressing the inherent interdependency of ethics and aesthetics, Schiller dealt with basic existential questions such as suffering, death, transience, the quest for truth, and the perception of the absolute. In poems such as the lovely "Nänie" ("Nenia"), written in 1796, he arrived at a final answer to questions posed in his early lyrics, replacing hopelessness and resignation with the achievement in art of a timeless unity of humanity's real and ideal dimensions.

In 1781, Schiller published "Die Entzückung an Laura" ("Rapture, to Laura") in Gotthold Stäudlin's *Schwäbischer Musenalmanach auf das Jahr 1782* (Swabian almanac of the muses for the year 1782). It was the first of six poems that have since become known as the Laura odes. The other five, including "Phantasie an Laura" ("Fantasy, to Laura"), "Laura am Klavier" ("Laura at the Piano"), "Vorwurf an Laura" ("Reproach, to Laura"), "Das Geheimnis der Reminiscenz" ("The Mystery of Reminiscence"), and "Melancholie an Laura" ("Melancholy, to Laura"), appeared for the first time in Schiller's *Anthology for the Year 1782*. As a group, these poems present Schiller's metaphysics of love. They are a product of creative reflection rather than intimate experience. When Schiller left the military academy, he had in fact had few encounters with women, and all of his early works reveal a lack of realistic perception of the opposite sex.

"Rapture, to Laura" sets the tone for the odes in its portrayal of love as a force that links the real world with the cosmic realm of absolutes. Schiller employs well-developed images of sight and sound as the outward manifestations of love, with visual contacts playing an especially important role in the communication of feeling. The gaze and what the poet can see in the eyes of his imagined Laura transform him, granting him the ability to move from his own reality into the ideal domain symbolized by the young woman. The last stanza of the poem defines her glances and the love that they represent as a clearly comprehended creative influence that has the power to vivify even inanimate stone.

The external tension between the physical and the spiritual receives special emphasis in the lyric structure of "Fantasy, to Laura," in which bodily and mental activities are juxtaposed in alternate stanzas and lines. As in all the Laura odes, the two realms are bonded together through the force of love, without which the world would disintegrate into a mechanical chaos. This poem, however, emphasizes the unresolved parallelism between sexual love, presented in the literary formulations of *Sturm und*

Drang, and the philosophical love of Enlightenment thought, causing the concept of love as such to remain somewhat ambiguous.

In "Laura at the Piano," Schiller developed a more precise representation of love as a metaphysical phenomenon. Consistent with his ultimate goal of natural harmony, love appears not so much as a personal experience with the feminine, but as a manifestation of the creative power of the masculine through which man masters all the cosmos. The dual character of love thus comes to symbolize the opposed forces of chaos and creation that mold the universe. A key to Schiller's message in "Laura at the Piano" lies once more in Laura's ability, through her very presence, to move her lover into a unified transcendent realm. The scope of this act is divine, and her being emerges as a subtle "proof" for the existence of God.

The notion of conflicting polarities is so basic to the Laura poems that even love has its own antagonist: death. Schiller's manner of coming to grips with the latter accords the odes a distinct kinship with his early elegies, including "Elegie auf den Tod eines Jünglings" ("Elegy to the Death of a Young Man") and "Trauer-Ode" ("Ode of Mourning"). In "Melancholy, to Laura," the death motif receives its most powerful illumination in the baroque imagery of the beloved's decay. Laura is presented here as a symbol for the entirety of earthly existence, which rests on "mouldering bones." Even her beauty is not immune to the ravages of death. In the struggle between the optimism of love and the finality of death, death triumphs, devaluating mortality as it ends all human striving for happiness. This conclusion anticipates the pessimistic mood of the famous poem "Resignation." Although not specifically dedicated to Laura, "Resignation" may be regarded as the thematic culmination of the ideas presented in the odes, a culmination that is encapsulated in a single stanza of the lengthy poem. There, in harshly vivid imagery, the poet tears his Laura bleeding from his heart and gives her to the relentless judge, eternity, in payment for the hope of peace beyond the grave.

Perhaps the most interesting symbol of death in "Resignation" appears in the poem's second stanza in the silent god who extinguishes the poet's torch. He is a precursor of more carefully refined images that Schiller based on models from Greek and Roman antiquity and employed in the powerful philosophical lyrics of his classical period. This personification of death signals a transition that occurred in the poet's creative orientation during the mid-1780's. By the time the first version of "The Gods of Greece" was printed in Wieland's periodical *Der teutsche Merkur,* Schiller had abandoned his metaphysics of love in favor of a poetic search for man's lost golden age. The characteristics of this new approach are a juxtapostion of the ancient and modern worlds, renewal of classical aesthetic and ethical values, and an appeal for the creation of a unity of sensual and spiritual experience in art.

The two variants of "The Gods of Greece," published in 1788 and 1793, respectively, have in common their focus on the concept of beauty. In the first version, Schiller presented a justification of sensual beauty, couching his arguments in a defense of ancient polytheism against modern monotheism and rationalism. The Christian God in His roles of avenger, judge, and rational defender of truth is too strict for the natural world. For that reason, Schiller advocated return to an order of existence based on feeling. From the notion that the Greek gods symbolize divine perfection in things earthly, a kind of theophany informs the world created by the poem, although the second rendering places heavier emphasis on the timelessness of beauty.

The carefully nurtured inner tension of "The Gods of Greece" derives from its dual nature. It is at once a lament for the loss of man's earlier existence in nature and a song of praise for the potential immanence of the ideal within the real. In the past for which the poet longs, a closer harmony existed between the physical and spiritual realms, because the gods were more human and man was more divine. When the old gods were driven away by reason, however, they took with them everything of beauty and majesty, leaving the world colorless, empty, and devoid of spirit. The final lines of the respective versions offer two different resolutions of the problem. In the first, the poet issues a simple plea for the return of the mild goddess, beauty. The final form of the poem places the responsibility for beauty's timeless preservation squarely in the lap of the creative artist. Next to Goethe's drama *Iphigenie auf Tauris* (1787; *Iphigenia in Tauris*), "The Gods of Greece" in its two versions is the most important document of Germanized Greek mythology in classical German literature.

Most of Schiller's poems reflect the instructional orientation of his literary works as a whole. Early in his career, Schiller forcefully acknowledged the author's responsibility to move his reader toward personal, moral, and ethical improvement. The ballads that he wrote after 1795 are among the most successful didactic lyrics in all of German literature. They are masterful combinations of simplicity and clarity with vivid, engaging sensual imagery. The parabolic ballads, among them "Der Taucher" ("The Diver"), "Der Handschuh" ("The Glove"), "Der Kampf mit dem Drachen" ("The Battle with the Dragon"), and "Die Bürgschaft" ("The Pledge"), reveal the inherent nobility of the human soul when tested in circumstances that threaten life itself. Each presents a variation on the problem of the individual's response to extraordinary challenge or temptation, laying bare the inner motivations for action and glorifying the deed that is based on ideal and principle rather than on material gain. In "The Diver," the implications and consequences of free will are central to the story of a young man who retrieves from the sea a golden chalice, its own reward for the daredevil act, then perishes in a second venture, when the prize is the king's lovely daughter. "The Battle with the Dragon" explores the dilemma of choice between noble intent and obedience. A heroic knight defies the command of his order's leader and slays a terrible monster that has ravaged the countryside. He then meekly accepts expulsion from the order as the penalty for disobedience, thereby redeeming himself. Friendship as a moral force is the primary focus of "The Pledge," Schiller's rendering of the famous Greek legend of Damon and Pythias.

Typically, the verse parables have a two-part structure that pairs an obviously rash, foolish, and dangerous act with a reasoned deed of noble sacrifice through which the central figure ascends to a higher moral plane. In the popular ballad "The Glove," the knight Delorges is asked by Kunigunde to retrieve her glove from the arena, where she has purposely dropped it among bloodthirsty beasts of prey. Delorges demonstrates his stature as a man, not when he faces the tiger to obtain the glove, but when he subsequently rejects Kunigunde's favors. It is not physical courage but the spiritual act of overcoming self that provides the measure of personal worth in this and similar ballads.

Like the parable poems, "The Cranes of Ibycus" is a dramatic, didactic short story in verse form. Its orientation, however, differs markedly from that of the works which stress the importance of heroic self-mastery. In its examination and defense of art as an active moral force in society, "The Cranes of Ibycus" forms a bridge between the ballads and Schiller's more abstract philosophical lyrics, while providing a concise vindication of his own approach to the drama. The ballad describes the murder of Ibycus by two men. A flock of cranes flying overhead witnesses the crime and later reappears over an outdoor theater where the criminals sit watching a play. Caught up in the mood of the drama, the criminals forget themselves and respond to the sight of the cranes, thereby revealing themselves to the crowd. More than a simple examination of problems of guilt and atonement, the lyric work juxtaposes audience reaction to stage events with the behavior of the villain-spectators to shatter the border between theater and reality. The scene is transformed into a tribunal which has the power to bring criminals to justice, thereby influencing events in the external world.

Schiller's most famous ballad, "The Song of the Bell," is also the most ambitious of his poetic works. In some 425 lines of verse, the poet projects the broad spectrum of man's mortal existence against the background of the magnificent bell's creation. Alternating stanzas of varying length parallel the process of casting the bell with characteristic events of life. Birth and death, joy and tragedy, accomplishment and destruction—all find their symbolic counterparts in the steps taken by the artisans to produce a flawless artifact. The imagery is vividly real, earthy, and natural, presenting the everyday world in a practical frame with which the reader readily identifies. At the same time, the stylized presentation successfully underscores the possibility of harmony between man's physical environment and the ideal domain of the mind.

In many respects, "The Song of the Bell" represents the culmination of Schiller's poetic art. The effective integration of the poem's two threads of description and discussion is a clear realization of the creative unity that he sought to achieve in all of his literary works. In his classical ballads, Schiller at last achieved the resolution of tensions caused by the opposing forces that play upon man as he searches for personal meaning. Like "The Cranes of Ibycus," "The Song of the Bell" assigns to art an ultimate responsibility for man's attainment of peace through productive interactions between his absolute and his temporal essence. The finished bell's very name, Concordia, symbolizes the final accord of material and spiritual values that was for Schiller the goal of both literature and life.

Other literary forms · Although Friedrich Schiller wrote poetry throughout most of his life, the bulk of his oeuvre belongs to other genres. He became especially famous for his powerful dramatic works. Among the most important of his ten major plays are *Die Räuber* (1781; *The Robbers*, 1792), *Don Carlos, Infant von Spanien* (1787; English translation, 1798), *Maria Stuart* (1800; *Mary Stuart*, 1801), and *Wilhelm Tell* (1804; *William Tell*, 1841). During the early part of his career, his writings brought him little income, and poverty forced him to turn to fiction for a broader audience. *Der Verbrecher aus verlorener Ehre* (1786, 1802; *The Criminal in Consequence of Lost Reputation*, 1841) and the serialized novel *Der Geisterseher* (1789; *The Ghost-Seer: Or, The Apparitionist*, 1795) were among the most successful of these endeavors. While a professor of history at the University of Jena, he wrote a number of historical books and essays, and during the early 1790's, he published a variety of theoretical and philosophical studies on aesthetics, ethics, and literature. His *Briefe über die ästhetische Erziehung des Menschen* (*On the Aesthetic Education of Man*) and *Über naive und sentimentalische Dichtung* (*On Naïve and Sentimental Poetry*) are among the most significant treatises on literature and art written in Germany during the second half of the eighteenth century. His extensive correspondence with Johann Wolfgang von Goethe is the high point in the several volumes of his letters that have been collected and published since his death.

Select works other than poetry

DRAMA: *Die Räuber*, pb. 1781 (*The Robbers*, 1792); *Die Verschwörung des Fiesko zu Genua*, pr., pb. 1783 (*Fiesco: Or, The Genoese Conspiracy*, 1796); *Kabale und Liebe*, pr., pb. 1784 (*Cabal and Love*, 1795); *Don Carlos, Infant von Spanien*, pr., pb. 1787 (*Don Carlos, Infante of Spain*, 1798); *Wallensteins Lager*, pr. 1798 (*The Camp of Wallenstein*, 1846); *Die Piccolomini*, pr. 1799 (*The Piccolominis*, 1800); *Wallensteins Tod*, pr. 1799 (*The Death of Wallenstein*, 1800); *Wallenstein*, pr. 1799, pb. 1800 (trilogy that includes previous three works); *Maria Stuart*, pr. 1800 (English translation, 1801); *Die Jungfrau von Orleans*, pr. 1801 (*The Maid of Orleans*, 1835); *Die Braut von Messina: Oder, Die feindlichen Brüder*, pr., pb. 1803 (*The Bride of Messina*, 1837); *Wilhelm Tell*, pr., pb. 1804 (*William Tell*, 1841); *Historical Dramas*, pb. 1847; *Early Dramas and Romances*, pb. 1849; *Dramatic Works*, pb. 1851.

NONFICTION: *Die Schaubühne als eine moralische Anstalt betrachtet*, 1784 (*The Theater as a Moral Institution*, 1845); *Historischer Kalender für Damen*, 1790, 1791; *Geschichte des dreissigjährigen Krieges*, 1791-1793 (3 volumes; *History of the Thirty Years War*, 1799); *Über den Grund des Vergnügens an tragischen Gegenständen*, 1792 (*On the Pleasure in Tragic Subjects*, 1845); *Über das Pathetische*, 1793 (*On the Pathetic*, 1845); *Über Anmut und Würde*, 1793 (*On Grace and Dignity*, 1875); *Briefe über die ästhetische Erziehung des Menschen*, 1795 (*On the Aesthetic Education of Man*, 1845); *Über naïve und sentimentalische Dichtung*, 1795 (*On Naïve and Sentimental Poetry*, 1845); *Über das Erhabene*, 1801 (*On the Sublime*, 1845); *Briefwechsel Zwischen Schiller und Goethe*, 1829 (*The Correspondence Between Schiller and Goethe*, 1845); *Aesthetical and Philosophical Essays*, 1845; *Schillers Briefwechsel mit Körner von 1784 bis zum Tode Schillers*, 1847 (*Schiller's Correspondence with Körner*, 1849).

MISCELLANEOUS: *Sämmtliche Werke*, 1812-1815 (12 volumes; *Complete Works in English*, 1870).

Lowell A. Bangerter

Bibliography · A classic study of Schiller in English is Thomas Carlyle, *The Life of Friedrich Schiller*, 1845. More recent general treatments of Schiller and his work include H. B. Garland, *Schiller*, 1949; William Witte, *Schiller*, 1949; E. L. Stahl, *Friedrich Schiller's Drama, Theory, and Practice*, 1954; R. D. Miller, *Interpreting Schiller*, 1986; and T. J. Reed, *Schiller*, 1991. More specialized studies include Stanley Sephton Kerry, *Schiller's Writings on Aesthetics*, 1961; R. D. Miller, *The Drama of Schiller*, 1963, and *Schiller and the Ideal of Freedom*, 1970; Philip Kain, *Schiller, Hegel, and Marx*, 1982; and Juliet Sychrava, *Schiller to Derrida: Idealism in Aesthetics*, 1989.

SIR WALTER SCOTT

Born: Edinburgh, Scotland; August 15, 1771
Died: Abbotsford, Scotland; September 21, 1832

Poetry · *The Eve of Saint John: A Border Ballad,* 1800 · *The Lay of the Last Minstrel,* 1805 · *Ballads and Lyrical Pieces,* 1806 · *Marmion: A Tale of Flodden Field,* 1808 · *The Lady of the Lake,* 1810 · *The Vision of Don Roderick,* 1811 · *Rokeby,* 1813 · *The Bridal of Triermain: Or, The Vale of St. John, in Three Cantos,* 1813 · *The Lord of the Isles,* 1815 · *The Field of Waterloo,* 1815 · *The Ettrick Garland: Being Two Excellent New Songs,* 1815 (with James Hogg) · *Harold the Dauntless,* 1817

Achievements · Sir Walter Scott's literary reputation still rests on thirty novels. Few twentieth century readers and scholars have been interested in his poetry or have taken the time to examine the distinct stages of his literary career. With the publication of *Waverley* in 1814, Scott's literary life as a novelist began and his period of intense poetic production terminated. At the outset, then, one is tempted to view the poetry only in the context of its effect on the fiction—or, from another perspective, the effect of Scott the poet on Scott the novelist.

Ample reason exists, however, for studying the poetry on its own merits, for the imaginative power to be found in Scott's metrical romances, lyrics, and ballads. Some contemporary scholars support the claims of their Victorian predecessors, who argued that Scott, among all of his "British" contemporaries, emerged as the first writer of the Romantic movement. Indeed, although literary historians correctly offer William Wordsworth's *Lyrical Ballads* (1798)—and its significant "Preface"—as the key to under-standing British Romanticism, Scott's *The Lay of the Last Minstrel,* published seven years later, reached a far wider audience (in both England and Scotland) than Wordsworth's collection and achieved a more noticeable impact among the poet's contemporaries than did the earlier work. In fact, no previous English poet had managed to produce a work that reaped such large financial rewards and achieved so much popular acclaim.

Interestingly enough, Scott's poetic achievements came in a form radi-cally different from those qualities that marked the traditional "giants" of his age—Wordsworth, Samuel Taylor Coleridge, John Keats, Percy Bysshe Shelley, and Lord Byron. True, Scott considered, at a variety of levels, the prevalent Romantic themes: the rejection of scientific dogmatism, a return to the glamour of past ages, the discovery of happiness in primitivism rather than in modernity, the enjoyment of emotion, a basic belief in humanitarianism. He rejected, however, the radical sentiments of the Romantic movement. By nature and upbringing a conservative, Scott clung to Tory politics and to the established Church of England rather than rising up in actual or intellectual rebellion against such institutions. He had little or no interest in mysticism, overzealous passion, or the dark unconscious. Scott's poetry is distinguished by its considerable clarity and directness; it is the product of a gentlemanly and reasonably satisfied attitude

Library of Congress

toward promoting the values of his own social class. He did rush back into an imaginary past to seek out heroes and adventurers whom he found lacking in his own early nineteenth century cultural and artistic environment. Such escapes, however, never really detracted from his belief in the challenge of the present intellectual life and the present world, where, if everything else failed, courage would support the intellectually honest competitor.

Chronologically, Scott belongs with the early Romantics; culturally and intellectually, he occupies a middle ground between Scotland and England, and therein, perhaps, lies his ultimate contribution to poetry in English. He captured, first in the poems and later in his prose fiction, the essence of Scottish national pride; that pride he filtered through the physical image of Scotland, through its varied and conflicting scenery and its traditional romantic lore. The entire area—joined politically to Great Britain in 1707, but still culturally free and theologically independent— stimulated and intensified his creative genius and supplied the substance first for his poetry, then for his prose fiction. Nevertheless, Scott remained distinctly aware of England and receptive to the demands of the English public—his largest reading audience. For them he translated the picturesqueness of the Highlands and the Lowlands, the islands and the borders. While photographing (or "painting," as his contemporaries maintained), through his imagination, the language and the sentiment of Scotland, Scott gave to his English readers scenes and characters that could be observed as partly English. His poetry has a freshness, a frankness, a geniality, and a shrewdness peculiar to his own Scottish Lowlands. Still, as observers of that part of the world quickly appreciate, there is little difference between a southern Scotsman and a northern Englishman—which, in the end, may also be an apt commentary on Scott's poetry.

Biography · The fourth surviving son of Walter Scott and Anne Rutherford, Walter Scott was born on August 15, 1771, in a house in the College Wynd, Edinburgh. At the age of eighteen months, the infant contracted a fever while teething and, in the end, lost the use of his right leg. The circumstance became noteworthy not only for its effect on Scott's personality and his writing, but also as the first fully authenticated case of infantile paralysis in medical history. After the failure of various attempts to remedy the malady, Scott's father sent him to Sandy Knowe, near Kelso (Roxburgh), to live with his grandfather (Robert Scott) and his uncle (Thomas). Although the five years spent there contributed little or nothing toward curing the boy's lameness, they provided some experiences with lasting influence: subjection to republican and Jacobite prejudices; songs and legends taught to him by his grandmother (Barbara Haliburton); a trip to the spas at Bath, with a stopover at London on the way; sea-bathing at Prestonpans, near Edinburgh (site of one of the key engagements of the Jacobite uprising of 1745), where he learned of the German wars from an old veteran of Invernahyle, one Captain Dalgetty.

In 1778, the boy returned to his father's house in George's Square, Edinburgh, and later that year entered the high school at Edinburgh. From his principal tutor, a strict Presbyterian named James Mitchell, Scott gained a knowledge of Scottish church history, while his mother encouraged him to read William Shakespeare. His health, however, continued to be a problem, so again the elder Scott sent his son off, this time to Kelso to live with an aunt, Jenny Scott. During his half-year's stay there, he met James Ballantyne and the blind poet Thomas Blacklock; there, also, he read James Macpherson's Ossianic poems, Edmund Spenser's *The Faerie Queene* (1590-1596), and Thomas Percy's *Reliques of Ancient English Poetry* (1765). Most important, however, he began to collect ballads, a form and a tradition that would remain with him and influence his own literary and cultural directions. By November, 1783, Scott had prepared himself sufficiently to begin studies at Edinburgh University; he pursued only those disciplines, however, that aroused his interest (law, history, romantic legends, and literature). Further illness reduced his stamina, and his education was interrupted once more when he apprenticed himself to his father, copying legal documents. Eventually he did manage to earn a degree in law (1792) and gain admission to the Scottish bar.

Although Scott did indeed practice law and, after a reasonable period as a novice, did manage to earn a fair income from his labors, his interest focused more sharply than ever on literature, ballads, and Scottish folklore. Thus, between 1792 and 1799–first merely as a companion to the sheriff-substitute of Roxburghshire, then as sheriff-deputy of Selkirkshire–he engaged in his "border raids," exploring the country, collecting ballads and tales, and generally enjoying the hospitality of many and various true and traditional Scottish characters. To that activity he added a deep interest in German literature; he learned the language (but not the formal grammar) well enough to read and to translate, publishing in 1799 an edition of Johann Wolfgang von Goethe's *Goetz von Berlichingen* (1774), one of that writer's earliest heroic creations in which an old knight bows to the forces of decay about him. Scott did not emerge as a public figure, however, until about six years later, when he published *The Lay of the Last Minstrel.* In rather quick succession he became a partner in and large contributor to James Ballantyne's publishing house, gained a permanent appointment (1806) as Clerk of Session at Edinburgh, and was a principal founder (along with John Murray the younger) of *The Quarterly Review*, the Tory rival to *The Edinburgh Review*. In 1813, he declined the honor of being named Poet Laureate of England in favor of Robert Southey. A year later his first novel, *Waverley*, was published.

As Sheriff of Selkirkshire, Scott went, in 1804, to live at Ashestiel, on the banks of the River Tweed (dividing England and Scotland); there he wrote, between 1805 and 1813, *The Lay of the Last Minstrel, Marmion, The Lady of the Lake, The Vision of Don Roderick, The Bridal of Triermain,* and *Rokeby*. In 1812 he had begun the construction of a baronial mansion at Abbotsford (near Melrose in Roxburghshire)—once known as the little farm of Cartleyhole belonging to the monks of Melrose. After taking up residence there he could, indeed, lay claim to the title of "Gentleman." He continued to reap financial benefits from his writing, and in 1820 he received a baronetcy. He would, however, be denied the luxury of lasting contentment. Economic depression swept the British Isles in 1825; a year later, the firm of John Ballantyne and Company collapsed, and Scott found himself being left responsible (morally and actually) for most of the publishing house's debts. Rather than declaring bankruptcy, the poet-novelist pressed forward on a number of literary projects in order to pay his creditors. To compound the emotional strain and the problems of failing health, Scott's wife, Charlotte Carpentier, died in the same year.

Thus, the last several years of Scott's life were marked by struggle and overwork; he was kept afloat, so to speak, on the strength of his pride and personal integrity. By 1831, his health had declined seriously and he took an Admiralty frigate on a sea voyage through the Mediterranean. He had been sent off from Abbotsford with a fresh sonnet by Wordsworth. While on board, he suffered a stroke of apoplexy resulting in paralysis and was forced to return to Abbotsford. There he lingered, from mid-July, 1832, until September 21, when he died quietly in the presence of all of his children.

Analysis · Sir Walter Scott's poetry, unlike that of his Romantic contemporaries, is vigorous, high-spirited, and unreflective. Scott delighted in war and pageantry, in the rich traditions of antiquity. As a Scottish poet born among a people who sought action, he was drawn to his heritage, to his connections with the border chieftains and the House of Buccleuch. Thus, his narrative poems and ballads reflect the character of a strong and proud man who dreamed of the ultimate masculine activities: of chivalry, adventure, the qualities of feudalism, and the military picturesqueness of another age.

Any survey of Scott the poet must consider his interest in the popular ballad, an interest that came naturally because of the love for the old, harsh times. Scott saw in the popular Scottish ballad a contrast to the relative serenity of his own early nineteenth century. He relished the clannish loyalties, the bravery, the cruelty, the revenge, and the superstitions of the old ballads. Thus, he began with "The Chase" and "William and Helen" (1796)–two translations from the German lyric poet (and, coincidentally, lawyer) Gottfried August Burger (1747-1794); next came three strange, almost mystical ballads contributed to Matthew Gregory "Monk" Lewis' *Tales of Wonder* in 1801: "Glenfinlas," "The Eve of St. John," and "The Gray Brother." His interest in the ballad reached its height–a scholarly as well as a poetic pinnacle–with *The Minstrelsy of the Scottish Border*, wherein Scott the editor and poet gathered and polished the best examples of what will always be considered the true literature of Scotland.

The ballad, however, was not to be the end-all for Scott the poet, but rather a springboard to other forms and variations of ballad themes. He turned his poetic attention to a series of complex and ornamental romances wherein, instead of the harshness and rusticity of the border, lords, ladies, and even clerics came forth to expound lofty themes in elevated language. Still, the stuff from which the popular ballads sprang is there. In *The Lay of the Last Minstrel*, for example, romantic love blends easily with magic, dwarfs, and goblins, while in *Marmion*, the early sixteenth century battle at Flodden Field in Northumberland, where the English, in 1513, defeated the Scots under James IV, allowed Scott to develop elaborate descriptions of conflict and chivalry, of the detailed instruments of warfare and the awesomeness of border castles. More important in terms of the ballad influence, *Marmion* draws considerable poetic life from its thoroughly romantic narrative–from intrigue, disguise, and unfaithfulness (both clerical and secular). *The Lady of the Lake* intensifies those actions, featuring Highland clans rushing to battle after being summoned by a fiery cross. Scott carried his readers on a tour of chieftain's lodge and king's court, setting the stage for James Fitz-James to reveal himself as King James and to restore the noble Ellen to her true love, Malcolm Graeme. Although the later poems–*The Vision of Don Roderick, Rokeby*, and *Harold the Dauntless*–reveal Scott as more than ready to abandon verse for prose fiction, the worlds of knighthood, sorcery, and the ancient bards and minstrels continued to fascinate him–no matter that the locales and circumstances seemed far removed from that wild terrain north of the River Tweed.

One must not too quickly assume that Scott's poetry contains little beyond historical or romantic re-creations. Although he, himself, readily admitted that his work did not rise to the levels of Wordsworth or Coleridge, he nevertheless remained a legitimate poet, not simply a compiler and reviser of historical verse tales. Scott fully realized the depth and complexity of human emotions; he chose, however, to portray the manifestations of those emotions within the context of his own historical knowledge and his own historical imagination. Thus, he could set forth value judgments and insights into history rather than simply displaying the past as mere background scenery. Scott knew only too well that he was living in the present—in a world marked by political and social revolution to which the romantic past must, for the sake of reason and order, subordinate itself. Nevertheless, history could continue to instruct the present; it could also amuse and it could momentarily ease the confusion within the minds of the poet's readers. History could help a restless and degenerate age to imagine the heroics of an older time.

With only a few exceptions, the poetry of Scott conveys action and excitement, for the poet had learned at an early age to master the conventions of narrative. But narration alone could not carry the essence of the poem. In *The Lady of the Lake*, he demonstrated the quality of painting lovely scenery, giving it dimension, and fusing it skillfully with the poetry of clan life. Scott opened the gates to the Scottish Highlands for his cultivated readers to the south. For the height of action and excitement, however, those same readers had to turn to *Marmion*, to the strong horse striding over green terrain in the fresh air, its shrill neighing and the sun's rays reverberating and reflecting from the shield and the lance of its rider. In fact, the poet stacked his details one upon the other in almost breathless fashion: "Green, sanguine, purple, red, and blue,/ Broad, narrow, swallow-tailed, and square,/ Scroll, pennon, pensil, brandrol."

The major weakness of Scott as a poet is his inability to create believable characters. Margaret of Branksome Hall (in *The Lay of the Last Minstrel*) exudes considerable charm, but she does little beyond fulfilling her function as the typical "fair maid," even amid a fast-paced series of armed encounters and magical spells. Roderick Dhu, Malcolm Graeme, and Lord James Douglas (*The Lady of the Lake*) appear active enough, but they have little else to do aside from their obvious responsibilities as fierce Highland chieftains, outlawed lords, and young knights. Also acting according to form (and little else) are Roland de Vaux (*The Bridal of Triermain*), Philip of Montham (*Rokeby*), and Edith of Lorn and Lord Ronald (both from *The Lord of the Isles*)—although Edith's disguise as a mute page, as well as the dangers she encounters, allows her some room for depth and variety. There is little doubt that Scott's best poetic characters assume the forms not of romantic heroes but of heroic scoundrels, such as the stately forger Marmion and the pirate Bertram Risingham (*Rokeby*), whose evil nature contains some elements of good. Scott addressed this problem himself, stating that no matter how hard he had tried to do otherwise, his rogues emerged as heroes. More accurately, the rogues had more life and depth than did the heroes.

Scott's ballads and verse tales are not, however, anchored to the issues of characterization, to the conflicts between good and evil, or even to the differences between heroes and villains. Virtually obliterating the shallowness of those characters, the poet's almost passionate love for the beauties of nature infuses practically every poem. In that sense, and within the context of his abilities to communicate that love to a relatively large and varied reading audience, Scott may indeed be identified with the early Romantic poets. Traditionally, his sophisticated English readership perceived Scotland—especially the Highlands—as a physical and intellectual wilderness; at best, readers of that day recalled only the Gothic descriptions of James Macpherson's Ossianic poems or the Addisonian sketches of the essayist Henry Mackenzie. Then, with *The Lay of the Last Minstrel*, *Marmion*, and *The Lady of the Lake*, Scott revealed the culture of his native land, and "Cold diffidence, and age's frost,/ In the full tide of my song were lost." He carried his readers on his poetic back "Across the furzy hills of Braid," through "all the hill with yellow grain," and over "To eastern Lodon's fertile plain"; through Scott's lines, his readers far to the south undertook a vicarious trek into a land that had been virtually shut off from their imaginations.

In addition to satisfying the imaginative needs of his Romantic readers, Scott conscientiously guided them through an almost microscopic study of physical nature, as if he were conducting a tour: going over each scene, textbook in hand, noting the various species of plants and shrubs, stones and rocks, surveying "each naked precipice,/ Sable ravine, and dark abyss" to uncover "Some touch of Nature's genial glow." For example, in the description of Lake Coriskin (in *The Lord of the Isles*), the landscape portrait captures the warmth of nature and the poet's feeling for color: In addition to the genial glow of nature, "green mosses grow" atop Benmore, while "heath-bells bud in deep Glencoe"—all of which serve up a sharp contrast to the "Black waves, bare crags, and banks of stone" that constitute the "bleakest" side of the mountain. Again, in depicting Edinburgh and the camp in *Marmion*, the poet directs his audience to the "rose on breezes thin" that clashes headlong with "Saint Giles's mingling din" as he strives to document the specifics of the distance (topographical and imaginative) "from the summit to the plain."

Critical response to Scott's poetry has ranged from kindness to indifference. Perhaps the fairest assessment of his poetry is Scott's own. He never aspired to equal Wordsworth or Coleridge or Byron; he wanted only to enjoy life and literature (indeed, even in that order), disclaiming everything beyond the love of Scotland and its traditions. That love obviously led him to poetry, as it did to prose fiction, to biography, to history, and to scholarly editing and collecting. When he finished with one of those aspects of the good, intellectual life, he simply went on to something else. Literary history must be prepared to accept Sir Walter Scott on his own terms and on that middle ground.

Other literary forms · Sir Walter Scott's literary reputation rests firmly on his monumental collection of Waverley novels, the final revision of which was issued, in forty-eight volumes, between 1829 and 1833. The novelist produced those classics on a regular basis during the last eighteen years of his life–beginning with the three-volume *Waverley: Or, 'Tis Sixty Years Since* in 1814 and concluding, shortly before his death, with *Count Robert of Paris* and *Castle Dangerous* (under the collective title *Tales of My Landlord*, fourth series), both in 1831. In addition to the novels, Scott also produced (or adapted) eight plays between 1799 and 1830: *Goetz of Berlichingen*, 1799 (translation); *The Iron Hand*, 1799 (translation); *Guy Mannering*, 1816; *Halidon Hill*, 1822; *Macduff's Cross*, 1823; *The House of Aspen*, 1829; *Auchindrane: Or, The Ayrshire Tragedy*, 1830; and *The Doom of Devorgoil*, 1830.

Scott's nonfiction prose includes *Provincial Antiquities of Scotland*, 1826; *Religious Discourses by a Layman*, 1828; *The History of Scotland*, 1829-1830; and *Letters on Demonology and Witchcraft*, 1830. He also produced three biographies of note: *The Life and Works of John Dryden*, first published in 1808 as part of his eighteen-volume edition of that poet's works; *The Memoirs of Jonathan Swift*, 1826 (originally included in the nineteen-volume *The Life of Jonathan Swift*, 1814); and *The Life of Napoleon Buonaparte: Emperor of the French, with a Preliminary View of the French Revolution*, 1827 (9 volumes). In addition, as editor of *Ballantyne's Novelist's Library* 1821-1824 (10 volumes) Scott wrote biographical essays on each writer in the series (including Henry Fielding, Tobias Smollett, Samuel Richardson, Ann Radcliffe, Charlotte Smith, and Fanny Burney); he published those sketches separately in 1825 (2 volumes).

Finally, Scott expended considerable energy on a long list of editorial projects carried out between 1799 and 1831: in addition to the works of John Dryden and Jonathan Swift and the *Novelist's Library*, one may note *Minstrelsy of the Scottish Border*, 1802 (2 volumes); *A Collection of Scarce and Valuable Tracts*, 1809-1815 (13 volumes); *Chronological Notes of Scottish Affairs from the Diary of Lord Fountainhall*, 1822; and *Lays of the Lindsays*, 1824.

Various editions of *The Journal of Sir Walter Scott* have appeared, beginning in 1890.

Select works other than poetry

LONG FICTION: *Waverley: Or, 'Tis Sixty Years Since,* 1814; *Guy Mannering,* 1815; *The Antiquary,* 1816; *The Black Dwarf,* 1816; *Old Mortality,* 1816; *Rob Roy,* 1817; *The Heart of Midlothian,* 1818; *The Bride of Lammermoor,* 1819; *A Legend of Montrose,* 1819; *Ivanhoe,* 1819; *The Monastery,* 1820; *The Abbot,* 1820; *Kenilworth,* 1821; *The Pirate,* 1821; *The Fortunes of Nigel,* 1822; *Peveril of the Peak,* 1823; *Quentin Durward,* 1823; *St. Ronan's Well,* 1823; *Redgauntlet,* 1824; *The Betrothed,* 1825; *The Talisman,* 1825; *Woodstock,* 1826; *The Fair Maid of Perth,* 1828; *Anne of Geierstein,* 1829; *Count Robert of Paris,* 1831; *Castle Dangerous,* 1831; *The Siege of Malta,* 1976.

SHORT FICTION: *Chronicles of the Canongate,* 1827.

DRAMA: *Halidon Hill,* pb. 1822; *Macduff's Cross,* pb. 1823; *The Doom of Devorgoil,* pb. 1830; *Auchindrane: Or, The Ayrshire Tragedy,* pr., pb. 1830.

NONFICTION: *The Life and Works of John Dryden,* 1808; *The Life of Jonathan Swift,* 1814; *Lives of the Novelists,* 1825; *The Life of Napoleon Buonaparte: Emperor of the French, with a Preliminary View of the French Revolution,* 1827.

TRANSLATIONS: *The Chase, and William and Helen: Two Ballads from the German of Gottfried Augustus Bürger,* 1796; *Goetz von Berlichingen,* 1799 (Johann Wolfgang von Goethe).

EDITED TEXTS: *Minstrelsy of the Scottish Border,* 1802-1803 (3 volumes); *A Collection of Scarce and Valuable Tracts,* 1809-1815 (13 volumes); *Chronological Notes of Scottish Affairs from the Diary of Lord Fountainhall,* 1822.

Samuel J. Rogal

Bibliography · The secondary literature on Scott is immense. Guides are James Clarkson Corson, *A Bibliography of Sir Walter Scott,* 1943, and Jill Rubenstein, *Sir Walter Scott: A Reference Guide,* 1978, supplemented by J. H. Alexander and David Hewitt, eds., *Scott and His Influence,* 1983, and their *Scott in Carnival,* 1993. The classic biography is John Gibson Lockhart, *Memoirs of the Life of Sir Walter Scott, Bart,* 1839. Modern accounts of the life and work include Edgar Johnson, *Sir Walter Scott: The Great Unknown,* 1970, David Daiches, *Sir Walter Scott and His World,* 1971, and John Sutherland, *The Life of Walter Scott: A Critical Biography,* 1995. W. E. K. Anderson, ed., *The Journal of Sir Walter Scott,* 1972, and James Corson, *Notes and Index to Sir Herbert Grierson's Edition of the Letters of Sir Walter Scott,* 1979, are invaluable. Jane Millgate, *Walter Scott: The Making of the Novelist,* 1984, and her *Scott's Last Edition: A Study in Publishing History,* 1987, relate the work to the publishing conditions of their time.

ANNE SEXTON

Born: Newton, Massachusetts; November 9, 1928
Died: Weston, Massachusetts; October 4, 1974

Poetry · *To Bedlam and Part Way Back*, 1960 · *All My Pretty Ones*, 1962 · *Selected Poems*, 1964 · *Live or Die*, 1966 · *Poems*, 1968 (with Thomas Kinsella and Douglas Livingston) · *Love Poems*, 1969 · *Transformations*, 1971 · *The Book of Folly*, 1972 · *The Death Notebooks*, 1974 · *The Awful Rowing Toward God*, 1975 · *45 Mercy Street*, 1975 · *Words for Dr. Y.: Uncollected Poems with Three Stories*, 1978 · *The Complete Poems*, 1981 · *Selected Poems of Anne Sexton*, 1988

Achievements · With little formal training in literature, Anne Sexton emerged as a major modern voice, transforming verse begun as therapy into poetic art of the first order. Important for refining the confessional mode, experimenting with new lyrical forms, and presenting themes from the female consciousness, Sexton's work has the controversial impact of any pioneering artist. Despite periodic hospitalization for depression ultimately culminating in her suicide a month before her forty-sixth birthday, Sexton contributed richly to her craft, receiving much critical recognition and traveling widely. Awarded fellowships to most of the major writing conferences, she worked closely with John Holmes, W. D. Snodgrass, Robert Lowell, Maxine Kumin, and others. She taught creative writing at Harvard, Radcliffe, and Boston University, and she served as editorial consultant to the *New York Poetry Quarterly* and as a member of the board of directors of *Audience* magazine. In 1963, her second collection of poetry, *All My Pretty Ones*, was nominated for a National Book Award; and in 1967, her fourth collection, *Live or Die*, received a Pulitzer Prize. Sexton also received a Guggenheim Fellowship in 1969 and many honorary degrees from major universities.

Although most critics believe the quality of her work deteriorated toward the end of her life, she had achieved by that time success with a new, highly personal voice in poetry and expanded the range of acceptable subjects to include the intimate concerns of women. In presenting the theme of female identity, Sexton began with a careful lyric formalism and then progressed throughout her career to experiment with open, dramatic forms, moving from the confessional to the surreal. She explored the limits of sanity and the nature of womanhood more fully than any poet of her generation.

Biography · The daughter of upper-middle-class parents, Anne Gray Harvey attended the public schools of Wellesley, Massachusetts, spent two years at Rogers Preparatory School, and one year at Garland Junior College, before marrying Alfred Muller Sexton, whose nickname "Kayo" provides the dedication for her first volume of poems. Although a strictly biographical approach to Anne Sexton's work is dangerously limiting, the significant events of her life serve as major subjects and impetus for her art.

After her marriage, she worked briefly as a model at the Hart Agency of Boston. Then, when she was twenty-five, her first daughter, Linda Gray Sexton, was born. The next year, Anne Sexton was hospitalized for emotional disturbance and several months later suffered the loss of her beloved greataunt, Anna Ladd Dingley, nicknamed "Nana," in various poems and remembrances. The next year, Joyce Ladd Sexton was born, but within months her mother was again hospitalized for depression culminating in a suicide attempt on her twenty-eighth birthday.

Following her first suicide attempt, Sexton began writing poetry on the advice of her psychiatrist, Dr. Martin, whose name appears in her first collection of poems. On the strength of her first work, she received a scholarship to the Antioch Writer's Conference where she worked with W. D. Snodgrass. Then she was accepted into Robert Lowell's graduate writing seminar at Boston University, soon developing friendships with Sylvia Plath, Maxine Kumin, and George Starbuck. The next year, both of Sexton's parents died in rapid succession. She continued her work, attending the Bread Loaf Writer's Conference and delivering the Morris Gray Poetry Lecture at Harvard, although she was hospitalized at intervals for pneumonia, an appendectomy, and an ovarectomy. In 1960, Sexton studied with Philip Rahv and Irving Howe at Brandeis University and developed a friendship with James Wright. She was appointed, with Maxine Kumin, to be the first scholars in poetry at the Radcliffe Institute for Independent Study. In 1962, she was again hospitalized for depression, but by the end of the year, she recovered and toured Europe on the first traveling fellowship of the American Academy of Arts and Letters. She also received a Ford Foundation grant for residence with the Charles Playhouse in Boston.

In 1966, Sexton began a novel that was never completed. She again attempted suicide in July, 1966. In August, she took an African safari with her husband, but in November, she was hospitalized again when she broke her hip on her thirty-eighth birthday. In May of that year, she received the Pulitzer Prize for *Live or Die* and the Shelley Award from the Poetry Society of America. She taught poetry as a visiting professor in many schools and received many honorary degrees before again attempting suicide in 1970. In 1973, she divorced her husband during another period of hospitalization for depression. Although she continued to write and teach despite frequent intervals of hospitalization, in 1974, she committed suicide by carbon monoxide poisoning in the garage of her home.

Analysis · Anne Sexton's poetry presents a search for self and meaning beyond the limits of conventional expression and form. Although viewing her work autobiographically limits critical understanding of it, readers discover in her work a chronicle of experience that is intensely personal and genuine. Her poems are confessional in that they present statements about impulses formerly unknown or forbidden. Begun for self-revelation in therapy and initially sustained for the possible benefit of other troubled patients, Sexton's poems speak with penetrating honesty about the experience of mental illness, the temptation of suicide, and the dynamics of womanhood. Although less strident in tone than the work of Sylvia Plath, Sexton's work occasionally alienates readers who, like James Dickey, find her work too personal for literary evaluation. At its best, however, Sexton's poetry develops the confessional lyric into an effective modern form.

In her first collection, *To Bedlam and Part Way Back*, scenes from an asylum are set against those of life before and after the speaker's hospitalization. The perspective of these early poems is a daring interior one, underscored by the book's epigraph taken from a letter of Arthur Schopenhauer to Johann Wolfgang von Goethe, including the phrase "But most of us carry in our heart the Jocasta who begs Oedipus for God's sake not to inquire further." Sexton's poems pursue the inquiry into the mental hospital and the mind of the patient as well. In the chantlike poem "Ringing the Bells," for example, Sexton projects the senseless rhythm of institutional life through the consciousness of a patient in the bell choir of a mental ward. The troubled women who "mind by instinct" assemble, smile, ring their bells when pointed to, and disperse, no better for their weekly music lesson. Another well-known portrayal of institutional life, "Lullaby," shows the figure of the night nurse arriving with the sleeping pills that, like splendid pearls, provide a momentary escape for the patients who receive them. Observing the moths which cling to window screen, the patient of "Lullaby" imagines that he will become like them after taking the sedative. "You, Doctor Martin" presents other figures in the mental hospital, including the large children who wait in lines to be counted at dinner before returning to the labor of making moccasins all day long. Although the portrayal of the mental hospital from an insider's perspective provides a fresh subject for experimental lyrics, Sexton's poems of the journey and return (suggested by the volumes title) are among her most complex and effective.

"The Double Image," for example, is a composite of experiences parallel to Sexton's own biography. In the poem, the speaker's hospitalization brings about a separation from her young daughter; the speaker's return to live in the home of her childhood coincides with the final illness of her own mother. Weaving together the present moment of her return home for a reunion with her daughter and events of the past, the speaker reflects on the guilt bounded by past and present sorrow. The three autumns explain her trouble better than any medical theories, and she finds that despair and guilt transform attempts at ordinary life into artifice. Portrait painting becomes a metaphor for control of time and emotions through the rest of the poem. Unable to adjust to the awkward period spent as a grown child in her parents' home, the speaker states repeatedly "I had my portrait done instead." The same response belongs to her mother, who cannot forgive the speaker's attempt at suicide and so chooses to have the daughter painted as a measure of control. A double image forms when the mother learns of her own incurable illness and has her portrait done "instead." The portraits, facing each other in the parental home, serve as a mirror reflection with the figure of the speaker's child moving between them. As the speaker had been "an awkward guest" returning to her mother's home, so the young daughter arrives "an awkward guest" for the reunion with her recovering mother. The child provides both a measure of final identity and guilt.

In "The Division of Parts," the bitterness of inheritance replaces grief as a response to the death of the speaker's mother. As in "The Double Image," the coincidence of the speaker's recovery with her mother's suffering suggests an apparent exchange of death for life. Equipped with the lost one's "garments" but not with grief, the speaker recalls the suffering of her mother, overshadowed now by the ceremonies of the Lenten season. Division of property replaces the concerns of the Christ who waits on the crucifix for the speaker.

Other poems in the first volume experiment with the voices of experience different from the poet's. "The Farmer's Wife," for example, reveals the isolation and loneliness of a young wife on an Illinois farm. The poem presents the ambivalence of the woman toward her husband, whose work and bed are her lifelong habit. "Unknown Girl in the Maternity Ward" attempts to voice the feelings of an unmarried girl who has just given birth. The emotions and imagery are generalized and undefined in presenting the setting of an urban hospital and the typical unmarried girl in trouble. According to Sexton, the poem marks a pivotal moment in her career, for after reading it, Robert Lowell advised her to develop the more personal voice that gives her finest poetry its power. A poem reflecting conflicting advice is "For John, Who Begs Me Not to Enquire Further." John Holmes, Sexton's teacher for a Boston University poetry workshop, recommended that she avoid the self-revelation becoming characteristic of her work. The directly personal voice won out, not only in this poem of apology to Holmes but also throughout her career. Another early poem, "Kind Sir: These Woods," indicates an awareness that readers in general may disapprove her probing of the psyche, "this inward look that society scorns." The speaker finds in her inward search, however, nothing worse than herself, "caught between the grapes and the thorns," and the search for herself continued to the end of her life.

An epigraph for Sexton's second collection, *All My Pretty Ones*, suggests a reason for the poet's insistence on inner exploration. According to a letter of Franz Kafka, "a book should serve as the ax for the frozen sea within us." Sexton similarly asserted in a later interview that "poems of the inner life can reach the inner lives of readers in a way that anti-war poems can never stop a war." The inner life revealed in *All My Pretty Ones* is primarily the experience of grief, the response to loss of the most precious others expressed in the lines from *Macbeth* (1606) that form the title. "The Truth the Dead Know" and the title poem deal with the death of Sexton's parents during the same year. The first poem eliminates personal references except for a dedication to the parents and simply contrasts the intensity of life and grief with the emptiness and stoniness of the dead. "All My Pretty Ones" addresses the lost father with memories of his belongings, his habits, and his hopes. Disposition of scrapbook photographs provides a way to accept and forgive the disappointments of the past, including the secret alcoholism his daughter can never forget.

The strongest poems of the second volume arise from Sexton's own experience. In "The Operation," the speaker's confrontation with death parallels the illness of her mother, and the speaker considers the uncertainty of life as much as the reality of death. Knowing that cancer, the disease of her mother, the "historic thief" that plundered her mother's home is now invading her own domain, the speaker proceeds helplessly through the preparations for surgery, the experience of losing consciousness, and the recovery phase in doubt of her survival. Then, pronounced better, perhaps cured, by the doctors, she is sent home like a child, the stitches in her abdomen reminding her of the lacing on a football ready for the game. A similar sense of vulnerability appears in "The Fortress," wherein the speaker admits to her sleeping child that a mother has no ability to control life and that eventually it will overtake the child through the suffering of "bombs or glands" ending in death. Beyond the sense of relationships, especially those connected with motherhood, controlling many of Sexton's poems, there looms a sense of dark knowledge gained through poetry as a secret or forbidden art. In "The Black Art," for example, the speaker asserts that a woman who writes will not fit into society, for she "feels too much, these trances and portents." Home, family, social life are inadequate expressions for the one who wishes to know and control the mysterious forces of existence. The poem recalls an earlier statement of identity, "Her Kind," in which the speaker presents herself as a witch who is lonely, misunderstood, insane, and unashamed to die in the course of her journey. The comparison of Sexton's poetry with the black arts places her work on the level of myth, particularly in her pursuit of death itself.

Live or Die, Sexton's third collection, marks a high point in her career for handling intimate or despairing material with sure control and an element of self-irony. The epigraph for this book, taken from Saul Bellow's *Herzog* (1964), records the admonition to "Live or die, but don't poison everything." Certainly, the poems of this group reflect the impulse toward love and life as well as the impulse toward despair and death. The institutional setting appears in the volume but so does the home and family relationships of Sexton. "Flee on Your Donkey," one of her best-known poems, develops the tension between the worlds of private and institutional life. In the poem, a flood of scenes from the hospital culminates in a desire to escape back to the normal world that patients enter the hospital to avoid. Similarly, in "For the Year of the Insane," structured as a prayer to Mary, the speaker struggles to escape her mental as well as physical confinement. No longer at peace in the refuge of therapy, a mind that believes itself "locked in the wrong house" struggles in vain for expression and release. Poems of similar desperation, "The Addict" and "Wanting to Die," develop other means of escape. The speaker of the former poem yearns for the hallucinatory realm where drugs parcel out moments of deathlike experience. "Wanting to Die," one of Sexton's best-known poems, strives to explain for the uninitiated the hunger for death haunting the potential suicide. The obsession with methods of dying replaces the desire for experience of life. Love itself becomes "an infection" to those seeking the secret pleasure that final escape from the body will bring.

Poems of the third collection that deal with survival include those concerned with children and birth. In "Little Girl, My String Bean, My Lovely Woman," the speaker identifies with the approaching womanhood of her daughter Linda, beautiful even in the uncertain changes adolescence creates. The poem celebrates the body in its growth and capacity for

becoming; the figure of mother and daughter share the mystery of repro-
duction that is spiritual, "a white stone," as well as physical, "laughter," and
joy. In "Pain for a Daughter," the mother discovers in her injured child's
suffering a universal misery that transcends their relationship. The child's
foot torn by the hoof of a horse, she cries out to God, not her mother, and
the isolation of the cry suggests not childhood misery but the future pangs
of childbirth and death itself. The decision to survive, for the moment at
least, appears in "Live," the final statement of the volume. The speaker
recounts a shift from life as a dark pretense or game to a moment when the
sun rose within her, illuminating the figures of her husband and daughters.
The speaker determines herself no longer the murderer she thought,
allowing the newborn Dalmatian puppies to live and deciding to survive
herself.

Love Poems, Sexton's fourth collection, examines the cycle of roles
women play in life and love. Poems of separation and return, for example,
include "Touch" and "Eighteen Days Without You," lyrics in which love
between a woman and her lover controls survival and existence beyond
their union. Throughout the volume, individual body parts achieve significance beyond their function in the physical realm. "Touch" begins, "For
months my hand had been sealed off/ in a tin box." Following the arrival
of her lover, life rushes into the fingers, spreading across the continent
in its intensity. Other celebrations of physical contact include "The Kiss,"
"The Breast," and "In Celebration of My Uterus." In this last poem, Sexton
develops a great song which a whole catalog of women sing as they go
about their daily work carrying the "sweet weight" of the womb. The
negative side of experience returns in poems such as "The Break," which
recounts the depression preceding a fall down the stairs which broke
Sexton's hip and forced another lengthy hospitalization. Although the
bones are sure to heal, the speaker's heart begins another building process to create a "death crèche," ready for the zeal of destruction when it
returns.

The theme of self-destruction is hidden in *Transformations,* Sexton's
collection of rewritten fairy tales narrated by a "middle-aged witch," the
poet's name for her persona in the tales. For some critics, this collection
provides a more objective scheme for Sexton's mythic quest; for others,
the subject matter is quaint and unoriginal. Certainly the retold tales are
entertaining and effective in the dark, modern twists Sexton creates. "Snow
White," for example, tortures the wicked queen without mercy before
returning to gaze triumphantly in her mirror "as women do." "Rumpelstilt-
skin" develops the figure of the dark one within, the doppelgänger trying
to escape every man. Failing to gain the queen's child, he splits in two, "one

part papa/ one part Doppelganger," completing the division of the psyche. "Briar Rose (Sleeping Beauty)" becomes a tortured insomniac after being awakened by her prince and never knows the sleep of death.

Sexton's last collections, *The Book of Folly, The Death Notebooks,* and *The Awful Rowing Toward God* contain many of her previous themes developed in experimental forms, including dramatic changes in style. Critics note a looser structure in the poems written late in Sexton's career; some believe it reflects a deterioration of her creative powers, while others find the experimentalism valuable for its innovation. One of the well-known late poems, "Hurry Up Please It's Time" reflects both the variety of thematic material, the variable stanza lengths, and the intrusion of dialogue, such as those between "Anne" and "The Interrogator." The poem reworks the approach of death and the obsessive derision of life on the part of the dying one. "Ms. Dog," one of Sexton's nicknames for herself and God spelled backward, figures in the poem as the troubled one facing guilt and rejection, the mystery and futility of death. In "Frenzy," another of the last poems, the speaker describes herself "typing out the God/ my typewriter believes in." Through the last years of Sexton's life, her writing sustained her even as her quest darkened. At the end of her life, she sought God when doctors, friends, and family were unable to help her; and her work reflected an outwardly religious search that had formerly been hidden. Although she never revealed that she found God within or without the lines of her poetry, she left behind a brilliant record of her heroic search.

Other literary forms · In addition to several articles on the craft and teaching of poetry, Anne Sexton authored a play that ran successfully at the American Place Theatre of New York and several children's books written in collaboration with Maxine Kumin. The play, *45 Mercy Street* (1969), presents the struggle of a woman named Daisy to find meaning in a past and present dominated by religious and sexual conflicts objectified as demons and disembodied voices. Its success suggests that the poet also had talent as a playwright, and critics find the thematic material important biographically and artistically in an analysis of Sexton's career. An important collection of her prose is *Anne Sexton: A Self-Portrait in Letters* (1977); also, a recording of twenty-four poems read by the poet is available as *Anne Sexton Reads Her Poetry,* recorded June 1, 1974.

Select works other than poetry

DRAMA: *45 Mercy Street,* pr. 1969.

NONFICTION: *Anne Sexton: A Self-Portrait in Letters,* 1977; *No Evil Star: Selected Essays, Interviews, and Prose,* 1985.

CHILDREN'S LITERATURE (with Maxine Kumin): *Eggs of Things*, 1963; *More Eggs of Things*, 1964; *Joey and the Birthday Present*, 1971; *The Wizard's Tears*, 1975.

Chapel Louise Petty

Bibliography · Diane Wood Middlebrook, *Anne Sexton: A Biography*, 1991, is considered "authoritative" by Sexton's daughter Linda, who also wrote her own reminiscence of family life (which was sometimes very loving, sometimes very dysfunctional) with her mother, *Searching for Mercy Street: My Journey Back to My Mother, Anne Sexton*, 1994. Diana Hume George, *Oedipus Anne: The Poetry of Anne Sexton*, 1987, a synthesis of Freudian and feminist approaches to Sexton, resembles much psychoanalytic literature on the poet. Various anthologies sample her changing reputation, including J. D. McClatchy, ed., *Anne Sexton: The Artist and Her Critics*, 1978; Francis Bixler, ed., *Original Essays on the Poetry of Anne Sexton*, 1988; Steven E. Colburn, ed., *Anne Sexton: Telling the Tale*, 1988; Diana Hume George, ed., *Sexton: Selected Criticism*, 1988; and Linda Wagner-Martin, ed., *Critical Essays on Anne Sexton*, 1989. Caroline King Barnard Hall, *Anne Sexton*, 1989, provides a methodical study of the poetry, book by book. Cameron Northouse and Thomas P. Walsh, *Sylvia Plath and Anne Sexton: A Reference Guide*, 1974, only covers scholarship through 1971, thus stopping before the flood began.

WILLIAM SHAKESPEARE

Born: Stratford-upon-Avon, England; April 23, 1564
Died: Stratford-upon-Avon, England; April 23, 1616

Poetry · *Venus and Adonis*, 1593 · *The Rape of Lucrece*, 1594 · *The Passionate Pilgrim*, 1599 (miscellany with poems by Shakespeare and others) · *The Phoenix and the Turtle*, 1601 · *A Lover's Complaint*, 1609 · *Sonnets*, 1609

Achievements · In addition to being the most renowned English-language dramatist, William Shakespeare wrote some of the greatest love poems in the language. His short erotic narratives, *Venus and Adonis* and *The Rape of Lucrece*, were typical examples of fashionable literary genres. Other minor poems include contributions to the miscellany *The Passionate Pilgrim* and *The Phoenix and the Turtle*, written for a collection of poems appended to *Love's Martyr* (1601), an allegorical treatment of love by Robert Chester. All of these pale alongside the sonnets, which, in an age of outstanding love poetry, attain a depth, suggestiveness, and power rarely duplicated in the history of mankind's passionate struggle to match desire with words.

Biography · William Shakespeare was born in the provincial town of Stratford-upon-Avon in 1564 and died there in 1616. He spent most of his adult life in the London theaters and quickly attained a reputation as a dramatist, actor, and poet. Shakespeare's company prospered under the reign of James I, and by the time of his retirement from playwrighting about 1612, Shakespeare had acquired a respectable fortune. His career as a poet, distinct from his more public career as a dramatist, was probably confined to perhaps a decade, between 1591 and 1601, although the sonnets were later collected and published (perhaps without his permission) in 1609. Because of the absurd controversies that grew, mainly in the nineteenth century, about whether Shakespeare actually existed, it is worthwhile pointing out that there are many official records (christening record, marriage license, legal documents, correspondence, and so on) which may be consulted by the skeptic.

Analysis · One of William Shakespeare's great advantages as a writer was that, as a dramatist working in the public theater, he was afforded a degree of autonomy from the cultural dominance of the court, his age's most powerful institution. All over Europe, even if belatedly in England, the

Library of Congress

courts of the Renaissance nation-states conducted an intense campaign to use the arts to further their power. The theater, despite its partial dependency on court favor, achieved through its material products (the script and the performance) a relative autonomy in comparison with the central court arts of poetry, prose fiction, and the propagandistic masque. When Shakespeare briefly turned to Ovidian romance in the 1590's and, belatedly, probably also in the 1590's, to the fashion for sonnets, he moved closer to the cultural and literary dominance of the court's taste–to the fashionable modes of Ovid, Petrarch, and Neoplatonism—and to the need for patronage. Although the power of the sonnets goes far beyond their sociocultural roots, Shakespeare nevertheless adopts the culturally inferior role of the petitioner for favor, and there is an undercurrent of social and economic powerlessness in the sonnets, especially when a rival poet seems likely to supplant the poet. In short, Shakespeare's nondramatic poems grow out of and articulate the strains of the 1590's, when, like many ambitious writers and intellectuals on the fringe of the court, Shakespeare clearly needed to find a language in which to speak—and that was, necessarily, given to him by the court. What he achieved within this shared framework, however, goes far beyond any other collection of poems in the age. Shakespeare's occasional poems are unquestionably minor, interesting primarily because he wrote them; his sonnets, on the other hand, constitute perhaps the language's greatest collection of lyrics. They are love lyrics, and clearly grow from the social, erotic, and literary contexts of his age. Part of their greatness, however, lies in their power to be read again and again in later ages, and to raise compellingly, even unanswerably, more than merely literary questions.

In his first venture into public poetry, Shakespeare chose to work within the generic constraints of the fashionable Ovidian verse romance. *Venus and Adonis* appealed to the taste of young aristocrats such as the Earl of Southampton to whom it was dedicated. It is a narrative poem in six-line stanzas, mixing classical mythology with surprisingly (and incongruously) detailed descriptions of country life, designed to illustrate the story of the seduction of the beautiful youth Adonis by the comically desperate aging goddess, Venus. It is relatively static, with too much argument to make it inherently pleasurable reading. Its treatment of love relies on Neoplatonic and Ovidian commonplaces, and it verges (unlike Christopher Marlowe's *Hero and Leander*, 1598, to which Shakespeare's poem is a fair but decidedly inferior fellow) on moralizing allegory, with Venus as flesh, Adonis as spiritual longing. The poem's articulation of the nature of the love that separates them is abstract and often unintentionally comic—although Shakespeare's characterization of Venus as a garrulous plump matron brings something of his theatrical power to enliven the poem. The poem was certainly popular at the time, going through ten editions in as many years, possibly because its early readers thought it fashionably sensual.

The Rape of Lucrece is the "graver labor" which Shakespeare promised to Southampton in the Preface to *Venus and Adonis*. Again, he combines a current poetical fashion—the complaint—with a number of moral commonplaces, and writes a novelette in verse: a melodrama celebrating the prototype of matronly chastity, the Roman lady Lucrece, and her suicide after she is raped. The central moral issue—that of honor—at times almost becomes a serious treatment of the psychology of self-revulsion, but the decorative and moralistic conventions of the complaint certainly do not afford Shakespeare the scope of a stage play. There are some fine local atmospheric effects which, in their declamatory power, occasionally bring the directness and power of the stage into the verse.

The Phoenix and the Turtle is an allegorical, highly technical celebration of an ideal love union: it consists of a funeral procession of mourners, a funeral anthem, and a final lament for the dead. It is strangely evocative, dignified, abstract, and solemn. Readers have fretted, without success, over the exact identifications of its characters. Its power lies in its mysterious, eerie evocation of the mystery of unity in love.

Probably more human ingenuity has been spent on Shakespeare's sonnets than on any other work of English literature. In his outstanding edition entitled *Shakespeare's Sonnets* (1978), Stephen Booth briefly summarizes the few facts that have led to a plethora of speculation on such matters as text, authenticity, date, arrangement, and, especially, biographical implications. The sonnets were first published in 1609, although numbers 138 and 144 had appeared in *The Passionate Pilgrim* a decade before. Attempts to reorder the sonnets have been both varied and creative, but none represents the "correct" order. Such attempts simply fulfill an understandable anxiety on the part of some readers to see narrative continuity rather than variations and repetition in the sonnets. The so-called "story" "behind" the sonnets has, as Booth puts it, "evoked some notoriously creative scholarship": speculation on the identity of the young man mentioned in many of the first 126 sonnets, of Mr. W. H., to whom the sequence is dedicated by the printer, of the so-called "Dark Lady" of sonnets 127-152, and of the rival poet of some of the earlier sonnets—all of these matters have filled many library shelves.

Such speculations—which reached their peak in critics and readers wedded to the sentimental Romantic insistence on an intimate tie between literary and historical "events"—are in one sense a tribute to the power of the sonnets. They are arguably the greatest collection of love poems in the English language, and they provide a crucial test for the adequacy of both the love of poetry and the sense of the fascinating confusion which makes up human love. In a sense, the sonnets are as "dramatic" as any of Shakespeare's plays inasmuch as their art is that of meditations on love, beauty, time, betrayal, insecurity, and joy. Each sonnet is like a little script, with (often powerful) directions for reading and enactment, with textual meanings that are not given but made anew in every performance, by different readers within their individual and social lives. What Sonnet 87 terms "misprision" may stand as the necessary process by which each sonnet is produced by each reader.

It is conventional to divide the sonnets into two groups: 1-126, purportedly addressed or related to a young man, and 127-152, to the so-called dark lady. Such a division is arbitrary at best—within each group there are detachable subgroups, and without the weight of the conventional arrangement many sonnets would not seem to have a natural place in either group. Sonnets 1-17 (and perhaps 18) are ostensibly concerned with a plea for a young man to marry; but even in this group, which many readers have seen to be the most conventional and unified, there are disruptive suggestions that go far beyond the commonplace context.

What may strike contemporary readers, and not merely after an initial acquaintance with the sonnets, is the apparently unjustified level of idealization voiced by many of the sonnets—an adulatory treatment of noble love which, to a post-Freudian world, might seem archaic, no matter how comforting. The continual self-effacement of the anguished lover, the worship of the "God in love, to whom I am confined" (110), the poet's claim to immortalizing "his beautie . . . in these blacke lines" (63), these idealizations are all born out of a world of serene affirmation. Some of the most celebrated sonnets, such as "Shall I compare thee to a summer's day" (18) or "Let me not to the marriage of true minds" (116), may even seem cloyingly affirmative, their texts seemingly replete, rejecting any subtextual challenges to their idealism.

In the two hundred years since Petrarch, the sonnet had developed into an instrument of logic and rhetoric. The Shakespearian sonnet, on the other hand, with its three quatrains and a concluding couplet, allows especially for the concentration on a single mood; it is held together less by the apparent logic of many of the sonnets (for example, the "when . . . then" pattern) than by the invitation to enter into the dramatization of a brooding, sensitive mind. The focus is on emotional richness, on evoking the immediacy of felt experience. Shakespeare uses many deliberately generalized epithets, indeterminate signifiers and floating referents which provoke meaning from their readers rather than providing it. Each line contains contradictions, echoes, and suggestions which require an extraordinary degree of emotional activity on the part of the reader. The couplets frequently offer a reader indeterminate statements, inevitably breaking down any attempt at a limited formalist reading. The greatest of the sonnets—60, 64, 129, as well as many others—have such an extraordinary combination of general, even abstract, words and unspecified emotional power that the reader may take it as the major rhetorical characteristic of the collection.

In particular lines, too, these poems achieve amazing power by their lack of logical specificity and emotional open-endedness. As Booth points out, many lines show "a constructive vagueness" by which a word or phrase is made to do multiple duty—by placing it "in a context to which it pertains but which it does not quite fit idiomatically" or by using phrases which are simultaneously illogical and amazingly charged with meaning. He instances "separable spite" in Sonnet 36 as a phrase rich with suggestion; another example is the way in which the bewilderingly ordinary yet suggestive epithets sit uneasily in the opening lines of Sonnet 64. Often a reader is swept on through the poem by a syntactical movement which is modified or contradicted by associations set up by words and phrases. There is usually a syntactical or logical framework in the sonnet, but so powerful are the contradictory, random, and disruptive effects occurring incidentally as the syntax unfolds that to reduce the sonnet to its seemingly replete logical framework is to miss the most amazing effects of these extraordinary poems.

Shakespeare is writing at the end of a very long tradition of using lyric poems to examine the nature of human love, and there is a weight of insight as well as of rhetorical power behind his collection. Nowhere in the Petrarchan tradition are the extremes of erotic revelation offered in such rawness and complexity. Northrop Frye once characterized the sonnets as a kind of "creative yoga," an imaginative discipline meant to articulate the feelings that swirl around sexuality. Most of the conventional *topoi* of traditional poetry are the starting points for the sonnets—the unity of lovers (36-40), the power of poetry to immortalize the beloved (18, 19, 55), contests between eye and heart, beauty and virtue (46, 141), and shadow and substance (53, 98, 101). As with Petrarch's *Rime* (after 1327) or Sir Philip Sidney's *Astrophel and Stella* (1591), it would be possible to create a schematic account of commonplace Renaissance thinking about love from the sonnets. To do so, however, would be to nullify their extraordinary power of creation, the way they force ejaculations of recognition, horror, or joy from their readers.

After half a century of existentialism, readers in the late twentieth century understood that one of the most urgent subjects of the sonnets is not the commonplaces of Renaissance thinking about love, nor even the powerful concern with the power of art, but what Sonnet 16 calls our "war upon this bloody tyrant Time." It is no accident that the "discovery" of the sonnets' concern with time and mutability dates from the 1930's, when the impact of Søren Kierkegaard, Friedrich Nietzsche, and the existentialists, including Martin Heidegger, was starting to be widely felt in England and America. The sonnets' invitation to see man's temporality not merely as an abstract problem, but as part of his inherent nature—what Heidegger terms man's "thrownness," his sense of being thrown into the world—seems central to a perception of the sonnets' power. Unpredictability and change are at the heart of the sonnets—but it is a continually shifting heart, and one that conceives of human love as definable only in terms of such change and finitude. The sonnets avoid the transcendentalism of Geoffrey Chaucer beseeching his young lovers to turn from the world, or of Edmund Spenser rejecting change for the reassurance of God's Eternity and His providential guidance of time to a foreknown, if mysterious, end. Shakespeare's sonnets rather overwhelm readers with questions and contradictions. In Sonnet 60, for example, time is not an impartial or abstract background. Even where it is glanced at as a pattern observable in nature or man, it is evoked as a disruptive, disturbing experience which cannot be dealt with as a philosophical problem. Some sonnets portray time as a sinister impersonal determinant; some thrust time at the reader as an equally unmanageable force of unforeseeable chances and changes, what Sonnet 115 calls man's "million'd accidents."

In Sonnet 15, it may be possible to enter into an understandable protest against time destroying its own creations (a commonplace enough Renaissance sentiment), and to accede to a sense of helplessness before a malignant force greater than the individual human being. When the sonnet tries, however, by virtue of its formally structured argument, to create a consciousness that seeks to understand and so to control this awareness, the reader encounters lines or individual words that may undermine even the temporary satisfaction of the aesthetic form. Such, for example is the force of the appalling awareness that "everything that grows/ Holds in perfection but a little moment." What is the application of "everything" or the emotional effect of the way the second line builds to a seemingly replete climax in "perfection" and then tumbles into oblivion in "but a little moment"? The sonnet does not and need not answer such questions. In a very real sense it cannot answer them, for readers can only acknowledge time's power in their own contingent lives. What is shocking is not merely the commonplace that "never-resting time leads summer on/ To hideous winter, and confounds him there" (5) but that each reading fights against and so disrupts the logical and aesthetic coherence of the reader's own sense of change and betrayal.

To attempt criticism of the sonnets is, to an unusual extent, to be challenged to make oneself vulnerable, to undergo a kind of creative therapy, as one goes back and forth from such textual gaps and indeterminancies to the shifting, vulnerable self, making the reader aware of the inadequacy and betrayal of words, as well as of their amazing seductiveness. Consider, for example, Sonnet 138. When one falls in love with a much younger person, does one inevitably feel the insecurity of a generation gap? What is more important in such a reading of the sonnets is the insistence that age or youthfulness are not important in themselves: It is the insistence itself that is important, not the mere fact of age—just as it is the anxiety with which a man or woman watches the wrinkles beneath the eyes that is important, not the wrinkles themselves. The note of insistence, in other words, is not attached merely to the speaker's age: It stands for an invitation to participate in some wider psychological revelation, to confess the vulnerability which people encounter in themselves in any relationship that is real and growing, and therefore necessarily unpredictable and risky.

Without vulnerability and contingency, without the sense of being thrown into the world, there can be no growth. Hence the poet invites the reader to accept ruefully what the fact of his age evokes—an openness to ridicule or rejection. The sonnet's insistence on being open to the insecurity represented by the narrator's age points not merely to a contrast between the speaker and his two lovers but rather to a radical self-division. This is especially so in the Dark Lady sonnets, where there is a savage laceration of self, particularly in the fearful exhaustion of Sonnet 129, in which vulnerability is evoked as paralysis. At once logically relentless and emotionally centrifugal, Sonnet 129 generates fears or vulnerability and self-disgust. Nothing is specified: The strategies of the poem work to make the reader reveal or recognize his own compulsions and revulsions. The poem's physical, psychological, and cultural basis forces the reader to become aware of his awful drive to repress words because they are potentially so destructive.

Even in the seemingly most serene sonnets there are inevitably dark shadows of insecurity and anxiety. In Sonnet 116, for example, the argument is that a love that alters with time and circumstance is not a true, but a self-regarding love.

The poem purports to define true love by negatives, but if those negatives are deliberately negated, the poem that emerges may be seen as the dark, repressed underside of the apparently unassailable affirmation of a mature, self-giving, other-directed love. If lovers admit impediments, and play with the idea that love is indeed love which "alters when it alteration finds," that it is an "ever-fixed mark" and, most especially, that love is indeed "time's fool," then the poem connects strikingly and powerfully with the strain of insecurity about the nature of change in human love that echoes throughout the whole collection. Such apparent affirmations may be acts of repression, an attempt to regiment the unrelenting unexpectedness and challenge of love. There are poems in the collection which, although less assertive, show a willingness to be vulnerable, to reevaluate constantly, to swear permanence within, not despite, transience—to be, in the words of St. Paul, deceivers yet true. Elsewhere, part of the torture of the Dark Lady sonnets is that such a consolation does not emerge through the pain.

In short, what Sonnet 116 represses is the acknowledgment that the only fulfillment worth having is one that is struggled for and which is independent of law or compulsion. The kind of creative fragility that it tries to marginalize is that evoked in the conclusion to Sonnet 49 when the poet admits his vulnerability: "To leave poor me thou hast the strength of laws,/ Since, why to love, I can allege no cause." This is an affirmation of a different order—or rather an acknowledgment that love must not be defined by repression and exclusion. Lovers can affirm the authenticity of the erotic only by admitting the possibility that it is not absolute. Love has no absolute legal, moral, or causal claims; nor, in the final analysis, can love acknowledge the bonds of law, family, or state—or if finally they are acknowledged, it is because they grow from love itself. Love moves by its own internal dynamic; it is not motivated by a series of external compulsions. Ultimately it asks from the lover the *nolo contendere* of commitment: do with me what you will. A real, that is to say, an altering, bending, *never* fixed and unpredictable love is always surrounded by, and at times seems to live by, battles, plots, subterfuges, quarrels, and irony. At the root is the acknowledgment that any affirmation is made because of, not despite, time and human mortality. As Sonnet 12 puts it, having surveyed the fearful unpredictability of all life, lovers must realize that it is even "thy beauty" that must be questioned. At times this thought "is as a death" (64), a "fearful meditation" (65)—that even the most precious of all human creations, will age, wrinkle, fade, and die. Just how can one affirm in the face of that degree of reality?

Under the pressure of such questioning, the affirmation of Sonnet 116 can therefore be seen as a kind of bad faith, a false dread—false, because it freezes lovers in inactivity when they should, on the contrary, accept their finitude as possibility. Frozen in the fear of contingency, which Sonnet 116 so ruthlessly represses in its insistent negatives, readers may miss Shakespeare's essential insight that it is in fact the very fragility of beauty, love, poetry, fair youth, and dark lady alike, that enhances their desirability. Paradoxically, it is precisely because they are indeed among the wastes of time that they are beautiful; they are not desirable because they are immortal but because they are irrevocably timebound. One of the most profound truths is expressed in Sonnet 64: "Ruin hath taught me thus to ruminate/ That Time will come and take my love away./ This thought is as a death, which cannot choose/ But weep to have that which it fears to lose." The power of such lines goes far beyond the serene platitudes of Sonnet 116. At his most courageous, man does not merely affirm, *despite* the forces of change and unpredictability which provide the ever-shifting centers of his life; on the contrary, he discovers his greatest strengths *because* of and within his own contingency. To accept rather than to deny time is to prove that man's deepest life ultimately does not recognize stasis but always craves growth, and that fulfillment is built not upon the need for finality, for being "ever fixed," but on the need to violate apparent limits, to push forward or die.

Against a sonnet such as 116, some sonnets depict love not as a serene continuation of life but rather as a radical reorientation. Readers are asked not to dismiss fears of limitation, but to affirm them. It is in the midst of contingency, when meditations are overwhelmed by the betrayals of the past, while "I sigh the lack of many a thing I sought,/ And with old woes new wail my dear Time's waste" (Sonnet 30), that love may open up the future as possibility, not as completion—so long as one accepts that it is time itself that offers such possibility, not any attempt to escape from it.

The typical Renaissance attitude to time and mutability was one of fear or resignation unless, as in Spenser, the traditional Christian context could be evoked as compensation; but for Shakespeare the enormous energies released by the Renaissance are wasted in trying to escape the burden of temporality. The drive to stasis, to repress experiences and meanings, is a desire to escape the burden of realizing that there are some transformations which love cannot effect. Ultimately, it is impossible to get inside a lover's soul no matter how much the flesh is seized and penetrated. The drive to possess and so to annihilate is a desire derived from the old Platonic ideal of original oneness, which only Shakespeare among the Renaissance poets seems to have seen as a clear and fearful perversion—it certainly haunts the lover of the Dark Lady sonnets and we are invited to stand and shudder at the speaker's Augustinian self-lacerations. In Sonnet 144 the two loves "of comfort and despair,/ Which like two spirits do suggest me still" are not just a "man right fair" and a "woman, colour'd ill": They are also aspects of each lover's self, the two loves that a dualistic mind cannot affirm and by which people may be paralyzed.

Throughout this discussion of the sonnets, what has been stressed is that their power rests on the seemingly fragile basis not of Shakespeare's but of their readers' shifting and unpredictable experiences. They are offered not in certainty, but in hope. They invite affirmation while insisting that pain is the dark visceral element in which man must live and struggle. Many of the Dark Lady sonnets are grim precisely because the lover can see no way to break through such pain. What they lack, fundamentally, is hope. By accepting that, for a time, "my grief lies onward and my joy behind" (Sonnet 50), the lover may be able, however temporarily, to make some commitment. Sonnet 124 is particularly suggestive, categorizing love as "dear," costly, not only because it is "fond," beloved, but also because it is affirmed in the knowledge of the world. Moreover, while it "fears not Policy" it is nevertheless "hugely politic." It is as if love must be adaptable, cunning, even deceptive, aware of the untrustworthiness of the world from which it can never be abstracted: "it nor grows with heat, nor drowns with showers." Finally, the poet affirms with a strong and yet strangely ironic twist: "To this I witness call the fools of Time,/ Which die for goodness, who have liv'd for crime." As Stephen Booth notes, Sonnet 124 "is the most extreme example of Shakespeare's constructive vagueness," its key the word "it," which, "like all pronouns, is specific, hard, concrete, and yet imprecise and general–able to include anything or nothing." "It" occurs five times, each time becoming more indeterminate, surrounded by sub-jectives and negatives: In this sonnet "composed of precisely evocative words in apparently communicative syntaxes which come to nothing and give a sense of summing up everything, the word *it* stands sure, constant, forthright, simple and blank." The blankness to which Booth points has been filled very specifically by generations of readers to force the poem into a repressive argument like that of Sonnet 116. For example, the key phrase "the fools of time" is usually glossed as local, historical examples of political or religious timeservers–but the phrase contains mysterious rever-berations back upon the lovers themselves. There is a sense in which men are *all* fools of time. When Sonnet 116 affirms that "Love's not Time's fool," it betrays a deliberate and fearful repression; an unwillingness to acknowledge that Love is not able to overcome Time; time is something that can be fulfilled only as it presents opportunity and possibility to us. People rightly become fools–jesters, dancers in attendance on Time, holy fools before the creative challenge of man's finitude–and men die, are fulfilled sexually, existentially, only if they submit themselves, "hugely politic," to the inevitable compromises, violence, and disruption which is life. Men "die for goodness" because in a sense they have all "lived for crime." People are deceivers yet true; the truest acts, like the truest poetry, are the most feigning.

The twelve-line Sonnet 126 is conventionally regarded as the culmina-tion of the first part of the sequence. Its serenity is very unlike that of 116. It acknowledges that, even if the fair youth is indeed Nature's "minion," even he must eventually be "rendered." Such realism does not detract from the Youth's beauty or desirability; it in fact constitutes its power.

Whether one considers the Fair Youth or the Dark Lady sonnets, then; whether one attempts to see a hidden order in the sonnets, or even if one wishes to see a story or some kind of biographical origin within them, perhaps their greatness rests on their refusal to offer even the possibility of solutions to the problems they raise. They disturb, provoke, and ask more than merely aesthetic questions; read singly or together, they make readers face (or hide from) and question the most fundamental elements of poetry, love, time, and death.

Other literary forms · William Shakespeare is perhaps the world's greatest dramatist—certainly, at the very least, the greatest to write in English. Of his thirty-seven plays, written over a career in the theater that spanned, roughly, the years 1588 to 1613, the most important are *Romeo and Juliet* (c. 1595-1596); *Henry IV, Parts I* and *II* (c. 1597-1598); *Hamlet, Prince of Denmark* (c. 1600-1601); *Othello, the Moor of Venice* (1604); *Measure for Measure* (1604); *King Lear* (c. 1605-1606); *Macbeth* (1606); *Antony and Cleopatra* (c. 1606-1607); *The Winter's Tale* (c. 1610-1611); and *The Tempest* (1611).

Select works other than poetry

DRAMA: *Henry VI, Part I*, wr. 1589-1590, pr. 1592; *Henry VI, Part II*, pr. c. 1590-1591; *Henry VI, Part III*, pr. c. 1590-1591; *Richard III*, pr. c. 1592-1593 (revised 1623); *The Comedy of Errors*, pr. c. 1592-1594; *The Taming of the Shrew*, pr. c. 1593-1594; *Titus Andronicus*, pr., pb. 1594; *The Two Gentlemen of Verona*, pr. c. 1594-1595; *Love's Labour's Lost*, pr. c. 1594-1595 (revised 1597 for court performance); *Romeo and Juliet*, pr. c. 1595-1596; *Richard II*, pr. c. 1595-1596; *A Midsummer Night's Dream*, pr. c. 1595-1596; *King John*, pr., c. 1596-1597; *The Merchant of Venice*, pr. c. 1596-1597; *Henry IV, Part I*, pr. c. 1597-1598; *The Merry Wives of Windsor*, pr. 1597 (revised c. 1600-1601); *Henry IV, Part II*, pr. 1598; *Much Ado About Nothing*, pr. c. 1598-1599; *Henry V*, pr. c. 1598-1599; *Julius Caesar*, pr. c. 1599-1600; *As You Like It*, pr. c. 1599-1600; *Hamlet, Prince of Denmark*, pr. c. 1600-1601; *Twelfth Night: Or, What You Will*, pr. c. 1600-1602; *Troilus and Cressida*, pr. c. 1601-1602; *All's Well That Ends Well*, pr. c. 1602-1603; *Othello, the Moor of Venice*, pr. 1604 (revised 1623); *Measure for Measure*, pr. 1604; *King Lear*, pr. c. 1605-1606; *Macbeth*, pr. 1606; *Antony and Cleopatra*, pr. c. 1606-1607; *Coriolanus*, pr. c. 1607-1608; *Timon of Athens*, pr. c. 1607-1608; *Pericles, Prince of Tyre*, pr. c. 1607-1608; *Cymbeline*, pr. c. 1609-1610; *The Winter's Tale*, pr. c. 1610-1611; *The Tempest*, pr. 1611; *The Two Noble Kinsmen*, pr. c. 1612-1613 (with John Fletcher); *Henry VIII*, pr. 1613 (with Fletcher).

Gary F. Waller

Bibliography · Because of the extensive range of Shakespeare studies since 1900, even a tentative bibliography would fill a number of pages and would require separate listings for the individual plays. Only general areas of study and criticism can be indicated here. The standard biography has become S. Schoenbaum's *William Shakespeare: A Compact Documentary Life*, 1977. See also E. K. Chambers, *William Shakespeare: A Study of Facts and Problems*, 2 vols., 1930; E. I. Fripp, *Shakespeare, Man and Artist*, 2 vols., 1938; Marchette Chute, *Shakespeare of London*, 1949; Mark Eccles, *Shakespeare in Warwickshire*, 1961; and Richard Dutton, *William Shakespeare: A Literary Life*, 1989.

General background studies include E. K. Chambers, *The Elizabethan Stage*, 4 vols., 1923; J. Dover Wilson, *Life in Shakespeare's England*, 1911, repr. 1968; Hardin Craig, *The Enchanted Glass*, 1936; Andrew Gurr, *Playgoing in Shakespeare's London*, 1987, and *The Shakespearean Stage*, 3d ed., 1992; and Stanley Wells, ed., *The Cambridge Companion to Shakespeare Studies*, 1986. For criticism see A. C. Bradley, *Shakespearean Tragedy*, 1904; G. Wilson Knight, *The Wheel of Fire*, 1930; H. B. Charlton, *Shakespearian Comedy*, 1938; Lily B. Campbell, *Shakespeare's 'Histories': Mirrors of Elizabethan Policy*, 1947; Northrop Frye, *A Natural Perspective: The Development of Shakespearean Comedy and Romance*, 1955; C. L. Barber, *Shakespeare's Festive Comedy*, 1959; Howard Felperin, *Shakespearean Romance*, 1972; and John Drakakis, *Alternative Shakespeares*, 1985. Valuable aids for the student are the Norton facsimile edition of *The First Folio Shakespeare*, prepared by Charlton Hinman, 1968; Oscar James Campbell and Edward G. Quinn, eds., *The Reader's Encyclopedia of Shakespeare*, 1966; Alfred Harbage, *A Reader's Guide to William Shakespeare*, 1963; Marvin Spevack, *A Complete and Systematic Concordance to the Works of Shakespeare*, 9 vols., 1968-1980; and Stanley Wells, ed., *Shakespeare: A Bibliographical Guide*, 1990.

PERCY BYSSHE SHELLEY

Born: Field Place, Sussex, England; August 4, 1792
Died: Off Viareggio, Italy; July 8, 1822

Poetry · *Original Poetry by Victor and Cazire*, 1810 (with Elizabeth Shelley) · *Posthumous Fragments of Margaret Nicholson*, 1810 · *Queen Mab: A Philosophical Poem*, 1813 (revised as *The Daemon of the World*, 1816) · *Alastor: Or, The Spirit of Solitude and Other Poems*, 1816 · *Mont Blanc*, 1817 · *The Revolt of Islam*, 1818 · *Rosalind and Helen: A Modern Eclogue, with Other Poems*, 1819 · *Letter to Maria Gisborne*, 1820 · *Epipsychidion*, 1821 · *Adonais: An Elegy on the Death of John Keats*, 1821 · *Hellas: A Lyrical Drama*, 1822 · *Posthumous Poems of Percy Bysshe Shelley*, 1824 (includes *Prince Athanase, Julian and Maddalo: A Conversation, The Witch of Atlas, The Triumph of Life, The Cyclops*, and *Charles the First*) · *The Masque of Anarchy*, 1832 · *Peter Bell the Third*, 1839 · *The Poetical Works of Percy Bysshe Shelley*, 1839 · *The Wandering Jew*, 1887 · *The Complete Poetical Works of Shelley*, 1904 (Thomas Hutchinson, editor) · *The Esdaile Notebook: A Volume of Early Poems*, 1964 (K. N. Cameron, editor)

Achievements · One of the six greatest English Romantic poets, Percy Bysshe Shelley is arguably the most versatile stylist among all English poets. His genius for versification enabled him to employ an astonishing variety of stanzaic patterns and poetic forms with equal facility. He had two basic styles, however—the sublime or rhapsodic, heard in such poems as *Alastor*, "Hymn to Intellectual Beauty," *Prometheus Unbound*, and *Adonais;* and the urbane or conversational style, found in poems such as *Julian and Maddalo: A Conversation, Letter to Maria Gisborne*, and *Epipsychidion*. In this latter mode, especially in the standard pentameter line with couplets, Shelley grew increasingly conservative prosodically, achieving a control almost neoclassical in balance and poise. Lyrical, unremitting intensity, however, is the defining quality of Shelley's verse.

Biography · In *Great Expectations* (1860-1861), Charles Dickens has the convict Magwitch put his life's story, as he says, into a mouthful of English—in and out of jail, in and out of jail, in and out of jail. Percy Bysshe Shelley's life falls into a similar pattern—in and out of love, in and out of love, in and out of love. Shelley admitted as much in a letter to John Gisborne, written the year he drowned in a boating accident, and expressive of a truth he discovered too late: "I think one is always in love with something or other; the error, and I confess it is not easy for spirits cased in flesh and blood to avoid it, consists in seeking in a mortal image the likeness of what is perhaps eternal." At the age of twenty-nine, Shelley was still looking for his antitype; he believed he had found her, at last, in a nineteen-year-old Italian girl imprisoned in a nunnery, and had written one of his greatest poems, *Epipsychidion*, in celebration, typically disregarding the impact the poem would have on his wife Mary. Mary, however, had been party to a similar emotional event five years earlier when Shelley had abandoned his first wife, Harriet Westbrook Shelley, then pregnant with his second child, to elope with Mary. Both times Shelley speculated that the women could live with him, together, in harmony—the first combination, wife Harriet as sister, lover Mary as wife; the second combination, as

Library of Congress

stated metaphorically in *Epipsychidion*, wife Mary as Moon, Teresa Viviani as Sun to Shelley's earth, with a comet, Claire Claremont, Mary's half-sister, zooming into their "azure heaven" as she willed.

One of Shelley's great biographers, Kenneth Neill Cameron, says that Shelley was rather ahead of his time, but most readers still find the facts of Shelley's love life disturbing. His vision of love is wonderful; his idealism that sought to change the world through love and poetry is wonderful; the reality of that vision and idealism translated into life was a disaster. Shelley knew it, and this awareness caused him to seek self-destruction.

His intense fits of love aside, Shelley could be the most thoughtful and loving of men. He was selfless, generous to a fault, a brilliant radical devoted to saving the world and just as passionately devoted to the pursuit of metaphysical truth. Edward John Trelawny provides a description of Shelley in his study, German folio open, dictionary in hand (Shelley always read literature in the original—Greek, Latin, Spanish, Italian, German—so that he could be sensitive to the style and linguistic nuances of the art), at 10 A.M., and the identical picture at 6 P.M., Shelley having hardly moved, forgetting he had not eaten, looking tired and pale. "Well," Trelawny said, "have you found it?," referring to some Truth Shelley sought. "Shutting the book and going to the window," Shelley replied, " 'No, I have lost it': with a deep sigh: 'I have lost a day.' "

Shelley was born into a family of landed gentry. His father Timothy was a Member of Parliament and his grandfather Bysshe Shelley was a very wealthy landowner. Shelley studied at Eton, where he rebelled against the hazing system; fell madly in love with a cousin, Harriet Grove; attended Oxford, briefly, until his expulsion for printing a pamphlet defending atheism; and completed his teenage years by eloping with sixteen-year-old Harriet Westbrook, the daughter of a wealthy merchant. Harriet and Shelley had two children, Ianthe and Charles, the latter born after Shelley had left Harriet to elope with Mary Godwin, the sixteen-year-old child of Mary Wollstonecraft, author of *A Vindication of the Rights of Woman* (1792), and William Godwin, author of *The Inquiry Concerning Political Justice and Its Influence on General Virtue and Happiness* (1793). After Harriet committed suicide by drowning, probably because of her pregnancy with another man's child, Shelley married Mary. The couple lived in England for a while, but left for Italy to protect Shelley's health and to escape the group of friends, including William Godwin, who had come to depend on Shelley for financial support.

In Italy, they settled near Lord Byron, who had fled England for his own personal reasons—a divorce and a child allegedly by his half-sister. Mary and Shelley had two children, Clara and William. When Clara died from an illness exacerbated by the traveling that Shelley forced upon his family in Italy, the lovelight seemed to wane in the Shelleys' marriage. The following year, 1819, Shelley's son died, and even greater despondency descended on them. Shelley was also disheartened by his ineffectiveness as a poet—no popularity, no audience, no hope of saving the world through his poetry. In *Adonais*, his eulogy for John Keats, Shelley tempts himself to put the things of this world aside, to die. On July 8, 1822, Shelley and Edward Williams set sail from Leghorn, too late in the afternoon considering their destination and with a storm pending. They drowned in the brief tempest. Several weeks later the two bodies were discovered on separate lonely beaches. In Shelley's pockets were a book of Sophocles and Keats's latest volume of poems, opened as if he had been reading. Byron, Trelawny, Leigh Hunt, and some Italian health officials cremated the bodies, Hellenic style, on the beach. Trelawny claims that Shelley's heart would not burn, or at least did not burn, and that he salvaged it from the ashes. Shelley, who likened the poet to fire and who prominently used the image of releasing one's fate to the stream, thus lived and died the myth of his poetry.

Analysis · Percy Bysshe Shelley mutedly noted in his Preface to *Prometheus Unbound* that he had "what a Scotch philosopher terms, 'a passion for reforming the world.' " One might think that this would have endeared his work at least to the reading public left of center and to later readers who value the reforming spirit in mankind. Yet Shelley was almost able to name his readers, they were so few, and today, of the six major poets who dominate the canon of British Romanticism—William Blake, William Wordsworth, Samuel Taylor Coleridge, Byron, Keats, and Shelley—it is still Shelley who remains the least popular. For one reason or another, and though Shelley will always have a cadre of eloquent apologists, dedicated scholars, and brilliant explicators, he is usually out of favor with a significant group of readers. He has been criticized for bad thinking, for bad writing, and for bad living. Devaluations of his thought and poetry have largely been overcome, but this last, especially when made by sensitive feminist readers who find his narcissistic theory of love stupidly, if not heartlessly, destructive to the women in his life, is difficult to refute, if one grants its relevance to his art. Shelley's theme of *self*-destructiveness leads to his poetry's most brilliant moments, but perhaps the weakness in Shelley's use of the antitype motif is that it fails to recognize even the possibility that the mate—the woman—exists in her own right, and that her likeness to the fiction of the poet's imagination might not be the best or safest evidence of her worth. In Lord Byron's *Manfred* (1817), the concept of the antitype is also used, but Byron is critical of the theme from the woman's point of view—Manfred has destroyed his lover, Astarte, with this dangerously egotistical love and madly strives to win her forgiveness. Shelley seems incapable of such a critique of his most important theme; therein may lie the weakness in his work. Except in this respect, Shelley was not in the least simpleminded concerning the problem of reforming the world according to his standards. Shelley desired more than the world could ever offer; he knew it, but he could not stop trying to close the gap between the ideal and the real, the vision and the fact. So powerful is his honesty that tension pervades his poetry, idealism playing against skepticism, irony hedging assertion. He ardently believed that man was perfectible, if man would only will it. At its most optimistic, his poetry seeks to arouse the reader's will to strive for perfection; at its most pessimistic, it is the poet's private struggle with the desire to escape through death.

One might take a poem of balanced oppsites as a synecdochic introduction to Shelley's thought and art. *Julian and Maddalo: A Conversation* presents the issues, the imagery that typically embodies them, and the quest to dissolve division in nature, society, and personal life. The conversants in this urbane, sophisticated debate are Julian, a thin disguise for Shelley, and Maddalo, or Lord Byron. Julian, the Preface suggests, is the idealist, "passionately attached to those philosophical notions which assert the power of man over his own mind, and the immense improvements of which, by the extinction of certain moral superstitions, human society may be yet susceptible." Maddalo is the card-carrying cynic, and the tragedy from Julian's point of view is that Maddalo is one of the few who might be capable of changing the world, if he would only will it. It is Maddalo's weakness to be proud; he does not think the world worth the effort. A maniac also enters the poem as a character who was destroyed through unrequited love. Finally, Maddalo's little daughter is the ever-present, romantic image of mankind's potential.

The poem opens with a vision of harmony. Julian and Maddalo have been riding along the Lido of Venice, a waste of a beach, at sundown, and Julian responds to the correspondence he senses between the inner and outer worlds:

> . . . I love all waste
> And solitary places; where we taste
> The pleasure of believing what we see
> Is boundless, as we wish our souls to be:
> And such was this wide ocean, and this shore
> More barren than its billows.

Not much later, Maddalo will offer a constricted image of the soul, but for now, Shelley allows his better half to continue. Disagreeing with earlier Romantic work of Wordsworth and Coleridge, which argued for the suffiency of man's relationship with nature, Julian/Shelley adds a companion to the landscape experience: "and yet more/ Than all, with a remembered friend I love/ To ride as then I rode." The friends are in perfect accord with each other as well as with nature. As they gallop along the beach, the wind brings the "living spray" into their faces, the blue heavens open, "stripped to their depths," and the waves send forth a "sound like delight . . ./ Harmonizing with solitude," carrying into their hearts "aereal merriment." The personal relationship is as perfect: "the swift thought,/ Winging itself with laughter, lingered not,/ But flew from brain to brain." As they turn homeward, however, division slowly enters the poem, beginning with a discussion on "God, freewill and destiny:/ Of all that earth has been or yet may be." Julian takes the brighter side, Maddalo, the darker. Shelley represents the argument metaphorically as two perceptions of landscape. Julian first offers a perception of the dissolution of the landscape's natural boundaries created by the light of the setting sun; Maddalo then counters with a brilliant image of the constricted soul and the madding passions, the bell of the insane asylum.

Julian first calls attention to the division between East and West, earth and sky. The Alps are a "heaven-sustaining bulwark reared/ Between the East and West"; only "half the sky/ Was roofed with clouds of rich emblazonry"; the sun pauses in a "rent" between the clouds; the hills are separate like a "clump of peaked isles." Then quite dramatically light begins to do its work of transformation:

> . . . as if the Earth and Sea had been
> Dissolved into one lake of fire were seen
> Those mountains towering as from waves of flame
> Around the vaporous sun, from where there came
> The inmost purple spirit of light, and made
> Their very peaks transparent.

This diffusion of water with fire, earth with air, air with fire, and water with earth, completed in the fleeting intensity of the sun's pause, becomes a vision of hope for human reconciliation through love. The sun's light is love and just as it can dissolve the perception of landscape boundaries so can the emotion dissolve boundaries in personal life and society. Nature teaches a lesson; even the city becomes a divine illusion, "Its temples and its palaces did seem/ Like fabrics of enchantment piled to Heaven."

Maddalo, however, is not taken by the vision. He insists on observing the sunset from a "better station." Between them and the sun is now imagined the madhouse, "A windowless, deformed and dreary pile," its bell tolling "In strong and black relief" for the maniacs to begin their evening prayers. Looking at his image of the bell and the asylum, Maddalo interprets:

> And such . . . is our mortality
> And this must be the emblem and the sign
> Of what should be eternal and divine—
> And like that black and dreary bell, the soul,
> Hung in a heaven-illumined tower, must toll
> Our thoughts and our desires to meet below
> Round the rent heart and pray—as madmen do
> For what? they know not,—till the night of death
> As sunset that strange vision, severeth
> Our memory from itself, and us from all
> We sought and yet were baffled!

If Byron literally spoke these lines, they are among the best lines of poetry he ever composed. The soul is no beach stretching to the horizon; it is finite, and dreary, and obfuscating. It provokes the heart with its spirituality to strive for the infinite in complete bewilderment, till death closes the quest. There is nothing eternal and divine; it is simply mortality at odds with itself. In the twilight, the "black bell became invisible" and the enchanted city "huddled in gloom," its ships, towers, palaces—emblems of commerce, church, and government—faded into the absurdity of night.

The following day, Julian argues that

> . . . it is our will
> That . . . enchains us to permitted ill—
> We might be otherwise—we might be all
> We dream of . . .
> Where is the love, beauty and truth we seek
> But in our mind? and if we were not weak
> Should we be less in deed than in desire?

Maddalo counters that such human weakness is incurable, that no matter how strong an argument Julian can make to prove the perfectibility of mankind, empirical evidence and experience will undermine it. Maddalo adduces as evidence the case of a maniac, who was like Julian an idealist but has been destroyed by unrequited love. Their visit to the maniac's cell in the asylum whose bell they had heard the preceding night reveals a man of rent heart, musing disjointedly and pathetically on his suffering. Still in love, he refuses to commit suicide because he does not want his former lover to feel responsible for his death. Julian feels that if he had the opportunity to befriend the man, he might save him, but the strength of Maddalo's argument has been felt. After many years, Julian returns to Maddalo's castle and learns from his grown daughter that the maniac's lover returned and he recovered; then, however, they separated once more. At Julian's entreaty, she reveals the whole story, but out of bitterness toward the world he refuses to disclose the resolution (as Shelley refuses to disclose it to his readers): "the cold world shall not know," concludes the poem. The debate has not resolved the issue. The maniac's recovery, although temporary, indicates that love is in the force that Julian has maintained, *if* one can sustain the will to love. Thus the poem returns to its starting point: clearly one can will to love, or, at least, act as if one loved, but constancy is the problem, as the maniac's lover indicates.

The same tensions which animate *Julian and Maddalo* inform Shelley's first major poem, *Alastor*. The poet-persona of *Alastor* begins as a happy youth. He seeks knowledge and truth from philosophy, nature, history, and travel, and experiences moments of high inspiration, as when, standing amidst the ruins of the cradle of civilization, "meaning on his vacant mind/ Flashed like strong inspiration, and he saw/ The thrilling secrets of the birth of time." On his quest he has been cared for by an Arab maiden, who brings food to him from her own plate and watches him dream innocently throughout the night, till to her father's tent she creeps "Wildered, and wan, and panting," but he does not recognize her love for him. Then, one night after leaving her locale, he has "a dream of hopes that never yet/ Had flushed his cheek." He dreams of his antitype, the perfect female of intellect, imagination, and sense to match his own. She speaks in low solemn tones of knowledge, truth, virtue, liberty; she next breathes the "permeating fire" of her pure mind in a song of passionate poetry; then, in the most erotic passage one will find in the Romantic canon, they join in sexual climax. She arises and the dreamer sees

> . . . by the warm light of their own life
> Her glowing limbs beneath the sinuous veil
> Of woven wind, her outspread arms now bare,
> Her dark locks floating in the breath of night,
> Her beamy bending eyes, her parted lips
> Outstretched, and pale, and quivering eagerly.

He receives her, "yielding to the irresistible joy,/ With frantic gesture and short breathless cry," folding his frame in "her dissolving arms." At the moment of climax, "blackness veiled his dizzy eyes, and night/ Involved and swallowed up the vision; sleep,/ Like a dark flood suspended in its course,/ Rolled back its impulse on his vacant brain."

One would wish to sleep forever to have such dreams, for how can such a dream be fulfilled? The world, which was once so beautiful to the poet, now appears vacant when he awakens. Cryptically, the narrator tells us that "The spirit of sweet human love has sent/ A vision to the sleep of him who spurned/ Her choicest gifts." Was the Arab maiden one of those gifts, or was she merely the catalyst of an awakening sexuality? Regardless, he now "eagerly pursues/ Beyond the realms of dream that fleeting shade," knowing that the realm beyond dream is most likely death. He moves madly through society and nature more to burn out than to seek a likeness of the veiled maid. When he tires or seeks infrequent nourishment, an image of the maid's eyes forces him on. In a passage that underscores the narcissism of his quest, the reflection of his own eyes in a fountain where he drinks provokes her shadowy presence.

He moves on, following a stream to its unknown source, for he has dimly perceived an analogue between "What oozy cavern or what wandering cloud" contain its waters and what mysterious source his own thoughts and visions may have. He finally stops in a virginal nook above the perilous mountain landscape and prepares to die. He is "at peace, and faintly smiling" as the crescent moon sets on his life: "His last sight/ Was the great moon," which as it declines finally shows only the tips of its crescent:

> . . . the alternate gasp
> Of his faint respiration scarce did stir
> The stagnate night:—till the minutest ray
> Was quenched, the pulse yet lingered in his heart.
> It paused—it fluttered.

The moon sets, and he dies. Why does his heart pause and flutter? Is he duped by the moon's tips appearing to be eyes, or does he smile faintly because he is aware of the irony? Or does he move from irony to the excitement of belief at the moment before final truth? The reader cannot know, but the poem's narrator finds little hope for the world when "some surpassing Spirit,/ Whose light adorned the world around it" dies an untimely death not with "sobs or groans,/ The passionate tumult of a clinging hope;/ But pale despair and cold tranquillity."

As he moved like a phantom through the landscape, the poet of *Alastor* recognized that nature provided a condition like love for its animate and inanimate beings—swans floating in pairs, "Ivy clasp[ing]/ The fissured stones with its entwining arms"—but that he belonged outside the circle.

Shelley could not maintain the romantic myth that, as Coleridge wrote in "This Limetree Bower My Prison," "Nature ne'er deserts the wise and pure," or, as Wordsworth wrote in "Lines Composed a Few Miles Above Tintern Abbey," "In nature and the language of the sense,/ [is] the anchor of my purest thoughts, the nurse,/ The guide, the guardian of my heart, and soul/ Of all my moral being." Shelley did write in his essay "On Love" that one seeks correspondence with nature when one is denied human love; he paraphrased an unknown source to the effect that, if one were in a desert, "he would love some cypress." As is evident in *Julian and Maddalo* and *Alastor*, Shelley preferred human companionship, because there is a force impelling the physical world which is antithetical to love. Shelley called this force Necessity, or physical determinism. *Mont Blanc* provides its principal image.

In what becomes a showdown of sorts between mind and matter, imagination and necessity, Shelley begins *Mont Blanc* by recognizing that mind shares with matter a significant feature. The sense impressions that flow through the mind's stream of thought are impelled by a force as mysterious as that which drives the river from its home in the clouds down the mountain's ravine. Is it the same force? Critics have struggled with this problem, for Shelley did not make the matter very clear, or perhaps it is as clear as possible without being reductive of a difficult metaphysical question. On the one hand, Shelley imagines the Power as residing above the world of mutability, "Remote, serene, and inaccessible," but not without profound effect on the world below. The Power's image is the mountain's summit, which none can see but which all can feel in the form of the forces it releases that destroy and preserve, its glaciers and its rivers. Its position is amoral, perfectly non-anthropomorphic. The glaciers wreak their havoc, "The dwelling-place/ Of insects, beasts, and birds" their spoil. "The race of man," too, "flies far in dread; his work and dwelling/ Vanished, like smoke before the tempest's stream." On the other hand, majestic rivers, such as the Arve of Mont Blanc, derive from the same source and are "The breath and blood of distant lands." Can the mind of man be a manifestation of such a power? This is the question to which the poem leads, but just as Shelley offers the answer in the final stanza, he undermines it.

Addressing the mountain he says, "The secret strength of things/ Which governs thought, and to the infinite dome/ of heaven is as a law, inhabits thee!" While thought may be governed by a psychological determinism, Shelley seems to imply a distinction between causally determined thought and the products of imagination—poetry and value. He stresses that "Mont Blanc yet gleams on high," above the vicissitudes of our world, where "In the calm darkness of the moonless nights,/ In the lone glare of day, the snows descend/ Upon that Mountain, none beholds them there," and without fanfare he begins describing, valuing, and symbolizing what he has just indicated none behold:

> Winds contend
> Silently there, and heap the snow with breath
> Rapid and strong, but silently! Its home
> The voiceless lightning in these solitudes
> Keeps innocently, and like vapour broods
> Over the snow.

The winds pile the snow for the coming glacier with the quality of "breath," because, while the glacier will bring death, its next state of being as river will bring life—"The breath and blood of distant lands." Likewise emphasizing the absent force of mind that now interprets and values the cold causality of the mountain's secret summit is the acknowledgement that all of this is happening "Silently . . ./ . . . but silently!" No ears, no sound; no perceiver, no value. The poem concludes: "And what were thou, and earth, and stars, and sea,/ If to the human mind's imaginings/ Silence and solitude were vacancy?"

Something in the human mind renders value, recognizes or makes meaning for this universe, or decides there is no meaning. These are acts of ultimate power; the rest is a "dull round," as the human mind itself may enact when it refuses to transcend the path of association with its power to create, to vision, and to will. Shelley does not make this case as forcefully as it is presented here, however; he concludes with a question, not the strong declarative the reader might wish. The imagining undermines the assertion of "The secret strength of things"; the surmise of the conclusion undermines the imagining. This ambivalence does not derive from some precious sense of caution, but from Shelley's genuine uncertainty.

Shelley's belief in the power of love was unequivocal, however, and *Prometheus Unbound* reveals on a mythic scale the transformation that will occur when love rather than fear and hatred binds relationships among nations and mankind. *Prometheus Unbound* is a psychological drama that, along with other works of the Romantic period, asserts the power of mind in transforming the world. The French Revolution having failed to rid France of despotism, British writers sought to fulfill by individual transformation the apocalyptic hopes it had aroused. The logic was simple: if the mind and heart of the reader could be changed, the world would be changed. Thus Wordsworth, the major poet of the period, writes at the height of his optimism: "Paradise, and groves/ Elysian, . . ./ . . . why should they be/ A history only of departed things" (Prospectus to *The Recluse*). The hope of the Romantics was not naïve, but rather a variation of an eternal hope to improve the world.

Shelley's promise was that if humanity could just will to love, everything wonderful would follow. Thus, Prometheus, the mythic champion of mankind, chained to a rock in the Indian Caucasus for three thousand sleepless years, finds that he no longer hates the tyrant, Jupiter, and as a consequence the universe swells with the love, the growth, and the energy of springtime.

Ironically, Prometheus' transformation begins, not more than fifty-five lines into the first act, as he dwells on the satisfaction he will feel when Jupiter is dethroned and made to kiss "the blood/ From [Prometheus'] pale feet," which could then trample him, except that he would disdain Jupiter too much to do so. Then he says: "Disdain? Ah no! I pity thee," for the suffering Jupiter will endure at his demise, and his pity leads to grief: "I speak in grief,/ Not exultation, for I hate no more,/ As then, ere misery made me wise." There is a significant relationship between Jupiter's power and Prometheus' hatred, Jupiter's demise and Prometheus' love: Though he has been the hero of mankind, Prometheus has been responsible for the tyranny of the universe, because he empowered Jupiter with his hate—in fact, willed the inflictions of Jupiter upon mankind. When he transcends his hatred to love, Jupiter inevitably falls. It is the dialectic of the master and the slave; the slave's willed obeisance gives the master his power. Prometheus recalls his curse, which began the reign of Jupiter, and the reader begins to understand one half of the dialectic.

On a literal level, perhaps it appears foolish that the sufferer could hold power over the oppressor, as Prometheus claims, but, if one considers the action on the psychological level, where Shelley intended the battle to be fought and won, one can understand that a mind indulging in hatred blights the potential joy of life. At some level, Prometheus understands this, and retracts his curse, yet he must still undergo a test from the furies (perhaps representing his historical consciousness) which brings to his sight the truth of mankind's condition. The Reign of Terror of the French Revolution, the rejection and murder of Christ, the general wave of personal violence and horror, are all summoned to reveal this darkest truth: "those who endure/ Deep wrongs for man, and scorn and chains, but heap/ Thousand-fold torment on themselves and him." The plight of mankind is absurdly tragic: "The good want power, but to weep barren tears./ The powerful goodness want: worse need for them./ The wise want love, and those who love want wisdom;/ And all best things are thus confused to ill."

Prometheus' response to this futility is: "Thy words are like a cloud of winged snakes/ And yet, I pity those they torture not." "Thou pitiest them?" the fury cries: "I speak no more," and vanishes defeated. Prometheus' love has endured. From this moment on, the action of the play moves forward, as if on its own pattern of necessity, to overthrow Jupiter and rejuvenate mankind. As love trickles down through the universe and the society of mankind, there are "thrones . . . kingless," men walking together without fawning or trampling, all "Scepterless, free, uncircumscribed." Though still subject to chance, death, and mutability, ruling over them like slaves, man is free, liberated consciousness, "The King/ Over himself." The "mind-forg'd manacles," to quote William Blake's "London," are sundered. The mind of man is now "an Ocean/ Of clear emotion/ A heaven of serene and mighty motion."

Yet, as wildly joyous and supremely optimistic as *Prometheus Unbound* is, the reader is warned at the close that even this mythic bliss cannot remain unguarded. Should the world fall again into its tyranny, the morality that will reincarnate her beauty, freedom, and joy again must be this:

> To suffer woes which Hope thinks infinite;
> To forgive wrongs darker than Death or Night;
> To defy Power which seems Omnipotent;
> To love, and bear; to hope, till Hope creates
> From its own wreck the thing it contemplates;
> Neither to change nor falter nor repent:
> This . . . is to be
> Good, great and joyous, beautiful and free;
> This is alone Life, Joy, Empire and Victory.

Prometheus Unbound is a difficult reading experience, a highly pitched lyric extended over four acts, without tonal relief, but it is essential reading for the student of Shelley and the Romantic period.

Part of Shelley's vision in *Prometheus Unbound* is that man would be passionate, "yet free from guilt or pain/ Which were, for his will made, or suffered them," and that women would be

> . . . gentle, radiant forms
> From custom's evil taint exempt and pure;
> Speaking the wisdom once they could not think,
> Looking emotions once they feared to feel
> And changed to all which once they dared not be.

Many might find Shelley a prophet of modern morality, or immorality, depending on point of view, but it is certain that even the most liberal in the nineteenth century could not quite live this ideal, not even Shelley's hand-picked women. In *Epipsychidion*, however, he allows himself a pure fantasy of relational perfection that celebrates his discovery, at last, of his antitype. The chief skepticism of the poem is not that he might be excessive in his rapture, but rather that language is not capable of adequately expressing his rapture, its object being perfection. The poem opens with a rhapsodic invocation without parallel in English literature, and struggles throughout with its diction to aggregate images and symbols that might invoke a rhetoric of infinity. Shelley has found the veiled maid of *Alastor*: "I never thought before my death to see/ Youth's vision thus made perfect. Emily,/ I love thee; . . . Ah me!/ I am not thine: I am a part of *thee*."

This perfect woman was Teresa Viviani, the teenage daughter of the governor of Pisa, who had confined her in a nunnery. The Shelleys became interested in her plight and this lovely victim of paternal tyranny inflamed Shelley's soul. He imagines how perfect it would be if Emily/Teresa could join him and Mary in a *ménage à trois*, for he has never been one of the "great sect,/ Whose doctrine is, that each one should select/ Out of the crowd a mistress or a friend,/ And all the rest, though fair and wise, commend/ To cold oblivion," though the moral code might demand such behavior. "True Love in this differs from gold and clay,/ That to divide is not to take away." Thus, if Mary would be the Moon–"The cold chaste Moon// Who makes all beautiful on which she smiles,/ . . ./ And warms not but illumines"–Emily would be the Sun and together they would form those spheres of influence "who rule this passive Earth,/ This world of live, this *me*." Finally, however, he and Emily both fly out of orbit, leaving the moon behind, to dwell in a paradisal isle.

Language cannot deal with the infinite limits of this vision: "The winged words on which my soul would pierce/ Into the height of love's rare Universe,/ Are chains of lead around its flight of fire.–/ I pant, I sink, I tremble, I expire!" Sympathetic readers of Shelley wince at these moments; his detractors triumph. Even Shelley was a bit embarrassed by the emotion of this poem, because the woman it celebrated finally married a boor. Shelley wrote to John Gisborne: "The 'Epipsychidion' I cannot look at." Mary Shelley also had a difficult time looking at it; *Epipsychidion* is the only poem in her excellent edition of Shelley's poems on which she does not comment.

Shelley often wore his heart on his sleeve for daws to peck at, to paraphrase William Shakespeare's Iago, especially in the great series of poems representing himself as the *poète maudit*, the suffering poet vainly striving to save those who reject him. "Hymn to Intellectual Beauty," "Ode to the West Wind," and *Adonais* constitute the constellation and farthest reaches of this personal myth. Of course there is a great deal of vanity involved. One perceives that the world is not perfect; one attempts to save it and fails, thereby proving that the world really is bad, even worse than one thought. One then strives harder, becoming more assured that one is needed and that one's work is essential, rejection feeding vanity in a wicked, self-defeating cycle. Throughout, one retains one's heroic self-image.

In "Hymn to Intellectual Beauty," Shelley describes the dynamics of his dedication to poetry. While on a youthful search for truth, in much the manner of the poet of *Alastor*, he calls on the "poisonous names with which our youth is fed," God, ghosts, and heaven, without success; he sees nothing, he hears nothing that responds to his metaphysical anxieties in a direct way. He experiences something, however, that profoundly moves him. As he muses deeply "on the lot/ Of life" within the context of nature's springtime regeneration, "Sudden, thy shadow fell on me;/ I shrieked, and clasped my hands in ecstasy." The shadow is that of the spirit of beauty, an inexpressible something that transiently brings value to life—life's only value—by evoking in the receiver, its guest, a pulse of spiritual joy. If it could be a permanent experience, "Man were immortal, and omnipotent." The poet says that his life has been dedicated to creating a medium for evoking this spiritual condition. He vows that he will dedicate his "powers/ To thee and thine—have I not kept the vow?" he asks the spirit. His hope has been that if others could be given the experience of spiritual ecstasy, the world would be reborn. The time he has spent in reading, thinking, writing—those hours know, he says, that joy never

> . . . illumed my brow
> Unlinked with hope that thou wouldst free
> This world from its dark slavery,
> That thou—O awful Loveliness,
> Wouldst give whate'er these words cannot express.

In seeking to suggest this evanescent condition, Shelley creates several of the most alluring similes in English, such as, in the fourth stanza: "Thou—that to human thought art nourishment,/ Like darkness to a dying flame!" As the mind is a fading coal, so the darkness intensified makes thought appear brighter, thereby nourishing its waning condition so that it does not appear to be waning at all. The loveliness of verse makes the mind seem as full of beauty and intensity as the moment of inspiration had promised. The poem's opening lines, however, are the ultimate of Shelleyan perfection: "The awful shadow of some unseen Power/ Floats though unseen amongst us!" It is "Like clouds in starlight widely spread,—/

Like memory of music fled,–/ Like aught that for its grace may be/ Dear, and yet dearer for its mystery." These lines are Shelley in his power, for no other poet has so effectively failed to express the inexpressible and thereby succeeded in his attempt to evoke it. While Shelley was curiously winning the battle of expression, however, he was losing the war.

Unlike the modern age, which conceded, in the words of W. H. Auden, that "poetry makes nothing happen," the Romantic and Victorian periods permitted their artists to believe that they could and ought to be effectual. Several seemed to be: Wordsworth, Charles Dickens, Alfred, Lord Tennyson, and Robert Browning had enormous moral influence. Shelley did not; in fact, Matthew Arnold, the great social and literary critic of Victorian England, likened Shelley to an "ineffectual angel, beating in the void his luminous wings in vain." In 1819, at the age of twenty-seven, Shelley wrote his most perfect poem on his ineffectuality. "Ode to the West Wind" is a prayer for power to further the vision of *Prometheus Unbound* in nineteenth century England and Europe, by a poet who has been battered with failure.

In its five terza rima sonnet stanzas, which describe the autumn of earth, sky, sea, and poet–the elements of earth, air, water, and fire–Shelley's impassioned ode takes the literal cycle of the seasons through metaphorical transformations to approach an answer to the question: "If rebirth happens in nature, can it happen in society, with my verse, like the west wind, as the catalyst of the transition from near death to new life?" The first and last stanzas are illustrative of the metaphorical union the poet seeks with the regenerative wind. Stanza one presents the west wind in its dual function of destroying and preserving, driving dead leaves "like ghosts from an enchanter fleeing," and blowing seeds to "their dark wintry bed" where they will "lie cold and low,/ Each like a corpse within its grave, until/ [the wind of spring] shall blow/ Her clarion o'er the dreaming earth" to awaken the seeds to life. Of course, the dead leaves have the function of preserving the seed beds.

In the final stanza, the poet prays that his "dead thoughts" might be driven "over the universe/ Like withered leaves to quicken a new birth!" His seeds are his words, and because he is the equivalent of fire, his words are likened to ashes and sparks–some merely functional, some inspirational–that are now dormant in the waning hearth that is his life. Thus, if his verse could be sufficiently empowered by spirit, like a wind, he might produce a conflagration through the blowing about of ashes and sparks. As the spring of stanza one had her clarion, his verse will be "to unawakened Earth/ The trumpet of a prophecy." "O Wind," he closes, "If Winter comes, can Spring be far behind?" Clearly, if those leaves of stanza one–"Yellow, and black, and pale, and hectic red,/ Pestilence-stricken multitudes"–which have been accurately interpreted as the suffering races of mankind, and those leaves of stanza five–the poet's "dead thoughts"– can both be set afire by the spark of the poet's verse, both may rise from the ashes to new life. The final question, however, is threatening to the dream, for though it is certain that spring follows winter in nature, it is not at all certain that if total spiritual darkness covers mankind, a springtime of recovery will follow.

In stanza four of "Ode to the West Wind," Shelley represents himself as praying to the wind "in my sore need": "Oh! lift me as a wave, a leaf, a cloud!/ I fall upon the thorns of life! I bleed!/ A heavy weight of hours has chained and bowed/ One too like thee: tameless, and swift, and proud." He finally shed the weight of hours to join, not the wind, for that is to be bound still in the world of process, change, and dying hopes, but a poet of his generation who preceded him into the realm "where the eternal are." His elegy for John Keats, *Adonais*, signaled the final shift of his quest from social and personal visions of resurrected worlds and discovered antitypes to transcendence of human life and care.

Shelley believed that Keats had been mortally wounded by a scurrilous review of his early work, *Endymion* (1818). "The savage criticism," he says in his Preface to *Adonais*, "produced the most violent effect on his susceptible mind; the agitation thus originated ended in the rupture of a blood-vessel in the lungs; a rapid consumption ensued, and the succeeding acknowledgements . . . of the true greatness of his powers, were ineffectual to heal the wound thus wantonly inflicted." This is not casebook medicine, but it does say something about the doctor who provides such an empathic diagnosis. Shelley self-consciously identified with Keats's early rejection and sought as well to identify with his early death.

Through the first thirty-seven stanzas of the poem, Shelley's narrator mourns Adonais' untimely death, culminating with the fancy of Shelley's image visiting the tomb in homage to a dead fellow-poet. The group of mourning poets stands aside to smile "through their tears" at this maudlin creature "Who in another's fate now wept his own." The muse, Urania, among the mourners for one of her most gifted, asks him his name; his response is to make "bare his branded and ensanguined brow,/ Which was like Cain's or Christ's." Then, in a moment of intense self-consciousness, Shelley disrupts this indulgent self-projection to criticize with truth–"Oh! that it should be so!" He is no important, mythical sufferer; though it has been his dream to be one, the comparison will not hold. Shortly, the poem moves to the second phase of its development, the realization that the living must not mourn for Adonais, who has "awakened from the dream of life," but for themselves: "*We* decay/ Like corpses in a charnel; fear and grief/ Convulse us and consume us day by day,/ And cold hopes swarm like worms within our living clay."

The second movement concludes with a pivotal question: "What Adonais is, why fear we to become?" The poem's third movement, stanzas 52-55, becomes darkly suicidal, but triumphant in its grasping of a new direction, a new vision. Life is imaged as a "dome of many-coloured glass" which "Stains the white radiance of Eternity,/ Until Death tramples it to fragments." Beyond Life is the Platonic "One," the blinding light of truth which mankind knows only from its shadows manifested in material form. "Die," the poet challenges, "If thou wouldst be with that which thou dost seek!" The beauties of natural, human, and aesthetic forms are "weak/ The glory they transfuse with fitting truth to speak." The challenge then becomes personalized as the poet addresses his heart, the image of his mortality and emotional life: "Why linger, why turn back, why shrink, my Heart?" Its hopes are gone, its love is gone, "what still is dear/ Attracts to crush, repels to make thee wither." The sky smiles, the wind whispers the invitation of Adonais: "oh, hasten thither,/ No more let Life divide what Death can join together." He feels the source of the fire he has represented as a poet, beaming, "Consuming the last clouds of cold mortality." Finally, the poem's concluding stanza aggregates the principal imagery of Shelley's major poetry to illustrate that throughout his work an undercurrent has been moving to this moment of poetic self-annihilation: the West Wind descends to blow. As in *Alastor*, the "spirit's bark is driven,/ . . . far from the trembling throng/ Whose sails were never to the tempest given"; the earth and skies, in contrast with the vision of *Julian and Maddalo*, are "riven" to accept the poet, rather than fused to involve him with a romantic vision of earth; he is now "borne darkly, fearfully, afar:/ Whilst burning through the inmost veil of Heaven,/ The soul of Adonais, like a star,/ Beacons from the abode where the Eternal are." The vision was shortly to descend to fact with Shelley's death by drowning.

Shelley admitted to a "passion for reforming the world." He sought an aesthetic medium that would inspire the will of man to close the gap between vision and reality. Shelley's art and thought are unique in the extremes that they bring to English literature; indeed, their fragile loveliness represents the hope and despondency possible only in an age that fervently believed in the infinite potential of man. He was a child of his age, and succeeding generations and imaginations will always need to be challenged by his visions.

Other literary forms · Except for *A Defence of Poetry* (1840), Percy Bysshe Shelley's essays are not classics of English prose, but they have influenced writers as diverse as George Bernard Shaw, H. G. Wells, and Bertrand Russell, and they are very useful as glosses on the poetry. "On Love," for example, introduces Shelley's concept of the "antitype," the perfect mate, uniquely suited to one's intellect, imagination, and sensory needs, a "soul within our soul," but purged of all one finds unsatisfactory within oneself. Love is defined as the attraction to the antitype. Shelley movingly describes this longing for a mirror image of perfection:

> If we reason, we would be understood; if we imagine, we would that the airy children of our brain were born anew within another's; if we feel, we would that another's nerves should vibrate to our own, that the beams of their eyes should kindle at once and mix and melt into our own, that lips of motionless ice should not reply to lips quivering and burning with the heart's best blood. This is Love.

Love, as the attraction toward refined idealism, figures as well in Shelley's theory of the formative power of poetry.

In *A Defence of Poetry*, he argues that "the great secret of morals is Love." Through identification with the "beautiful which exists in thought, action, or person, not our own," one becomes moral through the process of empathizing. Love is thus an act of the sympathetic imagination. Because poetry, and literature in general, enhances and exercises the ability to empathize, it is an agent of tremendous potential for the moral regeneration of mankind. It goes without saying that the poet thus has a high office in the government of morality; he is Shelley's "unacknowledged legislator." By this phrase Shelley did not primarily mean that poets are unacknowledged for the good they do, but rather that they themselves were not and could not be aware of the power of their beauty. Shelley's poet is not in control of his power, for, in the language of his great metaphor of the creative process,

> the mind in creation is as a fading coal which some invisible influence, like an inconstant wind, awakens to transitory brightness: this power arises from within, like the colour of a flower which fades and changes as it is developed, and the conscious portions of our natures are unprophetic either of its approach or its departure.

Hence, poets do not control their inspiration—in fact, when writing begins, the most intense phase of inspiration has already passed; they express more than they understand; they feel less than they inspire; they are "the influence which is moved not, but moves. Poets are the unacknowledged legislators of the World."

Select works other than poetry

LONG FICTION: *Zastrozzi: A Romance*, 1810; *St. Irvyne: Or, The Rosicrucian*, 1810.

DRAMA: *The Cenci*, pb. 1819; *Prometheus Unbound: A Lyrical Drama in Four Acts*, pb. 1820; *Oedipus Tyrannus: Or, Swellfoot the Tyrant*, pb. 1820; *Hellas: A Lyrical Drama*, pb. 1822; *Charles the First*, pb. 1824 (fragment).

NONFICTION: *The Necessity of Atheism*, 1811 (with Thomas Jefferson Hogg); *An Address to the Irish People*, 1812; *Declaration of Rights*, 1812; *A Letter to Lord Ellenborough*, 1812; *Proposals for an Association of . . . Philanthropists*, 1812; *A Refutation of Deism, in a Dialogue*, 1814; *History of a Six Weeks' Tour Through a Part of France, Switzerland, Germany, and Holland*, 1817 (with Mary Shelley); *A Proposal for Putting Reform to the Vote Throughout the Kingdom*, 1817; *An Address to the People on the Death of the Princess Charlotte*, 1817?; *Essays, Letters from Abroad, Translations, and Fragments*, 1840; *A Defence of Poetry*, 1840; *Shelley Memorials*, 1859; *Shelley's Prose in the Bodleian Manuscripts*, 1910; *Note Books of Shelley*, 1911; *A Philosophical View of Reform*, 1920; *The Letters of Percy Bysshe Shelley*, 1964 (2 volumes; Frederick L. Jones, editor).

TRANSLATIONS: *The Cyclops*, 1824 (of Euripides' play); *Ion*, 1840 (of Plato's dialogue); "The Banquet Translated from Plato," 1931 (of Plato's dialogue *Symposium*).

MISCELLANEOUS: *The Complete Works of Percy Bysshe Shelley*, 1926-1930 (10 volumes; Roger Ingpen and Walter E. Peck, editors); *Shelley's Poetry and Prose: Authoritative Texts and Criticism*, 1977 (Donald H. Reiman and Sharon B. Powers, editors).

Richard E. Matlak

Bibliography · The standard biography is Newman Ivey White, *Shelley*, 2 vols., 1940. See also Edward Dowden, *The Life of Percy Bysshe Shelley*, 2 vols., 1886; Jean Overton Fuller, *Shelley: A Biography*, 1968; and Richard Holmes, *Shelley: The Pursuit*, 1975. Of great importance is Kenneth Neill Cameron, ed., *Shelley and His Circle, 1773-1822*, 6 vols., 1973.

For criticism see Carl Henry Garbo, *The Magic Plant*, 1936; Carlos Baker, *Shelley's Major Poetry*, 1948; Richard Harter Fogle, *The Imagery of Keats and Shelley*, 1949; Harold Bloom, *Shelley's Mythmaking*, 1959; Earl R. Wasserman, *Shelley: A Critical Reading*, 1971; Kenneth Neill Cameron, *Shelley: The Golden Years*, 1974; Karsten Engleberg, *The Making of the Shelley Myth: An Annotated Bibliography of Criticism of Percy Bysshe Shelley 1822-1860*, 1988; and Karen A. Weisman, *Imageless Truths: Shelley's Poetic Fictions*, 1994.

SIR PHILIP SIDNEY

Born: Penshurst, England; November 30, 1554
Died: Arnhem, The Netherlands; October 7, 1586

Poetry · *Astrophil and Stella*, 1591 (pirated edition printed by Thomas Newman), 1598 (first authorized edition) · *Certaine Sonnets*, 1598 · *The Psalmes of David, Translated into Divers and Sundry Kindes of Verse*, 1823 (with Mary Sidney Herbert, Countess of Pembroke) · *The Complete Poems of Sir Philip Sidney*, 1873 (2 volumes) · *The Poems of Sir Philip Sidney*, 1962 (William A. Ringler, Jr., editor) · *The Psalms of Sir Philip Sidney and the Countess of Pembroke*, 1963 (J. C. A. Rathmell, editor)

Achievements · "Our English *Petrarke Sir Philip Sidney* . . . often comforteth him selfe in his sonnets of Stella, though dispairing to attaine his desire." Thus Sir John Harington in 1591, and generations of readers have similarly sighed and sympathized with Astrophel's tragicomic enactment of "poore Petrarch's long deceased woes." In literary history, *Astrophel and Stella* marks a poetical revolution no less than William Wordsworth's *Lyrical Ballads* (1800) or T. S. Eliot's *The Waste Land* (1922); the poem is the product of a young, ambitious poet, acting upon his impatience with the poetry he criticized in his manifesto, *Defence of Poesie*. "Poetry almost have we none," he wrote, "but that lyrical kind of songs and sonets," which "if I were a mistresse would never persuade mee they were in love." Sidney has also had a special place in England's broader cultural history. Part of his fascination has been the ways succeeding ages have appropriated him: as a lost leader of the golden Elizabethan age, Victorian

Library of Congress

gentleman, anguished Edwardian, committed existentialist, apolitical quietist, even a member of the Moral Majority. Like all great writers, Sidney and his works have been continually reinterpreted by successive ages, his poems and his life alike inscribed into different literary, political, and cultural discourses. As contemporary scholars have become more attuned to both the linguistic and ideological complexity of Renaissance literature generally and to the new possibilities of contemporary critical methods, Sidney's writing has been seen, both in its seemingly replete presence and its symptomatic gaps and absences, as central to an understanding of Elizabethan poetry and culture.

None of Sidney's poetry was published in his lifetime, and yet along with his other writings it circulated among a small coterie of family and court acquaintances during the 1580's. Sidney's vocations were those of courtier, statesman, Protestant aristocrat, and patriot before that of a poet, and his poetry encourages the piecing together of a more problematic Sidney than that afforded by conventional hagiography. Sidney's writings often served, as A. C. Hamilton argues, "as a kind of outlet for political interests, compensating for the frustrations and failures" of his life: "problems that prove insurmountable in his career" were transposed and wrestled with in his fictions.

Sidney's major poetic work, *Astrophel and Stella*, in particular marks the triumphant maturity of Elizabethan court poetry, the belated but spectacular adaption of Petrarchanism to English aristocratic culture. It remains one of the most moving, delightful, and provocative collections of love poems in the language, all the more powerful in its impact because of the variety of needs that strain within it for expression—erotic, poetic, political, religious, cultural. One may read it, as Harington did, as the expression of thwarted, obsessive love, but it opens itself, like its author, to much richer readings, which reinforce Sidney's position as the central literary and cultural figure in the English Renaissance before William Shakespeare.

Biography · Sir Philip Sidney was born into one of England's leading aristocratic families. His father was one of Elizabeth I's most loyal civil servants, serving as Lord President of Wales and Lord Deputy of Ireland. On his mother's side, Sidney was related to the influential Leicester family, one of the major Protestant powers in the country. He was educated under the stern Calvinist Thomas Ashton at Shrewsbury School, along with his lifetime friend and biographer Fulke Greville; in 1568 he went to Oxford, but he left without a degree in 1571 and in 1572 went on a Grand Tour through Europe, where he was introduced to and widely admired by major European scholars and statesmen, especially by leading Huguenot and

German Protestants. In 1575 he returned to England and joined Elizabeth's court. He contributed a masque, *The Lady of May*, to one of the royal entertainments in 1578 and was employed by the Queen in a number of minor matters. Unfortunately, he alienated Elizabeth, partly because he was so forthright in his support of European and English Protestant ideals and partly because of his own personal charisma. In a stormy career at court, he alternated between periods of willing service and periods of retirement to his sister's house at Wilton, near Salisbury, where an increasing number of Elizabethan poets, intellectuals, and thinkers were gathering—almost as an alternative to the Queen's court. In 1580 he quarreled with the Earl of Oxford over whether the Queen should consider marrying the French Catholic Duke of Anjou. His advice on the matter was ignored, or played down, and he contemplated going illegally to the New World. Elizabeth's attitude to the man the English court so much admired (almost as much as many Europeans) was an ambivalent one: Sidney was probably too much a man of outspoken principle to be of use to her in her devious political dealings.

Sidney's literary career therefore developed in part out of the frustrations of his political career. Most of his works were written in his periods of chosen, or enforced, retirement to Wilton, and often grew out of discussions with friends such as Fulke Greville and Edward Dyer and his sister, Mary. He looked at the poetry being written in England, contrasted it most unfavorably with that of European courts, and so set out deliberately, by precept and example, to improve it. The result was an outburst of writing that marked a literary revolution: *Defence of Poesie*, probably started by 1579, was a sophisticated, chatty, and persuasive theoretical treatment. *Astrophel and Stella*, written in 1581-1582, is the first major Petrarchan sonnet collection written in English; the continually revised romance, *Arcadia*, dedicated to his sister, was started in 1578, and was still being revised shortly before his tragic death in the Battle of Zutphen in 1586. Sidney was given a hero's funeral in London. Monarchs, statesmen, soldiers, and poets from all over Europe sent condolences, wrote memorials, and for the next sixty years or so Sidney's person, prestige, and power hung over the English court and culture as a reminder of how the Renaissance ideal of the courtier could be combined with Protestant piety.

Analysis · Sir Philip Sidney was educated to embrace an unusual degree of political, religious, and cultural responsibility, yet it is clear from his comments in *Defence of Poesie* that he took his literary role as seriously. Both this critical treatise and his *Astrophel and Stella* are manifestos—not only of poetic but also of broader cultural practice. Both look forward to a long-needed renaissance of poetry and culture generally. For Sidney, poetry and its broader social uses were inseparable. Indeed, it is only with distortion that one can separate a "literary" from a "social" text, even with a Petrarchan love sequence such as *Astrophel and Stella*. Like other Elizabethan court poets, Sidney's poetry was written within a structure of power, and it tries to carve out a discursive space under ideological pressures which attempted to control and direct the languages by which the court operated. The court was more than a visible institution for Sidney and his contemporaries: It was a felt pressure which attempted to fix and determine all that came within its reach. Sidney's life and poetry are especially interesting examples of how the Elizabethan court's power operated upon poetry. The court poets—for example, Sir Walter Raleigh, or the Earl of Oxford—acted as spokesmen for the court's values, and yet inevitably the strains and tensions of their roles show through in their poetry. Poetry was both an expression of the power of the court and a means of participating in that power. Where a poem like Raleigh's "Praised be Diana's Fair and Harmles Light" shows the court contemplating its own idealized image, Sidney's poetry has a more uneasy relation to the court's power. Although on the surface his writing appears to embody, in Terry Eagleton's words, a "moment of ideological buoyancy, an achieved synthesis" of courtly values, Sidney's own position in the court makes his poetry an especially revealing instance of the struggles and tensions beneath the seemingly replete surface of the court and court poetry alike.

More than any of his contemporaries before John Donne and Shakespeare, Sidney's poetry evokes a felt world of bustling activity, psychosocial pressure, cultural demand—in short, the workings of power upon literary and historical discourse. The institutions that shape the poetry—the court, its household arrangements, its religious and political controversies—are evoked in the tournaments (41), the gossip of "curious wits" (23) and "courtly nymphs" (54), and make up an atmosphere of energetic worldliness. What distinguishes Sidney's poetry is the forceful way that something more than the glittering surface of the court energizes it. Despite his posthumous reputation as the perfect Renaissance courtier, Sidney's public career was one of political disappointment and humiliation; he seems to have been increasingly torn between public duty and private desire, much in the way the hero of his sonnet sequence is.

As Richard McCoy has shown, all Sidney's works are permeated with the problem of authority and submission. Like himself, all his heroes (including Astrophel) are young, noble, well-educated and well-intentioned, but as they become aware of the complexities and ambiguities of the world, they become diverted or confused, and Sidney finds himself caught between compassion and condemnation of their activities. In *Arcadia*, Sidney attempted to solve in fiction many of the tensions that beset his life, and *Astrophel and Stella* similarly served as an outlet for political and social frustration. In the prose romance, Sidney's narrative irresolution and (in an early version) premature and repressive closure reveal deep and unsettling doubts; similarly, the ambivalences and hesitations, the shifting distance between poet and character, the divided responses to intellectual and emotional demands in *Astrophel and Stella*, articulate Sidney's ambivalent roles within the court.

One of the fundamental influences which give Sidney's life and poetry their particular cast is Protestantism. Indeed, perhaps the most potent factor disrupting the repleteness of the court poetic was Sidney's piety and his struggle with creating a Protestant poetic. In A. C. Hamilton's phrase, Sidney was "a Protestant English Petrarch." Unlike his close friend Fulke Greville, for whom a radical Augustinian suspicion of metaphor and writing itself consistently undermined poetry's value, Sidney tried to hold together what in *Defence of Poesie* he terms man's "erected wit" and his "infected will." Indeed, what Sidney perhaps uniquely brought to the Petrarchan lyric was a self-conscious anxiety about the tension between courtly celebration and Protestant inwardness, between the persuasiveness and rhetoric and the self-doubt of sinful man, between the insecurity of man's word and the absolute claims of God's.

The tension in Sidney's writing between the courtly and the pious, John Calvin and Baldassare Castiglione, disrupts *Astrophel and Stella* most interestingly. Sidney's own theory sees poetry focusing on the reformation of will and behavior, and it is possible to read his own sequence as an exemplum of the perils of erotic love, or, in Alan Sinfield's words, "the errors of unregulated passion." Sidney displays Astrophel deliberately rejecting virtue, treating Stella as a deity in a "direct challenge to Christianity" and to right reason. His cleverness is displayed in trying to avoid or repel the claims of reason and virtue, and the outcome of the sequence is the inevitable end of self-deception. The inwardness of *Astrophel and Stella*—not necessarily, it should be noted, its supposed autobiographical dimension, but its concern with the persona's self-consciousness, even self-centeredness, as lover, poet, courtier—is thus a fascinating blend of Petrarchan convention and Protestant self-concentration, and one which points to a distinctive late sixteenth century strain within the inherited vocabulary and rhetoric of the poet in his role in the court.

When Sidney returned from his Grand Tour, he looked back across the Channel to the sophisticated academies and court circles which were encouraging writers, scholars, and musicians, and which were united by a synthesis of Christian, usually Protestant, piety and high Neoplatonism. The French academies, in particular, displayed a self-consciousness that distinguished them very strongly from the medieval courts. Shortly after Sidney's return, his sister Mary became the Countess of Pembroke and established at Wilton what one of her followers was to term a "little Court," dedicated to continuing the renaissance of English courtly culture. Sidney's whole literary career became a frustrated attempt to realize a new role for the court poet, one based upon the integrity and responsibility of values which he was unable to embody in his public life, and which more and more he poured into his writing. His remark to the Earl of Leicester that he was kept "from the courte since my only service is speeche and that is stopped" has wider application than to its occasion, the French marriage crisis. It articulates a frustration toward the traditional subservience of a poet to the court, a stubborn insistence on forging a distinctive role for the poet.

Part of the fascination Sidney has traditionally evoked is what is often perceived as his ability to balance opposite ideological, rhetorical, or vocational demands upon him. Certainly in *Defence of Poesie* and *Astrophel and Stella* the elements of such a dialectic can be found. The promise of divinity that Astrophel perceives in Stella's eyes is, in Sidney's sympathetic comedy, wittily undermined by his self-consciousness, bashfulness, physical overeagerness, and human imperfection. In *Defence of Poesie*, Sidney describes poetry as a fervent reaching for the sublime, veiling truth in order to draw its reader toward it, and asserts that the power to move and so to bring about an enactment of poetry's transforming powers certainly lies within man's godlike nature. Yet for Sidney there was the seemingly inseparable problem of man's "infected will," and the reformed emphasis on man's depravity and the untrustworthiness of the mind seems to have posed crucial problems for him and for the possibility of creating a Protestant poetic. While elements of an opposition between rhetoric and truth, humanism and piety, Calvin and Castiglione, can be isolated, despite his most anxious intentions, Sidney does not manage to hold them together satisfactorily. In fact, his very fascination for later ages and his centrality for understanding sixteenth century poetry are grounded in such contradictions. "Unresolved and continuing conflict," in Stephen Greenblatt's phrase, is a distinctive mark of Renaissance culture, and Sidney's is a central place in that culture.

The versification of the Psalms, started by Sidney about 1579 and revised and completed by his sister, the Countess of Pembroke, after his death, comprises the first post-Reformation religious lyrics that combine the rich emotional and spiritual life of Protestantism with the new rhetorical riches of the secular lyric. There are distinctive Protestant notes—a strong stress on election in Psalm 43, echoing Théodore Bèze's and Calvin's glosses rather than the original text, for example—and other Psalms, where a strain of courtly Neoplatonism is highlighted, notably in Psalm 8, which (like Pico della Mirandola rather than Calvin) presents man as a privileged, glorious creation "attended" by God, an "owner" of regal and "crowning honour." Man emerges as a free and wondrous being, like his creator, "freely raunging within the Zodiack of his owne wit," as Sidney put it in *Defence of Poesie.* Here Sidney juxtaposes, without integrating them, the great contraries of his age.

It is now generally believed that the Psalms were originally drafted by Sidney early in his career, perhaps about 1579. Also written in this early period are a number of miscellaneous poems, including the so-called "certain sonnets" and many of the poems inserted into *Arcadia.* These are mainly of interest for showing Sidney's eager experimentation—with quantitative verse, pastoral dialogue, song, metrical and stanzaic patterns, and above all the appeal to the feelings of the reader, notably in "Leave me, O Love, which reachest but to dust" and the magnificent double sestina from *Arcadia,* "Yee Gote-heard Gods."

Sidney's most sustained and most celebrated work is his sonnet sequence *Astrophel and Stella,* probably written in 1582, which dramatizes a frustrated love affair between a courtier and an admired lady. As Germaine Warkentin has shown, Sidney may have been tinkering with his "Certain Sonnets" during 1581-1582, abandoning them the next summer "to compose one of the three most distinguished sonnet sequences of the English Renaissance." Certainly *Astrophel and Stella* conveys an intensity that suggests a short burst of concentrated writing.

This sequence of 108 sonnets and eleven songs anatomizes the love of a young, restless, self-conscious courtier, Astrophel, for a lady, Stella, his star. His purpose is set out in the opening sonnet, in which he claims, "I sought fit words to paint the blackest face of woe/ Studying inventions fine, her wits to entertaine." The reader is taken into the familiar world of Petrarchan convention and cliché: Astrophel the doubting, self-conscious, aggressive lover; Stella, the golden-haired, black-eyed, chaste and (usually) distant and (finally) unobtainable lady. The figures are equally familiar—debates between Hope and Absence, denials of loving at first sight, the frustrated desire alleviated by writing, the beautiful woman with the icy heart who pitilessly resists siege, and the final misery of the lover who ends his plaints in anguish, swearing in the end by all he has left, her "absent presence." Like the best *Petrarchisti,* Sidney makes the traditional motifs intensely dramatic. For the first time in English poetry since Geoffrey

Chaucer, C. S. Lewis suggests, "a situation is not merely written about: it is created, presented, so as to compel our imaginations." Earlier Petrarchan poets such as Thomas Wyatt had conveyed urgency and conversational informality, but, read as a whole, English poetry had not, since Chaucer, been distinguished by such continual, even restless, conflict and energy.

Modern critics, reacting against earlier impressionistic, Romantic criticism, have shown how the energy and variety of Sidney's poetry rests on a thorough exploitation of the riches of Renaissance rhetoric—through his use of apostrophe, dialogue, irony, shifts in decorum, and modulations of voice. As Ringler points out, perhaps "the most valuable product of his studies and disputations in Oxford was the thorough training he received in logic and formal classical rhetoric"; to these he added intense study and practice in ways of loosening the rhythmic movement of English line and working within the formal demands of stanzaic and metrical form. By a thorough familiarity with the conventional techniques of Renaissance love verse—which he parodies in 6, 9, and 15, for example—Sidney works within the eloquent courtly poetic, mocking and adapting it where necessary. Sidney uses his poems as workshops, experimenting with a great variety of stanzaic patterns and with devices such as inversion and feminine rhyme. Above all, he tries continually to juxtapose the movement of formal verse with an immediacy of idiom and logical development to involve his reader in the often tortuous movements of his character's broodings, arguments, and self-deceptions. Especially notable is the lightness and wit with which even Astrophel's most tortured self-examination is presented. Parody, the exaggerated use of erotic or literary clichés and puns, are all obvious enough, but the whole sequence is characterized by a sophisticated playfulness—the outrageous puns on "touch" in 9 leading to the self-pity (Astrophel's, not Sidney's) of the last line, the tongue-in-cheek anguish of the sonnets on Cupid, and the uproariousness of some of the erotic sonnets. Above all, the humor of the poet, indulging in his own mastery of language and able to dramatize his character, invites his readers to share his enjoyment at the varied follies and complexities of human love.

If the Petrarchan tradition and the resources of Elizabethan rhetoric afforded Sidney a wonderfully flexible and rich poetic vehicle, there is nevertheless something limiting, even disturbing, about the literary mode in which he is working. Petrarchanism purports to be about love, and specifically about the obsession of a lover for a lady before whom he feels inferior, humble, and yet ennobled. Paradoxically, the sonnets become a weapon in an attempted mastery of the woman and their focus is exclusively upon the anguish and achievements of the male lover. The conventions of Petrarchanism are those of a male-dominated society and its rhetorical strategies serve to elevate the woman only to subjugate her.

As Ann Jones and Peter Stallybrass have argued, "to Stella, Astrophel may speak of love as service," but outside his devotion to friends, "he can suggest a sub-text of masculine domination." Within the struggle for mastery, rhetoric and erotic convention alike becomes means of domination. Stella herself is, like other Petrarchan mistresses, reduced to a disconnected set of characteristics, acknowledged only as they are manipulable or impinge on her lover's consciousness. She is entirely the product of her poet-lover's desires. *Astrophel and Stella* is a theater of desire in which the man has all the active roles, and in which she is silent or merely iconic, most present when she refuses him or is absent. Astrophel does not want—although it is arguable that Sidney might—to call into question the power of his anguish or the centrality of his struggles of conscience, yet it seems legitimate to ask what Stella might reply to Astrophel's earnest self-regarding pleas for favor. Even if her replies are not "in" most of the poems (and where they are, as in Song 8, they are reported through Astrophel), what might she say? Is her silence the repression of the character or of Sidney? Does her silence reflect a whole cultural blindness that fixes women as objects of gaze and analysis within a society they did not invent and could not control? When one considers in these ways how the dynamics of Sidney's text function, once again one finds "literary" and "cultural" texts interacting.

An older criticism faced (or perhaps avoided) these issues by focusing on the biographical "origins" of the sequence. In part an outcome of the Romantic valorization of poetry as the overflow of sincerity or genuine experience, criticism sentimentalized the obvious connections between Sidney's life and the fiction of Astrophel and Stella into a poetic *roman à clef.* Undoubtedly, Sidney plays with his reader's curiosity about some kind of identification between himself and Astrophel and between Stella and Lady Penelope Rich (née Devereux) to whom as a youth Sidney's family nearly arranged a betrothal and in whom he may possibly (though there is no firm evidence either way) have had more than a literary interest. Sidney certainly builds into his sequence references to his career, to his father, to contemporary politics, to his friends, and—of most interest to the curious—to Lady Rich's name in two sonnets (24, 37) which were omitted from the first publication of the collection, perhaps for fear of embarrassing repercussions. Even so, the relationship between Sidney and his characters and between the events of his life and those seemingly within his poems should not be simplified. Just as Sidney manages simultaneously to have much in common with Astrophel, be sympathetic with him, and yet to criticize or laugh at him, so the gap between Stella and the historical Lady Rich is even wider—at best one can regard some of the references to Stella as sly or wistful fantasies. As to whether Sidney and Lady Rich were sexually involved, *Astrophel and Stella* gives no firm evidence.

A more rewarding approach is to try to trace the way the poems are traversed by a variety of overlapping and in many cases contradictory influences, including court politics, the psychology of love, poetry, rhetoric, and Christianity. Within its confusions, tensions, and contradictons, *Astrophel and Stella* highlights the diverse and often contradictory pressures and possibilities which constitute the situation of an Elizabethan poet and lover. One of the distinctive possiblities of Petrarchanism was to set the traditional medieval debate on the nature of love in terms of the lover's psychology and within the demands of the codes of courtly behavior. Part of the fascination Petrarch had for English poets in the late sixteenth century was their puzzlement about how the Petrarchist conventions might fit their experiences. The prestige and suggestiveness of Petrarchanism allowed poets to examine not only the relationship between love and poetry, but also the way its worldview, its rich schematization of human experience, and their own changing social and individual realities intersected.

One of the dominant concerns of the sequence is undoubtedly that of the problems and difficulties of erotic experience—although depicted entirely from the male viewpoint. *Astrophel and Stella* typically focuses on the "thrownness" of love—on the lover finding himself within a preexisting structuring of experience, a "race" that "hath neither stop nor start" (23), but which continually disrupts his sense of a preexistent self. Sexuality becomes an object to be examined, supervised, confessed, and transformed into poetry. It should be noted, however, that the "self" that is put into question in *Astrophel and Stella* is not, or not primarily, that of Sidney. The poet offers his poems to an audience of sympathetic listeners as a mirror less of his experiences than of theirs. The intellectual tensions observable in *Astrophel and Stella* are dramatized as paradigms, the effect of which is to highlight the readers' or hearers' awareness of their own experiences. Sidney's poems work upon their readers, suggesting and manipulating although never compelling into meaning. At times he refers to quite specific members of his audience—to other lover-poets in 6, in which Astrophel distinguishes his own "trembling voice" and the sincerity of his love from those of other lovers and so provokes them to respond by praising their own mistresses or talents. At times his suffering hero will ostensibly address a rather special audience—"I Stella's ears assayl, invade her ears," he says in Sonnet 61; or he (or Sidney) will address a friend (as in Sonnet 14), and even occasionally himself (as in 30). Yet the most important audience is unnamed: the readers who, through the poem's history, will read them, meditate upon and act out their drama.

Surveying the history of Sidney criticism, especially in the past forty years, one discovers a curious anxiety to find a coherent, sequential organization not merely made possible by the poems, but as a required means of reading them. *Astrophel and Stella* is thus often read as if it were a poetic novel. C. S. Lewis cautions against treating the Petrarchan sequence as if it were "a way of telling a story"; *Astrophel and Stella* is, he says, "not a love story but an anatomy of love," while Max Putzel speaks of the poems' "careful disorder." On the other hand, A. C. Hamilton argues that "the sonnets are organized into a sequence with a unifying structure," and other critics have written of what they see as careful structure and sequence. In Hamilton's scheme, sonnets 1-12 form an introduction, 13-30 concentrate on Astrophel's isolation, with 41-68 concerned with his moral rebellion, 71-85 with his attempt at seduction, and the remainder with his failure. Such divisions differ radically among the proponents of a narrative structure; in short, if a reader wishes to find a narrative development and final irresolution rather than an exercise in love's variety, then *Astrophel and Stella* is open to such a reading. Perhaps the most satisfying sequential reading of the collection is that by Ann Rosalind Jones, who stresses that although it is possible (and peculiarly satisfying) to see Astrophel as undergoing a gradual disintegration and loss of control, Sidney's sequence does not use the linking devices of other poets, such as Dante or Maurice Scève, which might strongly encourage a reading of the sequence as a growth in self-knowledge. Even when one constructs a sequence, it is primarily characterized by an unstable, eddying movement, "dramatically *dis*ordered," as Jones argues. "Even at the end of his experience," Astrophel can "predict the course of his writing no better than the course of his love" and so each sonnet becomes a new starting place. In short, while *Astrophel and Stella* allows for a linear development, it does not force one upon a reader, encouraging one just as readily to view Astrophel's experience as unpredictable, random, and even as an exemplum of failure.

One recurring pattern is a tension between the demands of the public world of politics and responsibility and the private world of erotic desire. In many sonnets, Astrophel presents love in terms of a debate between traditional abstractions such as desire and reason, love and duty. Part of the reader's enjoyment lies in watching him, through Sidney's fond but penetrating perspective, indulging himself in false logic (52) or in seeing his dutifully constructed arguments against love undermined by the simple appearance of his beloved, as in 5, 10, or in the amusing self-contradictions of 47. Astrophel tries in vain to keep his two worlds and their demands separate. He claims that love gives him a private place, a sense of self from which the demands of courtly responsibility are shown to be trivial, but caught between conflicting worlds of self-indulgence and political responsibility, he ends by succeeding in neither. The reader watches him corrupting his avowedly pure love into sensuality by the deviousness of political rhetoric. In Sonnet 23 he appears to reject the world, but in Sonnet 69 he expresses Stella's conditional encouragement of his advances in terms of the court's own language. Since, he argues, she has "of her high heart giv'n" him "the monarchie," as a king, he too can take some advantage from that power.

At the root of Astrophel's self-deception is the structure of Petrarchanism itself, which, as John Stevens and others have pointed out, was at once a literary convention and a very serious courtly game, one "in which three powerful discourses meet and join hands: love, religion, and politics." *Astrophel and Stella* is based on a formula by which the man is subjected to his lady while, at the same time, the situation enables him to pour forth his eloquence in an attempt to influence her. The relationship is parallel to the relationship between courtier and monarch—built on absolute loyalty and subjection, frustration and rejection—interlaced with devious manipulation for the favors of the capricious, distant beloved. Thus while Astrophel speaks of the "joy" inspired by Stella and of his own "noble fire," he is attempting to manipulate Stella's vulnerability, seeking power over her in the way the devious courtier seeks hidden but real power over the monarch. In terms of sexual politics of the Renaissance court, Astrophel's world is one shared primarily by other male courtiers, using language as a means of domination and treating women as subject to their desire, much in the way courtiers themselves were at the mercy of the monarch.

Thus the reader watches Astrophel indulging himself in small subtle ways—playing on grammar in 63, twisting Stella's words, speaking openly to her in a kind of "manic playfulness," and allowing (or being unable to prevent) the emergence of the underlying physicality of his desires in a series of fantasies of seduction (71, 72, 74, 79, 80, 81). The songs serve especially well to highlight the wish-fulfillment of Astrophel's frustrations—especially the dramatization in Song 5 of Astrophel's self-involvement, and the graceful fantasy of Song 8, viewed wistfully by the narrator from a distance and culminating in Sidney's clever and moving breaking down of the distance between narrator and character in the final line, where he confesses that "my" song is broken.

As the sequence draws to its inevitably inconclusive end, Astrophel's fantasies become less and less realizable. He indulges in self-pity and then more realistically accepts the end of the relationship, vacillating between joy and grief, optimism and despair, dedication and unfaithfulness. As Hamilton points out, the mutability of human love which haunts so many Elizabethan sonnet sequences, especially Shakespeare's, enters Sidney's only indirectly, but where he immerses himself in the intensity of the living moment, as the sequence ends, he realizes he is "forever subject to love's tyranny, a victim of *chronos* forever caught in time's endless linear succession."

Readings of *Astrophel and Stella* inevitably point to it as a quintessential ideological and literary struggle, where a variety of impulses struggle for mastery. Like the best love poems, it asks its readers to look at themselves. Stella herself, the guiding metaphor of the sequence, is distinguished by her nature, behavior, influence, and power, always requiring, like a text, interpretation. Astrophel, like the reader of his creator's sequence, is an exegete of love. "What blushing notes doest thou in margin see," he asks, and goes on, as all readers do with the whole sequence, to choose his own convenient misunderstanding of Stella. Astrophel may state that all his "deed" is to "copy" what in Stella "Nature writes" (3) or assert that "Stella" is, literally, the principle of love in the cosmos (28), and that the words he utters "do well set forth my mind" (44), but Sidney knows, as his readers do, that love and its significance and its expression in language are far more complex matters.

Astrophel and Stella is what Roland Barthes terms a "playful" text, one that depends strongly on its audience, inviting participation both to reproduce the process, intellectual and emotional, by which the poem's struggles came to be verbalized and to go beyond them, adding one's own preoccupations. *Astrophel and Stella* has a capacity to invade its readers, to direct and inform their responses, but as well, to open them to an awareness that it functions only through a process of deliberate reciprocity. It is this joyful welcome to its readers that makes it such a landmark in English poetry.

Other literary forms · Although Sir Philip Sidney's best-known work is *Astrophel and Stella*, his major work, the one to which he devoted most of his literary energy and much of his political frustration, was *Arcadia* (originally entitled *The Countess of Pembroke's Arcadia*). This long, much-revised epic prose romance was written and revised between 1578 and 1586; it was first published in an unfinished version in 1590, again in 1593 in a revised and imperfect version, and repeatedly in many editions for more than a century. The equivalent in prose of Edmund Spenser's *The Faerie Queene* (1590-1596), it is an encyclopedic romance of love, politics, and adventure, incorporating many stories and discussions of philosophical, theological, erotic, and psychological issues. Almost as important is Sidney's critical treatise, *Defence of Poesie* (1595; published in another edition as *An Apologie for Poetry*), written about 1580, and setting forth in a seductive, if never quite logically coherent argument, a celebration of the nature and power of poetry, along with some prescriptive (and perceptive) comments on the current malaise of English poetry, drama, and the literary scene generally. Other works Sidney wrote include *The Lady of May* (1578), a pastoral entertainment; the first forty-four poems in a translation of the Psalms, later revised and completed by his sister Mary; a number of other miscellaneous poems, prose treatises, and translations, mainly designed to further the cause of the Protestant faction in Elizabeth's court.

Select works other than poetry

LONG FICTION: *Arcadia*, 1590, 1593, 1598 (originally entitled *The Countess of Pembroke's Arcadia*).

DRAMA: *The Lady of May*, pr. 1578 (masque); "Fortress of Perfect Beauty," pr. 1581 (with Fulke Greville, Lord Brooke; Phillip Howard, the earl of Arundel; and Baron Windsor of Stanwell).

NONFICTION: *Defence of Poesie*, 1595 (also published as *An Apologie for Poetry*).

MISCELLANEOUS: *Miscellaneous Prose of Sir Philip Sidney*, 1973.

Gary F. Waller

Bibliography · *The Sidney Newsletter and Journal* and *English Literary Renaissance* regularly issue bibliographies of current research. Another bibliography is Donald Stump et al., *Sir Philip Sidney: Annotated Bibliography (1554-1984)*, 1994. A useful biography is Katherine Duncan-Jones, *Sir Philip Sidney: Courtier Poet*, 1991. Critical studies include Dennis Kay, ed., *Sir Philip Sidney: An Anthology of Modern Criticism*, 1987; Arthur F. Kinney, ed., *Sidney in Retrospect*, 1988; M. J. B. Allen et al., eds., *Sir Philip Sydney's Achievements*, 1990; Alan Hager, *Dazzling Images*, 1991.

GARY SNYDER

Born: San Francisco, California; May 8, 1930

Poetry · *Riprap*, 1959 · *Myths and Texts*, 1960 · *Hop, Skip, and Jump*, 1964 · *Nanao Knows*, 1964 · *The Firing*, 1964 · *Riprap, and Cold Mountain Poems*, 1965 · *Six Sections from Mountains and Rivers Without End*, 1965 · *A Range of Poems*, 1966 · *Three Worlds, Three Realms, Six Roads*, 1966 · *The Back Country*, 1967 · *The Blue Sky*, 1969 · *Sours of the Hills*, 1969 · *Regarding Wave*, 1970 · *Manzanita*, 1972 · *The Fudo Trilogy: Spel Against Demons, Smokey the Bear Sutra, The California Water Plan*, 1973 · *Turtle Island*, 1974 · *All in the Family*, 1975 · *Axe Handles*, 1983 · *Left out in the Rain: New Poems 1947-1986*, 1986 · *No Nature: New and Selected Poems*, 1992 · *Mountains and Rivers Without End*, 1996

Achievements · Before "ecology" had become a password of political correctness, Gary Snyder was devising a program of study designed to create a language of environmental advocacy; after many trendy westerners had long since recoiled from the rigors of Eastern thought, Snyder completed a curriculum of apprenticeship in Japan and went on to develop an American version of Zen applicable to his locality; as Native American life and lore gradually seeped into the area of academic interest, Snyder continued his examinations of the primal tribal communities that lived in harmony with the North American land mass for pre-Columbian millennia and worked to apply their successes to contemporary life; while hippies and dropouts returned to the button-down corporate culture after a brief dalliance with a countercul-

Raku Mayers

ture, Snyder built his own home at the center of a small community that endures as an example of a philosophical position in action; and most of all, while some of the other voices that arose during the post-"Howl" renaissance of the New American Poetry have become stale or quaint, Snyder's use of a clear, direct, colloquial but literature-responsive language made it possible for his concerns to reach, touch, and move a substantial audience through his poetry.

Snyder's varied interests have given him extensive material for his poems, but the appeal of his work is not dependent on a program calculated to educate or persuade. Much more than argument, the poetry is an outgrowth of the processes of Snyder's life—his work, his family, his intellectual and athletic interests, his cultural convictions, and his rapport with the landscape. He has been able to illustrate effectively how art and life can be intertwined in a reciprocal interchange that does not depend on academic procedures or traditional schools (while not denying their usefulness as well), an interchange that enriches and expands both realms, and in this he joins Herman Melville (the sailor), Henry David Thoreau (the naturalist), Ralph Waldo Emerson (the philosopher and teacher), and Walt Whitman (the celebrator) in a line of American artists whose work was, in a profound sense, the spiritual and aesthetic expression of their life's focus. *Turtle Island* won the Pulitzer Prize in 1975.

Biography · Gary Snyder was born in San Francisco in 1930, the son of Harold Alton and Lois Wilkie Snyder. His parents moved back to their native Pacific Northwest in 1932, where they settled on a dairy farm near Puget Sound in Washington. Snyder's mother moved to Portland, Oregon, to work as a newspaper-woman when Snyder was twelve, and reared Snyder and his younger sister Anthea as a single parent, insisting that Snyder commute downtown to attend Lincoln High, the most intellectually demanding school in the Portland system. In 1947, he received a scholarship to Reed College, where he devised a unique major in anthropology and literature. Early in his college years, he joined the outdoor groups the Mazamas and the Wilderness Society and took up backcountry hiking and skiing and snowpeak mountaineering. His first poems were published in the Reed College literary magazine. He lived in an old house shared by a dozen other students similarly interested in art and politics, including the poets Philip Whalen and Lew Welch, who became his close friends. Snyder wrote for *The Oregonian* newspaper at night and spent the summer of 1950 on an archaeological dig at old Fort Vancouver in Washington. At about that time, he was briefly married to Allison Gass, a fellow student.

Upon graduation from Reed, Snyder completed one semester of graduate studies in linguistics at Indiana University before transferring to the University of California at Berkeley to study Oriental languages. During the summers of the years he pursued graduate work, he took a job first as a fire-watcher in the Cascade mountains and later, after he was fired in the McCarthy-era hysteria of 1954, as a choker-setter for the Warm Springs Lumber Company. Utilizing skills in woodcutting he had learned from his family and neighbors, Snyder "was often supporting himself" in his student years, and his first accomplished poems were related to these experiences as well as to his work on a trail crew in Yosemite in 1955.

That fall, Snyder met Allen Ginsberg and Jack Kerouac and became involved in the exploding art scene in San Francisco, where he took part in the historic Six Gallery reading where Ginsberg read "Howl" in public for the first time. Snyder followed this extraordinary performance with his own poetry in a very different vein and was also successful in capturing the attention of the audience. He and Kerouac shared a cabin in Mill Valley, California, through that winter and spring, and then Snyder traveled to Kyoto, Japan, to take up residence in a Zen temple, beginning a twelve-year sojourn in Japan that was broken by a nine-month hitch as a crewman on the tanker *Sappa Creek* and a brief return to San Francisco in 1958. His translations from the Chinese poet Han-shan, who lived in the seventh century, were published in the *Evergreen Review* in 1958 as "Cold Mountain Poems," and his first collection, *Riprap*, was published by Cid Corman's Origin Press in Japan in 1959.

Working as a part-time translator and researcher of Buddhist texts, Snyder eventually became a student of Rinzai Zen under Oda Sesso, Roshi (master), and established contacts with activist groups concerned with ecology, women's issues, and world peace. His next collection, *Myths and Texts*, was published in 1960, the same year he married the poet Joanne Kyger. In 1962, he traveled to India with Ginsberg, Peter Orlovsky, and Kyger, and his association with the poet Nanao Sakaki drew him into artistic circles in Tokyo in 1964. He returned to the United States to teach at Berkeley in 1965, won a Bollingen grant, and returned to Japan. His marriage with Kyger was over when he met Masa Uehara, a graduate student in English, and they were married in 1967.

With his wife and his son, Kai, who was born in Kyoto, Snyder returned to the Western Hemisphere, settling in the northern Sierra Nevada mountains, where he built a home (called "Kitkitdizze," meaning "mountain misery") in 1970 with a crew of friends. His first book of poems reflecting his commitment to his native country, *Turtle Island* (from an old Native American name for the continent), was published in 1974 and won the Pulitzer Prize. During this time, Snyder was traveling to universities three or four months a year to read poetry, working on the needs of his immediate mountain community, and serving the state of California as the chairman of its Arts Council. At the end of the decade, he published a collection called *The Real Work: Interviews and Talks, 1964-1979* (1980), and in 1983, he published *Axe Handles*, poems written during the previous ten years. In 1985, he joined the English department at the University of California at Davis, where he taught literature and ecological matters, and he began to travel widely, visiting Hawaii, Alaska, China, and parts of Europe to speak "on the specifics of Buddhist meditation, ecological practice, language and poetics, and bioregional politics." The poems he had written but left uncollected were published in *Left Out in the Rain: New Poems 1947-1985*. In 1988, he was divorced from Masa Uehara and married Carole Koda, and in 1990, he completed a book that presented a program for personal renewal and planetary conservation called *The Practice of the Wild*. That same year, a compilation of comments, reminiscences, poems, and assorted other statements was published by the Sierra Club under the title *Gary Snyder: Dimensions of a Life* in celebration of the poet's sixtieth birthday. In his seventh decade, Snyder continues work on his "poem of process," *Mountains and Rivers Without End*, and trains students at Davis to deal with environmental crises. The hero figure Kerouac patterned after Snyder in *The Dharma Bums* (1958), "Japhy Ryder," has become the source of wisdom, the poet Gary Snyder, now grown into an elder of the tribe.

Analysis · Among many evocative statements about his life and work, a particularly crucial one is Gary Snyder's claim that

> As a poet, I hold the most archaic values on earth. They go back to the late Paleolithic; the fertility of the soil, the magic of animals; the power-vision in solitude, the terrifying initiation and rebirth; the love and ecstasy of the dance, the common work of the tribe.

The social and philosophical principles he has expressed are the fundamental credo of his convictions as a man and an artist. He uses the word "archaic" to suggest "primal" or "original"—the archetype or first pattern from which others may evolve. His citation of the late Paleolithic era as source-ground stems from his belief that essential lessons concerning human consciousness have been learned and then lost. Thus Snyder devotes much time to the study of ancient (and primitive) cultures. The values he holds stand behind and direct his poetry, as it is drawn from his studies and experiences. His values include a respect for land as the source of life and the means of sustaining it; a respect for all sentient creatures and for the animalistic instincts of humans; a recognition of the necessity for the artist to resist social pressure in order to discover and develop power from within; an acknowledgement of the necessity for participation in both communal ritual and individual exploration of the depths of the subconscious to transcend the mundane and risk the extraordinary; an acceptance of the body and the senses—the physical capabilities, pleasures, and demands of the skin; and a feeling for the shared labor of the community, another version of "the real work" that unites the individual with a larger sense and source of meaning. Neither the poet as solitary singer nor as enlightened visionary is sufficient without the complex of relationships that joins the local, the bioregional, and ultimately the planetary in an interdependent chain of reliance, support, and enlightened use of resources. It is with these values in mind that Snyder defines an ethical life as one that "is mindful, mannerly and has style," an attitude that is crucial to the accomplishment of "the real work."

Each of these precepts has an important analogue in the technical execution of the poems themselves. As Jerome Rothenberg has observed, "where I continue to see him best is as he emerges from his poems." Poetically, then, "the fertility of the soil" is worthless without the labor that brings it to fruition, and as Snyder has commented, "the rhythms of my poems follow the rhythms of the physical work I'm doing and life I'm leading at any given time—which makes the music in my head which creates the line." The linkage between the rhythmic movement of the body, the larger rhythmic cycles of the natural world, and the structure of words in a particular poem follows the precepts that Charles Olson prescribed in the landmark "Projective Verse" essay (1950), and Snyder, like Ginsberg, Robert Creeley, and others, has always favored the creation of a particular shape or form to suit the purpose of the poem under attentive development. The rhythms of a particular poem are derived from an "energy-mind-field-dance" that, in turn, often results from labor designed to capitalize on the life of the earth.

Similarly, when Snyder speaks of "the magic of animals," he is identifying one of his central subjects, and the images of many of his poems are based on his observations of animals in the wild. The importance of wilderness and the manner in which animals seem to interact instinctively with their natural surroundings are, for Snyder, keys to his conception of freedom. The magic of their existence is part of a mystery that humans need to penetrate. Thus, as image and subject animals and their ways are an important part of the "etiquette of freedom" Snyder's work serves.

The concept of the "power vision in solitude" is derived from both the shamanistic practices that Snyder has studied in primitive societies and the varieties of meditation he has explored in his research into and expressions of Buddhist thought. Its immediate consequence in poetry is the necessity for developing a singular, distinct voice, a language with which one is comfortable, and a style that is true to the artist's entire life. For Snyder, this has meant learning to control the mood of a poem through tonal modulation, matching mood to subject and arranging sequences of poems that can sustain visionary power as well as intimate personal reflection. "The terrifying initiation and rebirth" is a corollary of the power vision. It implies that once a singular voice has been established, it must be followed according to the patterns of its impulsive organization—in other words, to its points of origin in the subconscious. Snyder speaks of the unconscious as "our inner wilderness areas," and sees in the "depths of the mind" the ultimate source of the imagination. The exploration of the wilderness within is vital to the image-making function of poetry.

The "love and ecstasy" Snyder speaks of stems from the revolt that Snyder and his colleagues led against the stiff, formal, distant academic poetry favored by critics in the 1950's, and its application has been to influence the colloquial nature of his language, to encourage the use of primitive techniques such as chant to alter perceptive states, to permit the inclusion of casual data from ordinary existence to inform the poem, and, most of all, to confront the most personal of subjects with honesty and self-awareness. There is a discernible narrative consciousness present in Snyder's poetry even when he avoids—as he generally does—personal pronouns and definite articles. Yet his resistance to cultural authority is balanced by his praise for the "common work of the tribe," the artistic accomplishment that he treasures. As he has said, "I feel very strongly that poetry also exists as part of a tradition, and is not simply a matter of only private and personal vision." Explaining his interests in Ezra Pound, William Carlos Williams, Wallace Stevens, John Milton, and others, Snyder says he wants "to know *what* has been done, and to see *how* it has been done. That in a sense is true craft." Almost paradoxically, considering his emphasis on originality, he advocates (and practices) extensive examination of multidisciplinary learning, explaining that knowledge of the past saves one "the trouble of having to repeat things that others have done that need not be done again. And then also he knows when he writes a poem that has never been written before."

Snyder's first two collections, *Riprap* and *Cold Mountain Poems*—which were published together initially in 1965 and reached a "fourth incarnation" in 1990—are evidence of the writing and thinking that Snyder had been doing through the mid-1950's. *Riprap* took shape while Snyder was working on a backcountry trail crew in 1955, and its title is at first a description of "stone laid on steep, slick rock to make a trail for horses in the mountains," then a symbol of the interlinkage of objects in a region and a figure for the placement of words in a poetic structure. It serves to connect language and action, reflective thought and the work that generates it. The poems in the collection are dedicated to the men Snyder worked with, the "community" of cohesion and effort he joined, men who knew the requirements of the land and who transmitted their skills through demonstration. *Riprap* includes elements of the oral tradition Snyder intersected, and the title "celebrates the work of the hands" while some of the poems "run the risk of invisibility" since they tried "for surface simplicity set with unsettling depths." Poems like "Above Pate Valley" and "Piute Creek" begin with direct description of landscape and move toward an almost cosmic perspective concerning the passage of time across the land over geological epochs. The specific and the eternal coalesce:

> Hill beyond hill, folded and twisted
> Tough trees crammed
> In thin stone fractures
> A huge moon on it all, is too much.
> The mind wanders. A million
> Summers, night air still and the rocks
> Warm. Sky over endless mountains.
> All the junk that goes with being human
> Drops away, hard rock wavers.

Poetry, as Snyder put it in "Burning: No. 13" from *Myths and Texts*, is "a riprap on the slick road of metaphysics," helping one find meaning and explaining why one reads "Milton by Firelight" (the title of another poem) and finds new versions of hell and "the wheeling sky" in the Sierras.

The *Cold Mountain Poems* are "translations" (in the Poundian sense) from Han-shan, a hermit and poet of the T'ang dynasty, and they represent Snyder's identification with a kind of nature prophet at home in the wild as well as his inclination to isolate himself from those aspects of American (or Western) society he found abhorrent until he could fashion a program to combat the social ills he identified. As in most effective translations, there is a correspondence in sensibility between the two artists, and Snyder's comfort with the backcountry, as well as his growing sense of a cross-cultural and transepochal perspective, may be seen in lines such as

> Thin grass does for a mattress,
> The blue sky makes a good quilt.
> Happy with a stone underhead
> Let heaven and earth go about their changes.

Calling Han-shan a "mountain madman" or "ragged hermit," Snyder expresses through the translations his admiration for a kind of independence, self-possession, and mindful alertness that he saw as a necessity for psychic survival in the Cold War era, a husbanding of strength to prepare for a return to the social struggle. "Mind solid and sharp," he says, he is gaining the vision to "honor this priceless natural treasure"—the world around him ("the whole clear cloudless sky")—and the insight ("sunk deep in the flesh") to understand the complementary wonder within.

Written at about the same time as *Riprap, Myths and Texts* is Snyder's first attempt to organize his ideas into an evolving, complex structural framework. In it, Snyder's wilderness experience is amplified by the use of Pacific Coast Indian texts, which are set as a kind of corrective for the exploitation and destruction of the environment that Snyder sees as the result of misguided American-European approaches to nature. The crux of the matter is the failure of Judeo-Christian culture to recognize the inherent sacredness of the land, and Snyder uses what he feels is a kind of Buddhist compassion and a Native American empathy as a corrective thrust. The three books of the collection are called "Logging"—which uses the lumber industry as an example of "technological drivenness" that destroys resources and shows no respect for the symbolic or ritualistic aspect of the living wilderness; "Hunting"—which explores the intricate relationship between the hunter and the quarry (and between mind and body) in primitive societies; and "Burning"—which is somewhat less accessible in its intriguing attempt to find or chart a symbolic synthesis that integrates the mythic material Snyder has been presenting into a universal vision of timeless cycles of destruction and rebirth.

As Snyder defines the terms, in a preliminary fashion, the myths and texts are the "two sources of human knowledge—symbols and sense-impressions." The larger context at which he aims—the "one whole thing"—is built on the power of individual poems, such as "Logging: No. 8," in which the logged ground is likened to a battlefield after a massacre; "Logging: No. 3," in which the lodgepole pine is treated as an emblem of nature's enduring vitality; "Logging: No. 13," in which a fire-watcher reports a fire ("T36N R16E S25/ Is burning. Far to the west") and seems more interested in the abstract beauty of the landscape than in any specific situation; and among several hunting songs, the exceptional "No. 6," which carries the dedication, "*this poem is for bear.*"

Snyder read the original version of "The Woman who Married a Bear" in an anthropology text at Reed College and was fascinated by the interaction of the human and animal cultures. He devotes a chapter to the story in *The Practice of the Wild* (1990), lamenting that "the bears are being killed, the humans are everywhere, and the green world is being unraveled and shredded and burned by the spreading of a gray world that seems to have no end." His poem is placed at the convergence of several cultures and is structured by the different speaking voices—not specifically identified but clear from tone and context. First, in a quote from the anthropological text, the bear speaks: "As for me I am a child of the god of the mountains." Then, a field scientist speaks, observing the data:

> You can see
> Huckleberries in bearshit if you
> Look, this time of year
> If I sneak up on the bear
> It will grunt and run.

This relatively matter-of-fact, outside position is replaced by a tale of the girl who married a bear: "In a house under the mountain/ She gave birth to slick dark children/ With sharp teeth, and lived in the hollow/ Mountain many years." A shift has been made to the Native American culture, and what follows is the burden of the legend, as the girl's tribe goes to reclaim her. The next voice is the hunter addressing the bear:

> honey-eater
> forest apple
> light-foot
> Old man in the fur coat, Bear! come out!
> Die of your own choice!

Now the poet enters, turning the tale (text) into poetry (myth): "Twelve species north of Mexico/ Sucking their paws in the long winter/ Tearing the high-strung caches down/ Whining, crying, jacking off." Then the tale continues, as the girl's brothers "cornered him in the rocks," and finally the "voice" of the bear-spirit speaks, as through a shaman perhaps, in the "Song of the snared bear":

> "Give me my belt.
> "I am near death.
> "I came from the mountain caves
> "At the headwaters,
> "The small streams there
> "Are all dried up.

In a deft conclusion, Snyder reduces the dramatic tension by the interposition of the disarmingly personal. As if inspired by the story, he begins to imagine himself a part of the Paleolithic hunter culture: "I think I'll go hunt bears." Yet he is too solidly grounded in reality to go beyond a reading of the text: "Why shit Snyder,/ You couldn't hit a bear in the ass/ with a handful of rice." Although, of course, in the poem, he has hit the target squarely by assimilating the different voices (as different strands of culture) into his own modern version of the myth.

During the 1950's, Snyder began work on a "poem of process" somewhat akin to Pound's *Cantos* (1970) or Williams' *Paterson* (5 vols., 1946-1958) that he called *Mountains and Rivers without End*. The first division was published in six sections in 1965, and Snyder explained that it was structured by "very close correspondences between the external and internal landscape," and that he was moving back and forth, "breaking down the limit between the psychic and physical," as Tzetvan Todorov puts it in *The Fantastic* (1973). The title was taken from a Chinese scroll that progressed horizontally, apparently into a future "without end." Other sections have appeared through the years in various journals, and Snyder in conversation with David Robertson in 1989 remarked that the finished product would take a new shape and that the poems should be treated individually until the sequence is completed. Snyder has conceded that the separate sections contain a great deal of information, but hopes that eventually "there will be enough reverberations and echoes from the various sections so that it will be self-informing." In discussing his method, he has emphasized the use of a *ku* or key phrase in each section, such as the third line from the last in "Bubbs Creek Haircut," which has the phrase "double mirror waver"—an image of infinite regression and reflection that is at the crux of Buddhist thinking concerning mutual interdependence. This is similar to his technique of raising questions in one section that are answered in a later one, and Snyder has stressed the necessity for creating a sufficient body of the poem before the total framework could be seen, even by the poet.

With *Regarding Wave*, Snyder's work turned from the mythic and philosophical toward the intimate and immediately personal. He had begun a family (his son Kai was born in 1968) and returned to the United States, and the poems recall his last days in the Far East and his sense of how he had to proceed after returning to his native land at a time of strife and turmoil. The family poems are celebratory, written in wonder, open and exuberant in the first flush of parenthood, expressing his delight with his wife Masa and their infant son. There are poems that are like meditations on the sensual: "Song of the View," "Song of the Tangle," or "Song of the Taste," and poems that are drawn from the experience of rearing a child, like "The Bed in the Sky" or "Kai, Today," which is an awestruck reflection on the act of birth, or the supramundane "Not Leaving the House," in which Snyder admits "When Kai is born/ I quit going out," and justifies his inward angle of view by concluding "From dawn til late at night/ making a new world of ourselves/ around this life."

Yet since Snyder found in his return to the New World beyond "ourselves" that the political situation in America in 1969 was troubling ("Off the coast of Oregon/ The radio is full of hate and anger"), and even before landing was warned that "beards don't make money," he began to plan the outlines of a life as a poet and activist in the United States. The effects of his action become more clear in his next collection, but the cast of his mind is apparent in the transitional "What You Should Know to Be a Poet," which calls together what he had learned from his life to that point:

> all you can about animals as persons
> the names of trees and flowers and weeds
> names of stars, and the movements of the planets
> and the moon.

> your own six senses, with a watchful and elegant mind

and then blends it with a kind of resolution to confront the bestial nature of humans in order to prepare to engage the evil at large in the world, as expressed in the crucial central stanza beginning, "kiss the ass of the devil." From that point, the poem alternates positive aspects of existence ("& then love the human: wives husbands and friends") with an acceptance of the trials and burdens of life ("long dry hours of dull work swallowed and accepted/ and livd with and finally lovd") until it concludes with an unsettling sense of the future, "real danger. gambles. and the edge of death."

Snyder's ambivalent feelings about living in America are again expressed in the hilarious "Smokey the Bear Sutra," in which the familiar symbol of the forest service is depicted as a kind of Asiatic avenging demon protecting the environment and resisting polluters. Published in 1973 as a part of *The Fudo Trilogy*—a pamphlet that included "The California Water Plan" (a section of *Mountains and Rivers*) and "Spel Against Demons"—it combines Snyder's serious concerns about the environment and his continuing pursuit of Asiatic culture with his characteristically engaging high good humor. The chant, "Drown their butts; soak their butts" is presented in mock seriousness as a mantra of righteousness, while Smokey is depicted more as a lovable child's pet than the fierce scourge of evil that the archetype suggests. The comic conception works to keep Snyder's considerable anger under control, so that he does not turn his poetry into polemic. By then fully involved in the bioregional movement and committed to the local community of San Juan Ridge, where he had built a home,

Snyder in the early 1970's followed a dual course in his poetry. The overarching theme of his work was to protect and preserve "Turtle Island–the old/new name for the continent, based on many creation myths," and it was expressed in "poems that speak of place, and the energy-pathways that sustain life" and in poems that decry the forces of destruction unleashed by the stupidity of "demonic killers" who perpetrate "aimless executions and slaughterings."

These poems were published under the title *Turtle Island* (1974), sold more than 100,000 copies, and won the Pulitzer Prize. Among the most memorable poems Snyder has written, the ones that explore the "energy pathways" sustaining life include the unique "The Bath"–a Whitmanesque rapture in appreciation of the body that challenges the latent Puritanism and fear of the skin in American society by describing in loving detail the physical wonder of his son, his wife, and himself in a bath. The sheer glory of the body glowing with health and the radiant reflection of the natural world around them build toward a feeling of immense physical satisfaction and then toward a complementary feeling of metaphysical well-being. The frankness of the language may be difficult for some readers, but Snyder's tasteful, delicate, and comfortable handling of it makes his declaration "this is our body," an echoing chorus, an assertion of religious appreciation. In an even more directly thankful mode, the translation of a Mohawk "Prayer for the Great Family" unites the basic elements of the cosmos in a linked series of gemlike depictions, concluding with one of Snyder's essential ideas: that there is an infinite space "beyond all powers and thoughts/ and yet is within us-/ Grandfather Space/ The Mind is his Wife." Other expressions of "eternal delight" include "By Frazier Creek Falls," "Source," and "The Dazzle," as well as many poems in the book's last section, a kind of basic history primer called "For the Children," that convey considerable emotion without lapsing into obvious emotional tugging.

The more overtly political poems and sketches tend to be somber, frequently employing a litany of statistics to convey grim information that needs little additional comment, but in "The Call of the Wild," Snyder's anger is projected in language purposefully charged with judgmental fervor. Avoiding easy partisanship, Snyder condemns, first, "ex acid-heads" who have opted for "forever blissful sexless highs" and hidden in fear from what is interesting about life. His image of people missing the point of everything by living in trendy "Geodesic domes, that/ Were stuck like warts/ In the woods" is as devastating as his cartoon conception of advanced technology declaring "a war against earth" waged by pilots with "their women beside them/ in bouffant hairdos/ putting nail-polish on the/

gunship cannon-buttons." Snyder did not publish another book of poems until 1983, when *Axe Handles* was issued by North Point Press.

The poems in *Axe Handles* have a reflective tone, moving inward toward the life Snyder has been leading in his local community, to which he dedicated the collection. His concerns do not change, but in a return to the more spare, lyrical poems of *Riprap*, Snyder condenses and focuses his ideas into "firm, clean lines of verse reminiscent of Ezra Pound's *Rock-Drill* cantos," according to critic Andrew Angyal. The title has a typically dual meaning, referring to language as an instrument for shaping meaning and to the entire meaning of tools in human life. The theme of "cultural continuity" is presented in terms of Snyder's passing his knowledge on to his family, friends, and readers and is explicitly explained in the parable of the title poem. The book evokes an ethos of harmony in cycles of renewal and restoration, rebirth and reconsideration. Snyder moves beyond his specific criticism of human social organizations in the late twentieth century and toward, in Angyal's words, his "own alternative set of values in communal cooperation, conservation, and a nonexploitative way of life that shows respect for the land." The compression and density of Snyder's thinking are evident in the poem "Removing the Plate of the Pump on the Hydraulic System of the Backhoe," which reads in entirety

> Through mud, fouled nuts, black grime
> it opens, a gleam of spotless steel
> machined-fit perfect
> swirl of intake and output
> relentless clarity
> at the heart
> of work.

The pursuit of "relentless clarity" in everything characterizes Snyder's life and art, but the pressures of the search are alleviated by his congenial nature and sense of humor. While emphasizing the importance of Zen "mindfulness," Snyder has also stressed that "a big part of life is just being playful." In accordance with this approach, Snyder has kept dogmatic or simplistic solutions out of his work and has cherished the wild and free nature of humankind. In "Off the Trail," which he wrote for his wife Carole Koda, he envisions a life in which "all paths are possible" and maintains that "the trial's not the way" to find wisdom or happiness. "We're off the trail,/ You and I," he declares, "and we chose it!" That choice—the decision to go against the grain "to be in line with the big flow"—has led to a poetry of "deeply human richness," as Charles Molesworth puts it in his perceptive study of Snyder's work, in which "a vision of plenitude" leads to a "liminal utopia, poised between fullness and yet more growth." This utopian conception is, as the poet sees the universe, composed of elements that are "interconnected, interpenetrating, mutually reflecting, and mutually embracing." In making these connections, Snyder's poetry remains firmly grounded on the human values he sees as the fundamentals of existence. As he has said, "In a visionary way, what we would want poetry to do is guide lovers toward ecstasy, give witness to the dignity of old people, intensify human bonds, elevate the community and improve the public spirit."

Other literary forms · Gary Snyder's pioneering journal of personal environmental discovery, *Earth House Hold* (1969), was subtitled *Technical Notes and Queries to Fellow Dharma Revolutionaries*, a descriptive invitation to examine the treasure of the planet and to consider how it might be employed for the benefit of all living species. It represents the culmination of the work Snyder began nearly two decades before when he conceived of a major in literature and anthropology at Reed College, and its somewhat tentative, propositional format expresses the spirit of a movement that recognized the destructive aspects of modern industrial society and sought alternative approaches to the questions of planetary survival. Although Snyder was sometimes referred to disparagingly as "a kind of patron saint of ecology" by critics trapped in more conventional social arrangements, his interest in the environment has proved to be as perceptive and enduring as his best poetry, and the publication of *The Practice of the Wild* (1990) has deepened the context of his interests, offering the wisdom and experience of a lifetime spent living in and thinking about the natural world. The book is a linked series of reflective essays, and its amiable, reasonable tone—similar to Snyder's conversational voice in his interviews, most notably those collected in *The Real Work: Interviews and Talks, 1964-1979* (1980)—permits the power of his intellectual insights, his scholarly investigations, and his political theories to reach an audience beyond the experts he hopes to equal in his argument. Combining energetic conviction and poetic eloquence, Snyder's essays are intended to be a "genuine teaching text" and "a mediation on what it means to be human." They demonstrate his philosophy of composition as it reveals a poetics of existence and have been written to stimulate "a broad range of people and provide them with historical, ecological and personal vision."

Select works other than poetry

NONFICTION: *Earth House Hold: Technical Notes and Queries to Fellow Dharma Revolutionaries*, 1969; *The Old Ways*, 1977; *He Who Hunted Birds in His*

Father's Village: The Dimensions of a Haida Myth, 1979; *The Real Work: Interviews and Talks, 1964-1979,* 1980; *Passage Through India,* 1983; *The Practice of the Wild,* 1990; *Gary Snyder Papers,* 1995; *A Place in Space: Ethics, Aesthetics, and Watersheds,* 1995.

                                                                                    Leon Lewis

Bibliography · Written for students and general readers, Patrick Murphy's *Understanding Gary Snyder,* 1992, is a useful overview of Snyder's work and influences with detailed explications of his work. Murphy also edited *Critical Essays on Gary Snyder,* 1991, which contains eighteen lengthy examinations of Snyder's career. Bob Steuding's *Gary Snyder,* 1976, also written for general readers, is equally useful for its analysis of Snyder's work up to *Turtle Island.* Jon Halper, ed., *Gary Snyder: Dimensions of a Life,* 1991, is an appreciation of Snyder's life and works with sixty-eight reminiscences, reviews, analyses, and essays by friends, family members, fellow poets, and Snyder himself. This book contains numerous photographs of Snyder and his circle. Katherine McNeil's *Gary Snyder: A Bibliography,* 1983, is a detailed, extensive, annotated listing of works by and about Snyder, including books, articles, poems, recordings, translations, and criticism, indexed with publishers' notes and notes on composition by Snyder. See also Tim Dean, *Gary Snyder and the American Unconscious: Inhabiting the Ground,* 1991; and Robert Jordan Schuler, *Journeys Toward the Original Mind: The Long Poems of Gary Snyder,* 1994.

STEPHEN SPENDER

Born: London, England; February 28, 1909
Died: London, England; July 16, 1995

Poetry · *Nine Experiments, by S. H. S.: Being Poems Written at the Age of Eighteen,* 1928 · *Twenty Poems,* 1930 · *Poems,* 1933, 1934 · *Vienna,* 1935 · *The Still Centre,* 1939 · *Selected Poems,* 1940 · *Ruins and Visions,* 1942 · *Spiritual Exercises (To Cecil Day Lewis),* 1943 · *Poems of Dedication,* 1947 · *Returning to Vienna 1947: Nine Sketches,* 1947 · *The Edge of Being,* 1949 · *Collected Poems, 1928-1953,* 1955 · *Inscriptions,* 1958 · *Selected Poems,* 1964 · *The Generous Days,* 1971 · *Recent Poems,* 1978 · *Collected Poems, 1928-1985,* 1985 · *Dolphins,* 1994

Achievements · Several of Stephen Spender's poems stand among the most poignant of the twentieth century. Those anthology pieces with which his name is most often associated—"Not Palaces, an Era's Crown," "Beethoven's Death Mask," "I think continually of those who were truly great," "The Express," "The Landscape near an Aerodome" and "Ultima Ratio Regum"—have helped achieve for Spender greater recognition than for any of the other British poets who came into prominence in the late 1920's and early 1930's, with the notable exception of W. H. Auden. Spender's stature rests also on his peculiar position among poets writing through the Great Depression and after World War II. More than the others, he emerged as an authentic voice bridging the modernist and postwar periods. Even during the 1930's—when Auden was the leader of the loose confederation of young writers to which he and Spender belonged—it was Spender who in poem after poem voiced most honestly and movingly the tensions informing the writing of poetry in that troubled time. When Auden and Christopher Isherwood departed for America in 1939, Spender remained as the foremost representative of the liberal values and lyric intensity which had marked the best poetry of the prewar years. Later—especially with the death of the other figures making up the so-called Auden Group—Spender's verse, as well as his prose, took on special interest, as a last link between contemporary British literature and an earlier period crucial to its development.

In many respects Spender's outlook and poetry scarcely changed after the 1930's. While many critics regarded such want of development as a mark of failure, in a sense it represents a strength. Presumably, Spender saw little reason to change his poetic method or to go beyond those indisputably successful poems of his early adulthood because for him the fundamental problems—poetic, political, and personal—hardly changed since that time. Interestingly, an audience that grew up scarcely aware of Spender's poetic achievement became fascinated by Spender the essayist and lecturer. Because his most characteristic pronouncements to this more recently acquired audience were closely related to the viewpoint revealed in the early poems, they suggest the continuing value of those poems, not merely as artifacts from an increasingly distant past but as permanent sources of interest and pleasure.

Biography · Stephen Harold Spender was born in London on February 28, 1909. His father was Harold Spender, a noted journalist and lecturer, and his mother was Violet Hilda Schuster Spender, a painter and poet. The death of Spender's mother when he was fifteen and of his father two years later, in 1926, brought the four children, of whom he was the second-oldest, under the care of his maternal grandmother, a pair of great-aunts, and an uncle.

After attending University College School in London, Spender went to University College, Oxford, in 1928, leaving in 1930 without a degree. Having begun to write poetry in childhood and having determined to be a poet, he sought out the somewhat older W. H. Auden even before beginning at Oxford. Their friendship, marked by a mutual awareness of their differences in temperament and outlook, apparently developed rapidly; Spender himself published Auden's first book of poems in 1928 on the same handpress he used to bring out his own first book. He spent the summer vacation of 1929 in Germany, meeting many young Germans and observing social and political developments that would set the stage for the next decade.

The 1930's were a time of tremendous literary activity for the young Spender, periodically punctuated by travels throughout Europe. He achieved prominence as a leading member of the group of rising young writers clustered around Auden. Although Spender has claimed a singular position among the Auden group, during that time he behaved in a fashion broadly similar to that adopted by the others, briefly joining the Communist Party in 1936 and traveling to Spain in 1937 to observe the Civil War from the Republican side, and publishing poems and essays supporting a radical viewpoint and warning of the growing Nazi menace. By late 1939 he had joined Cyril Connolly as coeditor of *Horizon*, a post he held until 1941. The war years also saw Spender in the National Fire Service and later in the Foreign Service. In 1941, he married Natasha Litwin, his 1936 marriage to Agnes Marie Pearn having ended in divorce.

After World War II, Spender focused on numerous writing, editing, and translating projects, on extensive travel and university lecturing—particularly in the United States—and on his family life. From 1953 to 1966, he served as coeditor of *Encounter*, resigning when he learned of the Central Intelligence Agency's financing of that magazine. Spender's many public and literary honors include being named a Companion in the Order of the British Empire (C.B.E.) in 1962, receiving the Queen's Gold Medal for Poetry in 1971, and being given an Honorary Fellowship to University College, Oxford, in 1973. In 1970, he was appointed to the chair of English literature in University College, London. Spender died in London on July 16, 1995.

Analysis · Stephen Spender seems always to have struck his readers as halting. Even in the relatively confident writing of his youth, he was the most likely of the Auden Group to avoid the extreme pronouncements to which his seemingly more self-assured contemporaries—especially Auden himself—were prone. Taken as a whole, his poetry appears to reflect a perpetual debate, an unresolved tension over what can be known, over what is worth knowing, and over how he ought to respond as a poet and as a citizen of a modern society. Taken separately, his poems—particularly the best and most representative ones—exhibit an attraction or a movement sometimes toward one side of an issue, and sometimes toward the other. Almost always, however, such commitment at least implies its opposite.

This tension itself may account for the continuing appeal of so many Spender lyrics, decades after they were written and after their historical context had passed. Obviously they conform to the demand for irony and ambiguity begun in the late 1920's by I. A. Richards and William Empson and prolonged until recently by their American counterparts, the New Critics. In this respect, if not in others, Spender established a link with the seventeenth century Metaphysical wits so admired by T. S. Eliot. The qualifying tendency of Spender's poetry connects him also with the postwar movement among a younger generation of British poets—notably Philip Larkin, Donald Davie, and Kingsley Amis—who have taken issue with Eliot's modernist ambitions and with Dylan Thomas' romantic gesturing.

The tentativeness of Spender's writing connects with so many diverse and often opposing tendencies in modern literature because it has its roots in the Romanticism underlying all modern literature. Like Romanticism, Spender's verse embraces a variety of conflicting impulses. Whether to write about private subjects or to take on more public concerns, and whether to adopt a personal or an impersonal stance toward the selected subjects, become central problems for Spender. He finds himself at some times, and in some poems, drawn to life's simple, civilian joys; at other times he is moved toward the grand actions of politics. Stylistically, he can be seen vacillating between directness and obliqueness, literalness and figurativeness, and realism and imagism. The conflicting pulls of pragmatism and idealism so evident throughout his career suggest a sympathy with virtually all strains of Western philosophy, especially since René Descartes. Underlying this inability, or unwillingness, to project a set posture is the drive toward inwardness seen in nineteenth century literature, a drive at once hastened and opposed by the great Romantics. The legacy of this drive and its attendant struggle constitute much of the drama played out in Spender's poems.

His writing in the 1930's suggests the same sort of shift evident in the other Auden poets and in many prose writers, such as George Orwell. It suggests, too, a process more of accretion than of drastic change, since the seeds of Spender's discontent with the posture of his earlier political poems lay in the poems themselves. Auden's poetry probably encouraged the young Spender to move from the unfocused idealism of his teens and to write more about the real world. Spender's poetry thus became noticeably contemporary in reference, with urban scenes and crowds, to the point that he could devote entire poems to a speedy train ("The Express") or an airship ("The Landscape near an Aerodrome").

Just as Auden found Spender too romantic, Spender found Auden too cool and detached from the often grim world which Auden had induced him to consider in his poems. Even at his most topical, even when most under Auden's influence, Spender refused to indulge in Audenesque wit or satiric bite. The characteristic feeling of the *Poems* of 1933 is one of commitment and seriousness. Where Auden might concentrate on the ridiculousness of society, Spender concentrates on society's victims and their suffering.

"Moving through the silent crowd" illustrates well the understated poignancy of which Spender was capable at this time in his career. Nearly empty of metaphor, it gains its effect through Spender's emphasis on emblematic detail and through the development of saddening irony. He frames the poem with his own vantage point, from which he observes the idle poor. The first stanza turns on his intimation of "falling light," which represents for him the composite disillusionment and wasted potential of the men silent in the road. In the second, he notices the cynicism implicit in such gestures as shrugging shoulders and emptying pockets. Such a scene leads him, in the final two stanzas, to develop the irony of the situation and to hint at a radical political stance. He notes how the unemployed resemble the wealthy in doing no work and sleeping late. Confessing jealousy of their leisure, he nevertheless feels "haunted" by the meaninglessness of their lives.

An equally strong element of social conscience colors many other Spender poems written before 1933. Generally they exhibit more elo-quence and metaphorical sweep than the rather terse "Moving through the silent crowd." For example, in "Not palaces, an era's crown" he catalogs those purely intellectual or aesthetic considerations which he must dismiss in favor of social action. Such action he significantly compares to an energized battery and illustrates in a bold program of opposition to social and political tyranny. The short, forceful sentences of the poem's second section, where this program is described, contrast with the longer, more ornate syntax of the beginning. The hunger that Spender hopes to eradi-cate is of a more pressing order than that addressed by aesthetics or vague idealism, which he characterizes as sheer indolence. Only in the poem's final line, once his moral and political ambitions have been fully ex-pressed, can he permit himself a Platonic image, as light is said to be brought to life.

Such insistence upon social reform, shading into radical political action, probably peaked in the period of 1935 to 1938, when *Vienna* and *Trial of a Judge* were appearing. Perhaps more notable than Spender's eventual repudiation of the unsuccessful *Vienna* is the fact that in so many of the shorter poems written during these years, especially those concerned with Spain, he turned increasingly from the public subjects, the outwardly directed statements, and the didactic organization marking the earlier poems. Where his critique of life in England might be construed as supportive of Communism, the picture he draws of Spain during the Civil War largely ignores the political dimension of the struggle and focuses instead on the suffering experienced by civilians in all regions and of all political persuasions. While a strain of political idealism continues, the enemy is no longer simply capitalism or even Adolf Hitler; rather, for Spender it has become war and those persons responsible for inflicting a state of war on the helpless and innocent.

One of his most effective poems from Spain, "Ultima Ratio Regum," exhibits a didactic form, even ending with a rhetorical question; but it carefully avoids condemnation or praise of either side. Read without consideration for Spender's original reasons for going to Spain, his angry and moving account of a young Spaniard's senseless death by machine-gun fire condemns the Republicans no less than the Insurgents and ultimately centers on the impersonality of modern war, which reduces to statistical insignificance a formerly alive and sensitive young man. Similarly, "Thoughts During an Air Raid" deals with Spender's own feelings while taking cover and with the temptation to regard oneself as somehow special and therefore immune from the fate threatening all other people in time of war. If Spender here argues for a more collective consciousness, it is but a vague and largely psychological brotherhood. As in "Ultima Ratio Regum," the viewpoint here is wholly civilian and pacifist. Even "Fall of a City," which clearly and sadly alludes to a Republican defeat, suggests more the spirit of freedom which Spender sees surviving the fall than any political particulars or doctrine attending that spirit. There Spender derives his residual hope not from a party or concerted action, but from the simple handing down of memories and values from an old man to a child. If anything, this poem reflects a distrust of large-scale political ideologies and action and of the dishonesty, impersonality, and brutality that they necessarily breed.

In his autobiography Spender writes of having been puzzled by civilian enthusiasm for both sides in the Spanish struggle. Like Orwell, he was also disturbed by Republican atrocities against civilians. Such disillusioning discoveries no doubt contributed to the reluctance with which he viewed England's struggle against the Nazis even after the war had begun. Conceding the need to counter the German threat, Spender in his war poems nevertheless stressed the pain, rather than the glory, of that necessity. Such was his perception of that pain that he found it necessary in "The War God" to ask and answer questions which, after Munich or the invasion of Poland, even the most war-wary Englishman probably would no longer have considered. One almost gets the impression that Spender is concerned with convincing, or reminding, himself more than anyone else of the reasons behind the war, so obvious is the logic of the poem. Even "Memento," his more effective response to the death camps, betrays the same lingering pacifism as its surreal images describe the victims' horror and helplessness.

Perhaps Spender's most remarkable—and his most reluctant—war poem is his response to the fall of France, "June 1940." Even as Britain is most threatened, he finds it necessary and appropriate to invoke the ghost of World War I to express his skepticism about the impending defense against Hitler. The first section of the poem combines a lyrical description of the delights of the English summer with suggestions of the war's distance from that pastoral scene. Spender has the "grey" survivors of the earlier war note the difference between the trench fighting of their youth and the newer, more mechanized European war of which they have heard only very little. He shows boys bicycling around village war memorials and the Channel "snipping" England from France. The scene and mood change drastically in the next section, with the slightly surreal account of the "caterpillar-wheeled blond" charging over birds' nests in France that very day, and with the lengthy series of voices arguing the need to counter the Nazi horde with armed resistance. Such arguments persuade the old soldiers, sitting in their deck chairs since the poem's beginning, that the struggle against Germany is just and that the alternative is an imprisoned England.

Even so, Spender characterizes the old veterans' response as "disillusioned" to prepare the reader for the poem's audacious ending. In six short lines he overturns the style, the premises, and the conclusion of the earlier dialogue. A dead soldier from the Great War suddenly testifies to the purgatory of guilt to which participation in that earlier struggle against Germany has doomed him, to imply that the arguments justifying the current war represent only a seductive parallel to earlier warmongering, and that even defeating Hitler will not wholly justify the impending struggle or absolve the English of war guilt. While the conclusion implied by the logic of the poem may not be that England ought to surrender, it certainly cuts very thin any moral advantage the English might claim in resisting. Again Spender ultimately focuses his attention on the burden—in this case a moral one—placed on the individual by collective action.

"June 1940" represents only the most blatant evidence of Spender's departure from the spirited socialism and anti-Nazism of his earlier poems. The general drift of his writing after 1934 had been clearly in that direction. His poems had dealt increasingly with personal problems and situations. In *Forward from Liberalism* (1937), he had articulated his dissatisfaction with the socialist creed, a dissatisfaction based principally upon what he saw as the necessary antipathy to the individual person which politics, and especially leftist politics, inevitably aroused. Before too long he was able, in *The Creative Element: A Study of Vision, Despair, and Orthodoxy Among Some Modern Writers* (1953), to attribute his earlier political orthodoxy to liberal guilt induced by the misery of the poor during the Great Depression.

The ease with which such renunciation and self-analysis seems to have come after the late 1930's suggests the limited nature of Spender's commitment to politics even when he seemed most political. The tension between individual and collective viewpoints which becomes central to the Spanish Civil War poems and to "June 1940" is at least implicit in most of his earlier writing, as well.

It is true that in his criticism Spender repeatedly questions the wisdom of the modernists' avoidance of politics, particularly by T. S. Eliot and William Butler Yeats, whom he so admired as a young man. In this regard,

"An Elementary School Classroom in a Slum" constitutes Spender's gloss on Yeats's "Among School Children," first in the type of school the younger poet chooses to visit, and second in his refusal to turn the visit into an occasion for personal theorizing, as Yeats did. Spender's allusion to "Sailing to Byzantium"–where he asserts that he will not transform the street beggars into "birds" on his "singing-tree"–attacks Yeats even more directly.

The grammar of this assertion, however–indeed, of many ostensibly political statements by the young Spender–guarantees, perhaps intentionally, some confusion of purpose and does so so often that it seems reflective of a confusion in Spender himself. "In railway halls, on pavement near the traffic" is the very poem in which he seems to mock Yeats for the Irishman's indifference to public affairs. The poem is governed by an "I" whose statement of poetic intent ultimately reflects more on himself than on the plight of the poor. Not only does the subject of the poem thus become poetry–something that Spender could deplore in Yeats–but also in a sense the poet becomes the hero. This is not to criticize Spender, but merely to point out, ironically, how much his focus approaches Yeats's after all. The first-person perspective of so many other early Spender poems ties the public to the private and prevents any purely political orientation from taking over.

"Moving through the silent crowd" illustrates even more strikingly this same tension. While the observed poor are rendered sympathetically, the reader can never forget the observer. The marked return, in the final stanza, to his viewpoint and his troubles–where three of four lines begin with "I'm," and where each of the parallel clauses develops the poet's dilemma–clearly raises a question as to the ultimate object of sympathy here. This does not mean that the poem reflects merely self-pity or that Spender might not want to get outside himself; however, the poem finally becomes an exposure not only of poverty, but also of the poet's inability to close the perceived gap between himself and the poor. He concludes with a sense of his distance from them; all he can do is sympathize and be "haunted" by them. Because he appears as helpless as they, though in a somewhat different sense, his helplessness becomes at least as important as theirs as the subject of the poem. Without the personal perspective, the poem seems to ask, Of what validity is political or social criticism? At the same time, the poem's fixation with the observer's perspective places in serious doubt the efficacy of whatever criticism he may construct.

Another dimension of Spender's uncertainty comes in his treatment of contemporary civilization, particularly in those celebrated early poems dealing with technology. Although Auden probably influenced Spender in this direction, Spender seems never to have been so comfortable as Auden with the up-to-date world, particularly as an element of his poetry. Such discomfort largely escaped his first readers, who found his apparent acceptance of material progress a welcome departure from old-fashioned nature poetry. A. Kingsley Weatherhead rightly suggests, in *Stephen Spender and the Thirties* (1975), that many writers of that decade wrote a covert kind of nature poetry even as they purported to repudiate the values of the Georgian poets. They did so, Weatherhead says, by taking a critical look at contemporary civilization and thereby implying retreat as the only viable alternative.

While this no doubt is true of Spender, his retreat often takes very subtle forms. Sometimes it resides largely in the terms with which he commends an aspect of twentieth century technology. "The Express," for example, appears to celebrate the beauty and speed of a fast-moving train and, thus, to confirm the benefits of modern applied science. An examination of the poem's progression, however, reveals considerable dissatisfaction with the external world for which the train has been manufactured. Perhaps the whole idea of a lyric poem's appropriating something so utilitarian as an express train might seem an implied criticism of utility; certainly Walt Whitman's "To a Locomotive in Winter" and Emily Dickinson's "I like to see it lap the miles" can be seen as backhanded compliments. Even so, Spender's train poem seems of a different order in that it places the train much more realistically—with references to stations, to gasworks, and to Edinburgh. A good deal of the poem's language is very literal. Even Spender's initial nonliteral description ascribes utility to the train's beginning: It is cast as a queen issuing a "plain manifesto" to her subjects.

The image of such public action yields to more private behavior in the poem's second sentence, where "she" is said to "sing" with increasing abandon as she gathers speed. In the third and final sentence, she sings enraptured, exceeding the bounds of nature by flying in her music. The shape of the poem is thus the progression of its metaphors. Because that progression is vertical—away from the earth, into a state of Platonic grace suggested by music, again reminiscent of Yeats—the poem becomes a celebration of imaginative and self-absorbed retreat from the mundane and empirical reality in which the express actually resides. Even as Spender praises the train, he gives equal praise to a place where the express could not possibly exist. The two objects of praise coexist, as do the two kinds of language by which they are represented. There is no evidence that the speaker of the poem—significantly not represented as "I"—does not believe he is praising the express on its own terms. On the other hand, the progression of the terms he uses, particularly the metaphors, suggests that he in fact admires principles quite antipathetic to those upon which the express runs, and that perhaps he can find the express tolerable only by transforming it into something it is not and cannot be.

Poems such as "The Express," "The Landscape near the Aerodrome," and "Pylons" suggest a flight from the material values upon which modern popular culture is founded. In this they can have even greater pertinence now than when they were written. An examination of other early poems suggests a wish, or at least a need, to escape the human element as well. For all of their apparent humanism, they propose a withdrawal from the very society that Spender would help redeem, and confirm the Marxist critique of Romanticism as an elevation of private concerns at the expense of the public good. They bring to mind, too, Hugh MacDiarmid's indictment of the Auden group's ultimate lack of political commitment.

Certainly, it seems no accident that Spender wrote so much about Romanticism and especially about Percy Bysshe Shelley. His discussion of the modern poet's difficulties in reconciling the Romantic ideal of the individual imagination and sensibility with a public, collective age seems almost an abstract of poems such as "Without that one clear aim, the path of flight" or "From all these events, from the slum, from the war, from the boom." In the first of these, a sonnet, Spender complains of being choked and imprisoned by social reality, of needing desperately to escape on the "wings" of poetry. So politically suspect a motive for writing, which he reinforces by other Platonic images suggestive of Shelley, informs the second poem. There Spender expresses a faith, not in reformist action, but in the power of time to obliterate the memory not only of wrongdoing but also of those who would correct it. What might have horrified Thomas Hardy thus consoles Spender. In "Perhaps," he takes comfort in the more escapist position that troubling public events may be only fantasies. Even "I think continually of those who were truly great," so often cited as the epitome of 1930's selflessness, suggests that Spender's characteristic way of coping with social problems is to forget them: to ignore the present by dreaming of the "truly great."

Individual poems and the collective poetry of Spender rarely show him consistent in this regard. His struggle with the irreconcilables of individual and group, private and public, and realism and idealism have their stylistic level, as elegances of metaphor and syntax frequently accompany and undermine his call for action in the present. To an age grown increasingly aware of the limitations, if not the futility, of collective behavior and of the traps into which both leader and follower can fall, Spender poses the dilemma of the morally and socially sensitive individual. For this reason he commands a not inconsiderable place among the poets of this century.

Other literary forms · Although best known for his poetry, Stephen Spender wrote a considerable body of drama, fiction, criticism, and journalism. The first of his six plays, *Trial of a Judge* (1938), was his contribution to the Group Theatre effort, in which his friend W. H. Auden was so heavily involved, and reflected the young Spender's socialist outlook. Most of the others—notably *Danton's Death* (1939), which he wrote with Goronwy Rees; *Mary Stuart* (1957), taken from the J. C. F. Schiller play; and *Rasputin's End* (1963), a libretto to music by Nicholas Nabokov—likewise dealt with broadly political situations and problems. Spender's published fiction consists of a collection of stories, *The Burning Cactus* (1936); a novel, *The Backward Son* (1940); and two novellas, *Engaged in Writing* and *The Fool and the Princess* (published together in 1958).

Spender's nonfiction prose comprises more than a dozen books, as well as hundreds of essays contributed to periodicals. The critical works have dealt mostly with the issues and problems of modern literature, beginning with essays written for *The Criterion* in the 1930's and *The Destructive Element: A Study of Modern Writers and Beliefs* (1935), and continuing through his study of T. S. Eliot (1975) and the selection of essays from various periods of Spender's career entitled *The Thirties and After* (1978). Especially notable among his other critical books are *The Struggle of the Modern* (1963), a study of modernism's complicated relationship to twentieth century literature in general, and *Love-Hate Relations: A Study of Anglo-American Sensibilities* (1974), which examines the connections between American and English literary sensibilities. Spender's journalistic writings include *Citizens in War and After* (1945) and *European Witness* (1946). He also published an autobiography, *World Within World: The Autobiography of Stephen Spender* (1951).

Select works other than poetry

LONG FICTION: *The Backward Son*, 1940; *The Temple*, 1988.

SHORT FICTION: *The Burning Cactus*, 1936; *Engaged in Writing and The Fool and the Princess*, 1958.

DRAMA: *Trial of a Judge*, pr. 1938; *Danton's Death*, pr. 1939 (with Goronwy Rees); *To the Island*, pr. 1951; *Mary Stuart*, pr. 1957; *Lulu*, pr.1958; *Rasputin's End*, pb. 1963; *Oedipus Trilogy: A Play in Three Acts Based on the Oedipus Plays of Sophocles*, pr. 1983.

NONFICTION: *The Destructive Element: A Study of Modern Writers and Beliefs*, 1935; *Forward from Liberalism*, 1937; *Citizens in War and After*, 1945; *European Witness*, 1946; *Poetry Since 1939*, 1946; *World Within World: The Autobiography of Stephen Spender*, 1951; *Shelley*, 1952; *The Creative Element: A Study of Vision, Despair, and Orthodoxy Among Some Modern Writers*, 1953; *The*

Making of a Poem, 1955; *The Struggle of the Modern*, 1963; *Love-Hate Relations: A Study of Anglo-American Sensibilities*, 1974; *Eliot*, 1975; *The Thirties and After*, 1978; *Journals, 1939-1983*, 1985.

Bruce K. Martin

Bibliography · Three notable books published in the early 1990's are David Hugh, *Stephen Spender: A Portrait with Background*, 1992; Michael O'Neill, *Auden, MacNeice, Spender: The Thirties Poetry*, 1992; and Sanford V. Sternlich, *Stephen Spender*, 1992. A very useful annotated bibliography is Hemant Balvantrao Kulkarni, *Stephen Spender: Works and Criticism*, 1976, a reliable guide to selecting secondary sources about both Spender's life and his work. Kulkarni also wrote an excellent study of Spender, *Stephen Spender: Poet in Crisis*, 1970. A handy reference for Spender's poetry is A. T. Tolley, *The Early Published Poems of Stephen Spender: A Chronology*, 1967. Also useful are the essays, autobiographies, and novels of Spender's friend Christopher Isherwood, among them the essay "Stephen Spender," in *Exhumations*, 1966, and his autobiographies, *Christopher and His Kind, 1929-1939*, 1977, and *Lions and Shadows*, 1938. One of the best studies of Spender's early works is Andrew Kingsley Weatherhead, *Stephen Spender and the Thirties*, 1975, which is particularly useful in interpreting Spender's poems and motives. A. T. Tolley, *The Poetry of the Thirties*, 1975, examines the early poetry. It is complemented by Surya Nath Pandey, *Stephen Spender: A Study in Poetic Growth*, 1982, which compares Spender's early and mature work. For Spender's political and social ideals, see Elton E. Smith, *The Angry Young Men of the Thirties*, 1975. A fascinating study of the connection between Spender's poetry and politics is J. J. Connors, *Poets and Politics: A Study of the Careers of C. Day Lewis, Stephen Spender, and W. H. Auden in the 1930's*, 1976. See also Derek Stanford, *Stephen Spender, Louis MacNeice, Cecil Day Lewis: A Critical Essay*, 1969.

EDMUND SPENSER

Born: London, England; c. 1552
Died: London, England; January 13, 1599

Poetry · *The Shepheardes Calender*, 1579 · *The Faerie Queene*, 1590, 1596 · *Complaints*, 1591 · *Daphnaïda*, 1591 · *Colin Clouts Come Home Againe*, 1595 · *Astrophel*, 1595 · *Amoretti*, 1595 · *Epithalamion*, 1595 · *Fowre Hymnes*, 1596 · *Prothalamion*, 1596 · *The Poetical Works of Edmund Spenser*, 1912 (J. C. Smith and Ernest de Selincourt, editors)

Achievements · The inscription on Edmund Spenser's monument hails him as "the Prince of Poets in his time," but his reputation as "poet's poet" continued among his Romantic peers three centuries later. What was praised and imitated changed with time, but the changes themselves suggest the extent of Spenser's achievements. His popularity among his contemporaries was documented not only in commentaries written during his lifetime but also in William Camden's account of Spenser's funeral, during which mourning poets threw into his tomb their elegies and the pens with which they had written these tributes. Among his fellow Elizabethans, Spenser first gained renown as a love poet, a pastoral writer, and a restorer of the native language—all three of these roles already enacted in his early work, *The Shepheardes Calender*, in which he demonstrated the expansiveness of rural dialect and English unadulterated with continental vocabulary. Later, in a more courtly work, *The Faerie Queene*, Spenser still sought variety in language more through native archaisms than through foreign idiom. Despite its simplicity of diction, *The Shepheardes Calender* contained an elaborate academic apparatus that demanded recognition for its author as a serious poet. The fact that Spenser took his work seriously was also manifested in various levels of satire and in metrical experimentation which strengthened what Philip Sidney described as his "poetical sinews."

Seventeenth century imitators echoed Spenser's allegorical and pastoral elements, his sensuous description, and his archaic phrasing. These early Spenserians, however, did not fully comprehend their model. Their servile imitations of surface themes and complex metrical forms temporarily diminished Spenser's reputation and probably stimulated later eighteenth century parodies. The serious side of Spenser, however, gradually received more notice. In *Areopagitica* (1644), for example, John Milton extolled him as "a better teacher than Scotus or Aquinas," and when the neoclassicists praised him, it was primarily for allegorical didacticism. In the nineteenth century, admiration of Spenser's moral allegory yielded to delight in his metrical virtuosity and the beauties of his word-pictures. When such great Romantics as Sir Walter Scott, Lord Byron, and John Keats imitated the Spenserian or "Faerie Queene" stanza form, they demonstrated anew the strength and flexibility of Spenser's metrical inventiveness. Modern holistic criticism continues to find deeper levels of Spenserian inventiveness in structural intricacy, allegorical ingenuity, and both narrative and descriptive aptness.

Biography · If allusions in his own poetry can be read autobiographically, Edmund Spenser was born in London in 1552, apparently into a mercantile

Library of Congress

family of moderate income. In 1561, the Merchant Taylors' School opened with Richard Mulcaster as its first headmaster, and in that same year or shortly afterward Spenser was enrolled, probably as a scholarship student. From Mulcaster, Spenser learned traditional Latin and Greek, and also an awareness of the intricacies and beauties of the English language unusual among both schoolboys and schoolmasters of that time. Later, Spenser as "Colin Clout" paid tribute to Mulcaser as the "olde Shephearde" who had made him "by art more cunning" in the "song and musicks mirth" that fascinated him in his "looser yeares." Even before Spenser went to Cambridge, fourteen of his schoolboy verse translations had been incorporated into the English version of Jan van der Noot's *Theatre for Worldlings* (1569).

At Pembroke College, Cambridge, Spenser took his B.A. degree in 1573 and his M.A. in 1576; little else is known about his activities during that period except that he made several lifelong friends, among them Gabriel Harvey and Edward Kirke. Both Harvey and Kirke were later among Spenser's prepublication readers and critics, and Kirke today remains the most likely candidate for the role of "E. K.," the commentator whose glosses and arguments interpret enigmatic passages in *The Shepheardes Calender*. The Spenser-Harvey letters reveal young Spenser's theories on poetry and also his hopes for the patronage of Philip Sidney and Sidney's uncle, the Earl of Leicester, Queen Elizabeth's favored courtier. Harvey's greetings to a woman, whom he addresses as "Mistress Immerito" and "Lady Colin Clout," also suggest that Spenser was married about 1580; nothing more is known of the first wife, but there are records of a son and a daughter at the time of Spenser's second marriage to Elizabeth Boyle in 1594.

When Spenser found himself unable to gain an appointment as a Fellow at Cambridge, he accepted the post of secretary to John Young, Bishop of Rochester. In 1580, he went to Ireland as secretary for Arthur Lord Grey, the newly appointed Lord Governor. When Grey was recalled from Ireland two years later because his policies did not control the Irish rebellion as the English court desired, Spenser remained behind. For several years he moved into minor offices in different sections of the country; about 1589, he became "undertaker" of Kilcolman, an estate in Cork. As an "undertaker," Spenser received a grant of land previously confiscated from an Irish rebel, agreeing to see to the restoration of the estate and to establish tenant farmers on it. Love for Kilcolman is reflected in his poetry even though his days there were shadowed by litigation with an Irish neighbor who claimed the property and by a new outbreak of rebellion which eventually destroyed the estate and forced him to leave Ireland about a month before his death in 1599.

With the exception of *The Shepheardes Calender*, all of Spenser's major poetry was written in Ireland. The landscape and the people of his adopted country are reflected in imagery and allusions; political and economic conditions appear in various guises, perhaps nowhere so strongly and pervasively as in Book V of *The Faerie Queene*, the Book of Justice. Although Spenser lived most of his adult life far from the court of Elizabeth, he maintained constant contact with events and friends there. His strongest bid for court recognition came in *The Faerie Queene*, with its creation of Gloriana, the Fairyland reflection of the living Queen of Britain, who rewarded him for his portrait of her by granting him an annual pension. Two of Queen Elizabeth's favorites played major roles in Spenser's later years: Sir Walter Raleigh and Robert, Earl of Essex. Raleigh, who owned an estate neighboring Spenser's Kilcolman, frequently encouraged the poet's work in a general way and, if there is any validity in Spenser's famous prefatory letter, influenced specific changes in the structure of *The Faerie Queene*. Essex financed the poet's funeral and his burial in the Poet's Corner of Westminster Abbey in 1599.

Analysis · By an eclectic mingling of old traditions, Edmund Spenser created new poetry—new in verse forms, in language, and in genre. From the Middle Ages, Spenser had inherited complex allegorical traditions and a habit of interlacing narrative strands; these traditions were fused with classical myth and generic conventions, some of them transformed by continental imitators before they reached Spenser. This fusion of medievalism and classicism was in turn modified by currents of thought prevalent in Tudor England, especially by the intense nationalism that manifested itself in religion, language, politics, and international affairs.

To some extent, Spenser's poetic development evolved naturally from his deliberate selection of Vergil as his model. Like Vergil, he started his published career with pastoral eclogues; like him, too, he turned, in his last major work, from shepherds to great heroes. Before Spenser evoked classical muses in his epic, however, the tradition of Vergil had picked up romantic coloring and allegorical overtones from continental epics, especially Ludovico Ariosto's highly allegorized *Orlando furioso* (1532). Spenser himself announced the three-way pattern adopted for *The Faerie Queene*: "Fierce wars and faithful loves shall moralize my song." Long after Spenser's death his admirers continued to compare him with Vergil, often to Spenser's advantage. Vergil provided stimulus not only for the pastoral and epic genres in which Spenser wrote his two major works but also for the mythical allusions that permeate most of his work and for the serious use of poetry, especially in political and religious satire and in the reflection of nationalistic pride. Vergil's exaltation of Augustus and the Roman Empire accorded well with the nationalism of Elizabethan England, a nationalism poetically at its zenith in *The Faerie Queene.*

Vergil's sobriquet "Tityrus" became for Spenser a means of double praise when he hailed his fourteenth century predecessor Geoffrey Chaucer as an English Tityrus, the "God of shepheards." Rustic language, interlocked narratives, and experiments in vernacular quantitative verse forms in *The Shepheardes Calender* all reflect Chaucerian influence; in a less direct way, the vogue of courtly love in medieval and Renaissance literature was also channeled partly through Chaucer. During the two centuries between Chaucer and Spenser, love poetry became permeated with a blend of Petrarchan and Neoplatonic elements. Petrarchan lovers taught Spenser's shepherds to lament over their ladies' cruelty, to extol their beauty, and to describe their own pains, anxieties, and ecstasies with conventional images. The more sensuous aspects of love remained central to many of the *Amoretti* sonnets and to several set pieces in *The Faerie Queene,* such as Acrasia's Bower of Bliss and Busiranes' Mask of Cupid; but idealistic Neoplatonic concepts also emerged here. Such Neoplatonic concepts undergird the *Fowre Hymnes.* The first two hymns praise erotic human love and the inspirational force of feminine beauty; the other two deprecate these more earthly powers, elevating in their place the heavenly love and beauty of Christ, the source of all true human love and beauty.

In *The Faerie Queene,* too, idealistic Neoplatonic elements assume more pervasive significance than do Petrarchan motifs. The Platonic identification of the good and the beautiful, for example, is often manifest, especially in Gloriana, Una, and Belphoebe; and the true and false Florimels of Books III-V exemplify true and false beauty, the former inspiring virtuous love and marriage and the second inciting sensuous lust. Although Books III and IV are called the Books of Chastity and Friendship, their linked story dramatically demonstrates variant forms of love. The concept of love as either debilitating or inspiring reflects one of the mythical traditions transmitted from antiquity through the Middle Ages: the double significance of Venus as good and evil love. As the goddess of good, fruitful love, Venus herself frequents the Garden of Adonis, where nature is untouched by deceptive art, where spring and harvest meet, and where love flourishes joyfully. In her own temple, Venus listens to the sound of "lovers piteously complaining" rather than rejoicing.

Renaissance pageantry and Tudor emblem books contributed to the pictorial quality with which Spenser brought myths to life—classical tales, rustic folklore, and his own mythic creations. One of the most picturesque of Spenser's new myths describes the "spousals" of the Thames and

Medway rivers, a ceremony attended by such "wat'ry gods" as Neptune and his son Albion; by other rivers, remote ones such as the Nile and the Ganges, Irish neighbors such as the Liffey and the Mulla, and streams that paid tribute to one of the betrothed rivers; and by Arion, accompanied by his dolphin and carrying the harp with which he provided wedding music. Scenes like these exemplify the artistry with which Spenser created new poetry out of old traditions.

Classic and contemporary models, rural and courtly milieu, universal and occasional topics–from such a mixture Spenser formed his first major work, the "little booke," which he dedicated to Sidney and which he signed "Immerito," the Unworthy One. *The Shepheardes Calender* went through five editions between 1579 and 1597, none of them bearing Spenser's name. Such anonymity fits common Renaissance practice, but it may also have had additional motivation from Spenser's awareness of sensitive topical allusions with too thin an allegorical veil. Contemporary praise of Spenser indicates that by 1586 the anonymity was technical rather than real. In his twelve eclogues, one for each month of the year, Spenser imitated conventions that Renaissance writers attributed to Vergil and to his Greek predecessors: debates between rustic speakers in a rural setting, varied by a singing match between shepherds, a lament for the death of a beloved companion, praise of the current sovereign, alternating exultation and despair over one's mistress, and veiled references to contemporary situations. A fifteenth century French work, translated as *The Kalender and compost of Shepherds*, probably suggested to Spenser not only his title but also the technique of emblematic illustration, the application of zodiacal signs to everyday life and to the seasons, and the arrangement of instructional commentary according to the months. Barbabe Googe's *The Zodiake of Life* (1565) strengthened the satirical and philosophical undertone of the calendar theme.

Despite the surface simplicity connoted by its nominal concern with shepherds, Spenser's book is a complex work. Not the least of its complexities are the paraphernalia added by "E. K.": the dedicatory epistle, the introductory arguments (for the whole book and for each eclogue), and the glosses. Although the initials themselves make Spenser's Cambridge friend Edward Kirke the most likely person to designate as the mysterious commentator, the Renaissance love for name-games does not exclude other possible solutions of the identity puzzle. Even Spenser himself has been suggested as a candidate for the enigmatic role. Many of E. K.'s annotations supply information essential to an understanding of the poet's cryptic allusions, to the identification of real-life counterparts for the characters, and occasionally to a modernization of archaic diction. Some annotations, however, are either accidentally erroneous or pedantically misleading: for example, several source references and the etymology for "aeglogues." E. K. derives the term "eclogues" from "Goteheardes tales" rather than from "conversations of shepherds," the more usual Renaissance understanding of the term; in actuality, "eclogues" are etymologically short selections which convention came to associate with pastoral settings.

The twelve separate selections could have produced a sense of fragmentation, but instead they create a highly unified whole. The most obvious unifying device is the calendar framework, which gives to the individual poems their titles and their moods. Another source of unity lies in the shepherd characters who appear repeatedly, especially Colin Clout, a character borrowed from the Tudor satirist John Skelton and used by Spenser as his own persona. Colin appears in four of the eclogues and is the topic of conversation in three others; his friendship for Hobbinol (identified by E. K. as Harvey), and his love for Rosalind (unidentified) provide a thread of plot throughout the twelve poems. Moreover, the figure of Colin represents the whole life of "everyman"–or at least every poet–as he passes from the role of "shepherd boy" in "January" to that of the mature "gentle shepherd" in "December."

In his general argument, E. K. establishes three categories for the topics of the eclogues: plaintive, recreative, and moral. The four selections which E. K. classifies as plaintive are those in which Colin's is the main voice. "January" and "June" are laments about his futile love for Rosalind; "December," too, is a conventional love plaint, although it adds the dimension of Colin's approaching death. "November," one of the most highly structured eclogues, is a pastoral elegy for Dido, the daughter of one "greate shephearde" and the beloved of another "greate shepheard Lobbin." E. K. pleads ignorance of the identity of both shepherds, but most critics identify "Lobbin" as a typical anagram for Robin (Robert Dudley) plus Leicester, thus suggesting a covert allusion to a love interest of Elizabeth's favorite, the Earl of Leicester.

The first of the three recreative selections, "March," is a sprightly, occasionally bawdy, discussion of love by two shepherd boys. "April" starts out with a description of Colin's lovesickness but then moves on to an encomium on "fayre Elissa, Queene of shepheardes all," a transparent allusion to Queen Elizabeth. The singing contest in "August" gives Spenser an opportunity to exploit shifting moods and an intricate variety of metrical patterns.

It is sometimes difficult to interpret the satire in the eclogues which E. K. classes as "moral" because of the ambivalence of the dialogue structure itself and because of the uncertain implications of the fables included in four of the five moral selections. Besides, misperception on the part of the characters or the commentator can be part of the comedy. In "May," "July," and "September," different pairs of shepherds discuss religious "shepherds," making clear allusions to contemporary churchmen. In contrast to the sometimes vehement satire in these religious eclogues, the debate on youth and age in "February" has a light, bantering tone. As a statement of Spenser's views on poetry, "October" is perhaps the most significant "moral" eclogue. When the disillusioned young poet Cuddie complains that his oaten reeds are "rent and wore" without having brought him any reward, the idealistic Piers tries to convince him that glory is better than gain. He encourages Cuddie to leave rustic life, to lift himself "out of the lowly dust," but Cuddie complains that the great worthies that "matter made for Poets on to play" are long dead. The ambivalence of the pastoral debate is particularly evident here because the two voices apparently represent a conflict within Spenser himself. The inner Piers has an almost Platonic vision of poetry and sees potential inspiration in the active life of the court; but the inner Cuddie, fearing the frustrations of the poet's role, resigns himself to the less conspicuous, less stimulating rural life.

In a sequel to the eclogues, *Colin Clouts Come Home Againe,* Colin describes to his friends a trip to London, apparently a reflection of Spenser's trip to make arrangements for the publication of *The Faerie Queene.* The question-and-answer format allows Colin to touch on varied topics: the level of poetic artistry in London, conventional satire of life at court, topographical poetry about the "marriage" of two Irish rivers, and Platonic deification of love. Although this more mature Colin is less critical of court life than the earlier one had been, Ireland rather than England is still "home" to him.

Any study of *The Faerie Queene* must take into account the explanatory letter to Raleigh printed in all early editions under the heading: "A Letter of the Author's, Expounding his Whole Intention in the course of this Work. . . ." The fact that the letter was printed at the end rather than the beginning of the first edition (Books I-III only) suggests that Spenser was writing with a retrospective glance at what was already in the printer's press, even though he was also looking toward the overall structure of what had not yet been assembled. Raleigh had apparently requested such an explanation, and Spenser here clarified elements which he considered essential to understanding his "continued Allegory of dark conceit." These elements can be summarized as purpose, genre, narrative structure, and allegorical significance.

In carrying out his purpose "to fashion a gentleman or noble person in

vertuous and gentle discipline," Spenser imitated other Renaissance conduct books which set out to form representatives of different levels of polite
society, such as those peopled by princes, schoolmasters, governors, and
courtiers. By coloring his teaching with "historical fiction," Spenser obeyed
Horace's precept to make poetry both useful and pleasing; he also followed
the example of classic and Renaissance writers of epic by selecting for the
center of that fiction a hero whose historicity was overlaid by legend:
Arthur. Theoretically, an epic treats a major action of a single great man,
while a romance recounts great deeds of many men. Kaleidoscopic visions
of the deeds of many great knights and ladies within the separate books
superimpose a coloring of romance, but the overall generic designation of
The Faerie Queene as "epic" is possible because Arthur appears in the six
books as a unifying hero. Through Arthur, the poet also paid tribute to his
sovereign, whose family, according to the currently popular Tudor myth,
claimed descent from Arthur's heirs.

Although the complexity of the poem stems partly from the blending of
epic and romance traditions, Spenser's political concern added an even
greater complication to his narrative structure. He wanted to create a
major role by which he could pay tribute to a female sovereign in a genre
that demanded a male hero. From this desire came two interlocked plot
lines with Gloriana, the Faerie Queene, as the motivating force of both: the
young Arthur "before he was king" was seeking as his bride the beautiful
Queen of Fairyland whom he had seen in a vision; meanwhile, this same
queen had sent out on quests twelve different knights, one for each book
of the epic. At strategic points within these separate books Arthur would
interrupt his quest to aid the currently central figure. Since Spenser completed only six of the proposed twelve books, the climatic wedding of
Arthur and Gloriana never took place and the dramatic dispersion and
reassembling of Gloriana's knights occurred only in the poet's explanation, not in his poem.

Patterns of allegory, like patterns of narrative, intertwine throughout the
poem. By describing his allegory as "continued," Spenser did not imply
that particular meanings were continuously retained but rather that central
allegories recurred. In the letter to Raleigh, for example, Spenser explains
that in his "general intention" Gloriana means glory, but in a more
"particular" way she is "the glorious person" of Elizabeth. Spenser is not
satisfied to "shadow" Elizabeth only as Gloriana. In the letter and in the
introduction to Book III, he invites Elizabeth to see herself as both
Gloriana and Belphoebe, "In th'one her rule, in th'other her rare chastity."
Less pointedly, she is also "shadowed" in Una, the image of true religion
(Book I); in Britomart, the beautiful Amazonian warrior (Books III-V); and

in Mercilla, the just queen (Book V). The glories of Elizabeth thus appear as a pervasive aspect of the "continued allegory," even though they are represented by different characters. Allegorical continuity also comes from Spenser's plan to have his twelve knights as "patrons" of the "twelve private moral virtues" devised by Aristotle, with Arthur standing forth as the virtue of magnificence, "the perfection of all the rest." The titles of the six completed books indicate the central virtues of their heroes: holiness, temperance, chastity, friendship, justice, and courtesy.

Historical and topical allusions appear frequently. Only when such allusions link references to Arthur and Gloriana, however, do they form a continuous thread of allegory. In the Proem to Book II, "The Legend of Sir Guyon, or of Temperance," Spenser encourages Elizabeth to see her face in the "fair mirror" of Gloriana, her kingdom in the "land of faery," and her "great ancestry" in his poem. In Canto X he inserts a patch of "historical fiction" in which Arthur and Guyon examine the chronicles of Briton kings and elfin emperors, the first ending with the father of Arthur, Uther Pendragron, and the second with Tanaquil, called "Glorian . . . that glorious flower." Spenser prefaces his lengthy account of British history (stanzas 5-69) with a tribute to his own "sovereign queen" whose "realm and race" had been derived from Prince Arthur; he thus identifies the realm of the "renowned prince" of this story as the England of history. The second chronicle describes an idealized land where succession to the crown is peaceful, where the elfin inhabitants can trace their race back to Prometheus, creator of Elf (Adam) and Fay (Eve), and where Elizabeth-Gloriana can find her father and grandfather figured in Oberon and Elficleos. The "continued" historical allegory looks to the wedding of Arthur and Gloriana as blending real and ideal aspects within England itself.

Topical political allegory is most sustained in Book V, "The Legend of Artegall, or of Justice." In this book Elizabeth appears as Queen Mercilla and as Britomart; Mary Stuart as Duessa (sentenced by Mercilla) and as Radigund (defeated in battle by Britomart): Arthur Lord Grey as the titular hero, Artegall; the Earl of Leicester as Prince Arthur himself in one segment of the narrative. Several European rulers whom Elizabeth had either opposed or aided also appear in varied forms. Contemporary political problems are reflected in the story of Artegall's rescue of Irena (Ireland) from the giant Grantorto (literally translated as "Great Wrong"), usually allegorically identified as the Pope. Spenser's personal defense of Lord Grey shows through the naïve allegory of Canto XII, where Artegall, on the way back to Faery Court, is attacked by two hags, Envy and Detraction, and by the Blatant Beast (Calumny). Spenser thus suggests the cause of the misunderstandings that led to Elizabeth's recalling Grey from Ireland. Elizabeth's controversy with Mary Stuart, doubly reflected in Book V, also provides a significant level of meaning in Book I, "The Legende of the Knight of the Red Crosse, or of Holinesse."

A closer look at the tightly structured development of Book I shows more clearly Spenser's approach to heroic and allegorical poetry in the epic as a whole. On the literal level of romantic epic, Gloriana assigns to an untrained knight the quest he seeks: the rescue of the parents of a beautiful woman from a dreaded dragon. The plot traces the separation of Red Cross and Una, Red Cross's travels with the deceptive Duessa (duplicity), Una's search for Red Cross, the reunion of Una and her knight, the fulfillment of the quest, and the betrothal of hero and heroine. Vivid epic battles pit Red Cross against the serpentine Error and her swarming brood of lesser monsters, against a trio of evil brothers (Sansfoy, Sansjoy, and Sansloy), against the giant Orgoglio (from whose dungeon he must be rescued by Prince Arthur), and eventually against one of the fiercest, best-described dragons in literature. In Canto X, Red Cross learns his identity as Saint George, changeling descendant of human Saxon kings rather than rustic elfin warrior. Red Cross's dragon-fight clearly reflects pictorial representations of Saint George as dragon-slayer.

All three levels of allegory recognized by medieval exegetes are fully developed in Book I: typical, anagogical, and moral. Typically, Una is the true Church of England, and Elizabeth is the protector of this Church; Duessa is the Church of Rome and Mary Stuart, its supporter. Red Cross is both abstract holiness defending truth and a figure of Christ himself. Arthur, too, is a figure of Christ or of grace in his rescue of Red Cross—here a kind of Everyman—from Orgoglio, the forces of Antichrist.

Anagogical or apocalyptic elements appear primarily in sections treating Duessa and the dragon and in Red Cross's vision of heaven. Duessa, at her first appearance, reflects the description of the scarlet woman in the Revelation of Saint John, and the mount given her later by Orgoglio is modeled on the apocalyptic seven-headed Beast. The mouth of the great dragon of Canto XI belches forth flames like those often pictured erupting from the jaws of hell in medieval mystery plays. Red Cross is saved from the dragon by his contacts with the Well of Life and the Tree of Life, both borrowed from Revelation. Before Red Cross confronts the dragon, he has an apocalyptic vision of the New Jerusalem, a city rivaling in beauty even the capital of Fairyland, Cleopolis.

The moral level provides the most "continued" allegory in Book I. Red Cross-Everyman must develop within himself the virtue of holiness if he is eventually to conquer sin and attain the heavenly vision. When holiness is accompanied by truth, Error can be readily conquered. When holiness, however, is deceived by hypocrisy (Archimago), it is easily separated from truth and is further deceived by duplicity (Duessa) masquerading as fidelity (Fidessa). Tempted to spiritual sloth, Red Cross removes his armor of faith and falls to pride (Orgoglio). He must then be rescued from the chains of this sin by grace (Prince Arthur), must be rescued from Despair by truth, and must be spiritually strengthened in the House of Holiness, conducted by Dame Caelia (heaven) and her daughters Fidelia, Speranza, and Charissa (faith, hope, and charity). Only then can he repent of his own sins and become holy enough to conquer sin embodied in the dragon.

If Book I best exemplifies self-contained, carefully structured allegorical narrative, Books III and IV exemplify the interweaving common in medieval and early Renaissance narrative poetry. Characters pursue one another throughout the two books; several stories are not completed until Book V. In fact, Braggadochio, the cowardly braggart associated with false Florimell in this section, steals Guyon's horse in Book II and is judged for the crime in Book V. Belphoebe, too, introduced in a comic interlude with Braggadochio in Book II, becomes a central figure in the Book of Chastity. Belphoebe blends the beauty of Venus (Bel) with the chastity of Diana (Phoebe); her twin sister, Amoret, is a more earthly representation of Venus, destined to generate beauty and human love. Britomart, the nominal heroine of Book III, embodies the chastity of Belphoebe in her youth but the generative love of Amoret in maturity. Despite complex and not always consistent allegorical equations applicable to these central characters, Spenser moves them through their adventures with a delicate interlacing of narrative and allegorical threads typical of the romantic epic and its most entertaining level.

The sonnet sequence *Amoretti* ("little love poems") and the *Epithalamion* (songs "on the marriage bed") together provide a poetic account of courtship and marriage, an account which tradition links to actualities in Spenser's relationship with Elizabeth Boyle, whom he married in 1594. References to seasons suggest that the "plot" of the sonnet sequence extends from New Year's Day in one year (Sonnet 4) through a second New Year's Day (Sonnet 62) to the beginning of a third winter in the closing sonnet (Sonnet 89), a time frame of about two years. Several sonnets contain references which tempt readers to autobiographical interpretations. In Sonnet 60, "one year is spent" since the planet of "the winged god" began to move in the poet; even more significantly, the poet refers to the "sphere of Cupid" as containing the forty years "wasted" before this year. By simple arithmetical calculations, biographers of Spenser have deduced from his assumed age in 1593 his birth in 1552. Two sonnets refer directly to his work on *The Faerie Queene*: Sonnet 33 blames on his "troublous" love his inability to complete the "Queen of Faery" for his "sacred empress" and Sonnet 80 rejoices that having run through six books on Fairyland he can now write praises "low and mean,/ Fit for the handmaid of the Faery Queen."

Collectively and individually the *Amoretti* follow a popular Renaissance tradition established by Petrarch and imitated by numerous English sonneteers. In metrical structure, Spenser's sonnets blended Italian and English forms. The five-rhyme restriction in the Italian octave-plus-sestet pattern (abbaabba cdecde) was adapted to fit the English pattern of three quatrains plus couplet; instead of the seven rhymes used in most English sonnets, the interlocked rhymes of the Spenserian quatrains created a more intricate, as well as more restricted, form (abab bcbc cdcd ee).

Although Spenser's metrical pattern was innovative, most of his conceits and images were conventional; for example, love is related to a judicial court (Sonnet 10) and to religious worship (Sonnets 22 and 68); the beloved is a cruel causer and observer of his pain (Sonnets 20, 31, 41, 42, and 54) and the Neoplatonic ideal of beauty (Sonnets 3, 9, 45, 61, 79, and 88); love is warfare (Sonnets 11, 12, 14, and 57), a storm (Sonnet 46), sickness (Sonnet 50), a sea journey (Sonnet 63). The poet at times promises the immortality of fame through his praise (Sonnets 27, 29, 69, 75, and 82); at other times he simply rejoices in the skill which enables him as poet to offer his gift of words (Sonnets 1 and 84). Even the kind of praise offered to his beloved is traditional. In Sonnet 40, "An hundred Graces" sit "on each eyelid" and the lover's "storm-beaten heart" is cheered "when cloudy looks are cleared." Elsewhere, eyes are weapons (Sonnets 7, 16, and 49) and a means of entanglement (Sonnet 37). The beloved is a "gentle deer" (Sonnet 67) and a "gentle bee" caught in a sweet prison woven by the spider-poet (Sonnet 71); but she is also a cruel panther (Sonnet 53) and a tiger (Sonnet 56). Physical beauties are compared to precious metals and gems (Sonnet 15), to sources of light (Sonnet 9), and to the sweet odors of flowers (Sonnet 64). Classical myths color several sonnets, identifying the beloved with Penelope, Pandora, Daphne, and the Golden Apples of Hercules (Sonnets 23, 24, 28, and 77) and the poet-lover with Narcissus, Arion, and Orpheus (Sonnets 35, 38, and 44).

In typical Petrarchan fashion, the lyrical moments in the *Amoretti* fluctuate between joy and pain, between exultation over love returned and anxiety over possible rejection. The sequence ends on a note of anxiety not in keeping with a set of poems conceived as a prelude for the glowing joy of the *Epithalamion*. Despite clear references to the 1592-1594 period of Spenser's life, it seems unlikely that all eighty-nine sonnets were written during this period or that all were originally intended for a sequence in praise of Elizabeth Boyle. The *Epithalamion*, however, is clearly Spenser's celebration of his own wedding at Kilcolman on St. Barnabas' Day (June 11), 1594.

In its basic form and development, this marriage song is as conventional as the sonnets with which it was first published; but it is also original and personal in its variations on tradition. Classical allusions, for example, are countered by the homely invocation to nymphs of the Irish river and lake near Spenser's home (lines 56-66), by the imprecation against the "unpleasant choir of frogs still croaking" in the same lake (line 349), and by some of the attendants: "merchants' daughters," "fresh boys," and childlike angels "peeping in" the face of the bride. Although allusions to classical gods and goddesses heighten the lyric mood, other elements retain a more personal touch.

Structurally, Spenser adapted the *canzone* form. As used by Dante and Petrarch, the *canzone* consisted of a series of long stanzas followed by a short stanza (a *tornata*) responding to the preceding stanzas. Within the stanzas one or more three-foot lines varied the basic five-foot line; the *tornata*, too, had one short line. A. Kent Hieatt has demonstrated in *Short Time's Endless Monument* (1960) the ingenuity with which Spenser varied the basic *canzone* structure to reflect units of time in general and to relate poetic divisions with night/day divisions on the longest day of the year in southern Ireland. Hieatt points out that variations in verse form correspond to days in the year (365 long lines), hours in the day (24 stanzas), spring and fall equinoxes (parallel diction, imagery, and thought in stanzas 1-12 and 13-24), degrees of the sun's daily movement (359 long lines before the *tornata*, corresponding to 359 degrees of the sun's movement as contrasted with 360 degrees of the stars' movement), and the division between waking and sleeping hours (indicated by a change in the refrain at the end of stanza 17). It is variations within stanza 17 that most personalize the time element to make the "bedding" of the bride occur at the point in the poem representing nightfall on the poet's wedding day, the day of the summer solstice in southern Ireland. At the end of the stanza, the refrain, which had for sixteen stanzas been describing the answering echo of the woods, changes to "The woods no more shall answer, nor your echo ring": all is quiet so that the poet-bridegroom can welcome night and the love of his bride.

The collection of moralizing, melancholy verse entitled *Complaints* reflects an as yet not fully developed artistry in the author. Although published in the aftermath of fame brought by *The Faerie Queene*, most of the nine poems were probably first drafted much earlier. The most significant poem in this volume was probably the satirical beast fable, "Prosopopoia: Or, Mother Hubberd's Tale." Following the tradition of Giovanni Boccaccio and Geoffrey Chaucer, the poet creates a framework of tale-tellers, one of whom is "a good old woman" named Mother Hubberd. In Mother Hubberd's story, a Fox and an Ape gain personal prosperity through the gullibility of farmers, the ignorance and worldliness of clergymen, and the licentiousness of courtiers. About two-thirds of the way through, the satire turns more specifically to the concern of England in 1579 with a possible marriage between the twenty-four-year-old Duc d'Alencon and Queen Elizabeth, then forty-six. The marriage was being engineered by Lord Burleigh (the Fox of the narrative) and by Jean de Simier, whom Elizabeth playfully called her "Ape." This poem, even more than *The Shepheardes Calender,* demonstrates Spenser's artistic simplicity and the Chaucer-like irony of his worldview. Burleigh's later hostility to Spenser gives evidence of the pointedness of the poet's satiric barbs. "Virgil's Gnat" also exemplifies a satiric beast fable, this time with Leicester's marriage as the target, hit so effectively that Spenser himself was wounded by Leicester's lessened patronage. In "Muiopotmos: Or, The Fate of the Butterfly," beast fable is elevated by philosophical overtones, epic machinery, and classical allusions. Some type of personal or political allegory obviously underlies the poem, but critical interpretations vary widely in attempting to identify the chief figures, the Spider and the Butterfly. Despite such uncertainty, however, one message is clear: life and beauty are mutable.

Mutability permeates *Complaints;* it is even more central to the posthumous fragment known as the "Mutabilitie Cantos." The publisher Matthew Lownes printed these two cantos as "The Legend of Constancy," a fragmentary Book VII of *The Faerie Queene.* Lownes's identification of these two cantos with the unfinished epic was apparently based on similar poetic form, an allusion to the poet's softening his stern style in singing of hills and woods "mongst warres and knights," and a reference to the records of Fairyland as registering mutability's genealogy. There are, however, no knights, human or elf, in these cantos. Instead, Jove and Nature represent allegorically the cosmic principle of Constancy, the permanence that underlies all change. Despite the philosophical victory of Nature, one of the most effective extended passages in the cantos represents change through a processional pageant of the seasons, the months, day and night, the hours, and life and death.

The principle of underlying permanence applies to Spenser's works as well as to the world of which he wrote. In his shepherds and shepherdesses, his knights and ladies, his own personae, and even in the animal figures of his fables, images of Everyman and Everywoman still live. Time has thickened some of the allegorical veils that conceal as well as reveal, language then new has become archaic, and poetic conventions have become freer since Spenser's poetry first charmed his contemporaries. Despite such changes, however, the evocative and creative power that made Spenser "the Prince of Poets in his time" remains constant.

Other literary forms · Like most Renaissance writers, Edmund Spenser usually prefaced his poems with dedicatory letters that complimented the recipients and also provided helpful interpretations for other readers. Further indications of Spenser's theories about "English versifying" appear in his correspondence with Gabriel Harvey: *Three Proper, and Wittie, Familiar Letters* (1580) and *Foure Letters and Certaine Sonnets* (1586). Although *A View of the Present State of Ireland* was written in 1596, it was not published until 1633, thirty-four years after the author's death. In this treatise, Spenser presented a clear picture of Elizabethan Ireland and its political, economic, and social evils. The serious tone of this work deepens the significance of the Irish allusions and imagery throughout Spenser's poetry.

Select works other than poetry

NONFICTION: *Three Proper, and Wittie, Familiar Letters,* 1580; *Foure Letters and Certaine Sonnets,* 1586; *A View of the Present State of Ireland,* 1633 (written in 1596).

MISCELLANEOUS: *The Works of Edmund Spenser: A Variorum Edition,* 1932-1949 (Edwin Greenlaw et al., editors).

Marie Michelle Walsh

Bibliography · See A. C. Hamilton's *Essential Articles for the Study of Edmund Spenser,* 1972; Judith Dundas' *Spider and the Bee: The Artistry of Spenser's "Faerie Queene,"* 1985; Harold Bloom's edition of collected essays, *Edmund Spenser,* 1986; Harry Berger's *Revisionary Play: Studies in the Spenserian Dynamics,* 1988; S. K. Heninger's *Sidney and Spenser: The Poet as Maker,* 1989; Sean Kane's *Spenser's Moral Allegory,* 1989; Donna Gibbs's *Spenser's "Amoretti": A Critical Study,* 1990; A. C. Hamilton's *Spenser Encyclopedia,* 1990; John N. King's *Spenser's Poetry and the Reformation Tradition,* 1990; Kenneth Borris' *Spenser's Poetics of Prophecy in "The Faerie Queene V,"* 1991; John Rooks's *Love's Courtly Ethic in "The Faerie Queene": From Garden to Wilderness,* 1992; Patrick Cheney's *Spenser's Famous Flight: A Renaissance Idea of a Literary Career,* 1993; Robert Lane's *Shepheardes Devises: Edmund Spenser's "Shepheardes Calender" and the Institutions of Elizabethan Society,* 1993; and John Steadman's *Moral Fiction in Milton and Spenser,* 1995.

WALLACE STEVENS

Born: Reading, Pennsylvania; October 2, 1879
Died: Hartford, Connecticut; August 2, 1955

Poetry · *Harmonium*, 1923, 1931 (with 14 additional poems) · *Ideas of Order*, 1935 · *Owl's Clover*, 1936 · *The Man with the Blue Guitar and Other Poems*, 1937 · *Parts of a World*, 1942 · *Notes Toward a Supreme Fiction* (Stevens)], 1942 · *Esthétique du Mal*, 1945 · *Transport to Summer*, 1947 · *The Auroras of Autumn*, 1950 · *Selected Poems*, 1953 · *The Collected Poems of Wallace Stevens*, 1954

Achievements · Although Wallace Stevens never has had as large an audience as that enjoyed by Robert Frost and did not receive substantial recognition until several years before his death, he is usually considered to be one of the best five or six twentieth century poets writing in English. *Harmonium* reveals a remarkable style—or, to be more precise, a number of remarkable styles. While critics praised, or more often condemned, the early poetry for its gaudiness, colorful imagery, flamboyant rhetoric, whimsicality, and odd points of view, one also finds in this volume spare Imagist poems as well as abstract philosophical poems which anticipate his later work. The purpose of his rhetorical virtuosity in *Harmonium* and in subsequent volumes was not merely to dazzle the reader but to convey the depth of emotion, the subtle complexity of thought, and the associative processes of the mind.

Strongly influenced by early nineteenth century English poets, Stevens became a modern Romantic who transformed and extended the English Romantic tradition as he accommodated it to the twentieth century world. *Harmonium* and subsequent volumes reveal his assimilation of the innovations of avant-garde painting, music, poetry, and philosophy. One finds in his canon, for example, intimations of Pablo Picasso, Henri Matisse, and Henri Bergson, and of cubism, Impressionism, Imagism, and Symbolism. Such influences were always subordinated to the poet's romantic sensibility, however, which struggled with the central Romantic problem—the need to overcome the gulf between the inner, human reality and outer, objective reality. A secular humanist who rejected traditional Christianity, arcane mysticism, and the pessimism of *The Waste Land* (1922) and the *Cantos* (beginning in 1925), he succeeded as a Romantic poet in the modern world. His contribution to poetry was recognized in 1950 with the award of the Bollingen Prize and in 1955 with the National Book Award and the Pulitzer Prize for *The Collected Poems of Wallace Stevens.* His reputation has continued to grow since his death in 1955.

Biography · On October 2, 1879, in Reading, Pennsylvania, Wallace Stevens was born to Garrett Barcalow Stevens and the former Margaretha Catherine Zeller. Wallace Stevens' father was a successful attorney who occasionally published poetry and prose in the local papers.

In 1897 Stevens was graduated from Reading Boys High School and enrolled at Harvard as a special student with the ambition to become a writer. He published stories and poetry in the *Harvard Advocate* and the *Harvard Monthly* and became acquainted with the poet and philosopher George Santayana, whose books provided support for his belief that in an agnostic age poetry must assume the role of traditional religion. After completing his special three-year course in English at Harvard, he joined the staff of the *New York Tribune,* but failed as a reporter.

In the fall of 1901 he entered the New York Law School and, after passing the bar three years later, began legal practice. He was not successful as a practicing attorney, however, and in 1908 he joined the New York office of the American Bonding Company. The next year he married Elsie Moll.

In 1916 Stevens joined the Hartford Accident and Indemnity Company and moved to Hartford, Connecticut, which was to be his permanent residence. He now led a double life. During the day he was a successful businessman, while at night and on weekends he was a poet. Few of his associates in the insurance world knew of his second career. Beginning in 1914 his work had begun to be published in *Poetry* and the other little magazines. At this time he became acquainted with an avant-garde group of writers and artists, including William Carlos Williams, Alfred Kreymborg, and Marcel Duchamp. His involvement in the business world, however, permitted only occasional participation in the activities of literary groups.

In 1923, at the age of forty-four, Stevens published his first volume of poetry. *Harmonium* was largely ignored by the critics, however, and he wrote only a few poems in the next five or six years. In 1924 his only child, Holly, was born, and subsequently he devoted his time to his family and to his business career. In 1931 Alfred A. Knopf reissued *Harmonium,* and in 1934 Stevens was promoted to vice-president of his insurance company. With his business career secure and with *Harmonium* receiving some recognition, he began to write and publish again. By the time *The Auroras of Autumn* appeared in 1950, his reputation had been firmly established. Even after the mandatory retirement age of seventy, he continued to work

at his insurance company, and rejected an offer to be the Charles Eliot
Norton lecturer at Harvard for the 1955-1956 academic year because he
felt that if he accepted he might be forced to retire. He died in 1955, two
months before his seventy-sixth birthday.

Analysis · Wallace Stevens frequently alludes to or quotes from the English
Romantics in his letters and in his essays, and there is little doubt that this
twentieth century poet is working within the Romantic tradition. The best
evidence for the contention that he is a twentieth century Romantic,
however, is his poetry. Repeatedly, one finds in his work the "reality-
imagination complex," as he calls it. While one can see the central beliefs
of William Wordsworth and John Keats in Stevens' poetry (celebration of
nature, acceptance of mutability, rejection of supernatural realms, and
belief in the brotherhood of man), the foundation of his Romanticism is
his Wordsworthian imagination. The function of this imagination in
Stevens' poetry is to make sordid reality, what Wordsworth calls "the
dreary intercourse of daily life," palatable without resorting to mysticism.
It is a difficult task; failure results in a profound alienation ("dejection" in
the language of the Romantics).

Stevens does not merely repeat what Wordsworth and Keats have
accomplished in their work but extends the Romantic tradition. He differs
from his predecessors in his radical nontranscendentalism. In a May 30,
1910, letter to his wife he quotes from Keats's "Epistle to John Hamilton
Reynolds": "It is a flaw/ In happiness, to see beyond our bourn,−/ It forces
us in summer skies to mourn,/ It spoils the singing of the Nightingale."
This idea is the premise of all Stevens' work. He takes the secular Romanticism of Wordsworth and Keats to its logical conclusion.

Stevens' poem "Of Modern Poetry" provides a good introduction to
both his theory and his method. The modern poem whose origin goes back
to the discursive odes of Wordsworth and Keats is "the poem of the mind
in the act of finding/ What will suffice." This modern meditation shows the
process of the mind confronting reality, searching for a secular solution to
the individual person's feeling of meaninglessness. Before the Romantic
period (1789-1832) this was not a major problem, and thus there was no
need for this type of meditation. Or, as Stevens says: "It has not always
had/ To find: the scene was set; it repeated what/ Was in the script." Now
the poet ("the actor") is "a metaphysician in the dark," the man of vital
imagination who seeks to redeem ugly reality and overcome his alienation
by secular meditation. It is a meditation which will not descend to negation
or ascend to supernaturalism ("below which it cannot descend,/ Beyond
which it has no will to rise").

The meditation utilizes conversational speech, "the real language of men," as Wordsworth says in the Preface to the *Lyrical Ballads* (1800), or the "speech of the place," as Stevens states here, and seeks its affirmation in everyday reality. Yet this "poem of the act of the mind" may create heightened moments in everyday reality, "spots of time," as Wordsworth calls them in *The Prelude* (1850). It is these "spots of time" that often allow the imagination to redeem reality by ordering it, enchanting it, transforming it, or creating a feeling of stasis, of permanence beyond time. By these heightened moments and by the process of the meditation itself, the imagination strives to rectify the individual's sense of loss.

In short, Stevens expands the Wordsworthian-Keatsian discursive act of the mind in a radical fashion. In a number of his acts of the mind the only unifying element is the solitary mind searching for what will suffice to ease its alienation. In these acts of the mind the imagination can create moments of illumination which help regenerate the poet—and regeneration is the central goal of modern meditations, those "poems of our climate."

"Poems of Our Climate" reveals the function and limitation of a spot of time in a secular Romantic meditation. In the first six lines of the poem the mind seizes a specific, seemingly ordinary moment and freezes it into a timeless moment, reminiscent of the stasis in the beginning of "Ode on a Grecian Urn." Unlike Keats however, Stevens does not linger over this moment that the imagination has endowed with meaning. He does not wait until the fourth stanza to grow disenchanted but instinctively feels that this cannot be a permanent state—"one desires/ So much more than that." The evanescent and heightened quality of the frozen moment ("The light/ In the room more like a snowy air,/ Reflecting snow") immediately becomes the monotony of "Cold, a cold porcelain, low and round,/ With nothing more than the carnations there."

Stevens must reject this "cold pastoral" because one needs more than purity ("this complete simplicity"). One does not want to be stripped of all his "torments." The vital individual (the "vital I") is "evilly compounded"—an identity forged out of a world of pains and troubles, of good and evil experience.

The spot of time is a temporary relief from the banality or ugliness of reality, but it cannot be a permanent state. The "never-resting mind" always feels the compulsion to return to reality to remediate and recompose it. "The imperfect is our paradise" might be Stevens' twentieth century reformulation of Keats's essential feeling in "Ode on Melancholy." Like Keats, he is ambivalent—both bitter and delighted over man's existence. Instinctively he desires to escape to an ideal state, but intellectually he realizes the impossibility of doing so. Man finds meaning only in human reality, which is by definition imperfect. Strip life of its torments and it becomes banality; conceal the dark side of existence or the "evil" aspects of one's nature and vitality is erased. Pure stasis untainted by life would be meaningless, and an art that mirrored this would be meaningless too. Stevens believes that art should express pain, struggle, and conflict, and thus he prefers the modern poets of "flawed words and stubborn sounds" to the "bawds of euphony." Stevens' poetry is a continual search; it is a continual oscillation between the depths of depression and heightened moments of affirmation. "[The mind] can never be satisfied, the mind, never" concludes Stevens in "The Well Dressed Man with a Beard."

Stevens sees external reality as the Other outside the self. "Large Red Man Reading" is a poem that reveals the crucial importance of the regenerative capacity of the imagination and the need to embrace the everyday world and reject the supernatural. As he seeks to reconcile himself to an earthly reality devoid of supernatural inclinations, Stevens contrasts the vital man of imagination (the large red man reading) with those who are "dead" to the imagination, "the ghosts." Ghosts as symbolic of those dead to the imaginative life occur elsewhere in his work. In "Disillusionment of Ten O'Clock," for example, Stevens complains that "the houses are haunted/ By white night-gowns" who do not "dream" (that is, imagine) of catching tigers "in red weather," as an old sailor does. In the ghostly realms of the modern world life is colorless—a dreary intercourse of daily life without imagination. In "Large Red Man Reading" the ghosts seem to recognize that a life without the imaginative interaction between the mind and reality is worthless. After leading a dull life on earth, they had hoped to find their paradise in heaven, but they have become dissatisfied with heaven ("the wilderness of stars") and returned to earth. They returned to hear the "large red man reading," for he is the vital individual of the imagination, a true giant in a paltry age. (Reading and study symbolize meditation, or the life of the imagination, in Stevens' poetry.)

In the course of the meditation it becomes clear why the ghosts have returned to earth. Heaven lacked the reality of earthly existence, its joys and its torments. The ghosts want to hear the large red man read from the "poem of life" in all its prosaic beauty and banality—"the pans above the stove, the pots on the table, the tulips among them." In contrast to the mythic abstraction of heaven, the ghosts would eagerly reach out for any sensory knowledge ("They were those that would have wept to step barefoot into reality"), even though this knowledge might mean pain ("run fingers over leaves/ And against the most coiled thorn") as well as pleasure. Stevens has mocked, with good-natured humor, the traditional belief that people desire to go to a paradisiacal heaven after dissatisfaction with the sinful, painful life on earth. The ghosts return to earth for the true paradise of an ever-changing sensuous reality ("being") heightened by the imagination ("reading").

The imagination's attempt to redeem reality is, however, not always completely successful—stalemate or even defeat are possibilities. Stevens is a darker poet than the critics have made him out to be—despite the fact that modern criticism has largely overcome the once popular cliché of the insouciant hedonist of impressionistic, pictorial poems. Often his poems of naturalistic celebration end on a tentative note of affirmation, for the ugly side of reality is an able match for the imagination; the mind can never completely transform reality into something purely positive. Furthermore, in a significant number of his acts of the mind, a sense of loss threatens to dominate. It is in these poems of "the whole of Harmonium," as he would have preferred to call his canon, that one finds a profound sense of loss ("the burden of the mystery," as both Wordsworth and Keats called it) as the very genesis of the work. In these works the imagination must grapple with "dejection," ascertain its causes or roots, and seek to resolve it as far as possible. These meditations of Stevens' are different from his others only in degree. Here, however, the imagination does not appear as potent as in his other acts, and spots of time do not seem to have the intensity, or the frequency, that one finds in his other meditations.

Stevens does not have only one attitude toward this sense of loss—and certainly not one type of "dejection" poem. His imagination takes a variety of forms and attitudes. It is probably a mistake to stress a chronological development in his attitude toward the burden of the mystery, although a case might be made for some lessening of humor and flamboyance and a gradual movement toward an autumnal tone during his career. Instead, one should stress the variety and complexity of his response. To show that his attitude toward the problem is much more complex than is usually thought, one must examine several of his poems, from his earliest to those written just before his death. Finally, it will also become clear that despite the sophistication of his responses to the problem, he was always a secular romantic who rejected the leap into transcendence and refused to submit to existential despair.

At the heart of "Sunday Morning" (1915) is a profound sense of loss, evoked by abandonment of traditional religious belief. Modern human beings can no longer justify suffering and death with Christian certitudes. This complicated meditative poem struggles with the problem at length, pondering questions that are central to Stevens' work. How does one dispel his anxiety when he realizes that all past mythologies are irrelevant? If there is no afterlife, how does one come to terms with death? Even as Keats did, Stevens overcomes his desire for the supernatural and puts his faith in humanist values.

"In the very Temple of Delight/ Veiled Melancholy has her sovran shrine," Keats had proclaimed in "Ode on Melancholy," and Stevens more vehemently reiterates this idea that life is process and there can be no separation of opposites, no separation of pleasure and pain. "Death is the mother of beauty," Stevens' speaker twice asserts in the course of the meditation. The very transiency of things makes them valuable; paradoxically, it is death that makes things beautiful. Stanza VI, reminiscent of Keats's "Ode on a Grecian Urn," shows that a heaven without mortality is a false paradise devoid of life. "Does ripe fruit never fall?" asks the frustrated speaker. The boughs will always hang heavy with fruit in "that perfect sky," and we can only "pick the strings of our insipid lutes" in this monotonous heaven, just as Keats's boughs will never shed their leaves and his bold lovers will always remain in the frustrating position of being poised over each other in the first stage of their lovemaking, a lovemaking of perpetual anticipation, not consummation.

Stevens believes that death is necessary for a true paradise because life can be enjoyed only when there are cycles of desire and fulfillment or disappointment. Death also has some positive value because it makes people aware of their common humanity, what Stevens significantly calls "heavenly fellowship." Wordsworth, in "Lines Composed a Few Miles Above Tintern Abbey" and "Ode: Intimations of Immortality from Recollections of Early Childhood," had expressed similar sentiments; but Stevens' attitude is more extreme. He supposes that the rejection of God results in a world that is intrinsically meaningless, whereupon one realizes that one must return to humankind as the only source of value.

"Sunday Morning" presents, in short, a radical humanism that Wordsworth and Keats had anticipated a century earlier. Instead of religion ("the thought of heaven") Stevens offers naturalistic reality, the "beauty of the earth." A person's emotional contact with nature is a substitute for rituals performed before an invisible deity. The only immortality that has any meaning for modern human beings, the poet argues, is the permanence of nature as felt in the seasonal cycle—nothing endures as "April's green endures." Depression and disillusionment are as natural as joy and hope, and memory of these opposite feelings helps form one's "soul" or identity. Echoing Keats, Stevens suggests that "all pleasures and all pains" are involved in one's responses to nature. In short, one's intense responses to external reality are "measures destined" for the "soul."

"A Postcard from the Volcano" (1936) is a meditation with a profound sense of loss at its foundation; about the precise nature of this loss, however, there is no critical agreement. The poem is as perplexing and intriguing as its bizarre title; to understand it, one must account for the sense of loss and explain the shift of tone at the end of the work.

"A Postcard from the Volcano" is divided into two parts by the ellipsis. The first part presents the problem: The poet feels dejected because he realizes that after his death the imaginative expression of his life in poetry will seem foreign to the new generation. The poet will have become an irrelevant ghost, such as Stevens has elsewhere mocked as the antithesis of the vital life of the imagination. The world of the past, especially that world interpreted by the poet's imagination, will become meaningless to the children of the present.

They will "pick up our bones" but will never be able to comprehend that these once had vitality and a keen sense of participation in the moment ("that these were once/ As quick as foxes on the hill"). They will not be able to perceive the impact of the past on the present, or realize how one can change his world through the manipulations of language. "We knew for long the mansion's look/ And what we said of it became/ A part of what it is."

Stevens pauses in his meditation. The pause seems to give birth to a new feeling—a change finally occurs when the mind swerves away from its dejection to a reconciling thought in the last two lines. While the poet's vision will seem irrelevant and "run down" to the children, it will also be one with "A tatter of shadows peaked to white,/ Smeared with the gold of the opulent sun." That is, they will feel intuitively some of the vitality of the dead poet's vision. They will not intellectually understand the world of the past (it will be a "shadow" to them), but some of the remnants of the past will seem "smeared with the gold of the opulent sun" and consequently reveal the vitalistic imagination of the dead poet.

In "The Course of a Particular" (1951) Stevens presents a bleak winter landscape. The speaker in this matter-of-fact meditation does not appear to be much concerned with the "nothingness of winter." In fact, the speaker seems to be intellectually aware of the sense of loss but to remain emotionally tranquil, as if he had become accustomed to it. While the nothingness of the winter landscape becomes a "little less" because the poet can accept it more each day, he still feels he should try to humanize the sense of loss. He tries and then pauses. The attempt is half-hearted—"there is a resistance involved."

The humanizing metaphor of the crying leaves does not make the scene more human or more real to him. He tries to imagine harshness and the human responses to it, but the attempt does not work. Stevens discovers here that he cannot rewrite Percy Bysshe Shelley's "Ode to the West Wind" in the 1950's. All he feels is a dull monotonous winter scene; he cannot despair over a cold, inanimate universe. In "Sunday Morning" the separation of the self from nature was the cause for alienation, but now Stevens simply takes the separation for granted. He cannot pretend to be part of nature, even for a moment; if he says he is part of nature he immediately feels "resistance." He can no longer make the effort. Instead of attempting ennobling interchange of the imagination and reality, he concentrates on the particulars of reality before him. Winter is merely winter, wind-blown trees, snow, and ice.

In the final two stanzas the poet tries to transform the scene, but the cry of the leaves has no supernatural ("divine") significance, nor mythic ("puffed out heroes") significance, nor human significance. The "crying" leaves are simply leaves being blown by the wind; they do not transcend their phenomenological meaning. To imagine them crying is unsatisfactory. Finally, the poet asserts that the cry is simply the shrill winter wind and concerns no one at all. The poet has accepted the nothingness of modern life; the cry of the leaves does not symbolize a sense of loss but is simply another detail of reality.

The sense of loss in "Farewell Without a Guitar" (1954) is subdued. In lesser hands, this poem would have quickly degenerated into sentimental melancholy or nostalgia. Yet Stevens, with his few spare images, evokes a genuine feeling; like Hemingway, he expresses the most elemental emotions by cutting language to the bone. To do otherwise would be to luxuriate in an excess of emotion.

In "Farewell Without a Guitar," he suggests that things have come to their natural finale. While there is a sense of loss, there is also a sense of completion and fulfillment implicit in the meditation. The poem is so titled because Stevens' farewell is not accompanied by the music of lush poetry. Loss (and acceptance of it) is evoked without gaudy imaginative embellishment.

The paradise of spring yields to the autumnal terminal—youth to death, gaudy exuberance to spare imagism, celebration to farewell. Autumn is described as "The thousand leaved red," suggesting its beauty and naturalness, not the desolation of bare trees and cold, lifeless days. "Thunder of light" in the second stanza presages the storm of the third stanza and suggests that this storm is a virile one, one of power, not enervation. The oxymoronic metaphor might also suggest a heightened consciousness of reality, a consciousness that occurs when one comes to the end of life. The riderless horse is an apt image for the symbolic death of the man of imagination, the end of the poet's career. Stevens had previously symbolized the romantic poet, or the man of imagination, as "a youth, a lover with phosphorescent hair,/ Dressed poorly, arrogant of his streaming forces," who madly passes by on his horse the literal-minded Mrs. Alfred Uruguay ("Her no and no made yes impossible") on her slow donkey.

There will be no more imaginative excursions now. Only memories and past acts of the mind remain. Yet this activity of the mind and the memory of the past sensory contact with reality ("The blows and buffets of fresh senses/ Of the rider that was") now seem to form "a final construction"–a kind of spot of time that serves as the only immortality one can know. Sensuous reality in the present is heightened by this "construction"–a construction created out of the interchange of past sensuous reality ("male reality"), the imagination ("that other"), and the instinct for affirmation of the romantic poet ("her desire").

The autumnal sense of loss, rooted in Stevens' realization that he has come to the end of his career, is really transformed into an acceptance of loss, the celebration of his own farewell; it is reminiscent of Keats's "To Autumn." Reality is viewed in its most sensuous aspects, and affirmed. Reality had also been accepted in "The Course of a Particular," but it hardly appeared positive there. In contrast, in Stevens' final poems, mere existence ("mere being" or a life of process) is accepted and found affirmative.

Stevens differs from most twentieth century poets in his romantic faith in the power of the imagination to affirm mundane reality, or at least to make it palatable. He sees the imagination as the source of man's salvation in a godless world. Tough-minded and skeptical, he is not the kind of Romantic abhorred by T. E. Hulme, Ezra Pound, and the Imagists. He is not a visionary Romantic in pursuit of transcendent realms; he believes that the modern poet can reside only in the everyday world.

In his book of essays *The Necessary Angel* (1951), he states that the poet must avoid "the hieratic" and must "move in the direction of the credible." Without completely immersing himself in a sordid everyday world or escaping to an ideal world, the twentieth century romantic strives for the necessary balance between the imagination and reality. In his Preface to William Carlos Williams' *Collected Poems, 1921-1931*, reprinted in *Opus Posthumous* (1957), Stevens gives the best description of the "romantic poet nowadays": "he is the hermit who dwells alone with the sun and moon, but insists on taking a rotten newspaper."

Other literary forms · Wallace Stevens' significant achievement is in his poetry, but he did write several experimental one-act verse plays, a number of essays on poetry, and numerous letters and journal notes which contain perceptive comments on his work. In 1916 he published in the magazine

Poetry his first one-act verse play, *Three Travelers Watch a Sunrise*, for which he received a special prize from *Poetry;* in 1920 the play was performed at the Provincetown Playhouse in New York. A second verse play, *Carlos Among the Candles*, was staged in New York in 1917 and later published, again in *Poetry*. A third play, *Bowl, Cat, and Broomstick*, was produced at the Neighborhood Playhouse in New York in the same year but was never published during the poet's life. Between 1942 and 1951 he gave a series of lectures on poetry at Princeton and other universities, and these were collected in *The Necessary Angel: Essays on Reality and the Imagination* (1951). Later essays, as well as a number of uncollected poems and plays, appeared in *Opus Posthumous* (1957). The poet wrote excellent letters, and his daughter, Holly Stevens, collected and edited the best of them in *Letters of Wallace Stevens* (1966). In *Souvenirs and Prophecies: The Young Wallace Stevens* (1977) she presented important entries from the poet's journal (1898-1914). Focusing upon the relationship between the imagination and reality, Stevens' canon is highly unified; the prose and the plays help illuminate the difficult poetry.

Select works other than poetry

DRAMA: *Three Travelers Watch a Sunrise*, pb. 1916; *Carlos Among the Candles*, pr. 1917; *Bowl, Cat, and Broomstick*, pr. 1917.

NONFICTION: *The Necessary Angel: Essays on Reality and the Imagination*, 1951; *Letters of Wallace Stevens*, 1966; *Souvenirs and Prophecies: The Young Wallace Stevens*, 1977.

MISCELLANEOUS: *Opus Posthumous*, 1957 (Samuel French Morse, editor).

Allan Chavkin

Bibliography · Biographical information may be found in Holly Stevens, *Souvenirs and Prophecies: The Young Wallace Stevens*, 1977. Extensive critical resources exist in books and periodicals. Most notable among critical books are James Baird, *The Dome and the Rock: Structure in the Poetry of Wallace Stevens*, 1968; Milton J. Bates, *Wallace Stevens: A Mythology of Self,* 1985; Lucy Beckett, *Wallace Stevens*, 1974; Michel Benamou, *Wallace Stevens and the Symbolist Imagination*, 1972; Richard Allen Blessing, *Wallace Stevens' "Whole Harmonium,"* 1970; Harold Bloom, *Wallace Stevens: The Poems of Our Climate*, 1977; Marie Borroff, ed., *Wallace Stevens: A Collection of Critical Essays*, 1963; Peter Brazeau, *Parts of a World: Wallace Stevens Remembered,* 1983; Merle E. Brown, *Wallace Stevens: The Poem as Act*, 1970; William Burney, *Wallace Stevens*, 1968; Robert Buttel and Frank Doggett, eds., *Wallace Stevens: A Celebration*, 1980; Frank Doggett, *Stevens' Poetry of Thought*,

1966; Doggett, *Wallace Stevens: The Making of the Poem*, 1980; Irvin Ehren-preis, ed., *Wallace Stevens: A Critical Anthology*, 1973; Frank Kermode, *Wallace Stevens*, 1960; Edward Kessler, *Images of Wallace Stevens*, 1972; David M. LaGuardia, *Advance on Chaos: The Sanctifying Imagination of Wallace Stevens*, 1983; A. Walton Litz, *Introspective Voyager: The Poetic Development of Wallace Stevens*, 1972; James Longenback, *Wallace Stevens: The Plain Sense of Things*, 1991; Peter L. McNarmara, ed., *Critics on Wallace Stevens*, 1972; Adalaide Kirby Morris, *Wallace Stevens: Imagination and Faith*, 1974; Samuel French Morse, *Wallace Stevens: Poetry as Life*, 1970; Robert Pack, *Wallace Stevens: An Approach to His Poetry and Thought*, 1958; Alan Perlis, *Wallace Stevens: A World of Transforming Shapes*, 1976; Joan Richardson, *Wallace Stevens: The Early Years*, 1986; Joseph N. Riddel, *The Clairvoyant Eye: The Poetry and Poetics of Wallace Stevens*, 1981; Ronald Sukenick, *Wallace Stevens: Musing the Obscure*, 1967; Helen Vendler, *Wallace Stevens*, 1986; and Susan B. Weston, *Wallace Stevens: An Introduction to the Poetry*, 1977.

ALFRED, LORD TENNYSON

Born: Somersby, England; August 6, 1809
Died: Near Haslemere, England; October 6, 1892

Poetry · *Poems, Chiefly Lyrical,* 1830 · *Poems,* 1832 (imprinted 1833) · *Poems,* 1842 · *The Princess,* 1847 · *In Memoriam,* 1850 · *Maud and Other Poems,* 1855 · *Idylls of the King,* 1859-1885 · *Enoch Arden and Other Poems,* 1864 · *The Holy Grail and Other Poems,* 1869 (imprinted 1870) · *Gareth and Lynette,* 1872 · *The Lover's Tale,* 1879 · *Ballads and Other Poems,* 1880 · *Tiresias and Other Poems,* 1885 · *Locksley Hall Sixty Years After, Etc.,* 1886 · *Demeter and Other Poems,* 1889 · *The Death of Œnone and Other Poems,* 1892

Achievements · During his lifetime Alfred, Lord Tennyson attracted a popular following seldom achieved by any poet in any age. While his first four volumes received little favorable attention, the publication of *In Memoriam* in 1850 brought him overnight fame, and his subsequent works were all best-sellers. His Victorian contemporaries liked all forms of his poetry: over sixty thousand copies of *In Memoriam* were sold in the first few months after publication; ten thousand copies of the Arthurian tales entitled *Idylls of the King* sold in the first week after publication in 1859, and the remainder of the first edition shortly thereafter; and the first edition, sixty thousand copies, of his volume of narrative poems and lyrics, *Enoch Arden and Other Poems* (1864) sold out shortly after it was published. His popularity continued until his death; twenty thousand copies of *Demeter and Other Poems* (1889) were sold before publication. Readers found in Tennyson's poetry excitement, sentiment, and moral solace; his works were a lighthouse in a stormy sea of social and moral uncertainty. Many turned to Tennyson as a teacher, seeing in his works a wisdom not available in churches, schools, or public institutions.

Perhaps because he was so popular in his own day, Tennyson became the primary target for scores of critics of the two generations that followed. Critics of the post-World War I era condemned Tennyson for pandering to public demands that poetry be "uplifting," that it contain a moral for public consumption, and that it avoid controversial subjects. During the years between the World Wars, it became fashionable to speak of "the two Tennysons"; critics condemned the public poet who preached jingoism and offered moral platitudes in works such as *Maud* and *Idylls of the King,* yet found much of value in the private poet, a morbid, introverted person

whose achievement lay in his lyrics, with their private symbolism developed to express personal anxieties and frustrations.

Critics writing since World War II have generally been more appreciative of the entire canon of Tennyson's poetry. Following the lead of Sir Charles Tennyson, whose sympathetic yet scholarly biography of his grandfather rekindled interest in Tennyson as a serious poet both in his public and private roles, scholars have reexamined *In Memoriam, Idylls of the King, The Princess,* and *Maud* and found them to be works of considerable artistic merit. "Ulysses" is regarded as a significant short poem; *Idylls of the King* has been called one of the truly great long poems of the language; and *In Memoriam* is considered one of the world's great elegies.

Biography · Alfred Tennyson was born at Somersby in the Lincolnshire district of England on August 6, 1809, the fourth of twelve children. His father, the Reverend George Tennyson, was a brooding, melancholic man, whose lifelong bitterness—inspired by his having been disinherited in favor of a younger brother—manifested itself in his behavior toward his family. Alfred was spared much of his father's wrath, however, because George Tennyson apparently recognized his fourth son's special brilliance and took pains to tutor him in history, science, and literature. Tennyson spent five years at Louth Grammar School (1815-1820), then returned home to continue his studies under his father's personal guidance.

Tennyson began writing poetry at an early age; at eight he was imitating James Thomson, at twelve he was writing romances in the manner of Sir Walter Scott. In 1827, the year he entered Trinity College, Cambridge, he and his brother Charles published *Poems by Two Brothers*.

At Cambridge, Tennyson was an undisciplined student. He was well received by his fellow students, however, and in 1829 he was elected a member of the Apostles, a club devoted to intellectual inquiry. Through this association he met Arthur Henry Hallam, who was to figure prominently in his life. In 1829, Tennyson won the Chancellor's medal for his poem "Timbuctoo," and in 1830 he published *Poems, Chiefly Lyrical*. In March 1831, George Tennyson died, and shortly afterwards Tennyson left Cambridge without a degree.

Tennyson's 1832 volume, *Poems*, like his earlier one, was treated rather roughly by reviewers. Their comments, coupled with the death of Hallam in 1833, caused him to avoid publication for ten years. Hallam's death was an especially severe blow to Tennyson. Hallam had been engaged to Tennyson's sister, and the two men had become very close friends. The poet suffered prolonged fits of depression after receiving the news of Hallam's death. Eventually, however, he was able to transform his grief into a series of lyrics which he published in 1850, entitling the elegy *In Memoriam A. H. H.*

During the years between Hallam's death and the publication of *In Memoriam*, Tennyson was far from inactive. He lived with his mother and other members of his family, assisting in their moves from Somersby to Tunbridge Wells, then to Boxley. During these years he spent time in London, Cornwall, Ireland, and Switzerland, gathering material for his poems. In 1834, he fell in love with Rosa Baring, and when that relationship cooled, he lighted upon Emily Sellwood, whose sister had married his brother Charles. Tennyson had no real means of supporting a family at that time, so he was forced to wait fourteen years to marry. He returned to publishing in 1842, issuing a two-volume set entitled simply *Poems;* it contained both new materials and revisions of previously published poems. In 1847, he published *The Princess,* a long narrative exploring the roles of men and women in modern society.

Months after *In Memoriam* appeared in May 1850, Tennyson's fortunes rose meteorically. In June of that year he married Emily Sellwood. In November, he was named poet laureate, succeeding the recently deceased Wordsworth. During his forty-two years as laureate, he wrote numerous poems commemorating various public events, among them some of his more famous works, including "Ode on the Death of the Duke of Wellington" (1852) and "The Charge of the Light Brigade" (1854). He came to be lionized by the British public, and even the Royal Family made numerous personal requests for him to commemorate events of importance.

The decade of the 1850's was a productive and important one. In 1855 Tennyson published *Maud and Other Poems;* in 1859 he brought out a volume containing the first four Arthurian stories that would be joined by eight others during the next twenty-five years to form *Idylls of the King.*

The Tennysons' first child was stillborn, but in 1852 Hallam Tennyson was born. The family moved to Farringford on the Isle of Wight in 1853. The following year a second son, Lionel, was born.

The remainder of Tennyson's life can be characterized as personally stable but artistically tumultuous. During the 1860's, 1870's, and 1880's, several collections of his poems were issued. The poet added eight new volumes to his growing list of works. Beginning in the mid-1870's, Tennyson turned to drama, writing several successful plays and taking great interest in the details of their production. In 1886 his son Lionel died while returning from India. His elder son, Hallam, remained with the poet, serving as a kind of secretary and executor. In the early months of 1892, Tennyson's health began to fail, and he died in bed in October of that year, his hand resting on a volume of Shakespeare.

Analysis · Always praised for his ability to create musical lyrics, Tennyson is now recognized as a master of a number of verse forms and a thinker who brooded deeply over the problems of his age, attempting to capture these problems and deal with them in his poetry. He is also credited with being one of the few poets whose works demonstrate a real assimilation of the poetic tradition that preceded him. His poems reflect an insight into the crises of his own age, as well as an appreciation of problems that have faced all men, especially the problems of death, loss, and nostalgic yearning for a more stable world.

Early works such as "The Palace of Art" and "The Two Voices" are clear examples of the kind of poem for which Tennyson traditionally has been acclaimed. In each, the poet presents a sensitive person who faces a crisis and is forced to choose between radical alternatives. In "The Palace of Art," the speaker must choose between self-indulgence in a world of artistic beauty and commitment to a life of service; in "The Two Voices," the speaker's choice is either to escape the harsh realities of an oppressive world through suicide, or to continue living with only the faintest glimmer of hope. Tennyson's highly regarded classical poem "The Lotos-Eaters" explores the same themes. For his subject, the poet drew on the incident in the *Odyssey* (c. 800 B.C.) in which Odysseus' men disembark in the paradisiacal land of the lotus-eaters and fall under the enchantment of the lotus fruit. The poem is also influenced by Edmund Spenser's *The Faerie Queene* (1590, 1596), where the figure of Despair argues for the same kind of languid repose that the mariners sing of in "The Lotos-Eaters." Tennyson uses all his powers of description and his special command of the language to select words and phrases whose tonal qualities and connotative meanings strongly suggest the sense of repose and stasis. The musical quality of the poem is enhanced by the meter, the effectiveness of caesura and enjambment, and the varying linelengths used throughout, especially the extensive use of long lines broken by numerous caesuras near the end of the lyric. "The Lotos-Eaters," a combination of narrative and choric song, describes the arrival of the mariners in a land that appears to be perpetually "afternoon," where "all things always seemed the same." Here the "wild-eyed melancholy Lotos-eaters" bring to the travelers the food that will dull their desire to continue on to Ithaca. Having partaken of the fruit of the lotus, the mariners begin to think of their homeland as merely a dream, too distant a goal, no longer worth striving for. As they lie on the beach, one suggests that they "return no more," and the others quickly take up the chant; their choric song, in eight sections, makes up the remainder of the poem. In the song, the mariners review the many hardships they have faced and the many more that await them if they continue their journey. About them they see that "all things have rest"; they ask "Why should we toil alone?" Rather than continue, they beg to be given "long rest or death, dark death, or dreamful ease." The poem's final statement is an exhortation to "rest, ye brother mariners, we will not wander more." It is unwise, however, to assume that the mariners' decision to opt for "dreamful ease" over a life of "toil" is Tennyson's own position. Rather, "The Lotos-Eaters" explores, from only one perspective, the dilemma of commitment versus retreat. The poet treats the same theme in many other poems in which the speaker takes a decidedly different view.

Tennyson's complex treatment of this theme of commitment to ideals can be seen in one of his most famous shorter works, "Ulysses." This poem also exemplifies numerous other characteristics common to much of Tennyson's poetry, particularly his use of irony. Indeed, in "Ulysses" the reader can see the glimmerings of the essentially ironic poetic form that emerged during the nineteenth century, made popular by Robert Browning—the dramatic monologue. "Ulysses" is a poem inspired by Tennyson's personal experiences; yet in the poem Tennyson transforms his experiences into a work of art that speaks of an issue that concerns all men. In "Ulysses," Tennyson is both typically Victorian and still a poet for all times. The call to action at the end of the poem and the emphasis on each man's "work" was no doubt appealing to the poet's contemporaries. In the twentieth century, under the scrutiny of critics more aware of the subtleties of Tennyson's ironic vision, the poem provides pleasure for its refusal to yield to a simplistic reading.

In "Ulysses" the reader discovers how Tennyson uses the poetic tradition, especially the legacy of classical and Renaissance poets. Like "The Lotos-Eaters," "Ulysses" is based in part on Homer's *Odyssey*. The classical epic is not the only source, however, for by the poet's own admission the poem owes much to the portrait of Ulysses in Dante's *Inferno*. In Dante's poem, Ulysses is found in hell, condemned as a deceiver for having led his men away from Ithaca in search of vain glories. That Tennyson chose to draw his own hero from sources that present such radically different views of Ulysses suggests that he wanted to create an ironic tension in his own work. In the *Inferno*, Ulysses tells Dante that, unable to remain at home, he was compelled by wanderlust to set forth in search of new adventures. The spirit of Homer's unconquerable quester is captured in Tennyson's poem, but Dante's condemned spirit is always there to remind the reader that there may be dangers in pursuing the ideal at the expense of other considerations.

When one first reads "Ulysses" one can easily be swept along by the apparent vigor of the hero's argument. His description of life in his native Ithaca, where he is "matched with an aged wife," forced to "meet and dole/ Unequal laws" in a land whose people he regards as "savage," makes it easy for the reader to understand Ulysses' wish to return to a life of seafaring adventure. Among these people Ulysses is not appreciated for the adventures that have caused him to "become a name" throughout the Mediterranean world. His experiences have become absorbed into the very fiber of his being; he reflects that "I am a part of all that I have met." Small wonder that the confines of his island home seem to imprison him! He realizes that his many exploits are only doorways to future experiences, an "arch" beyond which "gleams/ That untravelled world" he has yet to see. At home he finds himself becoming "dull," like a weapon left to "rust unburnished."

Realizing that he can no longer be happy as ruler in such a land, Ulysses declares that he will leave his "sceptre and the isle" to his son Telemachus, a man more capable and more patient than his father when operating in the "sphere/ Of common duties." Ulysses recognizes that he and his son are different—"He works his work, I mine"—and it is best for all if each man follow his own destiny. This difference is easy for the modern reader to accept, as it suggests a truism about human nature that those imbued with the Romantic desire for self-fulfillment find immediately palatable.

Having passed on his kingship to his son, Ulysses turns to the companions who have "toiled, and wrought, and thought" with him, and calls them to one last voyage. As night draws near, he urges them to embark once more in the ship that will carry them to lands where "some work of noble note, may yet be done." "'Tis not too late," he exhorts them, "to seek a newer world." His purpose is to "sail beyond the sunset" until he dies. The unextinguishable spirit of adventure, burning still in the heart of this old warrior, is summed up best in the closing lines, where he proclaims to those who accompany him that, although they are no longer young, they can still be men of "heroic hearts," "strong in will,/ To strive, to seek, to find, and not to yield."

Because the poem was composed shortly after the death of Tennyson's friend Arthur Henry Hallam, some critics have seen "Ulysses" as a statement of the poet's personal commitment to continue living and writing even after suffering a great personal tragedy that seemed to have robbed life of its meaning. Looking at himself as an old man who had been deprived of the spark of adventure and facing a fast-approaching death of his creative self, Tennyson chose to continue living and working. Only through an active commitment to life itself could he hope one day to see "the great Achilles," here meant to represent Hallam. Such a biographical interpretation is supported by Tennyson's comment, preserved in Hallam Tennyson's *Alfred, Lord Tennyson: A Memoir*, that "Ulysses" expressed his "feeling about the need of going forward, and braving the struggle of life" after Hallam's death.

The biographical interpretation can be supported in part by a close reading of the text. The resounding note of optimism, at least on the surface of the poem, is apparent. All of the images associated with life on the isle of Ithaca suggest dullness, a kind of death-in-life. Tennyson displays his mastery of the single line in his withering description of the people of Ithaca; ten monosyllables capture the essence of those whom Ulysses has come to despise: they "hoard, and sleep, and feed, and know not me." Here is avarice, indolence, a suggestion of animal satisfaction with physical ease, and, most important, a lack of appreciation for the man who has

raised himself from the multitude and won fame through bravery, cleverness, and other distinctly human qualities. Similarly, Tennyson has Ulysses
describe the life of wandering and the yearning for further adventures
in most appealing terms, both sensual and intellectual. Ulysses' is a "hungry heart"; he wishes to "drink/ Life to the less," having previously
"drunk delight of battle with my peers." In a single phrase borrowed from
Homer, Tennyson's Ulysses recalls the great struggle in which he first won
fame, far away from home on the "ringing plains of windy Troy." The
excitement of battle serves as a counterpoint to the dullness of life in
Ithaca. The hero's excitement is captured in his final exhortation, in which
the poet once again resorts to a line of monosyllables that bombard the
reader in staccato fashion: "To strive, to seek, to find, and not to yield."
Active verbs call the mariners to action and the reader to acceptance of the
hero's decision.

Despite the stirring note of optimism in this final line, however, the
poem cannot be accepted simply as another example of strident Victorian
rhetoric aimed at encouraging one to have faith in oneself and one's God
and press on in the face of uncertainties. In fact, when the uncertainties in
the poem are considered carefully, the reader begins to see another side of
the aged hero. Ulysses is certain of his boredom with having to govern the
"savage race" and of the resentment he harbors toward them because they
fail to honor him for his past exploits. What Ulysses will substitute for his
present life, and what good he will accomplish in leaving Ithaca, is not at
all clear. Some notable work "may yet be done," but he cannot be certain
that his new wanderings will lead to anything but death: "It may be that
the gulfs will wash us down," he cautions. Of course, he and his mariners
may "touch the Happy Isles" where they will be reunited with "the great
Achilles," but the chance of such a reunion is at best tenuous. In fact, such
a desire implies a kind of death wish, since Achilles has departed this life
for Elysium.

One may sympathize with Ulysses, seeing that his present life is unful-
filling, and agree that pursuing tenuous goals is better than stagnating. At
this point, though, one must recall that the dreary condition on Ithaca is
not related by the poet as factual, but rather is described by Ulysses
himself. Since the poem is dramatic in nature, only the hero's own word
provides a touchstone for judging things as they really are, and it is possible
that Ulysses' view is jaundiced. One must consider, too, that Tennyson
draws not only from Homer but also from Dante for his portrait of Ulysses;
the Dantean quality of the hero cannot be overlooked, and in the *Inferno*
Ulysses is found in hell, having led his mariners to their doom. In the
version of the *Inferno* that Tennyson probably read, that by H. F. Cary

(1805), Ulysses tells Dante that no familial feelings could overcome the "zeal" he had to explore the world, a feeling that he calls "man's evil and his virtue." Tennyson's Ulysses may also be a victim of this curse and blessing. Despite his pronounced enthusiasm for a life of heroic adventure, Ulysses may in fact merely be running away from his responsibilities. If the reader recalls from the *Odyssey* the hero's struggles to return to his wife and son, Ulysses' behavior in Tennyson's poem must appear a little suspect. The beloved and faithful Penelope is now scorned as an "aged wife." Telemachus, although praised for his sagacity and patience, is still not of the heroic mold.

A word of caution is in order here. In the past, critics have been quick to call Ulysses' description of his son a thinly disguised piece of sarcasm, but this reading smuggles twentieth century notions into a nineteenth century context. Words such as "blameless" and "decent" were not terms of disapprobation in the nineteenth century, nor would Tennyson have been denigrating Telemachus by pointing out that he worked best in the sphere of "common duties." In fact, in his other poetry and in the writings preserved in Hallam Tennyson's *Alfred, Lord Tennyson: A Memoir*, Tennyson clearly had great respect for men and women who served society at the expense of personal gratification. Precisely because the duties that Ulysses turns over to Telemachus are ones that Tennyson and his contemporaries considered important for the continuation of ordered society, Ulysses' decision to abdicate them makes his motives questionable. It is at least possible to see that behind the hero's rhetoric lies a clever scheme to convince his listeners, and the reader, that his actions are motivated by the highest intentions, when in fact he is abandoning a job he finds distasteful and difficult in order to pursue a life-style he finds more gratifying. Such a possibility makes it difficult to see Ulysses as a hero; rather, he appears to be an irresponsible villain for whom Tennyson and the critical reader can have little sympathy. That Tennyson would have held such a man in low regard is evident from his own remarks; as recorded in Hallam Tennyson's *Alfred, Lord Tennyson: A Memoir*, he once told a young aspirant to university life that a man "should embark on his career in the spirit of selfless and adventurous heroism and should develop his true self by not shirking responsibility."

In the light of this ambiguity, it is easy to construe Ulysses' real decision as an affirmation not of life but of death, and to see his desire to journey forth again as a kind of death-wish. Whether one adopts such a reading depends largely on the way one views the tone of the final segments of the poem, in which Ulysses states publicly his reasons for undertaking such a voyage. If this public harangue is merely a rhetorical pose intended to win over skeptical followers so that they will man the hero's ship on this futile journey, then "Ulysses" is a poem of deceit and despair, a warning to the reader of the hypnotic power of such rhetoric to sway listeners into a mood of naïve optimism. On the other hand, if one is convinced of the hero's sincerity in his call to strive, seek, find, and not yield, one cannot help considering "Ulysses" another of the many poems in which Tennyson offers hope and support to his fellow Victorians, tempering such optimism with the notion that one can never be absolutely certain whether the journey through life will lead to paradise or merely to death, adrift on an angry sea.

The dilemma may never be solved satisfactorily, for in "Ulysses," Tennyson is experimenting with a relatively new poetic form, the dramatic monologue, in which ambiguity and ironic distance are characteristic. Although "Ulysses" does not possess all the formal qualities of the dramatic monologue, it does contain the essentials. Situation and action are inferred only from the speech of the main character, and the reader's assessment of motives rests on his estimation of the character of the speaker. The hero's exhortation is intended not only to be heard by his fellow mariners but also to be overheard by the reader; one feels compelled to judge the merits of the hero's philosophy. What one brings to the poem—knowledge of the *Odyssey* or *The Divine Comedy*, or of Tennyson's life—may help to determine whether one should accept or reject Ulysses' call. In any case, the act of choosing demanded by the poem forces one to make a moral commitment of some kind. The need for making such judgments, and the complexities involved in making them, are matters which concern Tennyson in all of his poetry. The ambiguity of the poem is intentional, reflecting the dilemmas faced in the real world by Tennyson and his readers.

The same concerns that one finds in Tennyson's shorter compositions, such as "Ulysses," are also reflected in the poet's longer works. Tennyson wrote four long poems: *The Princess, In Memoriam, Maud,* and *Idylls of the King.* None of these is typical of traditional narrative poetry, and in several ways they anticipate the long poems of the twentieth century. All four are fragmented in some way; none tells a single story from a consistent perspective. *The Princess* is the most tightly constructed of Tennyson's long poems. In this medley a group of seven young men and women each create part of a tale about a Princess who has removed herself from the world of men to establish a college for women. Princess Ida and the Prince who comes to "rescue" her and win her love are the products not of a single creator but of seven, as each young person participating in the game adds to both story line and character development. As a result, the poem is actually two stories—that of the Princess whose tale is created by the young people, and that of the young people who are themselves very like the characters they create. Throughout the poem songs are interspersed to serve as counterpoint to the narrative and to highlight major themes.

Maud is also a medley. Here, however, the variation is in the verse form, and the fragmentary structure mirrors the nature of the hero, a man poised on the edge of disaster and dementia.

Idylls of the King, Tennyson's Arthurian poem, consists of twelve separate pieces tied together by the overarching structure provided by the legend itself—the rise and fall of Arthur and his Round Table. Within this framework individual idylls remain relatively self-contained units. The poet's examination of the downfall of a society that abandons its ideals is carried forward through an intricate patterning of repeated images and parallel scenes.

Tennyson's most fragmented long poem is the one for which he is best remembered and most praised. *In Memoriam* is a collection of more than 130 lyrics, composed by the poet over seventeen years and finally pieced together to record his reaction to the death of his dearest friend. Rather than being a continuous narrative, *In Memoriam* is a loosely assembled collage that, when read as a whole, reflects the varied emotions that one man experiences when prompted by the death of a loved one to face the reality of death and change in the world and the possibilities for life after death. Like "Ulysses," the poem is inspired by Tennyson's personal grief, yet it uses this personal experience as a touchstone for examining an issue that plagued Victorians: the ability to cling to faith in God and an afterlife in the face of the challenges of the new science.

The "I" of *In Memoriam* is not always to be identified with the poet himself; rather, as Tennyson himself said, the speaker is sometimes "the voice of the human race speaking thro' him [that is, the poet]." Nine years before Darwin published *Origin of Species*, Tennyson was questioning the value of the individual human life in the light of scientific discoveries proving that whole species of animals that once roamed the earth had long ago become extinct. In the much-anthologized middle section of *In Memoriam*, Tennyson's narrator observes of nature, "So careful of the type she seems,/ So careless of the single life," only to cry despairingly in the next lyric,

> "So careful of the type?" but no.
> From scarpéd cliff and quarried stone
> She cries, "A thousand types are gone:
> I care for nothing, all shall go."

Here is the "Nature, red in tooth and claw" that people in Tennyson's era, nurtured on faith in a benevolent God, found impossible to comprehend.

Tennyson sees his personal dilemma over the loss of Hallam and the larger problem involving the conflict between the biblical account of creation and scientific discoveries as essentially similar. The speaker of *In Memoriam* passes through several emotional stages: from grief and despair over his loss; to doubt, which presumes that all is not lost in death; to hope, based not solely on blind trust but also on "intuition," his sense that a higher Person exists to guide his life and the life of nature itself; to, finally, faith, an acceptance of the notion of immortality and permanence even in the face of changes in nature that the speaker cannot deny. In the poem, Tennyson's friend Hallam becomes a symbol of a "higher Race," a harbinger of a better life, one sent to earth ahead of his time to offer hope to all men that the changes and impermanences of life exhibit not chaos but rather a divine pattern of progress, a movement toward God himself. In terms that anticipate the twentieth century theologian and mystic, Pierre Teilhard de Chardin, Tennyson concludes his elegy with a tribute to his friend who appeared on earth "ere the times were ripe," and who now lives with the beneficent God who guides this process of evolution, "who ever lives and loves,/ One God, one law, one element,/ And one far-off divine event,/ To which the whole creation moves."

The note of optimism at the end of *In Memoriam* is achieved only after a great deal of agonizing doubt. In fact, T. S. Eliot believed that the strength of Tennyson's elegy lay not in its final affirmation of faith, but rather in the quality of its doubt. The fragmentary nature of the poem allows Tennyson to explore that doubt with much greater range and intensity than would a more typical narrative structure. For example, Section LX begins with two lines that refer directly to the speaker's grief over his lost friend: "He past; a soul of nobler tone:/ My spirit loved and loves him yet." The remaining fourteen lines, however, are an extended simile, in which the speaker compares his grief to the feelings of a young girl for a boy who is above her in social status. The girl's "heart is set/ On one whose rank exceeds her own." Seeing the young man "mixing with his proper sphere," and recognizing "the baseness of her lot," the girl experiences jealousy, without knowing what she should be jealous of, and envy of those who are fortunate enough to be near her beloved. She goes about her life in the "little village" that "looks forlorn" to her, feeling that her days are "narrow" as she performs her common household chores in "that dark house where she was born." From her friends she receives no pity (they "tease her" daily), and she is left alone at night to realize the impossibility of ever achieving the union she desires: "How vain am I," she weeps, "How should he love a thing so low?"

The link to the larger themes of the poem, the speaker's grief over the loss of his friend, is found most obviously in the lyric's opening lines. Once that link is established, the parallels between the feelings of the speaker and the young girl he describes in the remaining lines become apparent at numerous points. The different "spheres" in which the girl and her beloved live represent the difference the speaker sees between himself and his friend, whom he calls elsewhere the "herald of a higher race." The "little village" is the speaker's world, into which the dead friend will no longer come. The most important image used to link this lyric with the other sections of *In Memoriam* is the "dark house" in which the girl must pass her days. That image, first appearing in Section VII when the speaker stands before his friend's house in London shortly after learning that his friend has died, recurs in several other sections and always suggests the loss the speaker feels at his friend's death.

Section LX, then, is typical of many lyrics that Tennyson pieced together to form *In Memoriam*. In it, the speaker's grief, inexpressible in its magnitude, is made realizable by comparison with feelings that immediately touch the reader. One develops a sense of the speaker's loss, and his friend's greatness, through the process of empathetic association with more familiar feelings of loss and pain experienced in the sphere of everyday life. Similarly, when the speaker begins to understand that the loss of his friend should not be cause for despair, but rather for joy, that joy is transmitted to the reader by associating the speaker's feelings with traditional symbols of happiness–the three Christmas seasons that form important structural links within *In Memoriam* and the wedding celebration that closes the poem. The celebration of the wedding is a most appropriate close for this poem: the union of two lives to form a single unit from which new life will spring mirrors man's ultimate union with God, "To which the whole creation moves."

Other literary forms · Although Alfred, Lord Tennyson is best known today for his poetry, he wrote several dramatic works that were popular in his own day. His first play, *Queen Mary*, was published in 1875. From that time until his death he continued writing verse dramas: *Harold* (1876), *The Falcon* (1879), *The Cup* (1881), *Becket* (written in 1879, published in 1884), and *The Foresters* (1892). Most of these were staged very successfully. The renowned producer and actor Henry Irving starred opposite Ellen Terry in *The Cup*, which ran for more than 130 nights. Irving also produced *Becket* several times after Tennyson's death, achieving success in both England

and America. Generally speaking, however, his contemporaries' judgment that Tennyson was a greater poet than a dramatist has been confirmed by modern critics. Tennyson's only prose composition was also a play, *The Promise of May* (1882); it was not well received by theatergoers. Although he published no criticism in his lifetime, Tennyson, like most of his contemporaries, expressed his critical opinions of his own and others' works in his conversations and in numerous letters. Hallam Tennyson's two-volume *Alfred, Lord Tennyson: A Memoir* (1897) of his father prints many of these documents, and preserves as well many of Tennyson's conversations and remarks about literature.

Select works other than poetry

DRAMA: *Queen Mary*, pb. 1875; *Harold*, pb. 1876; *Becket*, wr. 1879, pb. 1884; *The Falcon*, pr. 1879 (one act); *The Cup*, pr. 1881; *The Foresters*, wr. 1881, pr., pb. 1892; *The Promise of May*, pr. 1882; *The Devil and the Lady*, pb. 1930 (unfinished).

NONFICTION: *The Letters of Alfred Lord Tennyson: Volume 1, 1821-1850*, 1981 (Cecil Y. Lang and Edgar F. Shannon, editors).

MISCELLANEOUS: *The Works of Tennyson*, 1907-1908 (9 volumes; Hallam, Lord Tennyson, editor).

Laurence W. Mazzeno

Bibliography · Biographies include Hallam, Lord Tennyson, *Alfred, Lord Tennyson: A Memoir*, 2 vols., 1897; Sir Charles Tennyson, *Alfred Tennyson*, 1949; Christopher Ricks, *Tennyson*, 1972; and Robert B. Martin, *Tennyson: The Unquiet Heart*, 1980. Criticism includes Paull F. Baum, *Tennyson Sixty Years After*, 1948; John Killham, ed., *Critical Essays on the Poetry of Tennyson*, 1960; Jerome H. Buckley, *Tennyson: The Growth of a Poet*, 1960; Ralph W. Rader, *Tennyson's Maude: The Biographical Genesis*, 1963; Clyde de L. Ryals, *Theme and Symbol in Tennyson's Poems to 1850*, 1964; George O. Marshall, *A Tennyson Handbook*, 1964; J. Philip Eggers, *King Arthur's Laureate*, 1971; John R. Reed, *Perception and Design in Tennyson's Idylls of the King*, 1971; Alan Sinfield, *The Language of Tennyson's "In Memoriam,"* 1971; John D. Rosenberg, *The Fall of Camelot*, 1973; D. J. Palmer, ed., *Tennyson*, 1975; W. David Shaw, *Tennyson's Style*, 1976; A. Dwight Culler, *The Poetry of Tennyson*, 1977; Alistair W. Thomson, *The Poetry of Tennyson*, 1986; and Herbert F. Tucker, *Tennyson and the Doom of Romanticism*, 1988.

DYLAN THOMAS

Born: Swansea, Wales; October 27, 1914
Died: New York, New York; November 9, 1953

Poetry · *Eighteen Poems*, 1934 · *Twenty-five Poems*, 1936 · *The Map of Love*, 1939 · *New Poems*, 1943 · *Deaths and Entrances*, 1946 · *Twenty-six Poems*, 1950 · *In Country Sleep*, 1952 · *Collected Poems, 1934-1952*, 1952 · *The Poems of Dylan Thomas*, 1971 (Daniel Jones, editor)

Achievements · Whatever else may be said about Dylan Thomas' poetry, it had the qualities needed to bring its author to the attention of the English-speaking world by the time he was twenty-two years old. Whether it was simply his tone, his subject matter, or a bit of both, Thomas' poems elicited a marked response in readers caught in a fierce economic depression. In any immediate sense, the poems were not optimistic; they sang of no golden age in the offing. Instead, mildly outrageous in subject matter and language, defiant of the ugly processes of life and death, and apparently even more defiant of conventional poetic forms, they seemed to project a knowledge of the inner workings of the universe denied to other mortals but toughly shared. Small wonder, then, that Thomas gained a hearing as poet and seer in the literary world and among general readers. While the first impact of *18 Poems* was slight, *Twenty-five Poems* established Thomas as a writer to be reckoned with. The book generated several critical questions. Did the world have a new John Keats on its hands, a

poet who came almost at once to literary maturity and whose works would be permanent; or was Thomas simply a minor poet who had struck a rich topical vein which would soon be exhausted; or was he, worst of all, as seemed to some most likely, a mere wordmonger whose obscure rantings would soon become mere curiosities, interesting, if at all, only to literary historians? Nearly five decades after *18 Poems*, Thomas has been firmly established as a true poet, but discussion of the ultimate value of his poetry continues. What is clear is that he had a strong hold on the public imagination for roughly two decades and, during that time, helped to shape the idea of what poetry is or can aspire to be.

Biography · Dylan Marlais Thomas is firmly identified in many minds as the Welsh poet par excellence, as the voice of modern Wales speaking in the bardic tradition of *The Mabinogion* (c. twelfth and thirteenth centuries) and in the Renaissance tradition of William Shakespeare's mystic, Owen Glendower. In fact, Thomas' poetry is scarcely Welsh at all. G. S. Fraser, in his excellent critical biography, *Dylan Thomas* (1965), points out that Thomas loved Wales without being especially Welsh. Jacob Korg remarked in his biography, *Dylan Thomas* (1965), that Thomas' life and times have only a limited relevance to his poetry, and what influence there is, is transformed into a personal inner world. "Fern Hill," "Over Sir John's Hill," and a few other poems are set in the countryside and seashore that Thomas knew, and "Hold Hand, These Ancient Minutes in the Cuckoo's Month" speaks accurately of the brutality of the Welsh winter and spring, but rarely does Thomas' poetry treat in any serious way either the real or mythical history and countryside of Wales, the realities of the depressed industrial Wales he knew as an adolescent, or the postwar Wales he returned to after the horrors of the London bombing or the triumph of the American tours. The rough and intimate life of the family and village he treats so graphically in other genres seems to lie outside his idea of poetic fitness.

Thomas was born and reared in Swansea, in southern Wales, east by a few miles from Carmarthen and its environs, Fern Hill and Laugharne, which were to play such an important part in his personal life. Swansea, urban and industrial, contrasts strongly with the idyllic Carmarthenshire. Thomas' immediate family consisted of his father, David John Thomas; his mother, Florence Thomas (née Williams); and an older sister, Nancy. He was liberally supplied with aunts, uncles, and cousins of all sorts, and shared the usual family closeness of the Welsh, though his wife, Caitlin, recorded in *Leftover Life to Kill* (1957) that he tried hard but unsuccessfully to free himself from its puritanical background.

Thomas' paternal grandfather was, among a number of other vocations, a poet, not especially distinguished, who took for himself the bardic name "Gwilym Marles." "Gwilym" is William and "Marles" was taken from the Welsh stream Marlais, which, in its proper spelling, later became Thomas' middle name. Thomas' father had poetic ambitions of his own and was determined that his son should have his chance to become a poet. Disappointed in his hope for a distinguished career in education, he had settled with some lasting bitterness for a schoolmastership in the south of Wales. Thomas' poem "Do Not Go Gentle into That Good Night" furnishes some measure of his bitterness at his father's lingering death from cancer, and of the son's reciprocation of the father's love.

Thomas' school days were unusual only in that he began to write poetry early. His close friend in grammar school was Daniel Jones, who was later to edit *The Poems of Dylan Thomas.* They wrote more than two hundred poems together, each contributing alternate lines–Jones odd, Thomas even.

Thomas left school in 1931 and worked until 1932 for the *South Wales Daily Post.* The period of his most intense activity as a poet had already begun in 1930 and was to extend to 1934. Daniel Jones calculated that during this period Thomas' output was four times greater than that of the last nineteen years of his life. Ralph Maud has edited the four so-called "Buffalo Notebooks," which contain working drafts of Thomas' poems from 1930 to August, 1933–except for the period of July, 1932, to January, 1933–publishing them, with other manuscript material, in *Poet in the Making: The Notebooks of Dylan Thomas* (1968). Maud has observed that Thomas came to think of these poems as a sort of mine of early drafts and drew upon them, generally with some revision, for a number of poems in *Twenty-five Poems;* he continued to do so until the notebooks were purchased in 1941 for what is now the Lockwood Memorial Library of the State University of New York at Buffalo.

Thomas' last two years in Swansea, 1932 to 1934, foreshadowed the importance of the theater in his life. Bill Read, in his too-lightly regarded biography, *The Days of Dylan Thomas* (1964), traces an active interest in acting and playwriting while Thomas was still in school, then details Thomas' journeyman experience in a community theater group, the Mumbles Stage Society. By all accounts, Thomas rapidly became a competent actor, but the bohemianism which was to mar his personal life had already become established and caused his expulsion from the group.

In 1933, Thomas began to place poems in British papers and magazines which had more than local circulation. In September, 1933, he began a correspondence with the future novelist Pamela Hanford Johnson, who eventually married another novelist, C. P. Snow. The correspondence ripened into a friendship, which in turn became a love affair after visits in 1934. In November, Thomas moved to London, the center of his activities until 1937.

18 Poems appeared in December, 1934. Although the book caused hardly a ripple, when it was followed in 1936 by *Twenty-five Poems*, Thomas' reputation was established, helped not a little when the book was received by the prestigious poet Edith Sitwell.

Twenty-five Poems contains a rich trove of some of Thomas' best work. The sonnet sequence "Altarwise by Owl-Light," for example, has still not been exhausted by critical study. The sequence is generally viewed as containing the elements which make Thomas' poetry at once difficult and rewarding: religious, overtly Christian, motifs; packed metaphor and imagery, some of it traditional, some of it esoteric in various ways; high style mixed with colloquial phrasing; and the always-present theme of life-and-death as a process centered on, informed by, and powered through, sexuality.

Perhaps the central event of Thomas' personal life was his meeting with Caitlin Macnamara at a London pub party in April, 1936. The daughter of the eccentric Yvonne Majolier and Francis Macnamara, Caitlin was immediately drawn to Thomas and the affair quickly became serious. By all accounts, Caitlin's temperament was as mercurial as Thomas' own. After a trip together to Cornwall, they married on July 11, 1937, in Penzance, without any visible means of support or any moral support from Thomas' family. They lived at first in Hampshire, southwest of London, with Caitlin's mother. It was a relatively happy and carefree time.

In the fall of 1938, Thomas and his wife moved to Wales, living at first with Thomas' parents, then alone in Laugharne, where their first son, Llewelyn, was born in January, 1939. In August, *The Map of Love* was published, complete with Augustus John's portrait of Thomas. This book contains a number of more or less surrealistic stories plus sixteen poems. In spite of the celebrated episode of Thomas' participation in the Surrealist Exhibition of June 26, 1936, where he read poetry and passed around a cup of strong tea, the notion that Thomas was at any time a surrealist writer has been thoroughly exploded. G. S. Fraser argued that *The Map of Love* generated the New Apocalypse movement, later the New Romanticism, which was, in turn, superficially influenced by Surrealism and Dadaism. H. H. Kleinman, in *The Religious Sonnets of Dylan Thomas* (1963), argued that Thomas could not have been a Surrealist because he was essentially nonliterary as a reader. Earlier than either, Marshall Stearns, in "Unsex the Skeleton: Notes on the Poetry of Thomas" (1944), placed a high value on

Thomas' poetry because of its originality and because of the influence it had on the Apocalypse group, specifically Henry Treese, G. S. Fraser, and J. F. Hendry. When Richard Church, a Dent publishing company official, objected to some of Thomas' poems as surrealistic, Thomas rejected the charge and described Surrealism as a "pernicious experiment" which was beneath him, adding that "every line of his poetry was to be understood by the reader thinking and feeling." In any case, the book was well received and contained at least two outstanding poems, the brittle elegy "After the Funeral (In Memory of Ann Jones)" and the splendid compact birthday piece, "Twenty-Four Years."

On September 3, 1939, Great Britain declared war against Nazi Germany, beginning a struggle from which the world as Thomas had known it would never reemerge. During the relatively quiet early stages, before the German drives in the spring of 1940 which led first to the evacuation of Dunkirk and then to the surrender of France, Thomas registered shock about the war and determined not to be involved in it. Called up for military service in April, just after *Portrait of the Artist as a Young Dog* was published, he was found unfit for service. In June, he moved to an artist's colony in the Cotswolds and thence to London in the fall. There began a long period of poverty and writing scenarios for war documentaries, an occupation which may have been emotionally damaging, but which also stood him in good stead as preparation for later participation in filmmaking. His personal life continued to be on the windy side of bohemianism, especially during the periods when Caitlin was in Wales. On March 3, 1943, his daughter Aeron was born while Caitlin was still in London. The Thomases were to have no more children until their second son, Colm, was born in Carmarthen on July 24, 1949.

The war years saw only a single slim volume of poetry produced, *New Poems.* Included in this book were several poems of first importance: "And Death Shall Have No Dominion," "The Marriage of a Virgin," "The Hunchback in the Park," the long and controversial "Ballad of the Long-Legged Bait," "Once Below a Time," "Deaths and Entrances," and one of his few war poems, "Among Those Killed in the Dawn Raid Was a Man Aged One Hundred." In spite of the title, the poems were not "new"; they were drawn from earlier publication in scattered periodicals.

In the spring of 1945, the European phase of the war was finished and the Thomases returned once more to Wales, settling this time in New Quay on the western coast and moving from there to Oxford in 1946, and finally, in the spring of 1949, to the Boat House in Laugharne, with which Thomas is, perhaps, most often associated. He produced one book of poetry during this period, *Deaths and Entrances.* Meanwhile, he was busy writing and acting for the British Broadcasting Corporation, writing filmscripts, and traveling abroad to Italy, Czechoslovakia, and, finally, America, on the first of four tours.

In August, 1950, after his return from America, *Twenty-six Poems* was published. This limited edition, printed by hand in Italy, signed by Thomas, and in all ways a pretentious production, signaled a new sort of arrival. Rather a large number of people were now willing to pay handsomely for the status conferred by owning a copy of a limited edition of his work.

The American tours were triumphs for Thomas. He appears to have basked in the adoration of American society and academic groups. From the detailed accounts of his mentor, John Malcolm Brinnin, recorded in his biographical *Dylan Thomas in America: An Intimate Journal* (1955), Thomas worked very hard while at the same time continuing to behave in off-hours in the feckless manner for which he was now notorious.

Even so, in February, 1952, a second handsome edition appeared, the six poems of *In Country Sleep.* This book was almost immediately eclipsed by the publication in November of Thomas' most important book, *Collected Poems, 1934-1952.* Again, the format was impressive and the edition included a number of specially bound copies. This volume includes nearly all of Thomas' poetry and forms the point of departure for any serious study of his work.

While the fourth American tour was under way, Thomas was taken ill in New York, lapsed into a coma, and died on November 9, 1953. He was buried on November 24 in St. Martin's Churchyard, Laugharne, Wales.

Analysis · Three poems will serve to illustrate, provisionally, the range in theme and technique of Dylan Thomas' poetry: "And Death Shall Have No Dominion," "Altarwise by Owl-Light," and "Over Sir John's Hill." All three deal with the life-in-death theme which permeates Thomas' work. The first is a very early poem, rather clear and personal in its statement; the second, consisting of ten sonnets treated as a single entity, involves a great deal of Christian material, though it is not incontrovertibly a Christian poem and presents many problems of analysis and interpretation; the third is a "Welsh" poem inasmuch as it is set in Wales and may well spring from Welsh folk material. While the middle poem is considered to be difficult, the last is sequentially clear in its narrative progression, panorama of images, and vivid descriptions.

"And Death Shall Have No Dominion" appears in the "Buffalo Notebooks" dated April, 1933, and was published in *The New English Weekly* on May 18, 1933, and in *Collected Poems, 1934-1952.* It consists of three stanzas, each beginning and ending with the phrase "And death shall have no dominion." The rhythm is based on a four-stress count with enough variations to intrigue the serious prosodist. These may involve eccentric massing of stresses, as in the title line, or stressing or not stressing the same word in a single line, as in "When their bónes are picked cleán and the cleán bones góne." Aside from the title-refrain, the poem does not lend itself to simple syllable count, though lines two and six consistently have eight syllables and line five has nine. The other four lines are more or less irregular. For the most part, the lines tend to fall irregularly into the iambic and anapestic patterns common to English versification. Alliteration runs throughout the poem. End rhyme, assonance, and consonance also play a part in the sound pattern. Lines two and three of the second stanza, for example, substitute alliteration for end rhyme with "windily" and "way," while "way" is assonant with "break" in line five. Moreover, "windily" is assonant with the first word of the following line, "twisting," which, in turn, is assonant with both words of the phrase "sinews give." More alliteration is found in line three in "lying long," and "lying" echoes "windings" in line two. Such intricacy of sound patterning is the rule in Thomas' poetry.

This rhythmical music contributes much to the readability and under-standing of the poem. Prosed, the first stanza says little more than that human beings will die in many ways and places and their bodies will return to the elements and be scattered. The elements, however, will live again because love will continue its purpose of regeneration, and death will not rule life. Of course, prosing cannot indicate the cosmic triumph of "They shall have stars at elbow and foot." The second paragraph works with images of sea death and of torture, and plays on the paradox that the broken will remain whole. The third stanza picks up a minor theme of madness and couples it with a wasteland setting. In spite of madness, in spite of burial and dissolution, the poem insists that something will continue to hammer the elements into life until the sun itself breaks down. Again, the prosing gives little notion of the desolation evoked by "Where blew a flower may a flower no more/ Lift its head to the blows of the rain."

In an essay in the *Explicator* (1956), Thomas E. Connolly professed to see both Christian and Platonic elements in the poem and suggested the influence of Percy Bysshe Shelley's *Adonais* (1821) and John Milton's "Lycidas" (1645) as well. The Christian note is at best vague, while the breaking down of the sun and the persistence with which the elements return to the flesh instead of to the godhead seems clearly enough to refute Platonism. Whatever the merits of the *Adonais* identification may be, Thomas' resources would be poor indeed if he had to depend on "Lycidas" for sea-drowning imagery. On the other hand, Korg agrees with Connolly's identification of Saint Paul's Epistle to the Romans as the source of the title-refrain and the language indicating that the dead in the sea will rise again. Korg rejects the idea that the lines Christianize the poem and sees them, instead, as part of a "more generalized mysticism."

"Altarwise by Owl-Light" is a much more difficult and controversial poem. The first seven of its ten sonnets were published in *Life and Letters Today* (1935) and the last three were published at various times during 1936 in *Contemporary Poetry and Prose.* They were printed later as a sequence in *Twenty-five Poems.*

The poems that make up "Altarwise by Owl-Light" are traditional sonnets mainly inasmuch as they have fourteen lines each; they do not follow the rhyme scheme of either the English or the Italian form. In fact, their rhyme is of the incidental and varied pattern characteristic of so much of Thomas' poetry. Terminal sounds are patterned, but hardly enough so to be considered formalized. The rhythm is equally irregular. Most lines contain five stressed syllables, many of them iambic, but that the overall pattern is dominated by iambs is doubtful. Even so, the poems are recognizable as variants of the twentieth century sonnet.

Elder Olson, in *The Poetry of Dylan Thomas* (1954), developed what must be by far the most intricate analysis of the poems' symbolism. He assembled charts to demonstrate that the poems are based on astrology, basically Herculean in identity. Although Olson's interpretation has been rejected for the most part by other critics, it hardly merits Jones's curt dismissal as "ludicrously complex decipherment." On a different tack, Bernard Knieger, in an essay in the *Explicator* (1956), offered an interpretation to counter a rather muddled one by R. N. Maud earlier in the same periodical. Knieger defined the themes of "Altarwise by Owl-Light" as being simultaneously Christian and sexual. E. H. Essig, again in the *Explicator* (1958), built on Olson's and Knieger's interpretations to demonstrate a fully Christian poetry. In 1965, G. S. Fraser rejected Olson's position out of hand and joined David Daiches in the opinion, expressed in *College English* (1954), that, although splendid in parts, the sonnets are, as wholes, "oppressive and congested." At the same time, he declared that the sonnets "are important because they announce the current orthodox Christian feeling . . . which was henceforth increasingly to dominate Thomas' work in poetry." The opinion is interesting in the face of Thomas' remark, reported by J. M. Brinnin in an article in the *Atlantic Monthly* (1955), that he now intended to write "poems in praise of God's world by a man who doesn't believe in God." Daniel Jones, perhaps, deserves the last word. He argued that "Altarwise by Owl-Light" could be termed "absolute poetry," held together, not by ordinary logic, but by a pattern of words and images joined by a common relationship with such things as "sex, birth, death, Christian and pagan religion and ritual." He saw the poem as "sustained by a single metaphor" and as beyond translation into other words or thoughts. Like Fraser, he saw the poem marking a change in Thomas' poetry, but unlike Fraser, he saw it as moving away from the extravagant expression of the earlier work and toward economy.

It is clear that "Altarwise by Owl-Light" demonstrates Thomas' concern for the life-death paradox taken on the grandest scale and illuminated, at least in part, by the Christian mythos. Also helpful is the understanding that the persona of the poems is a universalized character who is at once himself and the Christ who dies, and who is also all the human beings who have ever died and who will ever die. With their insistence upon the mysteries of life in death, mercy in destruction, God in man, the sonnets are quintessentially Thomas.

"Over Sir John's Hill" first appeared in *Botteghe Oscure* in 1949 and was later included in the *Collected Poems, 1934-1952*. Daniel Jones pointed out that the poem was written during Thomas' residence at Laugharne. The area of "Sir John's Hill" borders an estuary east of the outlet of the River Towy, a semiwilderness area supporting many wildfowl and birds of prey. The poem, then, reflects a setting which was intimately familiar to Thomas; even so, except for the place-names, the setting could be nearly any waste area in the world where land and a large body of water meet.

Jones's detailed study of the prosody of "Over Sir John's Hill" is interesting. He has noted the varied but exact patterning of the long and short lines based on a syllabic count, the longest line containing fifteen syllables, the shortest containing only one; lines of either thirteen and fourteen syllables, or four to six syllables are the most common line lengths. Jones also observed that the poem's four stanzas have a rhyme pattern of *aabbccbxdadxx*, *a*, *b*, *c*, and *d* being either full-rhymes or half-rhymes, and *x* indicating alliteration with first-syllable assonance. Jones considered the verse form to be representative of Thomas' work at its best and most mature. While he conceded that such intricacy is open to the charge of artificiality and that syllabic verse tends to be "easily overcome by the natural patterns of the English language, based upon combinations of weak and strong stresses," he argued that all artists must work within "self-imposed discipline."

While "Over Sir John's Hill" exists on many levels, it can be approached quite usefully from the point of view of allegory. Allegory works by having each actor's part function on several levels simultaneously in a linear story. The trick is to see that each actor functions differently, though interrelatedly, in several stories at once. Thus, an actor may be a bird, functioning as a bird, and a bird functioning as a mortal man, and a man functioning as an immortal soul, all at the same time. Put another way, one actor plays three parts in three stories, all fully coherent, in the telling of one tale. In "Over Sir John's Hill," there is a persona who narrates the action, observes it, and participates in it. The "young Aesop fabling" watches the drama of bird life and bird death on the estuary shortly before sunset. On the literal level, the persona watches while a hawk, during last light, is destroying sparrows. A fishing heron watches and grieves and the grief is echoed by the "tear" of the river. The bird life then settles down, an owl hoots, and the persona hears the sound of the river in the willows just before the plunge of night.

On the ethical level, "Over Sir John's Hill" is a grim sort of parody of the legal system and of institutionalized religion. The birds and the countryside echo human behavior. The hill itself represents a judge who has, on evidence which is never presented in the poem, reached a verdict of condemnation; thus, he is sitting with the symbol of the death sentence on his head, the "black cap of jackdaws." That the cap is formed of jackdaws is instructive. The jackdaw's habit of playing jokes on people is reflected in the term "gulled birds," which Thomas may have picked up from his interest in Jacobean tragedy. "Gulled," in that context, means "fooled" and here functions to undercut the quality of human justice. As jackdaws are also minor carrion birds, their use as a "black cap" heightens the grim note. The hawk represents the executioner, as is indicated by the adjective "tyburn," an allusion to the Tyburn Tree or Tyburn Elms, a thirteenth century place of execution on the River Tybourne and later the slang name for the gallows built near the site of London's Marble Arch. The identification is intensified by an immediate reference to "wrestle of elms" and the "noosed" hawk. The law, it would seem, chooses its victims at random, and the victims themselves are by nature young and silly, foredoomed and courting death. They sing "dilly dilly, come let us die," and are described by the persona and the heron as "led-astray birds." The saintly heron, at the ethical level, stands for the church, which observes the workings of human justice without protest, though it grieves for the victims. The heron, like the church, continues to carry on its own business in spite of the mundane horrors about it. On the ethical level, then, society is formal, filled with sorrow but not with mercy, and its conceptions of justice, death, and divinity are at once structured and casual.

The divine level is still more disquieting. The persona regards nature in an old-fashioned way, his words couched in fresh metaphor, as he describes nature as the Book in which divinity can be read. He opens "the leaves of water" and reads psalms there, and in a shell he reads "death."

He and the heron-church ask for God's mercy, the God who, in silence, observes the sparrow's "hail," a term implying not only the sparrows' song of praise but also the numbers in which their dead bodies pelt the earth. If the God of the poem is more merciful than the indifferent hill-judge, the poem does not say so. Of salvation and an afterlife there is no affirmation; the "lunge of night" seems dreadfully final, not Thomas' more usual affirmation of a circular process in which death is the entrance to life, in which life is repeated rather than translated to a divine realm. It may be that, after the war, Thomas was no longer able to see the cycle of nature as an endlessly repeating pattern. If "Over Sir John's Hill" is in fact a celebration, it is an unusually dark one, even for Thomas.

In placing Thomas as a poet, Howard Nemerov's conclusion, expressed in *The Kenyon Review* (1953), that "he has written a few beautiful poems" furnishes a good point of departure. In a way, that is the best that can be said for any poet, even the greatest. David Daiches, who denied a place of greatness to Thomas in his essay in *College English* (1954), said that "it is enough that he wrote some poems that the world will not willingly let die." Richard A. Werry, again in *College English* (1955), allowed Thomas' poetry greater depth than is generally granted, suggesting that at least a half dozen of his poems will last out the twentieth century. This is rather faint praise. Even if Thomas' poetry comes down to no more than that, a few lasting poems, still, to have caught the imagination and the spirit, if not fully the understanding, of the people who endured the Depression and World War II, to have embodied in his poetry a fearless, if bitter, search for reality and a limited hope in a world bereft of its traditional theological certainties, is no mean feat. This much, at least, Thomas achieved.

Other literary forms · Dylan Thomas wrote one novel, *The Death of the King's Canary* (1976), in collaboration with John Davenport. His stories and collections of stories include the very popular, essentially autobiographical, *Portrait of the Artist as a Young Dog* (1940) and many posthumous publications. Scripts include the extremely popular *Under Milk Wood* (1954); *The Doctor and the Devils* (1953), which has been translated into German, Czech, and Spanish and was republished with four additional scripts in 1966; and *Quite Early One Morning* (1954), which has variant English and American versions. Thomas' letters are rich with biographical materials and critical insights. There are three important collections: *Letters to Vernon Watkins* (1957), written to, and edited by, Vernon Watkins, his friend and fellow poet; *Selected Letters of Dylan Thomas* (1966), edited by Constantine FitzGibbon, his "official" biographer; and *Twelve More Letters by Dylan Thomas* (1969), a limited edition supplemental to the FitzGibbon collection. Many other articles, poems, letters, scripts, and stories are widely scattered in manuscripts, anthologies, newspapers, and magazines. Whether a complete bibliography, much less an inclusive edition, of Thomas' work can ever be made is an open question. J. Alexander Rolph's *Dylan Thomas: A Bibliography* (1956) and Ralph Maud's *Dylan Thomas in Print: A Bibliographical History* (1970) are important efforts in this direction.

Select works other than poetry

LONG FICTION: *The Death of the King's Canary*, 1976 (with John Davenport).

SHORT FICTION: *Portrait of the Artist as a Young Dog*, 1940; *Selected Writings of Dylan Thomas*, 1946; *A Child's Christmas in Wales*, 1954; *Adventures in the Skin Trade and Other Stories*, 1955; *A Prospect of the Sea and Other Stories*, 1955; *Early Prose Writings*, 1971; *The Followers*, 1976; *The Collected Stories*, 1984.

DRAMA: *Under Milk Wood: A Play for Voices*, pr. 1953 (public reading), pr. 1954 (radio play), pb. 1954, pr. 1956 (staged; musical settings by Daniel Jones).

SCREENPLAYS: *Three Weird Sisters*, 1948 (with Louise Birt and David Evans); *No Room at the Inn*, 1948 (with Ivan Foxwell); *The Doctor and the Devils*, 1953; *The Beach at Falesá*, 1963; *Twenty Years A'Growing*, 1964; *Rebecca's Daughters*, 1965; *Me and My Bike*, 1965; *"The Doctor and the Devils" and Other Scripts*, 1966 (two screenplays and one radio play).

RADIO PLAYS: *Quite Early One Morning*, 1944; *The Londoner*, 1946; *Return Journey*, 1947; *Quite Early One Morning*, 1954 (twenty-two radio plays).

NONFICTION: *Letters to Vernon Watkins*, 1957 (Vernon Watkins, editor); *Selected Letters of Dylan Thomas*, 1966 (Constantine FitzGibbon, editor); *Poet in the Making: The Notebooks of Dylan Thomas*, 1968 (Ralph Maud, editor); *Twelve More Letters by Dylan Thomas*, 1969 (FitzGibbon, editor).

B. G. Knepper

Bibliography · The authorized biography, Constantine FitzGibbon's *The Life of Dylan Thomas*, 1965, was superseded by Paul Ferris' *Dylan Thomas*, 1978, which deconstructs the Thomas legend, and George Tremlett's revisionist biography, *Dylan Thomas: In the Mercy of His Means*, 1992, which resurrects the poet's image. Also of note are John Malcolm Brinnin's *Dylan Thomas in America*, 1955, and Caitlin Thomas' *Leftover Life to Kill*, 1957. See also *Dylan Thomas: The Collected Letters*, 1985, edited by Paul Ferris. Excellent critical studies include Jacob Korg's *Dylan Thomas*, 1965; William T. Moynihan's *The Craft and Art of Dylan Thomas*, 1966; and William York Tindall's *A Reader's Guide to Dylan Thomas*, 1962. See also *Critical Essays on Dylan Thomas*, 1989, edited by Georg Gaston.

TU FU

(in Pinyin transliteration, Du Fu)

Born: Possibly Tu-ling, China; 712
Died: Near T'an-chou, China; 770

Poetry · Approximately 1,450 poems of varying lengths, collected through the years in frequently revised and reprinted anthologies and collections such as *Tang Shi san bai shou,* 1763 (*The Jade Mountain: A Chinese Anthology,* 1929), and *Chuan Tang Shi,* 1706. An English-language collection is *Tu Fu: Selected Poems,* 1962

Achievements · Born during the T'ang Dynasty (618-907), the classical period in Chinese literary history, Tu Fu was one of four poets whose greatness marked the era. Some fifty thousand poems from that period have survived, the large number resulting primarily from the talents of these four men. Wang Wei was basically a nature poet; Po Chü-yi, a government official whose poetry often reflected official concerns; and Li Po, probably the best known of all Chinese poets, a poet of the otherworldly or the sublime. Tu Fu seemed to sum up all of these men's works with the wide range of topics and concerns which appear in his poems.

One of Tu Fu's major contributions to Chinese literature was his extensive "occasional" verse—poems inspired by a journey or by a mundane experience such as building a house. Many of Tu Fu's occasional poems were addressed to friends or relatives at some special time in their lives. Distant relatives who held official positions and achieved distinction would receive a laudatory poem. These poems could also be addressed to special friends. Tu Fu traveled much in his life, both by choice and involuntarily, relying on friends to shelter and support him, because, for the majority of his life, he was without an official governmental position and salary. His poems would therefore be addressed to these persons as expressions of gratitude and friendship on the occasion of his visit.

Poems about nature abounded during the T'ang period, and Tu Fu contributed extensively to this genre as well. In contrast to Li Po, who followed the Taoist philosophy of withdrawal from the world, Tu Fu was very much a poet of everyday life, both in his response to nature and to the physical world and in his active engagement in the social and political life of his times. Indeed, it has been said that Tu Fu's poetry provides a running history of the Chinese state during his era.

Finally, Tu Fu was a master of poetic form; his verse forms were as varied as his content. During the T'ang period, the *ku-t'i* (old forms) in Chinese poetry coexisted with the *lü-shih* (new forms). The old, or "unregulated," forms placed no restrictions on the word tones used in the verse; they did not limit the number of lines in a poem; and they did not require verbal parallelism. The new forms, or "regulated verse," however, were much more demanding. They mandated certain tonal patterns, especially in rhyme words, a requirement which markedly affected word choice; they usually restricted the total number of lines in a poem; and they utilized verbal parallelism. Each of these two major categories of Chinese poetry was also divided into subcategories depending on the meter, which in Chinese poetry depends on the number of words in each line rather than on stressed and unstressed syllables, as in Western poetry. Tu Fu adeptly used both old and new forms in his verse, justifying in this respect as in every other his reputation as "the Master."

Biography · Tu Fu's life could best be described as one of frustration. Although his mother's family was related to the imperial clan, and both his father and grandfather held official positions in the government, much of Tu Fu's life was spent in poverty. Unable to pass the examination for entrance into official service, Tu Fu remained a "plain-robed" man, a man without official position and salary, more often than not. His poems from the mid-730's allude to "the hovel" in which he lived on the outskirts of the capital while the court members resided in the splendor of the palace. One of Tu Fu's sons died from starvation in 755 because of the family's poverty, and the poet's sadness and anguish caused by his son's death is reflected in several of Tu Fu's poems.

Tu Fu was born in Honan Province, possibly in Tu-ling, in 712. His natural mother died at an early age, and Tu Fu's father remarried, eventually adding three brothers and a sister to the family. Tu Fu was apparently a very precocious child. In his autobiography, he states unabashedly that at the age of seven he pondered "only high matters" and wrote verses about beautiful birds, while other children his age were dealing with puerile subjects such as dogs and cats. At an early age, Tu Fu also mastered a great number of the characters which make up written Chinese. He was writing so extensively by the age of nine, he claims, that his output could easily have filled several large bags. Not much else is known about Tu Fu's early years. As would be expected, he was schooled in literary matters in preparation for entrance into official service. A firsthand knowledge of the many facets of Chinese life and the geography of the country also became a part of Tu Fu's education: He traveled for about three years before taking the official examination for public service. His poetry of this period reflects the experiences and sights he encountered while traversing the country-side.

In 735, at the age of twenty-three, Tu Fu finally took the test to enter government service, and failed. Apparently there was something in Tu Fu's writing style, in the way he handled the Chinese characters, which did not suit the examiners. This setback in Tu Fu's plans ushered in the first of several important phases in his life. Since the poet had failed the examination and was without a position, he resumed his travels. During these travel years, several significant changes occurred in his life. His father died in 740, which prompted a series of poems on the theme of life's imperma-nence. This event was followed by Tu Fu's marriage to a woman from the Ts'ui clan, a marriage which ultimately produced two sons and four daughters for the poet. Finally, and probably most important in terms of his literary work, Tu Fu met Li Po in 744.

Following the Taoist tradition, Li Po, who was ten years Tu Fu's senior, had become a "withdrawn" poet after his banishment from the court. As such, he represented a viewpoint opposite to that of Tu Fu concerning a literate man's obligations to Chinese society at that time. Tu Fu's poetry exhibits his grappling with these contending views. He was sometimes attracted to the simple lifestyle of Li Po, but the Confucian ethic under which Tu Fu had been reared persevered, and he returned to the capital in 746, eleven years after his first attempt, to repeat the test for an official position. He failed again; this time, according to the historians, one of the emperor's officials was afraid that new appointees to the bureaucracy would weaken the latter's power in the court, so he saw to it that *everyone* who took the examination failed. The frustration and humiliation resulting from this second failure to pass the examination, perhaps heightened by the fact that his younger brother had taken and passed the examination earlier, did not seem to deter Tu Fu from his goal of securing an official post. Although he was forced to move outside the capital with his family and to rely on support from friends and relatives to survive, Tu Fu seemingly resolved to gain an official position through another route, this time by ingratiating himself with important people who could aid his quest.

Wei Chi was one such person. As an adviser to the emperor, he was in a position to help Tu Fu when the occasion arose. Tu Fu was also well acquainted with Prince Li Chin, a pleasure-loving, undisciplined figure who was an embarrassment to the court. The prince had a great apprecia-tion for literature, however, and after Tu Fu wrote several poems dealing with "The Eight Immortals of the Wine Cup," as the prince and his coterie were called, the prince took a special liking to the poet. Because of these friendships, Tu Fu's name was heard around the court, and when he wrote the "Three Great Ceremonies" poems, their excellence and their laudatory treatment of the emperor engendered imperial recognition and favor. A third examination for an official position ensued as a result. Whether Tu Fu passed or failed this one was of little consequence; finally, at the age of forty-four, he was given an official position by imperial decree. (Li Po's position with the court had also been established by imperial decree, because he had refused to take the civil-service exam as a matter of principle.) Ironically, Tu Fu refused the position. It apparently involved moving to a distant western district; because the position required him to be a part of the police administration, it would also have involved beating people for infractions of the law, something Tu Fu was not inclined to do. The poet's refusal found some sympathy in the court, and he was appointed instead to the heir apparent's household. Thus, the years 755 and 756 stand as pivotal ones in Tu Fu's life: He received his first official position in the government after many years of struggle, and, strangely enough, he gave up that position because he rapidly grew to dislike the servile aspects of the job. Amid all of this, the An Lu-shan Rebellion began.

For the remainder of his life, Tu Fu was one of the many who endured the misfortunes of this war. When the Rebellion began in 756, the emperor was forced to flee the capital, as did Tu Fu. The latter's poems from that period depict the many defeats of the imperial army. Once he had established his family in the relative safety of Fu-chou in the north, Tu Fu set out to join the "Traveling Palace" of the displaced emperor, but he was captured by rebel forces and taken back to the capital, which they occupied. Held by the rebels for several months, he finally escaped and joined the Traveling Palace as a censor, an official responsible for reminding the emperor of matters which required his attention. During this period, Tu Fu did not hear from his family for more than a year, and he wrote possibly the most famous poem in Chinese literature, a love poem to his wife and children entitled "Moonlit Night."

The capital was retaken the next year, 757, and Tu Fu was reunited with his family. His "Journey North" describes the effects of the war on the Chinese people and countryside, and his homecoming to his family. With the government reestablished in the capital, Tu Fu returned there with his family for official service. This period of service was also short-lived; he once again grew tired of the bureaucratic life and its constraints. Floods and the war had devastated the countryside around the capital, so Tu Fu took his family west to flee the war and to find food. The war, however, also spread to the west, and as a result, Tu Fu once again shifted his family, this time southward to Ch'eng-tu, five hundred miles from the fighting.

The time he spent in the south has been labeled Tu Fu's "thatched hut" period. This was something of a pastoral period in his life, during which he seemed to emulate Li Po and the Taoist ethic to some degree. The war, however, persisted both in the countryside and in Tu Fu's poems. The rebellion finally spread even to the south, and Tu Fu was forced to leave his thatched hut in 765. He spent the remaining five years of his life in restless travel, cataloging in poetry his journeys and the events he witnessed. Tu Fu, "the Master," died in 770, at the age of fifty-eight, as he traveled the Hsiang River looking for a haven from the ill health and ill times which had beset him.

Analysis · Tu Fu's poetry deals with a multitude of concerns and events. His verses express the moments of self-doubt and frustration which plagued the poet, such as when he failed the civil-service examinations or when he became increasingly afflicted by physical ailments later in life, referring to himself in one verse as an "emaciated horse." Tu Fu's poems also deal with painting and the other arts, and they often employ allusions to outstanding figures in China's literary and political past to comment on contemporary conditions. It is, however, in his poems addressed to family and friends and in his nature poems that the substance and depth of his verse can be most clearly seen.

Among Tu Fu's finest poems are those which express his love for friends and family. Poems addressed to friends constituted both a literary and a social convention in China during the T'ang period. In literate society, men sought one another for friendship and intellectual companionship, and poems of the "address and answer" variety were often composed by the poet. Several examples occur in the poems which Tu Fu wrote either to or about Li Po, his fellow poet. After the two met in 744, they traveled together extensively, and a firm bond, both personal and scholarly, was established between them. In one poem commemorating the two poets' excursion to visit a fellow writer, Tu Fu explained his feeling toward Li Po: "I love my Lord as young brother loves elder brother/ . . . Hand in hand we daily walk together." In "A Winter Day," Tu Fu writes that "Since early dawn I have thought only of you [Li Po]," thoughts which may have been both pleasant and painful for Tu Fu as he grappled with the question of whether he wanted to continue his quest for a governmental position or follow Li Po's example and become a "withdrawn" poet. Tu Fu also highly praised Li Po's verses. In a later poem, "the Master" laments the fact that Li Po has become unstable, but he also rejoices in the gift of Li Po's talent:

"My thoughts are only of love for his talent./ Brilliant are his thousand poems."

The concern and admiration which Tu Fu felt and expressed poetically were not directed solely to other poets. Many of his poems of this type were addressed to longtime friends. "For Wei Pa, in Retirement" is one example which not only expresses Tu Fu's friendship for Wei Pa but also describes the life stages the two have passed through together. The poet comments on how briefly their youth lasted, observing that "Though in those days you were not married/ Suddenly sons and daughters troop in." The two friends have not seen each other for twenty years, "both our heads have become grizzled," and Tu Fu knows that the next day will separate them again. He is elated, however, by the "sense of acquaintance" his friend revives in him, and the poet captures that sense in his verse.

Tu Fu was separated from his family several times, sometimes by the war, sometimes by economic conditions. His most famous poem, "Moonlit Night," expresses his deep concern for his wife as "In her chamber she alone looks out/ . . . In the sweet night her cloud-like tresses are damp/ In the clear moonlight her jade-like arms are cold." The poet wonders how long it will be before "we two nestle against those unfilled curtains/ With the moon displaying the dried tear-stains of us both?" Essentially a love poem for the poet's wife, "Moonlit Night" was an unconventional work in its time. Wives in ancient China were seen primarily as pieces of reproductive machinery, with no intellectual capabilities. A poet might lavish great sentiment in verse on a male companion, but tender thoughts concerning a wife were rarely expressed in poetry.

In true classical fashion, Tu Fu was also a nature poet. He could portray nature in an idyllic vein, as in "The River by Our Village," in which the poet describes how "Clear waters wind around our village/ With long summer days full of loveliness/ Fluttering in and out from the house beams the swallows play/ Waterfowl disport together as everlasting lovers." These lines reflect the contentment of Tu Fu's pastoral or "thatched hut" period; he ends the poem by asking: "What more could I wish for?"

While many of Tu Fu's nature poems are distinguished by their vivid evocation of landscapes and wildlife for their own sake, he also treats nature symbolically. In "The Winding River," falling blossoms signify the changing of the seasons and cause the poet to "grieve to see petals flying/ Away in the wind." This evidence of mutability engenders further reflection; as the poet watches "Butterflies going deeper and deeper/ In amongst the flowers, dragon-flies/ Skimming and flicking over the water," he is reminded that "Wind, light, and time ever revolve," that the only constant factor in life is change. In turn, the poet is led to reflect on the inconsequential and often futile nature of his and other men's ambitions: "why should I be lured/ By transient rank and honours?" Nature instructs him "to live/ Along with her" in a rich and full harmony rather than existing in the pale semblance of living which men have created for themselves.

Because of the range of his sympathy, Tu Fu has been compared to William Shakespeare: Both were able to encompass in their works the whole teeming life of their times. Although Tu Fu's declaration that "In poetry I have exhausted human topics" may seem an overstatement, his many poems and their varied concerns seem almost to justify such a claim.

Kenneth A. Howe

Bibliography · Considering Tu Fu's stature, there is surprisingly little critical material about him in English. The most valuable study in English is the clear and highly readable one by William Hung, *Tu Fu: China's Greatest Poet*, 1952, which includes a volume of notes and incorporates translations of 374 poems. A. R. Davis' *Tu Fu*, 1971, is more general and concise, addressing simply the often complicated problems of form and theme. An excellent chapter on Tu Fu illustrated with fine translations may be found in Stephen Owen's *The Great Age of Chinese Poetry: The High T'ang*, 1981. Those who wish to approach Tu Fu in the original will find David Hawkes's *A Little Primer of Tu Fu*, 1967, an invaluable help; even the strictly Western reader will find much of value. More recent studies include David R. McCraw's *Du Fu's Laments from the South*, 1992, and David Lattimore's "Tu Fu" in *The Indiana Companion to Traditional Chinese Literature*, edited by William H. Nienhauser, Jr., 1986.

PAUL VALÉRY

Born: Sète, France; October 30, 1871
Died: Paris, France; July 20, 1945

Poetry · *La Jeune Parque*, 1917 (*The Youngest of the Fates*, 1947; also known as *The Young Fate*) · *Album de vers anciens*, 1920 (*Album of Early Verse*, 1971) · *Charmes, ou poèmes*, 1922 (*Charms*, 1971)

Achievements · The honors bestowed upon Valéry by the French people attest the veneration in which he was held by his fellow countrymen. His talents were also recognized by many outside France. Not only was he instrumental in acquainting the rest of the world with French culture, but also he enjoyed an international reputation as a literary figure and as a keen analyst of politics and culture. For a number of years, he served on the Committee on Intellectual Cooperation of the League of Nations. In 1935, he became a member of the Academy of Sciences of Lisbon. Highly respected by the British and the Portuguese, he received honorary degrees from the universities of Oxford (1931) and Coimbra (1937). Valéry was the last member of a trio of poets with similar aesthetic ideals and compositional practices (the others were Charles Baudelaire and Stéphane Mallarmé); he was the last major French poet to use the strict rules of French versification. The Surrealist poets, for example, although finding much to admire in his work, preferred other methods of poetic composition, such as automatic writing.

Although Valéry left no literary disciples to practice his aesthetic ideals, his works and literary philosophy interested and stimulated such diverse

literary figures as T. S. Eliot, Rainer Maria Rilke, Jorge Luis Borges, and Jean-Paul Sartre. Tzvetan Todorov and other structuralists share with Valéry an interest in the relationship between the component elements of a work, although Valéry focuses on the *process* of composition rather than on the analysis of the resulting literary discourse. Todorov credits Valéry with redefining the word "poetics" to emphasize literary language rather than rules of rhyme and versification. Others, such as New Novelist Jean Ricardou, find Valéry's aesthetic in accord with their rejection of the subjectivity, the false sense of "psychology," the insistence upon verisimilitude, and the lack of compositional rigor which they find characteristic of the traditional novel. Thus, Valéry still speaks to a wide range of writers and readers, and the beauty of his poetry, the incisive observations and lucid prose of his notebooks, and the continuing influence of his literary theories assure his continued importance in French literature.

Biography · Paul Valéry was born October 30, 1871, in the small French seaport of Sète. His childhood was bathed in the sunlight, blue sky and water, and salt air of this Mediterranean setting. The young Valéry disliked intensely the regimented nature of his schoolwork and spent much of his free time studying subjects which greatly interested him: painting, architecture, and poetry, especially that of Baudelaire, Théophile Gautier, and Victor Hugo. Valéry's first poems were composed in 1884, at the age of thirteen.

In that same year, Valéry's family moved to Montpellier. The year 1887 was marked by his father's death; in 1888, he entered law school at the university in Montpellier. His first published poem, "Rêve," appeared in 1889 in a small literary review. During this period, Valéry spent many hours studying mathematics (an interest which he maintained all his life), physics, and music (he especially admired the music of Richard Wagner, which had a grandeur he judged both "visceral" and "structural").

In 1890, Valéry met Pierre Louÿs, a young Symbolist poet and editor. Louÿs was to have a great impact on Valéry's future; not only did he help to further Valéry's literary reputation, but also he introduced the young man to others who were to play significant roles in his life. An introduction to Louÿs' uncle, André Gide, sparked a lasting friendship and voluminous correspondence which was to span the next fifty years. Louÿs also introduced his friend to Mallarmé. For Valéry, Mallarmé's works exemplified such perfection of form and control of language that all other poetry seemed inferior by comparison. In their subsequent correspondence, Mallarmé praised the young poet's work, and, perhaps as a result of this encouragement, Valéry's literary output increased dramatically; several of his poems soon appeared in print in Louÿs' literary review, *La Conque,* and elsewhere.

Valéry's literary career had hardly begun, however, when he chose to turn away from poetry as his primary occupation in favor of a life of study and contemplation. His biographers have sought to explain this action by referring to a growing predeliction for introspection among young French intellectuals, to their common dislike of the then-popular naturalistic novel and of objective and descriptive Parnassian poetry, to Valéry's feelings of inferiority in the face of the poetic perfection of his master, Mallarmé, and to Valéry's unrequited (and undeclared) love for a married woman, which left him frightened of his inability to control his strong feelings. No doubt these factors affected Valéry, but his decision in 1892 to devote his life to the cultivation of his intellect can just as easily be seen as a natural consequence of his introspective nature. His decision was greatly influenced by the intellectual and poetic theories of Edgar Allan Poe, which portrayed poetry as creating certain calculated effects. Valéry believed that the techniques required to produce these effects suppressed rather than expanded the intellect; thus, although he had already written several hundred poems, he concluded that the best path toward intellectual growth and wisdom was that of the thinker rather than the artist.

Thus began the period in Valéry's life somewhat erroneously termed the "Great Silence." For the next twenty years or so, he occasionally wrote and published, and he carried on an active social life, often frequenting Mallarmé's Tuesday evening salons and attending concerts and plays. In 1900, he married Jeannie Gobillard, niece of the Impressionist painter Berthe Morisot; the couple had three children. His main occupation during the years from 1892 to 1912, however, was the systematic and dispassionate study of the human mind. Charles Whiting indicates the great extent to which Valéry's method resembled that of René Descartes, in its insistence on intellectual independence, a rigorous method, the founding of all knowledge and certainty within the self, and the "ambition for reducing the process of the mind to measurable quantities." Perhaps in emulation of Leonardo da Vinci, Valéry began keeping a series of notebooks, in which he inscribed mathematical equations, aphorisms, ideas and their developments, bits of verse, and so on. By the time of his death, he had filled almost twenty-nine thousand pages.

During this period, the workings of international politics did not escape Valéry's attention. A prophetic essay on the threat posed by modern Germany, first published in England in 1897, was reprinted in France in 1915, and stirred the public's curiosity about Valéry. He published other works as well, including the essay "L'Introduction à la méthode de Léonard da Vinci" ("Introduction to the Method of Leonardo da Vinci") in 1895 and the philosophical tale "La Soirée avec Monsieur Teste" ("An Evening with Monsieur Teste") in 1896; the protagonist of the latter, Monsieur Teste, in many ways embodies Valéry's ideals of pure intellect and creative genius.

Although Valéry's family connections permitted him the leisure to pursue his interests, in 1897, he assumed a somewhat tedious clerkship with the War Ministry, and in 1900, he became private secretary to Mr. Edouard Lebey of the Havas Press Association. Valéry found the job with Lebey most stimulating, and it left him with ample free time for his own intellectual pursuits.

In 1912, André Gide and the publisher Gaston Gallimard urged Valéry to prepare a collection of his poetry for publication. Reluctant at first, he finally began to edit and revise his early poems (eventually published in 1920 as the *Album of Early Verse*) and to compose a new poem, *The Young Fate*, which was published in 1917. The poem was astonishingly successful in spite of its extreme hermeticism; it secured Valéry's reputation as a great poet, and it is still considered one of the finest French poems of the twentieth century.

His work on *The Young Fate*, originally intended by Valéry as his farewell to poetry, inspired him to write other poems. In 1920, "Le Cimetière marin" ("The Graveyard by the Sea") appeared, and 1922 saw the publication of *Charms*, a collection of poems written between 1917 and 1921 (a new edition of *Charms* was published in 1926). Although Valéry continued to compose poetry, these collections contain most of his best work.

The death of Edouard Lebey, in 1922, made Valéry resolve henceforth to earn his living as a freelance intellectual. Valéry's name was everywhere prominent: He became a noted lecturer; produced pamphlets, prefaces, dedications, and new editions of his poems; and wrote the texts of two verse-ballets and a cantata. He was a brilliant essayist whose topics embraced art, philosophy, literature, and social and political criticism. One of his best-known essays, "La Crise de l'esprit" ("The Crisis of the Mind"), published in France in 1919, eloquently warned that the modern world's self-destructive tendencies could condemn it to join the Babylons and Ninevehs of the past; it included one of Valéry's most oft-quoted phrases: "Nous autres, civilisations, nous savons maintenant que nous sommes mortelles" ("We other civilizations, we know now that we are mortal").

His reputation ever-growing, Valéry was elected to the Académie Française in 1925; he became a *chevalier* of the Legion of Honor in 1923 and was subsequently promoted to more prestigious ranks. In 1933, he was named administrator of the Centre Universitaire Méditerranéen, at

Nice, and he was appointed to a Chair of Poetics at the Collège de France in 1937.

Although his opposition to the Vichy government in World War II and his courageous public eulogy for the French Jewish philosopher Henri Bergson exposed Valéry to harassment by the German authorities during the occupation of France, it was typical of his generous spirit to speak out after the war in defense of three accused collaborators.

By 1945, Valéry was suffering from cancer; although very ill, he managed to complete the poetry course he had taught every winter since 1937 at the Collège de France. He died on July 20, 1945, at the age of seventy-three. Honored with a state funeral as one of France's greatest men, he was buried in his native Sète, in the cemetery which was the setting for one of his best-known poems, "The Graveyard by the Sea."

Analysis · Paul Valéry's youthful views about poetry, which were anti-Romanticist and somewhat cynical, led him to reject literature as his primary occupation and to lead instead a life of contemplation and study, which he hoped would enable him to understand better the relationships among the phenomena of the world. When he eventually realized that universal knowledge was unattainable and that individual facets of reality could not be frozen or studied in isolation, he began to write poetry again. Where he had earlier rejected the Romantic and Platonic notion of Muse-inspired poetry, he came to grant inspiration its place in the creative process. Perhaps he found in poetry that synthesis of world experience which he had hoped to find in his studies of scientific phenomena. In any case, the years devoted to such study had produced in Valéry a vigorous and finely honed mind, and he perceived in poetry not only a rewarding exercise of the intellect but also the nearest approach that human beings could make to expressing the ineffable.

Valéry's poetic theories grew out of his strong interest in the workings of human psychology. His model of mental functioning, reflecting the findings of the then relatively new science of psychiatry, portrayed a network of constantly changing interactions of words, feelings, motor impulses, sensations, stimuli, responses, and so on. He thus saw human identity as infinitely varied rather than possessed of an unchanging essence. In Valéry's psychological model, various functions are continually interacting, but only the intellect has a transcendent understanding of them, although it has no control over many of the organism's functions. Moreover, the intellect of a scientist is likely to interpret a given electrical stimulus differently from the way the intellect of a musician or a poet would interpret it. This recognition of the variety among human intellects and of the primal authority of instinctive responses led Valéry to relinquish his earlier faith in calculated technique, a faith which had been influenced in part by Poe's ideas about the ability of a technically skilled poet to manipulate the emotions of his readers and to produce specific predictable effects in all readers.

Valéry connected this model of psychological functioning to a theory of poetry by postulating that the intellect, when stimulated, tends to interpret and classify the information it receives as quickly as possible, in order to return to its habitual state of rest. In terms of this model, prose differs from poetry because the goal of prose is to transmit information; effective prose presents data in such a way that the information is easy to process, is easily extractable from its form, which is relatively unimportant except as a container, a vehicle. The goal of poetry, on the other hand, is to increase internal excitation and awareness and to resist the intellect's attempts to classify and return to a resting state. Valéry therefore sought to create a poetry with "subjects" so fragile and elusive that they would simultaneously charm and mystify the intellect, and that would be presented in forms so compelling to the intellect that they would themselves become part of the message. To summarize Valéry's psychopoetic theory, one could say that rhythm, sound, the use of metaphor and other tropes, and the emotive aspects of language in general serve to increase and sustain the involvement of the subconscious mind and the physical body in the reading process. The interplay of images, memories, ideas, melodies, and sensations prolongs the pleasurable state of internal excitement and delays closure by the intellect, which, captivated by the poem's form, returns to it repeatedly, seeking to prolong or renew its experience.

This view of aesthetic experience has its implications for the poet as well as for the reader. Valéry recognized that the genesis of his poems was usually to be found not in a conscious decision to compose a poem upon a particular subject but rather in those verses, couplets, sentence fragments, or insistent rhythmic or sound patterns which came to him as "gifts" from that modern Muse, the unconscious. At the same time, these "inspired" verses needed to be refined by the poet's technical and analytical skills, and integrated with other verses, fashioned more by skill than by inspiration, so as to form a seamless, aesthetic whole. To be successful, Valéry believed, a poem must present difficulties for the poet as well as for the reader; he preferred to work with traditional poetic forms with fixed rhyme schemes and other compositional requirements, because he found that his struggles with these obstacles often produced new and unexpectedly beautiful networks of meaning and sometimes altered the original thrust of the poem.

Valéry was concerned with aesthetic process more than with aesthetic results. In his view, the stimulation and prolongation of aesthetic pleasure which a poem provides is as important for the poet as for the reader. While he is engaged in the creative process, the poet experiences the intellectual growth, spiritual insight, and emotional release that poetic creation stimulates as it keeps the poet's intellect from returning to a state of equilibrium. Because he believed that it was the poetic process and not the end product that provided aesthetic stimulation, Valéry never considered his poems finished, and he was constantly revising his work. He claimed in his essay "Au sujet du *Cimetière marin*" ("On 'The Graveyard by the Sea,' " published in a bilingual edition of "The Graveyard by the Sea" by the University of Texas Press, 1971) that the published form of that poem merely represented its state on the day it was taken away from him by the editor of the *Nouvelle Revue française.*

Although he never felt that poetry could be a product of purely spontaneous composition, Valéry's youthful conception of poetry as a series of calculated effects controlled by the poet was tempered as he matured. He came to believe in the role of inspiration and mystery in the poetic process, as it operated on the intellect of both poet and reader; he believed that the aesthetic experience was so rich and complex that the intellect could never fully contain or understand it.

This aesthetic individualism colored Valéry's attitude toward his readers; he believed that, just as a poet's unique identity marks his poem, so will different readers' identities color their responses to it. He was therefore generous with his critics; although he may have been privately amused by some interpretations, he gave his official blessing to such endeavors, saying, "My poetry has the meaning that people give to it."

Valéry may have been troubled, however, by those critics who sought to reduce his poems to prose summaries. In his own writings, he often stated that a poem cannot be summarized any more than can a melody, that the beauty and power of poetry stem precisely from the fact that it cannot be put into prose without disintegrating. This problem in poetic theory is illustrated by what Valéry and two well-known critical interpreters have said about "The Graveyard by the Sea," a poem characteristic of Valéry's work in terms of its contemplative mood, its philosophical themes, its formal perfection, and its harmonious and evocative language.

Perhaps his best-known poem, "The Graveyard by the Sea" was written following Valéry's years of contemplation and study. First published in 1920, it portrays human consciousness becoming aware of itself in relation to time, death, and the expanse of the cosmos. The speaker in the poem ponders this interior vastness of consciousness in an ironic setting: a cemetery overlooking the sea, surrounded by tombstones, under the noon blaze of an apparently motionless sun.

"The Graveyard by the Sea" is composed of twenty-four stanzas of six decasyllabic lines each, with a rhyme scheme of *aabccb*. Valéry resurrected the decasyllabic line, which had been all but abandoned by French poets in favor of the more flowing Alexandrine. Although he welcomed the difficulties posed by the ten-syllable line, he did not consciously choose it. In his essay "On 'The Graveyard by the Sea,' " he states that the poem's genesis took the form of certain unintelligible decasyllabic "murmurings," and he became obsessed with the idea of arranging them into six-line stanzas connected by a network of correspondences and tonal contrasts. The intricate requirements of this form prompted him to seek his subject matter in familiar childhood memories, in the sea and sunlight of his Mediterranean birthplace, Sète. These elemental images led him directly to the contemplation of death.

The composition of "The Graveyard by the Sea" thus resembled the composition of a piece of music, in which the melodic motifs—the ideas— are often the *last* aspects of the composition to take shape. Valéry's essay on this poem stresses his belief that ideas simply do not play the same role in poetry that they do in prose; he conceives of "pure poetry" as a nonreferential network of infinite resonances that profoundly touch the reader's sensibility and cannot be summarized in prose. Elsewhere, however, he acknowledged that this ideal of pure poetry was an impossibility, that actual poems are always combinations of "fragments of pure poetry enclosed in the matter of a discourse," and that readers need some thematic or narrative material to guide them through a poem.

An oft-quoted explication of "The Graveyard by the Sea" which attempts to provide just such a guide is that of Sorbonne professor Gustave Cohen. His *Essai d'explication du "Cimetière marin"* (1933), is largely an elucidation of the poem's thematic development. It regards the poem as the recounting of a philosophical journey, a sort of classical tragedy in four acts, with three characters: Nonbeing, or Nothingness (symbolized by the seeming immobility of the noonday sun); human consciousness (represented by the sea), torn between its desire to unite with Nonbeing and its drive to change and create; and the speaker (whom Cohen calls the author), who is alternately a spectator and a participant in a drama which will irrevocably mark his life.

In Cohen's act 1 (stanzas 1-4), the speaker, transfixed by the sun's unwavering gaze, surveys the sailboats and the sea below him. Seen through the tree branches and tombstones, they resemble a roof covered with doves: "This tranquil roof where doves are walking." All *seems* motionless, and one feels the speaker's longing to be forever absorbed into the eternal.

The second act (stanzas 5-8) depicts the author's serene acceptance of his inevitable death. Stanza 5 exquisitely describes the loss of corporeal form and the separation of body and soul at death as the slow melting in the mouth of a piece of fruit which then releases a flood of fragrant juices: "As a fruit dissolves into a taste/ changing its absence to deliciousness/ within a palate where its shape must die." The speaker gradually realizes that despite the attraction of eternal changelessness, the essence of human existence is one of constant change. In the finale to this section, Cohen sees the speaker as aware of the vastness of his own consciousness as it exists in that moment of anticipatory emptiness before a poem is born: "Between the void and the pure event,/ I await the echo of my hidden depths."

In the third section (stanzas 9-18), Cohen sees the speaker rejecting the Christian promise of eternal life, and anticipating instead the permanent loss of individuality, sensuality, and awareness that is the fate of the dead, who have forever "melted into a dense absence." He now realizes that his very individuality is what defines him as alive.

Cohen's act 4 (stanzas 19-24) is entitled "Triumph of the Momentary, of the Successive, of Change and of Poetic Creation." The speaker recognizes that he cannot deny life; the worm which relentlessly gnaws the living is the worm of consciousness, which will not let him rest: "He lives on life, it's me he never quits!" The speaker is troubled momentarily by Zeno's paradoxes, but a fresh breath of salty air prompts him to brush aside his incertitude. The once-calm sea's curling waves reveal the creative energy constantly boiling beneath its surface; it is likened to the Hydra which swallows its own tail, a symbol of infinity and renewal. The poet's mind also boils with creative fervor; the poem ends with the speaker's vigorous acceptance of life and with a call to the waves to shatter the tranquil sea/roof where the dove/sails had been pecking.

Interpretations such as Cohen's, helpful as they are in understanding the poem, were subsequently faulted for dealing too little with the language and structure of the poem and for providing no basis for an assessment of its aesthetic quality. One such critique of this thematic approach to Valéry was that of Bernard Weinberg, whose well-known study of "The Graveyard by the Sea" in *The Limits of Symbolism* (1966) focuses instead on the poem's structure. Weinberg demonstrates how its principal metaphor develops from an initial state of apparent equilibrium in which sea, cemetery, and spectator seem to be equivalent, through a middle ground in which this balance is threatened and then disrupted, to the end, where the idea of balance is foregone and movement and change are embraced. Paying close attention to the lexical aspects of the poem's language (although neglecting the phonic and rhythmic aspects), Weinberg shows how the repetition and interplay of polyvalent words and images result in a tightly woven unity born out of poetic rather than logical necessity. For example, in his discussion of Valéry's use of Zeno's paradox of infinitely dividing distance (stanza 21), Weinberg shows how Valéry's language simultaneously recalls the poem's opening image of a sun fixed in the sky at high noon and introduces an upcoming allusion to the disparity between substance and shadow. In a later observation, Weinberg demonstrates how the poem's ending is linked to its beginning: The pantherskin surface of the sea, spotted with "thousands and thousands of idols of the sun," echoes the "thousand tiles" of the opening sea/roof image; *idole* is a further instance of the recurring religious vocabulary which first appears early in the poem and continues throughout ("temple," *idolâtre*, and so on); the image of the Hydra swallowing its tail recalls the earlier mention of the "forever-recommencing sea" ("The sea, the sea perpetually renewed!").

Concentrating mainly on the poem's diction and the development of its principal metaphor, Weinberg postulates that the presence and placement of every word and image in the poem have a structural justification deriving from and contributing to the poem's unity. Thus, he is able to conclude that "The Graveyard by the Sea" is an excellent poem, because it presents itself to the reader as "a consistent, consecutive, and unified whole."

Several decades of critical distance allow one to see not only the complementarity and differences in the interpretations of Cohen and Weinberg, but also certain shared limitations inherent in their approaches. Analyses of "The Graveyard by the Sea" that emphasize resolution (Cohen's) or unity (Weinberg's) or progression (both authors') tend to exclude or deemphasize references in the poem to circularity and repetition and to those enigmas of existence which forever resist integration into a unified whole.

In the course of this poem, the reader does indeed witness the evolution of the speaker's thought to a point of decision, but the poem's vocabulary and imagery reveal this progression to coexist with references to repetition and circularity. In the poem's twenty-four stanzas, there are twenty-three words containing the prefix "re- ." The opening image shows the speaker in a moment of contemplative repose following a previous interval of thought/ action and contemplation. Cyclical resonances characterize the poem's major images: The sun suggests the alternation of day and night, the Earth's orbit around the sun, and also evokes the representation of time as circularity (another critic, Bernard Vannier, sees "The Graveyard by the

Sea" as a clock, with its twenty-four hours/stanzas each divided into sixty minutes/feet); the massive solidity of the "forever recommencing sea" is counterbalanced by the oscillation of the waves and the ebb and flow of the tide ("The change of the murmuring shores"); death, too, is portrayed not only as an end but also as the beginning of a cycle ("All goes under the earth, and re-enters the game!").

The image of the Hydra biting its tail (stanza 23) symbolizes a circularity in which endings are contained within beginnings, and vice versa. This same sense of connection and continuity can be seen in the poem's opening and closing stanzas; one has an initial impression of absolute stasis eventually giving way to absolute motion, but each state is linked to and anticipates its opposite. The calm opening stanzas of the poem subtly suggest movement beneath the surface; the sea, seen as a "tranquil roof," "pulses" (*palpite*) in the sunlight, and peace "seems to conceive itself" in this moment of repose. Conversely, coloring the speaker's closing mood of affirmation are hints that he still struggles against the forces of inertia, hesitation, and doubt: "The wind rises! . . . One must attempt to live!/ The immense air opens and closes my book,/ The powdery waves dare to surge over the rocks!") Beginnings in endings also appear in the speaker's closing exhortation to the waves to "break the tranquil roof where the sails were pecking"—a reprise of the poem's opening image. The two notions of circularity and progression are thus fused; insofar as this poem represents the universal experience of every individual who confronts the inifinite, the speaker's ultimate decision to embrace life is as much a re-solution (a solving again) as it is a resolution.

But what of those elements that resist resolution or integration into a system, those paradoxes that confound the human mind? The speaker in the poem longs for the oblivion of nonbeing. As long as he is alive and changing, he will never know this peace; finding peace in death, he will also lose it, for he will lose all awareness. The vastness of nonbeing is pure and yet impure; changeless and sufficient unto itself, it needs an imperfect, changing human consciousness ("The flaw in [its] great diamond") to recognize and reflect its perfection. The speaker longs to merge with the absolute but cannot in his present form cross the boundary which separates him from the infinite. The poem abounds in images juxtaposed without being merged: in the cemetery, the living visit the dead, but there is no contact; the sea meets the land but remains forever separate; any substance which reflects the light has a dark half always in shadow. It should be noted, too, that the poem's protagonist does not ever resolve Zeno's paradoxes; in the end he impetuously allows his vital life-instincts to override the obstacles created by thought and logic.

It seems inappropriate to seek total unity and complete resolution in a poem in which paradox enjoys the status of a theme. According to Zeno's paradoxes, motion cannot exist, and a moving object can never arrive at its destination—yet arrows have been known to pierce their targets. Faced with things beyond comprehension, the living man is afforded a glimpse of infinite vastness; he, like the noonday sun in the poem's opening, "rests above the abyss."

This state of suspension, "between the void and the pure event," brings to mind the similar state which Zen masters seek to produce in their disciples by means of the koan, an enigmatic question which has no answer but the contemplation of which can lead to spiritual enlightenment. In "The Graveyard by the Sea," it is the contemplation of evocative language and poetic enigma that produces a sense of vastness and mystery. Explications that place too great an emphasis on unity and resolution risk stifling other, more elusive echoes which are equally a part of the poem's seductive charms.

Other literary forms · Paul Valéry's diverse and copious writings include plays, such as *Mon Faust* (1946; *My Faust*); musical drama such as *Amphion* (1931), *Sémiramis* (1934), and *Cantate du Narcisse* (1939; *The Narcissus Cantata*); dialogues such as *Eupalinos, ou l'architecte* (1921; *Eupalinos: Or, The Architect*) and *L'Âme et la danse* (1925; *Dance and the Soul*); the witty Monsieur Teste series; essays on a wide range of subjects; translations (such as that of Vergil's *Eclogues*, 43-37 B.C.); numerous book prefaces, speeches, and university lectures; and an extensive correspondence with many illustrious contemporaries, such as André Gide and Stéphane Mallarmé. Dwarfing this work in terms of volume alone are the nearly twenty-nine thousand pages of his notebooks, which he kept from 1894 until his death in 1945. They record his thoughts on such diverse subjects as psychology, mathematics, culture, and literary theory, and are considered to contain some of the most beautiful prose ever written in the French language. Virtually the only literary form which Valéry did not attempt was the novel. He considered the genre, with its contradictory demand to create a fictional reality, to be alien to his sensibilities, once remarking that he was incapable of composing a work which began with a line such as "The Marquise went out at five o'clock."

Select works other than poetry

SHORT FICTION: "La Soirée avec Monsieur Teste," 1896 ("An Evening with Monsieur Teste," 1925).

DRAMA: *Amphion*, pr., pb. 1931 (musical drama; English translation,

1960); *Sémiramis*, pr., pb. 1934 (musical drama; English translation, 1960); *Cantate du Narcisse*, pr. 1939 (musical drama; *The Narcissus Cantata*, 1960); *Mon Faust*, pb. 1946 (*My Faust*, 1960).

NONFICTION: *Eupalinos; Ou, L'Architecte*, 1921 (dialogue; *Eupalinos: Or, The Architect*, 1932); *Variété*, 1924-1944 (5 volumes); *L'Âme et la danse*, 1925 (dialogue; *Dance and the Soul*, 1951); *Analecta*, 1926 (*Analects*, 1970); *Regards sur le monde actuel*, 1931 (*Reflections on the World Today*, 1948); *Degas, danse, dessin*, 1938 (*Degas, Dance, Drawing*, 1960); *Les Cahiers*, 1957-1961.

MISCELLANEOUS: *Selected Writings*, 1950; *The Collected Works of Paul Valéry*, 1956-1975 (15 volumes).

Janet L. Solberg

Bibliography · Although fewer in number than those in French, good critical studies of the life and work of Paul Valéry do exist in English, among them Walter Putnam, *Paul Valéry Revisited*, 1995. Earlier sources for biographical information as well as criticism and interpretation are Theodora Bosanquet, *Paul Valéry*, 1974; Charles Whiting, *Paul Valéry*, 1978; Henry Grubbs, *Paul Valéry*, 1968; Agnes Mackay, *The Universal Self: A Study of Paul Valéry*, 1961; and James Lawler, *The Poet as Analyst: Essays on Paul Valéry*, 1974. Works dealing primarily with literary criticism and theory include Geoffrey Hartman, *The Unmediated Vision: An Interpretation of Wordsworth, Hopkins, Rilke, and Valéry*, 1966; Charles Davy, *Words in the Mind: Exploring Some Effects of Poetry, English and French*, 1965; *The Poetic Theory of Paul Valéry* by W. N. Ince, 1961; Francis Scarfe, *The Art of Paul Valéry*, 1954; and T. S. Eliot, *A Brief Introduction to the Method of Paul Valéry*, 1924.

CÉSAR VALLEJO

Born: Santiago de Chuco, Peru; March 16, 1892
Died: Paris, France; April 15, 1938

Poetry · *Los heraldos negros*, 1918 (*The Black Heralds*, 1990) · *Trilce*, 1922 (English translation, 1973) · *Poemas en prosa*, 1939 (*Prose Poems*, 1978) · *Poemas humanos*, 1939 (*Human Poems*, 1968) · *España, aparta de mí este cáliz*, 1939 (*Spain, Take This Cup from Me*, 1974) · *Obra poética completa*, 1968 · *Poesía completa*, 1978 · *The Complete Posthumous Poetry*, 1978 · *Selected Poems*, 1981

Achievements · Finding an authentic language in which to write has always represented a fundamental problem for Latin American writers, since it became evident that the language inherited from the Spanish conquerors could not match Latin American reality. The problem of finding such a language goes hand in hand with that of forging a separate cultural identity. An important attempt at renovating poetic language was made by the Spanish American *Modernistas* around the turn of the century, but their verse forms, imagery, and often exotic subject matter were also becoming obsolete by the time Vallejo reached maturity. It was thus up to him and his contemporaries to find a language that could deal with contemporary concerns involving war, depression, isolation, and alienation. Although hardly recognized in his lifetime, Vallejo did more than perhaps any other poet of his generation to provide an idiom that would at once reflect the Spanish tradition, his own Peruvian heritage, and the contemporary world. Aware of his heritage from Spain's great writers of the past, he blended traditional poetic vocabulary and tropes with homely Peruvian idioms and even the language of children. Where the result was still inadequate, he made up new words, changed the function of old ones, and incorporated a lexicon never before seen in poetry, often savaging poetic convention.

Vallejo's gradual conversion to Marxism and Communism is of great interest to those attempting to understand how collectivist ideals may shape poetry. The evolution of his ideology continues to be studied intensively by many individuals committed to bettering the conditions of poverty and alienation about which Vallejo wrote so eloquently—conditions which still exist in Latin America and other parts of the world. His unflinchingly honest search for both linguistic and moral solutions to the existential anguish of modern man gives his poems universal validity, while their density and complexity challenge critics of the most antithetical modes.

Biography · César Abraham Vallejo was born in Santiago de Chuco, a primitive "city" of some fourteen thousand inhabitants in Peru's northern mountains that could only be reached by a rail trip and then several days ride on mule or horseback. Both of his grandfathers had been Spanish priests and both of his grandmothers native Peruvians of Chimu Indian heritage. His parents were literate and of modest means; his father was a notary who became a subprefect in the district. Francisco de Paula Vallejo and María de los Santos Mendoza were an upright and religious pair whose marriage produced twelve offspring and who were already middle-aged when their youngest child, César, was born. In his writings, Vallejo was often to remember the security and warmth of his childhood home—games with three of his older siblings, and particularly with his mother, who might have been especially indulgent with her sensitive youngest child.

At age thirteen, Vallejo left Santiago de Chuco to attend high school in Huamachuco, another mountain village, where he received an introduction to literature and began scribbling verses. Economic difficulties prevented him from continuing the university studies that he had begun in the larger coastal cities of Trujillo and Lima in 1911. The young man first went to work in a nearby tungsten mine—an experience that he would later draw upon for his Socialist Realist novel *El tungsteno*—and then on a coastal sugar plantation. While there, he observed the tightly structured hierarchy that kept workers in misery while the middle class, to which he himself belonged, served the needs of the elite. In 1913, he returned to the University of Trujillo and was graduated two years later, having written a master's thesis entitled *El romanticismo en la poesía castellana.* For the next few years, he studied law in Trujillo, supporting himself by becoming a first-grade teacher. One of his pupils, Ciro Alegría, later to become an important novelist, described Vallejo in those days as lean, sallow, solemn, and dark-skinned, with abundant straight black hair worn somewhat long, brilliant dark eyes, a gentle manner, and an air of sadness.

During these years, Vallejo became familiar with the writings of Ralph Waldo Emerson, José Rodó, Friedrich Nietzsche, Miguel de Unamuno y Jugo, Walt Whitman, and the early Juan Ramón Jiménez. Vallejo also read the poems of two of the leading Spanish-American *Modernistas*, Rubén Darío and Julio Herrera y Reissig, as well as those of Peruvian poets of the day. Vallejo declaimed his own poems—mostly occasional verse—at various public ceremonies, and some of them appeared in Trujillo's newspapers.

Critical reception of them ranged from the cool to the hostile, since they were considered to be exaggerated and strange in that highly traditional ambience. Vallejo fell in love with a young Trujillo girl, Zoila Rosa Cuadro, the subject of several poems included in *Los heraldos negros*. The breakup of this relationship provided one motive for his departure, after he had obtained a law degree, for Lima in 1918. There he found a position teaching in one of the best elementary schools and began to put the finishing touches on his first volume of poems.

Vallejo was soon in love with the sister-in-law of one of his colleagues, a woman identified only as "Otilia." A number of the *Trilce* poems, which he was writing at the time, deal with this affair. It ended when the poet refused to marry the woman, resulting in the loss of his job. This crisis was compounded by the death of his mother, a symbol of stability whose loss made him feel like an orphan. For some time, Vallejo had thought of going to Paris, but he decided to return first to his childhood home in Santiago de Chuco. During a national holiday, he was falsely accused of having been the instigator of a civil disturbance and was later seized and imprisoned for 112 days despite the public protests of many Peruvian intellectuals. The experience affected him profoundly, and the poems that he wrote about it (later published in *Trilce*) testify to the feeling of solidarity with the oppressed that he voiced for the first time. While in prison, he also wrote a number of the sketches to appear in *Escalas melografiadas*. In 1923, he sailed for Europe, never again to return to Peru.

While Vallejo's days in Lima had often been marked by personal problems, in Paris he experienced actual penury, sometimes being forced to sleep in the subway. Eventually, he found employment in a press agency, but only after a serious illness. He began to contribute articles to Lima newspapers, made friends with a number of avant-garde artists, and journeyed several times to Spain, where he was awarded a grant for further study. Increasingly concerned with injustice in the world, he made his first trip to Russia in 1928 with the intention of staying. Instead, he returned within three weeks, living soon afterward with a Frenchwoman, Georgette de Philippart, who was later to become his wife. With some money that had come to her, the pair set out on a tour by train through Eastern Europe, spending two weeks in Moscow and returning by way of Rome. As Vallejo's enthusiasm for Marxism was apparent in his newspaper articles, he found them no longer welcome in Lima, and in 1930, he was ordered to leave France because of his political activity. Once again in Spain, he wrote several plays and the novel *El tungsteno* and published *Rusia en 1931*, the only one of his books to sell well. No publisher could be found for several other works. After a third and final visit to Russia as a delegate to the International Congress of Writers, he wrote *Rusia ante el segundo plan quinquenal* and officially joined the Communist Party.

In 1932, Vallejo was permitted to return to Paris, where he tried unsuccessfully to publish some new poems. In 1936, the Spanish Civil War broke out, and Vallejo became an active supporter of the Republic, traveling to Barcelona and Madrid to attend the Second International Congress for the Defense of Culture. He visited the battlefront and learned at first hand of the horrors suffered by the Spanish people in the war. Returning to Paris for the last time, he poured his feelings into his last work, *España, aparta de mí este calíz* (1939; *Spain, Take This Cup from Me*). In March, 1938, he became ill. Doctors were unable to diagnose his illness, and Vallejo died a month later on Good Friday, the day before the troops of Francisco Franco won a decisive victory in Spain.

Analysis · One of the unique qualities of César Vallejo's poetry—one that makes his work almost impossible to confuse with that of any other poet in the Spanish language—is his ability to speak with the voice and sensibility of a child, whether as an individual orphaned by the breakup of a family or as a symbol of deprived and alienated human beings everywhere. Always, however, this child's voice, full of expectation and hope, is implicitly counterposed by the adult's ironic awareness of change and despair. Inseparable from these elements is the poet's forging of a language capable of reflecting the register and the peculiarly elliptical reasoning of a child and, at the same time, revealing the hermetic complexity of the adult intellectual's quest for security in the form of truth. The poetry that is Vallejo's own answer to these problems is some of the most poignant and original ever produced.

The lines of Vallejo's subsequent development are already evident in his first volume, *Los heraldos negros*, a collection of sixty-nine poems grouped under various subtitles. As critics have observed, many of these poems reflect his involvement with Romantic and *Modernista* poetry. They are conspicuous in many cases for their descriptions of idyllic scenes in a manner that juxtaposes words of the Peruvian Sierra and the vocabulary of Symbolism, including religious and erotic elements. Vallejo did not emphasize rhyme and rhythm to the extent that some *Modernistas* did, but most of these early poems are framed in verse forms favored by the latter, such as the Alexandrine sonnet and the *silva*. While demonstrating his impressive mastery of styles already worked out by others, he was also finding his own voice.

This originality is perhaps most evident in the last group of poems in *Los heraldos negros*, entitled "Canciones de Hogar" ("Home Songs"), poems dealing with the beginning of Vallejo's sense of orphanhood. In "A mi hermano Miguel in memoriam" ("To My Brother Miguel in Memoriam"), the poet relives a moment of the childhood game of hide-and-seek that he used to play with his "twin heart." Speaking to his brother, Vallejo announces his own presence in the part of the family home from which one of the two always ran away to hide from the other. He goes on to remind his playmate of one day on which the latter went away to hide, sad instead of laughing as he usually was, and could not be found again. The poem ends with a request to the brother to please come out so as not to worry "mama." It is remarkable in that past and present alternate from one line to the next. The language of childhood, as well as the poet's assumed presence at the site of the events, lends a dramatic immediacy to the scene. At the same time, the language used in the descriptive passages is clearly that of the adult who is now the poet. Yet in the last verse, the adult chooses to accept literally the explanation that the brother has remained in hiding and may finally respond and come out, which would presumably alleviate the mother's anxiety and make everything right once more. The knowledge that the poet is unable (or refuses) to face the permanent alteration of his past may elicit feelings of tragic pathos in the reader.

"Los pasos lejanos" ("The Distant Steps") recalls the poet's childhood home in which his parents, now aged, are alone—the father sleeping and the mother walking in the orcahrds. Here, the only bitterness is that of the poet himself, because he is now far away from them. He in turn is haunted by a vision of his parents as two old, white, and bent roads along which his heart walks. In "Enereida," he imagines that his father has died, leading to a regression in time so that the father can once again laugh at his small children, including the poet himself, who is again a schoolboy under the tutelage of the village priest.

Many of the poems in *Los heraldos negros* deal with existential themes. While religious imagery is pervasive, it is apparent that the poet employs it to describe profane experiences. Jean Franco has shown that in speaking of "the soul's Christs" and "Marías who leave" and of Communions and Passions, Vallejo trivializes religious language rather than attempting to inflate the importance of his own experiences by describing them in religious terms. As well as having lost the security and plenitude of his childhood home, the poet has lost the childhood faith that enabled him to refer in words to the infinite.

In the title poem, "Los heraldos negros" ("The Black Messengers"), he laments life's hard blows, harder sometimes than man can stand. He concludes that these blows come from the hatred of God, that they may be the black heralds sent by Death. In "Los dados eternos" ("The Eternal

Dice"), God is a gambler throwing dice and may as easily cast death as life. In fact, the Earth itself is His die. Now worn to roundness, it will come to rest only within the sepulchre. Profane love is all that is left; while the beloved may now be pure, she will not continue to be so if she yields to the poet's erotic impulses. Love thus becomes "a sinning Christ," because man's nature is irrevocably physical. Several poems allude to the poet's ideal of redeeming himself through brotherly love, a thematic constant in Vallejo's work, yet such redemption becomes difficult if not impossible if man is lonely and alienated. In "Agape," the poet speaks of being alone and forgotten and of having been unable therefore to "die" for his brother. "La cena miserable" ("The Wretched Supper") tells of the enigma of existence in which man is seen, as in "Agape," as waiting endlessly for spiritual nurture, or at least for some answer concerning the meaning of life. Here, God becomes no more than a "black spoon" full of bitter human essence, even less able than man to provide needed answers. Man's life is thus meaningless, since he is always separated from what he most desires—whether this be the fulness of the past, physical love, God's love, or brotherly love.

Even in the poems most laden with the trappings of *Modernismo,* Vallejo provides unusual images. In "El poeta a su amada" ("The Poet to His Beloved"), he suggests that his kiss is "two curved branches" on which his beloved has been "crucified." Religious imagery is used with such frequency that it sometimes verges on parody, and critics agree that in playing with language in this way Vallejo is seeking to highlight its essential ambiguity, something he continues to do in *Trilce* and *Human Poems,* even while totally abandoning the imagery of *Modernismo.* Such stripping away of excess baggage is already visible in *Los heraldos negros.* Antitheses, oxymorons, and occasional neologisms are also to be noted. While the great majority of the poems are elegantly correct in terms of syntax—in marked contrast to what is to become the norm in *Trilce*—there are some instances of linguistic experimentation, as when nouns are used as adjectives. In "The Distant Steps," for example, the mother is described as being "so soft, so wing, so departure, so love." Another device favored by the poet in all of his later poems—enumeration—is also present. Finally, traditional patterns of meter and rhyme are abandoned in "Home Songs," with the poetic emotion being allowed to determine the form.

In spite of these formal adumbrations and in spite of the fact that *Los heraldos negros* is not a particularly transparent work, there is little in it to prepare the reader for the destruction of language in the hermetic density of *Trilce,* which came along only three years later. These were difficult years for the poet, in which he lost his mother, separated from Otilia, and spent what he was later to refer to as the gravest moments of his life in the Trujillo jail. All the anguish of these events was poured into the seventy-seven free-verse poems of his second major work. If he suffered existentially in *Los heraldos negros* and expressed this suffering in writing, it was done with respect for traditional verse forms and sentence structure, which hinted at an order beyond the chaos of the poet's interior world. In *Trilce*, this order falls. Language, on which "logical assumptions" about the world are based, is used in such a way as to reveal its hollowness: It, too, is cut loose and orphaned. Abrupt shifts from one metaphorical sphere to another make the poems' internal logic often problematic.

A hint of what is to come is given in the title, a neologism usually taken to be a hybrid of *tres* (three) and *dulce* (sweet), an interpretation which is in accord with the poet's concern about the ideal number expressed in several poems. It is not known, however, what, if any, concrete meaning the poet had in mind when he coined the word; it has become a puzzle for readers and critics to solve. It is notable that in "interpreting" the *Trilce* poems, critics often work out explications that seem internally consistent but that turn out to be related to a system diametrically opposed to the explication and system of some other critic. It is possible, however, to say with certainty that these poems deal with a struggle to do something, bridge something, say something. Physical limits such as the human body, time, space, and numbers often render the struggle futile.

Two of the thematic sets of *Trilce* for which it is easiest to establish concrete referents are those dealing with the poet-as-child and those dealing with his imprisonment. In Poem III, the poet once again speaks in the voice of a child left at home by the adults of the family. It is getting dark, and he asks when the grown-ups will be back, adding that "Mama said she wouldn't be gone long." In the third stanza, an ironic double vision of years full of agonizing memories intrudes. As in "To My Brother Miguel in Memoriam," the poet chooses to retain the child's faith, urging his brothers and sisters to be good and obey in letter and spirit the instructions left by the mother. In the end, it is seen that the "leaving" is without remedy, a function of time itself; it eventually results in the poet's complete solitude without even the comfort of his siblings. In Poem XXIII, the mother, the only symbol of total plenitude, is seen as the "warm oven" of the cookies described as "rich hosts of time." The nourishment provided by the mother was given freely and naturally, taken away from no one and given without the child's being obliged. Still, the process of nurturing leads to growing up and to individuation and alienation. Several poems mythicize the process of birth but shift so abruptly to demythicize human existence that the result is at first humorous. In Poem XLVII, a candle is lighted to protect the mother while she gives birth, along with another for the babe who, God willing, will grow up to be bishop, pope, saint, "or perhaps only a columnary headache." Later, in *Human Poems*, there is a Word Incarnate whose bones agree in number and gender as it sinks into the bathtub ("Lomo de las sagradas escrituras"/"Spine of the Scriptures").

In Poem XVIII, the poet surveys the four walls of the cell, implacably closed. He calls up a vision of the "loving keeper of innumerable keys," the mother, who would liberate him if she could. He imagines the two longer walls as mothers and the shorter ones as the children each of them is leading by the hand. The poet is alone with only his two hands, struggling to find a third to help him in his useless adulthood. In Poem LVIII, the solid walls of the cell seem to bend at the corners, suggesting that the poet is dozing as a series of jumbled thoughts produce scenes in his mind that follow no easy logical principle of association. The poet sees himself helping the naked and the ragged, then dismounting from a panting horse that he also attempts to help. The cell is now liquid, and he becomes aware of the companions who may be worse off than he. Guilt suddenly overwhelms him, and he is moved to promise to laugh no more when his mother arises early to pray for the sick, the poor, and the prisoners. He also promises to treat his little friends better at play, in both word and deed. The cell is now boundless gas, growing as it condenses. Ambiguously, at the end, he poses the question, "Who stumbles outside?" The openness of the poem is similar to that of many others in *Trilce*, and it is difficult to say what kind of threat to the poet's resolutions is posed by the figure outside. Again, the poetic voice has become that of a child seeking to make all that is wrong in the world right once more by promising to be "a good boy." Of course, he is not a child at all, as the figure outside may be intended to remind both him and the reader. The result is once again a remarkable note of pathos tinged with poignant irony.

Many of *Trilce*'s poems deal with physical love and even the sexual act itself. "Two" seems to be the ideal number, but "two" has "propensities of trinity." Clearly, the poet has no wish to bring a child into the world, and sex becomes merely an act of organs that provides no solution to anything. While the poet seems to appreciate the maternal acts performed by his lover, he fails to find any transcendental satisfaction in the physical relationship, even though he is sad when it is over.

An important theme that emerges in *Trilce* and is developed more fully in *Human Poems* and *Spain, Take This Cup from Me* is that of the body as text. In Poem LXV, the house to which the poet returns in Santiago seems to be his mother's body. Parts of the body—the back, face, shoulder, eyes, hands, lips, eyelashes, bones, feet, knees, fingers, heart, arms, breasts, soles of the feet, eyelids, ears, ribs—appear in poem after poem, reminding the reader of human and earthly functions and the limitations of man.

In many ways, *Trilce* resembles the poetry of such avant-garde movements as Surrealism, Ultraism, and Creationism in the boldness of its images, its unconventional vocabulary, and its experimentation with graphics. Vallejo did have very limited exposure to some of this poetry after he reached Lima; his critics, however, generally agree that *Trilce* was produced independently. While Vallejo may have been encouraged to experiment by his knowledge of European literary currents, his work coincides with them as an original contribution.

As far as is known, the poems after *Trilce* were written in Europe; with very few exceptions, none was published until 1939, a year after the poet's death, when they appeared under the title *Human Poems*. While Vallejo's life in Peru was far from affluent, it must have seemed easy in comparison with the years in Paris, where he often barely subsisted and suffered several illnesses. In addition, while he did see a new edition of *Trilce* published through the intervention of friends in 1931, and while his *Rusia en 1931* did go into three editions during his lifetime, he could never count on having his writings accepted for publication.

Human Poems, considered separately from *Spain, Take This Cup from Me*, is far from being a homogeneous volume, and its final configuration might have been different had it been Vallejo who prepared the final edition rather than his widow. Generally speaking, the poems that it includes deal with ontological anguish whose cause seems related to physical suffering, the passage of time, and the impossibility of believing that life has any meaning. In fact, *Human Poems* examines suffering and pain, with their corollaries, poverty, hunger, illness, and death, with a thoroughness that few other works can match. At times, the anguish seems to belong only to the poet, now not only the orphan of *Trilce* but alienated from his fellow-man as well. In "Altura y pelos" ("Height and Hair"), the poet poses questions: "Who doesn't own a blue suit?/ Who doesn't eat lunch and board the streetcar// Who is not called Carlos or any other thing?/ Who to the kitty doesn't say kitty kitty?" The final answer given is "Aie? I who alone was solely born." At least two kinds of irony seem to be involved here. The activities mentioned are obviously trivial, but neither is it easy to be alone. In the well-known "Los nueve monstruos" ("The Nine Monsters"), the poet laments the abundance of pain in the world: "Never, human men/ was there so *much* pain in the chest, in the lapel, in the wallet/ in the glass, in the butcher-shop, in arithmetic!" and "never/ . . . did the migraine extract so much forehead from the forehead!" Pain drives people crazy "in the movies,/ nails us into the gramophones,/ denails us in bed."

The poem concludes that the "Secretary of Health" can do nothing because there is simply "too much to do."

"The Nine Monsters" is representative of several features of *Human Poems.* The language is extremely concrete, denoting things that are inseparable from everyday existence. Much of the poem consists of lists, continuing a device for which the poet had already shown a disposition in his first work. Finally, the logic of the systems represented by the items named is hard to pin down, so that it is somewhat reminiscent of child logic in its eccentricity. Again and again, Vallejo's remarkable sensibility is demonstrated beyond any preciosity or mere posturing.

One reason for the poet's alienation is that he sees men as engaged in trivial occupations and as being hardly more advanced on the evolutionary scale than pachyderms or kangaroos, whereas he himself aspires to rise above his limitations. In "Intensidad y altura" ("Intensity and Height"), he tells of his desire to write being stifled by his feeling "like a puma," so that he might as well go and eat grass. He concludes, "let's go, raven, and fecundate your rook." He thus sees himself condemned not to rise above the purely mundane. Religion offers no hope at all. In "Acaba de pasar el que vendrá . . ." ("He Has Just Passed By, the One Who Will Come . . ."), the poet suggests that "the one who will come"–presumably the Messiah–has already passed by but has changed nothing, being as vague and ineffectually human as anyone else.

While the majority of these posthumously published poems convey utter despair, not all of them do. Although the exact dates of their composition are generally unknown, it is natural to associate those that demonstrate growing concern for others with Vallejo's conversion to Marxist thought and eventually to Communism. In "Considerando en frío . . ." ("Considering Coldly . . ."), speaking as an attorney at a trial, the poetic voice first summarizes the problems and weaknesses of man's humanity (he "is sad, coughs and, nevertheless,/ takes pleasure in his reddened chest/ . . . he is a gloomy mammal and combs his hair"). Then, however, he announces his love for man. Denying it immediately, he nevertheless concludes, "I signal him,/ he comes,/ I embrace him, moved./ So what! Moved . . . Moved. . . ." Compassion thus nullifies "objectivity." In "La rueda del hambriento" ("The Hungry Man's Wheel"), the poet speaks as a man so miserable that his own organs are pulled out of him through his mouth. He begs only for a stone on which to sit and a little bread. Apparently ignored, aware that he is being importunate, he continues to ask, disoriented and hardly able to recognize his own body. In "Traspié entre dos estrellas" ("Stumble Between Two Stars"), the poet expresses pity for the wretched but goes on to parody bitterly Christ's Sermon on the

Mount ("Beloved be the one with bedbugs,/ the one who wears a torn shoe in the rain"), ending with a "beloved" for one thing and then for its opposite, as if calling special attention to the emptiness of mere words. It is possible to say that in these poems the orphan has finally recognized that he is not alone in his orphanhood.

Although first published as part of *Human Poems, Spain, Take This Cup from Me* actually forms a separate, unified work very different in tone from the majority of the other posthumous poems—a tone of hope, although, especially in the title poem, the poet seems to suspect that the cause he has believed in so passionately may be lost. In this poem, perhaps the last that Vallejo wrote, the orphan—now all human children—has found a mother. This mother is Spain, symbol of a new revolutionary order in which oppression may be ended. The children are urged not to let their mother die; nevertheless, even should this happen, they have a recourse: to continue struggling and to go out and find a new mother.

Another contrast is found in the odes to several heroes of the Civil War. Whereas, in *Human Poems*, man is captive of his body and hardly more intelligent than the lower animals, *Spain, Take This Cup from Me* finds him capable of true transcendence through solidarity with his brothers and the will to fight injustice. A number of poems commemorate the battles of the war: Talavera, Guernica, Málaga. Spain thus becomes a text—a book that sprouts from the bodies of an anonymous soldier. The poet insists again and again that he himself is nothing, that his stature is "tiny," and that his actions rather than his words constitute the real text. This may be seen to represent a greatly evolved negation of poetic authority, first seen in *Los heraldos negros* with the repeated cry, "I don't know!"

Nevertheless, *Spain, Take This Cup from Me* rings with a biblical tone, and the poet sometimes sounds like a prophet. James Higgins has pointed out certain images that recall the Passion of Christ and the New Jerusalem, although religious terminology, as in all of Vallejo's poetry, is applied to man rather than to divinity. While Vallejo continues to use techniques of enumeration, which are often chaotic, and while he uses concrete nouns (including many referring to the body), he also employs abstract terms—peace, hope, martyrdom, harmony, eternity, greatness. The sense of garments, utensils, and the body's organs stifling the soul is gone and is replaced by limitless space. In Vallejo's longest poem, "Himno a los voluntarios de la República" ("Hymn to the Volunteers for the Republic"), a panegyric note is struck.

One of Vallejo's most immediately accessible poems, "Masa" ("Mass"), tells almost a parable of a dead combatant who was asked by one man not to die, then by two, and finally by millions. The corpse kept dying until surrounded by all the inhabitants of the Earth. The corpse, moved, sat up and embraced the first man and then began to walk. The simplicity of the story and of its narration recalls the child's voice in *Trilce*, promising to cease tormenting his playmates in order to atone for the world's guilt. In this piece, as well as in all Vallejo's last group of poems, however, the irony is gone.

It is thus possible to see the completion of a cycle in the four works. Disillusionment grows in *Los heraldos negros*, and then alienation works its way into the language itself in *Trilce*. *Human Poems* is somewhat less hermetic than *Trilce*, but life is an anguished nightmare in which the soul is constrained by the ever-present body that seems to be always wracked with pain. Only in *Spain, Take This Cup from Me*, with the realization that men are brothers who can end their common alienation and suffering by collective action, does the poet regain his lost faith and embark upon a positive course. The orphan relocates the lost mother, whom he now sees to be the mother of all, since all men are brothers. The true significance of Vallejo's poetry, however, surely lies in his honesty in questioning all established rules of poetic expression, as well as the tradition of poetic authority, in order to put poetry fully in touch with the existential prison-house of twentieth century man.

Other literary forms · César Vallejo wrote fiction, plays, and essays, as well as lyric poetry, although his achievement as a poet far outstrips that in any other genre. His short stories—many of them extremely brief—may be found in *Escalas melografiadas* (1923; musical scales). A novella, *Fábula salvaje* (1923; primitive parlance), is a tragic idyll of two rustic lovers. *Hacia el reino de Los Seiris* (1967; toward the kingdom of the Sciris), set in the time of the Incas, is usually described as a novel, despite its brevity. *El tungsteno* is a proletarian novel with an Andean setting that was written in 1931, the year Vallejo joined the Communist Party. Another story, *Paco Yunque* (1969), is about the mistreatment of a servant's son by a classmate who happens to be the master's son.

Vallejo became interested in the theater around 1930, but he destroyed his first play, "Mampar." Three others, *Moscú contra Moscú*—later changed to *Entre las dos orillas corre el río* (the river flows between two banks)—*Lock Out*, and *Colacho hermanos* (Colacho brothers), never published during the poet's lifetime, are now available in *Teatro completo* (1979, complete theatrical work). His long essay, *Rusia en 1931: Reflexiones al pie del Kremlin* (1931; reissued in 1965), was followed by *Rusia ante el segundo plan quinquenal* (1965); *Contra el secreto profesional* (1973); and *El arte y la revolución* (1973). His master's thesis, *El romanticismo en la poesía castellana*, was published in 1954.

Select works other than poetry

LONG FICTION: *Fábula salvaje*, 1923 (novella); *El tungsteno*, 1931 (*Tungsten*, 1988).

SHORT FICTION: *Escalas melografiadas*, 1923; *Hacia el reino de Los Seiris*, 1967; *Paco Yunque*, 1969.

DRAMA: *La piedra cansada*, pb. 1979; *Colacho hermanos: O, presidentes de América*, pb. 1979; *Lock-Out*, pb. 1979; *Entre las dos orillas corre el río*, pb. 1979.

NONFICTION: *Rusia en 1931: Reflexiones al pie del Kremlin*, 1931, 1965; *El romanticismo en la poesía castellana*, 1954; *Rusia ante el segundo plan quinquenal*, 1965; *El arte y la revolución*, 1973; *Contra el secreto profesional*, 1973.

Lee Hunt Dowling

Bibliography · *César Vallejo: The Complete Posthumous Poetry*, translated by Clayton Eshleman and José Rubia Barcia, 1978, apart from offering translations of the later poems, contains a helpful introduction to Vallejo's work. Jean Franco's study *César Vallejo: The Dialectics of Poetry and Silence*, 1976, remains the best introduction to Vallejo's work. James Higgins' *The Poet in Peru: Alienation and the Quest for a Super-Reality*, 1982, contains a good overview of the main themes of Vallejo's poetry. Christiane von Buelow, "Vallejo's 'Venus de Milo' and the Ruins of Language," *PMLA* 104 (January, 1989), provides a close analysis that convincingly shows how Vallejo's poetry dismembers the very structure of language itself. R. K. Britton, "Love, Alienation, and the Absurd: Three Principal Themes in César Vallejo's *Trilce*," *Modern Language Review* 87 (July, 1992), demonstrates how Vallejo's poetry expresses the anguished conviction that humankind is simply a form of animal life subject to the laws of a random, absurd universe.

VERGIL

(Publius Vergilius Maro)

Born: Andes, Italy; October 15, 70 B.C.
Died: Brundisium, Italy; September 21, 19 B.C.

Poetry · *Eclogues*, 43-37 B.C. (also known as *Bucolics*; English translation, 1575) · *Georgics*, c. 37-29 B.C. (English translation, 1589) · *Aeneid*, c. 29-19 B.C. (English translation, 1553)

Achievements · Vergil is considered by many to be the greatest poet of ancient Rome, and his influence reaches well into the modern era of Western poetry. Vergil mastered three types of poetry: pastoral (*Eclogues*), didactic (*Georgics*), and national epic (*Aeneid*). This mastery is reflected in the final words of his epitaph, "cecini pascua, rura, duces" ("I sang of shepherds, farmlands, and national leaders"). Vergil's fame was assured even in his own lifetime, as Tibullus, Sextus Propertius, and Horace praised and emulated him. He was his own harshest critic, and it was his dying wish that the unfinished *Aeneid* be destroyed. The Emperor Augustus himself intervened, however, and the poem was rescued and edited by Varius and Tucca in 17 B.C. The works of Vergil influenced Ovid and Manilius, and Vergil's epic craft established a tradition which was followed by Lucan, Statius, Silius Italicus, and Valerius Piaccus. Writers of satire, epigram, and history, such as Juvenal, Martial, Livy, and Tacitus, also show the influence of Vergil's thought, language, and prosody. The first critical edition of the *Aeneid*, the work of Probus, appeared in the time of Nero, and the Verona scholia also

Library of Congress

record interpretations based on editions by Cornutus, Velius Longus, and Asper in the late second century A.D. By this time, the poetry of Vergil had become a school manual, used for teaching grammar, rhetoric, and language.

In the fourth and fifth centuries A.D., Nonius and Macrobius discussed and quoted the works of Vergil. The tradition of *centos* soon arose, in which poets employed clever rearrangements of lines of Vergilian poetry to create poems with new meanings. The admiration of Vergil's works eventually approached a kind of worship, with the superstitious practice of consulting random lines of his poetry as one might consult an oracle.

Dante and John Milton both studied Vergil, and their great epics owe much to his works, especially the *Aeneid*. John Dryden called the *Georgics* "the best poems of the best poet"; Alfred, Lord Tennyson, described Vergil's hexameters as "the stateliest measures ever moulded by the lips of man."

Vergil's achievement is therefore enormous. He raised the dactylic hexameter to new levels of grandeur, he elevated the Latin language to new beauty, and he set new standards for three types of poetry. Perhaps his greatest achievement lies in the vision of the imperial grandeur of Rome depicted in the *Aeneid*.

Biography · Publius Vergilius Maro was born on October 15, 70 B.C., in Andes, an Italian town located near present-day Mantua. He was not born to Roman citizenship, but the franchise was later granted to his native province. His early education took place at Cremona and at Mediolanum, now called Milan. Like most promising young men of his era, Vergil eventually made his way to Rome, where he studied philosophy, rhetoric, medicine, and mathematics; he also completed preparation for the legal profession, although he spoke only once as an advocate. At this time, he also made the acquaintance of the poets who remained from Catullas' circle and absorbed from them the Alexandrian ideals of poetry. In 41 B.C., the farm belonging to Vergil's family was confiscated and given to the soldiers of Mark Anthony. According to tradition, this personal catastrophe, referred to in eclogues 1 and 9, was remedied by Octavian himself (after 23 B.C., the emperor Augustus) in response to a personal appeal by Vergil, but many scholars believe the loss of the farm was permanent; the references in the *Eclogues* are subject to interpretation. It was during this period, from about 43 to 37 B.C., that Vergil wrote the ten *Eclogues*, working first in Northern Italy and later in Rome. The success of the *Eclogues* resulted in an introduction to Maecenas, Octavian's literary adviser, and this personal connection assured financial support for Vergil's literary activities and provided an entrée into the circle of Rome's best writers and poets.

In 38 or 37 B.C., Vergil met the great Roman poet Horace and arranged for Horace to meet Maecenas. It was at this time that the two poets and their colleagues, Varius and Tucca, participated in the famous journey to Brundisium described in Horace's *Satires* (35, 30 B.C.). From that point on, Vergil lived and wrote in Southern Italy, at a country house near Nola and at Naples. From 37 to 29 B.C., he worked slowly on the *Georgics*, a didactic poem in four books which instructs the reader in various aspects of agriculture and animal husbandry. Finally, in 29 B.C., Vergil began his greatest undertaking, the *Aeneid*, an epic poem which describes the journey of the hero, Aeneas, from the ruins of Troy to the west coast of Italy; in the poem, Aeneas' son Iulus is linked to the Julian clan from which the emperor Augustus claimed descent. The writing of this poem also proceeded laboriously. In 19 B.C., Vergil embarked on a journey to Greece and the East, during which he hoped to polish and revise his epic. During his journey, he fell ill at Megara; shortly after reaching Brundisium, the port city on the east coast of Italy which serves as the gateway to Greece, he died. He was buried at Naples, and his dying request for the unrevised *Aeneid* to be destroyed was fortunately countermanded by the orders of Augustus.

Little is known of the character of Vergil, except that he was a shy and reclusive man who never married. He was also of weak physical constitution, often ill. The main source of information about Vergil's life and character is the biography by Aelius Donatus, from the fourth century.

Analysis · In order to understand more fully the poetry of Vergil, his works should be considered in the light of two relationships: his literary connection with the Greek poetry on which his works are modeled and his personal and ideological connection with the builders of the Roman Empire. Vergil, like most Roman artists, worked within genres invented by the Greeks, but he also left on his works a uniquely Roman imprint. It was his great genius that he was able to combine both Greek and Roman elements so effectively.

Vergil's earliest major work was a group of ten short poems called the *Eclogues*, or the *Bucolics*. The poems are set in an idealized Italian countryside and are populated by shepherds. Vergil has clearly modeled the poems on the thirty idylls of Theocritus, a Greek poet of about 310 to 250 B.C. who lived primarily in Sicily. The *Eclogues* are, in fact, the most highly imitative of Vergil's three works, although the Roman element asserts itself clearly. In the first eclogue, which is one of the most Roman, Vergil tells of two shepherds, Tityrus and Meliboeus. Tityrus has retained his farm in the face of confiscation, and he relaxes among his sheep while Meliboeus, ejected from his fields, drives his weary livestock to new pastures. Tityrus expresses his gratitude to the young Octavian, whom he depicts as a god. Here, Vergil uses the Theocritean framework, but the content of the poem reflects Vergil's own private and public Roman experience. Eclogue 2, by contrast, follows Theocritus in both form and substance. Here, the shepherd Corydon bemoans his failure to win Alexis, imitating Polyphemus' lament of the cruelty of Galatea in the *Idylls* (third century B.C.). Similarly, the capping contest between shepherds Menalcas and Damon in Eclogue 3 closely follows idylls 4 and 5.

Eclogue 4 is perhaps the most famous, as well as the most Roman. Here, the shepherd format has been abandoned. The poem honors the consulship of Vergil's early local patron, Asinius Pollio, during which the former governor helped negotiate the Treaty of Brundisium. Welcoming the hope of peace, Vergil predicts the coming of a new Golden Age. His ideas about the cycle of ages are based on a number of sources, including the Sybilline Books and the "ages of man" in Hesiod. Because the new era of peace is here connected with the birth of a child, scholars of the Middle Ages believed that the poem held a messianic message, predicting the birth of Christ. Present-day scholars disagree about the identity of the young child: Some argue that Vergil refers here to the children of Pollio, who were born around this time, while others believe that the poem expresses hope for the future offspring of Mark Anthony and Octavia, or perhaps of Octavian and his new wife, Scribonia. In any case, the language of the eclogue is sufficiently vague to preclude any clear identification.

Eclogue 5 returns once again to the Theocritean format: Two shepherds, Mopsus and Menalcas, engage in a contest of amoebaean verse (poetry written in the form of a dialogue between two speakers). They sing of the death and deification of Daphnis, also a shepherd, and in so doing they reprise the song of Idyll 1. Eclogue 6 maintains the pastoral theme: Two shepherds catch Silenus (a mythological woodland deity with horse's ears and tail) and induce him to sing of the world's creation and other legends. The preface to this poem, however, deals with more Roman matters: Vergil dedicates the poem to Varus, the man who succeeded Pollio as legate in the region of Vergil's birthplace. Apparently the new legate had urged the poet to write an epic; here the poet demurs. Eclogue 7, like eclogues 2, 3, and 5, adheres to the Theocritean model: Melliboeus tells of a contest between shepherds Thyrsis and Corydon.

Eclogue 8, like Eclogue 4, is dedicated to Pollio. Two shepherds sing an amoebaeic: Damon grieves over the faithlessness of Nisa, and Alphesiboeus sings of a young woman's attempts to secure the love of Daphnis by magic charms. The latter topic has as its model Idyll 2 of Theocritus, but the ethos is Roman. Eclogue 9 returns to the farm confiscations discussed in Eclogue 1. Shepherd Moeris has been ejected from his farm; shepherd Lycidas expresses surprise, since he had thought that the poetry of Menalcas (Vergil's persona) had secured the safety of all the farms of the region. The collection concludes with Eclogue 10, in which Gallus (a real-life Roman) grieves for the loss of an actress named Lycoris.

Critics agree that these poems, although very artificial, are exercises which show the power of a great poet early in his development. Eclogues 2, 3, 5, and 7, among the first written, follow the Theocritean model rather closely, working within the conventionalized framework of the pastoral genre. Other eclogues introduce matters closer to Vergil's life and times, such as the farm confiscations dealt with in eclogues 1 and 9 (and alluded to in 6) and the problems of Gallus in Eclogue 10. *Eclogues* offers the promise of greater works to come, and this promise is redeemed first in the *Georgics* and later in the *Aeneid.*

The *Georgics* comprise four books of dactylic hexameter verse on the subject of farming and animal husbandry. The basic Greek model is Hesiod's *Works and Days*, (c. 700 B.C.); however, Vergil's sources for the *Georgics* also include the Alexandrian scientific poets and the Roman Epicurean poet, Lucretius. The *Georgics* are very Italian, and the Hesiodic model provides only a form and an outline: The poet distances himself from his model to a much greater degree than in the *Eclogues.* Vergil's own words suggest that Maecenas, the great Augustan literary patron, suggested the subject matter of this poem. Augustus' vision of the new order, the Pax Romana, had as its cornerstone a revival of "old Roman" virtues, religion, and the simple agrarian life. The *Georgics*, then, aimed to present the simplicity and beauty of Italian country life as an important element of Augustus' new empire. Once again, Vergil is working with a Greek model and Roman ideas, but in the *Georgics* the model is less intrusive and the Italian element predominates.

Book 1 of the *Georgics* deals with the farming of field crops and the relationship of weather and constellations to this pursuit. Vergil stresses the importance of Jupiter and of Ceres, the goddess of agriculture. Near the end of the book, the discussion of weather phenomena leads the poet to a description of the ominous cosmological omens that accompanied the assassination of Julius Caesar in 44 B.C.; Vergil closes the book by expressing his hope that Augustus will save Rome and by expressing his regret that years of civil war have prevented the people of Italy from peacefully farming their lands.

In book 2, Vergil treats the matter of vines and trees, especially the olive tree. He instructs the reader on the propagation, growth, planting, and tending of these plants. Technical discussions of soils, vines, and proper seasons are included, and here the Hesiodic and Alexandrian models are evident, although not predominant. Praise for the agriculture of Italy leads to praise of the country as a whole, and then of its chief, Augustus. The book concludes with a paean to the life of the farmer, especially as contrasted with the life of war. The themes of Augustus' new order find eloquent voice.

Book 3 of the *Georgics* takes up the subject of cattle and their deities. At the beginning of the book, Vergil tells the reader that Maecenas urged the writing of the *Georgics*, and Vergil also promises future works in praise of Augustus and Rome. Following these literary comments, the poet once again turns to technical matters: care of broodmares, calves, and racing foals; the force of love among animals; sheep and goats; and the production of wool, milk, and cheese. A discussion of disease in sheep leads into the very famous and poignant description of the plague, based on similar passages in Lucretius and Thucydides.

In book 4, Vergil turns to the subject of bees and beekeeping. He discusses the location of hives, the social organization of bees, the taking of honey, and the very ancient practice of obtaining a new stock of bees by using the carcass of a dead animal. The book closes with the stories of Aristaeus and Arethusa, and finally of Orpheus.

The matter of sources, then, is much more complex in the *Georgics* than in the *Eclogues*. The *Georgics* reveal a wide variety of sources and a poet who is more confident and thus more willing to depart from his models. Vergil's relationship to Maecenas, Augustus, and the new Roman order manifests itself both in the overall intent of the poem and in specific passages. The artificial landscape of the *Eclogues* yields to the reality and beauty of the Italian countryside.

The final and most important work of Vergil's career was the twelve-book hexameter epic called the *Aeneid*. Vergil wished to pay homage to the great Greek epics of Homer (the *Iliad* and the *Odyssey*, both c. 800 B.C.) and Apollonius Rhodius (the *Argonautica*, third century B.C.), but Vergil also sought to create a work that would supplant the work of Ennius and glorify the Rome of his own day and its leader, Augustus. The solution lay in telling the mythological story of Aeneas, a Trojan hero who fought on the losing side in the great Trojan War. Homer mentions that Aeneas was purposefully rescued by the gods, and a firm post-Homeric tradition told of the hero's subsequent journey to Italy. Vergil, then, would tell the story of Aeneas' travels and of the founding of the Roman race, and in so doing would remain close to the Homeric era; at the same time, prophetic passages could look forward to the Rome of Vergil's lifetime, and the poem overall would stress Roman virtues and ideals. In the figure of Aeneas, Vergil had discovered the perfect transition from the Homeric world in which epic was rooted to the Augustan era of his own day.

The first six books tell of the wandering journey of Aeneas and his men from Troy to the western coast of Italy, a voyage which was impeded by false starts, the anger of the goddess Juno, and Aeneas' own fears, hesitations, and weaknesses. Vergil chose as his basic model for these books Homer's *Odyssey*, also a tale of wandering. Since books 6 through 12 of the *Aeneid* describe the battles between Aeneas and the Italic tribes which opposed him, the poet here emulated the *Iliad*, an epic of war. Indeed, the opening phrase of the *Aeneid*, "I sing of arms and of the man" ("Arma virumque cano"), sets forth this two-part plan very clearly.

Book 1 begins with an introduction in which Vergil states his aim: He will tell of the deeds and sufferings of Aeneas, a man driven by destiny, whose task is to found the city of Rome in the face of strong opposition from Juno, the queen of the gods, whose anger is rooted in past insults (the judgment of Paris, the rape of Ganymede) as well as future offenses (the defeat of Carthage by Rome) of which the gods have advance knowledge. The actual narrative begins not at Troy but *in medias res*. Aeneas and his Trojan remnant are off the coast of Sicily, about to sail to Italy, when Juno conspires with Aeolus to cause a storm at sea. When the hero finally appears for the first time, he is cold and frightened, wishing that he had died at Troy. It is at once obvious that Aeneas is no courageous Homeric hero, but a man who must learn through difficulty to understand obedience to destiny and dedication to duty–the very Roman quality of *pietas*, or piety. Indeed, the first six books of the epic demonstrate Aeneas' growing maturity and piety, which increase as he comes to understand fate's grand plan for the future of Rome.

Neptune soon intervenes, calming the wild seas; this act is described in terms of a unique simile–Neptune and the seas are compared to a statesman using words to calm a rebellious mob–which surely is a vague allusion to the great Augustus ushering in an era of peace on the heels of decades of civil war. Aeneas' party finds harbor in North Africa, and the scene quickly changes to Olympus, where Venus complains bitterly to Jupiter about the way her son is being treated. The king of the gods responds with a prophecy: He tells of Aeneas' Italian wars; of the founding of Alba Longa by Aeneas' son Iulus (also called Ascanius); of Romulus and Remus; of the boundless future empire; of Julius Caesar; and, finally, of the new era of peace. Augustus is not explicitly named, but the final lines refer to his Pax Romana, the era of Roman peace. In the short term, Jupiter arranges for

Aeneas to receive a warm welcome in Carthage in the person of Queen Dido. Dido's history is related, and it is remarkably similar to that of Aeneas: She, too, is the widowed leader of a group of refugees, from Tyre, and her people have found their new home, which they are building happily, like bees in summer. The leaders meet, and their mutual sympathy is soon deepened through the machinations of Venus and Cupid; Dido falls in love with Aeneas.

Dido arranges a welcoming banquet for her guests, and after dinner Aeneas agrees to tell the story of the fall of Troy, his escape, and his subsequent wanderings in the Mediterranean basin. Books 2 and 3, then, constitute a flashback, the device also used in the *Odyssey*. In these books Vergil adheres more clearly to his sources than elsewhere in the epic. Book 2, which relates the fall of Troy, relies on the epic cycle, of which only fragments have survived to modern times. Aeneas loses his wife, Creusa, but he escapes carrying his father, Anchises, on his shoulders, bearing the household gods, and holding his son, Ascanius, by the hand. The stories of Laocoön and Cassandra, the death of Priam, and the figure of Helen all derive from the Greek tradition, but Aeneas' ultimate acceptance of destiny and the picture of his devotion to father and son serve to underline ideals and values that are distinctly Roman. Book 3, the narrative of Aeneas' wanderings, contains many episodes based on the *Odyssey* and a few which come from Apollonius. The Trojans make several erroneous attempts to find their new homeland, but omens and progressively clearer prophecies keep them on the track of destiny. Aeneas is warned by Helenus to seek further prophetic information in Italy from the Cumaen Sibyl. The monsters of Greek epic appear, interspersed with more realistic episodes. The book concludes with the most painful incident of all, the death of Anchises. Thus, Aeneas concludes his recollection of the past, a narrative based on the Greek models but heavily laden with Roman ideas of destiny, perseverance, and devotion to duty.

Book 4, perhaps the most famous in the *Aeneid*, tells of the ill-fated love of Dido and Aeneas. Dido's frenzied emotion is pitted against Aeneas' growing *pietas*. Drawing on book 3 of Apollonius' *Argonautica*, Vergil tells the tragic tale. Fire and wound imagery convey Dido's passion in a subjective manner. Through the machinations of the goddesses, the two leaders find themselves driven by a rainstorm, which interrupts a formal hunt, to the same cave. Here they enjoy a sexual union which Vergil surrounds with perverted wedding imagery. Aeneas and Dido live together openly, but only Dido perceives the relationship as a marriage. Aeneas has made no lasting commitment, and, worse, the outside world is offended by their conduct. Iarbas, an earlier and unsuccessful suitor of Dido, prays to

Jupiter for satisfaction; as a result, Mercury is dispatched to remind Aeneas of his duty. Aeneas at first tries to hide his impending departure, but this fails, and the confrontation which follows does not change the hero's mind. Obeying the call of destiny, Aeneas leaves Carthage. Dido has lost her self-respect and the respect of her people and their neighbors. She commits suicide on a pyre, abandoning her kingdom and her sister Anna. Roman virtue has defeated the passion of the foreign queen, and Aeneas has triumphed over his own weaknesses.

Book 5 describes the funeral games for Anchises and is clearly based on book 23 of the *Iliad*. Like Homer, Vergil uses the games to show his hero in the role of leader and judge. Later in the book, a mutiny of the women in Aeneas' party, incited by Juno, is put down, but most of the ships are burned. A portion of the party elects to remain in Sicily, and Aeneas' father appears in a night vision, urging him to come to the underworld. The book closes with the death of the helmsman Palinurus, which offers a fitting transition to book 6, the narrative of Aeneas' journey to the underworld.

Aeneas arrives at Cumae, meets the Sibyl, and hears a short-term prophecy of events in Italy: He will marry a new wife, but there will be more bloodshed, and Juno will continue to hinder Aeneas' progress. Before Aeneas can descend to the underworld, there are lengthy preliminaries, perhaps aimed at emphasizing the difficulty of a mortal's descent to Hades: Aeneas must obtain the golden bough, a sign of fortune's favor; he must perform the requisite sacrifices; and he must bury his dead comrade Misenus. Finally, Aeneas is permitted to descend to an underworld based largely on book 11 of the *Odyssey*, as well as on folk tradition. After encountering the traditional creatures of the underworld, including the ferryman Charon, Aeneas meets a succession of three figures from his past, beginning with the most recent: First, there is Palinurus the helmsman; next, in the Fields of Mourning, Aeneas finds the silent Dido, who turns away from the hero to the comfort of her first husband, Sychaeus; and, finally, Deiphobus, a Trojan warrior, describes his own death amid the sack of Troy. Through these three encounters, Aeneas makes his peace with the past, an essential preparation for his greeting of the future later in the book. An interlude follows, during which the Sibyl describes Tartarus, the place where the guilty are punished; here again, Vergil relies on Homer and folk tradition.

Aeneas moves on to the Elysian fields and a tearful reunion with Anchises. This portion of the book has many different sources, among them Lucretius' Epicureanism, Pythagorean doctrines of the transmigration of souls, Platonism, and Orphism. Here, mythology yields to history and philosophy. Anchises explains the future to Aeneas, but this prophecy is more detailed than any thus far. Moreover, Anchises is able to illustrate his words by showing Aeneas the souls of the great future Romans as they line up for eventual ascent to the upper world. Here, in the exact center of the epic, a powerful passage reiterates the history of Rome as future prophecy. We meet the Alban kings and Romulus, and then the chronological order is interrupted for the highly emphatic introduction of Augustus himself: It is predicted that he will renew the Golden Age in Latium, and elaborate phrases describe the new boundaries of the Roman Empire under his rule. Aeneas is reminded that his own courage is needed if all of this is to come about.

The history lesson now resumes with the early Roman kings who followed Romulus—Numa, Tullius, Ancus Marcius—and then the Tarquin kings from Etruria. The heroes of the early Republic, such as Brutus and Camillus, follow, and then the chronology is once again interrupted for the introduction of Caesar and Pompey and an admonishment against the evils of civil war. The list of Romans resumes with Mummius, Aemilius Paulus, and other great warriors; the emphasis here is on those whose victories expanded the Empire. Anchises closes with a generalized description of the fields of endeavor in which Romans will achieve greatness—sculpture, oratory, and astronomy—but he isolates leadership and government as the unique responsibility of Rome toward the world. One last shade remains to be named, and that is Marcellus, Augustus' nephew and heir, who showed great promise but died very young. Aeneas then departs from the underworld, through the gate of sleep, taking with him a new and more complete understanding of Roman destiny and his duty to fulfill that destiny; his growth as a man is complete, and in the remaining books he fights an enemy which is purely external.

Book 7 begins the "Iliadic" portion of the *Aeneid*, which describes the war in Latium; Vergil marks the new subject with a second invocation to the Muse and calls his new subject "a greater theme" and "a greater labor." Avoiding Circe's island, the Trojans sail the coast and enter the Tiber River. The mood is tranquil and calm as Vergil introduces the new cast of characters: King Latinus, an older man, who has one child; his daughter Lavinia, much sought after as a wife; Queen Amata; and Turnus, a Rutulian king and relative of Amata, and Amata's preferred choice among Lavinia's suitors. The omens, however, argue against Turnus and in favor of a heretofore unknown foreign prince. The Trojans, meanwhile, have disembarked on the banks of the Tiber, where a serendipitous omen makes clear that they have, at long last, found their future home. Aeneas and his men are received warmly by Latinus, who offers both alliance and the hand of Lavinia; the Latin king has some understanding of fate and of his own role in Rome's destiny.

The founding of Rome, however, is not so easy a task: Aeneas' relentless enemy, Juno, greets the happy welcome and the new alliance with rage. She searches out Allecto, a gruesome Fury, and sends her to kindle the anger of Amata, using a snake to stir up the queen's emotions. Amata passionately opposes the alliance, the marriage, and the slight to Turnus; she is compared to a top, a madly spinning child's toy, and she passes her fury on to the other matrons of Latium. Allecto moves on to infect Turnus with jealousy, hatred, and lust for war. Once again, Roman piety is opposed by *furor* (passion), here represented by Allecto, Amata, and Turnus; the main symbols of *furor* are snakes and fire—as used earlier in connection with Dido's passion. Still, Allecto's work is not yet complete: She virtually assures the coming of war by inducing Iulus, Aeneas' son, to wound a stag which is the favorite of a girl called Silvia. Silvia summons the men of the region, and the conflict bursts into armed struggle. Latinus withdraws into his palace, and Juno takes the final irrevocable step of forcing open the gates of the temple of Janus, nothing less than formal declaration of war. (Vergil's own times witnessed the closing of those gates, an event which Augustus saw as his greatest achievement.) The book concludes with a catalog of the Latin allies: the impious Mezentius and his son Lausus; Camilla, a female warrior patterned after Penthesilea, the Amazon fighter and Trojan ally described in the epic cycle; and Turnus himself, decked out for war. The catalog, a Homeric device, introduces the characters who will fight in the books that follow, thereby increasing interest in future events. Thus concludes the book which began so differently, on a tranquil note of sunrise, the Tiber, alliance, and betrothal.

Aeneas must also seek allies for the imminent battle, and to that end he sails up the Tiber to Etruria. This journey and the visit with King Evander provide the subject for book 8. En route to Etruria, the omen of the white sow marks for Aeneas the future site of Rome. When the Trojans arrive, they find Evander's people celebrating an ancient feast in honor of the victory of Hercules over the brigand Cacus. Vergil devotes many lines of verse to the retelling of this tale, partly because it conforms to the Augustan theme of civilization overcoming savagery, and partly because Aeneas must learn and assume the customs of Italy as he leaves his Trojan past behind him. Evander offers his guests a brief tour of the area, pointing to future Roman landmarks and discussing the history and lore of central Italy. The Etruscan also provides background information about Mezentius and agrees to an alliance with Aeneas, sending a contingent of warriors led by his own son, Pallas.

In the meantime, Aeneas' mother, Venus, has urged her husband, Vulcan, god of fire and metalworking, to create arms for Aeneas. Vergil follows Homer (in *Iliad*, book 18) in offering a lengthy description of his hero's shield, but whereas the Homeric shield depicted scenes of the human condition, universal in their implication, Aeneas' weapon offers a lesson in Roman history: Ascanius is depicted with his offspring; the wolf suckles Romulus and Remus; the Romans carry off the Sabine women; Romulus and Tatius make peace; Horatius and Manlius perform their heroic exploits; and Rome's enemies are punished in Hades. In the center of the shield is depicted the raging battle of Actium, the naval conflict of 31 B.C. in which Augustus (then Octavian) defeated Mark Anthony while Anthony's foreign wife, Cleopatra, fled; the gods of war surround the scene. Other panels show Augustus celebrating his triumph and consecrating temples that honor the far-flung boundaries of his empire. Aeneas does not understand everything on the shield, but he lifts it high, signaling his willingness to take on the responsibility of Rome's destiny.

Book 9 is contemporaneous with book 8, describing events in Latium during Aeneas' absence. Iris, Juno's messenger, inflames Turnus to begin the battle: They attack the Trojan fleet. At the urging of Cybele, the mother goddess, the ships are rescued and metamorphosed into sea nymphs. The frightened Rutulians withdraw, ending the day of battle. That night, Nisus and Euryalus, two Trojans bound by special friendship, volunteer to cross enemy lines in order to reach Aeneas. In a scene based on the *Iliad*, book 10, the night raid ends in catastrophe: Both are killed, although their mutual devotion prevails even in the face of death. Cruel Turnus beheads the two Trojans and impales the heads on pikes as prizes of battle, much to the despair of Euryalus' mother. As the battle continues, Ascanius prevails, killing the insolent Numanus; Turnus, too, enjoys a moment of glory, killing Pandarus, before he escapes by leaping into the Tiber. The book is very reminiscent of the *Iliad* in its gory battle descriptions, but Vergil adds his own imprint with a series of wild animal similes.

Book 10 opens with a council of the gods: Venus and Juno bicker, and Jupiter refuses to take sides. Back in Latium, the weary Trojans are cheered by the return of Aeneas, who brings with him Evander's men and a host of Etruscan allies. The battle resumes, led by Turnus, Mezentius, and Mezentius' son Lausus on the side of Latium, and Aeneas, Pallas, and Iulus on the side of Troy. Turnus kills Pallas and puts on his sword belt, spurring Aeneas to furious deeds of battle; Aeneas' rage at Turnus, however, is frustrated by Juno, who removes Turnus from the battle. In a confrontation with Mezentius, Aeneas kills Lausus and then the repentant Mezentius himself, promising first to bury his enemy. The material of the book is again very Iliadic, but the compassion of Aeneas for friend and foe alike and the emphasis on the father-and-son relationship are very Roman.

Book 11 begins with a truce, during which Evander poignantly receives the corpse of his son, and both sides mourn their dead. The Latins hold a council of war, and it is reported that Diomedes, a Greek hero now living in Italy, will not aid their cause: The years at Troy have made him weary of war, and he respects the renowned piety of Aeneas. A rancorous discussion between Turnus and the Latin Drances is interrupted by the news that Aeneas and his allies are on the march. The battle now resumes, with Turnus guarding the city while the warrior maiden Camilla advances against the cavalry. Camilla excells in battle but is mortally wounded by Arruns; Opis, a nymph attending Diana, avenges Camilla's death, killing Arruns.

In book 12, Turnus, now wounded, speaks with Latinus. He pleads for an opportunity to face Aeneas in single combat. Amata and Lavinia weep, and Latinus favors appeasement, but Turnus and Aeneas agree to a duel. Aeneas prays, divulging his plan for equality of Trojans and Latins and respect for Latin custom. But the compact for single combat is broken when Juturna, a nymph and sister of Turnus, incites the Rutulians and one of them hurls a javelin. Aeneas is wounded as he shouts for both sides to remain calm and respect the truce, but the battle erupts, and Aeneas, now a martyr to the cause of peace and respect for law, is healed by his mother and soon returns to the fray. When the battle reaches the walls, Amata, believing Turnus to be dead, kills herself. As the confict approaches its climax, Jupiter and Juno reach an agreement: Juno will withdraw from the battle and cease her harassment of the Trojans, and the newly unified nation of Trojans and Latins will be called Latins using Latin language and Latin dress. Juno will be worshiped and honored by the pious new nation. Juturna, too, withdraws from the conflict, and Aeneas confronts Turnus. The Rutulian is wounded and he surrenders all claim to Lavinia. Aeneas is moved by Turnus' words of acceptance, but a glance at Pallas' sword belt, now worn by Turnus, spurs him to deliver the mortal blow. The epic closes with the flight of Turnus' shade to the world of the dead.

Book 12 completes the portrait of Aeneas as the personification of Roman leadership: He is strong yet compassionate; he obeys and upholds the law; his victory promises to spare the conquered and honor their laws and customs. The confused Trojan fugitive of book 1 has made his peace with his Trojan past and has evolved into a pious, devoted, and progressive leader—a symbol of the glory of Augustan Rome. Turnus, too, commands respect in this book. He possesses all the natural vigor of primitive Italy, which, once harnessed by just government, provides an important component of Roman greatness.

The works of Vergil are thus characterized by a creative tension between deference to Greek models and allegiance to Roman history and values. In the *Eclogues*, Vergil was still striving to find the correct balance, but in the *Georgics* and in the *Aeneid* he skillfully infused the old Greek forms with the moods and themes of his own day. Augustus' new vision of peace and empire found eloquent expression in the timeless hexameters of Rome's greatest poet.

Laura M. Stone

Bibliography · Three good studies are John W. Mackail, *Virgil,* 1931; William F. J. Knight, *Roman Vergil,* 1944; and Michael C. Putnam, *Virgil's Pastoral Art: Studies in the Eclogues,* 1970. More recent works on specific themes include R. D. Williams and T. S. Pattie, *Virgil: His Poetry Through the Ages,* 1982 (with a good introduction for generalists); R. O. A. M. Lyne, *Words and the Poet: Characteristic Techniques of Style in Vergil's "Aeneid,"* 1989; Ian McAuslan and Peter Walcot, eds., *Virgil,* 1990; and Theodore Ziolkowski, *Virgil and the Moderns,* 1993, on the influence of Vergil on twentieth century writers, especially between the world wars, written from a "modernist" perspective. A number of celebratory collections on specific issues were published following the bimillennial anniversary of Vergil's death; noteworthy ones include Charles Martindale, ed., *Virgil and His Influence,* 1984, and Craig Kallendorf, ed., *Vergil, the Classical Heritage,* 1993.

PAUL VERLAINE

Born: Metz, France; March 30, 1844
Died: Paris, France; January 8, 1896

Poetry · *Poèmes saturniens*, 1866 · *Fêtes galantes*, 1869 (*Gallant Parties*, 1912)
· *La Bonne Chanson*, 1870 · *Romances sans paroles*, 1874 (*Romances Without
Words*, 1921) · *Sagesse*, 1881 · *Jadis et naguère*, 1884 · *Amour*, 1888 · *Parallèle-
ment*, 1889, 1894 · *Femmes*, 1891 · *Bonheur*, 1891 · *Chansons pour elle*, 1891 ·
Liturgies intimes, 1892 · *Odes enson honneur*, 1893 · *Élégies*, 1893 · *Dans les
limbes*, 1894 · *Épigrammes*, 1894 (English translation, 1977) · *Chair, dernière
poésies*, 1896 · *Invectives*, 1896 · *Hombres*, 1903 (English translation, 1977) ·
Selected Poems, 1948 · *Femmes/Hombres*, 1977 (includes English translation of
Femmes and *Hombres*)

Achievements · Paul Verlaine is universally recognized as one of the great
French poets of the nineteenth century. His name is associated with those
of his contemporaries Charles Baudelaire, Arthur Rimbaud, and Stéphane
Mallarmé. His most famous and frequently anthologized poems, such as
"Chanson d'automne" ("Song of Autumn"), "Mon rêve familier" ("My
Familiar Dream"), "Clair de lune" ("Moonlight"), and "Il pleure dans mon
coeur" ("It Is Crying in My Heart"), are readily recognized and often
recited by persons with any knowledge of French poetry. Many of his
poems, including those cited, have been set to music by serious composers.
  Verlaine's admirers include both saints and sinners, for Verlaine is at
once the author of one of the most beautiful collections of religious poetry
ever published and the writer of some explicitly erotic poems. During his
lifetime, Verlaine's poetic genius was recognized by only a handful of poets
and friends. His penchant for antisocial and occasionally criminal behavior (he was jailed twice for potentially murderous attacks) undoubtedly
contributed to his lack of commercial success or popular recognition
during his lifetime. By the end of his life, he had gained a small measure
of recognition and received some income from his royalties and lecture
engagements.

Biography · Paul Marie Verlaine was born in Metz, France, on March 30,
1844, the only child of Captain Nicolas-Auguste Verlaine and Elisa Dehée
Verlaine. The family moved often during Verlaine's first seven years, until
Captain Verlaine retired from the army to settle in Paris. Verlaine attended

the Lycée Bonaparte (now Condorcet) and received his *baccalauréat* in 1862.

Verlaine's adoring mother and equally adoring older cousin Elisa Moncomble, whose death in 1867 affected him profoundly, spoiled the sensitive child, encouraged his demanding capriciousness and helped him to become a selfish, immature, unstable young man.

After his *baccalauréat*, he worked in an insurance office and then found a clerical job in municipal government, which he kept until 1870. In 1863, he published his first poem, "Monsieur Prudhomme." He met Catulle Mendès, an editor of the literary magazine *Le Parnasse contemporain*, in which Verlaine published eight poems. In 1866, he published his first volume of poetry, *Poèmes saturniens*, and in 1869 a second volume, *Gallant Parties*.

Alcoholism began to take its toll on his personal life. Twice in drunken rages he threatened to kill his mother. His family tried to marry him to a strong-willed cousin, a fate which he avoided by proposing to Mathilde Mauté, whom he married in 1870 and who inspired his third volume of poetry, *La Bonne Chanson*.

Having served as press officer to the Commune of Paris during the 1870 insurrection, Verlaine subsequently fled Paris and lost his government job. He helped to found a new journal, *La Renaissance*, in which he published many of the poems included in his 1874 volume, *Romances Without Words*.

Verlaine's drinking and his friendship with Arthur Rimbaud led to violent domestic scenes. Following several fights and reconciliations with Mathilde, Verlaine ran off to Brussels with Rimbaud in July, 1872. During the following year, the two poets lived together in Brussels and London and then returned to Brussels. On July 10, 1873, Verlaine, in a drunken rage, fired a revolver at Rimbaud, who had threatened to leave him. Verlaine was convicted of armed assault and sentenced to two years in prison.

In prison, Verlaine converted to a mystical form of Catholicism and began to write the poems for the volume *Sagesse*, published in 1881. After his release in 1875 and until 1879, he held teaching positions in England and France. He formed a sincere and probably chaste relationship with one of his students, Lucien Létinois. They attempted a joint farming venture which failed and then returned to Paris, where Verlaine tried to get back his old government job but was turned down because of his past record. This disappointment, coupled with the sudden death of Lucien in 1883, caused Verlaine to become profoundly discouraged.

After another ill-fated farming venture, Verlaine abandoned himself for a long period to drinking and sordid affairs. A drunken attack on his mother cost him a month in prison in 1885. During his last ten years, his economic distress was somewhat eased by his growing literary reputation. He continued writing and published several more significant volumes of verse.

From 1890 to his death in 1896, Verlaine moved in and out of several hospitals, suffering from a swollen, stiffened leg, the terminal effects of syphilis, diabetes, rheumatism, and heart disease. He lived alternately with two women who cared for him and exploited him. During his last years, he was invited to lecture in Holland, Belgium, and England.

Analysis · In two articles on Baudelaire published in *L'Art* in 1865, Paul Verlaine affirms that the overriding concern of a poet should be the quest for beauty. Without denying the role of inspiration and emotion in the process of poetic creation, Verlaine stresses the need to master them by poetic craftsmanship. Sincerity is not a poetic virtue. Personal emotion must be expressed through the combinations of rhyme, sound, and image which best create a poetic universe in which nothing is the result of chance.

The most obvious result of Verlaine's craftsmanship is the musicality of his verse. Sounds flow together to create a sonorous harmony which repetitions organize and structure as in a musical composition. In his 1882 poem "L'Art poétique," Verlaine gives a poetic recipe which begins with the famous line, "Music above everything else." He goes on to counsel using odd-syllabled lines, imprecise vocabulary and imagery (as if veiled), and nuance rather than color. The poet should avoid wit, eloquence, and forced rhyme. Poetic verse should be light and fugitive, airborne and slightly aromatic. The poem ends with the somber warning, "Anything else is literature."

The subject matter of Verlaine's carefully crafted poetry is frequently his personal experience, certainly dramatic and emotionally charged material. The prologue to *Poèmes saturniens* reveals his consciousness of his miserable destiny. Throughout the rest of his poetry, he narrates the various permutations of his self-fulfilling expectation of unhappiness. "Moonlight," which serves as a prologue to his second volume of verse, presents gallant eighteenth century lovers "who don't appear to believe in their happiness." This skepticism clouds the fugitive moments of happiness throughout Verlaine's poetic pilgrimage. *La Bonne Chanson* is Verlaine's homage to marital bliss. Poem 17, filled with images of love and faithfulness, begins and ends with the question, "Isn't it so?" Poem 13 ends with a similar worry: "A vain hope . . . oh no, isn't it so, isn't it so?" In *Sagesse*, which proposes Catholic mysticism as the ultimate form of happiness, the fear of a return to his old ways haunts the poet's peaceful communion with God.

Because sex, love, God, and wine all fail to provide a safe haven from his saturnine destiny, Verlaine must seek another refuge. What he finds, perhaps not entirely consciously, is sleep. With surprising frequency the final images of Verlaine's poems are images of sleep; many of his musical pieces are thus lullabies whose delicate, soothing images—from which color, laughter, pompousness, loudness, and sharpness have been banished—lead the poet's battered psyche to the unthreatening harbor of sleep. Often, a maternal figure cradles the poet's sleep or stands watchfully by. In many poems in which the sleep motif is not explicit, the imagery subsides at the end of the poem, leaving an emptiness or absence analogous to the oblivion of sleep.

Verlaine's first volume of poetry was published by Lemerre in November, 1866, at the author's expense. It drew very little critical or popular attention. The title refers to the astrological contention, explained in the prologue, that those like Verlaine who are born under the sign of Saturn are doomed to unhappiness, are bilious, have sick, uneasy imaginations, and are destined to suffer.

The volume is the work of a very young poet, some of the poems having been written as early as 1861. They are consequently of uneven quality, but among them is the poem "My Familiar Dream," which is perhaps the most frequently anthologized of all of Verlaine's poems and which, according to Verlaine's friend and admirer H. Suquet, the poet preferred to all his others. It is a haunting evocation of an imaginary woman who loves the poet, who understands him, and who is capable of soothing his anguish.

The central section of the volume, entitled "Paysages tristes" ("Sad Landscapes"), contains the most "Verlainian" of the poems: vague, melancholy landscapes, inspired by his memories of the Artois region, whose fading colors, forms, and sounds reflect the poet's soul and whose ultimate disappearance translates as an innate desire for oblivion.

The first of these poems, "Soleils couchants" ("Setting Suns"), a musical poem of sixteen five-syllable lines, describes a rising sun so weakened that it casts a sunsetlike melancholy over the fields, inspiring strange reddish ghosts in the poet's imagination. The short, odd-syllabled lines create a musical effect reinforced by alliteration and repetition—the phrase "setting suns," for example, is repeated four times in a poem about dawn!

"Promenade sentimentale" ("Sentimental Walk") presents a twilight scene through which the wounded poet passes. The vaguely lit water lilies that glow faintly through the fog in the evening light are swallowed up by the shroudlike darkness in the poem's final image.

"Nuit du Walpurgis classique" ("Classical Walpurgis Night") is full of allusions. Phantoms dance wildly throughout the night in a landscape designed by Johann Wolfgang von Goethe, Richard Wagner, Antoine Watteau, and André Le Nôtre. At dawn's approach, the Wagnerian music fades and the phantoms dissolve, leaving "absolutely" nothing except "a correct, ridiculous, charming Le Nôtre garden." Another noteworthy tone poem, "Chanson d'automne" ("Song of Autumn"), a melodic eighteen-line lyric composed of four- and three-syllable lines, combines *o*'s and nasal sounds to reproduce a melancholy autumn wind which carries off the mournful poet like a dead leaf.

Verlaine's first collection of verse reveals the influence of Baudelaire, Victor Hugo, Charles Leconte de Lisle, Théodore de Banville, and Théophile Gautier—and of Verlaine's young friends Louis de Ricard and Joseph Glatigny. It is a carefully crafted and original volume, demonstrating that at twenty-four Verlaine had already mastered the art of poetry and discovered most of the themes of his later works.

The mid-nineteenth century's rediscovery of the paintings of Watteau is confirmed by several works dedicated to that artist and to his times, including one by the Goncourt brothers, *L'Art du 18ème siècle*, which undoubtedly had a strong influence on Verlaine's choice of this subject and his interpretation of it. During the composition of the poems of *Gallant Parties*, Verlaine undoubtedly consulted some of the published reproductions of Watteau's works as well as his one painting in the Louvre's collection, *Embarkation for Cythère*, a vast work devoted to eighteenth century gallantry, its rites, costumes, myths, poetry, and fashionable devotees. These aristocratic gallants and the characters from *The Italian Comedy*, also painted by Watteau, come alive in Verlaine's second published volume of poetry.

The often-anthologized "Moonlight" opens the volume and sets the mood. This musical evocation of the songs and dances of the masked characters and the relationship between their costumes and their souls insists upon the underlying sadness of both. The gallant aristocrats are somewhat sad beneath their fantastic disguises because they do not really believe in the love and life of which they sing. Their dispersed song is absorbed by the moonlight.

These same characters sing, dance, walk, skate, and love through the rest of the volume, sometimes assuming stock character names from commedia del l'arte—Pierrot, Clitandre, Cassandre, Arlequin, Colombine, Scaramouche, and Pulcinella—and sometimes classical names—Tircis, Aminte, Chloris, Eglé, Atys, Damis.

The landscapes of *Gallant Parties* are very different physically and psychologically from those of the *Poèmes saturniens*. They are sculpted, landscaped, arranged, and peopled. Paths are lined by rows of pruned trees and mossy benches. Fountains and statues are harmoniously placed around well-kept lawns. The relationship between the characters and the landscape is no longer a natural sympathetic mirroring. Nature has been artificially subdued to reflect the characters' forced gaiety and becomes a mocking image of the vanity of their pursuits. One of the obvious formal characteristics of the volume is the presence of dialogue and monologue, couched in the artificial, erotic language of gallantry. There are many allusions to "former ecstasies," "infinite distress," and "mortal languors."

The volume's overriding pessimism is orchestrated by the arrangement of the poems. The latent sadness of the apparently carefree gallants in "Moonlight" becomes the dominant feeling in the second half of the work. While humorous love play and inconsequential erotic exchanges dominate the first half, several disturbing images—such as the statue of a snickering faun who anticipates eventual unhappiness and the sad spectacle of a statue of Cupid overturned by the wind—foreshadow the volume's disastrous conclusion, the poem "Colloque sentimentale" ("Sentimental Collo-quium"), in which a ghostly "form" tries to recall a past sentimental adventure. The cold, solitary park, witness to the scarcely heard dialogue, swallows up the desperate efforts to recall a past love as well as the negations of those efforts. One of the lovers tries unsuccessfully to awaken memories of their past love, which the other negates repeatedly: "Do you remember our former ecstasy?" "Why do you want me to remember it?" "Does your heart still beat at the sound of my name?" "No."

The Franco-Prussian War of 1870 and the Commune separated Verlaine from his Parnassian friends and led him toward new friendships and a new form of poetry, toward a modernistic vision which replaced the artificiality of Parnassian inspiration with an attempt to capture the essence of contem-porary life. During 1872 and 1873, Verlaine wrote the poems of *Romances Without Words*, which was published in 1874. All the poems precede the episode with Rimbaud which resulted in Verlaine's imprisonment. The period was emotionally difficult for Verlaine. Torn between love for Mathilde and dependence on Rimbaud, Verlaine was tormented by his vacillations. *Romances Without Words* fuses his new poetic ideal with his personal struggle.

The sad, lilting songs which make up the first part of the volume, entitled "Ariettes oubliées" ("Forgotten Melodies"), includes one of the most frequently quoted of Verlaine's poems, "It Is Crying in My Heart," in which the gentle sound of the rain falling on the town echoes the fall of tears within his heart. A more interesting poem, however, is the musical twelve-line poem "Le Piano que baise une main frêle" ("The Piano Kissed by a Fragile Hand"), in which the light, discreet melody rising from the piano corresponds to the faintness in the fading evening light of the visual impression of slight hands on a barely discernible piano. A series of vague, fleeting adjectives seep out of the perfumed boudoir to disappear through a slightly opened window into a small garden. The hushed sonorities of the poem coincide with the diminished intensity of the images. One remark-able phrase in the tenth line embodies both the musical effects and the characteristic tone of Verlaine's verse: "fin refrain incertain" ("delicate, uncertain refrain").

While the influence of music on Verlaine's poetry is certain, the impor-tance of painting is no less significant. *Gallant Parties* is to a great extent a tribute to the painting of Watteau. The "Paysages belges" ("Belgian Land-scapes") which Verlaine paints into *Romances Without Words* are a tribute to the Impressionist school of painting, whose birth corresponds with the date of composition of the collection. Verlaine knew Édouard Manet and Ignace Henri Fantin-Latour and was certainly interested in their technique. The impressionistic Belgian landscapes which Verlaine has painted are carefree and gay, carrying no reflection of the shadow of Mathilde which haunts the rest of the volume. The first poem in the section, "Walcourt" (a small, industrial town in Belgium), reflects the gaiety of the two vagabond poets (Verlaine and Rimbaud) in a series of brightly colored images which flash by, without help of a verb, in lively four-syllabled lines: tiles and bricks, ivy-covered homes, and beer drinkers in outdoor bars.

The gaiety of the Belgian countryside is interrupted by a bitter poem, "Birds in the Night" (original title in English), which Verlaine had first entitled "La Mauvaise Chanson" ("The Bad Song") as an ironic counterpart to his previous book of poems, *La Bonne Chanson*, devoted to marital bliss. "Birds in the Night" accuses Mathilde of a lack of patience and kindness, and of treachery. The suffering poet offers his forgiveness. The poem suggests a singular lack of understanding of the real causes of their marital discord.

The last section of *Romances Without Words* contains visions of Verlaine's London experience, but the image of Mathilde pierces through the local color with haunting persistence. All six of the poems have English titles. The most interesting is "Green," in which the poet presents to his mistress fruits, flowers, leaves, branches, and then his heart, which he commends to her care. The poem ends with the desire for a restful oblivion upon the woman's breast.

Only seven of the poems in *Sagesse* were actually composed while Verlaine was in prison. The rest were written between the time of his release in 1875 and the spring of 1880. The volume was published at the end of that year. The title refers to Verlaine's intention to live virtuously according to the principles of his new faith and should perhaps be translated not as "wisdom" but as "good behavior." The volume is divided into three parts, the first of which dwells on the difficulty of converting to a virtuous life, the almost daily battles with overwhelming temptation. The second part narrates the poet's mystic confrontation with God, primarily through a cycle of ten sonnets. The last part describes the poet's return to the world and contains many of the themes and images of his earlier nature poetry. These poems are not overtly religious; the prologue to this part, "Désormais le sage, puni" ("Henceforth, the Virtuous, Punished"), explains the virtuous poet's return to a contemplative love of nature.

Poems 6 and 7 of the first part, both sonnets, are the most poetic of Verlaine's evocations of the contrast between his former and his present preoccupations. Poem 6 presents his former joys as a line of clumsy geese limping off into the distance on a dusty road. Their departure leaves the poet with a welcome emptiness, a peaceful sense of abandonment as his formerly proud heart now burns with divine love. Poem 7 warns of the prevailing appeal of the "false happy days" which have tempted his soul all day. They have glowed in his memory as "long hailstones of flame" which have symbolically ravaged his blue sky. The last line of the poem exhorts the poet's soul to pray against the storm to forestall "the old folly" which threatens to return.

Three of the most moving poems of the third part were written in prison, one on the very day of Verlaine's sentencing: "Un Grand Sommeil noir" ("A Great Black Sleep"). This poem, as well as "Le Ciel est, par-dessus le toit" ("The Sky Is, Beyond the Roof") and "Gaspard Hauser chante" ("The Song of Kaspar Hauser"), sings of the poet's despair, plaintively expressing his selfpity, his regrets, and his total sense of shock in the early days of his imprisonment. The third part of *Sagesse* also contains two of Verlaine's most finely crafted sonnets. "L'Espoir luit comme un brin de paille dans l'étable" ("Hope Glistens Like a Blade of Straw in a Stable") is perhaps his most Rimbaldian and most obscure poem. An unidentified protector speaks to the poet reassuringly as he rests in a country inn. The voice is maternal and encourages the poet to sleep, promising to cradle him. The voice shoos away a woman whose presence threatens the poet's rest. The poem opens and closes with a fragile image of glistening hope, which, in the final line, opens up into a hoped-for reflowering of the roses of September.

The sonnet "Le Son du cor" ("The Sound of the Hunting Horn") is perhaps the best example of Verlaine's poetic art. It was written before his imprisonment, probably in the spring of 1873. This very musical poem blends the sound of the hunting horn, the howling of the wind, and the cry of a wolf into a crescendo which subsides to a mere autumn sigh as the falling snow blots out the last colors of the setting sun. The painful notes of the opening stanza are completely obliterated as day gives way to a cradling, monotonous evening.

Other literary forms · Most of Paul Verlaine's other published works are autobiographical writings and critical articles on contemporary poets. During his lifetime, he published two plays which were performed, *Les Uns et les autres* (1884; the ones and the others) and *Madame Aubin* (1886), and one short story, *Louise Leclercq* (1886). A collection of seven other short stories, *Histories comme ça* (1903; stories like that), was published posthumously.

The most significant of his critical writings were published under the title *Poètes maudits* (1884; cursed poets), which includes articles on Tristan Corbière, Arthur Rimbaud, Stéphane Mallarmé, Villiers de L'Isle-Adam, and others. Verlaine's *Confessions* (*Confessions of a Poet*, 1950) was published in 1895. Many of his previously unedited writings were published posthumously in a 1903 edition of his works, which includes several autobiographical pieces as well as some original ink drawings. All of his prose works were published in the 1972 Pléiade edition.

Select works other than poetry

SHORT FICTION: *Louise Leclercq*, 1886; *Histoires comme ça*, 1903.

DRAMA: *Les Uns et les autres*, pr. 1884; *Madame Aubin*, pr. 1886.

NONFICTION: *Poètes maudits*, 1884; *Mes hôpitaux*, 1891; *Quinze jours en Hollande*, 1892; *Mes prisons*, 1893; *Confessions*, 1895 (*Confessions of a Poet*, 1950); *Les Mémoires d'un veuf*, 1896; *Charles Baudelaire*, 1903; *Critiques et conférences*, 1903; *Souvenirs et promenades*, 1903; *Voyage en france par un français*, 1903.

Paul J. Schwartz

Bibliography · An excellent biographical study in English is Joanna Richardson, *Paul Verlaine*, 1971. Other important biographies in English include Alfred Carter's *Paul Verlaine*, 1971, and Charles Chadwick's *Paul Verlaine*, 1973. A solid analysis of style and structure is Adam Antoine's *The Art of Paul Verlaine*, 1963. For a thorough analysis of the importance of Verlaine as a Symbolist in France, an influence on Rimbaud and Baudelaire, and a contributor to postmodern American poetry, see Lawrence M. Porter's *The Crisis of French Symbolism*, 1990. See also David Hillery, *Verlaine: Fixing an Image*, 1988. Older but still relevant studies include Edmond Lepelletier, *Paul Verlaine: His Life–His Work*, translated by E. M. Lang, 1909, and Lawrence Hanson and Elizabeth Hanson, *Verlaine: Fool of God*, 1957.

ROBERT PENN WARREN

Born: Guthrie, Kentucky; April 24, 1905
Died: Stratton, Vermont; September 15, 1989

Poetry · *Thirty-Six Poems*, 1935 · *Eleven Poems on the Same Theme*, 1942 · *Selected Poems 1923-1943*, 1944 · *Brother to Dragons: A Tale in Verse and Voices*, 1953 · *Promises: Poems 1954-1956*, 1957 · *You, Emperors, and Others: Poems 1957-1960*, 1960 · *Selected Poems: New and Old, 1923-1966*, 1966 · *Incarnations: Poems 1966-1968*, 1968 · *Audubon: A Vision*, 1969 · *Or Else—Poem/Poems 1968-1974*, 1974 · *Selected Poems 1923-1975*, 1976 · *Now and Then: Poems 1976-1978*, 1978 · *Being Here: Poetry 1977-1980*, 1980 · *Rumor Verified: Poems 1979-1980*, 1981 · *Chief Joseph of the Nez Percé*, 1983 · *New and Selected Poems 1923-1985*, 1985

Achievements · Robert Penn Warren was undoubtedly one of the most honored men of letters in American history. Among his numerous awards and honors were a 1936 Houghton-Mifflin Literary Fellowship for his first novel, *Night Rider;* Guggenheim fellowships for 1939-1940 and 1947-1948; and Pulitzer prizes for his novel *All the King's Men* (1947) and the poetry volume *Now and Then* (1979). (He was the only person to have won a Pulitzer for both fiction and poetry.) He also won the National Book Award for poetry with the volume *Promises* in 1958, the National Medal for Literature (1970), and the Presidential Medal of Freedom (1980). He was one of the first recipients of a so-called genius grant, a Prize Fellowship from the MacArthur Foundation, in 1981. In 1986 he was selected to be the first poet laureate of the

Washington Post/D.C. Public Library

United States, and he served in that distinguished capacity until age and ill health required him to resign the position in 1987.

Biography · Robert Penn Warren was born on April 24, 1905, amid the rolling hills of the tobacco country of southwestern Kentucky, in the town of Guthrie; he was the son of Robert Franklin Warren, a businessman, and Anna Ruth (Penn) Warren. He spent his boyhood there, and summers on his grandparents' farm in nearby Trigg County. Both grandfathers were Confederate veterans of the Civil War, and he was often regaled with firsthand accounts of battles and skirmishes with Union forces. The young Warren grew up wanting to be a sea captain, and after completing his secondary education in neighboring Clarksville, Tennessee, he did obtain an appointment to the United States Naval Academy at Annapolis.

A serious eye injury prevented his attending, however, and in 1920 Warren matriculated instead at Vanderbilt University in Nashville, set on becoming an electrical engineer. In his freshman English class, Warren's interest took a fateful turn as the young professor John Crowe Ransom and another, advanced student, Allen Tate, introduced him to the world of poetry. The two were at the center of a campus literary group called the Fugitives, and Warren began attending their meetings and soon was contributing to their bimonthly magazine, *The Fugitive*, which he edited in his senior year. Under the tutelage of Tate and Ransom, he became an intense student not only of earlier English poets, particularly the Elizabethans and such seventeenth century Metaphysical poets as John Donne and Andrew Marvell, but also of the contemporary schools that were emerging from the writings of older poets such as A. E. Housman and Thomas Hardy, as well as from the work of William Butler Yeats and T. S. Eliot.

Warren was graduated summa cum laude from Vanderbilt in 1925, taking a B.A. degree, and he continued his graduate studies at the University of California at Berkeley, from which he obtained an M.A. in 1927. He then enrolled in another year of graduate courses at Yale University and went on to spend two years as a Rhodes Scholar at the University of Oxford in England, which awarded him a B.Litt. degree in 1931.

While at Oxford, Warren completed his first published book, *John Brown: The Making of a Martyr* (1929), which took a rather callow, Southerner's view of the legendary hero of the abolitionist cause. When Paul Rosenberg, one of the editors of the *American Caravan* annual, invited him to submit a story, Warren "stumbled on" fiction writing, as he later recounted the incident. The result, "Prime Leaf," a story about labor troubles among tobacco growers back in his native Kentucky, would later find fuller expression in his first published novel, *Night Rider*.

Back in the United States, Warren joined the Agrarian movement, an informal confederation of many of his old Fugitive colleagues who were now espousing a return to agrarian, regional ideals in a Depression-ravaged America that was rapidly becoming more and more industrialized, urbanized, and, at least inasmuch as the images generated by popular culture were concerned, homogenized.

After teaching for a year as an assistant professor of English at Southwestern College in Memphis, he became, in 1931, an acting assistant professor of English at Vanderbilt. He remained there until 1934, when he moved on to accept a position at Louisiana State University in Baton Rouge. After promotion to associate professor in 1936, Warren took a full professorship at the University of Minnesota in 1942.

In 1935, while at Louisiana State, Warren had cofounded *Southern Review*, an influential journal with which he would remain until it folded in 1942. From 1938 to 1961, meanwhile, Warren served on the advisory board of another prestigious quarterly, *Kenyon Review*.

In 1930 Warren had married Emma Brescia, whom he divorced in 1951, shortly after accepting a position as professor of playwriting at the School of Drama of Yale University. On December 7, 1952, Warren married the writer Eleanor Clark, by whom he would father his two children, Rosanna, born in 1953, and Gabriel, born in 1955. Warren left his position with the drama school in 1956, but in 1961 he returned to New Haven, Connecticut, to rejoin the Yale faculty as a professor of English. From that time onward he made his home in nearby Fairfield and summered in Stratton, Vermont.

Warren continued his distinguished career as a teacher, poet, novelist, critic, editor, and lecturer virtually to the end of his long life. In February, 1986, the Librarian of Congress named him the first official poet laureate of the United States, a position he held until 1987. On September 15, 1989, the poet died at his summer home in Stratton. He was eighty-four years old.

Analysis · Robert Penn Warren was blessed twice over. He was a son of and grew up in a region of the country renowned for its love of the land and devotion to earthy folk wisdom and the art of storytelling. There was also a love of language, particularly the fustian spirit of the orator and the preacher, based on a deep, dark respect for the Word, orotund and oracular.

Added to that, however, Warren spent his formative years in a world that was making the transition from the comparative bucolic and optimistic sensibilities of the late nineteenth century to the frenzied, fearful, frenetic pace of the post-World War I 1920's. Poetry was being called into service by young people everywhere to try to explain what had happened, or at least give it manageable shape. T. S. Eliot's *The Waste Land* (1922) set the tone. At Vanderbilt among his fellow Fugitives, Warren was quickly put in touch with the new poetry that was emerging.

It is this combination of effects and influences that made Warren's poetry and gave it its vision. From the first, he hovered between the old and new—the mannered style, the modern flip; the natural scene, the symbolic backdrop; the open gesture, the hidden motive; original sin, the religion of humankind. This peculiar vantage point scored his vision, for it allowed him to know at first hand what his age was surrendering at the same time that it allowed him to question the motives for the surrender and the terms of the victory, the name of the enemy—or, better yet, his face.

Warren can bring the personal into the most profound metaphysical musings without blinking an eye or losing a beat, because finally the source of all vision, at least for Warren, is the darkest of selves at the heart of one's being, the unknown brother who shares not only one's bed but also one's body and makes, or so it seems, one's decisions. Self-discovery is Warren's trail, and the reader who follows it discovers that while it begins in coming to grips with the painful processes of caring in an uncaring world, it concludes in accepting caring as a moral obligation rather than merely a state of mind or soul. Like most twentieth century poets, Warren was really trying to reinvigorate the heroic ideal.

The early poem "To a Face in a Crowd" echoes the world-weary angst typical of the period, the 1920's, by rendering an urban apocalypse in the bleak, stark terms of lonely souls lost in vacant vistas, finding their meager consolations in passing strangers who may—or may not—be spiritual kindred with similar dreams and like despairs. It is night, and adjectives and nouns collide in a litany of pessimism and negativism: "lascivious," "lust," "bitter," "woe," "dolorous," "dim," "shroud." This vision is mitigated, however, by the markedly poetic tone of the language: "Brother, my brother, whither do you pass?/ Unto what hill at dawn, unto what glen. . . . ?" While there is hope, the speaker seems to be saying that the idyllic interlude is no longer a viable option; instead, "we must meet/ As weary nomads in this desert at last,/ Borne in the lost procession of these feet."

Among these early poems, "The Return: An Elegy" is by far the most successful effort, for in it Warren eschewed the derivative and imitative tone, mood, and theme of poems such as "To a Face in the Crowd" and found what time would prove to be the beginnings of his own voice and vision.

The setting is simple, though not at first easily discerned: in a Pullman as the train carries the speaker back home to the hills to attend his mother's funeral. Sentiment is kept at bay, almost with a vengeance, it might seem: "give me the nickels off your eyes/ . . . / then I could buy a pack of cigarettes." Only an occasional, italicized lapse into poeticized feeling—"*does my mother wake*"—among the details of the rugged mountain-country landscape that the speaker intersperses with his thoughts gives the sense that a profound emotional turmoil is seething beneath the modernist "flip": "Pines drip without motion/ The hairy boughs no longer shake/ Shaggy mist, crookbacked, ascends."

As the poem continues, however, the reader is gradually forced to realize that it is the tension between the speaker's grief and his desire not to sentimentalize his loss that give the poetry its incredible and peculiarly modern motive power: "*the old fox is dead/* what have I said." Thus, the speaker earns the right to lapse into the unabashed sentiment, at poem's end, of "this dark and swollen orchid of my sorrow."

This rare ability to combine the most enduring verbal expressions of human feelings with the most fleeting of contemporary realities and attitudes in a poetry that magically maintains its precarious balance between traditional poetic tone and style and the most ragged-edged and flippant of modern sensibilities continued to give Warren's work its own shape and direction as he expanded his range in the 1930's and 1940's. In "Pursuit," for example, his vision of the urban landscape has hardly improved, but it is peopled with three-dimensional emblems of a faltering, seeking humanity—"the hunchback on the corner," "that girl the other guests shun," "the little old lady in black." "Original Sin: A Short Story," meanwhile, places the reader in Omaha and the Harvard Yard and speaks of as cosmopolitan an image as "the abstract Jew," yet it ends its commentary on humanity's fated failings with country images of "the backyard and . . . an old horse cold in pasture."

So much is in keeping, of course, with the social and literary ideals that the original Fugitives formulated when they coalesced into the Agrarian movement. Their notion was that American democracy was not an urban but a rural phenomenon, forged by a link between the people and the land. In this regard, regionalism—the countryman's sense of place and of a devotion to his people—was not a pernicious thing but involved the very health of the nation, a health that the increasing pressures toward homogeneity of people and culture in sprawling urban centers could not only threaten but perhaps even destroy. Poets such as Warren became spokespersons both for that lost agrarian ideal and for the simple country folk forced by economic necessity into the anonymity of large cities, where they lived at the edge of squalor and struggled to maintain their small-town dignities.

Warren combines all these themes and concerns in "The Ballad of Billie Potts." As the speaker recounts the story of Big Billie, his wife, and their son, Little Billie, he mixes in long, parenthetical sections in which he seems to be addressing himself rather than the readers, urging himself to return—as if he could—to the life-styles of those hillbillies "in the section between the rivers," where they were poor by urban standards but rich in spirit, in faith in themselves, and in the power of familial love. In the lost idyll mode reminiscent of William Wordsworth's "The Ruined Cottage" and "Michael," the story of Little Billie's travails and his parents' despair when circumstances force the boy to leave "his Pappy in Old Kaintuck/ And [head] West to try his luck" is really a twentieth century throwback's yearnings for what were simpler and certainly more communal times. For him now there is only the endless urban tedium, the vacant, lonely sameness, maddeningly monotonous and vaguely threatening: "And the clock ticked all night long in the furnished room/ And would not stop/ And the *El*-train passed on the quarters with a whish like a terrible broom/ And would not stop."

Warren never ceased to contrast the earthiness of country values and country life with the mind-forged manacles that constrain the individual within the modern industrial landscape. At the heart of his vision, however, is a sense of the sad wasting of time and of love that mortality forces one constantly to consider. Clearly the problem is not "out there"; it is within us. The increasing urbanization of America is not the enemy, then, it is simply the latest battlefield—not the disease, but the symptom. The disease is life, and the ageless enemy is our insatiable need to try to make it make sense, to try to make it hurt less.

For Warren, then, one can hope only to keep oneself spiritually and emotionally—and painfully—alive in a world that tends undeniably toward death and decay. His villains become those who deny that life is hardship as much as those who visit hardships on others. Behind the indictment, though, there is always the lance of forgiveness, aimed as much at the heart of the speaker who dreads the pain of his feelings as much as at the iniquities that arouse it.

As the poet himself became a father and middle-aged, children rather than the lonely crowd figured more and more as the best emblems of the tragic core of the human condition, as well as of the human capacity to endure and transcend. The poetry consequently finds its locus more and more in personal experience, the day to day providing sufficient grist for the poet's thinking and feeling mill.

"The Child Next Door," from the prize-winning volume *Promises: Poems 1954-1956*, focuses not on the child "who is defective because the mother," burdened with seven already, "took a pill," but on an older sister, who is twelve and "beautiful like a saint," and who takes care of "the monster all day":

> I come, and her joy and triptych beauty and joy stir hate
> —Is it hate?—in my heart. Fool, doesn't she know that the process
> Is not that joyous or simple, to bless, or unbless,
> The malfeasance of nature or the filth of fate?

Warren's unstinting, almost embarrassing honesty as he records his feelings and attitudes, an honesty exercised in his poetry from as early as "The Return," gains him an edge of intimate moral ambiguity in this more mature poetry. The present poem concludes: "I think of your goldness, of joy, how empires grind, stars are hurled,/ I smile stiff, saying *ciao*, saying *ciao*, and think: this is the world." Whether that is the expression of a bitter resignation or a casual dismissal or a measure of joyful acceptance, the speaker will give no clue: "this is the world." Readers are left to measure the size of their own hearts and thereby experience both the pain of observing life too closely and, if they wish, the expiation of letting it go.

By now a cosmopolitan himself, a Yale professor with an Oxford degree and summer home in Vermont, the boy who is father to the man did not forget the Kentucky hill-country source of his vision. In reminiscences such as "Country Burying (1919)," the autobiographical rather than symbolical and metaphysical seems to prevail, but there is still a telling tale. The poem is a requiem for all those lost "boy's afternoon[s]" when life was so present, even there amid tokens of death, and the mind more receptive, but the spirit would be somewhere else: "Why doesn't that fly stop buzzing—stop buzzing up there!" Apologies to Emily Dickinson aside, those were a boy's thoughts in 1919: in the poem they are some measure of the adult's remorse as he reached midcentury with the century. Now there is not only the pain of the present to endure; there is the pain of the past, its loss, as well.

This sense of remorse was never absent from Warren's poetry, but now it is outspoken and unremitting, and it becomes a major motivating factor in the later poetry. *Brother to Dragons*, a historical novel in verse written in the form of a play that the author calls a poem, is the apex of all Warren's previous pessimism, displaying little of his often-whimsical capacity to turn heel but not turn coat on caring too much for the human condition. In the largest sense, the poem is a severe indictment of the human animal. With some liberties but no real distortion of the facts, it recounts the tale of Lilburn Clarke, a Kentuckian who in the early nineteenth century brutally murdered a black slave over a trifling offense. Beyond the tragic scope of those facts, there was an even more tragic rub in Warren's view: Clarke was the nephew of Thomas Jefferson, himself a paradoxical figure who could pen the Declaration of Independence and still be a slaveholder, and who believed in the perfectibility of humankind.

Warren, who appears himself as a character in the poem by carrying on a pointed philosophical debate with Jefferson, used the bare bones of the story to call into question the worth, let alone the authenticity, of all human ideals. Still, in the lengthy monologue with which the poem concludes, he insists that despite this sorry record of human endeavor in the name of ideals that are always betrayed, "we must argue the necessity of virtue."

By the time the 1950's ended, Warren had established a new metier as a social commentator with an equally self-accusatory eye. In *You, Emperor, and Others*, the public and the private, the man and the child, the father and the son all find expression. "Man in the Street," with its singsong rhythms and nursery-rhyme, choruslike echoes, hits the gray flannel suits with their black knit ties and Brooks Brothers shirts not where they live but where they work, where each of them somehow makes accommodations with the vacuities of the corporate world. If it is a vision that virtually lends an air of nostalgic romance to an early poem such as "To a Face in the Crowd," "Mortmain" harks back to "The Return." It is the speaker's father who is dying now, but the irreverent flippancy of the earlier poem is not even there to be turned away from: "All things . . . // Were snatched from me, and I could not move,/ Naked in that black blast of his love." It is a poem in five parts, and in the last of those, "A Vision: Circa 1880," he imagines his father as a boy, "in patched britches and that idleness of boyhood/ Which asks nothing and is its own fulfillment." The poem ends with a turn to pure lyricism, without any reaching out to metaphysical solutions or conceits, merely the wholly verbal bounty of language giving life to dead time in images of a present, natural splendor.

Warren published seven additional volumes of poetry from 1960 to 1980, and the lyrical mode itself intensified into the speculative tone that he apparently could not abandon. Still, as he reminds the reader in the 1968 volume, *Incarnations*, "You think I am speaking in riddles./ But I am not, for// The world means only itself" ("Riddle in the Garden"). In *Audubon*, meanwhile, he asks, "What is love," and reminds the reader that "one name for it is knowledge," as if attempting to justify his lifelong preoccupation with trying to understand human beings and their place on earth and in the universe.

As the poet grew older, mortality became even more of an obsessive theme, and the issues of time past and time present, the poet now having a wealth of experience to draw upon, found even more expression in this new admixture of a metaphysical lyricism. In "Paradox," for example, from the "Can I See Arcturus from Where I Stand?" section of *Selected Poems, 1923-1975*, stargazer man is brought down to earth, or at least a sense of his limits, when he confronts a retelling of Zeno's paradox of the arrow and its unreachable goal. The natural simplicity and personal quality of the setting—a run on a beach that causes the speaker to recollect an earlier spirited chase—remove from the poem the bane of a *de profundis* that often intruded into Warren's most youthful metaphysical flights; the information is presented not as insight but as the sort of everyday truth any feeling, thinking person might draw from experience, should he or she care to. Indeed, the poem is finally a tender love lyric worthy, in its formal rhapsodic effect, of A. E. Housman:

> I saw, when your foot fulfilled its stride,
> How the sand, compressed, burst to silver light,
> But when I had reached that aureoled spot
> There was only another in further stride.

This bringing all vision down to earth is best exemplified in a late poem such as "Last Meeting." It is another hill-country recollection; the poet, now by all accounts elderly, recalls being back home once and meeting an elderly woman who had known him as a boy. Now she too is dead. "All's changed. The faces on the street/ Are changed. I'm rarely back. But once/ I tried to find her grave." He failed, he explains, but promises that he will yet succeed. Still, "It's nigh half a lifetime I haven't managed,/ But there must be enough time left for that." People's failures are little things, he seems to be saying toward the end of his creative life, and because Warren has done such an incredible job of exploring them in every other permutation throughout his long career, the reader should pay heed to the conclusions he reaches. People's failures, no matter how great, are little things; it is the burden of remorse they carry for them that is great.

Like Thomas Hart Benton, who painted the great vistas of Western deserts in his later years, Warren turns to the overlooked and the insignificant to find beauty and, in it, significances he may have missed. In "Arizona Midnight," "dimly I do see/ Against that darkness, lifting in blunt agony,/ The single great cactus." He strains to see the cactus; "it has/ its own necessary beauty." One must see through the apparent agony into the heart of the thing and seek out the beauty there, rather than pausing too long to reflect only on the tragic surface—which one can see only dimly, in any event.

It is no wonder, then, that one of Warren's last completed volumes was *Chief Joseph of the Nez Percé*. Here he returns to the tragic record that is the

past, to betrayal and injustice and the bitter agony of exile despite one's
having "done the right thing." Yet this time, in Joseph's enduring the
arrogance of office and the proud man's contumely, Warren finds an
emblem of triumph despite apparent defeat. Now he can see history not as
irony, filled with the tragic remorse that looking back can bring, but as
process and as "sometimes, under/ The scrutinizing prism of Time,/
Triumphant." It seems to be the declaration of a total peace, and one
cannot help but hear, as Warren surely must have hoped one would,
echoing behind those words Chief Joseph's own: "I will fight no more
forever."

Other literary forms · In an era when poets are often as renowned and
influential as critics, Robert Penn Warren nevertheless stands out inasmuch
as he achieved success on two creative fronts, having as great a critical
reputation as a novelist as he has as a poet. This accomplishment is not
limited to the production of one singular work or of a sporadic body of
work; rather it is a sustained record of development and achievement
spanning more than three decades. His fiction includes the novels *Night
Rider* (1939), *At Heaven's Gate* (1943), *All the King's Men* (1946), *World Enough
and Time: A Romantic Novel* (1950), *Band of Angels* (1955), *The Cave* (1959),
Wilderness: A Tale of the Civil War (1961), and *Flood: A Romance of Our Time*
(1964), and there is also a short-story collection, *The Circus in the Attic and
Other Stories* (1947). There can be no doubt that *All the King's Men*, a highly
fictionalized and richly wrought retelling of the rise and fall, by assassination, of the demagogic Louisiana governor Huey Long, has justifiably
attained the status of an American classic; it is not only Warren's best novel
but also his best-known work. The story of Willie Stark, the country-boy
idealist who becomes far worse an exploiter of the public trust than the
corrupt professional politicians he at first sets his heart and soul against,
embodies many of Warren's most persistent themes, in particular the
fumbling process self-definition becomes in a universe awry with irony and
a world alive with betrayal and mendacity. Made into an Oscar-winning
film, the novel was also very successfully adapted as a play by Warren in
the 1950's.

Warren's considerable influence on the life of letters in twentieth century America was also exercised in a series of textbooks that he edited
jointly with the noted critic Cleanth Brooks. The first, *An Approach to
Literature* (1936), coedited as well by John Thibault Purser, was followed
by *Understanding Poetry: An Anthology for College Students*, edited by Warren
and Brooks, in 1938, and *Understanding Fiction*, also edited by Warren and
Brooks, in 1943. These texts utilized the practices (just then being formu-

lated) of New Criticism, which encouraged a close attention to the literary text as a self-contained, self-referring statement. It is certain that several generations of readers have had their entire attitude toward literature and literary interpretation determined by Warren and Brooks's effort, either directly or through the influence of teachers and critics whose values were shaped by these landmark works.

Select works other than poetry

LONG FICTION: *Night Rider*, 1939; *At Heaven's Gate*, 1943; *All the King's Men*, 1946; *World Enough and Time: A Romantic Novel*, 1950; *Band of Angels*, 1955; *The Cave*, 1959; *Wilderness: A Tale of the Civil War*, 1961; *Flood: A Romance of Our Time*, 1964.

SHORT FICTION: *The Circus in the Attic and Other Stories*, 1947.

NONFICTION: *John Brown: The Making of a Martyr*, 1929; *Modern Rhetoric*, 1949 (with Cleanth Brooks).

EDITED TEXTS: *An Approach to Literature*, 1936 (with Cleanth Brooks and John Thibault Purser); *Understanding Poetry: An Anthology for College Students*, 1938 (with Brooks); *Understanding Fiction*, 1943 (with Brooks).

Russell Elliott Murphy

Bibliography · To understand Warren's literary context, see *The Fugitives*, 1958, by John M. Bradbury; *The Fugitive Group*, 1959, by Louise Cowan; and *The Burden of Time*, 1965, by John L. Stewart. Two books by Victor Strandberg, *The Poetic Vision of Robert Penn Warren*, 1977, and *A Colder Fire*, 1965, are useful for understanding Warren's poetry. There are many studies of the Warren canon: Leonard Casper, *Robert Penn Warren: The Dark and Bloody Ground*, 1960; Charles H. Bohner, *Robert Penn Warren*, 1964; L. Hugh Moore, *Robert Penn Warren and History*, 1970; Barnett Guttenberg, *Web of Being*, 1975; Marshall Walker, *Robert Penn Warren: A Vision Earned*, 1979; James Justus, *The Achievement of Robert Penn Warren*, 1981; Katherine Snipes, *Robert Penn Warren*, 1983; Hugh M. Ruppersburg, *Robert Penn Warren and the American Imagination*, 1990; William Bedford Clark, *The American Vision of Robert Penn Warren*, 1991; and Joseph R. Millichap, *Robert Penn Warren: A Study of the Short Fiction*, 1992.

WALT WHITMAN

Born: West Hills, New York; May 31, 1819
Died: Camden, New Jersey; March 26, 1892

Poetry · *Leaves of Grass*, 1855, 1856, 1860, 1867, 1871, 1876, 1881-1882, 1889, 1891-1892 · *Drum-Taps*, 1865 · *Passage to India*, 1871 · *After All, Not to Create Only*, 1871 · *As a Strong Bird on Pinions Free*, 1872 · *Two Rivulets*, 1876 · *November Boughs*, 1888 · *Good-bye My Fancy*, 1891 · *Complete Poetry and Selected Prose*, 1959 (James E. Miller, editor)

Achievements · Walt Whitman's stature rests largely on two major contributions to the literature of the United States. First, although detractors are numerous and the poet's organizing principle is sometimes blurred, *Leaves of Grass* stands as the most fully realized American epic poem. Written in the midst of natural grandeur and burgeoning materialism, Whitman's book traces the geographical, social, and spiritual contours of an expanding nation. It embraces the science and commercialism of industrial America while trying to direct these practical energies toward the "higher mind" of literature, culture, and the soul. In his Preface to the first edition of *Leaves of Grass*, Whitman referred to the United States itself as "essentially the greatest poem." He saw the self-esteem, sympathy, candor, and deathless attachment to freedom of the common people as "unrhymed poetry," which awaited the "gigantic and generous treatment worthy of it." *Leaves of Grass* was to be that treatment.

As James E. Miller points out in his edition of Whitman's *Complete Poetry and Selected Prose* (1959), the poet's second achievement was in language and poetic technique. Readers take for granted the modern American poet's emphasis on free verse and ordinary diction, forgetting Whitman's revolutionary impact. His free verse form departed from stanzaic patterns and regular lines, taking its power instead from individual, rolling, oratorical lines of cadenced speech. He subordinated traditional poetic techniques, such as alliteration, repetition, inversion, and conventional meter, to this expansive form. He also violated popular rules of poetic diction by extracting a rich vocabulary from foreign languages, science, opera, various trades, and the ordinary language of town and country. Finally, Whitman broke taboos with his extensive use of sexual imagery, incorporated not to titillate or shock, but to portray life in its wholeness. He determined to be the poet of procreation, to celebrate the elemental and primal life

The National Portrait Gallery

force that permeates humans and nature. Thus, "forbidden voices" are unveiled, clarified, and transfigured by the poet's vision of their place in an organic universe.

Whitman himself said he wrote but "one or two indicative words for the future." He expected the "main things" from poets, orators, singers, and musicians to come. They would prove and define a national culture, thus justifying his faith in American democracy. These apologetic words, along with the early tendency to read Whitman as "untranslatable," or barbaric and undisciplined, long delayed his acceptance as one of America's greatest poets. In fact, if judged by the poet's own test of greatness, he is a failure, for he said the "proof of a poet is that his country absorbs him as affectionately as he has absorbed it." Whitman has not been absorbed by the common people to whom he paid tribute in his poetry. Today, however, with recognition from both the academic community and such twentieth century poets as Hart Crane, William Carlos Williams, Karl Shapiro, and Randall Jarrell, his *Leaves of Grass* has taken its place among the great masterworks of American literature.

Biography · Walt Whitman (christened Walter) was born in West Hills, Long Island on May 31, 1819. His mother, Louisa Van Velsor, was descended from a long line of New York Dutch farmers, and his father, Walter Whitman, was a Long Island farmer and carpenter. In 1823, the father moved his family to Brooklyn in search of work. One of nine children in an undistinguished family, Whitman received only a meager formal education between 1825 and 1830, when he turned to the printing trade for the next five years. At the age of seventeen he began teaching at various Long Island schools and continued to teach until he went to New York City to be a printer for the *New World* and a reporter for the *Democratic Review* in 1841. From then on, Whitman generally made a living at journalism. Besides reporting and freelance writing, he edited several Brooklyn newspapers, including the *Daily Eagle* (1846-1848), the *Freeman* (1848-1849), and the *Times* (1857-1859). Some of Whitman's experiences during this period influenced the poetry that seemed to burst into print in 1855. While in New York, Whitman frequented the opera and the public library, both of which furnished him with a sense of heritage, of connection with the bards and singers of the past. In 1848, Whitman met and was hired by a representative of the New Orleans *Crescent*. Although the job lasted only a few months, the journey by train, stagecoach, and steamboat through what Whitman always referred to as "inland America" certainly helped to stimulate his vision of the country's democratic future. Perhaps most obviously influential was Whitman's trade itself. His flair for action and vignette, as well as descriptive detail, surely was sharpened by his journalistic writing. The reporter's keen eye for the daily scene is everywhere evident in *Leaves of Grass*.

When the first edition of his poems appeared, Whitman received little money but some attention from reviewers. Included among the responses was a famous letter from Ralph Waldo Emerson, who praised Whitman for his brave thought and greeted him at the beginning of a great career. Whitman continued to write and edit, but was unemployed during the winter of 1859-1860, when he began to frequent Pfaff's bohemian restaurant. There he may have established the "manly love" relationships which inspired the "Calamus" poems of the 1860 edition of *Leaves of Grass*. Again, this third edition created a stir with readers, but the outbreak of the Civil

War soon turned everyone's attention to more pressing matters. Whitman himself was too old for military service, but he did experience the war by caring for wounded soldiers in Washington, D.C., hospitals. While in Washington as a government clerk, Whitman witnessed Lincoln's second inauguration, mourned over the president's assassination in April, printed *Drum-Taps* in May, and later added to these Civil War lyrics a sequel, which contained "When Lilacs Last in the Dooryard Bloom'd."

The postwar years saw Whitman's reputation steadily increasing in England, thanks to William Rossetti's *Selections* in 1868, Algernon Swinburne's praise, and a long, admiring review of his work by Anne Gilchrist in 1870. In fact, Mrs. Gilchrist fell in love with the poet after reading *Leaves of Grass* and even moved to Philadelphia in 1876 to be near him, but her hopes of marrying Whitman died with her in 1885. Because of books by William D. O'Connor and John Burroughs, Whitman also became better known in America, but any satisfaction he may have derived from this recognition was tempered by two severe blows in 1873. He suffered a paralytic stroke in January, and his mother, to whom he was very devoted, died in May. Unable to work, Whitman returned to stay with his brother George at Camden, New Jersey, spending summers on a farm at Timber Creek.

Although Whitman recuperated sufficiently to take trips to New York or Boston, and even to Colorado and Canada in 1879-1880, he was never again to be the robust man he had so proudly described in early editions of *Leaves of Grass*. His declining years, however, gave him time to revise and establish the structure of his book. When the seventh edition of *Leaves of Grass* was published in Philadelphia in 1881, Whitman had achieved a total vision of his work. With the money from a Centennial edition (1876) and an occasional lecture on Lincoln, Whitman was able by 1884 to purchase a small house on Mickle Street in Camden, New Jersey. Although he was determined not to be "house-bound," a sunstroke in 1885 and a paralytic stroke in 1888 made him increasingly dependent on friends. He found especially gratifying the friendship of his secretary and companion, Horace Traubel, who recorded the poet's life and opinions during these last years. Despite the care of Traubel and several doctors and nurses, Whitman died of complications from a stroke on March 26, 1892.

Analysis · An approach to Walt Whitman's poetry profitably begins with the "Inscriptions" to *Leaves of Grass*, for these short, individual pieces introduce the main ideas and methods of Whitman's book. In general, they stake out the ground of what Miller has called the prototypical New World personality, a merging of the individual with the national and cosmic, or universal, selves. That democratic principles are at the root of Whitman's views becomes immediately clear in "One's-Self I Sing," the first poem in *Leaves of Grass*. Here, Whitman refers to the self as a "simple separate person," yet utters the "word Democratic, the word En-Masse." Citizens of America alternately assert their individuality—obey little, resist often—and yet see themselves as a brotherhood of the future, inextricably bound by the vision of a great new society of and for the masses. This encompassing vision requires a sense of "the Form complete," rejecting neither body nor soul, singing equally of the Female and Male, embracing both realistic, scientific, modern humankind and the infinite, eternal life of the spirit.

Whitman takes on various roles, or engages in what Raymond Cook calls "empathic identification" (*Walt Whitman Review*, 1964), to lead his readers to a fuller understanding of this democratic universal. In "Me Imperturbe," he is at ease as an element of nature, able to confront the accidents and rebuffs of life with the implacability of trees and animals. As he suggests in *Democratic Vistas*, the true idea of nature in all its power and glory must become fully restored and must furnish the "pervading atmosphere" to poems of American democracy. Whitman must also empathize with rational things—with humanity at large and in particular—so he constructs what sometimes seem to be endless catalogs of Americans at work and play. This technique appears in "I Hear America Singing," which essentially lists the varied carols of carpenter, boatman, shoemaker, woodcutter, mother, and so on, all "singing what belongs to him or her and to none else" as they ply their trades. In longer poems, such as "Starting from Paumanok," Whitman extends his catalog to all the states of the Union. He intends to acknowledge contemporary lands, salute employments and cities large and small, and report heroism on land and sea from an American point of view. He marks down all of what constitutes unified life, including the body, sexual love, and comradeship, or "manly love." Finally, the poet must join the greatness of love and democracy to the greatness of religion. These programs expand to take up large parts of even longer poems, such as "Song of Myself" or to claim space of their own in sections of *Leaves of Grass*.

Whitman uses another technique to underscore the democratic principle of his art: He makes the reader a fellow poet, a "camerado" who joins hands with him to traverse the poetic landscape. In "To You," he sees the poet and reader as passing strangers who desire to speak to one another and urges that they do so. In "Song of the Open Road," Whitman travels the highways with his "delicious burdens" of men and women, calling them all to come forth and move forever forward, well armed to take their places in "the procession of souls along the grand roads of the universe."

His view of the reader as fellow traveler and seer is especially clear in the closing lines of the poem:

> Camerado, I give you my hand!
> I give you my love more precious than money,
> I give you myself before preaching or law;
> Will you give me yourself? will you come travel with me?
> Shall we stick by each other as long as we live?

Finally, this comradeship means willingness to set out on one's own, for Whitman says in "Song of Myself" that the reader most honors his style "who learns under it to destroy the teacher." The questions one asks are one's own to puzzle out. The poet's role is to lead his reader up on a knoll, wash the gum from his eyes, and then let him become habituated to the "dazzle of light" that is the natural world. In other words, Whitman intends to help his reader become a "poet" of insight and perception and then release him to travel the public roads of a democratic nation.

This democratic unification of multiplicity, empathic identification, and comradeship exists in most of Whitman's poems. They do not depend on his growth as poet or thinker. Yet, in preparing to analyze representative poems from *Leaves of Grass*, it is helpful to establish a general plan for the various sections of the book. Whitman revised and reordered his poems until the 1881 edition, which established a form that was to remain essentially unchanged through succeeding editions. He merely annexed materials to the 1881 order until just before his death in 1892, then authorized the 1892 version for all future printings. Works originally published apart from *Leaves of Grass*, such as *Drum-Taps* or *Passage to India*, were eventually incorporated in the parent volume. Thus, an analysis of the best poems in five important sections of this final *Leaves of Grass* will help delineate Whitman's movement toward integration of self and nation, within his prescribed portals of birth and death.

"Song of Myself," Whitman's great lyric poem, exemplifies his democratic "programs" without diminishing the intense feeling that so startled his first readers. It successfully combines paeans to the individual, the nation, and life at large, including nature, sexuality, and death. Above all, "Song of Myself" is a poem of incessant motion, as though Whitman's energy is spontaneously bursting into lines. Even in the contemplative sections of the poem, when Whitman leans and loafs at his ease observing a spear of summer grass, his senses of hearing, taste, and sight are working at fever pitch. In the opening section he calls himself "nature without check with original energy." Having once begun to speak, he hopes "to cease not till death." Whitman says that although others may talk of the beginning and the end, he finds his subject in the now—in the "urge and urge and urge" of the procreant world.

One method by which Whitman's energy escapes boundaries is the poet's ability to "become" other people and things. He will not be measured by time and space, nor by physical form. Rather, he effuses his flesh in eddies and drifts it in lacy jags, taking on new identities with every line. His opening lines show that he is speaking not of himself alone but of all selves. What he assumes, the reader shall assume; every atom of him, and therefore of the world, belongs to the reader as well. In Section 24, he represents himself as a "Kosmos," which contains multitudes and reconciles apparent opposites. He speaks the password and sign of democracy and accepts nothing which all cannot share. To stress this egalitarian vision, Whitman employs the catalog with skill and variety. Many parts of "Song of Myself" list or name characters, places, occupations, or experiences, but Section 33 most clearly shows the two major techniques that give these lists vitality. First, Whitman composes long single-sentence movements of action and description, which attempt to unify nature and civilization. The poet is alternately weeding his onion patch, hoeing, prospecting, hauling his boat down a shallow river, scaling mountains, walking paths, and speeding through space. He then follows each set of actions with a series of place lines, beginning with "where," "over," "at," or "upon," which unite farmhouses, hearth furnaces, hot-air balloons, or steamships with plants and animals of land and sea. Second, Whitman interrupts there long listings with more detailed vignettes, which show the "large hearts of heroes"—a sea captain, a hounded slave, a fireman trapped and broken under debris, an artillerist. Sections 34-36 then extend the narrative to tales of the Alamo and an old-time sea fight, vividly brough forth with sounds and dialogue. In each case, the poet becomes the hero and is actually in the scene to suffer or succeed.

This unchecked energy and empathy carry over into Whitman's ebullient imagery to help capture the physical power of human bodies in procreant motion. At one point Whitman calls himself "hankering, gross, mystical, nude." He finds no sweeter flesh than that which sticks to his own bones, or to the bones of others. Sexual imagery, including vividly suggestive descriptions of the male and female body, is central to the poem. Although the soul must take its equal place with the body, neither abasing itself before the other, Whitman's mystical union of soul and body is a sexual experience as well. He loves the hum of the soul's "valved voice" and remembers how, on a transparent summer morning, the soul settled its head athwart his hips and turned over on him. It parted the shirt from the poet's "bosom-bone," plunged its tongue to his "bare-strip heart," and reached until it felt his beard and held his feet. From this experience came peace and the knowledge that love is fundamental to a unified, continuous creation. Poetic metaphor, which identifies and binds hidden likenesses in nature, is therefore emblematic of the organic world. For example, in answering a child's question, "What is the grass?" the poet offers a series of metaphors that join human, natural, and spiritual impulses:

> I guess it must be the flag of my disposition, out
> of hopeful green stuff woven.
> Or I guess it is the handkerchief of the Lord,
> A scented gift and remembrancer designedly dropt,
> Bearing the owner's name someway in the corners, that we
> may see and remark, and say *Whose?*

The grass becomes hair from the breasts of young men, from the heads and beards of old people, or from offspring, and it "speaks" from under the faint red roofs of mouths. The smallest sprout shows that there is no death, for "nothing collapses," and to die is "luckier" than anyone had supposed. This excerpt from the well-known sixth section of "Song of Myself" illustrates how image-making signifies for Whitman a kind of triumph over death itself.

Because of its position near the beginning of *Leaves of Grass* and its encompassing of Whitman's major themes, "Song of Myself" is a foundation for the volume. The "self" in this poem is a replica of the nation as self, and its delineation in the cosmos is akin to the growth of the United States in the world. Without putting undue stress on this nationalistic interpretation, however, the reader can find many reasons to admire "Song of Myself." Its dynamic form, beauty of language, and psychological insights are sufficient to make Whitman a first-rate poet, even if he had written nothing else.

The passionate celebration of the self and of sexuality is Whitman's great revolutionary theme. In "Children of Adam" he is the procreative father of multitudes, a champion of heterosexual love and the "body electric." In "From Pent-Up Aching Rivers," he sings of the need for superb children, brought forth by the "muscular urge" of "stalwart loins." In "I Sing the Body Electric," he celebrates the perfection of well-made male and female bodies. Sections 5 and 9 are explicit descriptions of sexual intercourse and physical "apparatus," respectively. Whitman does not shy away from the fierce attraction of the female form, or the ebb and flow of "limitless limpid jets of love hot and enormous" that undulate into the willing and yielding "gates of the body." Because he sees the body as sacred, as imbued with divine power, he considers these enumerations to be poems of the soul as much as of the body. Indeed, "A Woman Waits for Me" specifically states that sex contains all—bodies and souls. Thus, the poet seeks warm-blooded and sufficient women to receive the pent-up rivers of himself, to start new sons and daughters fit for the great nation that will be these United States. The procreative urge operates on more than one level in "Children of Adam"—it is physical sex and birthing, the union of body and soul, and the metaphorical insemination of the poet's words and spirit into national life. In several ways, then, words are to become flesh. Try as some early Whitman apologists might to explain them away, raw sexual impulses are the driving force of these poems.

Whitman's contemporaries were shocked by the explicit sexual content of "Children of Adam," but modern readers and critics have been much more intrigued by the apparent homosexuality of "Calamus." Although it is ultimately impossible to say whether these poems reflect Whitman's homosexual associations in New York, it is obvious that comradeship extends here to both spiritual and physical contact between men. "In Paths Untrodden" states the poet's intention to sing of "manly attachment" or types of "athletic love," to celebrate the need of comrades. "Whoever You Are Holding Me Now in Hand" deepens the physical nature of this love, including the stealthy meeting of male friends in a wood, behind some rock in the open air, or on the beach of some quiet island. There the poet would permit the comrade's long-dwelling kiss upon the lips and a touch that would carry him eternally forth over land and sea. "These I Singing in Spring" refers to "him that tenderly loves me" and pledges the hardiest spears of grass, the calamus-root, to those who love as the poet himself is capable of loving. Finally, two of Whitman's best lyrics concern this robust but clandestine relationship. "I Saw in Louisiana a Live-Oak Growing" is a poignant contrast between the live oak's ability to "utter joyous leaves" while it stands in solitude, without companions, and the poet's inability to live without a friend or lover near. There is no mistaking the equally personal tone of "When I Heard at the Close of the Day," probably Whitman's finest "Calamus" poem. The plaudits of others are meaningless and unsatisfying, says Whitman, until he thinks of how his dear friend and lover is on his way to see him. When his friend arrives one evening, the hissing rustle of rolling waves becomes congratulatory and joyful. Once the one he loves most lies sleeping by him under the same cover, face inclined toward him in the autumn moonbeams and arm lightly lying around his breast, he is happy.

Other short poems in "Calamus," such as "For You O Democracy," "The Prairie Grass Dividing," or "A Promise to California," are less obviously personal. Rather, they extend passionate friendship between men to the larger ideal of democratic brotherhood. Just as procreative love has its metaphorical implications for the nation, so too does Whitman promise to make the continent indissoluble and cities inseparable, arms about each other's necks, with companionship and the "manly love of comrades." Still other poems move this comradeship into wider spans of space and time. "The Moment Yearning and Thoughtful" joins the poet with men of Europe and Asia in happy brotherhood, thus transcending national and continental boundaries. "The Base of All Metaphysics" extends this principle through historical time, for the Greek, Germanic, and Christian systems all suggest that the attraction of friend to friend is the basis of civilization. The last poem in the "Calamus" section, "Full of Life Now," completes Whitman's panoramic view by carrying friendship into the future. His words communicate the compact, visible to readers of a century or any number of centuries hence. Each seeking the other past time's invisible boundaries, poet and reader are united physically through Whitman's poetry.

"Crossing Brooklyn Ferry" is the natural product of Whitman's idea that love and companionship will bind the world's peoples to one another. In a sense it gives the poet immortality through creation of a living artifact: the poem itself. Whitman stands motionless on a moving ferry, immersed in the stream of life and yet suspended in time through the existence of his words on the page. Consequently, he can say that neither time nor place nor distance matters, because he is with each reader and each fellow traveler in the future. He points out that hundreds of years hence others will enter the gates of the ferry and cross from shore to shore, will see the sun half an hour high and watch the seagulls floating in circles with motionless wings. Others will also watch the endless scallop-edged waves cresting and falling, as though they are experiencing the same moment as the poet, with the same mixture of joy and sorrow. Thus, Whitman confidently calls upon the "dumb ministers" of nature to keep up their ceaseless motion—to flow, fly, and frolic on—because they furnish their parts toward eternity and toward the soul.

Techniques match perfectly with these themes in "Crossing Brooklyn Ferry." Whitman's frequent repetition of the main images—sunrise and sunset, ebb and flow of the sea and river, seagulls oscillating in the sky—reinforces the belief in timeless, recurring human experience. Descriptions of schooners and steamers at work along the shore are among his most powerful evocations of color and sound. Finally, Whitman's employment of pronouns to mark a shift in the sharing of experiences also shows the poem's careful design. Whitman begins the poem with an "I" who looks at the scenes or crowds of people and calls to "you" who are

among the crowds and readers of present and future. In Section 8, however, he reaches across generations to fuse himself and pour his meaning
into the "you." At the end of this section, he and others have become "we,"
who understand and receive experience with free senses and love, united
in the organic continuity of nature.

The short section of *Leaves of Grass* entitled "Sea-Drift" contains the first
real signs of a more somber Whitman, who must come to terms with
hardship, sorrow, and death. In one way, this resignation and accommo-
dation follow the natural progression of the self from active, perhaps
callow, youth to contemplative old age. They are also an outgrowth of
Whitman's belief that life and death are a continuum, that life is a symphony of both sonatas and dirges, which the true poet of nature must
capture fully on the page. Whereas in other poems the ocean often signifies
birth and creation, with fish-shaped Paumanok (Manhattan) rising from the
sea, in "Tears" it is the repository of sorrow. Its white shore lies in solitude,
dark and desolate, holding a ghost or "shapeless lump" that cries streaming, sobbing tears. In "As I Ebb'd with the Ocean of Life," Whitman is
distressed with himself for daring to "blab" so much without having the
least idea who or what he really is. Nature darts upon the poet and stings
him, because he has not understood anything and because no human ever
can. He calls himself but a "trail of drift and debris," who has left his poems
like "little wrecks" upon Paumanok's shores. Yet, he must continue to
throw himself on the ocean of life, clinging to the breast of the land that is
his father, and gathering from the moaning sea the "sobbing dirge of
Nature." He believes the flow will return, but meanwhile he must wait and
lie in drifts at his readers' feet.

"Out of the Cradle Endlessly Rocking" is a fuller, finally more optimistic, treatment of the poet's confrontation with loss. Commonly acknowledged as one of Whitman's finest works, this poem uses lyrical language
and operatic structure to trace the origin of his poetic powers in the
experience of death. Two "songs" unite with the whispering cry of the sea
to communicate this experience to him. Central to the poem is Whitman's
seaside reminiscence of a bird and his mate, who build and tend a nest of
eggs. When the female fails to return one evening, never to appear again,
the male becomes a solitary singer of his sorrows, whose notes are "translated" by the listening boy-poet. The bird's song is an aria of lonesome
love, an outpouring carol of yearning, hope, and finally, death. As the boy
absorbs the bird's song, his soul awakens in sympathy. From this moment
forward, his destiny will be to perpetuate the bird's "cries of unsatisfied
love." More important, though, Whitman must learn the truth that this
phrase masks, must conquer "the word" that has caused the bird's cries:

> Whereto answering, the sea,
> Delaying not, hurrying not,
> Whisper'd me through the night, and very plainly before daybreak,
> Lisp'd to me the low and delicious word death,
> And again death, death, death, death.

Whitman then fuses the bird's song and his own with death, which the sea, "like some old crone rocking the cradle," has whispered to him. This final image of the sea as old crone soothing an infant underscores the central point of "Out of the Cradle Endlessly Rocking": Old age and death are part of a natural flux. Against the threat of darkness, one must live and sing.

Like the tone of "Sea-Drift," darker hues permeate Whitman's Civil War lyrics. His experiences as a hospital worker in Washington, D.C. are clearly behind the sometimes wrenching imagery of *Drum-Taps*. As a wound dresser he saw the destruction of healthy young bodies and minds at first hand. These spectacles were in part a test of Whitman's own courage and comradeship, but they were also a test of the nation's ability to survive and grow. As Whitman says in "Long, Too Long America," the country had long traveled roads "all even and peaceful," learning only from joys and prosperity, but now it must face "crises of anguish" without recoiling and show the world what its "children enmasse really are." Many of the *Drum-Taps* lyrics show Whitman facing this reality, but "The Wound Dresser" is representative. The poet's persona is an old man who is called upon years after the Civil War to "paint the mightiest armies of earth," to tell what experience of the war stays with him latest and deepest. Although he mentions the long marches, rushing charges, and toils of battle, he does not dwell on soldiers' perils or soldiers' joys. Rather, he vividly describes the wounded and dying at battlegrounds, hospital tents, or roofed hospitals, as he goes with "hinged knees and steady hand to dress wounds." He does not recoil or give out at the sight of crushed heads, shattered throats, amputated stumps of hands and arms, the gnawing and putrid gangrenous foot or shoulder. Yet, within him rests a burning flame, the memory of youths suffering or dead.

Confronted with these horrors, Whitman had to find a way to surmount them, and that way was love. If there could be a positive quality in war, Whitman found it in the comradeship of common soldiers, who risked all for their fellows. In "As Toilsome I Wander'd Virginia's Woods," for example, Whitman discovers the grave of a soldier buried beneath a tree. Hastily dug on a retreat from battle, the grave is nevertheless marked by a sign: "Bold, cautious, true, and my loving comrade." That inscription remains with the poet through many changeful seasons and scenes to follow, as evidence of this brotherly love. Similarly, "Vigil Strange I Kept on the Field One Night" tells of a soldier who sees his comrade struck down in battle and returns to find him cold with death. He watches by him through "immortal and mystic hours" until, just as dawn is breaking, he folds the young man in a blanket and buries him in a rude-dug grave where he fell. This tale of tearless mourning perfectly evokes the loss caused by war. Eventually, Whitman finds some ritual significance in these deaths, as though they are atonement for those yet living. In "A Sight in Camp in the Daybreak Gray and Dim," he marks three covered forms on stretchers near a hospital tent. One by one he uncovers their faces. The first is an elderly man, gaunt and grim, but a comrade nevertheless. The second is a sweet boy "with cheeks yet blooming." When he exposes the third face, however, he finds it calm, of yellow-white ivory, and of indeterminable age. He sees in it the face of Christ himself, "dead and divine and brother of all." "Over the Carnage Rose Prophetic a Voice" suggests that these Christian sacrifices will finally lead to a united Columbia. Even though a thousand may have to "sternly immolate themselves for one," those who love one another shall become invincible, and "affection shall solve the problems of freedom." As in other sections of *Leaves of Grass*, Whitman believes the United States will be held together not by lawyers, paper agreements, or force of arms, but by the cohesive power of love and fellowship.

"When Lilacs Last in the Dooryard Bloom'd," another of Whitman's acknowledged masterpieces, repeats the process underlying *Drum-Taps*. The poet must come to terms with the loss of one he loves—in this case, the slain President Lincoln. Death and mourning must eventually give way to consolation and hope for the future. Cast in the form of a traditional elegy, the poem traces the processional of Lincoln's coffin across country, past the poet himself, to the president's final resting place. To objectify his emotional struggle between grief on the one hand and spiritual reconciliation with death on the other, Whitman employs several vivid symbols. The lilac blooming perennially, with its heart-shaped leaves, represents the poet's perpetual mourning and love. The "powerful fallen star," which now lies in a "harsh surrounding could" of black night, is Lincoln, fallen and shrouded in his coffin. The solitary hermit thrush that warbles "death's outlet song of life" from a secluded swamp is the soul or spiritual world. Initially, Whitman is held powerless by the death of his departing comrade. Although he can hear the bashful notes of the thrush and will come to understand them, he thinks only of showering the coffin with sprigs of lilac to commemorate his love for Lincoln. He must also warble his own song before he can absorb the bird's message of consolation. Eventually, as he sits amidst the teeming daily activities described in Section 14, he is struck by the "sacred knowledge of death," and the bird's carol thus becomes intelligible to him. Death is lovely, soothing, and delicate. It is a "strong deliveress" who comes to nestle the grateful body in her flood of bliss. Rapt with the charm of the bird's song, Whitman sees myriad battlecorpses in a vision—the debris of all the slain soldiers of the war—yet realizes that they are fully at rest and unsuffering. The power of this realization gives him strength to loose the hand of his comrade. An ever-blooming lilac now signifies renewal, just as death takes its rightful place as the harbinger of new life, the life of the eternal soul.

Whitman's deepening concern with matters of the spirit permeates the last sections of *Leaves of Grass.* Having passed the test of Civil War and having done his part to reunite the United States, Whitman turned his attention to America's place in the world and his own place in God's design. As he points out in "A Clear Midnight," he gives his last poems to the soul and its "free flight into the wordless," in order to ponder the themes he loves best: "Night, sleep, death and the stars." Such poems as "Chanting the Square Deific" and "A Noiseless Patient Spider" invoke either the general soul, the "Santa Spirita" that pervades all of created life, or the toils of individual souls, flinging out gossamer threads to connect themselves with this holy spirit.

In *A Reader's Guide to Walt Whitman* (1970), Gay Wilson Allen finds this late Whitman too often pathetically didactic and unpoetic, but he points out that the poet was still able to produce fine lyrics in his old age. One of these successful poems, "Passage to India," announces Whitman's intention to join modern science to fables and dreams of old, to weld past and future, and to show that the United States is but a "bridge" in the "vast rondure" of the world. Just as the Suez Canal connected Europe and Asia, Whitman says, America's transcontinental railroad ties the Eastern to the Western sea, thus verifying Columbus' dream. Beyond these material thoughts of exploration, however, lies the poet's realm of love and spirit. The poet is a "true son of God," who will soothe the hearts of restlessly exploring, never-happy humanity. He will link all human affections, justify the "cold, impassive, voiceless earth," and absolutely fuse nature and humankind. This fusion takes place not in the material world but in the swelling of the soul toward God, who is a mighty "centre of the true, the good, the loving." Passage to these superior universes transcends time and space and death. It is a "passage to more than India," through the deep waters that no mariner has traveled, and for which the poet must "risk the ship, ourselves and all."

Whitman also uses a seagoing metaphor for spiritual passage in "Prayer of Columbus," which is almost a continuation of "Passage to India." In the latter, Whitman aggressively flings himself into the active voyage toward God, but in "Prayer of Columbus" he is a "batter'd, wreck'd old man," willing to yield his ships to God and wait for the unknown end of all. He recounts his heroic deeds of exploration and attributes their inspiration to a message from the heavens that sped him on. Like Columbus, Whitman is "old, poor, and paralyzed," yet capable of one more effort to speak of the steady interior light that God has granted him. Finally, the works of the past fall away from him, and some divine hand reveals a scene of countless ships sailing on distant seas, from which "anthems in new tongues" salute and comfort him. This implied divine sanction for his life's work was consolation to an old poet, who, at his death in 1892, remained largely unaccepted and unrecognized by contemporary critics and historians.

The grand design of *Leaves of Grass* appears to trace self and nation neatly through sensuous youth, crises of maturity, and soul-searching old age. Although this philosophical or psychological reading of Whitman's work is certainly encouraged by the poet's tinkering with its structure, many fine lyrics do not fit into neat patterns, or even under topical headings. Whitman's reputation rests more on the startling freshness of his language, images, and democratic treatment of the common American citizen than on his success as epic bard. Common to all his poetry, however, are certain major themes: reconciliation of body and soul, purity and unity of physical nature, death as the "mother of beauty," and above all, comradeship or love, which binds and transcends all else. In fact, Whitman encouraged a complex comradeship with his readers to bind his work to future generations. He expected reading to be a gymnastic struggle and the reader to be a re-creator of the poem through imaginative interaction with the poet. Perhaps that is why he said in "So Long" that *Leaves of Grass* was no book, for whoever touches his poetry "touches a man."

Other literary forms · Walt Whitman published several important essays and studies during his lifetime. *Democratic Vistas* (1871), *Memoranda During the War* (1875-1876), *Specimen Days and Collect* (1882-1883, autobiographical sketches), and the *Complete Prose Works* (1892) are the most significant. He also tried his hand at short fiction, collected in *The Half-Breed and Other Stories* (1927), and a novel, *Franklin Evans* (1842). Many of his letters and journals have appeared either in early editions or as parts of the New York University Press edition of *The Collected Writings of Walt Whitman* (1961-1984; 22 volumes).

Select works other than poetry

LONG FICTION: *Franklin Evans,* 1842.

SHORT FICTION: *The Half-Breed and Other Stories,* 1927.

NONFICTION: *Democratic Vistas,* 1871; *Memoranda During the War,* 1875-1876; *Specimen Days and Collect,* 1882-1883; *Complete Prose Works,* 1892; *Calamus,* 1897 (letters; Richard M. Bucke, editor); *The Wound Dresser,* 1898 (Richard M. Bucke, editor); *Letters Written by Walt Whitman to His Mother, 1866-1872,* 1902 (Thomas B. Harned, editor); *An American Primer,* 1904; *Walt Whitman's Diary in Canada,* 1904 (William S. Kennedy, editor); *The Letters of Anne Gilchrist and Walt Whitman,* 1918 (Thomas B. Harned, editor).

MISCELLANEOUS: *The Collected Writings of Walt Whitman,* 1961-1984 (22 volumes).

Perry D. Luckett

Bibliography · There are numerous biographies and critical studies of Whitman's life and work, some dating from the 1890's. Interesting and useful biographies have been written by Gay Wilson Allen, *The Solitary Singer: A Critical Biography of Walt Whitman,* 1955; Justin Kaplan, *Walt Whitman: A Life,* 1980; and Paul Zweig, *Walt Whitman: The Making of the Poet,* 1984. Two important critical works are by Gay Wilson Allen, *The New Walt Whitman Handbook,* 1986, and James E. Miller, Jr., *Walt Whitman,* updated ed., 1990.

RICHARD WILBUR

Born: New York, New York; March 1, 1921

Poetry · *The Beautiful Changes and Other Poems*, 1947 · *Ceremony and Other Poems*, 1950 · *Things of This World*, 1956 · *Poems 1943-1956*, 1957 · *Advice to a Prophet and Other Poems*, 1961 · *Loudmouse*, 1963 (juvenile) · *The Poems of Richard Wilbur*, 1963 · *Walking to Sleep: New Poems and Translations*, 1969 · *Digging for China*, 1970 · *Opposites*, 1973 (juvenile) · *The Mind-Reader: New Poems*, 1976 · *Seven Poems*, 1981 · *New and Collected Poems*, 1988 · *More Opposites*, 1991 · *Runaway Opposites*, 1995 (children's poetry) · *The Disappearing Alphabet*, 1998 (juvenile)

Achievements · Eschewing any obvious poetic version or formal, personal set of guidelines, Richard Wilbur has come to be regarded as a master craftsman of modern poetry. Although he sees himself as an inheritor of the vast wealth of language and form used by poets before him, Wilbur has consistently striven to create and maintain his own artistic signature and control over his own work. Having begun his career immediately after World War II and having been exposed to what has been called "the Beat generation," Wilbur creates his poetry from an intriguing blend of imaginative insights and strict adherence to the niceties of conventional poetics. His is not the poetry of confession or hatred readily exemplified by Sylvia Plath, nor is it hallucinatory or mystical as is much of Allen Ginsberg's work.

Wilbur began to write poetry because the war prompted him to confront the fear and the physical and spiritual detachment brought about by a world in upheaval. He says that he "wrote poems to calm [his] nerves." It is this sense of imposed order on a disorderly world that has caused some readers to think of Wilbur's poetry as a distant investigation into human life addressed to a small, educated audience and delivered by a seemingly aloof but omniscient observer. Nearly all Wilbur's poems are metrical, and many of them employ rhyme. Perhaps if a feeling of detachment exists, it comes not from Wilbur the poet but from the very standards of poetic expression. Every persona established by a poet is, in Wilbur's words, "a contrived self." This voice is the intelligent recorder of experience and emotion. It is Wilbur's voice in the sense that, like the poet, the persona discovers relationships between ideas and events which are grounded in concrete reality but which lead to abstracted views of nature, love, endurance, and place. He uses concrete images—a fountain, a tree, a hole in the floor—to explore imagination. His flights into imagery are not sojourns into fantasy; they are deliberate attempts to be a witness to the disordered and altogether varied life around him.

Wilbur achieves brilliantly what he sees poetry doing best: compacting experience into language that excites the intellect and vivifies the imagination. His voice and the cautious pace at which he works are not to be taken as self-conscious gestures. They are, to use his word, matters demanding "carefulness." He finds "gaudiness annoying, richness not." Wilbur's poetry is rich; it is wealthy in imagery and plot and rhythmic movement. He seems to believe that language cannot be guarded unless it

Constance Stuart Larrabee

is used to carry as much meaning as it can possibly bear. This freedom with language is not prodigal but controlled. Betraying poetry's ancestry would be anarchy for Wilbur. At the heart of his canon is the verbal liberty he finds in formalism. Consequently, in each line he hopes that at least one word will disturb the reader, providing a freedom found only within the architectonics of poetry's conventions. His poems enjoy humor and quiet meditation, and they lend themselves easily to being read aloud. Because of the freedom the rules of poetry give to them, Wilbur's poems are energetic, and his persona, peripatetic.

Honored with degrees from numerous colleges and universities, Wilbur has also been the recipient of Guggenheim Fellowships (1952-1953, 1963) and the Prix de Rome (1954). *Things of This World* was awarded the Pulitzer Prize, the National Book Award, and the Edna St. Vincent Millay Memorial Award. In 1964, he was a corecipient of the Bollingen Prize for his translation of *Tartuffe*. In 1987 he was named Poet Laureate of the United States, an honor that was soon followed by the Aiken Taylor Award for Modern American Poetry.

Biography · Born to Lawrence and Helen Purdy Wilbur, Richard Purdy Wilbur was reared in a family which was moderately interested in art and language. His father was an artist, and his mother was a daughter of an editor with the *Baltimore Sun*. His maternal great-grandfather was also an editor and a publisher who established newspapers supporting the Democratic platform. In 1923, the family moved to a farm in North Caldwell, New Jersey, and Wilbur and his brother enjoyed their childhoods investigating nature, an activity which remained a strong focal point in his poems. His father's painting and his mother's link with newspapers led him at times to think of becoming a cartoonist, an artist, or a journalist. His love of cartooning continued, for he illustrated *Opposites* with bold line drawings. His interests were many, however, and he was encouraged by his family to explore any talents he wished. After graduating from Montclair High School in 1938, he entered Amherst College, where he edited the newspaper and contributed to *Touchstone*, the campus humor magazine. He spent summers hoboing around the country.

After graduation in 1942, Wilbur married Charlotte Hayes Ward (with whom he had four children), joined the Enlisted Reserve Corps, and saw active duty in Europe with the 36th Infantry Division. At Cassino, Anzio, and the Siegfried line, he began writing poetry seriously, embarking on what he called creation of "an experience" through a poem. He sent his work home where it remained until he returned from the war to pursue a master's degree in English at Harvard. The French poet André du Bouchet read the poems, pronounced Wilbur a poet, and sent the works to be published. They were released as *The Beautiful Changes and Other Poems* in 1947; the same year Wilbur received his degree from Harvard and was elected to the Society of Fellows.

His status as a poet established, Wilbur began his teaching career. From 1950 to 1954, he was an assistant professor of English at Harvard. Then, from 1954 to 1957, he served as an associate professor at Wellesley College; during that time his award-winning *Things of This World* was published. In 1957, he went to Wesleyan University as a professor of English. He stayed there until 1977, when he accepted the position of writer-in-residence at Smith College. He divided his time between Key West, Florida, and the Berkshire Mountains near Cummington, Massachusetts, where he occupied himself doing things which he said were "nonverbal so that I can return to language with excitement and move toward language from kinds of strong awareness for which I haven't instantly found facile words. It is good for a writer to move into words out of the silence, as much as he can."

Analysis · If readers were to limit their interest in Richard Wilbur's poetry to a discussion of imagery, they would misunderstand and distort some of the basic premises upon which he builds his poetry. Just as he sees each of his poems as an independent unit free of any entanglement with other poems in a collection or with a superimposed, unifying theme, so he views the creation of a poem as an individual response to something noticed or deeply felt. Because all worthwhile poetry is a personal vision of the world, Wilbur heightens the tension and irony found in his poems by establishing a voice enchanted by what is happening in the poem but controled so that the persona is nearly always a reasonable voice recording details and events in an entirely believable way. His sense of decorum, then, plays a major role in creating the relationship between reader and poet.

Readers often react to Wilbur's decorum in one of two ways: either they laud the fictive persona as a trustworthy human being, lacking deceit, or they hear him speaking from a plateau which is at best inaccessible to the reader because it is too distant from the mundane. Wilbur's decorum actually creates a median between these two extremes. Like Robert Frost, Wilbur believes that poetry must present shared experiences in extraordinary ways. His persona is not directed toward readers solely as readers of poetry. Rather, the voice is aimed sharply at defining the experiences that both readers and poet hold in common. Wilbur never talks *at* the reader, but rather, he addresses himself to the human condition. Often his voice is much more vulnerable and humorous than readers admit. Many of his poems are reminiscent of soliloquies. A reader may come to the poems the way a person may discover a man talking out loud to himself about personal experiences, all the while using the most imaginative, sonorous language to describe them. At his best, Wilbur provides moments when readers can recognize the deep humanity which runs through his work.

Although he looks for no overriding idea or central metaphor when he organizes a collection, Wilbur does return to themes which are at the heart of human life: nature, love, a sense of goodness and contentment, the search for direction, the need to feel a part of a larger unknown, a wider life. All of these topics are spiritual concerns. Unlike Edgar Allan Poe, whom he sees as a writer who ignores reality to construct a world colored by the fantastic, Wilbur grounds his spiritual wanderings in the world that readers know. In this respect, he is capturing what is abstract in the mesh of concrete imagery, a feat also successfully accomplished by Frost and Emily Dickinson.

Perhaps nowhere else do Wilbur's major themes so intelligently and ironically coalesce as in "Lamarck Elaborated," a poem dealing not only with nature and love but also with the inner and outer worlds that human beings inhabit. Humanity's place in these two worlds and its ability to balance them provide a common experience for both poet and reader. The inner world of the human being, represented by the senses and the intellect, perceives the outer world framed by nature which, in turn, has the power to shape the human's ability to interpret what he or she senses to be the physical world. Chevalier de Lamarck, a French naturalist whose life straddles the seventeenth and eighteenth centuries, believed that the environment causes structural changes that can be passed on genetically. Although humans may assign names to the animals, plants, and objects that surround them, they are unable to control the changes which may occur in nature and which may, in turn, change them. Humankind has adapted to nature. Paradoxically, humanity's attempts at analyzing the natural state of things leads us to "whirling worlds we could not know," and what humans think is love is simply an overwhelming desire causing dizziness. The poem's voice records the human obsession with its place in a scheme it wishes to dominate but cannot. Literally and figuratively, the balance between the inner and outer worlds "rolls in seas of thought."

The balance implied in "Lamarck Elaborated" is also investigated in "Another Voice." Here Wilbur probes the soul's ability to do good when humankind's nature is often to do bad. How can the soul feel sympathy when evil has been committed? How can it transform violence into "dear concerns"? Can the "giddy ghost" do battle with malevolence? Wilbur seems to suggest that the soul's response should be one of endurance as it acknowledges evil without becoming evil. The soul may not be able to rid itself of its "Anxiety and hate," two powerful forces, but neither will it relinquish its quiet sympathy which serves as a witness for compassion.

Although "Another Voice" may conjure up a spirit of resignation as the poet ponders the weaknesses of the human soul, Wilbur's poetry contains many examples of contentment, complete happiness, and mature acknowledgement of human limitations. Wilbur reminds his readers that human beings cannot be or do all that they might wish to become or accomplish. "Running," "Patriot's Day," and "Dodwells Road" form a thematic triptych in which Wilbur muses about the stages of life and the reactions human beings have to these stages. The first poem is an account of the persona's memories of his boyhood and the abandonment that running provided. In the second, the persona is an observer of the Boston Marathon and of "Our champion Kelley who would win again,/ Rocked in his will, at rest within his run." The third poem presents the persona as both participant and observer. Having taken up the sport of jogging, as if to reaffirm his physical well-being, the speaker runs out of the forest and is brought to a halt by "A good ache in my ribcage." He feels comfortable in the natural setting surrounding him, a "part of that great going." The shouts of two boys (possibly the persona's sons) and the barking of a dog break the quiet, and the speaker finds delight in their running and leaping. In a gesture as inevitable as it is moving, the speaker gives the "clean gift" of his own childhood, his own vigor, to the boys.

The voice that Wilbur assumes in his poems is often that of a person discovering or attempting to discover something unknown or removed. Usually the epiphany that the persona undergoes is centered around ordinary conditions or experiences. Sometimes the enlightenment produces extraordinary insights into human nature, the fragility of life, or the inexorable passage of time. A poem which manages to evoke poignancy, humor, and fear is "A Hole in the Floor," in which the speaker stands directly above an opening a carpenter has made "In the parlor floor." The use of the word "parlor" brings to mind turn-of-the-century home life, a certain quaintness and security. Now that this *sanctum sanctorum* has been defiled, the speaker stares into the hole to view an unexpected scene. He is poised on the brink of a discovery and compares himself with Heinrich Schliemann, the excavator of Troy and Mycenae. He sees in the hole the vestiges of the house's origins: sawdust, wood shavings "From the time when the floor was laid."

Wilbur heightens the mythological tone of the poem by comparing the shavings to the pared skins of the golden apples guarded by the Hesperides in the garden on the Isles of the Blest. Although in the dim light the curly lengths of shaved wood may seem "silvery-gold," they remain concrete reminders of the carpenter's trade and of the creation of the structure in which the speaker now stands. If he senses that something primordial has been uncovered, he cannot quite convey his feelings. The speaker, of course, has given in to his own curiosity and wishes to be the explorer of unknown territories, the uncoverer of what had been private and hidden, but, at the same time, close by. Reveling in his investigation of the joists and pipes, he finally wonders what it is he thought he would see. He brings his consciousness back to the steady, mundane world of the parlor and upbraids himself for his curiosity and romanticism. He asks himself if he expected to find a treasure or even the hidden gardens of the Hesperides. Perhaps, he ponders, he has come face-to-face with "The house's very soul."

Unlike Frost's figure who is content to kneel by a well, see his own reflection, and then catch a glimmer of something at the bottom, Wilbur's speaker understands that what he discovers or believes he has discovered is something beyond the orderly, formal restrictions imposed upon him by the parlor. Somehow, the hidden realm on which the house stands adds an importance to what can in fact be known. Paradoxically, what the persona knows is his inability to fathom the unknowable, that "buried strangeness/ which nourishes the known." The parlor suddenly becomes "dangerous" because its serenity rests on uncertainty, darkness, and private beginnings. The "buried strangeness" not only resides at the foundation of the house, but it is also found in any human construction, a building, a passion, a theory, or a poem.

"A Hole in the Floor" is further representative of Wilbur's poetry because it balances two opposites, and these contraries work on several levels: curiosity and expectation, the known and the unknown, and reality and imagination. It is a complex and beautifully crafted poem. Other poems which also investigate the balance between opposites include "Another Voice," "Advice to a Prophet," "Gemini," "Someone Talking to Himself," and "The Writer." Wilbur's obvious pleasure in riddles is another example of this taut balance between the unknown and the known, the question and the answer, the pause and the reply. In addition, *Opposites*, charming and witty as it is, has this same tense equilibrium built into it.

The contrast between opposing ideas is probably most evident in what could be called Wilbur's "two-voice" poems, those in which he presents "two voices going against each other. One is a kind of lofty and angelic voice, the other is a slob voice, and these are two parts of myself quarreling in public." The poem "Two Voices in a Meadow," which begins *Advice to a Prophet and Other Poems*, juxtaposes a milkweed's flexibility with a stone's tenacity. The milkweed yields to the wind's power to carry its cherubic seeds to the soil, and the stone attributes the solid foundation of heaven to its immovable nature. In "The Aspen and the Stream," the tree and the brook carry on a dialogue in which the aspen's metaphysics are countered by the stream's nononsense, literal approach to its place in the universal scheme of life.

Sometimes Wilbur's interest in opposites takes the form of a study of reconciliation through religion. Such poems as "Water Walker" and "A Christmas Hymn" suggest his concern with religious doctrine and its influence on private action and public thought. At other times, the balance is jarred because the persona is duped into believing something false or is misled because of naïveté. A more gullible person than the one in "A Hole in the Floor," the character in "Digging for China" burrows into the earth thinking that he can reach China. The speaker digs and digs to no avail, of course, and becomes obsessed and then delirious, "blinking and staggering while the earth went round." Admitting his folly, he confesses that "Until I got my balance back again/ All that I saw was China, China, China." He returns to whatever balance he may have known before his futile attempt to reach the Orient, but he enjoys no enlightenment of the spirit.

The tense balance between knowledge and ignorance may appear in Wilbur's poems when the persona is confronted with an abstraction so amorphous and foreign that it cannot adequately be defined, as in "A Hole in the Floor." At other times, Wilbur allows his characters to confront ideas, events, or feelings which are much more readily and vividly recognized. In such cases, the emotions, although private, have a larger, perhaps a more cosmic significance added to them; these are shared emotions, easily identifiable because nearly all human beings have experienced them. Even if humanity stands on the edge or the margins of experience, it is from time to time thrust squarely into life's demands and responsibilities. Wilbur elucidates this idea in poems such as "Marginalia," in which "Things concentrate at the edges," and "Our riches are centrifugal."

Two poems which combine both the experience of living life fully and the experience of participating at its edges are "Boy at the Window" and "The Pardon." Both have titles which would befit paintings, and, indeed, Wilbur presents concrete stories colored and framed by his language and the structure of the poems themselves. Each has as its main character a boy who is both witness and participant. "Boy at the Window" is reminiscent of a classic Italian sonnet in its form and meter, although Wilbur divides the two sections into equal parts of eight lines each. Looking out from a window toward a snowman he has built, the boy is confronted by the "god-forsaken stare" of the figure "with bitumen eyes." The structure of the poem reinforces the balanced stares given by the boy and the snowman.

Safe and warm, the boy intuitively knows that the snowman is an "outcast" from the world that the boy, himself, enjoys. The boy, however, does not mourn for the snowman; rather, the snowman "melts enough to drop from one soft eye/ A trickle of the purest rain, a tear." Surrounded as he is by "light" and "love," the boy understands, perhaps for the first time, fear and dread. The poem provides a quiet moment when the boy in his silence recognizes something about sin and futility and innocence and contentment. With its blending of childhood trust and energy with a maturer reflection on humankind's fall from grace, it evokes much the same mood as Dylan Thomas' "Fern Hill."

"The Pardon" has as its plot a boy's confrontation with the death of his dog. At first he refuses to accept the event and tries to mask the experience just as "the heavy honeysuckle-smell" masks the odor of the decaying body. Admitting fear and the inability to "forgive the sad or strange/ In beast or man," the child cannot bring himself to bury the dog he loved "while he kept alive." After the boy's father buries the dog, the child sleeps and dreams of the dog's coming toward him. The boy wants to "call his name" to ask "forgiveness of his tongueless head." His attempts are checked, however, and he feels betrayed by his horror and his guilt. The poem is told from the perspective of a grown man who is remembering his childhood. Knowing the gesture may be ludicrous or ineffective, he "begs death's pardon now." Whether redemption occurs or the guilt is lifted is not told, but the very act of confronting this long-ago event is in itself a mature gesture of reconciliation and remorse, covered, perhaps, with shame and embarrassment. The rhyme scheme of the poem also suggests the persona's growing control over the incident, a control made possible by the passing of years and the accumulation of experience. The boy lacked a perspective; the man he has become provides it. Like his father before him, the speaker hopes to have the strength and the will to bury the dog, if not literally, then at least symbolically. As the persona moves toward this strength, the rhyme scheme, chaotic at the poem's beginning, settles into an obvious, harmonious pattern which parallels the speaker's growing dominance over his sorrow.

Wilbur is known and admired for his short poems whose imagery and subjects are compacted by his mastery of language and poetic convention. As if to reaffirm his commitment to the richness of these standards, his later collections have included long, dramatic monologues which remind readers of the oral tradition in poetry. "Walking to Sleep" and "The Mind-Reader" are poems which invite Wilbur's audience to explore the frontier, the wilderness of conscious thought and subconscious ruminating. The poems are both accessible and cryptic. Nowhere else has Wilbur created such sustained narrations, such talkative, complex tellers of his tales. In fact, he has noted that "Walking to Sleep" requires eight minutes to read aloud. The narrators are both conjurers and straightforward friends. Readers wish to believe them, but, at the same time, their manipulative language and their careful choice of details and information suggest an artifice. Both poems deal with the equilibrium between what is private, sleep and thought, and what is public, consciousness and action. Readers are led through the poems by the narrators who help the audience balance its way as if on a tightrope. In addition, the poems seem to be inviting readers to lose themselves in their own minds, an activity calling for leisure, courage, and an eagerness to embrace the unknown and the uncontrollable.

On its surface, "Walking to Sleep" is a sensuous account of sleep, sweeping from scene to scene, mirroring the act of dreaming. It begins *in medias res*, and readers are asked to have the poise of a queen or a general as they give themselves over to sleep and, more important, to the devices of the poem itself. Wilbur explores in ways that are whimsical, horrifying, and provocative the images that appear to a sleeper and to a poet as well. The poem may well be an exploration into the origins of poetry, and the narrator-poet may be speaking to himself as much as he is to an audience. His only direct warning to himself and his readers is the speaker's suggestion that the imagination never be allowed to become too comfortable; it must remain "numb" with a "grudging circumspection." Readers can feel the rhythms of sleep and love, creativity, and balance in the poem just as vividly as they sense the rhythms of meter, imagery, humor, and resignation. The poem is a masterful work controled by the limitless power of the human imagination.

"The Mind-Reader" deals with a man who thinks other people's thoughts. The narrator describes himself as a person condemned to finding what is lost, remembering what is forgotten, or foreseeing what is unknown. He is able to manipulate his listeners and his followers because of their superstitious awe of his ability, of which they are afraid to disprove. He confesses that he "sometimes cheats a little," admitting that he has no clear, easy answers to give to questions about love, careers, or doubts. He sees his duties as being those of a listener rather than those of a man capable to prescience, and he wonders if "selfish hopes/ And small anxieties" have replaced the "reputed rarities of the soul." The irony in the poem is underscored when the speaker turns to his readers and asks them a question of huge, religious proportions. Like his audience, he now longs for guidance, "some . . . affection" capable of discovering "In the worst rancor a deflected sweetness." Ironically, he dulls his mind with drink and satiates himself with "concupiscence." To the great question of whether a gentle, proper, and completely honest, cosmic mind-reader exists, he has no answer.

In the past, Wilbur's craft has been narrowly defined as the poetry of a mind set apart from the everyday world that human beings inhabit. Although his interest in balance is evident, his keen insight into contraries and the inner and outer lives of his characters is equally important to an understanding of what he is attempting in his poems. His work focuses on the enlightenment of the human spirit, but it never denies the darker impulses or fears which are brought to bear when doubt, resignation, or apathy appear as challenges to the harmony that civilized humankind strives to achieve. His poems are not so much reaffirmations of the beauty of life as they are records of an attempt at order, an order certainly suggested by the conventions of poetry. These conventions govern a poetic talent whose use of subject, meter, rhyme, and imagery provokes the senses and provides an ordinary understanding of life in an extraordinary and uncompromising way.

Other literary forms · In addition to his success as a poet, Richard Wilbur has won acclaim as a translator. Interspersed among his own poems are translations of Charles Baudelaire, Jorge Guillén, François Villon, and many others. His interest in drama is most notably shown in his translations of four Molière plays: *Le Misanthrope* (1955, *The Misanthrope*); *Tartuffe* (1963); *École des femmes* (1971, *The School for Wives*); and *Les Femmes savantes* (1978, *The Learned Ladies*). In 1957, Random House published *Candide: A Comic Operetta* with lyrics by Wilbur, book by Lillian Hellman, and score by Leonard Bernstein. Wilbur admits that he attempted to write a play in 1952, but he found its characters unconvincing and "all very wooden." He turned to translating Molière, thinking he "might learn something about poetic theater by translating *the master*." Wilbur has edited several books, including *A Bestiary*, with Alexander Calder (1955); *Poe: Complete Poems* (1959); and *Shakespeare: Poems*, with coeditor Alfred Harbage (1966). In 1976, Wilbur published *Responses, Prose Pieces: 1953-1976*, a collection of essays which he describes as containing "some prose by-products of a poet's life." Most of his manuscripts are in the Robert Frost Library at Amherst College. His early work is housed in the Lockwood Memorial Library at the State University of New York at Buffalo.

Select works other than poetry

DRAMA: *Candide: A Comic Operetta*, pr. 1956 (lyrics; book by Lillian Hellman, music by Leonard Bernstein).

DRAMA TRANSLATIONS: *The Misanthrope*, 1955 (Molière); *Tartuffe*, 1963 (Molière); *The School for Wives*, 1971 (Molière); *The Learned Ladies*, 1978 (Molière); *Andromache*, 1982 (Jean Racine); *Four Comedies*, 1982 (Molière); *Phaedra*, 1986 (Racine); *The School for Husbands*, 1991 (Molière); *The Imaginary Cuckold: Or, Sgarnarelle*, 1993 (Molière); *Amphitryon*, 1995 (Molière).

NONFICTION: *Responses: Prose Pieces, 1953-1976*, 1976; *On My Own Work*, 1983; *Conversations with Richard Wilbur*, 1990 (William Butts, editor); *The Catbird's Song: Prose Pieces, 1963-1995*, 1997.

EDITED TEXTS: *A Bestiary*, 1955; *Poe: Complete Poems*, 1959; *Shakespeare: Poems*, 1966; *The Narrative Poems and Poems of Doubtful Authenticity*, 1974.

Walter B. Freed, Jr.

Bibliography · The most inclusive work on Wilbur is Bruce Michelson, *Wilbur's Poetry: Music in a Scattering Time*, 1991. For Wilbur's personal views see William Butts, ed., *Conversations with Richard Wilbur*, 1990. An entire issue of *Renascence* 45 (Fall, 1992/Winter, 1993) is devoted to Wilbur's poetry. Other significant periodical articles include Bruce Bower, "Richard Wilbur's Difficult Balance, *The American Scholar* 60 (Spring, 1991), and Peter Harris, "Poetry Chronicle: Forty Years of Richard Wilbur, the Loving Work of an Equilibrist," *The Virginia Quarterly Review* 66 (Summer, 1990).

WILLIAM CARLOS WILLIAMS

Born: Rutherford, New Jersey; September 17, 1883
Died: Rutherford, New Jersey; March 4, 1963

Poetry · *Poems*, 1909 · *The Tempers*, 1913 · *Al Que Quiere!*, 1917 · *Kora in Hell: Improvisations*, 1920 · *Sour Grapes*, 1921 · *Spring and All*, 1923 · *Last Nights of Paris*, 1929 (translation of Philippe Soupault · with Elena Williams) · *Collected Poems, 1921-1931*, 1934 · *An Early Martyr and Other Poems*, 1935 · *Adam & Eve & The City*, 1936 · *The Complete Collected Poems of William Carlos Williams, 1906-1938*, 1938 · *The Broken Span*, 1941 · *The Wedge*, 1944 · *Paterson*, 1946-1958 · *The Clouds*, 1948 · *Selected Poems*, 1949 · *Collected Later Poems*, 1950, 1963 · *Collected Earlier Poems*, 1951 · *The Desert Music and Other Poems*, 1954 · *A Dog and the Fever*, 1954 (translation of Pedro Espinosa · with Elena Williams) · *Journey to Love*, 1955 · *Pictures from Brueghel*, 1962 · *Selected Poems*, 1985 · *The Collected Poems of William Carlos Williams: Volume I, 1909-1939*, 1986 · *The Collected Poems of William Carlos Williams: Volume II, 1939-1962*, 1988

Achievements · William Carlos Williams' recognition was late in coming, although he received the Dial Award for Services to American Literature in 1926 for the "Paterson" poem and the Guarantor's Prize from *Poetry* in 1931; Louis Zukofsky's Objectivist number of *Poetry* in 1931 featured Williams. The critics, other poets and writers, as well as the public, however, largely ignored his poetry until 1946, when *Paterson*, Book I appeared. From that time on, his recognition increased steadily. He was made a Fellow of the Library of Congress, 1948-1949, and appointed Consultant in Poetry to the Library of Congress in 1952, even though he never served because of political opposition to his alleged left-wing principles. In 1948 he received the Russell Loines Award for *Paterson*, Book II, and in 1950 the National Book Award for *Selected Poems* and *Paterson*, Book III; in 1953 he shared with Archibald MacLeish the Bollingen Prize for excellence in contemporary verse. Finally, in May, 1963, he was awarded posthumously the Pulitzer Prize and Gold Medal for Poetry for *Pictures from Brueghel*.

Biography · William Carlos Williams was born in Rutherford, New Jersey, on September 17, 1883. His father (William George Williams) was an Englishman who never gave up his British citizenship, and his mother

(Raquel Hélène Rose Hoheb, known as "Elena") was a Puerto Rican of Basque, Dutch, Spanish, and Jewish descent. His father was an Episcopalian who turned Unitarian and his mother was Roman Catholic. He was educated at schools in New York City and briefly in Europe and was graduated with a medical degree from the University of Pennsylvania in 1909. After an internship in New York City and graduate study in pediatrics in Leipzig, he returned to his native Rutherford, where he practiced

Irving Wellcome

medicine until he retired. In 1909 he proposed to Florence (Floss) Herman and in 1912 they were married. Their first son, William Eric Williams, was born in 1914 and their second, Paul Herman Williams, in 1916.

Williams, a melting pot in himself, had deep roots as a second-generation citizen of the United States. From early in his life he felt that the United States was his only home and that he must possess it in order to know himself. Possessing the America of the past and the present would enable him to renew himself continually and find his own humanity. Unlike many writers of his generation who went to Europe, such as his friend Ezra Pound, Williams committed himself to living in America because he believed he had to live in a place to be able to grasp it imaginatively.

Williams met Ezra Pound when they were both at the University of Pennsylvania; their friendship was fierce and uneven throughout their lives. While at the University, he also met Hilda Doolittle (H. D.) and the painter Charles Demuth. In his early poetry, he imitated Pound and the Imagists, accepting the Imagist credo as presented in *Poetry*. His natural inclination was to treat things directly with brevity of language and without conventional metrics. He was also influenced by his painter friends, particularly by the cubists and the expressionists. Modern painters filled their canvases with mechanisms, and Williams called a poem a "machine made of words." During 1915 and 1916, he attended literary gatherings with the *Others* group and met Alfred Kreymborg, Marianne Moore, and Wallace Stevens.

He began writing poetry in a poetic wasteland that did not want new or experimental poetry. The poets who had been popularly admired were the three-name poets so greatly influenced by the English tradition. Walt Whitman was not regarded highly and Emily Dickinson was unknown.

Although he devoted much of his time to being a full-time physician in Rutherford, Williams was a prolific writer—a poet, short-story writer, novelist, playwright, essayist, and translator. He was neglected both by the general public and by the literary establishment for most of his career, and often in his frustration he erupted against his critics and other practicing poets. With the publication of *Paterson*, Book I, in 1946, however, he began to receive the recognition he felt he deserved.

During most of the last fifteen years of his life, he continued to write even though he was not in good health. In 1948, when he was sixty-five years old, he suffered a heart attack, and in 1951 he had his first stroke, which was followed by another serious one a year later. The next year he was hospitalized because of severe depression. Finally, in 1961, two years before his death, he gave up writing after he suffered a series of strokes. On March 4, 1963, at the age of seventy-nine, he died in Rutherford, where he had been born and had lived all his life.

Analysis · Like Walt Whitman, William Carlos Williams attempted to create an American voice for American poetry. Both Whitman and Williams wanted to record the unique American experience in a distinctively American idiom, a language freed from the constraints of traditional English prosody. Whitman, as Williams says in his autobiography, broke from the traditional iambic pentameter, but he had only begun the necessary revolution. It was then up to Williams to use "the new dialect" to continue Whitman's work by constructing a prosody based on actual American speech.

Williams' search for a new language using the American idiom was intertwined with his search for a new poetic measure. Although he wanted to recover the relationship between poetry and the measured dance from which he believed it derived, his concept of measure is elusive. He believed that Whitman's free verse lacked structure. Williams sought a new foot that would be fairly stable, yet at the same time was variable, a foot that was not fixed but allowed for variation according to what the language called for. While the traditional poetic foot is based on the number of syllables in a line, Williams based his poetic foot on "a measure of the ear." The proper measure would allow him to present the American idiom as controlled by the rhythm of American speech.

When Williams wrote his early poems, he had not yet developed his own poetical theory; he first wrote conventionally and then according to the Imagist credo. He created some very good pictures of "things" and his poems achieved a reality of their own, but they did not go beyond the particulars to express universal truths—something that involves more than merely recreating data.

In "The Red Wheelbarrow," for example, all the reader is left with is the picture of the red wheelbarrow and the white chickens beside it standing in the rain. In "Poem" the cat climbs over the jam closet into the empty flower pot; Williams conveys nothing more than this picture. Other examples of Williams' poems of this period include "The Locust Tree in Flower" (the locust tree in flower is sweet and white, and brings May again), "Between Walls" (behind the hospital in the cinders of the courtyard shine the pieces of a broken green bottle), and "This Is Just to Say" (the poet tells his wife he has eaten the plums she was saving in the icebox).

In "To a Poor Old Woman," Williams does not convey any meaning beyond the picture he evokes of an old woman munching on a plum that she has taken from a bag she is holding in her hand. He does, however, experiment with the way he places the words of the line "They taste good to her" on the page. He repeats the line three times. First, he puts all the words on one line without a period at the end of the line; then he writes

"They taste good/ to her. They taste/ good to her." He is searching for the correct form to use—the elusive measure needed.

In the epic poem *Paterson*, Williams sought to cover the landscape of contemporary American society and to discover himself as an American poet. His twenty-year journey in *Paterson* is similar to that of Hart Crane in *The Bridge* (1930), Ezra Pound in the *Cantos* (1925-1972), and T. S. Eliot in *The Waste Land* (1922) and *Four Quartets* (1943). Just as Whitman revised the poems of *Leaves of Grass* (1855) continuously and frequently moved them from section to section within the volume, so Williams identified *Paterson* with his own continuing life as a poet.

Paterson consists of five books and a projected sixth; each book is made up of three sections. In "The Delineaments of the Giants" (*Paterson*, Book I, 1946), Mr. Paterson, as he wanders through the city Paterson, describes details of the town and the area around it: the valley, the Passaic Falls, and Garret Mountain. Williams creates a history for the city as he describes past and present inhabitants and events concerning both them and the city. In "Sunday in the Park" (*Paterson*, Book II, 1948), the persona walks through Garret Mountain Park on a Sunday afternoon; there he views the workers of Paterson in their Sunday leisure activities. "The Library" (*Paterson*, Book III, 1949) takes place in the library, where the persona searches to discover how best to express the aspects of the city of Paterson that he has described in the first two books. "The Run to the Sea" (*Paterson*, Book IV, 1951) takes place in two locales—New York City and an entrance to the sea. The first section consists mostly of dialogues between Corydon and Phyllis, and Phyllis and Paterson. The section involves Madame Marie Curie's discovery of uranium and a digressive discussion of economics in America. The final section of the fourth book presents accounts of events, mostly violent, concerning the inhabitants of Paterson; it ends with the persona and a dog headed inland after they have emerged from the sea. *Paterson*, Book V, which does not have a title, takes place in The Cloisters, a museum on the Hudson River in New York City. This book is shorter than the others and some critics refer to it as a coda to *Paterson*, Books I-IV. Having grown old, the persona contemplates the meaning of a series of unicorn tapestries in the museum.

Paterson can be difficult reading. The persona of the poem does not remain constant; moreover, "Paterson" refers to both the city and the man. There are a number of other personae in *Paterson* who are sometimes ambiguously fused. Paterson the city becomes Paterson the man, who is also a woman, who becomes the poet writing *Paterson*, who is also William Carlos Williams, a poet and a man.

In addition, Williams shifts from verse to prose without transitional devices, and there are many such shifts within verse passages, from persona to persona, and from subject matter to subject matter. The prose passages, sometimes taken directly from an exterior source, range from newspaper clippings and quotations from various books to letters by Williams' fictional personae.

Paterson is Williams' attempt to delineate his culture and to define himself poetically. The two quests are interrelated. Williams can present details of the America that he sees and describe aspects of its culture. He wants, however, to convey the truths in what he describes and the universals concerning his vision. To be able to do so, he must work out his poetic theory and discover himself as a poet.

In *Paterson*, Williams relied importantly on local particulars. First, he chose a city that actually existed. In *The Autobiography of William Carlos Williams* he writes of taking the city Paterson and working it up as a case, just as he worked up cases as a doctor. According to Joel Conarroe in *William Carlos Williams' "Paterson"* (1970), Paterson was a city that was similar to Williams' native Rutherford, but one that better possessed the characteristics that Williams needed for his poem. Paterson had existed since the beginning of America and therefore had a history. It was a very American city with a diverse population, about a third of which was foreign-born. Located on the Passaic River with the Passaic Falls, Paterson was bounded on one side by Garret Mountain. Partially because of these natural resources, it was one of the first industrial cities in America. Furthermore, its industry grew steadily and it was often the scene of well-known strikes. Fortunately for the action of the poem, Paterson also suffered a major fire, flood, and tornado.

Williams peoples his poem with persons who actually existed and uses events that actually occurred. Often, in the prose passages, he gives the specifics about the inhabitants and events. In *Paterson*, Book I, Williams develops a history for the city of Paterson. He tells the reader the number of inhabitants of each nationality living in Paterson in 1870. He describes some of the inhabitants. David Hower, for example, is a poor shoemaker who in February, 1857, while eating mussels, finds substances that turn out to be pearls. A gentleman in the Revolutionary Army describes a monster in human form, Pieter Van Winkle. His description is followed by the account of a 126-pound monster fish taken by John Winters and other boys. Mrs. Sarah Cumming, the wife of Reverend Hopper Cumming for two months, mysteriously disappears into the falls just after her husband turns from the cataract to go home. When the bridge that Timothy B. Crane built is being put across the falls, Sam Patch jumps to retrieve a rolling pin and thus begins his career as a famous jumper, a career that ends when he attempts to jump the falls of the Genesee River in 1829. The reader learns exactly what Cornelius Doremus owned when he died at eight-nine years of age and what each item was worth. At one time the men of Paterson ravage the river and kill almost all of its fish. Finally, the reader is told about Mr. Leonard Sandford, who discovers a human body near the falls.

In *Paterson*, Books II-V, Williams continues to present details about the geography, inhabitants, and events of Paterson; as the poem progresses, however, he relies less on prose from historical accounts in books and newspapers and more on letters, dialogues, and verse. The particulars also become more personally related to the fictional poet of the poem or to Bill (Dr. Williams). There are passages about the Indians who first lived in the area. Williams includes a tabular account of the specimens found when men were digging an artesian well at the Passaic Rolling Mill, Paterson, and an advertisement concerning borrowing money on the credit of the United States. Phyllis, an uneducated black woman, writes several letters to her father. Throughout the poem a woman poet (C. or Cress), another poet (A. G.), and Edward or E. D. (Edward Dahlberg) write letters to a person without a name, to Dr. Paterson, to Dr. Williams, and to Bill.

In addition to all of these particulars, Williams deals with aspects of American society. A major weakness of contemporary American culture is the inability of the individual to communicate with others and even with himself. In *Paterson*, Book I, Williams immediately introduces the problems with language faced by the inhabitants of Paterson. Industrialization is one of the sources of their difficulties; industrialization and materialism separate them from themselves and from each other. The people walk incommunicado; they do not know the words with which to communicate. It is as if they face an equation that cannot be solved, for language fails them. Although there is a torrent in their minds, they cannot unlock that torrent since they do not know themselves.

Sam Patch is an example of a man who dies incommunicado. Before he attempts to dive into the falls of the Genesee River, he makes a short speech. The words, however, are drained of meaning and they fail him. He disappears into the stream and is not seen until the following spring, when he is found frozen in ice, still locked in by his inability to communicate.

In the second part of *Paterson*, Book II, Williams describes Madame Curie's discovery of uranium, a discovery that he relates to the need in the United States for the discovery of a new credit system. This system would be like "the radiant gist" that Madame Curie discovered and would cure America's economic cancer, a condition contributing to man's inability to communicate. The lust for money and the industrialization of society cut man off from his roots and from other men.

Humanity's problems with language are reflected in the relationships between man and woman. The love of man and woman consummated in marriage should be a means of communication, but in contemporary society "divorce" is the common word: "The language/ is divorced from their minds." In *Paterson*, Book I, Williams tells of Mrs. Sarah Cumming, who after two months of marriage has everything to look forward to, but who mysteriously disappears into the falls after her husband turns his back on her. Marriage, then, is no answer to the problem of communication. The words locked in the "falls" of the human mind must be released. Immediately after the prose section about Mrs. Cumming comes the passage "A false language. A true. A false language pouring–a/ language (misunderstood) pouring (misinterpreted) without/ dignity, without minister, crashing upon a stone ear. At least/ it settled it for her."

In *Paterson*, Book II, as Paterson walks through Garret Mountain Park, the breakdown of language is reflected in the religious and sexual life of the Paterson workers as they spend their leisure time on a Sunday afternoon. A sermon by the itinerant evangelist Klaus Ehrens is a meaningless harangue; he does not communicate with those in the park. The relationship between man and woman is reduced to a sexual act of lust without meaning; it is not even an act that will produce children. Language and communication between male and female is exhausted. Ironically, B. is told in a letter by someone who has been caring for a dog that the dog *is* going to have puppies; animals, unlike humans, remain fertile.

The first section of *Paterson*, Book IV, is primarily a narrative consisting of dialogues between Corydon and Phyllis, and Phyllis and Paterson. In both relationships the participants fail to communicate successfully. Corydon is an old lesbian who is half-heartedly attempting to seduce Phyllis, a virgin. Paterson is also an unsuccessful lover of the young black nurse. Phyllis writes letters to her Pappy in uneducated English. In the last letter she tells him of a trip with Corydon to Anticosti–a name that sounds Italian but is French. The two women have a guide who speaks French with Corydon. Phyllis cannot understand what they are saying; she does not care, however, because she can speak her own language. The dialogues reveal relationships in which there is a potential for love and communication, but in which there is a failure to communicate.

Williams describes the predicament of Paterson, but he wants to convey the universals of American society and go beyond the "facts" to the "ideas." Being able to express the general through "things" is part of Williams' quest to define himself as a poet. *Paterson* is a search for the redeeming language needed to enable contemporary man to communicate; the quest itself, however, is valuable even if the redeeming language is not discovered.

In the "Preface" to *Paterson*, Williams states that the poem is the quest to find the needed language ("beauty") that is locked in his mind. Soon after, in *Paterson*, Book I, Williams indicates that he is attempting to determine "what common language to unravel." Mr. Paterson, the persona, will go away to rest and write. Thus, Williams begins his quest for the redeeming language.

Paterson, Book I, ends with a quotation from *Studies of Greek Poets* (1873) by John Addington Symonds in which Symonds discusses Hipponax's attempt to use a meter appropriate for prose and common speech. Symonds also notes that the Greeks used the "deformed verse" of Hipponax for subjects dealing with humanity's perversions. Thus, the Greek poets devised a prosody suitable to their society, just as Williams seeks a measure to express American society.

Throughout *Paterson*, several letters by the woman poet C., or Cress, interrelate the theme of humankind's failure to communicate, especially through heterosexual love, and the poet's function to solve this problem of language. The longest of her letters, covering six-and-one-half pages, appears at the end of *Paterson*, Book II. In it she complains about woman's wretched position in society. She is particularly upset about her relationship, or lack of relationship, with Dr. P. She has tried to communicate intimately and has shared thoughts with him that she has not shared with anyone else. He has rejected her. She accuses him of having used her; he has encouraged her first letters only because he could turn them into literature and use them in his poem. As long as her letters were only literature—a literature divorced from life—their relationship was satisfactory, but when she attempted to use her letters to communicate on a personal level, he turned his back on her. When her writings became an expression of herself, their friendship failed. She thus expresses an idea that E. D. had stated earlier in the poem—that the literary work and its author cannot be separated. An artist derives a unity of being and a freedom to be himself when he achieves a successful relationship between the externals, such as the paint, clay, or language that he uses, and his shaping of these externals.

In *Paterson*, Book II, the persona goes to the library to try to learn how, as a poet, to express the details of the city described in the first two books. The library contains many acts of communication, but all of them are from the past and will not serve the poet in his quest for the redeeming language that will free humankind and himself. The poet in the poem, and Williams himself by implication, have failed to communicate, both as poets and as people.

Briefly at the beginning of *Paterson*, Book III, Williams suggests the need for an "invention" without which the old will return with deadly repetitiveness. Only invention will bring the new line that in turn brings the new word, a word that is required now that words have crumbled like chalk. Invention requires the poet to reject old forms and exhausted words in order to find the new-measured language. Throughout this book there is destruction and violence. The natural disasters that occurred in Paterson (the flood, the fire, and the tornado) and made it necessary for the inhabitants to rebuild sections of the city suggest the poet's search in which he finds it necessary to destroy in order to create. The poet does not find what he is searching for, because both the invention and words are lacking. Nevertheless, he continues his search for "the beautiful thing."

Near the end of *Paterson*, Book III, the poet experiments with form and language. On one page Williams places the lines almost at random. It is as if someone has taped various typed lines carelessly on the page without making sure that the lines are parallel or that they make sense when read. There are numbers and words in both English and French. The reader is invited to consider the meanings evoked by "funeral *designed*," "plants," and "wedding bouquets." On the following page there are four passages in which the words are abbreviations meant to be a phonological representation of the words of an illiterate person. Immediately after these passages appears the tabular account of the specimens found when a water well is being dug. Water brings life and rebirth. The poet wants to unlock the language of the falls that had filled his head earlier and to create the new-measured language. He concludes that "*American poetry is a very easy subject to discuss for the/ simple reason that it does not exist.*"

In *Paterson*, Book IV, Williams returns to Madame Curie's "radiant gist"; the poet hopes to make a similar discovery in his poetry so that he can heal those who suffer from an inadequate language. The poet reminds himself that his "virgin" purpose is the language and that he must forget the past. At the end of the book he emerges from the sea, which has been presented in terms of violence, and heads inland eating a plum and followed by a dog that has also been swimming in the sea. Williams concludes that "This is the blast/ the eternal close/ the spiral/ the final somersault/ the end." Williams suggests process in this end; the end is a spiral similar to a Möbius strip in which the end is always a return to the beginning.

Again Williams interrelates the poet's art and the process of love. Both are a means of communication between man and woman and a way for a person to discover himself; both, he explains in *Paterson*, Book V, involve a paradox. The virgin's maidenhead must be violently destroyed in the sexual act for her to realize her potential to create another human being. The poet must destroy past forms to discover the form appropriate for his time; Williams must reject the language and form of past poetry to create the new-measured language that will express contemporary American society and provide for communication among men.

Paterson, Book V, contains a question-and-answer section in which Williams discusses his theory of poetry. Poetry is made of words that have been organized rhythmically; a poem is a complete entity that has a separate existence. If the poem is any good, it expresses the life of the poet and tells the reader what the poet is. Anything can be the subject of poetry. The poet in America must use the American idiom, but the manner in which the words are presented is of the greatest importance. Sometimes a modern poet ignores the sense of words. In prose, words mean what they say, but in poetry words present two different things: what they actually mean and what their shape means. Williams cites Pieter Brueghel as an artist who saw from two sides. Brueghel painted authentically what he saw, yet at the same time served the imagination. The measured dance, life as it is presented in art by the imagination, is all that humankind can know. The answer to the poet's quest is that "We know nothing and can know nothing/ but/ the dance, to dance to a measure/ contrapuntally,/ Satyrically, the tragic foot." The poet presents life in a form appropriate to the time in which he lives; he presents the particulars of life that are a contrast or interplay of elements directed by his sexual desires and need for love, his humanity.

It is in the poems that Williams wrote during the last ten years of his life that he achieves greatness—the poems collected in *The Desert Music and Other Poems, Journey to Love*, and *Pictures from Brueghel*. In these, he uses the new-measured language he had sought in *Paterson*, Books I-V; but, more importantly, he goes beyond "things" to "ideas." The poems are more than pretty subjects; in them he discovers "the beautiful thing."

Some of the best poems of this period are "The Descent," from *Paterson*, Book II; "Paterson: Episode 17," in *Paterson*, Book III; "To Daphne and Virginia"; "The Sparrow (To My Father)"; "A Negro Woman"; "Self-Portrait"; "The Hunters in the Snow"; "The Wedding Dance in the Open Air"; "The Parable of the Blind"; "Children's Games"; "Song," beginning "Beauty is a shell"; "The Woodthrush"; and "Asphodel, That Greeny Flower."

When Williams was asked in 1961 to choose his favorite poem for an anthology called *Poet's Choice*, he selected "The Descent" from *Paterson*,

Book II. He said that he had been using "the variable foot" for many years, but "The Descent" was the first in that form that completely satisfied him. "Asphodel, That Greeny Flower," from *Journey to Love,* is another poem in which Williams truly succeeds, and a discussion of that poem provides a good summary to a discussion of Williams' poetry.

In "Asphodel, That Greeny Flower" Williams uses his new-measured language, containing "fresh" words (the American idiom) written in a measure appropriate to his times and controlled by the rhythm of American speech ("the variable foot" in the triadic stanza). He is also concerned with creating a poem that has its own existence and is a "thing" in itself. Williams draws from the particulars of American life and his own life to evoke images of America and American culture; now that he has discovered the new-measured language, however, he can express universal truths about the United States and its culture. The poem at the same times expresses Williams' life as a poet and points to what he is and believes.

Williams uses his new-measured language to capture the flow of American speech as well as to reinforce and emphasize the content and meaning of the poem. For example, in one passage the measure of the lines suggests the urgency of the present, then slows into memory and reminiscence and finally into silence. At another point, Williams' measure gives the sense of the rolling sea. James Breslin in *William Carlos Williams: An American Artist* (1970) discusses in detail Williams' use of the American idiom presented in "the variable foot" and triadic stanza.

Williams uses natural details such as the asphodel, the honeysuckle, the bee, the lily, the hummingbird, apple blossoms, strawberries, the lily-of-the-valley, and daisies. He uses particulars from his own life: a trip he took with his wife, a time he was separated from her, and their wedding day. He makes references to his own poetry; a young artist likes Williams' poem about the broken green bottle lying in the cinders in the hospital courtyard and says he has heard about, but not read, Williams' poem on gay wallpaper.

The new-measured language enables Williams to draw from the facts and details of the local to reach the realm of the imagination and convey truths about humanity. He begins the poem by addressing the asphodel, but immediately, his "song" becomes one addressed to his wife of many years, not to the flower. Throughout the poem there is constant shifting between the image of the asphodel and Floss, as well as a fusing of the two particulars. The flower at times becomes a symbol. As Breslin explains, the poem is a continuing process as the "things" expand to the "ideas" beyond them, and the truths expressed contract back into the particular images.

The poem is a realistic love song that conveys the nature of the man who is the poet creating the poem. He asks his wife to forgive him because too often medicine, poetry, and other women have been his prime concerns, not her and their life together. The asphodel becomes a symbol of his renewed love for her in his old age. He can ask for her forgiveness because he has come to realize that love has the power to undo what has been done. Love must often serve a function similar to that of the poet, for the poet also must undo what has been done by destroying past forms in order to create new ones.

In "Asphodel, That Greeny Flower" Williams regrets that he has reached a time when he can no longer put down the words that come to him out of the air and create poems. Through the details of his poetry, he has attempted to express the general truths of the imagination. With his old age, however, he has gained knowledge that makes him optimistic. "Are facts not flowers/ and flowers facts/ or poems flowers/ or all words of the imagination,/ interchangeable?" "Flowers" or "facts," "poems" and "words of the imagination" are interchangeable, for everything is a work of the imagination. What is important is that love is a force of the imagination that rules things, words, and poems; love is life's form for poetry. Through love and poetry, all people will be able to communicate. Both love and works of the imagination, be they artistic endeavors or otherwise, are creative powers that are humanity's means of escaping death. This is the universal truth, the "idea" that Williams has come to, through the particulars of his poetry and his life.

Other literary forms · William Carlos Williams is best known for his poetry, but he did not limit himself to that form. His short-story collections include *The Knife of the Times and Other Stories* (1932), *Life Along the Passaic River* (1938), *Make Light of It: Collected Stories* (1950), and *The Farmers' Daughters: The Collected Stories of William Carlos Williams* (1961). Among his novels are *The Great American Novel* (1923), *A Voyage to Pagany* (1928), and the Stecher trilogy, composed of *White Mule* (1937), *In the Money* (1940), and *The Build-Up* (1952), and his best-known collection of plays is *Many Loves and Other Plays* (1961). He also wrote criticism and an autobiography. His essay collections include *In the American Grain* (1925) and *Selected Essays of William Carlos Williams* (1954). In addition, he and his mother translated Philippe Soupault's *Last Nights of Paris* (1929) and Don Francisco de Quevedo's *A Dog and the Fever* (1954).

Select works other than poetry

LONG FICTION: *The Great American Novel*, 1923; *A Voyage to Pagany*, 1928; *White Mule*, 1937; *In the Money*, 1940; *The Build-up*, 1952.

SHORT FICTION: *The Knife of the Times and Other Stories,* 1932; *Life Along the Passaic River,* 1938; *Make Light of It: Collected Stories,* 1950; *The Farmers' Daughters: The Collected Stories of William Carlos Williams,* 1961; *The Doctor Stories,* 1984.

DRAMA: *Many Loves and Other Plays,* pb. 1961.

NONFICTION: *In the American Grain,* 1925; *A Novelette and Other Prose,* 1932; *The Autobiography of William Carlos Williams,* 1951; *Selected Essays of William Carlos Williams,* 1954; *The Selected Letters of William Carlos Williams,* 1957; *The Embodiment of Knowledge,* 1974; *A Recognizable Image,* 1978; *William Carlos Williams, John Sanford: A Correspondence,* 1984; *William Carlos Williams and James Laughlin: Selected Letters,* 1989; *Pound/Williams: Selected Letters of Ezra Pound and William Carlos Williams,* 1996 (Hugh Witemeyer, editor).

Sherry G. Southard

Bibliography · An excellent general introduction to Williams' work remains James E. Breslin, *William Carlos Williams: An American Artist,* 1970. Paul Mariani's biography *William Carlos Williams: A New World Naked,* 1981, is also essential reading. Steven Gould Axelrod and Helen Deese, eds., *Critical Essays on William Carlos Williams,* 1995, is a solid collection of essays. Williams' important relationships with the modernist painters have been the subject of a number of studies, including Bram Dijkstra, *The Hieroglyphics of a New Speech,* 1969; Henry Sayre, *The Visual Text of William Carlos Williams,* 1983; Christopher MacGowan, *William Carlos Williams' Early Poetry: The Visual Arts Background,* 1984; and Peter Schmidt, *William Carlos Williams: The Arts, and Literary Tradition,* 1988. A highly readable and intelligent study of Williams' innovative poetics is Stephen Cushman, *William Carlos Williams and the Meanings of Measure,* 1986. General views of the poetry include Kelli A. Larson, *Guide to the Poetry of William Carlos Williams,* 1995; Donald W. Markos, *Ideas in Things: The Poems of William Carlos Williams,* 1994; and Daniel Morris, *The Writings of William Carlos Williams: Publicity for the Self,* 1995. Benjamin Sankey, *A Companion to William Carlos Williams' "Paterson,"* 1971, provides helpful background to the literary, personal, and geographical allusions in the poem. See also "William Carlos Williams," in J. Hillis Miller, *Poets of Reality,* 1966; Emily Wallace, *A Bibliography of William Carlos Williams,* 1968; and Joel Conarroe, *William Carlos Williams' "Paterson": Language and Landscape,* 1970.

WILLIAM WORDSWORTH

Born: Cockermouth, England; April 7, 1770
Died: Rydal Mount, England; April 23, 1850

Poetry · *An Evening Walk,* 1793 · *Descriptive Sketches,* 1793 · *Lyrical Ballads,* 1798 (with Samuel Taylor Coleridge) · *Lyrical Ballads, with Other Poems,* 1800 (with Coleridge, includes Preface) · *Poems in Two Volumes,* 1807 · *The Excursion,* 1814 · *Poems,* 1815 · *The White Doe of Rylstone,* 1815 · *Peter Bell,* 1819 · *The Waggoner,* 1819 · *The River Duddon,* 1820 · *Ecclesiastical Sketches,* 1822 · *Poems Chiefly of Early and Late Years,* 1842 · *The Prelude: Or, The Growth of a Poet's Mind,* 1850 · *Poetical Works,* 1940-1949 (5 volumes; Ernest de Selincourt and Helen Darbishire, editors)

Achievements · William Wordsworth was one of the leading English Romantic poets. Along with William Blake (1757-1827), Samuel Taylor Coleridge (1772-1834), Lord Byron (1788-1824), Percy Bysshe Shelley (1792-1822), and John Keats (1795-1821), Wordsworth created a major revolution in ideology and poetic style around 1800. The Romantic writers rebelled against the neoclassical position exemplified in the works of Alexander Pope (1688-1744) and Samuel Johnson (1709-1784). Although all such broad generalizations should be viewed with suspicion, it is generally said that the neoclassical writers valued restraint and discipline, whereas the Romantic poets favored individual genius and hoped to follow nature freely. Wordsworth's poetry praises the value of the simple individual, the child, the helpless, the working class, and the natural man. Such sentiments were explosive in the age of the French Revolution, when Wordsworth was young. He helped to define the attitudes which fostered the spread of democracy, of more humane treatment of the downtrodden, and of respect for Nature.

Biography · The northwestern corner of England, which contains the counties of Northumberland and Westmorland, is both mountainous and inaccessible. The cliffs are not as high as those in Switzerland, but they are rugged and the land is settled mainly by shepherds and by isolated farmers. The valleys have long, narrow, picturesque lakes, and so the region is called the English Lake District. William Wordsworth was born and lived much of his life among these lakes. Many of the English Romantic writers are sometimes called "lake poets" because of their association with this area.

Wordsworth was born in 1770 in the small town of Cockermouth in Cumberland. Although he later wrote about the lower classes, his own family was middle-class, and the poet never actually worked with his hands to make his living. His father was a lawyer who managed the affairs of the Earl of Lonsdale. The poet had three brothers (Richard, John, and Christopher) and a sister (Dorothy). For the first nine years of his life, the family inhabited a comfortable house near the Derwent River. William attended Anne Birkett's school in the little town of Penrith, where Mary Hutchinson,

whom he married in 1802, was also a student. His mother died when he was seven. The two brothers, William and Richard, then boarded at the house of Ann Tyson while attending grammar school in the village of Hawkshead.

Apparently this arrangement was a kindly one, and the boy spent much time happily roaming the nearby fields and hills. He also profited from the teaching of his schoolmaster William Taylor, who encouraged him to write poetry. In 1783 his father died and the family inheritance was tied up in litigation for some twenty years. Only after the death of the Earl of Lonsdale in 1802 was Wordsworth able to profit from his father's estate. With the help of relatives, he matriculated at St. John's College, Cambridge University. Although he did not earn distinction as a student, those years were fertile times for learning.

While he was a student at St. John's, between 1787 and 1791, the French Revolution broke out across the English Channel. During his summer vacation of 1790, Wordsworth and his college friend, Robert Jones, went on a walking tour across France and Switzerland to Italy. The young students were much impressed by the popular revolution and the spirit of democracy in France at that time. Wordsworth took his degree at St. John's in January, 1791, but had no definite plans for his future. The following November he went again to revolution-torn France with the idea of learning the French language well enough to earn his living as a tutor. Passing through Paris, he settled at Blois in the Loire Valley. There he made friends with Captain Michael Beaupuy and became deeply involved in French Republican thought. There, too, he fell in love with Annette Vallon, who was some four years older than the young poet. Annette Vallon and Wordsworth had an illegitimate daughter, Caroline, but Wordsworth returned to England alone in December, 1792, probably to try to arrange his financial affairs. In February, 1793, war broke out between France and England so that Wordsworth was not able to see his baby and her mother again until the treaty of Amiens in 1802 made it possible for him to visit them. His daughter was then ten years old.

In 1793 Wordsworth must have been a very unhappy young man: His deepest sympathies were on the side of France and democracy, but his own country was at war against his French friends such as Captain Michael Beaupuy; he was separated from Annette and his baby, and his English family associates looked on his conduct as scandalous; the Earl of Lonsdale refused to settle his father's financial claims, so the young man was without funds and had no way to earn a living, even though he held a bachelor's degree from a prestigious university. Under these conditions, he moved in politically radical circles, becoming friendly with William Godwin, Mary

Wollstonecraft, and Tom Paine. In 1793 he published his first books of poetry, *An Evening Walk* and *Descriptive Sketches.*

Wordsworth and his younger sister, Dorothy, were close friends. In 1795 the poet benefited from a small legacy to settle with her at Racedown Cottage in Dorset, where they were visited by Mary Hutchinson and Samuel Taylor Coleridge. In 1797 they moved to Alfoxden, near Nether Stowey in Somerset, to be near Coleridge's home. Here a period of intense creativity occurred: Dorothy began her journal in 1798 while Wordsworth and Coleridge collaborated on *Lyrical Ballads.* A walking trip with Dorothy along the Wye River resulted in 1798 in "Lines Composed a Few Miles Above Tintern Abbey." That fall, Coleridge, Dorothy, and Wordsworth went to study in Germany. Dorothy and the poet spent most of their time in Goslar, where apparently he began to write *The Prelude,* his major autobiographical work which he left unfinished at his death. Returning from Germany, he and Dorothy settled in Dove Cottage in the Lake District. In 1800 he completed "Michael" and saw the second edition of *Lyrical Ballads* published. With the end of hostilities in 1802. Wordsworth visited Annette Vallon and their daughter in France, arranging to make an annual child-support payment. Upon his return to England, he married Mary Hutchinson. During that year he composed "Ode: Intimations of Immortality from Recollections of Early Childhood."

In 1805 his brother John was drowned at sea. Wordsworth often looked upon Nature as a kindly force, but the death of his brother in a shipwreck may have been a powerful contribution to his darkening vision of Nature as he grew older. In 1805 he had a completed draft of *The Prelude* ready for Coleridge to read, although he was never satisfied with the work as a whole and rewrote it extensively later. It is sometimes said that when Wordsworth was a "bad" man, fathering an illegitimate child, consorting with revolutionaries and drug addicts, and roaming the countryside with no useful occupation, he wrote "good" poetry. When he became a "good" man, respectably married and gainfully employed, he began to write "bad" poetry. It is true that, although he wrote prolifically until his death, not much of his work after about 1807 is considered remarkable. In 1813 he accepted the position of Distributor of Stamps for Westmorland County, the kind of governmental support he probably would have scorned when he was younger. His fame as a writer, however, grew steadily. In 1842 when his last volume, *Poems Chiefly of Early and Late Years,* was published, he accepted a government pension of three hundred pounds sterling per annum, a considerable sum. The next year he succeeded Robert Southey as Poet Laureate of England. He died April 23, 1850, at Rydal Mount in his beloved Lake District.

Analysis · When the volume of poetry called the *Lyrical Ballads* of 1798 was published in a second edition (1800), William Wordsworth wrote a prose preface for the book which is the single most important statement of Romantic ideology. It provides a useful introduction to his poetry.

Wordsworth's Preface displays the idea of primitivism as the basis of the Romantic position. Primitivism is the belief that there is some primary, intrinsically good "state of nature" from which adult, educated, civilized humankind has fallen into a false or wicked state of existence. When Jean-Jacques Rousseau began *The Social Contract* (1762) with the assertion that "Man was born free, and yet we see him everywhere in chains," he concisely expressed the primitivist point of view. The American and French revolutions were both predicated on Romantic primitivism, the idea that man was once naturally free, but that corrupt kings, Churches, and social customs held him enslaved. The Romantic typically sees rebellion and breaking free from false restraint to regain a state of nature as highly desirable; Wordsworth's Preface shows him deeply committed to this revolutionary ideology. He says that he is going to take the subjects of his poems from "humble and rustic life" because in that condition humankind is "less under restraint" and the "elementary feelings" of life exist in a state of simplicity.

Many writers feel that serious literature can be written only about great and powerful men, such as kings and generals. Some writers apparently believe that wounding a king is tragic, while beating a slave is merely funny. Wordsworth's Preface firmly rejects such ideas. He turns to simple, common, poor people as the topic of his poetry because they are nearer a "state of nature" than the powerful, educated, and sophisticated men who have been corrupted by false customs of society. Many writers feel that they must live in the centers of civilization, London or Paris, for example, in order to be conversant with new ideas and the latest fashions. Wordsworth turns away from the cities to the rural scene. He himself lived in the remote Lake District most of his life, and he wrote about simple shepherds, farmers, and villagers. He explains that he chooses for his topics

> humble and rustic life . . . because, in that condition, the essential passions of the heart find a better soil in which they can attain their maturity, are less under restraint, and speak a plainer and more emphatic language; because in that condition of life our elementary feelings coexist in a state of greater simplicity, and consequently may be more accurately contemplated.

He sees a correspondence between the unspoiled nature of man and the naturalness of his environment. Romantic ideology of this sort underlies much of the contemporary environmentalist movement: the feeling that man ought to be in harmony with his environment, that Nature is beneficent, that man ought to live simply so that the essential part of his human nature may conform to the grand pattern of Nature balanced in the whole universe.

The use of the words "passion" and "restraint" in Wordsworth's quotation above is significant. English neoclassical writers such as Alexander Pope tended to be suspicious of human passions, arguing that anger and lust lead people into error unless such passions are restraint by right reason. For Pope, it is necessary to exercise the restraint of reason over passion in order for humankind to be morally good. "Restraint" is good; "passion" bad. Wordsworth reverses this set of values. Humanity's natural primitive feelings are the source of goodness and morality; the false restraints of custom and education are what lead humankind astray from natural goodness. In his Preface Wordsworth seems to be following the line of thought developed by Anthony Ashley Cooper, Earl of Shaftesbury (1671-1713) in his *An Inquiry Concerning Virtue or Merit* (1709). Shaftesbury asks his readers to imagine a "creature who, wanting reason and being unable to reflect, has notwithstanding many good qualities and affections,—as love to his kind, courage, gratitude or pity." Shaftesbury probably is thinking of creatures such as a faithful dog, a child too young to reason well, or a kindly mental defective. In such cases one would have to say that the creature shows good qualities, even though it lacks reasoning power. For Shaftesbury, then, to reason means merely to recognize the already existing good impulses or feelings naturally arising in such a creature. Morality arises from natural feeling, evidently present in creatures with little reasoning power.

Wordsworth's Preface is heavily influenced by Shaftesbury's argument. He turns to simple characters for his poems because they exhibit the natural, primary, unspoiled states of feeling that are the ultimate basis of morality. Wordsworth's characters are sentimental heroes, chosen because their feelings are unspoiled by restraints of education and reason: children, simple shepherds, and villagers, the old Cumberland Beggar, an idiot boy, Alice Fell, and so on. While William Shakespeare often puts a nobleman at the center of his plays and relegates the poor people to the role of rustic clowns, Wordsworth takes the feelings of the poor as the most precious subject of serious literature.

The Preface displays two kinds of primitivism. Social primitivism is the belief that humanity's state of nature is good and that it is possible to imagine a social setting in which humankind's naturally good impulses will flourish. Social primitivism leads to the celebration of the "noble savage,"

perhaps an American Indian or a Black African tribesman, who is supposed to be morally superior to the sophisticated European who has been
corrupted by the false restraints of his own society. Social primitivism was
one of the driving forces behind the French Revolution. The lower classes
rose up against the repression of politically powerful kings and destroyed
laws and restraints so that their natural goodness could flourish. Unfortunately, the French Revolution did not produce a morally perfect new man
once the corrupt restraints had been destroyed. Instead, the French Revolution produced the Reign of Terror, the rise of Napoleon to military
dictatorship, and the French wars of aggression against relatively democratic states such as the Swiss Republic. With unspeakable shock,
Wordsworth and the other Romantics saw the theory of social primitivism
fail in France. The decline of Wordsworth's poetic power as he grew older
is often explained in part as the result of his disillusionment with revolutionary France.

A second kind of primitivism in the Preface is psychological. Psychological primitivism is the belief that there is some level in the mind which
is primary, more certain than everyday consciousness. In the Preface,
Wordsworth says that humble life displays "the primary laws of our nature;
chiefly, as far as the manner in which we associate ideas." Here
Wordsworth refers to a very important Romantic idea, associational psychology, which developed from the tradition of British empirical philosophy—from John Locke's *Essay Concerning Human Understanding* (1690),
David Hume's *Enquiry Concerning Human Understanding* (1748), and especially David Hartley's *Observations on Man* (1749).

In Latin, the term *tabula rasa* means the blank wax tablet on which one
writes with a stylus. Associational psychologists assumed that the human
mind at birth is a *tabula rasa*, a blank surface of some impressionable
material such as wax or clay. On this surface, the human senses constantly
write their impressions of sight, sound, feeling, odor, and taste. All that is
in the mind are these impressions and the memories of them, called ideas.
Ideas are nothing more than memories of sensory experience. The mind,
however, has ideas it has never experienced, and the associationist must
explain them. In addition to simple ideas, which are merely memories of
experiences, there are complex ideas. One sees a horse, and one has ever
afterward the simple idea of a horse printed on the tablet of one's mind.

These simple ideas can be associated into more complex ideas. For
example, one can associate the idea of half a horse with the idea of half a
man and produce the complex idea of a centaur, even though one has
never seen one. The mind has in it a power of imagination which allows
the construction of complex ideas from simple experiences. These associa-

tions follow rules. Ideas are associated only through similarity, opposition, causality, or contiguity in space and time. Even the most complex ideas of right and wrong, the good and the beautiful, can be traced back to initial sensory experiences, involving pleasure and pain, and transformed by the associative power of the imagination. When Wordsworth speaks in the Preface to the *Lyrical Ballads* about tracing in his poems the "manner in which we associate ideas," he is endorsing the line of thought of the associational psychologists. Poems trace the process by which the mind works. They help people to understand the origins of their own feelings about what is good and bad by demonstrating the way impressions from nature strike the mind and by showing how the mind associates these simple experiences, forming complex attitudes about what proper conduct is, what fidelity and love are, what the good and the true are. In *The Prelude*, one of Wordsworth's main motives is to trace the history of the development of his own mind from its most elementary feelings through the process of association of ideas until his imagination constructs his complex, adult consciousness.

Wordsworth's Preface to the second edition of *Lyrical Ballads* set out a series of ideas which are central to the revolutionary Romantic movement, including both social and psychological primitivism, the state of nature, the "noble savage," the sentimental hero, the power of the imagination, and the association of ideas. These concepts are basic to understanding his poetry.

Wordsworth's "Lines Composed a Few Miles Above Tintern Abbey" (hereafter called simply "Tintern Abbey") was composed on July 13, 1798, and published that same year. It is one of the best-known works of the English Romantic movement. Its poetic form is blank verse, unrhymed iambic pentameter, in the tradition of John Milton's *Paradise Lost* (1667). In reading any poem, it is important to define its dramatic situation and to consider the text as if it were a scene from a play or drama and determine who is speaking, to whom, and under what circumstances. Wordsworth is very precise in telling the reader when and where these lines are spoken. Tintern Abbey exists, and the poet Wordsworth really visited it during a tour on July 13, 1798. Because the poem is set at a real point in history rather than once-upon-a-time, and in a real place rather than in a kingdom-far-away, it is said to exhibit "topographic realism." The speaker of the poem reveals that this is his second visit to this spot; he had been there five years earlier. At line 23 he reveals that he has been away from this pleasant place for a long time and, at lines 50-56, that while he was away in the "fretful stir" of the world he was unhappy. When he was depressed, his thoughts turned to his memory of this natural scene and he felt comforted.

Now, as the poem begins, he has come again to this beautiful site with his beloved younger sister, whom he names directly at line 121. The dramatic situation involves a speaker, or persona, who tells the reader his thoughts and feelings as if he were addressing his younger sister, who is "on stage" as his dramatic audience. Although the poem is autobiographical, so that the speaker resembles Wordsworth himself and the sister resembles Dorothy Wordsworth, it is better to think of the speaker and his listener as two invented characters in a little play. When William Shakespeare's Hamlet speaks to Ophelia in his play, the audience knows that Hamlet is not the same as Shakespeare, although he surely must express some of Shakespeare's feelings and ideas. So, too, the reader imagines that the speaker in "Tintern Abbey" speaks for Wordsworth, but is not exactly the same as the poet himself.

The poem displays many of the ideas stated in the Preface to the *Lyrical Ballads*. It begins with a description of a remote rural scene, rather than speaking about the latest news from London. In this rustic setting, the poet discovers some essential truths about himself. The first twenty-two lines describe the natural scene: the cliffs, orchards, and farms. This is a romantic return to Nature, the search for the beautiful and permanent forms which incorporate primitive human goodness. The speaker not only describes the scene, but also tells the reader how it generates feelings and sensations in him. In lines 23-56, the speaker says that his memory of this pure, natural place had been of comfort to him when he was far away. Lines 66-90 trace the speaker's memory of his process of growing up: When he first came among these hills as a boy, he was like a wild animal. He was filled with feelings of joy or fear by wild Nature. As a boy, nature was to him "a feeling and a love" which required no thought on his part. That childish harmony with nature is now lost. His childish "aching joys" and "dizzy raptures" are "gone by." As he fell away from his unthinking harmony with nature, his power of thought developed. This power is "abundant recompense" for the childish joys of "thoughtless youth." Now he understands Nature in a new way. He hears in nature "The still sad music of humanity." At line 95, he explains that his intellect grasps the purpose and direction of Nature, whereas his childish experience was more intense and joyous but incomplete. Now, as an adult, he returns to this natural scene and understands what he had only felt as a child, that nature is the source of moral goodness, "the nurse, the guide, the guardian of my heart, and soul of all my moral being."

At line 110, he turns to his younger sister and sees in her wild eyes his own natural state of mind in childhood. He foresees that she will go through the same loss that he experienced. She too will grow up and lose her unthinking harmony with the natural and the wild. He takes comfort in the hope that Nature will protect her, as it has helped him, and in the knowledge that the memory of this visit will be with her when she is far away in future years. Their experience of this pastoral landscape is therefore dear to the speaker for its own sake, and also because he has shared it with his sister. He has come back from the adult world and glimpsed primitive natural goodness both in the scene and in his sister.

The poem employs social and psychological primitivism. The rural scene is an imagined state of primitive nature where human goodness can exist in the child, like Adam in the garden of Eden before the Fall of Man. The poem shows how the primitive feelings of the boy are generated by the forms of nature and then form more and more complex ideas until his whole adult sense of good and bad, right and wrong, can be traced back to his elementary childish experiences of nature. Reason is not what makes beauty or goodness possible; natural feelings are the origin of the good and the beautiful. Reason merely recognizes what the child knows directly from his feelings.

Critics of Wordsworth point out that the "natural" scene described in the opening lines is, in fact, not at all "natural." Nature in this scene has been tamed by man into orchards, hedged fields, and cottage farms. What, critics ask, would Wordsworth have written if he had imagined Nature as the struggling jungle in the Congo where individual plants and animals fight for survival in their environmental niche and whole species are brought to extinction by the force of nature "red in tooth and claw?" If Wordsworth's idea of Nature is not true, then his idea of human nature will likewise be false. While he expects the French Revolution to lead to a state of nature in joy and harmony, in fact it led to the Reign of Terror and the bloodshed of the Napoleonic Wars. Critics of Romantic ideology argue that when the Romantics imagine Nature as a "kindly nurse," they unthinkingly accept a false anthropomorphism. Nature is not like a kindly human being; it is an indifferent or neutral force. They charge that Wordsworth projects his own feelings into the natural scene and thus his view of the human condition becomes dangerously confused.

"Michael: A Pastoral Poem" (hereafter called "Michael") was composed between October 11 and December 9, 1800, and published that same year. It is typical of Wordsworth's poetry about humble and rustic characters in which the sentiments or feelings of man in a state of nature are of central importance. The poem is written in blank verse, unrhymed iambic pentameter, again the meter employed in Milton's *Paradise Lost.* Milton's poem explores the biblical story of the Fall of Adam from the garden of Eden. Michael's destruction in Wordsworth's poem shows a general similarity to the tragedy of Adam in *Paradise Lost.* Both Michael and Adam begin in a natural paradise where they are happy and good. Evil creeps into each garden and, through the weakness of a beloved family member, both Adam and Michael fall from happiness to misery.

The poem "Michael" has two parts: the narrative frame and the tale of Michael. The frame occupies lines 1-39 and lines 475 to the end, the beginning and ending of the text. It relates the circumstances under which the story of Michael is told. The tale occupies lines 40-475, the central part of the text, and it tells the history of the shepherd Michael, his wife Isabel, and their son Luke. The frame of the poem occurs in the fictive present time, about 1800, whereas the tale occurs a generation earlier. The disintegration of Michael's family and the destruction of their cottage has already happened years before the poem begins. The frame establishes that the poem is set in the English Lake District and introduces the reader to the "I-persona" or speaker of the poem. He tells the story of Michael, and he knows the geography and history of the district. A "You-character" who does not know the region is the dramatic audience addressed by the "I-persona." In the frame, "I" tells "You" that there is a hidden valley up in the mountains. In that valley there is a pile of rocks, which would hardly be noticed by a stranger; but there is a story behind that heap of stones. "I" then tells "You" the story of the shepherd Michael.

Michael is one of the humble and rustic characters whose feelings are exemplary of the natural or primitive state of humankind. He has lived all his life in the mountains, in communion with Nature, and his own nature has been shaped by his natural environment. He is a good and kindly man. He has a wife, Isabel, and a child of his old age, named Luke. The family works from morning until far into the night, tending their sheep and spinning wool. They live in a cottage far up on the mountainside, and they have a lamp that burns late every evening as they sit at their work. They have become proverbial in the valley for their industry, so that their cottage has become known as the cottage of the evening star because its window glimmers steadily every night. These simple, hard-working people are "neither gay perhaps, nor cheerful, yet with objects and with hopes, living a life of eager industry." The boy is Michael's delight. From his birth, the old man had helped to tend the child and, as Luke grew, his father worked with him always at his side. He made a perfect shepherd's staff and gave it to his son as a gift. Now the boy has reached his eighteenth year and the "old man's heart seemed born again" with hope and happiness in his son.

Unfortunately, Michael suffers a reversal of his good fortune, for news comes that a distant relative has suffered an unforeseen business failure, and Michael has to pay a grievous penalty "in surety for his brother's son." The old man is sorely troubled. He cannot bear to sell his land. He suggests that Luke should go from the family for a time to work in the city and earn enough to pay the forfeiture. Before his beloved son leaves, Michael takes him to a place on the farm where he has collected a heap of stones. He tells Luke that he plans to build a new sheepfold there and asks Luke to lay the cornerstone. This will be a covenant or solemn agreement between the father and son: The boy will work in the city and meanwhile the father will build a new barn so that it will be there for the boy's return. Weeping, the boy puts the first stone in place, and he leaves the next day for his work far away. At first the old couple get a good report about his work, but after a time Luke "in the dissolute city gave himself to evil courses; ignominy and shame fell on him, so that he was driven at last to seek a hiding-place beyond the sea." After the loss of his son, Michael still goes to the dell where the pile of building stones lies, but he often simply sits the whole day merely staring at them, until he dies. Some three years later, his wife Isabel also dies and the land is sold to a stranger. The cottage of the Evening Star is torn down and nothing remains of the poor family's hopes except the straggling pile of stones which are the remains of the still unfinished sheepfold. This is the story that the "I-persona," who knows the district, tells to the "You-audience," who is unacquainted with the local history and geography.

The poem "Michael" embodies the ideas proposed in Wordsworth's Preface to the *Lyrical Ballads*. He takes a family of simple, rural people as the main characters in a tragedy. Michael is a sentimental hero whose unspoiled contact with nature has refined his human nature and made him a good man. Nature has imprinted experiences on his mind that his imagination has built into more and more complex feelings about what is right and wrong. The dissolute city, on the other hand, is confusing, and there Luke goes astray. From the city and the world of banking and finance, the grievous forfeiture intrudes into the rural valley where Michael was living in a state of nature, like a noble savage or like Adam before his fall.

The poem argues that nature is not a neutral commodity to be bought and sold. It is humanity's home. It embodies values. The poem demands that the reader consider Nature as a living force and demonstrates that once one knows the story of Luke, one never again can look on a pile of rocks in the mountains as worthless. That pile of rocks was a solemn promise of father and son. It signified a whole way of life, now lost. It was gathered for a human purpose, and one must regret that the covenant was broken and the sheepfold never completed. Likewise, all Nature is a covenant, an environment, filled with human promise and capable of guiding human feelings in a pure, simple, dignified, and moral way. The function of poetry (like the "I-persona's" story of Michael) is to make the reader see that nature is not neutral. The "I-persona" attaches the history of Michael to what otherwise might be merely a pile of rocks and so makes the "You-audience" feel differently about that place. Likewise, the poem as a whole makes the reader feel differently about Nature.

"Tintern Abbey" and "Michael" both explore the important question of how moral nature develops. What makes one good, virtuous, or proper? If, as the Preface argues, man is morally best when most natural, uncorrupted by false custom and education, then the normal process of growing up in the modern world must be a kind of falling away from natural grace. Wordsworth's "Ode: Intimations of Immortality from Recollections of Early Childhood" (hereafter called "Ode: Intimations of Immortality") is also concerned with the process of growing up and its ethical and emotional consequences. The poem is written in eleven stanzas of irregular length, composed of lines of varying length with line-end rhyme. The core of the poem is stanza V, beginning "Our birth is but a sleep and a forgetting." Here the poet discusses three stages of growth: the infant, the boy, and the man. The infant at birth comes from God, and at the moment when life begins the infant is still close to its divine origin. For this reason, the newborn infant is not utterly naked or forgetful, "but trailing clouds of glory do we come from God." The infant is near to divinity; "Heaven lies about us in our infancy," but each day leads it farther and farther from its initial, completely natural state. As consciousness awakens, "Shades of the prison house begin to close upon the growing boy." In other words, the natural feelings of the infant begin to become constrained as man falls into consciousness. A boy is still near to Nature, but each day he travels farther from the initial source of his natural joy and goodness. The youth is like a priest who travels away from his Eastern holy land, each day farther from the origin of his faith, but still carrying with him the memory of the holy places. When a man is fully grown, he senses that the natural joy of childish union with nature dies away, leaving him only the drab ordinary "light of common day" unilluminated by inspiration. This process of movement from the unthinking infant in communion with nature, through the stage of youth filled with joy and natural inspiration, to the drab adult is summarized in stanza VII, from the "child among his new-born blisses" as he or she grows up playing a series of roles "down to palsied Age."

The poem as a whole rehearses this progression from natural infant to adulthood. Stanzas I and II tell how the speaker as a child saw nature as glorious and exciting. "There was a time when meadow, grove, and stream . . . to me did seem apparelled in celestial light." Now the speaker is grown up and the heavenly light of the natural world has lost its glory. Even so, in stanza III, his sadness at his lost childhood joys is changed to joy when he sees springtime and thinks of shepherd boys. Springtime demonstrates the eternal rebirth of the world when everything is refreshed and begins to grow naturally again. The shepherd boys shouting in the springtime are doubly blessed, for they are rural characters, and, moreover, they are young, near the fountainhead of birth. In stanza IV the adult speaker can look on the springtime or on rural children and feel happy again because they signify the experience he has had of natural joy. Even though, as he says in stanza X, "nothing can bring back the hour of splendour in the grass, of glory in the flower," the adult can understand with his "philosophic mind" the overall design of the natural world and grasp that it is good.

The Prelude is Wordsworth's longest and probably his most important work. It is an autobiographical portrait of the artist as a young man. He was never satisfied with the work and repeatedly rewrote and revised it, leaving it uncompleted at his death. He had a fairly refined draft in 1805-1806 for his friend Coleridge to read, and the version he left at his death in 1850 is, of course, the chronologically final version. In between the 1805 and the 1850 versions, there are numerous drafts and sketches, some of them of the whole poem, while others are short passages or merely a few lines. When a reader speaks of Wordsworth's *The Prelude*, therefore, he or she is referring not so much to a single text as to a shifting, dynamic set of sometimes contradictory texts and fragments. The best edition of *The Prelude* is by Ernest de Selincourt, second edition revised by Helen Darbishire (Oxford University Press, 1959), which provides on facing pages the 1805-1806 text and the 1850 text. The reader can open the de Selincourt/Darbishire edition and see side by side the earliest and the latest version of every passage, while the editors' annotations indicate all significant intermediate steps.

The 1805 version is divided into thirteen books, while the 1850 version has fourteen. Book I, "Introduction, Childhood and Schooltime," rehearses how the poet undertook to write this work. He reviews the topics treated in famous epic poems, in Milton's *Paradise Lost*, Edmund Spenser's *The Faerie Queene* (1590, 1596), and other works. He concludes that the proper subject for his poem should be the process of his own development. He therefore begins at line 305 of the 1805 version to relate his earliest experiences, following the ideas explored above in "Tintern Abbey" and his "Ode: Intimations of Immortality." He traces the earliest impressions on his mind, which is like the *tabula rasa* of the associational psychologists.

"Fair seed-time had my soul, and I grew up/ Foster'd alike by beauty and by fear." He tells of his childhood in the lakes and mountains, of stealing birds from other hunters' traps, of scaling cliffs, and especially a famous episode concerning a stolen boat. At line 372, he tells how he once stole a boat and rowed at night out onto a lake. As he rowed away from the shore facing the stern of the boat, it appeared that a dark mountain rose up in his line of vision as if in pursuit. He was struck with fear and returned with feelings of guilt to the shore. Experiences like this "trace/ How Nature by extrinsic passion first peopled my mind." In other words, impressions of Nature, associated with pleasure and pain, provide the basic ideas which the imagination of the poet uses to create more and more complex attitudes until he arrives at his adult view of the world. The process described in the stolen boat episode is sometimes called the "discipline of fear."

Book II concerns "School-Time." It corresponds to the three stages of man outlined in "Ode: Intimations of Immortality": infant, youth, and adult. As in "Tintern Abbey," in *The Prelude*, Book II, Wordsworth explains that his early experiences of Nature sustained him when he grew older and felt a falling off of the infant's joyful harmony with the created universe. Book III deals with his "Residence at Cambridge University," which is like a dream world to the youth from the rural lakes: "I was a Dreamer, they the dream; I roamed/ Delighted through the motley spectacle." He talks of his reading and his activities as a student at St. John's College, concluding that his story so far has been indeed a heroic argument, as important as the stories of the ancient epics, tracing the development of his mind up to an eminence, a high point of his experience.

Book IV recounts his summer vacation after his first year of college, as he returns to the mountains and lakes of his youth, a situation comparable to the return of the persona in "Tintern Abbey" to the rural scene he had previously known. He notes the "inner falling-off" or loss of joy and innocence which seems to accompany growing up. Yet at line 344 he tells of a vision of the sun rising as he walked homeward after a night of gaiety and mirth at a country dance, which caused him to consider himself a "dedicated spirit," someone who has a sacred duty to write poetry. Later in this book he recounts his meeting with a tattered soldier returned from military service in the tropics and how he helped him find shelter in a cottage nearby. Book V is entitled simply "Books" and examines the role of literature in the poet's development. This book contains the famous passage, beginning at line 389, "There was a boy, ye knew him well, ye Cliffs/ And Islands of Winander." There was a youth among the cliffs of the lake district who could whistle so that the owls would answer him.

Once when he was calling to them the cliffs echoed so that he was struck with surprise and wonder. This boy died while he was yet a child and the poet has stood "Mute—looking at the grave in which he lies." Another recollection concerns the appearance of a drowned man's body from the lake.

Book VI, "Cambridge and the Alps," treats his second year at college and the following summer's walking tour of France and Switzerland. When the poet first arrived at Calais, it was the anniversary of the French Revolution's federal day. The young man finds the revolutionary spirit with "benevolence and blessedness/ spread like a fragrance everywhere, like Spring/ that leaves no corner of the land untouched." Frenchmen welcome the young Englishman as brothers in the struggle for freedom and liberty and they join in a common celebration. The Alps were a formidable barrier in the nineteenth century, seeming to separate the Germanic culture of Northern Europe from the Mediterranean. Crossing the Alps meant passing from one culture to a totally different one. Ironically, the poet records his errant climb, lost in the fog and mist, as he approached Italy, so that the English travelers cross the Alps without even knowing what they had done. Perhaps the crossing of the Alps unaware is like his observation of the French Revolution. The poet *sees* more than he *understands.* Book VII depicts the poet's residence in London. As one would expect, the city is unnatural and filled with all kinds of deformed and perverted customs, epitomized at the Bartholomew Fair, "a hell/ For eyes and ears! what anarchy and din/ Barbarian and infernal! t'is a dream/ Monstrous in colour, motion, shape, sight, sound."

Book VIII, "Retrospect—Love of Nature Leading to a Love of Mankind," is in contrast to Book VII. Opposed to the blank confusion of the city, Book VIII returns to the peaceful, decent rural scenes of the Lake District. It contrasts a wholesome country fair with the freak shows of London. Nature's primitive gift to the shepherds is beauty and harmony, which the poet first experienced there. Such "noble savages," primitive men educated by Nature alone, are celebrated as truly heroic.

Book IX tells of the poet's second visit to France and residence in the Loire Valley. It suppresses, however, all of the real biographical details concerning Wordsworth's affair with Annette Vallon and his illegitimate daughter. As he passes through Paris the poet sees "the revolutionary power/ Toss like a ship at anchor, rock'd by storms." He arrives at his more permanent home in the Loire Valley and makes friends with a group of French military officers there. One day as he wanders with his new friends in the countryside, he comes across a hunger-bitten peasant girl, so downtrodden that she resembles the cattle she is tending. His French companion

comments, "'Tis against *that* which we are fighting," against the brutaliza-
tion of humankind by the monarchical system. In later versions, at the
conclusion of this book, Wordsworth inserts the story of "Vaudracour and
Julia." This love story seems to stand in place of Wordsworth's real-life
encounter with Annette Vallon. Book X continues his discussion of his visit
to France, including a second visit to Paris while the Reign of Terror is in
full cry and the denunciation of Maximilien Robespierre takes place. This
book also traces his return to England and the declaration of war by
England against France, which caused the young Wordsworth deep grief.
The French Revolution was probably the most important political event in
the poet's life. His initial hopes for the French cause were overshadowed
by the outrages of the Reign of Terror. His beloved England, on the other
hand, joined in armed opposition to the cause of liberty. In the numerous
reworkings of this part of his autobiography, Wordsworth steadily became
more conservative in his opinions as he grew older. Book X in the 1805
text is split into Books X and XI in the 1850 version. In this section he
explains that at the beginning of the French Revolution, "Bliss was it in that
dawn to be alive,/ But to be young was very heaven." Yet the course of the
revolution, running first to despotic terror and ending with the rise of
Napoleon, brought Wordsworth to a state of discouragement and desolation.

Book XI in the 1805 text (Book XII in the 1850 version) considers how
one may rise from spiritual desolation: having lost the innocent joy of
primitive youth and having lost faith in the political aims of the French
Revolution, where can the soul be restored? At line 74, the poet tells how
"strangely he did war against himself," but Nature has a powerful restorative force. At line 258, he enters the famous "Spots of time" argument, in
which he maintains that there are remembered experiences which "with
distinct preeminence retain/ A vivifying Virtue" so that they can nourish
one's depleted spirits. Much as in "Tintern Abbey," a remembered experience of Nature can excite the imagination to produce a fresh vitality.
Book XII in the 1805 version (Book XIII in the 1850) begins with a
summary of Nature's power to shape one's imagination and taste:

> From nature doth emotion come, and moods
> of calmness equally are nature's gift,
> This is her glory; these two attributes
> Are sister horns that constitute her strength.

The concluding book tells of the poet's vision on Mt. Snowdon in Wales.
On the lonely mountain, under the full moon, a sea of mist shrouds all the
countryside except the highest peaks. The wanderer looks over the scene

and has a sense of the presence of divinity. Nature has such a sublime aspect "That men, least sensitive, see, hear, perceive,/ And cannot choose but feel" the intimation of divine power. In this way, Nature feeds the imagination, and a love of Nature leads to a sense of humanity's place in the created universe and a love for all humankind. The poem ends with an address to the poet's friend Coleridge about their mutual struggle to keep faith as true prophets of Nature.

It is often said that Wordsworth's *The Prelude*, written in Miltonic blank verse, is the Romantic epic comparable to *Paradise Lost* of Milton. Other critics point to a similarity between *The Prelude* and the *Bildungsroman*, or novel of development. *The Prelude* is subtitled the "Growth of a Poet's Mind" and bears considerable resemblance to such classic stories as Stendhal's *The Red and the Black* (1830), in which the author traces the development of the hero, Julien Sorel, as he grows up. Finally, most readers find an important pastoral element in *The Prelude*. The "pastoral" occurs whenever an author and an audience belonging to a privileged and sophisticated society imagine a more simple life and admire it. For example, sophisticated courtiers might imagine the life of simple shepherds and shepherdesses to be very attractive compared to their own round of courtly duties. They would then imagine a pastoral world in which shepherdesses with frilly bows on their shepherds' crooks and dainty fruits to eat would dally in the shade by fountains on some peaceful mountainside. Such a vision is termed pastoral because it contrasts unfavorably the life of the real author and audience with the imagined life of a shepherd. *The Prelude* makes such pastoral contrasts frequently: for example, in the depiction of rural shepherds in the Lake District compared with urban workers; in the comparison of the life of a simple child with that of the adult; and in the comparison of the working classes of France and England with their masters. The pastoral elements in *The Prelude* are a natural consequence of the primitivism in the poem's ideology.

Wordsworth is one of the recognized giants of English literature, whose importance is nearly equal to Milton's or Shakespeare's. Even so, his work has been the subject of sharp controversy from its first publication until the present. William Hazlitt in his *Lectures on the English Poets* (1818) argues that Wordsworth is afflicted with a false optimism and that his idea of Nature is merely a reflection of the human observer's feelings. Aldous Huxley in "Wordsworth in the Tropics" in *Holy Face and Other Essays* (1929) attacks the unnaturalness of Wordsworth's view of Nature. John Stuart Mill's *Autobiography* (1873), on the other hand, discusses the restorative power of Romantic poetry and the capacity of Wordsworth to relieve the sterility of a too "scientific" orientation. R. D. Havens' *The Mind of a Poet* (1941) provides a detailed study of *The Prelude*, and additional commentary can be found in Abbie Findlay Potts's *Wordsworth's Prelude* (1953) and Herbert Lindenberger's *On Wordsworth's Prelude* (1963).

The apparent decline of Wordsworth's poetic powers in his later years has occasioned much debate. Was he disillusioned with the course of the French Revolution so that he could no longer bear to praise humankind's primitive nature? Was he so filled with remorse over his affair with Annette Vallon that his inspiration failed? Was he a living demonstration of his own theory of the development of man from infant, to boyhood, to adult: that as man grows older he becomes more and more remote from the primitive feelings of the infant who comes into this world trailing clouds of glory, so that old men can never be effective poets? In any case, the young Wordsworth writing in the 1790's and the first decade of the nineteenth century was a voice calling out that life can be joyful and meaningful, that humanity's nature is good, and that man is not alone in an alien world, but in his proper home.

Other literary forms · In addition to his poetry, William Wordsworth's Preface to the second edition of his *Lyrical Ballads* is the single most important manifesto of the Romantic position in English, defining his ideas of the primary laws of Nature, the working of the imagination, the process of association of ideas, and the balance of passion and restraint in human conduct.

Select works other than poetry

NONFICTION: *The Prose Works of William Wordsworth*, 1876; *Letters of William and Dorothy Wordsworth*, 1935-1939 (6 volumes; Ernest de Selincourt, editor).

Todd K. Bender

Bibliography · The standard biography is Stephen Gill's *William Wordsworth: A Life*, 1989. See also Emile Legouis, *The Early Years of William Wordsworth, 1770-1798*, 1987; Edith Batho, *The Later Wordsworth*, 1933; George W. Meyer, *Wordsworth's Formative Years*, 1943; and Mary Trevelyan Moorman's two-volume *William Wordsworth*, vol. 1, *The Early Years, 1770-1803*, 1957, vol. 2, *The Later Years, 1803-1850*, 1965.

For criticism see Samuel Taylor Coleridge, *Biographia Literaria*, 1817; Matthew Arnold, *Essays in Criticism: Second Series*, 1888; Alfred North Whitehead, *Science and the Modern World*, 1925; Raymond Dexter Havens, *The Mind of a Poet*, 1941; Helen Darbishire, *The Poet Wordsworth*, 1950; and

G. H. Hartman, *Wordsworth's Poetry, 1787-1814*, 1965. Among those works whose interest in Wordsworth's work centers primarily on its reflection of the culture and politics of an era is Gary Harrison's *Wordsworth's Vagrant Muse: Poetry, Poverty, and Power*, 1994. Tracy Ware's "Historicism Along and Against the Grain: The Case of Wordsworth's 'Michael,' " *Nineteenth Century Literature* 49, no. 3 (1994), reflects responses of the New Historicists and post-structuralists, recommending finally a "dialogic criticism." Among other valuable analyses are David Perkins' "Wordsworth, Hunt, and Romantic Understanding of Meter," *Journal of English and Germanic Philology* 93, no. 1 (1994), and David P. Haney's "Poetry as Super-Genre in Wordsworth: Presentation and Ethics," *European Romantic Review* 5, no. 1 (1994).

SIR THOMAS WYATT

Born: Allington, England; 1503
Died: Sherborne, England; October, 1542

Poetry · *The Courte of Venus,* c. 1539 (includes 3 to 10 Wyatt poems) ·
Certayne Psalmes Chosen out of the Psalter of David, 1549 · *Songes and Sonettes,*
1557 (known as *Tottel's Miscellany,* Richard Tottel, editor; includes 90 to 97
Wyatt poems) · *Collected Poems of Sir Thomas Wyatt,* 1949 (Kenneth Muir,
editor) · *Sir Thomas Wyatt and His Circle: Unpublished Poems,* 1961 (Kenneth
Muir, editor) · *Collected Poems,* 1975 (Joost Daalder, editor)

Achievements · The best of the court poets who wrote under Henry VIII,
Sir Robert Wyatt stands at a crossroads in English poetry, looking both
backward and forward. His fluent native lyrics, perhaps written for musical
accompaniment, show direct continuity with medieval popular song and
with Chaucerian love imagery. At the same time, he opened the door to
the Renaissance in English poetry, importing Italian and French forms and
naturalizing them. His most influential innovation was the sonnet. Experimenting with translations from Petrarch's sonnets, he invented both the
Italian and the English or "Shakespearean" sonnet forms. His successors—among them the Earl of Surrey, Sir Philip Sidney, Samuel Daniel,
Michael Drayton, and William Shakespeare—adopted and refined the
sonnet form for their own famous sequences of love poems.

Wyatt introduced virtually every new stanza form that appeared in the
sixteenth century. As the first English satirist, he experimented with terza
rima, and in his epigrams with ottava rima. He also wrote several rondeaux
after French models. His verse translations from the Psalms are the finest
in the language, written at a time when English versions of biblical
literature were few.

Comments by his contemporaries and the high degree of preservation
of his works—he is, for example, by far the largest contributor to *Tottel's
Miscellany*—testify to his high reputation in his own day. When Wyatt wrote,
there were no formal standards of prosody in English. Soon after his death,
metrical regularity, which he had helped to establish, prevailed. Unfortunately, Tottel's editors blurred some of his most powerful effects by regu-
larizing his meter, and his younger and smoother contemporary, Surrey,
came to be regarded as a better poet. To critics of the eighteenth and
nineteenth centuries, Wyatt's poems, read in the light of their successors,

appeared rough and jarring. The twentieth century, with its interest in "organic" rhythm as opposed to fixed rules of meter, and in dramatic compression and conversational immediacy as opposed to formal diction, has reevaluated Wyatt and granted him precedence as the greatest poet of his age, not only as an innovator in form but as an original explorer of the effect on the individual mind of the insecurities and tensions inherent in love and politics.

Biography · (Sir) Thomas Wyatt was born into a family already in favor with the court. His father had served and prospered under Henry VII and Henry VIII, holding a series of important offices, and purchasing as his principal residence Allington Castle in Kent, where the poet was born. Young Wyatt made his first court appearance in 1516, and probably entered St. John's College, Cambridge, the same year. He was suitably married in 1520 to Elizabeth Brooke, the daughter of Lord Cobham, with whom he had a son; but in 1526, they separated because of her infidelity. He was sent on important diplomatic missions, in 1526 to France and in 1527 to Italy, where he traveled extensively.

It is plausibly conjectured that Wyatt was a lover of Anne Boleyn before her marriage to Henry VIII. Some of his poems were probably written to or about her, and his imprisonment in 1536 seems to have been connected with her downfall. He was quickly released to his father's custody, however, and continued to enjoy the king's favor. Knighted, he was sent as ambassador to Spain to improve relations between Henry and the Emperor Charles V and to prevent an alliance of the latter with France. On later embassies to France and Flanders, he continued this mission. In 1540, because of a shift in policy, his patron, Thomas Cromwell, was arrested and executed. Slanderous accusations found among Cromwell's papers led to Wyatt's imprisonment in 1541 and his subsequent preparations to reply to the charges. He was soon released, however, on condition that he leave his mistress, Elizabeth Darrell, who had borne him a son, and return to his wife. He continued to occupy important offices, serving as member of Parliament for Kent and Vice-Admiral of the Fleet. At about thirty-nine he died of a sudden fever contracted on a diplomatic mission to meet the Spanish envoy at Falmouth.

Analysis · Sir Thomas Wyatt was esteemed in his time for all the best qualities associated with the Renaissance courtier: military prowess, grace in art, skill in language, intelligence in council, and loyalty to his sovereign. The court of Henry VIII, himself a poet and musician, was receptive to the literary talents of such a man and capable of nourishing his worldly gifts, but the ways of politics and love were fraught with risks, as Wyatt's own career shows. It is against the background of this court, with its political and amorous intrigues, the insecurities of favor both in love and in worldly ambitions, that Wyatt's poetry can best be considered.

Wyatt is known primarily as a poet of love. The conventions of courtly love, deriving from twelfth century Provençal poetry, are the usual basis of his imagery. This tradition concerns the relationship between the great lady and her courtier "servant." Love is treated variously as sickness, servitude, worship, and war. The lover is in agony, the lady disdainful, her beauties idealized by comparisons with nature. The tradition reached Wyatt through two main sources, Geoffrey Chaucer and Francesco Petrarch, the Italian strain developing more fully the spiritual aspect of courtly love.

Wyatt's treatment of the tradition he inherited adapts to it the conditions of his own insecure times. He uses the love convention to speak not only of his lack of satisfaction in love but about his unhappiness at other aspects of ill fortune. Since a direct judgment on contemporary events could have been dangerous to his political career, even to his life, it is likely that Wyatt used the guise of a disappointed lover to interpret the sense of betrayal, the melancholy, and the insecurity inherent in his career. Life and death lay at the king's whim. Friendship was risky and tenuous, since the adherents of those who fell in favor were in danger themselves. Although Wyatt's own career was generally successful, he suffered two severe setbacks. From his prison cell he may have watched Anne Boleyn and her former lovers, his friends and acquaintances—persons once high in fortune and favor—go to the block. Later, his life was endangered by friendship with Thomas Cromwell. Such experiences fostered a deep sense of insecurity, which he expresses in several ways: by use of love conventions, in which he explores and comes to terms with the feeling of betrayal; by satire, in which he can compare the dangers and deceptions of court life with the peace of the country; and by seeking God's support, in his translations of the psalms. In all of his works, even in translations, it is clear that he is doing far more than merely following established forms. He is bringing stanzaic and rhythmic patterns, compression and directness of language, as well as the motif of disappointed love, to bear on the problems of expressing the strong and deep emotions of a sensitive individual, the complexities of a divided mind.

Looking at Wyatt's translations, one can see what kinds of changes he made to naturalize and individualize what he derived from his Italian models. It is impossible to determine an exact chronology for his poems, but it seems likely that those sonnet translations which are closest to their originals are earlier than those he adapts more fully to his own form and expression.

There was no equivalent in English of the sonnet form; Wyatt had to discover and invent it. For Petrarch's hendecasyllabic line, Wyatt devised a normally decasyllabic substitute, probably developed from Chaucerian models. Iambic pentameter was not, as it later was, a prescribed form, and Wyatt's lines must not be read as incompetent iambics. There are manuscript examples of his revisions away from metrical regularity, showing that the irregularity often criticized as "roughness" was intentional. Wyatt's line is open to variable stress which allows for dominance of speech rhythms and expression of nuances of feeling. While Petrarch's rhyme scheme divided the sonnet between octave in braced rhyme and sestet in alternative rhyme, Wyatt's three quatrains in braced rhyme allow for his rational progression of thoughts and images. The series of braced rhymes gives him several couplets with which to work as the poem progresses, to reinforce his contrasts and hammer home his feelings. He introduces a concluding couplet which he employs with great flexibility and variety of effect—unlike William Shakespeare, who too often used it lamely as a detached tag.

In several of the courtly love sonnets that Wyatt translates, he sharpens Petrarch's images and makes their expression more vivid while carefully pursuing an elaborate conceit. "The long love that in my thought doth harbor" explores love as war; Wyatt, who had participated in chivalric tournaments, conveys a vigorous, dramatic atmosphere of action in the field by use of energetic words and rhythmic pressure. "My galley charged with forgetfulness" pursues the conventional conceit of love as a ship in dangerous seas. Again, Wyatt achieves a feeling of energy, of rushing forward, opening with two run-on lines and blurring the Italian's sharp distinction between octave and sestet. This poem does not actually mention love, allowing wider application to the dangers of political life.

Another probably early translation shows how Wyatt uses courtly love conventions to focus attention more on the sufferer's state of mind than on the love situation. The original Petrarchan version of the sonnet "I find no peace, and all my war is done" appealed to Wyatt for its antithetical construction, portraying a divided mind; Wyatt's version shows how intricately he uses form to convey the sense of internal division. An essential aspect of much of his poetry is the "broken-backed" line, deriving from Anglo-Saxon through medieval lyric and still prevalent before metrical regularity became the norm. This line is divided sharply into two segments by a pronounced caesura. Each of the two resulting half-lines, containing two or three stresses, has an integrity related more to speech rhythm than to syllable counts. The divided lines point and balance the antitheses of the lover's internal division, but his balance is conveyed more intricately than in the original by the weaving together of phrases throughout the octave. The first three half-lines are parallel in structure: "I find," "I fear," "I fly." The first and last lines of the first quatrain are united by parallel sounds and structure: "and all my war is done," "and all the world I season"; a similar effect parallels the third line of the first quatrain and the second line of the second quatrain: "yet can I not arise," "yet can I scape no-wise." The imagery is traditional in the courtly love convention, but the structure dramatizes the tension in a mind whose suffering, itself, rather than the cause of his suffering, is the poem's focus.

Wyatt uses the conventions of the suffering lover but turns them around in "Was I never yet of your love grieved." Petrarch's lover, worn out with sighing, longs for death as a release and plans a beautiful sepulchre with his lady's name engraved on it; yet if she will be satisfied with his faithful love, he may survive. Wyatt says that he is *not* prepared to die and have a tomb with an inscription naming the lady as the cause of his demise. Such a tomb, in any case, far from being a monument to her, would be an indictment of her cruelty. Wyatt discards Petrarch's physical description of the tomb to focus on the lover's mood. That mood is one of independent cynicism: The lady may choose to accept his love and faith, but if she chooses instead to continue acting out her disdain, she will not succeed, and that will be her own fault. There is no Petrarchan veneration of the lady here. The lover, having exhausted himself trying, has reached the conclusion that the prize is really not worth the chase. Using the couplets formed by the braced rhyme of the quatrains, he produces a powerful stress on "past" in the third line, and increases the tension between the courtly love expectation and his own rebellion against it through the rhyme of "wearied" and "buried"—an association belied by the unexpected "not."

A sonnet of similar subject and tone, whose subtlety and smoothness show Wyatt's confidence in having made the form his own, is "Whoso list to hunt." The Petrarchan sonnet on which this is based has a visionary, dreamlike quality, picturing the lady as a white hind in a beautiful spring landscape disappearing from the poet's ken because Caesar (presumably God) has set her free (presumably by death). The tone of Wyatt's version is quite different. The mention of the hind is developed into an extended hunting metaphor. Instead of the solitary lover, he becomes a member of a crowd of hunters (suitors). He has thus introduced a dramatic situation, plunging into it abruptly and colloquially with direct address. The natural description of the original is replaced by the immediate, realistic atmosphere of the hunt, into which Petrarch's mention of the mind has led him: the pressing rivals, the net, the hot pursuit. His use of rhythm conveys this physical experience, as heavy stresses on the alliterated "Fainting I follow" suggest limping or labored breath, with the poet's abrupt about-face, the "turn" in the poem, coming in the middle of the sharply divided line. Wyatt attacks the artificiality of the courtly love tradition, remarking that to pursue this lady is "in vain," as in the preceding sonnet—a waste of effort. Unlike Petrarch's modest Laura, this lady is wild and spirited. She is inaccessible not because she is called by God but because she has already been claimed by his social superior (it is usually assumed that "Caesar" is Henry VIII, the hind Anne Boleyn). He further strains the convention by seeking reciprocity of affection, as opposed to one-sided worship of an ideal; to the Petrarchan lover, the pursuit, the service, is its own reward.

The structural pattern portrays the stages of the poet's argument: the first quatrain defining his plight; the second focusing more sharply on his feelings, from which he abruptly breaks; the third explaining why the case is hopeless; and the couplet giving the explanation an epigrammatic and ironic punch. With the awareness that pursuit of a highborn lady was often an essential stepping-stone to court favor, it is not straining interpretation to see in this particular love pursuit—in which idealized description of the lady has yielded to focus on the lover's feelings—a more general pursuit of fortune and success with the frustrations encountered in that struggle.

Some of Wyatt's lyrics seem to bear particular relation to his work on foreign models, such as the *strambotti* of the Italian poet Serafino de Ciminelli. Light in tone, the *strambotto* is an eight-line poem with six alternate rhymes and a concluding couplet. Examples in Wyatt's work are "Who hath heard of such cruelty before" and "Alas, madame! for stealing of a kiss?" Two of his finest lyrics which relate closely in mood to his sonnets and in form to his *strambotti* are "They flee from me that sometime did me seek" and "It may be good, like it who list." Both use three seven-line stanzas to portray intellectual or emotional development: A problem stated in the first stanza is reexamined in the third in the light of the second. Both have the rhyme scheme *ababbcc*.

In Wyatt's most famous poem, "They flee from me, that sometime did me seek," the description of a specific experience may in part function as a figure to express general feelings about good fortune and its loss. This is especially likely if—as is often assumed—the poem refers to Anne Boleyn. Although the situation is a conventional one of courtly love, the setting and experience are real and immediate, the diction that of everyday speech. The dominant image, like that of "Whoso list to hunt," is of animals, but it is uncertain what animal the poet has in mind: deer, birds, or simply women. The wild and bestial is contrasted with the tame, courtly, and civilized quality suggested by the words "gentle" and "gentleness." The main rhetorical device is a simple contrast of past with present tense, past joys with present loss. The use of "they" in the first line may point to a sense of desertion by all the speaker's friends, similar to that expressed in the epigram, "Lux, my fair falcon," in which an animal image is used in more complex fashion, as an ironic contrast between loyal animals and disloyal men. The men are ultimately seen as even lower on the animal scale than the falcons, as the men are compared to lice leaving a dead body.

The first stanza of "They flee from me" establishes the focal point of the speaker's mood, his sense of desertion. The remarkable second stanza recalls in minute detail and tingling immediacy a specific experience, in the light of which a new mood, irony, emerges in the third stanza. This final stanza begins with the rhythmic subtlety of abrupt conversational rhythm, the jolting caesura, and the insistence of many stressed monosyllables. In this line, the dream-vision of Petrarchan convention and the erotic dream of Chaucerian romance are banished. Once again the poet's insistence on reciprocity in affection has been violated, yet he reacts not with vengefulness or even rebellion, but with ironic detachment. He, with his humanity, his gentleness, has kept his part of the bargain. She, however, who once appeared "gentle, tame and meek," has now reverted to her wild animal nature. "Kindly" may be taken both in the sense of "according to nature" and ironically in its modern sense. The suggestion that *he* should be served better recalls ironically the courtly love tradition of the man's service to his lady on her pedestal, and thus Wyatt drives home again his insistence on reciprocity: Should service be given if not deserved? His conclusion is not, as in the courtly love tradition, and as the poem's opening suggests, one of sentimental agony, but musing, perhaps even amused understatement. One is left with a question: What does one deserve who repays loyalty with disloyalty? Yet there remains some sense of the reality and intensity of loss from the vividness of the scene described in the second stanza. Wyatt's ideal of a reciprocal and permanent love is more of this world than Petrarch's one-sided idealization, and its existence belies a charge against him of cynicism.

"It may be good, like it who list" opens with a striking colloquial tone in mid-conversation. The debate symbolized by this dramatic situation is an internal one: The poet is uncertain whether to believe signs of friendship or affection in words and looks. He would like to, but having seen so many changes in human favor, fears to commit himself. The form perfectly conveys the thought-movement, with its seesawing rhythm, produced by the broken-backed line, used with effect similar to that in "I find no peace, and all my war is done." Stanza one begins with half-lines strongly set off against each other by caesuras, on either side of which are stressed syllables, so that the movement seems to be first a pressing toward a decision, then a receding from it, a depiction in sound of the mind swinging back and forth between the desire to believe and the impulse to doubt—opposites that the poet cannot reconcile—with a question to reinforce his uncertainty. The second stanza states the doctrine of contrarieties more objectively, yet four lines of it maintain structurally and rhythmically the sensation of vacillation. The final stanza resolves the argument into another question, directed to the imaginary interlocutor, and the poet seems firmly to resolve the argument in the spondaic "Nay sir." The next line opening, "And yet," sets off the whole argument again, however, to leave it seesawing still in the concluding broken-backed line—"For dread to fall I stand not fast"—which has served as a refrain in the two preceding stanzas. The paradox is stressed in union by alliteration of opposite-meaning words, "fall" and "fast," which occupy corresponding positions in their respective half-lines.

The use of a refrain connects this poem with the other main lyrical form for which Wyatt is famous, sometimes called the "ballette." This form had its origin in popular song, toward which the musical impetus of Henry VIII's court drew the courtly minds of the time. Wyatt's ballettes probably had a social function: They may have been composed for musical accompaniment to be sung in company and were certainly circulated privately. They have short stanzas and simple meters, with short lines and often a refrain. Wyatt's tendency to compression is here at its finest, as he expresses strong and deep emotion in a simple manner and brief compass.

Wyatt's use of the refrain is exquisitely subtle and varied. He may, as in "Such hap as I am happed in," retain for the final line of each stanza the same rhythm and line length but alter the words of the refrain, then echo it at the beginning of the next stanza. By this means the intensity of feeling and the details of the mind's torture are progressively built up, until the poem comes to rest in its opening words, with the tortured mind drawn taut and caught in a circular trap, with no hope of escape. The poem's circularity depicts the speaker's plight.

He may repeat the same or similar words at the end of each stanza, letting them accumulate meaning and force in each recurrence from the stanza they follow, and progressively from all the preceding stanzas. "My lute awake" explores, with the subtle variations of its refrain, the relationship between the sufferer and his instrument. The first and final stanzas, almost identical, frame the poem, their minor variations exhibiting the effect of the mental progression through the intervening six. The second, third, and fourth stanzas explore the lover's plight, hinting at the possibility of retribution. The fifth, sixth, and seventh turn the tables and imagine the once-disdainful lady old and deserted, longing but daring not to express her desires (as he, ironically, is able to express his in the present poem). In the second two revenge stanzas, the poet discards the lute altogether and speaks for himself: "I have done" (finished) caring for you; you will suffer "as I have done." The sense of the opening refrain, "My lute be still, for I have done," is that the lover is finished with life. When he returns to echo it at the end, the accumulation of meanings makes it plain that he is finished with the lady. Though the last stanza echoes the first verbally, its sounds are brisker. The word "waste" now carries the full sense of time wasted in the love pursuit (similar to "As well as I may spend his time in vain" in "Whoso list to hunt"). The poet has moved from a pathetic opening through an emotional progression to a detached conclusion, a progress like that exhibited in "They flee from me." The poem has served to delineate the lover's hurt feelings and, in a way, to cure them.

Wyatt's satires and psalms explore in their own way his basic problem of insecurity in public and private life. The satires were probably written in a period directly following one of his imprisonments, when he was relegated or had temporarily retired to his home in Kent. There he examines at length, in epistolary form addressed to his closest friends, the contrasts between courtly and country virtues, comparing the simple honesty of the country to the practiced dissimulation of the court.

His own imprisonment and the death of Anne and her lovers had introduced a somber gloom, which he explored in shorter poems such as "Who list his wealth and ease retain," in which he urges sequestration and anonymity as a means of holding onto life and safety. In the satires, he moves forward from this position, working through his disillusion to a contentment derived from interior strengths and virtues. This process is similar to that of the love poems, in which he works from a mood of despair or grief to one of detachment.

The satires are based on the models of Luigi Alamanni, a contemporary Italian poet, whose terza rima Wyatt imitates, and on the satiric moods and techniques of Horace and Juvenal. The first satire especially ("Mine own John Poyntz") and the other two less overtly employ Wyatt's favorite antithetical manner, using it not to portray a divided mind but to contrast two lifestyles, public and private. Despite the difficulty of the verse form (there are far fewer available rhymes in English than in Italian), the opening of this poem based on Alamanni's tenth satire is smooth, collo-quial, and ruminative. As Wyatt catalogs the courtly vices, what stings him most, as in the love poetry, is the deceit which leads to a betrayal of friendship, of "gentleness": "The friendly foe with his double face/ [I cannot] Say he is gentle, and courteous there-withal." Two series of catalogs, the first of courtly "arts" that he cannot affect–five tercets beginning "I cannot"–and the second of foreign countries where he might be ("I am not . . . Nor am I") are joyously resolved both rhetorically and metrically in the regular iambic line, "But here I am in Kent and Christendom," where he invites Poyntz to visit him and share his attractive life of independence, hunting in good weather, reading in bad.

The second, and perhaps most attractive of the three satires, "My mother's maids, when they did sew and spin," again addressed to Poyntz, is the most effective, for instead of the catalog of vices paraded in the other two at some risk of monotony, it uses the Horatian fable of the town mouse and the country mouse to expound a moral. The language is appealingly homely, the approach intimate, and the poem's directness is assisted–like that of some of the love poems–by direct discourse: " 'Peep,' quod the other, 'sister I am here.'/ 'Peace,' quod the towny mouse, 'why speakest thou so loud?' " The moral is that man should content himself with and use well the lot assigned him and, instead of outward reward, seek inward peace. A religious note is introduced here as Wyatt asks of God a punishment for seekers after worldly gain–a punishment which resembles what he imagines for the lady in "My lute awake": that they shall behold virtue and regret their loss.

Wyatt's versions of seven psalms were probably written, like his satires, during or after one of his imprisonments. The narrative prologues that introduce them and the conception of them as expressions of penitence are derived from Pietro Aretino's prose translations into Italian. This framework probably appealed to Wyatt because it places the psalms in the context of David's love for Bathsheba and the resultant sickness of heart and soul which he strives to cure with the aid of his harp. The verse is powerful and fluid; the rhyme scheme, as in the satires, is terza rima. An examination of Psalm 38 ("O Lord, as I thee have both prayed and pray") shows how the psalms develop and continue the preoccupations expressed in the love poems and satires. As in the love poems, the focus of attention, the diction, rhetorical devices, and movement of the verse, is on depicting internal conflict, the movement of the suffering and divided mind: "O Lord, thou knowst the inward contemplation/ Of my desire, thou knowst my sighs and plaints,/ Thou knowst the tears of my lamentation." This might be part of a love lament. So might the following description of agony, where meter and imagery unite to depict a profound emotional crisis: "My heart panteth, my force I feel it quail,/ My sight, mine eyes, my look decays and faints." Broken-backed lines divided in two reinforce the poet's desperation as the second half-lines rhythmically duplicate each other. There follows a detailed description of the evils and dangers of courtly life: Friendship is betrayed, "kin unkind" desert him, slander assails him, he is in danger of his life. Like the lover, he fears rejection and seeks—this time with God—the succor of a reciprocal relationship.

The poet of individual consciousness has tested his strength against the courtly love tradition which, in its lack of reciprocity, fails him and against court manners which, in their lack of honesty and loyalty, appall him. He thus seeks reciprocity, trust, and affection by turning his "inward contemplation" to God.

Other literary forms · Sir Thomas Wyatt's *Plutarckes Boke of the Quyete of Mynde*, a prose translation of Plutarch's essay *Quiet of Mind*, which he read in Guillaume Budé's Latin version, was made at the request of Queen Katherine of Aragon and published in 1528—his only notable work published in his lifetime. His original prose works are interesting in their own right. The state papers contain several fine examples of his correspondence. His most polished prose works are the defense he prepared for his trial in 1541 and his two letters of moral advice to his son. These letters make explicit the moral stance which underlies his poems, especially extolling honesty, which comprises "wisdome, gentlenes, sobrenes, disire to do good, frendlines to get the love of many, and trougth above all the rest." Wyatt's prose is distinguished by its clarity and directness, its easy, colloquial use of language, its lively intelligence, and its wit. Often in the diplomatic letters he makes his style more immediate by using direct discourse to report conversations.

Select works other than poetry
ESSAY TRANSLATION: *Plutarckes Boke of the Quyete of Mynde*, 1528 (Plutarch).

Arthur Kincaid

Bibliography · Full-length studies include Stephen Merriam Foley, *Sir Thomas Wyatt*, 1990; Patricia Thomson, *Sir Thomas Wyatt and His Background*, 1964; Raymond Southall, *The Courtly Maker: An Essay on the Poetry of Wyatt and His Contemporaries*, 1964; and the older but valuable E. M. W. Tillyard, *Sir Thomas Wyatt: A Selection and a Study*, 1929. See also Douglas L. Peterson, *The English Lyric from Wyatt to Donne*, 1967. A brief cross-section of essays on Wyatt from the 1980's and early 1990's would include Cecile Williamson Cary, "Sexual Identity in 'They Flee from Me' and Other

Poems by Sir Thomas Wyatt," *Assays: Critical Approaches to Medieval and Renaissance Texts* 4 (1987); Diane M. Ross, "Sir Thomas Wyatt: Proverbs and the Poetics of Scorn," *The Sixteenth Century Journal* 18 (1987); Reed Way Dasenbrock, "Wyatt's Transformation of Petrarch," *Comparative Literature* 40 (1988); Ellen C. Caldwell, "Recent Studies in Sir Thomas Wyatt," *English Literary Renaissance* 19 (1989); Lisa M. Klein, "The Petrarchism of Sir Thomas Wyatt Reconsidered," in David G. Allen and Robert A. White, eds., *The Work of Dissimilitude: Essays from the Sixth Citadel Conference on Medieval and Renaissance Literature,* 1992; Catherine Bates, " 'A Mild Admonisher': Sir Thomas Wyatt and Sixteenth Century Satire," *Huntington Library Quarterly* 56 (1993); Perez Zagorin, "Sir Thomas Wyatt and the Court of Henry VIII," *Journal of Medieval and Renaissance Studies* 23 (1993); and Barbara L. Estrin, "Wyatt's Unlikely Likenesses: Or, Has the Lady Read Petrarch," in Peter C. Herman, ed., *Rethinking the Henrician Era: Essays on Early Tudor Texts and Contexts* (1994).

WILLIAM BUTLER YEATS

Born: Sandymount, near Dublin, Ireland; June 13, 1865
Died: Cap Martin, France; January 28, 1939

Poetry · *Mosada: A Dramatic Poem*, 1886 · *Crossways*, 1889 · *The Wanderings of Oisin and Other Poems*, 1889 · *The Countess Kathleen and Various Legends and Lyrics*, 1892 · *The Rose*, 1893 · *The Wind Among the Reeds*, 1899 · *In the Seven Woods*, 1903 · *The Poetical Works of William B. Yeats*, 1906, 1907 (2 volumes) · *The Green Helmet and Other Poems*, 1910 · *Responsibilities*, 1914 · *Responsibilities and Other Poems*, 1916 · *The Wild Swans at Coole*, 1917, 1919 · *Michael Robartes and the Dancer*, 1920 · *The Tower*, 1928 · *Words for Music Perhaps and Other Poems*, 1932 · *The Winding Stair and Other Poems*, 1933 · *The Collected Poems of W. B. Yeats*, 1933, 1950 · *The King of the Great Clock Tower*, 1934 · *A Full Moon in March*, 1935 · *Last Poems and Plays*, 1940 · *The Poems of W. B. Yeats*, 1949 (2 volumes) · *The Collected Poems of W. B. Yeats*, 1956 · *The Variorum Edition of the Poems of W. B. Yeats*, 1957 (P. Allt and R. K. Alspach, editors) · *The Poems*, 1983 · *The Poems: A New Edition*, 1984

Achievements · William Butler Yeats is generally regarded as the major English-speaking poet of the "modern" era (approximately 1890 to 1950). Some authorities go even further, designating him the most important twentieth century poet in any language. Purportedly, his work has generated more scholarly and critical commentary than that of any other modern writer, with the possible exception of William Faulkner. Here again, even greater claims have been voiced; perhaps more secondary material has been produced on Yeats than on any other English-speaking writer of any time in any genre, except William Shakespeare. Although in his late career and for some time thereafter he was overshadowed by the poetic and critical stature of T. S. Eliot, in the years since Eliot's death, Yeats's reputation has continued to grow whereas Eliot's has declined. Like most modern poets, writing in a period labeled the age of the novel, Yeats has been relatively obscure and inaccessible to the general reader, but among academicians his eminence has flourished, and, even more significant, his influence upon other poets has been both broad and deep. In fact, in recent decades he has become in such circles little less than a cult figure.

Even though he was never very robust, suffering from chronic respiratory problems and extremely poor eyesight throughout much of his adult life, W. B. Yeats lived a long, productive, and remarkably multifaceted life.

How one person could have been as completely immersed in as many different kinds of activity as he was is difficult to conceive. Throughout his life he was involved in occult pursuits and interests of one kind or another, a preoccupation which has long been considered by many authorities—especially early ones—as more an impediment than a contribution to his literary career. Of more "legitimate" significance, he was, with a handful of associates, a leading figure in the initiation of the related movements that have come to be known as the Irish Renaissance and the Irish Literary Revival.

The Nobel Foundation

Especially as a cofounder and codirector of the Irish National Theatre—later the famous Abbey Theatre—he was at the center of the literary movement, even aside from his prolific publication of poems, plays, essays, and reviews and the editorship of his sisters' artistically oriented Cuala Press. Moreover, between 1903 and 1932, Yeats conducted or participated in a series of five theater or lecture tours in America, thereby enhancing his renown in English-speaking countries on both sides of the Atlantic.

Major expressions of national and international recognition for such endeavors and achievements were forthcoming in the last decades of Yeats's life in such forms as honorary degrees from Queen's University (Belfast) and Trinity College (Dublin) in 1922, Oxford University in 1931, and Cambridge University in 1933; appointment as Senator for the newly established Irish Free State in 1922; and, most gratifying of all, the Nobel Prize in Literature in 1923. Furthermore, in 1935 Yeats was designated editor of the *Oxford Book of Modern Verse*, having declined previously an offer of knighthood in 1915 and an invitation to lecture in Japan in 1919. From young manhood, Yeats had lived and played out the role of the poet in society, gesturing, posing, and dressing for the part. In middle years and old age, he experienced genuine fulfillment of his dream and enjoyed self-realization as "the great man" of Anglo-Irish literature within his own lifetime.

Yeats's greatest accomplishment, however, was the achievement, in both his life and his work, of an astonishing singleness or oneness in the midst of myriad activities. Driven by an obsessive precept which he labeled "Unity of Being," he strove unceasingly to "hammer" his thoughts into "unity." Though never a masterful thinker in terms of logic or ratiocination, Yeats possessed unequivocal genius of the kind recognized by today's psychologists as imaginative or creative, if not visionary. In addition to an almost infallible gift for the precisely right word or phrase, he had a mind awesomely capacious in its ability to conceive and sustain complexly interwoven structures of symbolic suggestion, mythic significance, and allusive associations. He used these abilities to link poem to poem, poems to plays, and oeuvre to a self-consciously dramatic life, which was itself hardly other than a supremely sculpted *objet d'art.* By the time of his death at the age of seventy-three, Yeats had so completely interfused national interests, philosophical convictions, theories of symbolic art, and mythopoeic techniques of literary composition that he had indeed fulfilled his lifelong quest to master experience by wresting unity from multiplicity, achieving an intricately wrought identity of life and work in the midst of almost unimaginably manifold diversity.

Biography · The eldest son of an eldest son of an eldest son, William Butler Yeats was born on June 13, 1865, in Sandymount, Ireland, a small community on the outskirts of Dublin which has since been absorbed by that sprawling metropolis. His father, paternal grandfather, and great-grandfather Yeats were all graduates of Trinity College, Dublin, but only his father, John Butler Yeats, had begun his post-collegiate career in the city where he had studied. Both the great-grandfather and the grandfather had been clergymen of the Protestant Church of Ireland, the latter in County Down, near Northern Ireland, and the former at Drumcliff, near the west-Irish port town of Sligo, with which the poet is so thoroughly identified.

The reason for the identification with Sligo is that John Butler Yeats married the sister of his closest collegiate schoolmate, George Pollexfen, whose family lived in Sligo. Dissatisfied with the courts as a fledgling barrister, J. B. Yeats abandoned law and Dublin to follow in London his inclinations as a graphic artist in sketches and oils. The combination of limited finances and his wife's dislike of urban life resulted in numerous extended visits by her and the growing family of children back to Sligo at the home of the poet's maternal grandfather, a sea captain and partner in a shipping firm. Thus, Yeats's ancestral line doubled back upon itself in a sense. In the Sligo area he became acquainted with Yeats descendants of the Drumcliff rector, and in memory and imagination the west-Irish valley between the mountains Ben Bulben and Knocknarea was always his spiritual home.

Yeats's formal education was irregular, at best. His earliest training was in London at the hand of his father, who read to him from English authors such as Sir Walter Scott and William Shakespeare. He did not distinguish himself at his first school in London or at Erasmus High School when the family returned to Dublin in 1880. Declining to matriculate at Trinity in the tradition of his forebears, he took up studies instead at the Metropolitan School of Art, where he met George Russell (later Æ), who was to become a lifelong close acquaintance. Yeats soon found that his interests inclined more toward the verbal arts than toward the visual, however, and by 1885 he had discontinued his studies in painting and had published some poems. At this same relatively early time, he had also become involved in occult interests, being among the founders of the Dublin Hermetic Society.

In 1887, the family returned to London, where Yeats was briefly involved with the famous Madame Blavatsky's Theosophical Society. The years 1889 to 1892 were some of the most important in this crucially formative period of his life. He was active in the many diverse areas of interest that were to shape and color the remainder of his career. In rapid succession he became a founding member of the Rhymers Club (a young group of Pateresque fin de siècle aesthetes) and of the Irish Literary Society of London and the Irish Literary Society of Dublin (both devoted to reviving interest in native Irish writers and writing). He also joined the newly established Hermetic Order of the Golden Dawn, a Rosicrucian secret society in which he became an active leader for a number of years and of which he remained a member for more than two decades. In 1889 Yeats published *The Wanderings of Oisin and Other Poems* and became coeditor of an edition of William Blake's work, an experience that was to influence greatly much of his subsequent thought and writing. No event in this period, however, had a more dramatic and permanent effect upon the rest of his life than his introduction in the same year to Maud Gonne, that "great beauty" of Ireland with whom Yeats fell immediately and hopelessly in love. The love was largely unrequited, although Maud allowed the one-sided relationship to continue for a painfully long time throughout much of the poet's early adult life—in fact, even after her marriage and widowhood.

From this point on, Yeats's life was a whirlwind of literary, nationalistic, and occult activity. In 1896, he met Lady Augusta Gregory and John Synge, with both of whom he was later to be associated in the leadership of the Abbey Theatre, as well as in investigation of the folklore and ethos of west-Irish peasants. The purpose of the Abbey Theatre, as far as these three were concerned, was to produce plays that combined Irish interests with artistic literary merit. The acquaintance with Lady Gregory also initiated a long series of summer visits at her estate in Coole Park, Galway, where his aristocratic inclinations, as well as his frequently frail physical being, were nurtured. During parts of 1895 and 1896, Yeats shared lodgings in London briefly with Arthur Symons, of the Rhymers Club, who, as author of *The Symbolist Movement in Literature* (1899), helped to acquaint him further with the French symbolist mode. Actually, however, through his intimate relationships with Hermetic lore and the English Romantics—especially Blake and Percy Bysshe Shelley—Yeats was already writing poetry in a manner much like that of his continental contemporaries. Later in 1896, Yeats moved in to 18 Woburn Buildings, Dublin, which came to be his permanent residence, except for rather frequent travels abroad, for an extended period.

At about the turn of the century and just after, Yeats abandoned his pre-Raphaelite aestheticism and adopted a more "manful" style. Not wholly unrelated to this was his more outgoing involvement in the daily affairs of the nationalist theater movement. The fact should be remembered—for it is easy to forget—that at this time Yeats was in his late thirties, already moving into a somewhat premature middle age. In 1909 he met Ezra Pound, the only other major figure in the modernist movement with whom he was ever to develop an acquaintance to the point of literary interaction and influence. The relationship reached its apex in the years from 1912 to 1915, during which Pound criticized Yeats's romantic tendencies and, perhaps more important, encouraged the older poet's interest in the highly stylized and ritualistic Nō drama of Japan.

In the same years, another important aspect of Yeats's life and interests had been developing in new directions as well. Beginning about 1908-1909, his esoteric pursuits shifted from active involvement in the Order of the Golden Dawn to investigations in spiritism, séances, and "psychical research." This preoccupation continued until 1915 or 1916, at which point some biographers seem to indicate that it ended. Yet, in one sense, spiritism as an obsessive concern simply redoubled itself about this time upon the occasion of Yeats's late-life marriage, for his wife turned out to be the "mystic" par excellence, through whose mediumship came the ultimate flowering of his lifelong prepossession with occult aspects of human—and superhuman—experience.

After Maud Gonne MacBride's husband was executed for his participation in Dublin's 1916 Easter uprising, Yeats visited Maud in Paris and proposed to her, only to be rejected as upon previous occasions years before. He then became attracted to her daughter Iseult and proposed to her in turn. Once again rejected, he decided to marry an English woman whom he had known in occult circles for some years and who was a close friend of mutual acquaintances—Georgie Hyde-Less. On their honeymoon in 1917, Georgie began to experience the first of what came to be a voluminous and almost literally fantastic collection of "automatic writings," the basis of Yeats's famous mystic system, as elaborated in his book *A Vision.*

The various honors that Yeats received in the 1920's and 1930's have been outlined already under "Achievements." Ironically, from these same years, not earlier ones, came most of the poems and collections by which his importance as a major modern literary figure is to be measured. Two interrelated experiences were very likely the chief contributors to the newfound vigor, imagery, and stylistic devices characteristic of these late works—his marriage and the completion of his mystic system in *A Vision.* The nature and degree of indebtedness to the latter of these influences, however, has often been both misunderstood and overestimated. The connection can probably never be assessed with complete accuracy, whereas various other possible factors, such as his renewed interest in the writings of John Donne and Jonathan Swift, should not be ignored or minimized.

In 1926 and 1927, Yeats's health became a genuinely serious problem, and at times in the last dozen years of his life, to live seemed to him to be almost more difficult than to die. There can be little question that such prolonged confrontation with that ultimate of all human experiences is responsible for some of the combined profundity, choler, and—paradoxically—wit of his last poems and plays. During this period, winters were usually spent in various Mediterranean locales for climatic reasons. Death eventually came in the south of France in January, 1939. With characteristic doggedness, Yeats continued working to the very end; he wrote his last poem only a week before his death and dictated to his wife some revisions of a late poem and his last play after the onset of his final illness, only two days before he died. Because of transportation difficulties at the beginning of World War II, Yeats was initially buried at Roquebrune, France. His body was exhumed in 1948, however, and transported aboard an Irish corvette for reburial at Drumcliff Churchyard, as he had specified at the end of his valedictory poem, "Under Ben Bulben." As his friend and fellow author Frank O'Connor said upon the occasion, that event brought to its appropriate and symbolic conclusion a life which was itself a work of art long planned.

Analysis · The complexity and fullness of William Butler Yeats's life was more than matched by the complexity and fullness of his imaginative thought. There are few poets writing in English whose works are more difficult to understand or explain. The basic problems lie in the multiplicity and intricacies of Yeats's own preoccupations and poetic techniques, and all too often the reader has been hindered more than helped by the vagaries of criticism and exegesis.

A coincidence of literary history is partly responsible for the latter problem. The culmination and conclusion of Yeats's career coincided with the advent of the "New Criticism." Thus, in the decades following his death, some of his most important poems became exercise pieces for "explication" by commentators whose theories insisted upon a minimum of attention to the author's cultural background, philosophical views, personal interests, or even thematic *intentions* (hence their odd-sounding term "intentional fallacy"). The consequence has been critical chaos. There simply are no generally accepted readings for some of Yeats's major poems. Instead, there have been ingenious exegeses, charges of misapprehension, countercharges, alternative analyses, then the whole cycle starting over again—in short, interpretational warfare.

Fortunately, in more recent years, simultaneously with decline of the New Critical movement, there has been increasing access to Yeats's unpublished materials—letters, diaries, and especially the manuscript drafts of poems and plays—and more scholarly attention has been paid to the relationships between such materials and the probable themes or meanings in the completed works. Even so, critical difficulties of no small magnitude remain because of continuing widespread disagreement among even the most highly regarded authorities about the basic Metaphysical vision from which Yeats's poetic utterances spring, variously interpreted as atheism, pagan theism, quasi-Christian theism, Theosophy, sheer aestheticism, Platonic dualism, modern humanist monism, and existentialism.

Added to the problems created by such a critical reception are those deriving from Yeats's qualities as an imaginative writer. Probably the most obvious source of difficulty is the highly allusive and subtly symbolic mode in which Yeats so often expressed himself. Clearly another is his lifelong practice of infusing many of his poems and plays with elements of doctrine, belief, or supposed belief from the various occult sources with which he was so thoroughly imbued. Futhermore, as to doctrine or belief, Yeats was constantly either apparently or actually shifting his ground (more apparently than actually). Two of his better-known poems, for example, are appropriately entitled "Vacillation" and "A Dialogue of Self and Soul." In these and numerous others, he develops and sustains a running debate between two sides of an issue or between two sides of his own truth-seeking psyche, often with no clear-cut solution or final stance made unequivocally apparent. Related to this—but not simply the same—is the fact that Yeats tended to change philosophical or metaphysical views throughout a long career, again either actually or apparently, and, also again, sometimes more apparently than actually. One disquieting and obfuscating consequence of such mental habits is that one poem will sometimes seem flatly to contradict another, or, in some cases even aside from the dialogue poems, one part of a given poem may appear to contradict a different part of the same poem. Adjacent passages in the major piece "The Tower," involving apparent rejection of Plato and Plotinus alongside apparent acceptance of Platonic or Neoplatonic reincarnation and "translunar paradise," constitute a case in point.

To quibble at much length about Yeats's prevailing metaphysical vision is to indulge in delusive sophistry, however, if his more than moderate pronouncements on such matters in prose are taken at anything approaching face value. What emerges from the prose is the virtually unequivocal proposition that—having rejected orthodox Christianity—the poet developed his own theistic "religion." This ontology and cosmology is made from many pieces and parts of that almost unimaginably multiplex body of lore—exoteric and esoteric—sometimes referred to as the *Philosophia Perennis:* Platonism, Neoplatonism, Hermetic symbolism, spiritual alchemy, Rosicrucianism, and certain elements of cabalism. Moreover, as Yeats stated in several essays, he found still further parallel and supporting materials at almost every turn—in Jakob Boehme, Emanuel Swedenborg, and William Blake; in the folklore of the Irish peasantry; in classical mythology, Irish legends, and the seasonal rituals examined by Sir James Frazer; and in Asian and Oriental religions, among other places. In two different senses Yeats found in all these materials convincing bases for the perpetuation of his obsession with extracting unity from multiplicity. For one thing, all the similarities and parallels in theme and motif from the many diverse sources constituted in themselves a kind of unity within multiplicity. Furthermore, the "philosophies" involved were largely oriented toward oneness—Plato's Idea of the good, alchemy's distillation of the immutable *lapis* from the world of flux, Hermetism's theory of symbolic correspondences (as above, so below), Hinduism's Brahma, and so on.

In both thought and work, however, the unresolved opposites sometimes seem to loom as large as—or even larger than—the union itself. From this context came the so-called doctrine of the mask or antiself (though not actually wholly original with Yeats). From that in turn, or alongside it, came the concept of the daimon, "guardian genius," or minor deity for each human being, a concept fundamental to a number of the traditional sources already cited. The greatest of all possible unions, of course, was the ultimate one of humankind with God, natural with supernatural, or temporal with eternal. Because of the *scintilla* principle, however, also inherent in parts of the tradition (the universe's permeation with tiny fragments of godhead), the union of man and daimon became virtually equivalent to the ultimate divine union. This concept helps to explain a handful of otherwise misleading passages where Yeats occasionally seemed to be rejecting his usually dominant dualism for a momentary monism: For example, in "The Tower" man creates everything in the universe from his own soul, and in "Two Songs from a Play" whatever illuminates the darkness is from man's own heart. Such human wholeness and power, however, are not possible, Yeats would probably say, without communion with daimon.

In spirit, doctrine, or belief, then, Yeats remained preponderantly a romantic and a nineteenth century spiritualist as he lived on into the increasingly positivistic and empirically oriented twentieth century. It was in form, not content, that he gradually allowed himself to develop in keeping with his times, although he abjured *vers libre* and never wholly relinquished his attachment to various traditional poetic modes. In the direction of modernism, he adopted or employed at various times irregular rhythms (writing by ear, declaring his ignorance of the technicalities of conventional metrics), approximate rhymes, colloquial diction, some Donnean or "metaphysical" qualities, and, most important of all, symbolic techniques much like those of the French movement, though not from its influence alone. The inimitable Yeatsian hallmark, however, remained a certain romantic rhetorical quality (despite his own fulminations against rhetoric), what he called passionate syntax, that remarkable gift for just the right turn of phrase to express ecstatic emotional intensity or to describe impassioned heroic action.

To suggest that Yeats consistently achieved great poetry through various combinations of these thematic elements and stylistic devices, however, would be less than forthright. Sometimes doctrinal materials are indeed impediments. Sometimes other aspects of content are unduly personal or sentimental. At times the technical components seem to be ill-chosen or fail to function as might have been expected, individually or conjointly. Thoroughly capable of writing bad poetry, Yeats has by no means been without his detractors. The poems for which he is famous, however—even those which present difficulties of understanding—are masterpieces, alchemical transformations of the raw material of his art.

Probably the most famous of all Yeats's poems, especially from his early period and with popular audiences, is "The Lake Isle of Innisfree." A middle-income Dublin housewife of today, chosen at random, said upon mention of Yeats's name: "Oh, yes; I like his 'Lake Isle of Innisfree'; yes, I always did like 'The Lake Isle of Innisfree.'" Such popularity, as well as its representative quality among Yeats's early poems, makes the piece a natural choice for initial consideration here.

On the surface, there seems to be little that is symbolic or difficult about this brief lyric, first published in 1890. The wavering rhythms, syntactical inversions, and colorful but sometimes hazy images are characteristic of much of Yeats's youthful verse. So too are the Romantic tone and setting, and the underlying "escape motif," a thematic element or pattern that pervades much of Yeats's early work, as he himself realized and acknowledged in a letter to a friend.

The island of the title—real, not imaginary—is located in Lough Gill near the Sligo of Yeats's youth. More than once he mentioned in prose a boyish dream of living on the wooded isle much as Henry David Thoreau lived at Walden Pond, seeking wisdom in solitude. In other passages he indicates that while homesick in London he heard the sound of a small fountain in the window of a shop. The experience recalled Lough Gill's lapping waters, he says, and inspired him to write the poem. The most important factor for Yeats's emerging poetic vision, however, was his longstanding fascination with a legend about a supernatural tree that once grew on the island with berries that were food for the Irish fairy folk. Thus in the poet's imaginative thought, if not explicitly in the poem itself, esoteric or occult forces were at play, and in a figurative sense, at least, the escape involved was, in the words of the letter to his friend, "to fairyland," or a place much like it.

One of the most notable sources of praise for "The Lake Isle of Innisfree" was a letter from Robert Louis Stevenson in distant Samoa. Stevenson wrote that only two other passages of literature had ever captivated him as Yeats's poem did. Yeats himself said later that it was the earliest of his nonnarrative poems whose rhythms significantly manifested his own music. He ultimately developed negative feelings, however, about his autobiographical sentimentality and about instances of what he came to consider unduly artificial syntax. Yet in late life when he was invited to recite some of his own poems for radio programs, he more than once chose to include "The Lake Isle of Innisfree." Evidently he wished to offer to that audience what he felt it probably wanted to hear. Evidently he realized that the average Irish housewife or ordinary working man, then as later, would say in response to the name Yeats: "Oh, yes, I like his 'Lake Isle of Innisfree.'"

Technically, "Leda and the Swan" (1923) is a sonnet, one of only a few that Yeats ever composed. The spaces between quatrains in the octave and between the octave and the sestet—not to mention the break in line eleven—are evidently Yeats's innovations, characteristic of his inclination toward experimentation within traditional frameworks in the period of the poem's composition. The story from Greek mythology upon which the poem is based is well-known and much treated in the Western tradition. In the tale from antiquity, a Spartan queen, Leda, was so beautiful that Zeus, ruler of the gods, decided that he must have her. Since the immortals usually did not present themselves to humankind in their divine forms, Zeus changed himself into a great swan and in that shape ravished the helpless girl. The story has often been portrayed pictorially as well as verbally; Yeats himself possessed a copy of a copy of Michelangelo's lost painting on the subject. There has been considerable critical discussion of the degree of interrelationship between the picture or other graphic depictions and Yeats's poem, but to no very certain conclusion, except that Leda seems much less terrified in Michelangelo's visual version—where perhaps she might even seem to be somewhat receptive—than in Yeats's verbal one.

The poem has been one of Yeats's most widely praised pieces from the time of early critical commentaries in the first decade after his death. Virtually all commentators dwell upon the power, economy, and impact of the poem's language and imagery, especially in the opening sections, which seem to be concerned predominantly, if not exclusively, with mere depiction of the scene and events themselves. The poem's apparent simplicity, especially by Yeatsian standards, however, is decidedly deceptive. The greatest problem in interpretation is with the sestet's images of Troy in flames and with Agamemnon's death.

To understand the importance of these allusions to Greek history—and the deeper meanings of the poem—the reader must realize that Yeats intended the poem to represent the annunciation of a new era of civilization in his cyclic vision of history, the two-thousand-year-period of pagan polytheism that preceded the present age of Christian monotheism. As emphasized in Giorgio Melchiori's book *The Whole Mystery of Art* (1961), the poet later imaginatively balanced a second poem against "Leda and the Swan": "The Mother of God," in which another woman, Mary, is visited by another deity, the Holy Ghost, in the form of another bird, the divine dove, to initiate another period of history, the Christian era. The conscious intention of such a parallel between the two poems is attested by Yeats's having printed "Leda and the Swan" at the head of the chapter in *A Vision* entitled "Dove or Swan," with a sentence on the next page stating explicitly that he thought of the annunciation which began Grecian culture as having been made to Leda. Equally unequivocal evidences are Melchiori's citation of a letter in which Yeats called the poem a classic annunciation, Yeats's note for the poem that speaks of a violent annunciation, and the fact that the poem's first submission to a publisher was under the title "Annunciation."

This last-mentioned fact relates to another point of critical disagreement. In a note, Yeats says that the poem was written in response to a request from the editor of a political review. As he worked, though, the girl and the swan took over the scene, he says, and all politics fell away. Some commentators have accepted or reaffirmed this assertion, failing to realize that Yeats—intentionally or unintentionally—overstated the case. Bird and woman did indeed so dominate the poet's imagination in the first eight lines that one critical consequence has been undue attention to the language and imagery of the surface there. When one recalls, however, that the pre-Christian era in Yeats's system was governmentally monarchical or totalitarian while the present era was imagined (however erroneously) as predominantly democratic, the perception dawns that the affairs of Leda's progeny, especially Helen as a causal factor in the Trojan War and Clytemnestra as a figure involved in its aftermath, constitute, in truth, "politics" enough. Otherwise, the allusions to the burning city and deceased king would be gratuitous deadwood in the poem, unaccountable anomalies, which is just exactly what they remain in those analyses that disregard them or minimize their importance.

Even recognition and acceptance of the themes of annunciation and history do not reveal the poem's full complexity, however, as the average reader may well sense upon perusal of the final interrogative sentence. This concluding question seems to constitute a third unit in the piece, as well as the basis of some third level of significance. The traditional octave-sestet relationship of the Italian sonnet created for Yeats a division into two parts with two different but related emphases. It is his unconventional break in line eleven, however, which achieves a tripartite structure at the same time that it introduces the thematic bases for an amalgamating—if not resolving—unity for all three parts of the poem and for all their interrelated levels of symbolic implication.

If the octave can be said to focus predominantly upon the "surface" level of "Leda and the Swan," with the allusions to antiquity adumbrating a historical level, then the final question—a real one rather than the rhetorical sort with which Yeats sometimes concluded poems—can be seen as the introduction of a philosophical or metaphysical level. Given the possibility of such consort or interaction between the human and the divine, what supernatural effects—if any—are consequent for the mortal party? This issue, so relevant to the rest of this poem, is raised not only here or a few times in related pieces like "The Mother of God," but rather over and over again throughout the entirety of Yeats's canon. More than that, it is frequently voiced in those other places in surprisingly similar terms.

The possibility of union between humankind and God, between natural and supernatural, is probably the most persistent and pervasive theme in all of Yeats's oeuvre. It is the strongest of those threads woven throughout the fabric of his work which create the unity within multiplicity previously considered. It was also unquestionably the motivating factor in his relentlessly moving from one occult preoccupation to the other. Moreover, the conviction that artistic inspiration was one of the more readily observable manifestations of such divine visitation upon the human sensibility made Yeats philosophically a confessed Romantic for life, regardless of what modernist elements of style or technique he may have allowed to emerge in the poetry of his later years.

A major emblem for such miraculous converse, elsewhere in Yeats just as in "Leda and the Swan," is sexual union. In several prose passages, for example, he draws explicit parallels between human interaction with the daimon or semidivine guardian spirit and a man's relationship with his sweetheart or lover. In another place, he conjectures that the "mystic way" and physical love are comparable, which is not surprising in light of the fact that most of his occult sources employed the same analogy and frequently spoke of the moment of union—mortal with immortal—as the "mystic marriage." Yeats's utilization of this particular sexual symbology is apparent in pieces such as "Solomon and the Witch," "A Last Confession," "Chosen," and *The Player Queen*, among others. Equally relevant is the fact that Yeats repeatedly used birds as symbols of discarnate spirits or deities. Finally, the two motifs—sexual union as an analogue for supernatural union and avian symbolism for the divine—occur together in at least two works by Yeats other than "Leda and the Swan": the plays *At the Hawk's Well* (1916) and *The Herne's Egg* (1938), in the latter of which copulation between a woman and a great white bird is similarly fundamental to the piece's philosophical implications.

In Yeats's imaginative thought, such moments of transcendent union leave behind in the physical world some vestige of the divine condescension—the art object's "immortality" in the case of inspiration, for example. In more portentous instances, however, such as those imaged in "Leda and the Swan" and "The Mother of God"—with clear metaphorical interplay between the phenomena of creation and procreation, even if not voiced in so many words—the remnant is the conception of some demigod or incarnate divinity such as Helen or Christ, whose beauty, perfection, or power is so great that its presence on earth inaugurates a whole new cultural dispensation.

What one ultimately finds in "Leda and the Swan," then, is Yeats hammering out, in the midst of manifold antinomy, two kinds of unity at a single stroke. The three somewhat separate parts of the poem are joined in unity with one another, and, simultaneously, the poem as a unified whole is united to some of the most important themes that recur through-out his canon. This unity within multiplicity is achieved through Yeats's ingeniously imaginative manipulation of a single famous myth chosen from many that involve—either or both—godhead manifested in avian form and divine visitation upon humankind cast in the image of sexual conjuga-tion.

Almost as synonymous with Yeats's name as "The Lake Isle of Innis-free" is the unusual and foreboding poem "The Second Coming," which was composed in January, 1919, and first published in 1920. It is one of Yeats's few unrhymed poems, written in very irregular blank verse whose rhythms perhaps contribute to the ominous effect created by the diction and imagery. The piece has had a strange critical reception, deriving in part from the paradox that it is one of Yeats's works most directly related to the system of history in *A Vision*, but at the same time appears to offer reasonably accessible meanings of a significant kind to the average reader of poetry in English.

The more obvious "meanings," generally agreed upon, are implications of disorder, especially in the first section where the falcon has lost touch with the falconer, and impressions of horror, especially in the second section with its vision of the pitiless rough beast slouching through the desert. In the light of the date of composition, the validity of such thematic elements for both Yeats and his audience is immediately evident. World War I had just ended, leaving the Western world in that continuing mood of despondency voiced also in T. S. Eliot's *The Waste Land* (1922) (which shares with Yeats's poem the desert image) and in Gertrude Stein's—and Ernest Hemingway's—epithet of "a lost generation." In other words, de-spite the author's considerable further concerns, the piece on this level "caught a wave," as it were, so that it quickly came to be regarded by commentators and the author alike as prophetic—an attitude enhanced, of course, by the richly allusive title.

On a deeper level, "The Second Coming" is directly related to the cyclical conception of history which Yeats delineated in *A Vision*. As seen in the discussion of "Leda and the Swan," Yeats envisioned history in terms of two-thousand-year eras, each of which was ushered in by a portentous annunciation of some sort. If Zeus's descent upon Leda initiated the period from about 2000 B.C. to the year zero, and if the Holy Ghost's descent to Mary initiated the subsequent period from the year zero to approximately A.D. 2000, then in 1919 the poet could speculate that the next such annunciation might occur either just barely within his lifetime or else not very long thereafter. These two-thousand-year periods of culture were characterized, like so many other things in Yeats's imaginative thought, by opposition to each other, with the main oppositions in *A Vision* designated as "antithetical" (or "subjective") and "primary" (or "objective"). These labels, or "tinctures" as Yeats called them, are not always easy to define, but from reading his book one begins to sense their nature. In general, the antithetical is individualistic (self-centered), heroic, aristocratic, emotional, and aesthetic. It is concerned predominantly with inner being and is symbolized by a full moon. The primary, by contrast, is anti-individualistic (mass-oriented), saintly or sagelike, democratic, rational, and moral. It is associated mainly with external existence and is symbolized by either the sun or the dark of the moon. Yeats identified himself with the antithetical and associated many things that he disliked (such as democracy and "fact-finding" science) with the primary. Thus he favored the polytheistic era of Homeric and classical Greece (antithetical), whereas he rejected or spurned the moral and anti-individualistic monotheism (primary) which began with the birth of Christ.

Borrowing from Swedenborg and other esoteric sources, Yeats conceptualized the growth of these historical movements in terms of gyres or spirals, a feature of the system rather difficult to discuss without reference to diagrams. (One may see *A Vision* for diagrams in great sufficiency.) For the sake of convenience in depiction, the spirals (widening from vertex in larger and larger circles) are imaged as the outer "shells" surrounding them—that is, as cones. Furthermore, for purposes of two-dimensional representation on a book's page, each cone is usually regarded simply in terms of its profile—that is, as a triangle. However, since the entire system of *A Vision* is based on the proposition that the universe consists of numberless pairs of antinomies or contraries, no cone or triangle exists in isolation; instead, everyone is in locked interpenetration with an opposing cone or triangle, each with its vertex or narrowest point at the center of the other's widest expansion or base. Thus, Yeats conceived of the present two-thousand-year era not simply as one set of interlocked cones, but rather as two sets of one thousand years each, as is made quite explicit in the chapter that reviews history under the title "Dove or Swan." Thus, instead of the Christian gyre or cone sweeping outward toward its widest expansion at the year A.D. 2000, as most commentators seem to have assumed, the widest expansion of the triangle representing that "primary" religious dispensation occurred at about the year A.D. 1000, completely in keeping with the medieval Church's domination of virtually all aspects of life at that time. For the period following A.D. 1000, that religion's declining movement is represented by a contracting gyre, its base set against the base of its predecessor, forming, in two-dimensional terms, a figure that Yeats speaks of as shaped like an ace of diamonds. The Christian dispensation, then, is at the present time dwindling to its cone's or triangle's narrowest point, at the center of the opposing gyre's widest expansion, completely in keeping with the post-Darwinian upheaval in Victorian England about science's undermining the foundations of the Church, subsequent notions of the "death of God," and so on.

What, then, is spiraling outward to its widest expansion in the twentieth century, the falcon's gyring flight having swept so far from the falconer that "the centre cannot hold"? The answer to this question lies in recognition of a point that appears rather clearly at various places in *A Vision*. In Yeats's system of history, every cone representing a religious dispensation has as its interlocking counterpart a cone that represents the secular culture of the same period. Thus, the two movements, religious and secular, live each other's death and die each other's life, to use an expression from Heraclitus that Yeats repeated time and again, in creative pieces as well as in his discursive prose. The birth of Christ came, then, as Yeats indicates with unequivocal clarity, at the time of an "antithetical" secular or political phenomenon at the very height of its development, at the widest expansion of its cone—the Roman Empire. As the gyre representing the "primary" Christian religious movement revolved outward toward its widest expansion in the Middle Ages, the power of the Roman Empire gradually declined until it vanished at about A.D. 1000 (Yeats uses the year 1050 in "Dove or Swan"). Then both movements reversed directions, with primary Christianity beginning to dwindle at the same time that a new secular life of antithetical nature started and gyred outward up to the present day. This—the widest expansion of an antithetical secular or political gyre in the twentieth century—is almost certainly what Yeats identified with Fascism, not the new annunciation to come. Such a collapsing and reexpansion of the antithetical spirals in the two-thousand-year period since the birth of Christ—two one-thousand-year cones tip to tip—created what Yeats called an hourglass figure superimposed upon (or, more accurately, interlocked with) the diamond shape of Christianity's primary religious dispensation.

The crucial point in interpreting "The Second Coming" is that the annunciation of every new religious dispensation involves what Yeats calls an interchange of the tinctures. In other words, at 2000 B.C., at the year zero, and at A.D. 2000, religion changes from primary to antithetical in quality, or vice versa, while secular life and politics change tinctures just oppositely. (Yeats was explicit about identification of the secular with politics.) No such interchange occurs, however, at the initiation of new secular gyres, as at 1000 B.C. or A.D. 1000. At those points the expanding or collapsing gyres of both aspects of life—religious and secular—simply reverse directions without their tinctures changing from primary to antithetical or the other way around. The importance of this feature of the system for meanings in "The Second Coming" can hardly be overstated. The interchange is sudden and cataclysmic, causing such strife in human history as the Trojan War soon after the annunciation to Leda from Zeus or the widespread battles of the Roman Empire soon after the annunciation from the Holy Ghost to the Virgin Mary. The abrupt change near the end of the twentieth century, of the antithetical tincture from secular life's widely expanded cone to religion's extremely narrowed one (and, vice versa, of the primary tincture almost instantaneously from the nearly extinguished religious gyre to the widest expansion of the counterpoised secular or political gyre), could in and of itself be catastrophic enough to warrant most of the portentous imagery and diction in Yeats's poem. Fearful concerns even more specifically related to the system than that, however, were involved in the piece's genesis and evolution. The annunciation of a new religious dispensation, antithetical in nature, would not have been anticipated by Yeats with foreboding, for he simultaneously favored the antithetical tincture and held in low regard the existing primary religious movement which was to be displaced. The only disappointing thing for Yeats about the forthcoming antithetical religion was that it would have no more than its merest beginnings within his lifetime or shortly thereafter, reaching its fullest expansion as a historical gyre not until the year A.D. 3000. The sudden imposition upon the world of a primary political system, on the other hand, at its widest expansion from the very outset, was quite another matter.

What might constitute such an ultra-primary or super-"democratic" political phenomenon for the aristocratic-minded Yeats as he looked about the European world in 1919? Other than the last stages of World War I, one particular violent upheaval had just occurred: the Bolshevik Revolution. Communism was for Yeats the horrifying rough beast slouching through the postwar wasteland to be born, its politically primary hour come round exactly as predicted by the gyres and cycles of history available to him from the "automatic scripts" which his wife had begun to write out more than a year before the poem's composition.

While this interpretational conclusion can be reached through a careful reading of *A Vision*'s sections on history, its validity has been made virtually unequivocal by Jon Stallworthy's publication of the poem's manuscript drafts (originally in his book *Between the Lines: Yeats's Poetry in the Making*, 1963, and again with fuller transcription of some partially illegible passages in the journal *Agenda*, 1971/1972). Along with several other convincing clues in these drafts occurs one line that leaves little to the imagination: "The Germany of Marx has led to Russian Com." Working with these same unpublished drafts as well as other materials, Donald Torchiana has made a persuasive case for the proposition that what upset Yeats most of all was the possibility that Ireland's civil strife in this same period made his country a highly vulnerable tinderbox for the spread of Marxist factions or Communistic forces (*W. B. Yeats and Georgian Ireland*, 1966). A letter by Yeats written later in 1919 makes this thesis virtually incontrovertible. In it the poet states that his main concern was for Ireland to be saved from Marxist values, because he felt that their fundamental materialism could only lead to murder. Then he quotes a catch-phrase that seems to echo lines from "The Second Coming": "Can the bourgeois be innocent?"

The manuscripts reveal much else as well. They show, for example, that from its earliest inception–a brief prose draft of the opening portion–"The Second Coming" was a decidedly political poem, not one concerned with some antithetical religious annunciation. Even the highly effective–though intentionally ironical–religious allusions to Bethlehem and Christ's return emerged relatively late in the poem's development. Moreover, the politics of concern are plainly of the primary tincture; the word "mob" appears repeatedly. When the expression "surely" occurred for the first time, it was followed by "the great falcon must come." Yeats, however, having said in a much-quoted passage elsewhere that he often used large noble birds to represent the subjective or antithetical and beasts that run upon the ground to symbolize the objective or primary, realized his momentary drift toward depiction of the birth of an antithetical religious entity and struck the line. Then later came the famous beast, with its blank solar (primary) gaze.

Although it might shock some readers to think that Yeats would identify Christ with a beast, and with a political ideology such as Marxism, the point that should not be overlooked is that while Christ may be alternately sacred or secular in Yeats's imaginative thought, He is always unalterably "primary." *A Vision* is quite explicit in several places about Christ's being primary. The poem is therefore, about His second coming, although in a frighteningly unfamiliar secular guise: a mass-oriented and anti-individualistic political materialism that paradoxically corresponds to but simultaneously contravenes His previous mass-oriented and anti-individualistic spiritual teachings. After twenty centuries of religious equality urged by Christ the Lamb, a cataclysmic and leveling social anarchy is about to be loosed upon the world by Christ the Lion.

Composed in 1926 and published in 1927, "Among School Children" is another of Yeats's most widely acclaimed and extensively studied poems. The two most "famous" interpretative readings are by Cleanth Brooks in *The Well Wrought Urn: Studies in the Structure of Poetry* (1947) and John Wain in *Interpretations: Essays on Twelve English Poems* (1955). Although both essays are almost belligerently "New Critical," each sees as the overall theme the relationships between natural and supernatural, or between matter and spirit, and the ravages wrought upon humankind by the passage of time. Most other analyses tend to accept this same general meaning for the poem as a whole, although almost inevitably there have been some who see the subject as the triumph of art, or something of that sort. With this poem, the problems and difficulties of interpretation have been not so much with larger suggestions of significance as with individual lines or passages in their relationships—or supposed relationships—to the poem's broadest meanings. Such tendencies toward agreement about the piece's general thematic implications are fortunate since they are in keeping with Yeats's own comments in notes and letters: that physical or temporal existence will waste the youthful students and that the poem is one of his not infrequent condemnations of old age.

The inspirational matrix for the poem was literal enough—a visit by Yeats in his role as senator in the newly established Irish Free State to a quite progressive school administered by a Catholic convent. Given this information, the reader will have no problems with stanza I. (Any analysis, incidentally, which suggests that Yeats felt that the children depicted were being taught the wrong kinds of things is open to question, for Yeats subsequently spoke to the senate about the convent school in highly laudatory terms.) The next three stanzas, however, although they are generally thought to be less problematical than the last part of the poem, are somewhat more opaque than the casual-toned and low-keyed opening. In stanza II, the sight of the schoolchildren suddenly brings to the poet-senator's memory (with little transition for the reader) a scene in which a beautiful woman had told him of some childhood chastisement, probably by a schoolteacher. That memory, in turn, evokes for him a vision of what she must have looked like at such an age, perhaps not too much unlike the girls standing before him in the convent's hall.

There can be little doubt that the beautiful woman in question is the one by whom Yeats's aching "heart" was "driven wild" for a large part of his adult life—Maud Gonne. Time and time again throughout his canon, Yeats compares that special woman's almost divine or superhuman beauty to the beauty of Helen of Troy, who, in Greek mythology, was born to Leda after her visitation by Zeus. This information, then, helps to clarify such characteristically allusive terms in stanzas II through IV as "Ledaean body," "daughters of the swan," "every paddler's heritage," "Ledaean kind," and "pretty plumage." The alteration of Plato's parable (in the *Symposium*, probably one of the middle dialogues, where the basis of love is explained as the desire in divinely separated humankind for reunion in a sphere) to union in the white and yellow of a single egg, rather than the myth's division, also fits into this pattern of Ledaean imagery, at the same time that it looks forward to images and suggestions of generation or birth in subsequent stanzas.

Then, in stanza IV, with still another shift, the beautiful woman's present visage drifts before the poet's eyes. Surprisingly, despite the rather heavily connotative language of lines three and four, along with Yeats's comparison in the second quatrain of his own youth with his present old age (not to mention similar thematic implications in the entire poem), there has been some controversy about line one. The issue is whether Yeats meant to convey a vision of the woman still young and beautiful or, instead, ravaged by time and decrepitude. The word "Quattrocento," denoting fifteenth century Italian art and artists, might be taken to substantiate either side of such a debate, depending upon how it itself is construed; but along with virtually everything else in the stanza, the concluding–and later recurring–scarecrow image would seem to lend support to the suggestion of deterioration and decay.

If lines two through four of stanza V were removed, the stanza would not only be completely intelligible, but it would also be a rather concise statement of one of the poem's two main themes—the effects upon humankind of time's passage. Since lines two through four were included, however, along with other characteristically Yeatsian elements akin to them in subsequent stanzas, the poem's real difficulties begin to manifest themselves in its second half. In a note to the poem, Yeats indicates that the honey of generation is an image that he borrowed from Porphyry's essay "The Cave of the Nymphs," almost certainly with an intended symbolic suggestion, on one level, of the pleasures of sexual union. The same note, however, also indicates explicitly that the recollection mentioned is the soul's memory–à la William Wordsworth's "Ode: Intimations of Immortality"–of a prenatal condition higher and freer than earthly incarnation. At this point, Yeats's occult and esoteric beliefs that so many twentieth century critics have found difficult to accept enter the poem. Brooks's reaction, for example, is virtual incredulity. To make interpretational matters even worse, Yeats evidently employed the honey image ambiguously to relate also to "the drug," presumably physically procreated or temporal existence, which allows or causes the prenatal memory to fade. Both the note and the draft versions of the poem (reproduced in Thomas Parkinson's *W. B. Yeats: The Later Poetry*, 1964) suggest the likelihood of such intentional or semi-intentional ambiguity. All this, along with what is probably the poem's least felicitous line—"sleep, shriek, struggle . . ."—has led to considerable exegetical dispute about who or what was betrayed—mother or shape? The ambiguity seems less intentional in this particular case, however, and the drafts, along with a certain amount of common sense, tend to indicate the child, a soul entrapped in flesh by the mother's generatively honeyed act.

Stanza VI is perhaps not too difficult once the reader realizes that the final line is, in effect, appositionally related to the main nouns in the other seven lines. In other words, the generally accepted thrust of meaning is that even the greatest and presumably wisest of men come to be, in time, like elderly poet-senators and everyone else, dilapidated old scarecrows. There is, however, a bit more wit and symbolism at work—or at play—in the stanza. For one thing, Yeats has chosen men who were teachers or students or—in two cases—both in turn: Plato, Aristotle, Alexander the Great, and Pythagoras. Furthermore, three of these four men spent their lives contemplating and theorizing about the same crucial and fundamental aspects of human experience which are the subjects of the poem—the relationships between spirit and matter and between being and becoming.

The second half of stanza VII is the most problematical unit in the poem. The first quatrain, however, gives little trouble. With a pun on the word "images," Yeats refers both to pictures in the maternal mind's eye and to religious icons or statuary. The Presences of line five are what create interpretational difficulties, again because here Yeats's occult views become involved, views which too few exegetes have been willing to address even as accepted by the poet himself. Yeats's use of a capital *P* and the expression "self-born" (compare "self-sown," "self-begotten," and "miracle-bred" on the very next page of *The Collected Poems of W. B. Yeats*) should be clues that some kind of divinity is being apostrophized in this stanza about worship. That, in turn, can lead to recognition of a third level of meaning for the punword "images." The mask, the antiself, and especially the daimon (not synonymous terms, but kindred ones in Yeats's esoteric thought and vocabulary) were sometimes referred to as the image, for they are, like a mirror image, simultaneously like and yet exactly opposite to the human individual. Furthermore, with the daimon, that special semidivine guiding or misguiding spirit, each man or woman is involved in an exasperating attraction-repulsion relationship which explains the poet's emphasis upon heartbreak and mockery. Fleetingly known—in actuality or by analogy—through such heightened experiences as the earlier stanzas' sexual love (passion), religious love (piety), or maternal love (affection), these hatefully loving guardian geniuses draw humanity onward from the flesh toward spiritual glory at the same time that they do all they can to frustrate every inch of progress or enterprise along the way.

The first half of the closing stanza would be much more readily comprehensible if Yeats had retained his draft's version of the opening line, which began with the word "all" instead of "labor." That would have agreed with a draft line relating to the dancer, "all so smoothly runs," and would justify the status usually attributed to the concluding quatrain: perhaps the most successful of Yeats's famous passages whose antinomy-resolving symbols or images lift poet, poem, and reader above the strife of physical existence to a condition of triumphant affirmation or realm of artistically perfected unity. Dance and dancer are indivisibly—almost divinely—one. The tree—and the poem—are supremely organic wholes, greater than the sums of their parts. This seems to be Romantic lyricism at its transcendent best.

Such a conclusion, however, is too hasty. When its initial word was "all," the first quatrain of the final stanza rather plainly meant something like, "Life in this world is best when and where humankind achieves a balance between body and soul, between spirit and flesh." Yeats's eventual substitution of the word "labor," however, could well have been intended to add, among other things, the idea that such a balance is never easily come by nor readily sustained in this life. That would echo in one sense the feminine persona in "Adam's Curse," who says that women have to labor to become beautiful, as well as her interlocutor's rejoinder that subsequent to Adam's fall nothing very fine can be achieved or created without a great deal of labor. How, then, did the poet move so suddenly from the broken hearts and mockery of stanza VII to some rhapsodically evoked unity or triumph in the last four lines of stanza VIII? Perhaps the poem was never meant to suggest such a leap. There is, after all, no journey in this poem from one realm to another, as there is in "Sailing to Byzantium." The tree and the dancer are still very much in the sensuous physical realm. Perhaps the supposed transition has been only through some strange magic as unsavory to common sense as Yeats's occult inclinations were to the critics who have perpetrated this illusory transmutation. Perhaps, ironically, the un-Romantic critics have made Yeats much more Romantic in this particular poem than he ever intended to be. In all fairness, the point must be acknowledged, however, that Brooks and Wain themselves read the final stanza in much more neutral or negative terms than many of the commentators who have written subsequently. Almost unquestionably the chief influence upon numerous analyses of the final stanza in terms of transcendence and artistic unity has been Frank Kermode's book *Romantic Image* (1957), which takes the passage as a virtual epitome of the opposition-resolving powers of the symbolic mode, as the image of the Image.

"Among School Children" has a rather high incidence of puns and intentional ambiguities in addition to the ones already noted. The two most obvious further instances involve the words "labor" and "play," which have been commented upon both separately and together. Perhaps insufficient attention has been given, however, to possibilities of multiple meanings in that salient feature, the title. Yeats, an inveterate reviser, was well capable of changing a title if it no longer best suited the interests of his poem. Why would he have retained the title here if it did not fit the finished piece—the whole work as well as the opening portions? Some continuing concern with the symbolic implications of students and teachers has already been observed in stanza VI. Why would not or could not the same kind of thing be appropriate for that very important portion of the poem, its conclusion? Suppose, in contrast to prevalent interpretations of the last quatrain, that the questions asked there are real questions, such as schoolchildren ask, rather than rhetorical ones implying some transcendence or triumph over the rest of the poem's concerns. Like a staring schoolchild, man might well ask—in fact, for centuries he has asked—where the material world ends and the spiritual world begins, and how, in this temporal realm, he can separate the one from the other. The great rooted blossomer, then, may be more an emblem of the puzzles and problems studied in life's schoolroom than of some artistically achieved solution to them. Is man the newborn infant, the adolescent pupil, the youthful procreator, or the white-haired elder statesman—or none of these or all of these or more than all of these? In the face of such conundrums, all men are "among school children," seeking and inquiring, frequently without finding or being given reassuring answers.

No work in Yeats's canon has won more renown or elicited more controversy than the so-called Byzantium poems, "Sailing to Byzantium" (1927) and "Byzantium" (1930). Critical opinion as to which is poetically superior has been almost, if not quite, equally divided. There is almost universal agreement, however, that the earlier and more frequently reprinted piece, "Sailing to Byzantium," is the easier to understand.

Several authorities, in fact, have gone so far as to say that "Sailing to Byzantium" explains itself or needs no extensive clarification; but if such were actually the case, the amount of commentary that it has generated would clearly constitute an anomaly. If nothing else, the general reader ought to have some answer to the almost inevitable question, "Why Byzantium?" Though it does not provide every possible relevant response to such a query, a much-quoted passage from *A Vision* indicates some of the more important reasons why and how Yeats came to let that great Near Eastern city of medieval times represent in his imagination a cultural, artistic, and spiritual ideal. He believes, he says, that one might have found there "some philosophical worker in mosaic" with "the supernatural descending nearer to him than to Plotinus even," that in "early Byzantium" perhaps more than at any other time in history "religious, aesthetic and practical life were one." Artists of all kinds expressed "the vision of a whole people," "the work of many that seemed the work of one" and was the "proclamation of their invisible master."

While there is no question whatever that "Sailing to Byzantium" is a richly symbolic poem, its genesis apparently involved a more or less literal level which, even though it has not been ignored, may not have been stressed in all its particulars as much as might be warranted. Yeats was first exposed to Byzantine art during a Mediterranean tour in 1907 which included Ravenna, where he saw mosaics and a frieze in the Church of San Apollinare Nuovo which is generally regarded as the chief basis of imagery in stanza III of "Sailing to Byzantium." Years later, however, two factors coincided to renew his interest, one of them involving a voyage in certain respects interestingly akin to that in the poem. In the first half of the 1920's, Yeats had read rather widely about Byzantium in connection with his work on the historical "Dove or Swan" section of *A Vision.* Then in 1924, nearing sixty years of age, he became somewhat ill and suffered high blood pressure and difficulty in breathing. He was advised to stop work and was taken by his wife on another Mediterranean tour, this time seeking out other Byzantine mosaics, and similar craftsmanship that sharply contrasted art with nature, at places such as Monreale and Palermo, Sicily. As at least one commentator has pointed out, Yeats had no great regrets about leaving home at this time because of dissatisfaction with the political situation and depression about his health. The first legible words in the drafts of "Sailing to Byzantium" are "Farewell friends," and subsequent early portions make unequivocal the fact that "That country" in the finished poem is (or at least originally was) Ireland. Thus, the imaginative and poetic voyage of a sick old man leaving one locale for a more desirable one very probably had at least some of its antecedents in a rather similar actual journey a few years earlier.

Two symbolic interpretations of "Sailing to Byzantium" have been predominant by a considerable margin: Either the poem is about the state of the poet's spirit or soul shortly before and after death, or it is about the creative process and artistic achievement. A choice between the two might be said to pivot upon response to the question, "How ideal is the ideal?" In other words, does Byzantium represent this-worldly perfection on the aesthetic level or perfection of an even greater kind in a transcendent realm of existence? A not insignificant amount of the massive critical commentary on the poem (as well as on its sequel "Byzantium") has been in the way of a war of words about the "proper" reply to such a question, with surprisingly inflexible positions being taken by some of the combatants. Fortunately, however, a number of authorities have realized that there is no reason at all why both levels of meaning cannot obtain simultaneously and that, as a matter of fact, the poem becomes much more characteristically Yeatsian in its symbolic complexity and wealth of import if such a reading is accepted.

About 1926 or 1927 and thereafter, an apparent major change—with emphasis upon apparent—seems to have taken place in Yeats's attitude toward life. On the surface, "Sailing to Byzantium" may look and sound like the culmination of a long line of "escape" poems, while many poems or passages written after it seem to stress instead a plunge into the physicality of this world, even a celebration of earthly existence (as, for example, "A Dialogue of Self and Soul"). Even though Yeats continued to write poems very much concerned with transcendence, supernaturalism, and otherworldliness, he developed in his late career a "new" kind of poem. These poems were often short, were frequently presented in series or sequences, and were frequently—but not always—concerned with a particularly physical aspect of worldly existence, sex.

These poems also share other attributes, a number of them related to Yeats's revived interest at the time in the ballad form. One group is entitled, for example, *Words for Music Perhaps and Other Poems*, indicating their songlike qualities. In addition to the poems themselves being brief, the lines and stanza patterns are also short, the lines sometimes having as few as two stresses. Diction, syntax, and idiom are—again as in the ballad or folk song—colloquial and uncomplicated. Imagery, too, is earthy, sometimes stark or blunt. At times sound patterns other than rhyme contribute to the songlike effects, and some pieces, although not all, make effective use of the refrain as a device. In these verses Yeats has come a long way from the amorphous Pre-Raphaelitism of his early lyrics. In them, in fact, he achieves some of the most identifiably "modern" effects in his entire canon.

Related to that modernity is the fact that these late-life songs are anything but simple in content and meaning. Their deceptiveness in this regard has led some early critics to label them—especially the scatological ones—as tasteless and crude. More recent and perceptive analysts, however, have found them to be, in the words of one commentator, more nearly eschatological. What Yeats is doing thematically in such pieces, in fact, is by no means new to him. As in "Solomon and the Witch," "Leda and the Swan," and some other earlier pieces, he is using the sexual metaphor to explore some of the metaphysical mysteries of human existence. One significant difference, however, is that now the sexual experience itself sometimes seems to be regarded as something of a mystery in its own right.

Almost as well-known as Yeats himself is his fictive persona "Crazy Jane," evidently based compositely on two old Irish women from the poet's experience, one early, one late. Like Shakespeare's—and Yeats's—fools, however, Jane is usually "crazy like a fox." In her series of poems, in the "Three Bushes" sequence, and in poems such as "Chosen," "A Last Confession," "Her Anxiety," "Consolation," and "The Wild Old Wicked Man," Yeats considers or deals with sexuality and sexual imagery in some six or seven different, though frequently interrelated, ways. At times, the poet seems to vacillate or contradict himself from one poem to another, a habit that at first makes understanding these pieces rather difficult. After a while, however, the phenomenon can be recognized for what it is: Yeats's characteristic technique of shifting ground or altering angle of vision in order to explore his subject the more completely.

One basic use of the sexual image has already been seen: the union of man and woman is parallel to or representative of the union of natural with supernatural, human with divine, or man with daimon. In some of these poems, however, the union seems to be so overwhelming that it almost ceases to be mere symbol and becomes the thing in itself, as in the last stanza of "Chosen" or in an unpublished poem where even the gyres are laid to rest in the bed of love. On the other hand (and at the other extreme) are poems that suggest that sex just does not accomplish very much at all, as in "The Chambermaid's Second Song" (last in the "Three Bushes" sequence), where after mere physical pleasure man's spirit remains "blind as a worm." A poem of this kind echoes a reported statement by Yeats that the most unfortunate thing about coitus is the continuing "virginity of the soul." In between the two extremes are poems that see sex as little better than a *pis aller*—"Consolation," for example, or "The Wild Old Wicked Man," whose protagonist chooses "the second-best" upon "a woman's breast." Then there are poems that contemplate the pleasures or problems of sexuality in this life in the light of a Swedenborgian intercourse of the angels ("A Last Confession" and "Crazy Jane on the Day of Judgment") or the Hermetic paradigm—as above, so below ("Ribh Denounces Patrick," though this piece is not in the ballad tradition). Still other poems in the collection, instead of comparing bodies in this world with spirits in the otherworld, use sexual symbolism to ponder the conundrums of the body-soul relationship here on earth, a theme reminiscent of "Among School Children." The Lady's three songs in the "Three Bushes" series fall into this category. Finally, Yeats sometimes uses the transience of sexual experience to parallel the ephemeral nature of all human experience, especially such heightened moments as mystic vision or artistic inspiration. Such an ironic self-consuming quality inherent in the sex act is touched upon in the first stanza of "Crazy Jane and Jack the Journeyman" and in "Her Anxiety," among other places.

As indicated earlier in the biographical section, Yeats continued to work on poems and plays right down to the last day but one before his death. Although "Under Ben Bulben" was not his last poem, it was written quite consciously as a valedictory or testamentary piece in the summer and fall of 1938 when Yeats knew that death was not far away. While such a status for the poem has been widely recognized by authorities from a very early date, surprisingly little has been written about it until relatively recently.

Ben Bulben is the impressive west-Irish headland "under" whose shadow Yeats specified that his body be buried in the churchyard at Drumcliff where his great-grandfather had been rector a century earlier. In draft versions, "Under Ben Bulben" had two previous titles: "His Convictions" and "Creed." Furthermore, the opening lines that read "Swear by" in the finished poem originally read "I believe." Here, then, presumably, if anywhere, one should be able to find Yeats's final views on life and the human condition. Because the poem goes on, however, to indicate quite candid belief in the existence of supernatural spirits and, further still, in reincarnation or transmigration of the soul, modern critics who do not accept such quasi-religious views have evidently declined to take the piece very seriously. One apparent consequence has been that they have had little adequate basis for understanding or glossing the epitaph with which the poem concludes.

Ironically, the epitaph has been very often quoted: "Cast a cold eye/ On life, on death./ Horseman, pass by!" Exegetical commentary on these three lines, however, has been almost as rare as that on the larger poem. Explication has been so minimal and inconclusive, in fact, that as late as 1974 one spokesman, Edward Malins, asserted that determination of the epitaph's meaning and its intended audience "is anybody's guess." In terms of the framing poem's thesis of transmigration, however, along with evidence from other sources, the horseman can be identified as Yeats himself, a cosmic journeyer engaged in a vast round of cyclical deaths and rebirths, as outlined in *A Vision.* A cold eye is cast on both life and death because the point of possible release from the wheel of reincarnation to some ultimate beatific state such as that imaged in "Sailing to Byzantium" is at such great distance that the grave is little more than a way station on the cosmic odyssey. Thus, there is time or place for little more than a passing nod or glance toward either life or death. In the words of a passage from *A Vision* that is virtually a prose counterpart of the epitaph's verse, man's spirit can know nothing more than transitory happiness either between birth and death or between death and rebirth; its goal is to "pass rapidly round its circle" and to "find freedom from that circle."

The means of passing rapidly around *A Vision*'s great wheel is to live each incarnation properly "in phase." Failure in this endeavor can cause rebirth again into the same phase, thus slowing progress toward "freedom" or release. From his youthful days as a disciple of Walter Pater, Yeats had long regarded the living of life itself as an art. With the coming of *A Vision,* teleological impetus was added to this aesthetic conviction. In a note on "Sailing to Byzantium" from a radio script and in several poems, Yeats exclaims that he must "make his soul." In the terms of *A Vision,* then, once he knew the prescribed qualities of his current incarnation or phase on the wheel, he must shape and sculpt his very life until it becomes a concrete manifestation of that phase, a mythopoeic *objet d'art.*

In *Autobiographies,* on the other hand, Yeats states that when great artists were at their most creative the rest was not simply a work of art, but rather the "re-creation of the man through that art." Similarly, in a scrap of verse he said that whenever he remade a poem the real importance of the act was that, in the event, he actually remade himself. Thus emerged the ultimate unity. Yeats's life and his work became two sides of the one coin. The phenomena were mutually interdependent, the processes mutually interactive. As he forged his poems, Yeats also created his self. That created self, a living myth, was in turn the image reflected in his poetry, the center of vision embodied in the verbal constructs of his art.

Other literary forms · William Butler Yeats was a playwright as well as a poet. During certain periods in his career he devoted more time and energy to the composition, publication, and production of plays in verse or prose than to the writing of nondramatic poetry. These plays, excluding several early closet dramas, were republished singly or in various collections from 1892 through the year of his death. *The Collected Plays of W. B. Yeats* was published in 1934, and a "new edition with five additional plays" appeared in 1952 (London) and 1953 (New York), the former being the "basic text." The genuinely definitive publication, however, is the admirably edited *Variorum Edition of the Plays of W. B. Yeats* (1966).

In addition to poems and plays, Yeats published prolifically during the course of his life in almost every imaginable genre except the novel. In fact, the record of such publications is so complex that little more than the merest outline can be given here. Numerous prose tales, book reviews, nationalistic articles, letters to editors, and so on far exceeded poems and plays in volume in the early stages of Yeats's career. In 1908, *The Collected Works in Verse and Prose of William Butler Yeats*–including lyrics, narrative poems, stories, plays, essays, prefaces, and notes–filled eight volumes, of which only the first contained predominantly nondramatic poetry. Previously, stories and sketches, many of them based wholly or in part upon Irish folk tales, had been collected in *The Celtic Twilight* (1893) and *The Secret Rose* (1897). Rewritten versions of those tales from *The Secret Rose* that featured a roving folk poet invented by Yeats were later published as *Stories of Red Hanrahan* (1904). Similarly, relatively formal critical and philosophical essays were collected and published as *Ideas of Good and Evil* (1903), *The Cutting of an Agate* (1912), and *Essays, 1931-1936* (1937).

A slender doctrinal book, *Per Amica Silentia Lunae* (1918), is generally regarded as something of a precursor to *A Vision*. The first edition of *A Vision* itself, an exposition of Yeats's mystical philosophy, appeared in 1925. A considerably revised edition first published in 1937 has revealed to scholars that while the book unquestionably owes much to Mrs. Yeats's "automatic writing," as avowed, more than a little of its content is generally based upon Yeats's or his and his wife's earlier occult interests and contacts. In 1926, Yeats published a volume entitled *Autobiographies*. In 1938, an American edition entitled *The Autobiography of William Butler Yeats* was released, with the addition of several sections or units which had been published separately or in groups in the interim. Then, in 1955 a final British issue appeared with the original title and one subunit not included in the American edition. A posthumous supplement to *Autobiographies* is *Memoirs* (1972), combining the draft of an earlier unpublished autobiography with a complete transcription of the private journal from which Yeats had used only selected portions in the post-1926 versions of his original book. A large and carefully edited collection of Yeats's correspondence, *The Letters of W. B. Yeats*, was published in 1954, and various smaller collections of correspondence with certain people have been published from time to time since the poet's death.

Most of Yeats's major prose, other than *A Vision, Autobiographies*, and his editor's introduction to *The Oxford Book of Modern Verse* (1936), has been collected and republished in three volumes printed simultaneously in

London and New York. *Mythologies* (1959) includes *The Celtic Twilight, The Secret Rose, Stories of Red Hanrahan*, the three so-called Rosa Alchemica stories from 1897 (which involve Yeats's fictional personae Michael Robartes and Owen Aherne), and *Per Amica Silentia Lunae*. *Essays and Introductions* (1961) incorporates *Ideas of Good and Evil*, most of *The Cutting of an Agate, Essays, 1931-1936*, and three introductions written in 1937 for portions of a projected edition of Yeats's works which never materialized. *Explorations* (1962) brings together a number of miscellaneous items, most of them previously not readily accessible. There are three introductions to books of legend and folklore by Lady Augusta Gregory, introductions to some of Yeats's own plays, a sizable body of his early dramatic criticism, the essay "If I Were Four-and-Twenty," *Pages from a Diary Written in Nineteen Hundred and Thirty*, and most of the author's last prose piece *On the Boiler*, a potpourri including late political philosophy.

As to fiction not already mentioned, two stories from 1891—a long tale and a short novel—have been republished in a critical edition, *John Sherman & Dhoya* (1969), and a fine scholarly edition of Yeats's early unfinished novel, *The Speckled Bird* (published in a limited edition in Dublin in 1974), was printed in 1976 as an item in the short-lived *Yeats Studies* series. In another highly competent piece of scholarship, almost all of the previously mentioned early book reviews, nationalist articles, and so on, as well as some later essays, have been edited and republished relatively recently in *Uncollected Prose by W. B. Yeats*, volume 1 in 1970 and volume 2 in 1976. Finally, the bewildering mass of Yeats's unpublished materials—thousands of pages of working drafts, notebooks, proof sheets, personal and family letters and papers, occult documents, automatic scripts, and the like—were made available on microfilm by the poet's son, Senator Michael Yeats, in 1975. Two sets of these films are housed, one each, at the National Library of Ireland and the State University of New York at Stony Brook. With the generous permission of Yeats's daughter and son, Anna and Michael, scholars are currently studying, transcribing, and editing many of these materials. Several books that employ or reproduce portions of them have been published. The first of a projected multivolume collection of Yeats's letters, *The Collected Letters of William Butler Yeats: Volume I, 1865-1895*, was published in 1986. Most of the letters included are from Yeats's twenties, when he was passionately involved with furthering two causes: his own career and Irish literature as a whole.

Select works other than poetry

SHORT FICTION: *John Sherman and Dhoya*, 1891, 1969; *The Celtic Twilight*, 1893; *The Secret Rose*, 1897; *The Tables of Law. The Adoration of the Magi*, 1897;

Stories of Red Hanrahan, 1904; *Mythologies*, 1959.

DRAMA: *The Countess Cathleen*, pb. 1892; *The Land of Heart's Desire*, pr., pb. 1894; *Cathleen ni Houlihan*, pr., pb. 1902 (with Lady Augusta Gregory); *The Pot of Broth*, pr. 1902 (with Lady Gregory); *The Hour-Glass*, pr. 1903, pr. 1912 (revised); *The King's Threshold*, pr., pb. 1903 (with Lady Gregory); *On Baile's Strand*, pr. 1904; *Deirdre*, pr. 1906 (with Lady Gregory); *The Shadowy Waters*, pr. 1906; *The Unicorn from the Stars*, pr. 1907 (with Lady Gregory); *The Golden Helmet*, pr., pb. 1908; *The Green Helmet*, pr., pb. 1910; *At the Hawk's Well*, pr. 1916; *The Player Queen*, pr. 1919; *The Only Jealousy of Emer*, pb. 1919; *The Dreaming of the Bones*, pb. 1919; *Calvary*, pb. 1921; *Four Plays for Dancers*, pb. 1921 (includes *Calvary*, *At the Hawk's Well*, *The Dreaming of the Bones*, and *The Only Jealousy of Emer*); *The Cat and the Moon*, pb. 1924; *The Resurrection*, pb. 1927; *The Words upon the Windowpane*, pr. 1930; *The Collected Plays of W. B. Yeats*, pb. 1934, 1952; *The King of the Great Clock Tower*, pr., pb. 1934; *A Full Moon in March*, pr. 1934; *The Herne's Egg*, pb. 1938; *Purgatory*, pr. 1938; *The Death of Cuchulain*, pb. 1939; *Variorum Edition of the Plays of W. B. Yeats*, pb. 1966 (Russell K. Alspach, editor).

NONFICTION: *Ideas of Good and Evil*, 1903; *The Cutting of an Agate*, 1912; *Per Amica Silentia Lunae*, 1918; *Essays*, 1924; *A Vision*, 1925, 1937; *Autobiographies*, 1926, 1955; *A Packet for Ezra Pound*, 1929; *Essays, 1931-1936*, 1937; *The Autobiography of William Butler Yeats*, 1938; *On the Boiler*, 1939; *If I Were Four and Twenty*, 1940; *The Letters of W. B. Yeats*, 1954; *The Senate Speeches of W. B. Yeats*, 1960 (Donald R. Pearce, editor); *Essays and Introductions*, 1961; *Explorations*, 1962; *Ah, Sweet Dancer: W. B. Yeats, Margot Ruddock—a Correspondence*, 1970 (Roger McHugh, editor); *Uncollected Prose by W. B. Yeats*, 1970, 1976 (2 volumes); *Memoirs*, 1972; *The Collected Letters of William Butler Yeats: Volume I, 1865-1895*, 1986.

MISCELLANEOUS: *The Collected Works in Verse and Prose of William Butler Yeats*, 1908.

James Lovic Allen

Bibliography · Critical literature on Yeats is so extensive as to be daunting. Balachandra Rajan, *W. B. Yeats: A Critical Introduction*, 2d ed. 1969, is a notable short introductory study, though less substantial than Richard Ellmann, *The Identity of Yeats*, 2d ed. 1964, and T. R. Henn, *The Lonely Tower: Studies in the Poetry of W. B. Yeats*, 2d ed. 1965. A. N. Jeffares' *A New Commentary on the Poems of W. B. Yeats*, 1984, and *A Commentary on the Collected Plays of W. B. Yeats*, 1975, are particularly helpful commentaries. Three specialist critical studies of important areas in Yeats's work are Thomas Parkinson, *W. B. Yeats Self Critic: A Study of His Early Verse*, 1951, repr. 1971 with *The Later Poetry* and a new foreword; Jon Stallworthy, *Between the Lines: W. B. Yeats's Poetry in the Making*, 1963, corrected 2d ed. 1965; and Thomas R. Whitaker, *Swan and Shadow: Yeats's Dialogue with History*, 1964.

An excellent critical biography is Richard Ellmann, *Yeats: The Man and the Masks*, 1948, rev. ed. 1978, and Frank Tuohy, *Yeats: An Illustrated Biography*, 1976, rev. ed. 1991, supplements a straightforward narrative with many excellent illustrations. Harold Bloom's *William Butler Yeats*, 1970, is also valuable. More recent studies include Bernard G. Krimm, *William Butler Yeats and the Emergence of the Irish Free State, 1918-39*, 1981; Raymond Cowell, ed., *Critics on Yeats*, 1979, and *Sligo: Land of Yeats' Desire*, 1989; G. M. Harper, *The Making of Yeats's "A Vision,"* 3 vols., 1987; Phillip Marcus, *Yeats and the Beginning of the Irish Renaissance*, 2d ed. 1987; Carmel Jordan, *A Terrible Beauty: The Easter Rebellion and Yeats's "Great Tapestry,"* 1987; Denis Donoghue, *William Butler Yeats*, 1971, repr. 1989; R. J. Finneran, ed., *Editing Yeats's Poems: A Reconsideration*, 2d ed. 1990; Stan Smith, *William Butler Yeats: A Critical Introduction*, 1990; C. B. Bradford, ed., *Yeats at Work*, 1990; Margery Brady, *The Love Story of Yeats and Maud Gonne*, 1990; A. M. White and A. N. Jeffares, eds., *The Gonne-Yeats Letters, 1893-1938*, 1993; M. L. Rosenthal, *Running to Paradise: Yeats's Poetic Art*, 1993; Elizabeth Cullingford, *Gender and History in Yeats's Love Poetry*, 1993; Sylvia C. Ellis, *The Plays of William Butler Yeats*, 1994; and A. D. F. Macrae, *William Butler Yeats: A Literary Life*, 1994.

YEVGENY YEVTUSHENKO

Born: Stantsiya Zima, U.S.S.R.; July 18, 1933

Poetry · *Razvedchicki gryadushchego*, 1952 · *Tretii sneg*, 1955 · *Stantsiya Zima*, 1956 (*Zima Junction*, 1962) · *Shossye entuziastov*, 1956 · *Obeshchaniy*, 1957 · *Luk i lira*, 1959 · *Stikhi raznykh let*, 1959 · *Yabloko*, 1960 · *Vzmakh ruki*, 1962 · *Selected Poetry*, 1963 ·*Nezhnost*, 1962 · *Bratskaya GES*, 1965 (*Bratsk Station and Other New Poems*, 1966) · *The Poetry of Yevgeny Yevtushenko 1953-1965*, 1965 · *Kachka*, 1966 · *Yevtushenko: Poems*, 1966 · *Poems Chosen by the Author*, 1967 · *Idut belye snegi*, 1969 · *Stolen Apples*, 1971 · *Doroga Nomer Odin*, 1972 · *Poyushchaya dambra*, 1972 · *Otsovskiy slukh*, 1975 · *From Desire to Desire*, 1976 · *Ivanovskiye sitsi*, 1976 · *V Polniy Rost*, 1977 · *Golub' v Sant'iago*, 1978 (novel in verse; *A Dove in Santiago*, 1983) · *Tyazholive zemli*, 1978 · *The Face Behind the Face*, 1979 · *Ivan the Terrible and Ivan the Fool*, 1979 · *Invisible Threads*, 1981 (poems and photographs) · *Ty na planete ne odin*, 1981 · *The Poetry of Yevgeny Yevtushenko*, 1981 · *Grazhdane, poslushaite menia*, 1989 · *Early Poems*, 1989 · *Stikhotvoreniya i poemy*, 1990 · *The Collected Poems, 1952-1990*, 1991

Achievements · Yevtushenko's appeal to a popular audience began with his first verses, which appeared in a sports magazine, *Sovjetskiy sport*, in 1949. His early publications, full of autobiographical revelations, charmed his audiences by their freshness and sincerity. After Joseph Stalin's death in 1953, Yevtushenko began to address deeper social and political issues and became known as a dissident voice in Soviet literature. During the period of liberalization under Nikita Krushchev in the late 1950's and early 1960's, Yevtushenko's personal and political poetry appeared in numerous Soviet journals and newspapers, including *Sovjetskiy sport, Yunost*, where he was on the editorial board, *Komsomolskaya pravda, Molodaya gvardiya, Literaturnaya gazeta, Pravda, Znamya, Ogonyok, Rossiya, Novy mir*, and *Oktyabr*. When *Stikhi raznykh let* (poems of various years) appeared in 1959, twenty thousand copies were sold immediately. The 1962 collection *Vzmakh ruki* (a wave of the hand) enjoyed a sale of one hundred thousand copies.

Not all of Yevtushenko's poetry, however, was so widely appreciated. When the controversial "Babiy Yar" was published in *Literaturnaya gazeta* in 1961, many hostile articles appeared in the Soviet press, such as that of D. Starikov in *Literatura i zhizn*. It was during this same period that Yevtushenko wrote the script for Dmitri Shostakovich's controversial Thirteenth Symphony (1962), a work that uses the Babiy Yar incident as its

principal motif. Shortly thereafter, Yevtushenko began to
travel abroad, to France, England, and the United States
during the 1960's. This exposure made him one of the most
popular Soviet poets. Articles
about him as well as his poems appeared in *Paris-Match,
London Observer, Der Spiegel,
Time, Saturday Review, Holiday,
Life, Harper's Magazine,* and
many others. Known as a
dynamic reciter of poetry,
Yevtushenko has given many
poetry readings both in the
Soviet Union and abroad in a
vibrant, declamatory style. He
claims to have given 250 in
1961 alone.

Jean-Claude Bouis

Yevtushenko was still a prolific poet through the 1980's. He has traveled
widely and incorporated his observations and reactions into poetry, photography (*Invisible Threads,* 1981), attempts at film scenarios, drama, essays,
and a novel.

Biography · Yevgeny Alexandrovich Yevtushenko was born in Stantsiya
Zima, Siberia, U.S.S.R., on July 18, 1933, of mixed Ukrainian, Russian,
and Tartar blood. In his famous poem "Stantsia Zima" ("Zima Junction"),
he describes in detail this remote Siberian town on the Trans-Siberian
Railway about two hundred miles from Irkutsk and not far from Lake
Baikal. Both his grandfathers were victims of Stalinist purges, a fact which
helps to explain Yevtushenko's attitude toward Stalin. Yevtushenko's father was a geologist, and between the ages of fifteen and seventeen, young
"Zhenya," as he was familiarly called, accompanied his father on geological
expeditions to Kazakhstan and the Altai. His mother, of modest peasant
stock, worked as a singer in Moscow during and after the war.

As a young boy in Moscow, Yevtushenko began to read Russian and
foreign classics, familiarizing himself not only with the works of Leo
Tolstoy and Anton Chekhov, but also those of Alexander Dumas, Gustave
Flaubert, Friedrich Schiller, Honoré de Balzac, Dante, and many other
foreign authors. In 1941, he was evacuated to Stantsiya Zima, where he

developed his love for the Siberian taiga and his horror of war. When his parents were separated in 1944, he returned to Moscow with his mother. His education from 1944 to 1948 was very desultory, and when he was expelled from school at fifteen, he ran off to join his father in Siberia for two years.

Among Yevtushenko's many interests was sports, and it was not accidental that his first verses were published in a sports magazine. He met the editors Tarasov and Barlas, who became his first mentors, although his continued interest in reading led him to other models, especially Ernest Hemingway, Aleksandr Blok, Sergei Esenin, and Vladimir Mayakovsky. Yevtushenko wrote in the style of the times, paying lip service to Stalin until the latter's death in 1953.

The year 1953 was a turning point in Yevtushenko's life, for along with many others he experienced disillusionment with the Stalinist regime. With the coming of the "Thaw" in 1956, he began to write poetry against the former rulers and, gradually, for freedom. In 1954, he married Bella Akhmakulina, whom he himself describes as Russia's greatest living woman poet, although the marriage was doomed to failure. Yevtushenko's meeting with Boris Pasternak in 1957 brought him into contact with his greatest mentor.

In 1962, Yevtushenko began to travel abroad. His great success and popularity was temporarily interrupted by the publication in Paris of *A Precocious Autobiography* without the permission of the Soviet authorities, for which infraction his travel was curtailed. He subsequently made trips abroad, however, including one to the United States in 1966, where he gave many poetry readings and charmed audiences with his warm and dynamic personality. He also visited Cuba, which he admired greatly as exemplary of the revolutionary ideal. Later travels to Rome, Vietnam, Africa, Japan, Alaska, California, and Florida also inspired poems. He lists sixty-four countries that he visited up to 1981. His second marriage, to Galina Semyonovna, and the birth of a son greatly inspired his life and work.

Analysis · Although not the most original poet of the post-Stalinist era in the Soviet Union, Yevtushenko has shown himself to be one of the most significant. This is essentially because he has been able to put his finger on the pulse of the times. He became the spokesman for a new generation, not only in his native land but all over the world. Unflinchingly honest and sincere, he has spoken with clarity and courage on issues that threaten freedom. He is best known for his poems of protest, such as "Babiy Yar" and "Stalin's Heirs." In the tradition of Russian poetry, he sees himself invested with a mission and a message, and he proclaims it fearlessly. He directs his criticism not only against the cult of personality, anti-Semitism, and oppression in his own land, but he speaks out against the same abuses in other countries, especially in the United States. Images of Martin Luther King, John and Robert Kennedy, and Allison Krause of Kent State University appeared in his work in the 1970's; the perils of television and advertising, war in Northern Ireland, and the threat of nuclear weapons in poems of the late 1970's. "Freedom to Kill," "Flowers and Bullets," and "Safari in Ulster," among others, explore these themes.

Yevtushenko knows how to combine the social with the personal and how to move effortlessly from one to the other. His poetry is extremely autobiographical and one can read his life by exploring his verse. He tells whimsically of his Siberian childhood in Stantsiya Zima, in the poem by the same name; of his youth in Moscow; of his travels and disappointment in love; and of his family and child. He reflects on the idealism of youth and the fears of impending old age. He is especially sensitive to childhood, and can frequently combine his own experiences, a universal theme of childhood, and social observation. A typical poem is "Weddings," which recounts his folk dancing at ill-fated wartime weddings in Siberia.

A child of the North, Yevtushenko speaks best of nature when evoking the taiga, the lakes, and the rivers of Siberia, the smell of fresh berries or the blue glow of fresh snow in "Zima Junction," "Monologue of the Fox," and "The Hut." He is close to the sea, and often associates it with love, ("The Sea"), with women ("Glasha, Bride of the Sea"), and with contemporary problems, as in "Kachka" ("Pitching and Rolling"). Nature, however, is not the most common source of images for this contemporary poet, who prefers the city with its neon lights, the sound of jazz, and the smell of smog. He is especially fond of New York and records his impressions in many poems such as "New York Elegy," "Smog," and *Pod kozhey statuey sbobody.*

People, more than nature, dominate Yevtushenko's poetry. In the tradition of Fyodor Dostoevski, Anton Chekhov, and Maxim Gorky, the lowly and the downtrodden occupy an important place. Socialist Realism places an emphasis on the "people." Yevtushenko adopts this attitude, but he goes even further, showing genuine sympathy for the worker and the peasant, especially evident in *Bratsk Station,* in which he also speaks of the unmarried mother ("Nushka"). While extolling the humble and the poor he manifests hatred for the cruel overseer, the bully, or the compromiser. Such characters appear in "Babiy Yar," "Zima Junction," and "Song of the Overseers" in *Bratsk Station.* He detests hypocrisy and slavery in any form and denounces it loudly in Russia, the United States, South Africa, and anywhere else in the world.

Women occupy an important place in Yevtushenko's verse. In keeping with his sympathy for the peasant and workers, he dedicates many poems to the hardworking Russian woman, as in "The Hut." Old women in particular are among his favorites, such as the one who brings the red flowers of the taiga to the workers of Bratsk Station. The young innocent girl in love, such as "Masha," the mothers who work for their young children and are never appreciated, the dancer, the singer, all of these are living people who impart to Yevtushenko's works a strong dramatic quality.

The narrative, along with the lyric, is an important feature of Yevtushenko's poetry. He prefers the epic style, and "Zima Junction," *Bratsk Station,* and *Ivan the Terrible and Ivan the Fool* illustrate this tendency, although he often falls short of his goals. All of his verse is dynamic rather than static. Many of his shorter works have a balladlike quality; among these are "Glasha, Bride of the Sea," "Rhythms of Rome," and "Nushka" in *Bratsk Station.* Dialogue occurs frequently and enhances the dramatic effect of his verse. *Pod kozhey statuey sbobody,* partially prose and partially verse, was staged in Moscow as a play in 1973; it satirized Russia as well as the United States.

Yevtushenko claims as his masters Hemingway (to whom he dedicated one of his finest poems, "Encounter"), Esenin, Mayakovsky, and Pasternak, whom he knew personally and who offered friendly criticism of his early verse. The influence of Esenin and Mayakovsky is not always evident in his style, although at first glance he seems to be an avid disciple of Mayakovsky. Yevtushenko uses the "step lines" of Mayakovsky, but the verbal brilliance, bold speech, and innovation of the older poet are rarely evident. Yevtushenko employs a colloquial style, with many words borrowed from foreign languages. His poetry is filled with vivid twentieth century speech, with frequent sound effects, internal rhymes, and wordplay not always evident in English translations. He uses a wide variety of rhymes and rhythms, as well as free verse. His earlier poems tend to be freer than the poems of the late 1970's and early 1980's, which make use of regular meters and indulge in much less verbal experimentation. At all times he seems to write with ease and facility, although his poems frequently give the impression of too great haste. He is a prolific, spontaneous poet who writes without looking back and sometimes produces profound and startling insights.

Yevtushenko is a poet who wishes to be accessible to as many people as possible. He refuses poetic isolation and an elitist concept of art. In fact, he has chosen photography as a medium because its meaning is immediately obvious and it does not lose in translation. Above all, he is an apostle of human brotherhood. He believes in kindness and mutual under-standing. *Invisible Threads* captures this theme dramatically. He is satirical, disarmingly frank, yet idealistic and trusting. Images of Christ, the sea, African jungles, and neon lights all serve to highlight his essential opti-mism and hope for the future.

Yevtushenko's poetry falls roughly into three periods. The first, from 1952 to 1960, contains poems of youthful enthusiasm and is extremely autobiographical, as in "Zima Junction," "The Visit," and "Weddings." Memories of war and the child's inability to grasp its impact appear in "Weddings," "Party Card," and "A Companion." Since Yevtushenko had not begun his travels at this time, his inspiration was limited to Russia, centering especially on Moscow, Siberia, and Georgia. Although Yevtushenko was born long after the revolution and did not know it at first hand, he manifests amazing conviction and enthusiasm for its ideals. "Lies" and "Knights" are among the many typical examples. Lyricism, love, and, above all, human sympathy characterize this early period.

Perhaps the best and most important poem of this period is "Zima Junction," first published in the journal *Oktyabr* in 1956. It refers to a visit to his native village in 1953, after the death of Stalin, the Doctors' Plot, and the deposition of Lavrenti Beria. Relatives and friends in far-off Siberia are anxious to learn all the news at first hand from this Moscow visitor, who, they expect, has all the information and has known Stalin personally. He accepts their naïveté with humor and respect for their simple lives, while at the same time noticing how both he and they have changed, and how they too have anxieties beneath the apparent simplicity of their ways.

The return to Stantsiya Zima is the occasion for a retrospective glance at his own past and the past of his ancestors, as he recalls his great-grand-father's trip to Siberia from his peasant village in the Ukraine, and his grandfather's revolutionary idealism. Yevtushenko returns to the place where he was born not only for the past, but also for the future, to seek "strength and courage." He realizes that he, like the people of the village, has changed, and that it is difficult to decide wisely on a course of action. He personifies Stantsiya Zima, which speaks to him through the forest and the wheat, in some of his best nature images. The section "Berry-Picking" has frequently been reprinted separately.

Throughout the poem, local color abounds, and Yevtushenko's narra-tive quality emerges through images of such people as the barefoot berry picker, the garrulous fisherman, or the disappointed wife in the hayloft who complains of her ungrateful and inattentive husband. Yevtushenko's family such as Uncle Volodya and Uncle Andrei, simple laborers, contrast with Pankratov, "the ponderous didactic president." The wheat and the village speak to young Zhenya, who is on the uncertain threshold of manhood, urging him to explore the world over and to love people.

Although the poem consists of many isolated incidents, they are obviously linked by the village and its message of courage and hope. The style is simple and colloquial, interspersed with local Siberian and Ukrainian expressions. The dialogue is suited to the speaker, and the nature imagery is among Yevtushenko's best. Belief in revolutionary ideals is evident, and party ideology, although present, is sincere and unaffected. Yevtushenko began to acquire fame after publishing this poem, where the personal note becomes universal.

The poems of the 1970's show a broader scope and are mainly influenced by travel. Yevtushenko writes especially of the United States, Latin America, Cuba, Alaska, Hawaii, and Rome. He speaks out more freely against hypocrisy and loss of freedom, and addresses social and political abuses, of which "Babiy Yar" is the most significant example. At the same time, he professes strong patriotism, as evidenced in the lengthy *Bratsk Station*. The North, especially Siberia, is an inspiration for his work, especially *Kachka*. The personal and autobiographical theme returns in poems about love and loss of love. A more serious note is expressed in images of guilt, suffering, and repentance. Poems such as "Twist on Nails" and "Torments of Conscience" (published in English in *Stolen Apples*) express these themes through religious and dramatic imagery, of which one of the most striking examples is that of the pierced hands of the crucified Christ. These are poems of maturity and considerable depth and sensitivity in both the personal and the social order.

"Babiy Yar" was first published in the *Literaturnaya gazeta* in 1961. It is a poetic meditation on the tragic fate of the Jews in Eastern Europe, thirty-three thousand of whom were killed by the Germans in 1941 at Babiy Yar, a ravine near the city of Kiev. As an attack on Soviet anti-Semitism, the poem stimulated controversy in the Soviet press and provoked counterattacks from leading journalists, but Yevtushenko continued to publish. In the poem, Yevtushenko deplores the absence of a monument at Babiy Yar. One has subsequently been erected, without reference to the specific massacre of 1941.

The poem is not confined to Soviet anti-Semitism; it attacks prejudice against all peoples, but especially against Jews everywhere. In the poem, Yevtushenko, who is not Jewish himself, identifies with all the Jews of the past: those in ancient Egypt, Christ on the Cross, Alfred Dreyfus, Anne Frank. Amid the harsh indictment of those who killed the Jews, Yevtushenko inserts delicate poetry: "transparent as a branch in April." He emphasizes the need for all people to look at one another and to recognize their responsibility and their brotherhood. By poetic transfer, Yevtushenko sees in himself each of these murderers and accepts responsibility for the terrible massacre. With characteristic optimism, he expresses trust in Russia's international soul, which will shine forth when anti-Semitism is dead.

Bratsk Station was first published in the April, 1965, issue of *Yunost.* It is a long discursive poem of epic proportions: 5,000 lines divided into thirty-five unequal and loosely connected parts. The main idea, as expressed by Yevtushenko himself, is a "controversy between two themes: the theme of disbelief expressed in the monologue of the Pyramid and the theme of faith, expressed by Bratsk Station." The Bratsk project was launched in 1958. It is a gigantic hydroelectric station, and it also contains lumber mills and plants for pulp, cardboard, wood by-products, and aluminum. Located in central Siberia along the Angara River, it is one of the largest hydroelectric plants in the Soviet Union. Yevtushenko sees it as a monument to free labor and considers the manpower that constructed it and keeps it in operation as a symbol of brotherhood, expressed in the word "bratsk," which means "brotherly."

The essential conflict is expressed in the recurring dialogue between the Egyptian Pyramid and Bratsk Station. Yevtushenko sees the Pyramid as a construction of slaves, and therefore it has no faith in itself. Moreover, it maintains that all men will ultimately turn to slavery and that freedom is only an illusory dream. The Bratsk Station, on the other hand, extols the free labor that built it, for it is the daughter of Russia who has attained freedom through centuries of suffering. Yevtushenko's naïve interpretation of Egyptian history has provoked much criticism, notably from Andrei Sinyavsky in "In Defense of the Pyramid," where he maintains that Yevtushenko does not understand the significance of Egyptian society.

To illustrate the quest for freedom in the Russian soul, Yevtushenko evokes a number of events and heroes from Russian history, especially Stenka Razin, the Decembrists, and the followers of Mikhail Petrashevsky. To these he adds Russia's greatest writers, Alexander Pushkin, Tolstoy, Dostoevski, and the modern writers he so admires, Esenin and Mayakovsky, with a poem in the style of the latter. Finally, there are the unsung heroes of the people: Issy Kramer, the Light Controller, who still suffers from anti-Semitism; Sonka and Petka, the concrete pourers, and Nushka, the unwed mother. Yevtushenko relates that when he read his poem to the workers of Bratsk Station, mothers like Nushka held their children up to him, recognizing themselves in his poem.

Themes of socialism and patriotism abound in the poem, frequently exaggerated. Despite its loosely connected parts, the poem moves quickly, with dramatic and lively style and balladlike quality. There are echoes of "Babiy Yar" in the Light Controller and of "Zima Junction" in the images of the taiga and the Simbirsk Fair, and the work is autobiographical as well as political and social. It begins and ends with poetry. In the "Prayer Before the Poem," Yevtushenko invokes Pushkin, Mikhail Lermontov, Nikolai Nekrasov, Blok, Pasternak, Esenin, and Mayakovsky and asks for their gifts (mutually exclusive, claims Sinyavsky). The final section, "The Night of Poetry," evokes the Siberian custom of improvising poetry and delivering it to musical accompaniment. In the moment of recitation, Yevtushenko sees before him the great Russian heroes and writers of the past and experiences with them the glory of freedom symbolized by Bratsk Station.

The years from 1970 to 1981 show both a return to basic structures in theme and composition and a broadening of scope into various genres: photography, the theater, novel, and essay. As the father of a child, Yevtushenko again writes about childhood, as in "Father and Son," "Walk with My Son," and "A Father's Ear." Now approaching middle age, he writes more of death ("A Child's Grave," "Come to My Tomb") and speaks of his desire to live in all lands and be all types of people possible, but to be buried in Russia. The travel theme is still uppermost, with an emphasis on the Far East, where Vietnam becomes an important social and political question. Yevtushenko, always against war, continues to make an appeal to human brotherhood in Northern Ireland, South Africa, and between the United States and Russia.

Still drawn to the epic theme, Yevtushenko published *Ivanovskiye sitsi* in the journal *Avrora* in 1976. The title means literally "calico from Ivanovo," and refers to Ivanovo-Voznesensk, a large textile center important for the labor movement. In 1905, there was a strike there which led to the establishment of one of the first Soviets of Workers' Deputies. Yevtushenko is always fond of wordplay, and thus uses "Ivan" in several contexts. There is Ivan the Terrible, czar of Russia from 1533 to 1584, the symbol of autocracy in constant conflict with the people. Ivan the Fool is an important but composite character from folk epic and represents the growing popular consciousness. The poem glorifies the revolution and the proletariat and expresses faith in the consciousness of the working class, bearers of the Russian soul. Yevtushenko maintains, however, that the revolution extols heroes of all nations: Joan of Arc, John Brown, and Anne Frank, and aims for human brotherhood and a real International.

Invisible Threads, published in the United States and composed of poetry and photography, takes its inspiration from Edward Steichen's *Family of Man* exhibit and emphasizes the same theme. It contains poems from the late 1970's and addresses contemporary themes such as the threat of atomic warfare, the conflict in Northern Ireland, and the universal themes of birth and death, the former inspired by the birth of Yevtushenko's son in London. In the poem "Life and Death," a balladlike lyric, Life and Death exchange places. Death realizes that she is respected, if only because of fear, whereas Life is not. Yevtushenko pleads again for human dignity. Religious images are more evident than in the past, although Yevtushenko sees salvation among human beings on earth. He wishes to echo every voice in the world and "dance his Russian dance on the invisible threads that stretch between the hearts of men."

Other literary forms · Yevgeny Yevtushenko's works in prose include *A Precocious Autobiography* (1963), first published in the Paris periodical *L'Express*; *Talant est' chudo nesluchainoe* (1980; talent is not an accidental wonder), a collection of essays that are mainly on poetry, but also on music, film, and prose; *Yagodniye mesta* (1981; berry patches), a novel; and *Pod kozhey statuey sbobody* (1972; under the skin of the Statue of Liberty), a poetic drama.

Select works other than poetry

LONG FICTION: *Yagodniye mesta*, 1981 (*Wild Berries*, 1984); *Don't Die Before You're Dead*, 1995.

DRAMA: *Pod kozhey statuey sbobody*, pr. 1972.

NONFICTION: *Primechaniya k avtobiografii*, 1963 (*A Precocious Autobiography*, 1963); *Talant est' chudo nesluchainoe: Kniga statei*, 1980.

Irma M. Kashuba

Bibliography · Among the numerous English-language articles on Yevtushenko, see Vickie A. Babenko, "Women in Evtushenko's Poetry," *Russian Review* 36 (1977); Richard N. Porter, "Evtusenko's Jagodnye mesta: The Poet as Prose Writer," *Russian Language Journal* 40, no. 135 (Winter, 1986), which deals with the good and weak points of Yevtushenko's first novel; and Michael Pursglove, "Yevtushenko's *Stantsiya Zima*: A Reassessment," *New Zealand Slavonic Journal* 2 (1988), which successfully compares different versions of *Zima Junction*. R. R. Millner-Gullard offers a useful introduction to Yevtushenko, *Selected Poetry*, 1963, as does George Reavey to *The Poetry of Yevgeny Yevtushenko 1953-1965*, 1965. See also the entry on the poet in *Contemporary Authors, New Revision*, vol. 33.

GLOSSARY

Accented syllable: See *Stressed syllable*

Accentual meter: One of four base meters used in English (accentual, accentual-syllabic, syllabic, and quantitative), accentual meter is the system in which the occurrence of a syllable marked by a *stress* determines the basic unit, regardless of the number of unstressed syllables. In other words, it is the stresses that determine the metrical base. An example from modern poetry is "Blue Moles" by Sylvia Plath, the first line of which scans: "They're out of the dark's ragbag, these two." Because there are five stressed syllables in this accentually based poem, the reader can expect that many of the other lines will also contain five stresses. (See also *Scansion*)

Accentual-syllabic meter: By far the most common base meter for English poetry, accentual-syllabic meter measures the pattern of stressed syllables relative to the unstressed ones. In the first line of William Shakespeare's sonnet 130, "My mistress' eyes are nothing like the sun," there is a pattern of alternating unstressed with stressed syllables, although there is a *substitution* of an unstressed syllable for a stressed syllable at the word "like." In the accentual-syllabic system, stressed and unstressed syllables are grouped together into *feet*.

Allegory: One of the "figures of speech," allegory represents an abstract idea in concrete imagery, almost always in the form of a humanized character. Gluttony, for example, might be allegorized by a character who eats all the time, while Christian love might be allegorized by a character who does charitable deeds. The traditional use for allegory is to make it possible for the poet to show how abstract ideas affect real people who are in contact with them, or how abstract emotions affect each other within a human being.

Alliteration: When consonant repetition is focused at the beginning of syllables, the repetition is called alliteration, as in: "Large mannered motions of his mythy mind." Alliteration is used when the poet wishes to focus on the details of a sequence of words and to show relationships between words within a line. Because a reader cannot easily skim over an alliterative line, it is conspicuous and demands emphasis.

Allusion: When a reference is made to a historical or literary event whose story or outcome adds dimension to the poem, then poetical allusion occurs. "Fire and Ice" by Robert Frost, for example, alludes to the biblical account of the flood and the prophecy that the next destruction will come by fire, not water. Without recognizing the allusion and understanding the biblical reference to Noah and the surrounding associations of hate and desire, the reader cannot fully appreciate the poem.

Anacrusis: The opposite of *truncation,* anacrusis occurs when an extra unstressed syllable is added to the beginning or end of a *line,* as in the line: "their shoul/ders held the sky/suspended." This line is described as iambic tetrameter with terminal anacrusis. Anacrusis is used to change a rising meter to falling, and vice versa, in order to change the reader's emotional response to the subject.

Anapest: One of six standard rhythmic units in English poetry, the anapestic foot associates two unstressed syllables with one stressed syllable, as in the line, "With the sift/ed, harmon/ious pause." The anapestic foot is one of the three most common in English poetry and is used to create a highly rhythmical, usually emotional, line.

Approximate rhyme: The two categories of approximate rhyme are assonance and half rhyme (or slant rhyme). Assonance occurs when words with identical vowel sounds but different consonants are associated. "Stars," "arms," and "park" all contain identical *a* (and *ar*) sounds, but because the consonants are different the words are not *full rhymes.* Half rhyme or slant rhymes contain identical consonants but different vowels, as in "fall" and "well." "Table" and "bauble" constitute half rhymes; "law," "cough," and "fawn" assonate.

Assonance: See *Approximate rhyme*

Ballad: The ballad stanza, a type of *quatrain,* may alternate its rhyme scheme as *abab* or *abcb.* If all four lines contain four feet each (*tetrameter*), the stanza is called a "long ballad"; if one or more of the lines contain only three feet (trimeter), it is called a "short ballad." Ballad stanzas, which are highly *mnemonic,* originated with verse adapted to singing. For this reason, the poetic ballad is well suited for presenting stories. Popular ballads are songs or verse which tell tales, usually impersonal, and they usually impart folk wisdom. Supernatural events, courage, and love are frequent themes, but any experience which appeals to common people is acceptable material. A famous use of the ballad form is *The Rime of the Ancient Mariner* (1798), by Samuel Taylor Coleridge.

Ballade: The French "ballade," a popular and sophisticated form, is commonly (but not necessarily) composed of an eight-line stanza rhyming *ababbcbc.* Early ballades usually contained three stanzas and an *envoy,* commonly addressed to a nobleman, priest, or the poet's patron, but no consistent syllable count. Another common characteristic of the ballade is a refrain that occurs at the end of each stanza.

Base meter (or metrical base): Poems in English and in most European languages which are not *free verse* are written in one of four base meters (*accentual, accentual-syllabic, syllabic,* or *quantitative*), measured by the number, pattern, or duration of the syllables within a line or stanza. Rhythm in verse occurs because of *meter,* and the use of meter depends upon the type of base into which it is placed.

Blank verse: Although many variations can occur in the *meter* of blank verse, its *base meter* is iambic pentameter. Blank verse lines are unrhymed, and are usually arranged in *stichic* form (that is, not in stanzas). Most of Shakespeare's plays are written in blank verse; in poetry it is often used for subject matter that requires much narration or reflection. In both poetry and drama, blank verse elevates emotion and gives a dramatic sense of importance. Although the base meter of blank verse is iambic pentameter, the form is very flexible, and *substitution, enjambment,* feminine endings, and extra syllables can relax the rigidity of the base. The flexibility of blank verse gives the poet an opportunity to use a formal structure without seeming unnecessarily decorous. T. S. Eliot's "Burnt Norton" is a modern blank-verse poem.

Cadence: The rhythmic speed or tempo with which a line is read is its cadence. All language has cadence, but when the cadence of words is forced into some pattern, it then becomes *meter,* thus distinguishing poetry from prose. A *prose poem* may possess strong cadence, combined with poetic uses of imagery, symbolism, and other poetic devices.

Caesura: When the poet imposes a pause or break in the poem, with or without punctuation marks, a caesura has occurred. The comma, question mark, colon, and dash are the most common signals for pausing, and these are properly termed "caesuras"; pauses may also be achieved through syntax, *lines, meter, rhyme,* and the sound of words. The type of punctuation determines the length of the pause. Periods and question marks demand full stops; colons take almost a full stop; semicolons take a long pause; commas a short pause. The end of a line usually demands some pause even if there is no punctuation.

Cinquain: Any five-line stanza, including the *mad-song* and the *limerick,* is a cinquain. Cinquains are most often composed of a *ballad* stanza with an extra line added to the middle.

Conceit: One of several types of *metaphor,* the term "conceit" is used for comparisons which are highly intellectualized. A conceit may therefore be said to be an extended, elaborate, or complex metaphor. The term is frequently applied to the work of the Metaphysical poets, notably John Donne.

Connotation: Words convey meaning through their sound, through their formal, *denotative* definitions, through their use in context, and through connotation. When a word takes on an additional meaning other than its denotative one, it achieves connotation. The word "mercenary," for example, simply means a soldier who is paid to fight in an army not of his own region, but connotatively a mercenary is an unprincipled scoundrel who kills for money and pleasure, not for honor and patriotism. Connotation is one of the most important devices for achieving *irony,* and readers may be fooled into believing a poem has one meaning because they have missed connotations which reverse the poem's apparent theme.

Consonance: When the final consonants of stressed syllables agree but the preceding vowels are different, consonance occurs. "Chair/star" is an example of consonance, since both words end with *r* preceded by different vowels. Terminal consonance creates half or slant rhyme (see *Approximate rhyme*). Consonance differs from *alliteration* in that the final consonants are repeated rather than the initial consonants. In the twentieth century consonance became one of the principal rhyming devices, used to achieve formality without seeming stilted or old-fashioned.

Consonants: Consonants (all letters except the vowels, *a, e, i, o, u,* and sometimes *y*) are among the most important sound-producing devices in poetry. There are five basic effects that certain consonants will produce: resonance, harshness, plosiveness, exhaustiveness, and liquidity. Resonance, exhaustiveness, and liquidity tend to give words—and consequently the whole line if several of these consonants are used—a soft effect. Plosiveness and harshness, on the other hand, tend to create tension. Resonance is the property of long duration produced by nasals, such as *n* and *m*, and by voiced fricating consonants such as *z*, *v*, and the voiced *th*, as in "them." Exhaustiveness is created by the voiceless fricating consonants and consonant combinations, such as *h*, *f*, and the voiceless *th* and *s*. Liquidity results from using the liquids and semivowels *l*, *r*, *w*, and *y*, as in the word "silken." Plosiveness occurs when certain consonants create a stoppage of breath before releasing it, especially *b*, *p*, *t*, *d*, *g*, *k*, *ch*, and *j*.

Controlling image/controlling metaphor: Just as a poem may include as structural devices form, theme, action, or dramatic situation, it may also use imagery for structure. When an image runs throughout a poem, giving unity to lesser images or ideas, it is called a "controlling image." Usually the poet establishes a single idea and then expands and complicates it; in Edward Taylor's "Huswifery," for example, the image of the spinning wheel is expanded into images of weaving until the reader begins to see life as a tapestry. Robert Frost's "The Silken Tent" is a fine example of a controlling image and *extended metaphor*.

Couplet: Any two succeeding lines that rhyme form a couplet. Because the couplet has been used in so many different ways, and because of its long tradition in English poetry, various names and functions have been given to types of couplets. One of the most common is the decasyllabic (tensyllable) couplet. When there is an *end-stop* on the second line of a couplet, it is said to be "closed"; an *enjambed* couplet is "open." An end-stopped decasyllabic couplet is called a "heroic couplet," because the form has often been used to sing the praise of heroes. The heroic couplet was widely used by the neoclassical poets of the eighteenth century. Because it is so stately and sometimes pompous, the heroic couplet invites satire, and many poems have been written in "mock heroic verse," such as Alexander Pope's *The Rape of the Lock* (1712). Another commonly used couplet is the octasyllabic (eight-syllable) couplet, formed from two lines of iambic tetrameter, as in "L'Allegro" by John Milton: "Come, and trip as we go/ On the light fantastic toe." The light, sing-song tone of the octasyllabic couplet also invited satire, and in the seventeenth century Samuel Butler wrote one of the most famous of all satires, *Hudibras*, in this couplet. When a couplet is used to break another rhyme scheme, it generally produces a summing-up effect and has an air of profundity. Shakespeare found this characteristic particularly useful when he needed to give his newly invented Shakespearean *sonnet* a final note of authority and purpose.

Dactyl: The dactyl, formed of a stress followed by two unstressed syllables (´ ˘ ˘), is fairly common in isolated words, but when this pattern is included in a line of poetry, it tends to break down and rearrange itself into components of other types of feet. Isolated, the word "méan-ĭng-lĕss" is a dactyl, but in the line "Pŏlíte/méanĭng/lĕss wórds," the last syllable becomes attached to the stressed "words" and creates a *split foot,* forming a *trochee* and an *iamb.* Nevertheless, a few dactylic poems do exist. "Ăftér thĕ/pángs ŏf ă/déspĕrăte/lóvĕr," is a dactyllic line.

Denotation: The explicit formal definition of a word, exclusive of its implications and emotional associations (see *Connotation*), is its denotation or denotative meaning.

Depressed foot: Occasionally, two syllables occur in a pattern in such a way as to be taken as one syllable without actually being an *elision,* thus creating a depressed foot. In the line: "Tŏ éach thĕ boúl/dĕrs (thăt hăve)/fállĕn/tŏ éach" the *base meter* consists of five iambic feet, but in the third foot there is an extra syllable which disrupts the meter but does not break it, so that "that have" functions as the second half of the iambic foot.

Diction: John Dryden defined diction concisely as the poet's "choice of words." In Dryden's time, and for most of the history of English verse, the diction of poetry was elevated, sharply distinct from everyday speech. Since the early twentieth century, however, the diction of poetry has ranged from the banal and the conversational to the highly formal, and from obscenity and slang to technical vocabulary, sometimes in the same poem. The diction of a poem often reveals its persona's values and attitudes.

Dieresis: Caesuras which come after the foot (see *Split foot* for a discussion of caesuras which break feet), called "dieresis" (although the technical name is seldom used), can be used to create long pauses in the *line,* and they are often used to prepare the line for *enjambment.*

Dramatic dialogue: When two or more personae speak to each other in a poem or a play, they engage in dramatic dialogue. Unlike a *dramatic monologue,* both characters speak, and in the best dramatic dialogues, their conversation leads to a final resolution in which both characters and the reader come to the same realization at the same time.

Dramatic irony: See *Irony*

Dramatic monologue: In dramatic monologue, the narrator addresses a silent persona who never speaks but whose presence greatly influences what the narrator tells the reader. The principal reason for writing in dramatic monologue form is to control the speech of the major persona through the implied reaction of the silent one. The effect is one of continuing change and often surprise. In Robert Browning's "My Last Duchess," for example, the duke believes that he is in control of the situation, when in fact he has provided the emissary with terrible insights about the way he treated his former duchess. The emissary, who is the silent persona, has asked questions which the duke has answered; in doing so he has given away secrets. Dramatic monologue is somewhat like hearing one side of a telephone conversation in which the reader learns much about both participants.

Duration: The measure of quantitative meter is the duration or length of the syllables. Duration can alter the tone and the *relative stress* of a line and influence meaning as much as the *foot* can.

Elegy: The elegy and pastoral elegy are distinguishable by their subject matter rather than their form. The elegy is usually a long, rhymed, *strophic* poem whose subject is meditation upon death or a lamentable theme, while the pastoral elegy uses the natural setting of a pastoral scene to sing of death or love. Within the pastoral setting the simplicity of the characters and the scene lends a peaceful air despite the grief the narrator feels.

Elision: The two types of elision are synaeresis and syncope; they occur when a poet who is attempting to maintain a regular *base meter* joins two vowels into a single vowel or omits a vowel altogether. In the line "Of man's first disobedience, and the fruit" the "ie" in "disobedience" is pronounced as a "y" ("ye") so that the word reads dis/o/bed/yence, thereby making a five-syllable word into a four-syllable word. This process of forming one vowel out of two is synaeresis. When a vowel is dropped altogether, rather than combining two into one, it is called "syncope," as when "natural" becomes "nat'ral" and "hastening" becomes "hast'ning." Less frequent uses of elision are to change the sound of a word, to spell words as they are pronounced, and to indicate dialect.

Emphasis: Through a number of techniques, such as *caesura,* the *line, relative stress, counterpointing,* and *substitution,* poets are able to alter the usual emphasis or meaning of words. Whenever the meter of a poem is intentionally altered through one of these techniques, certain words or an entire line will be highlighted or emphasized for the purpose of calling attention to the most important parts of the poem.

End rhyme: See *Rhyme*

End-stop: When a punctuated pause occurs at the end of a line, the line is said to be "end-stopped." The function of end-stops is to show the relationship between lines and to create *emphasis* on particular words or lines. End-stopping in rhymed poems creates more emphasis on the rhyme words, which already carry a great deal of emphasis by virtue of their rhymes. *Enjambment* is the opposite of end-stopping.

Enjambment: When a line is not *end-stopped*—that is, when it carries over to the following line—the line is said to be "enjambed," as in John Milton's: "Avenge, O Lord, thy slaughtered saints, whose bones/ Lie scattered on the Alpine mountains cold." Enjambment is used to change the natural emphasis of the *line,* to strengthen or weaken the effect of *rhyme,* or to alter *meter.*

Envoy: Generally, an envoy (or envoi) is any short poem or stanza addressed to the reader as a beginning or end to a longer work. Specifically, the envoy is the final stanza of a sestina or a *ballade* in which all the rhyme words are repeated or echoed.

Extended metaphor: When *metaphors* are added to one another so that they run in a series, they are collectively called an "extended metaphor." Robert Frost's poem "The Silken Tent" uses an extended metaphor; it compares the "she" of the poem to the freedom and bondage of a silken tent. (See also *Controlling image/controlling metaphor*)

Eye rhyme: Words that appear to be identical because of their spelling but that sound different are known as "eye rhymes." "Bough/enough/cough" and "ballet/pallet" are examples. Because of changes in pronunciation, many older poems appear to use eye rhymes but do not. For example, "wind" (meaning moving air) once rhymed with "find." Eye rhymes which are intentional and do not result from a change in pronunciation may be used to create a disconcerting effect.

Falling rhyme: Rhyme in which the correspondence of sound comes only in the final unstressed syllable, which is preceded by another unstressed syllable, is known as a "falling rhyme." T. S. Eliot rhymes "me-tic-u-lous"

with "ri-dĭc-ŭ-loŭs" and creates a falling rhyme. (See also *Feminine rhyme;*
Masculine rhyme)

Falling rhythm: A line in which feet move from stressed to unstressed
syllables (*trochaic* or *dactyllic*) is said to "fall," as in this line from "The
Naming of Parts": "Glistens/lĭke cór/al ĭn/áll of thĕ/néighborĭng/gárdens."
Because English and other Germanic-based languages naturally rise, im-
posing a falling rhythm on a rising *base meter* creates *counterpointing.*

Feminine rhyme: Feminine rhyme occurs when (1) a line's final accented
syllable is followed by a single unaccented syllable and (2) the accented
syllables rhyme, while the unaccented syllables are phonetically identical,
as with "flĭck-ér/snĭck-ér " and "fín-gĕrs/mă-lín-gĕrs." Feminine rhymes
are often used for lightness in tone and delicacy in movement.

First person: This *point of view* is particularly useful in short lyrical poems,
which tend to be highly subjective, taking the reader deep into the narrator's thoughts. First-person poems normally, though not necessarily, signal
the use of the first person through the pronoun "I," allowing the reader
direct access to the narrator's thoughts or providing a character who can
convey a personal reaction to an event. (See also *Third person*)

Foot/feet: The natural speech pattern in English and other Germanic-based
languages is to group syllables together in family units. In English, the
most common of these rhythmic units is composed of one unstressed
syllable attached to one stressed syllable (an *iamb*). When these family
groups are forced into a line of poetry, they are called "feet" in the
accentual-syllabic metrical system. In the line "Mў mĭs/trĕss' eýes/ are
nóth/ĭng lĭke/ thĕ sún" there are four iambic feet ($\smallsmile$ $'$) and one pyrrhic foot
($\smallsmile$ $\smallsmile$), but in the line "Thére whére/ thĕ vĭnes/ clĭng crĭm/sŏn ŏn/ thĕ wáll"
there are three *substitutions* for the iamb—in the first, third, and fourth feet.
The six basic feet in English poetry are the iamb ($\smallsmile$ $'$), *trochee* ($'$ $\smallsmile$), *anapest*
($\smallsmile\smallsmile$ $'$), *dactyl* ($'$ $\smallsmile\smallsmile$), *spondee* ($'$ $'$), and *pyrrhus* ($\smallsmile$ $\smallsmile$).

Form: The form of a poem is determined by its arrangement of lines on
the page, its base meter, its rhyme scheme, and occasionally its subject
matter. Poems which are arranged into *stanzas* are called "strophic," and
because the strophic tradition is so old a large number of commonly used
stanzas have evolved particular uses and characteristics. Poems which
run from beginning to end without a break are called *stichic.* The form of
"pattern poetry" is determined by its visual appearance rather than by

lines and stanzas, while the definition of *free verse* is that it has no discernable form. Some poem types, such as the sestina, *sonnet*, and *ode*, are written in particular forms and frequently are restricted to particular subject matter.

Found poetry: Found poetry is created from language which is "found" in print in nonliterary settings–on menus, tombstones, fire extinguishers, even on shampoo bottles. Any language which is already constructed, but especially language which appears on artifacts that characterize society, such as cereal boxes, provides the material from which the found poem is created. The rules for writing a found poem vary, but generally the found language is used intact or altered only slightly.

Free verse: A poem that does not conform to any traditional convention, such as meter, rhyme, or form, and that does not establish any pattern within itself, is said to be a free verse poem. There is, however, great dispute over whether "free" verse actually exists. Eliot said that by definition poetry must establish some kind of pattern, and Frost said that "writing free verse is like playing tennis with the net down." However, some would agree with Carl Sandburg, who insisted that "you can play a better game with the net down." Free verse depends more on cadence than on meter.

Ghazal: The ghazal is a poetic form based on a type of Persian poetry. A ghazal is composed of couplets, often unrhymed, that function as individual images or observations but that also interrelate in sometimes subtle ways.

Haiku: Haiku is a Japanese form which appeared in the sixteenth century and is still practiced in Japan. A haiku consists of three lines of five, seven, and five syllables each; in Japanese there are other conventions regarding content which are not observed in Western haiku. The traditional haiku took virtually all of its images from nature, using the natural world as a *metaphor* for the spiritual.

Half rhyme: See *Approximate rhyme*

Heroic couplet: See *Couplet*

Hymn stanza: See *Ballad*

Hyperbole: When the poet deliberately overstates in order to heighten the reader's awareness, he is using hyperbole. As with *irony*, hyperbole works because the reader can perceive the difference between the importance of the dramatic situation and the manner in which it is described.

Iamb: The basic *foot* of English speech, the iamb associates one unstressed syllable with one stressed(˘ ′). The line "So long/as men/can breathe/or eyes/can see" is composed of five iambs. In the line "A cold/coming/we had/of it," a trochaic foot (a *trochee*) has been substituted for the expected iamb in the second foot, thus emphasizing that this is a "coming" rather than a "going," an important distinction in T. S. Eliot's "The Journey of the Magi."

Iambic pentameter: Iambic pentameter is a very common type of poetic *line* in English. It consists of five iambic feet together in a line (a foot is a two-syllable grouping). The following two lines by Thomas Wyatt are in iambic pentameter: "I find no peace and all my war is done,/ I fear and hope, I burn and freeze like ice." (See also *foot*; *iamb*)

Identical rhyme: Identical rhyme occurs when the entire final stressed syllables contain exactly the same sounds, such as "break/brake," or "bear" (noun), "bear" (verb), "bare" (adjective), "bare" (verb).

Imagery: Imagery is traditionally defined as the verbal simulation of sensory perception. Like so many critical terms, "imagery" betrays a visual bias: it suggests that a poetic image is necessarily visual, a picture in words. In fact, however, imagery calls on all five senses, although the visual is predominant in many poets. In its simplest form, an image re-creates a physical sensation in a clear, literal manner, as in Robert Lowell's lines, "A sweetish smell of shavings, wax and oil/ blows through the redone bedroom newly aged" ("Marriage"). Imagery becomes more complex when the poet employs *metaphor* and other figures of speech to re-create experience, as in Seamus Heaney's lines, "Right along the lough shore/ A smoke of flies/ Drifts thick in the sunset" ("At Ardboe Point"), substituting a fresh metaphor ("A smoke of flies") for a trite one (a cloud of flies) to help the reader visualize the scene more clearly.

Interior monologue: A first-person representation of a persona's or character's thoughts or feelings. It differs from a *dramatic monologue* in that it deals with thoughts rather than spoken words or conversation.

Internal rhyme: See *Rhyme*

Irony: Irony is among the three or four most important concepts in modern literary criticism. Although the term originated in classical Greece and has been in the vocabulary of criticism since that time, only in the nineteenth and twentieth centuries has it assumed central importance. The term is used in many different contexts with an extraordinary range of meanings, eluding precise definition. In its narrowest sense, irony is a figure of speech in which the speaker's real meaning is different from (and often exactly opposite to) the apparent meaning. In Andrew Marvell's lines, "The Grave's a fine and private place,/ But none I think do there embrace" ("To His Coy Mistress"), the speaker's literal meaning—in praise of the grave—is quite different from his real meaning. This kind of irony, the easiest to define, is often called "verbal irony." Another kind of irony is found in narrative and dramatic poetry. In the *Iliad* (c. 800 B.C.), for example, the reader is made privy to the counsels of the gods, which greatly affect the course of action in the epic, while the human characters are kept in ignorance. This discrepancy between the knowledge of the reader and that of the character (or characters) is called "dramatic irony." Beyond these narrow, well-defined varieties of irony are many wider applications.

Limerick: The limerick is a comic five-line poem rhyming *aabba* in which the third and fourth lines are shorter (usually five syllables each) than the first, second, and last lines, which are usually eight syllables each. The limerick's *anapestic* base makes the verse sound silly; modern limericks are almost invariably associated with bizarre indecency or with ethnic or anticlerical jokes.

Line: A line has been defined as a poetical unit characterized by the presence of *meter*, and lines are categorized according to the number of feet (see *Foot/feet*) they contain. A pentameter line, for example, contains five feet. This definition does not apply to a great deal of modern poetry, however, which is written in *free verse*. Ultimately, then, a line must be defined as a typographical unit on the page that performs various functions in different kinds of poetry.

Lyric poetry: The two ancient roots of poetry are the narrative and lyric traditions. Narrative poetry, such as the *Iliad*, relates long stories, often historical, which preserve information, characters, and values of a culture. Lyric poetry developed when music was accompanied by words, and although the "lyrics" were later separated from the music, the characteristics of lyric poetry have been shaped by the constraints of music. Lyric poems are short, adaptable to metrical variation, and usually personal compared with the cultural functions of narrative poetry. Lyric poetry sings of the self, exploring deeply personal feelings about life.

Mad-song: The mad-song—verse uttered by the presumably insane—usually expresses a happy, harmless, inventive sort of insanity. The typical rhyme scheme of the mad-song is *abccb*, and the unrhymed first line helps to set a tone of oddity and unpredictability, since it controverts the expectation that there will be a rhyme for it. The standard mad-song has short lines that help suggest benign madness, since "simple" people are associated with uncomplicated sentence patterns.

Masculine rhyme: Masculine rhyme occurs when rhyme exists in the stressed syllables. "Men/then" constitute masculine rhyme, but so do "af-ter-noons/spoons." Masculine rhyme is generally considered more forceful than *feminine rhyme*, and while it has a variety of uses, it generally gives authority and assurance to the line, especially when the final syllables are of short duration.

Metaphor: Metaphor, like *irony*, is one of a handful of key concepts in modern literary criticism. Like irony, the term "metaphor" is used in such a wide variety of contexts that a precise, all-encompassing definition is impossible. In its narrowest sense, metaphor is a figure of speech in which two strikingly different things are identified with each other, as in "the waves were soldiers moving" (Wallace Stevens). A metaphor contains a "tenor" and a "vehicle." The tenor is the subject of the metaphor, and the vehicle is the *imagery* by which the subject is presented. In D. H. Lawrence's lines, "Reach me a gentian, give me a torch/ let me guide myself with the blue, forked torch of this flower" ("Bavarian Gentians"), the tenor is the gentian and the vehicle is the torch. This relatively restricted definition of metaphor by no means covers the usage of the word in modern criticism. Some critics argue that metaphorical perception underlies all figures of speech. Others dispute the distinction between literal and metaphorical description, saying that language is essentially metaphorical. The term "metaphor" has become widely used to identify analogies of all kinds in literature, painting, film, and even music.

Meter: Meter is the pattern of language when it is forced into a *line* of poetry. All language has rhythm; when that rhythm is organized and regulated in the line so as to affect the meaning and emotional response to the words, then the rhythm has been refined into meter. Because the lines of most poems maintain a similar meter throughout, poems are said to have a *base meter.* The meter is determined by the number of syllables in a line and by the relationship between them.

Metonymy: When an object which is closely related to an idea comes to stand for the idea itself, such as saying "the crown" to mean the king, "metonymy" is being used. The use of a part of an object to stand for the entire object, such as using "heart" to mean a person, is called "synecdoche." Metonymy and synecdoche are used to emphasize a particular part of the whole or one particular aspect of it.

Mnemonic verse: Poetry in which rhythmic patterns aid memorization but are not crucial to meaning is called "mnemonic verse." Ancient bards were able to remember long poems partly through the use of stock phrases and other mnemonic devices.

Mock-heroic: See *Couplet.*

Narrator: The terms "narrator," "persona," and "speaker" are roughly synonymous. They all refer to who is doing the talking—or observing or thinking—in a poem. Lyric poetry most often consists of the poet expressing his or her own personal feelings directly. Other poems, however, may involve the poet adopting the *point of view* of another person entirely. In some poems—notably in a *dramatic monologue*—it is relatively easy to determine that the narrative is being related by a fictional (or perhaps historical) character, but in others it may be more difficult to identify the "I."

Occasional verse: Broadly defined, occasional verse includes any poem written for a specific occasion, such as a wedding, a birthday, a death, or a public event. Edmund Spenser's *Epithalamion* (1595), which was written for his marriage, and John Milton's "Lycidas," which commemorated the death of his schoolmate Edward King, are examples of occasional verse, as are W. H. Auden's "September 1, 1939" and Frank O'Hara's "The Day Lady Died."

Ode: The ode is a *lyric* poem which treats a unified subject with elevated emotion, usually ending with a satisfactory *resolution.* There is no set *form* for the ode, but it must be long enough to build intense emotional response. Often the ode will address itself to some omnipotent source and will take on a spiritual hue. When explicating an ode, readers should look for the relationship between the narrator and some transcendental power to which the narrator must submit in order to find contentment. Modern poets have used the ode to treat subjects which are not religious in the theological sense but which have become innate beliefs of society.

Ottava rima: Ottava rima is an eight-line *stanza* of *iambic* pentameter, rhyming *abababcc*. Probably the most famous English poem written in ottava rima is Lord Byron's *Don Juan* (1819-1824), and because the poem was so successful as a spoof, the form has come to be associated with poetic high jinks. However, the stanza has also been used brilliantly for just the opposite effect, to reflect seriousness and meditation.

Oxymoron: Closely related to *paradox*, an oxymoron occurs when two paradoxical words are placed in juxtaposition, such as "wise fool" or "devilish angel."

Paradox: A paradox is a statement that contains an inherent contradiction. It may be a statement that at first seems true but is in reality contradictory. It may also be a statement that appears contradictory but is actually true or that contains an element of truth that reconciles the contradiction.

Pentameter: A type of rhythmic pattern in which each line consists of five poetic feet. (See also *Accentual-syllabic meter; Foot/feet; Iamb; Iambic pentameter; Line*)

Persona: See *Narrator*

Point of view: Point of view may be simply defined as the eyes and other senses through which readers experience the situation of a poem. As with fiction, poems may be related in the *first person*, second person (unusual), or *third person*. (The presence of the words "I" or "we" indicates singular or plural first-person narration.) Point of view may be limited or omniscient. A limited point of view means that the narrator can see only what the poet wants him or her to see, while from an omniscient point of view the narrator can know everything, including the thoughts and motives of others.

Prose poem: The distinguishing feature of the prose poem is its typography: It appears like prose on the page, with no line breaks. There are no formal characteristics by which a prose poem can be distinguished from a piece of prose. Many prose poems employ rhythmic repetition and other poetic devices not normally found in prose, but others use such devices sparingly if at all. Prose poems range in length from a few lines to three or four pages; most prose poems occupy a page or less.

Pun: A pun occurs when words which have similar pronunciations have entirely different meanings. By use of a pun the speaker establishes a connection between two meanings or contexts that the reader would not ordinarily make. The result may be a surprise recognition of an unusual or striking connection, or, more often, a humorously accidental connection.

Pyrrhus: When two unstressed syllables comprise a foot, it is called a pyrrhus or a pyrrhic foot, as in the line "Appear/and dis/appear/in the/blue depth/of the sky," in which foot four is a pyrrhus.

Quatrain: Any four-line stanza is a quatrain; aside from the *couplet,* it is the most common stanza type. The quatrain's popularity among both sophisticated and unsophisticated readers suggests that there is something inherently pleasing about the form. For many readers, poetry and quatrains are almost synonymous. Balance and antithesis, contrast and comparison not possible in other stanza types are indigenous to the quatrain.

Regular meter: A *line* of poetry that contains only the same type of *foot* is said to be regular. Only the dullest of poems maintains a regular meter throughout, however; skillful poets create interest and *emphasis* through *substitution.*

Relative stress: When more emphasis is placed on one syllable in a pattern than on another, that syllable is said to be "stressed." Once the dominant stress in the line has been determined, every other syllable can be assigned a stress factor relative to the dominant syllable. The stress factor is created by several aspects of prosody: the position of the syllable in the *line,* the position of the syllable in its word, the surrounding syllables, the type of vowels and consonants which constitute the syllable, and the syllable's relation to the *foot, base meter,* and *caesura.* Since every syllable will have a different stress factor, there could be as many values as there are syllables, although most prosodists *scan* poems using primary, secondary, and unstressed notations. In the line "I am there like the dead, or the beast" the anapestic base meter will not permit "I" to take a full stress, but it is a more forceful syllable than the unstressed ones, so it is assigned a secondary stress. Relative to "dead" and "beast," it takes less pressure; relative to the articles in the line, it takes much more.

Resolution: Generally, a resolution is any natural conclusion to a poem, especially to a short *lyric* poem which establishes some sort of dilemma or conflict that the narrator must solve. Specifically, the resolution is the octave stanza of a Petrarchan *sonnet* or the couplet of a Shakespearean sonnet in which the first part of the poem presents a situation which must find balance in the resolution.

Rhyme: Rhyme is a correspondence of sound between syllables within a line or between lines whose proximity to each other allows the sounds to be sustained. Rhyme may be classified in a number of ways: according to the sound relationship between rhyming words, the position of the rhyming words in the line, and the number and position of the syllables in the rhyming words. Sound classifications include full rhyme and approximate rhyme. Full rhyme is defined as words that have the same vowel sound, followed by the same consonants in their last stressed syllables, and in which all succeeding syllables are phonetically identical. "Hat/cat" and "laughter/after" are full rhymes. Categories of *approximate rhyme* are *assonance, slant rhyme, alliteration, eye rhyme,* and *identical rhyme.*

Rhyme classified by its position in the line includes end, internal, and initial rhyme. End rhyme occurs when the last words of lines rhyme. Internal rhyme occurs when two words within the same line or within various lines recall the same sound, as in "Wet, below the snow line, smelling of vegetation" in which "below" and "snow" rhyme. Initial rhyme occurs when the first syllables of two or more lines rhyme. (See also *Masculine rhyme; Feminine rhyme*)

Rhyme scheme: Poems that establish a pattern of rhyme have a "rhyme scheme," designated by lowercase (and often italicized) letters. The letters stand for the pattern of rhyming sounds of the last word in each line. For example, the following A. E. Housman quatrain has an *abab* rhyme scheme.

> Into my heart an air that kills
> From yon far country blows:
> What are those blue remembered hills,
> What spires, what farms are those?

As another example, the rhyme scheme of the poetic form known as *ottava rima* is *abababcc.* Traditional stanza forms are categorized by their rhyme scheme and *base meter.*

Rime royal: The only standard seven-line stanza in English prosody is rime royal, composed of iambic pentameter lines rhyming *ababbccc.* Shakespeare's *The Rape of Lucrece* (1594) is written in this form. The only variation permitted is to make the last line hexameter.

Rondeau: One of three standard French forms assimilated by English prosody, the rondeau generally contains thirteen lines divided into three groups. A common stanzaic grouping rhymes *aabba, aabR, aabbaR,* where the *a* and *b* lines are tetrameter and the *R* (refrain) lines are dimeter. The rondel, another French form, contains fourteen lines of trimeter with alternating rhyme (*abababa bababab*) and is divided into two stanzas. The rondeau and rondel forms are always light and playful.

Rondel: See *Rondeau*

Scansion: Scanning is the process of assigning *relative stresses* and meter to a line of poetry, usually for the purpose of determining where variations, and thus emphasis, in the *base meter* occur. Scansion can help explain how a poem generates tension and offer clues as to the key words. E. E. Cummings's "singing each morning out of each night" could be scanned in two ways: (1) singing/each morn/ing out/of each night or (2) sing/ing each/morning/out of/each night. Scansion will not only affect the way the line is read aloud but will also influence the meaning of the line.

Secondary stress: See *Relative stress*

Seguidilla: Like the Japanese haiku, the Spanish seguidilla is a mood or imagistic poem whose success hinges on the reader's emotional recognition or spiritual insight. Although there is no agreement as to what form the English seguidilla should take, most of the successful ones are either four or seven lines with an alternating *rhyme scheme* of *ababcbc.* Lines 1, 3, and 6 are trimeter; lines 2, 4, 5, and 7 dimeter.

Shakespearean sonnet: See *Sonnet*

Simile: Loosely defined, a simile is a type of *metaphor* that signals a comparison by the use of the words "like" or "as." Shakespeare's line "My mistress' eyes are nothing like the sun" is a simile that establishes a comparison between the woman's eyes and the sun.

Slant rhyme: See *Approximate rhyme*

Sonnet: The most important and widely used of traditional poem types, the sonnet is almost always composed of fourteen lines of iambic pentameter with some form of alternating rhyme, and it contains a turning point that divides the poem into two parts. The two major sonnet types are the "Petrarchan" (or "Italian") sonnet and the "Shakespearian" sonnet. The original sonnet form, the Petrarchan (adopted from the poetry of Petrarch), presents a problem or situation in the first eight lines, the "octave," then resolves it in the last six, the "sextet." The octave is composed of two *quatrains* (*abbaabba*), the second of which complicates the first and gradually defines and heightens the problem. The sestet then diminishes the problem slowly until a satisfying resolution is achieved.

During the fifteenth century, the Italian sonnet became an integral part of the courtship ritual, and most sonnets during that time consisted of a young man's description of his perfect lover. Because so many unpoetic young men had generated a nation full of bad sonnets by the end of the century, the form became an object of ridicule, and the English sonnet developed as a reaction against all the bad verse being turned out in the Italian tradition. When Shakespeare wrote "My mistress' eyes are nothing like the sun," he was deliberately negating the Petrarchan conceit, rejoicing in the fact that his loved one was much more interesting and unpredictable than nature. Shakespeare also altered the sonnet's formal balance. Instead of an octave, the Shakespearean sonnet has three quatrains of alternating rhyme and is resolved in a final couplet. During the sixteenth century, long stories were told in sonnet form, one sonnet after the next, to produce "sonnet sequences." Although most sonnets contain fourteen lines, some contain as few as ten (the curtal sonnet) or as many as seventeen.

Speaker: See *Narrator*

Split foot: A split foot occurs when the natural division of a word is altered as a result of being forced into a metrical base. For example, the words "poínt/ĕd," "lád/dĕr," and "stíck/ĭng" have a natural falling rhythm, but in the line "Mý lóng/twŏ-poínt/ĕd lăd/dĕr's stíck/ĭng thrŏugh/ă tree" the syllables are rearranged so as to turn the falling rhythm into a rising meter. The result of splitting feet is to create an uncertainty and delicate imbalance in the line.

Spondee: When two relatively stressed syllables occur together in a foot, the unit is called a "spondee" or "spondaic foot," as in the line "Appéar/and dis/appeár/in thĕ/blúe dépth/ŏf thĕ ský."

Sprung rhythm: If *accentual meter* is taken to its extreme, one can never predict the patterns of succeeding stresses: It is possible only to predict a prescribed number of stresses per line. This unpredictability characterizes sprung rhythm, first described near the end of the nineteenth century by Gerard Manley Hopkins. In sprung rhythm "any two stresses may either follow one another running, or be divided by one, two, or three slack syllables."

Stanza: When a certain number of lines are meant to be taken as a unit, that unit is called a "stanza." Although a stanza is traditionally considered a unit that contains rhyme and recurs predictably throughout a poem, the term is also sometimes applied to nonrhyming and even irregular units. Poems that are divided into fairly regular and patterned stanzas are called "strophic"; poems that appear as a single unit, whether rhymed or un-rhymed, or that have no predictable stanzas, are called "stichic." Both strophic and stichic units represent logical divisions within the poem, and the difference between them lies in the formality and strength of the interwoven unit. Stanza breaks are commonly indicated by a line of space.

Stichic verse: See *Stanza*

Stress: See *Relative stress*

Strophic verse: See *Stanza*

Substitution: Substitution, one of the most common and effective methods by which the poet can emphasize a foot, occurs when one type of foot is replaced by another within a *base meter*. For example, in the line "Thy lífe/a lóng/ déad cálm/ŏf fíxed/repóse," a spondaic foot (′ ′) has been substituted for an iambic foot (˘ ′). Before substitution is possible, the reader's expectations must have been established by a base meter so that a change in those expectations will have an effect. (See also *Foot/feet*; *iamb*; *spondee*)

Syllabic meter: The system of meter which measures only the number of syllables per line, without regard to stressed and unstressed syllables, is called syllabic meter.

Symbol: Loosely defined, a symbol is any sign that a number of people agree stands for something else. Poetic symbols cannot be rigidly defined; a symbol often evokes a cluster of meanings rather than a single specific meaning. For example, the rose, which suggests fragile beauty, gentleness, softness, and sweet aroma, has come to symbolize love, eternal beauty, or virginity. The tide traditionally symbolizes, among other things, time and eternity. Modern poets may use personal symbols; these take on significance in the context of the poem or of a poet's body of work, particularly if they are reinforced throughout. For example, through constant reinforcement swans in William Butler Yeats's poetry come to mean as much to the reader as they do to the narrator.

Synaeresis: See *Elision*

Synecdoche: See *Metonymy*

Tenor: See *Metaphor*

Terza rima: Terza rima is a three-line stanzaic form in which the middle line of one stanza rhymes with the first line of the following stanza, and whose rhyme scheme is *aba bcb cdc*, and so on. Since the rhyme scheme of one stanza can be completed only by adding the next stanza, terza rima tends to propel itself forward, and as a result of this strong forward motion it is well suited to long narration.

Theme: Loosely defined as "what a poem means," theme more specifically refers to recurring elements. The term is sometimes used interchangeably with "motif." A motif is any recurring pattern of images, symbols, ideas, or language and is usually restricted to the internal workings of the poem. Thus, one might say that there is an animal motif in William Butler Yeats's poem "Sailing to Byzantium." Theme, however, is usually more general and philosophical, so that the theme of "Sailing to Byzantium" might be interpreted as the failure of human attempts to isolate oneself within the world of art.

Third person: Third-person narration exists when a poem's narrator, or speaker, has not been part of the events described and is not probing his or her own relationship to them; rather, the speaker is describing what happened without the use of the word "I" (which would indicate first-person narration). A poet may use a third-person *point of view*, either limited or omniscient, to establish a distance between the reader and the subject, to give credibility to a large expanse of narration, or to allow the poem to include a number of characters who can be commented on by the narrator.

Tone: Strictly defined, tone is the expression of a poet's attitude toward the subject and persona of the poem as well as about him- or herself, society, and the poem's readers. If the ultimate aim of art is to express and control emotions and attitudes, then tone is one of the most important elements of poetry. Tone is created through the denotative and connotative meanings of words and through the sound of language (principally, *rhyme, consonants,* and *diction*). Adjectives such as "satirical," "compassionate," "empathetic," "ironical," and "sarcastic" are used to describe tone.

Trochee: One of the most common feet in English poetry, the trochee associates one stressed syllable with one unstressed syllable (′ ˘), as in the line: "Double/double toil and/trouble." Trochaic lines are frequently *substituted* in an iambic *base meter* in order to create counterpointing. (See also *Foot/feet*; *iamb*)

Truncation: Truncation occurs when the last, unstressed syllable of a falling line is omitted, as in the line: "Tyger,/tyger/burning/bright," where the "ly" has been dropped from bright."

Vehicle: See *Metaphor*

Verse: The term "verse" has two or three different applications. It is a generic term for poetry, as in *The Oxford Book of English Verse* (1939). Verse also refers in a narrower sense to poetry that is humorous or superficial, as in "light verse" or "greeting-card verse." Finally, "verse" is sometimes used to mean *stanza* or *line.*

Verse drama: Drama which is written in poetic rather than ordinary language and which is characterized and delivered by the *line* is called "verse drama." Verse drama flourished during the eighteenth century, when the *couplet* became a standard literary form.

Verse paragraph: A division created within a stichic poem (see *Stanza*) by logic or syntax, rather than by form, is called a "verse paragraph." These are important for determining the movement of a poem and the logical association between ideas.

Villanelle: The villanelle, like the *rondeau* and the rondel, is a French verse form that has been assimilated by English prosody. It is usually composed of nineteen lines divided into five tercets and a quatrain, rhyming *aba, bba, aba, aba, abaa.* The third line is repeated in the ninth and fifteenth lines. Dylan Thomas's "Do Not Go Gentle into That Good Night" is a modern English example of a villanelle.

TIME LINE

c. 800 B.C.   Homer, 494
612 B.C.   Sappho, 1029
518 B.C.   Pindar, 852
70 B.C.   Vergil, 1233
65 B.C.   Horace, 524
43 B.C.   Ovid, 821
701   Li Po, 617
712   Tu Fu, 1200
1265   Dante, 255
1304   Petrarch, 841
1343   Chaucer, Geoffrey, 191
1503   Wyatt, Sir Thomas, 1330
1552   Raleigh, Sir Walter, 918
  Spenser, Edmund, 1146
1554   Sidney, Sir Philip, 1105
1564   Shakespeare, William, 1072
1572   Donne, John, 299
1593   Herbert, George, 470
1608   Milton, John, 746
1621   Marvell, Andrew, 692
1644   Matsuo Bashō, 705
1648   Cruz, Sor Juana Inés de la, 236
1688   Pope, Alexander, 886
1749   Goethe, Johann Wolfgang von, 399
1757   Blake, William, 77
1759   Burns, Robert, 153
  Schiller, Friedrich, 1041
1770   Hölderlin, Friedrich, 483
  Wordsworth, William, 1310
1771   Scott, Sir Walter, 1053
1772   Coleridge, Samuel Taylor, 208
1788   Byron, George Gordon, Lord, 165
1792   Shelley, Percy Bysshe, 1085
1795   Keats, John, 559
1797   Heine, Heinrich, 459
1803   Emerson, Ralph Waldo, 334
1806   Browning, Elizabeth Barrett, 125
1807   Longfellow, Henry Wadsworth, 627

1808   Nerval, Gérard de, 793
1809   Poe, Edgar Allan, 874
  Tennyson, Alfred, Lord, 1174
1812   Browning, Robert, 137
1819   Whitman, Walt, 1268
1821   Baudelaire, Charles, 44
1822   Arnold, Matthew, 20
1830   Dickinson, Emily, 285
1842   Mallarmé, Stéphane, 670
1844   Hopkins, Gerard Manley, 507
  Verlaine, Paul, 1247
1854   Rimbaud, Arthur, 964
1865   Yeats, William Butler, 1342
1869   Robinson, Edwin Arlington, 976
1871   Valéry, Paul, 1207
1874   Frost, Robert, 364
  Lowell, Amy, 639
1875   Rilke, Rainer Maria, 953
1878   Sandburg, Carl, 1017
1879   Stevens, Wallace, 1162
1880   Apollinaire, Guillaume, 9
1883   Williams, William Carlos, 1296
1885   Lawrence, D. H., 591
  Pound, Ezra, 903
1886   H. D., 434
1887   Moore, Marianne, 760
1888   Eliot, T. S., 318
  Ransom, John Crowe, 929
1889   Akhmatova, Anna, 1
1891   Mandelstam, Osip, 679
  Sachs, Nelly, 1009
1892   Millay, Edna St. Vincent, 724
  Vallejo, César, 1220
1894   Cummings, E. E., 244
1895   Graves, Robert, 421
1896   Breton, André, 106
1898   García Lorca, Federico, 376
1899   Crane, Hart, 224
1902   Hughes, Langston, 536
1904   Neruda, Pablo, 780
1905   Warren, Robert Penn, 1257

1907 Auden, W. H., 31
1908 Roethke, Theodore, 988
1909 Spender, Stephen, 1134
1910 Olson, Charles, 810
1911 Bishop, Elizabeth, 66
     Miłosz, Czesław, 732
1913 Rukeyser, Muriel, 1000
1914 Berryman, John, 55
     Paz, Octavio, 823
     Thomas, Dylan, 1188
1917 Brooks, Gwendolyn, 114
     Lowell, Robert, 650
1919 Ferlinghetti, Lawrence, 348
1920 Celan, Paul, 183
     Nemerov, Howard, 771
1921 Wilbur, Richard, 1284

1922 Larkin, Philip, 578
1923 Levertov, Denise, 604
1926 Bly, Robert, 96
     Ginsberg, Allen, 386
     Merrill, James, 713
1928 Sexton, Anne, 1063
1929 Rich, Adrienne, 940
1930 Hughes, Ted, 546
     Snyder, Gary, 1119
1932 Plath, Sylvia, 861
1933 Yevtushenko, Yevgeny, 1374
1939 Heaney, Seamus, 445
1942 Olds, Sharon, 803
1950 Forché, Carolyn, 356
1951 Graham, Jorie, 413

NOTABLE POETS

GEOGRAPHICAL INDEX

AUSTRIA
Rilke, Rainer Maria, 953

CHILE
Neruda, Pablo, 780

CHINA
Li Po, 617
Tu Fu, 1200

ENGLAND
Arnold, Matthew, 20
Auden, W. H., 31
Blake, William, 77
Browning, Elizabeth Barrett, 125
Browning, Robert, 137
Byron, George Gordon, Lord, 165
Chaucer, Geoffrey, 191
Coleridge, Samuel Taylor, 208
Donne, John, 299
Eliot, T. S., 318
Graves, Robert, 421
Herbert, George, 470
Hopkins, Gerard Manley, 507
Hughes, Ted, 546
Keats, John, 559
Larkin, Philip, 578
Lawrence, D. H., 591
Levertov, Denise, 604
Marvell, Andrew, 692
Milton, John, 746
Pope, Alexander, 886
Raleigh, Sir Walter, 918
Shakespeare, William, 1072
Shelley, Percy Bysshe, 1085
Sidney, Sir Philip, 1105
Spender, Stephen, 1134
Spenser, Edmund, 1146
Tennyson, Alfred, Lord, 1174
Thomas, Dylan, 1188
Wordsworth, William, 1310
Wyatt, Sir Thomas, 1330

FRANCE
Apollinaire, Guillaume, 9
Baudelaire, Charles, 44
Breton, André, 106
Mallarmé, Stéphane, 670
Nerval, Gérard de, 793
Rimbaud, Arthur, 964
Valéry, Paul, 1207
Verlaine, Paul, 1247

GERMANY
Goethe, Johann Wolfgang von, 399
Heine, Heinrich, 459
Hölderlin, Friedrich, 483
Sachs, Nelly, 1009
Schiller, Friedrich, 1041

GREECE
Homer, 494
Pindar, 852
Sappho, 1029

IRELAND
Heaney, Seamus, 445
Yeats, William Butler, 1342

ITALY
Dante, 255
Horace, 524
Ovid, 821
Petrarch, 841
Vergil, 1233

JAPAN
Matsuo Bashō, 705

MEXICO
Cruz, Sor Juana Inés de la, 236
Paz, Octavio, 832

PERU
Vallejo, César, 1220

POLAND
Mandelstam, Osip, 679
Miłosz, Czesław, 732

ROMANIA
Celan, Paul, 183

RUSSIA
Akhmatova, Anna, 1
Mandelstam, Osip, 679
Yevtushenko, Yevgeny, 1374

SCOTLAND
Burns, Robert, 153
Scott, Sir Walter, 1053

SPAIN
García Lorca, Federico, 376

UNITED STATES
Auden, W. H., 31
Berryman, John, 55
Bishop, Elizabeth, 66
Bly, Robert, 96
Brooks, Gwendolyn, 114
Crane, Hart, 224
Cummings, E. E., 244
Dickinson, Emily, 285
Eliot, T. S., 318
Emerson, Ralph Waldo, 334
Ferlinghetti, Lawrence, 348
Forché, Carolyn, 356
Frost, Robert, 364

Ginsberg, Allen, 386
Graham, Jorie, 413
H. D., 434
Hughes, Langston, 536
Levertov, Denise, 604
Longfellow, Henry Wadsworth, 627
Lowell, Amy, 639
Lowell, Robert, 650
Merrill, James, 713
Millay, Edna St. Vincent, 724
Moore, Marianne, 760
Nemerov, Howard, 771
Olds, Sharon, 803
Olson, Charles, 810
Plath, Sylvia, 861
Poe, Edgar Allan, 874
Pound, Ezra, 903
Ransom, John Crowe, 929
Rich, Adrienne, 940
Robinson, Edwin Arlington, 976
Roethke, Theodore, 988
Rukeyser, Muriel, 1000
Sandburg, Carl, 1017
Sexton, Anne, 1063
Snyder, Gary, 1119
Stevens, Wallace, 1162
Warren, Robert Penn, 1259
Whitman, Walt, 1268
Wilbur, Richard, 1284
Williams, William Carlos, 1296

WALES
Thomas, Dylan, 1188

SUBJECT INDEX

Aa

Abbey Theatre, 1346
"About Marriage" (Levertov), 612
About the House (Auden), 40
"Ache of Marriage, The" (Levertov), 612
Acmeist poets, 1, 683
"Adam and the Sacred Nine" (Hughes), 556
"Addict, The" (Sexton), 1068
"Address to the Deil" (Burns), 159
Adonais (Shelley), 1101
Adorno, Theodor, 187, 861
Advice to a Prophet and Other Poems (Wilbur), 1290
Aeneid (Vergil), 1238-1246
"Affliction" (Herbert), 474
Africa (Petrarch), 849
"After Apple-Picking" (Frost), 368-371
Afternoon of a Faun, The (Mallarmé), 672
Age of Anxiety, The (Auden), 38
"Agonie, The" (Herbert), 474
Agrarianism, 930, 1261
"Ajanta" (Rukeyser), 1004
Akhmatova, Anna, 1-8, 682
Alastor (Shelley), 1092
Albatross, 214
Alcools (Apollinaire), 9, 13, 16
All My Pretty Ones (Sexton), 1067
All the King's Men (Warren), 1266
"All the Soul Indrawn . . ." (Mallarmé), 672
"Allegro, L'" (Milton), 749
"Almond Blossom" (Lawrence), 599
"Altar, The" (Herbert), 475
"Altarwise by Owl-Light" (Thomas), 1195-1196
"America" (Ginsberg), 391
America: A Prophecy (Blake), 88
"American Scholar, The" (Emerson), 346, 1024
"Among School Children" (Yeats), 1360-1364

Amores (Ovid), 824-826
Amoretti (Spenser), 1157-1158
"Ancient Torso of Apollo" (Rilke), 960
"And Death Shall Have No Dominion" (Thomas), 1193
"Andrea del Sarto" (Browning), 146
"Annabel Lee" (Poe), 879
Annie Allen (Brooks), 120
Anniversaries (Donne), 311
Anno Domini MCMXXI (Akhmatova), 4
"Another Voice" (Wilbur), 1288
Anthology for the Year 1782 (Schiller), 1044
"Antiphon" (Herbert), 477
Anti-Semitism, Soviet, 1380
Antschel, Paul. *See* Celan, Paul
"anyone lived in a pretty how town" (Cummings), 251
"Apogee of Celery" (Neruda), 787
Apollinaire, Guillaume, 9-19
"Apollonius of Tyana, A Dance, with Some Words, for Two Actors" (Olson), 815
Apollonius Rhodius, 1238
"Apparently with no surprise" (Dickinson), 293
Arcadia (Sidney), 1107, 1117
Archaeologist of Morning (Olson), 818
Arnold, Matthew, 20-30
"Ars poetica?" (Miłosz), 741
Art of Love (Ovid), 826-828
Art of Poetry, The (Horace), 524
"As Children Together" (Forché), 362
"As I Walked Out One Evening" (Auden), 37
Asbaje y Ramírez de Santillana, Juana Inés de. *See* Cruz, Sor Juana Inés de la
Ash Wednesday (Eliot), 329
Ask Your Mama (Hughes), 542
"Asphodel, That Greeny Flower" (Williams), 1307
"Assassination Raga" (Ferlinghetti), 352, 354

Astrophel and Stella (Sidney), 1106, 1111-1117
"At Luca Signorelli's *Resurrection of the Body*" (Graham), 418
"At the Indian Killer's Grave" (Lowell), 656
"At Woodward's Gardens" (Frost), 371
Atta Troll (Heine), 464
"Aubade," (Larkin), 588
Auden, W. H., **31-43**, 1134
"Auld Lang Syne" (Burns), 160
Aurélia (Nerval), 797
Aurora Leigh (Browning), 133
Auschwitz, 187, 862
"Autobiography" (Ferlinghetti), 352
"Autumnal, The" (Donne), 305
Awful Rowing Toward God, The (Sexton), 1070
Axe Handles (Snyder), 1131

Bb

"Babiy Yar" (Yevtushenko), 1380
"Bad Blood" (Rimbaud), 970
"Ballad of Billie Potts, The" (Warren), 1262
"Ballad of the Little Square" (García Lorca), 380
"Banquet, The" (Herbert), 474
"Bard's Epitaph, A" (Burns), 160
Bashō, Matsuo. *See* Matsuo Bashō
Basoalto, Neftalí Ricardo Reyes. *See* Neruda, Pablo
"Bat, The" (Roethke), 992
"Bath, The" (Snyder), 1130
"Batter my heart, three-personed God" (Donne), 313
Baudelaire, Charles, **44-54**
"Bavarian Gentians" (Lawrence), 601
"Beacons" (Baudelaire), 48
Beatrice, 257, 259
"Because I could not stop for Death" (Dickinson), 296
Belaia staia (Akhmatova), 4
Belfry of Bruges and Other Poems, The (Longfellow), 632
Bell Jar, The (Plath), 861
"Bells for John Whiteside's Daughter" (Ransom), 931
"Bells in Winter" (Miłosz), 742

"Bells of San Blas, The" (Longfellow), 631
"Berry-Picking" (Yevtushenko), 1379
Berryman, John, **55-65**
Bestiary (Apollinaire), 13, 15
"Beyond the Alps" (Lowell), 657
"Birches" (Frost), 371
"Bird, The" (Paz), 836
Birds, Beasts and Flowers (Lawrence), 595
"Birds of Passage" (Longfellow), 633
Bishop, Elizabeth, **66-76**
"Bishop Blougram's Apology" (Browning), 144
"Bishop Orders His Tomb at St. Praxed's Church, The" (Browning), 143
Black Arts Movement, 114
Black Mountain poets, 812
Black Mountain Review, 811
"Blackstone Rangers, The" (Brooks), 121
Blake, William, **77-95**
Blanco (Paz), 838
"Blind Singer, The" (Hölderlin), 490
"Blossoming of the Solitary Date-Tree, The" (Coleridge), 222
"Blue Rock" (Rich), 950
Blue Swallows, The (Nemerov), 774
"Blues Fantasy" (Hughes), 540
Bly, Robert, **96-105**
"Bobo's Metamorphosis" (Miłosz), 740
Boccaccio, 205
"Bog Oak" (Heaney), 450
"Bogland" (Heaney), 449
Bonaparte, Napoleon, 175
Book of Ahania, The (Blake), 91
"Book of Ephraim, The" (Merrill), 717
Book of Hours, The (Rilke), 956
Book of Los, The (Blake), 90
Book of Songs (Heine), 463
Book of the Duchess (Chaucer), 196
Book of Thel, The (Blake), 84
"Born Yesterday" (Larkin), 582
"Boy at the Window" (Wilbur), 1291
Bradstreet, Anne, 61
"Brahma" (Emerson), 342
Bratsk Station (Yevtushenko), 1381
Braving the Elements (Merrill), 716

"Bread and Wine" (Hölderlin), 488, 491
"Break of Day" (Donne), 308
Breaking Open (Rukeyser), 1007
Breasts of Tiresias, The (Apollinaire), 11
Breton, André, **106-113**
"Bride and Groom Lie Hidden for Three Days" (Hughes), 555
Bridge, The (Crane), 227
Brodsky, Joseph, 8
Brooks, Gwendolyn, **114-124**
Brother to Dragons (Warren), 1263
Browning, Elizabeth Barrett, **125-136**, 140-141
Browning, Robert, 127, **137-152**, 906
Bucolics (Vergil), 1235-1238
"Building, The" (Larkin), 581, 586
"Buried Life, The" (Arnold), 26
"Burning" (Snyder), 1126
"Burning of Paper Instead of Children, The" (Rich), 946
"Burning the Tomato Worms" (Forché), 359
Burns, Robert, **153-164**
"Burnt Norton" (Eliot), 330
"Butterfly" (Sachs), 1011, 1014
"By Candlelight" (Plath), 869
"Bye-Child" (Heaney), 451
Byron, George Gordon, Lord, **165-182**
"Byzantium" (Yeats), 1364

Cc

"Cake, The" (Baudelaire), 53
"Calamus" (Whitman), 1276
"Call of the Wild, The" (Snyder), 1130
Calligrammes (Apollinaire), 17
Callimachus, 524
"Canonization, The" (Donne), 306
Canterbury Tales, The (Chaucer), 201-205
Cantos (Pound), 908-912
"Cape Hatteras" (Crane), 231
"Capital" (Paz), 837
"Carcass, A" (Baudelaire), 49
"Carrion Comfort" (Hopkins), 521
Casa Guidi Windows (Browning), 132
"Cat-Goddesses" (Graves), 429
Cathay (Pound), 907
Cave Birds (Hughes), 555

Celan, Paul, **183-190**, 1011
"Chained Stream, The" (Hölderlin), 490
Change of World, A (Rich), 942
Changing Light at Sandover, The (Merrill), 714, 720
Charms (Valéry), 1210
Chaucer, Geoffrey, **191-207**, 1150
"Che Guevara" (Lowell), 663
Chetki (Akhmatova), 2
"Chicago *Defender* Sends a Man to Little Rock, The" (Brooks), 120
Chicago Poems (Sandburg), 1025
Chicago Renaissance, 1019
Chief Joseph of the Nez Percé (Warren), 1265
"Child Next Door, The" (Warren), 1262
"Child of Europe, A" (Miłosz), 739
Childe Harold's Pilgrimage (Byron), 166, 170, 172-177
"Childe Roland to the Dark Tower Came" (Browning), 147
"Children of Adam" (Whitman), 1275
Chimères, Les (Nerval), 798
"Chiron" (Hölderlin), 488, 490
"Chorus of the Stones" (Sachs), 1013
Christabel (Coleridge), 218
"Church, The" (Herbert), 473
"Church Going" (Larkin), 583
Cibber, Colly, 900
"Circe" (H. D.), 441
"City in the Sea, The" (Poe), 882
City Lights press and bookstore, 350
Civil War, 1279
"Clearances" (Heaney), 457
"Clearing the Title" (Merrill), 721
"Clerk's Tale, The" (Chaucer), 204
"Climbing the Peak of Mount T'ai-po" (Li Po), 621
Cocktail Party, The (Eliot), 331
Cold Mountain Poems (Snyder), 1124
Coleridge, Samuel Taylor, **208-223**, 1313
"Collar, The" (Herbert), 476
"Colonel, The" (Forché), 361
Columbus, Christopher, 228
Complaints (Spenser), 1159
Comus (Milton), 750

Concentration camps, World War II, 186-187, 1012
"Concord Hymn" (Emerson), 345
Coney Island of the Mind, A (Ferlinghetti), 352
"Consider" (Auden), 36
"Considering Coldly . . ." (Vallejo), 1229
"Constantly Risking Absurdity" (Ferlinghetti), 352
"Cool Web, The" (Graves), 426
Cornhuskers (Sandburg), 1025
"Cotter's Saturday Night, The" (Burns), 157
"Counsels" (Miłosz), 741
"Counting Small-Boned Bodies" (Bly), 99
Country Between Us, The (Forché), 358, 361
"Course of a Particular, The" (Stevens), 1169
Courtship of Miles Standish, The (Longfellow), 636
Crane, Hart, **224-235**
"Cranes of Ibycus, The" (Schiller), 1050
"Crazy Jane on the Day of Judgment" (Yeats), 1367
"Creation Myth on a Moebius Band" (Nemerov), 775
Creeley, Robert, 812
Crepusculario (Neruda), 783
Cromwell, Oliver, 694
"Crossing Brooklyn Ferry" (Whitman), 1277
Crow (Hughes), 552-553
"Crusoe in England" (Bishop), 74
Cruz, Sor Juana Inés de la, **236-243**
"Culture and Anarchy" (Arnold), 30
Culture and Anarchy (Arnold), 24
Cummings, E. E., **244-254**
Cure for Love (Ovid), 826

Dd
Dadaism, 108
"Daddy" (Plath), 871
Dante, **255-284**, 1179
"Darien" (Graves), 429
Davidson, Donald, 930

Day by Day (Lowell), 666
"Days" (Emerson), 341
"Days of 1935" (Merrill), 716
Dead and the Living, The (Olds), 806
"Dead Gallop" (Neruda), 786
"Dead Pan, The" (Browning), 131
"Death Fugue" (Celan), 186
Death of a Naturalist (Heaney), 445
"Death of the Hired Man" (Frost), 368
Death's Duell (Donne), 315
"Decade, A" (Lowell), 647
Defence of Poesie (Sidney), 1105
Defence of Poetry, A (Shelley), 1102
"Dejection" (Coleridge), 219
"Deliria I" (Rimbaud), 971
"Deliria II" (Rimbaud), 970
"Depths, The" (Levertov), 607
"Descent, The" (Williams), 1306
"Desdichado, El" (Nerval), 328, 799
Desert Music, The (Williams), 1306
"Despondency" (Arnold), 24
Devotions upon Emergent Occasions (Donne), 303, 314
Dial, The, 760, 762
Diamond Cutters, The (Rich), 943
Dice Thrown Never Will Annul Chance (Mallarmé), 677
Dickinson, Emily, **285-298**
"Digging" (Heaney), 447
"Digging for China" (Wilbur), 1291
Dinggedicht (thing poem), 957
"Diotima" (Hölderlin), 487
"Discipline" (Herbert), 478
"Distant Steps, The" (Vallejo), 1224
Divine Comedies (Merrill), 714
Divine Comedy, The (Dante), 262-283
Divine Tragedy, The (Longfellow), 636
Diving into the Wreck (Rich), 946
"Divinity School Address" (Emerson), 343
"Dockery and Son" (Larkin), 585
"Dog" (Ferlinghetti), 353
Dog Beneath the Skin, The (Auden), 41
"Dolphin," (Lowell), 665
Dolphin, The (Lowell), 653, 665
Don Juan (Byron), 177-180
Donne, John, **299-317**, 695
Doolittle, Hilda. *See* H. D.

Door into the Dark (Heaney), 447
"Double Image, The" (Sexton), 1066
"Dover Beach" (Arnold), 28
Drafts and Fragments of Cantos CX-CXVII (Pound), 913
Dramatic Lyrics (Browning), 141
Dramatic monologue, 137, 141
Dream of a Common Language, The (Rich), 947
Dream Songs, The (Berryman), 60, 63
Drum-Taps (Whitman), 1279
"Drunken Boat, The" (Rimbaud), 966
"Dry Salvages, The" (Eliot), 330
Du Fu. *See* Tu Fu
Duino Elegies (Rilke), 960-961
Duncan, Robert, 812
Dunciad, The (Pope), 900
"Duns Scotus's Oxford" (Hopkins), 519
"During the Eichmann Trial" (Levertov), 607

Ee

"Each and All" (Emerson), 343
"Eagle in New Mexico" (Lawrence), 598
Eagle or Sun? (Paz), 836
"East Coker" (Eliot), 330
"Ecstasy, The" (Donne), 307
"Effort at Speech Between Two People" (Rukeyser), 1004
Eichmann, Karl Adolf, 607
Eimi (Cummings), 253
El Salvador, 357
El Salvador: Requiem and Invocation (Levertov), 610
"Elegy to the Memory of an Unfortunate Lady" (Pope), 894
Elemental Odes, The (Neruda), 787
"Elf King" (Goethe), 404, 408
Eliot, T. S., 300, **318-333**
"Emerald, The" (Merrill), 716
Emerson, Ralph Waldo, **334-347**, 1024, 1270
"End of a Year" (Lowell), 665
End of Beauty, The (Graham), 415
English Bards and Scotch Reviewers (Byron), 171
Enormous Room, The (Cummings), 253

"Entrance to Wood" (Neruda), 787
"Eolian Harp, The" (Coleridge), 211
Epinikia (Pindar), 852
Epipsychidion (Shelley), 1098
Epistle from Eloisa to Abelard (Pope), 895
"Epistle to a Young Friend" (Burns), 160
Epistle to Dr. Arbuthnot (Pope), 899
Epistles (Horace), 534
Epithalamion (Spenser), 1157-1158
Epodes (Horace), 528-529
"Equilibrists, The" (Ransom), 936
"Eros Turannos" (Robinson), 980-983
Erosion (Graham), 416
Essay on Criticism, An (Pope), 890
Essay on Man, An (Pope), 895
"Eternal Dice, The" (Vallejo), 1225
"Euclid Alone Has Looked on Beauty Bare" (Millay), 727
Europe: A Prophecy (Blake), 89
Evangeline (Longfellow), 635
"Eve of St. Agnes, The" (Keats), 569-572
"Express, The" (Spender), 1142
Extravagaria (Neruda), 790

Ff

Faerie Queene, The (Spenser), 1146, 1153-1157
Fall of America, The (Ginsberg), 396
Fall of Hyperion, The (Keats), 567
"Fantasy" (Nerval), 796
Far Field, The (Roethke), 996
"Farewell Without a Guitar" (Stevens), 1170
Fata Morgana (Breton), 112
Fatal Interview (Millay), 727
"Fate" (Olds), 806
Faust (Goethe), 402
"Fears in Solitude" (Coleridge), 219
"Felix Randal" (Hopkins), 519
Ferlinghetti, Lawrence, **348-355**
Field Work (Heaney), 454
Fine Clothes to the Jew (Hughes), 541
"Fire and Ice" (Frost), 374
Fire Screen, The (Merrill), 715
Fireside poets, 628
"First Dream" (Cruz), 241

"First Night" (Olds), 806
"Fish, The" (Bishop), 68
"Fish, The" (Moore), 764
Fisher King, 327
"Fisherman, The" (Goethe), 404
"Fishnet" (Lowell), 665
"Fission" (Graham), 419
Flaccus, Quintus Horatius. *See* Horace
"Flea, The" (Donne), 307
"Flee on Your Donkey" (Sexton), 1068
"Fleeing" (Sachs), 1014
"Flight, The" (Levertov), 614
Flowering of the Rod, The (H. D.), 439
Flowers of Evil (Baudelaire), 47
"Fog" (Sandburg), 1025
"Follower" (Heaney), 447
"For a Dead Lady" (Robinson), 980
"For A' That and A' That" (Burns), 160
For Lizzie and Harriet (Lowell), 664
"For the Marriage of Faustus and Helen" (Crane), 226
For the Time Being (Auden), 34
"For the Union Dead" (Lowell), 660
For the Union Dead (Lowell), 659
"For Wei Pa, in Retirement" (Tu Fu), 1205
Forché, Carolyn, **356-363**
Ford, Ford Madox, 591
Four Quartets (Eliot), 330
Four Zoas, The (Blake), 80, 89, 92
Free Union (Breton), 111
French Revolution, 1316, 1326
French Revolution, The (Blake), 88
"From an Airplane" (Akhmatova), 6
"From an Old House in America" (Rich), 947
"From the New World" (Graham), 419
"From the Oriental Notebook" (Akhmatova), 6
Frost, Robert, 68, **364-375**, 1025
"Frost at Midnight" (Coleridge), 213
Fugitive poets, 929, 1258
"Funeral Rites" (Heaney), 453

Gg

"Gacela of the Flight" (García Lorca), 380
Gallant Parties (Verlaine), 1252
Gallipoli, 550
"Ganymed" (Goethe), 406
García Lorca, Federico, **376-385**
"Garden, The" (Marvell), 697-700
"Gates, The" (Rukeyser), 1007
Gathering the Tribes (Forché), 358, 360
Gaudete (Hughes), 554
Gautier, Théophile, 795
"Gazing at Yellow Crane Mountain" (Li Po), 623
"Geese, The" (Graham), 414
Georgics (Vergil), 1238
Germany: A Winter's Tale (Heine), 464
"Gerontion" (Eliot), 325
"Ghazals" (Rich), 945
Gide, André, 1208
"Gifts of Rain" (Heaney), 450
Ginsberg, Allen, 351, **386-398**
Girl in Winter, A (Larkin), 589
"Give All to Love" (Emerson), 343
Glass, Philip, 388
"God" (Lawrence), 600
"God and the Bayadere, The" (Goethe), 409
"God's Grandeur" (Hopkins), 518
"Gods of Greece, The" (Schiller), 1045, 1048
Goethe, Johann Wolfgang von, **399-412**, 1041
"Going, Going" (Larkin), 586
Gold Cell, The (Olds), 807
Golden Legend, The (Longfellow), 636
"Golden Verses" (Nerval), 801
"Golem Death!" (Sachs), 1013
Góngora y Argote, Luis de, 376
Gonne, Maud, 1345
"Good Friday, 1613" (Donne), 314
Good Morning, America (Sandburg), 1026
Gorenko, Anna Andreyevna. *See* Akhmatova, Anna
Graham, Jorie, **413-420**
"Grauballe Man, The" (Heaney), 453
"Grave, A" (Moore), 764
Graves, Robert, **421-433**, 548
"Graveyard by the Sea, The" (Valéry), 1213-1218
"Green charm of human life" (Cruz), 240

Gregory, Lady Augusta, 1345
Gypsy Ballads (García Lorca), 381
Gyres, 1358

Hh

H. D., **434-444**
"Hallelujah" (Sachs), 1014
"Hamatraya" (Emerson), 342
"Happily Neighing, the Herds Graze"
    (Mandelstam), 683
Harlem Renaissance, 538
Harmonium (Stevens), 1162
"Haunted Palace, The" (Poe), 883
Haw Lantern, The (Heaney), 457
Hawk in the Rain, The (Hughes), 549
Heaney, Seamus, **445-458**
Heart of Darkness (Conrad), 329
"Heautontimoroumenos"
    (Baudelaire), 52
"Hebrew Melodies" (Heine), 467
Heine, Heinrich, **459-469**
Helen in Egypt (H. D.), 438, 441
"Her Pure Fingernails on High
    Offering Their Onyx" (Mallarmé),
    674
Herbert, George, **470-482**
"Here Lies a Lady" (Ransom), 936
"Herman Melville" (Auden), 38
"Hermes of the Ways" (H. D.), 440
Herodias (Mallarmé), 675
Higginson, Thomas Wentworth, 287
His Toy, His Dream, His Rest
    (Berryman), 56
History (Lowell), 664
History of the World, The (Raleigh), 918
Hölderlin, Friedrich, **483-493**
"Holdfast, The" (Herbert), 477
"Hole in the Floor, A" (Wilbur), 1289
"Hollow Men, The" (Eliot), 329
Holocaust, 1012
Homage to Mistress Bradstreet
    (Berryman), 61
Homage to Sextus Propertius (Pound),
    907
"Home After Three Months Away"
    (Lowell), 658
"Home Songs" (Vallejo), 1223
"Homeland" (Hölderlin), 485
Homer, **494-506**, 1238

Honey and Salt (Sandburg), 1027
Hopkins, Gerard Manley, **507-523**
Horace, **524-535**, 1235
"Horseshoe Finder, The"
    (Mandelstam), 687
Hours of Idleness (Byron), 170
Hous of Fame (Chaucer), 197
"How Annandale Went Out"
    (Robinson), 984-985
"Howl" (Ginsberg), 386, 389
Hugh Selwyn Mauberley (Pound), 908
Hughes, Langston, **536-545**
Hughes, Ted, **546-558**, 864
Human Poems (Vallejo), 1228
"Humble Bee, The" (Emerson), 345
"Hunting" (Snyder), 1126
"Hunting: No. 6" (Snyder), 1126
"Huntress" (H. D.), 438
"Hurrahing in Harvest" (Hopkins), 517
"Hurry Up Please It's Time" (Sexton),
    1070
Hybrids of Plants and of Ghosts
    (Graham), 415
"Hymn to Freedom" (Hölderlin), 489
"Hymn to Immortality" (Hölderlin),
    486, 489
"Hymn to Intellectual Beauty"
    (Shelley), 1098
Hyperion (Keats), 564-567
"Hyperion's Song of Destiny"
    (Hölderlin), 487
"Hypocrite Women" (Levertov), 612

Ii

I, Claudius (Graves), 422
"I Felt a Funeral, in my Brain"
    (Dickinson), 294
"I Have Forgotten the Word I Wanted
    to Say" (Mandelstam), 685
"I know that He exists" (Dickinson),
    291
"I like to see it lap the Miles"
    (Dickinson), 289
"I Remember, I Remember" (Larkin),
    583
"I Saw in Louisiana a Live-Oak
    Growing" (Whitman), 1276
"i sing of Olaf glad and big"
    (Cummings), 251

"I Sing the Body Electric" (Whitman), 1275

"I taste a liquor never brewed" (Dickinson), 292

"Idyll" (Roethke), 993

Idylls of the King (Tennyson), 1184

"If poisonous minerals" (Donne), 313

"If Synthia be a Queene, a princes, and supreame" (Raleigh), 923

Igitur (Mallarmé), 676

Iliad (Homer), 494, 501-504, 1239

Illuminations (Rimbaud), 972-975

Imagist poets, 434, 639, 642, 904, 1298

"Imperialism" (Graham), 419

"Importance of Elsewhere, The" (Larkin), 586

"In a Station of the Metro" (Pound), 904

"In Distrust of Merits" (Moore), 766

"In Excelsis" (Lowell), 647

In Memoriam (Tennyson), 1174-1175, 1184-1186

"In Memory of W. B. Yeats" (Auden), 31

"In Petersburg We Shall Meet Again" (Mandelstam), 686

"In Salvador, 1978-80" (Forché), 362

"In the Blue Distance" (Sachs), 1015

"In the City" (Matsuo Bashō), 710

"In the Eyes of the Gods" (Breton), 110

"In the Grave No Flower" (Millay), 728

"In the Lovely Half-Light" (Breton), 111

"In the Mecca" (Brooks), 120

"In the Mountains" (Li Po), 623

"In the Village" (Bishop), 75

"In the Waiting Room" (Bishop), 73

"In Tonga" (Levertov), 612

"In vayne my Eyes, in vayne yee waste your tears" (Raleigh), 923

Inferno (Dante), 262-265, 267, 271, 274, 276-277, 280

Inner Room, The (Merrill), 722

"Innisfree." *See* "Lake Isle of Innisfree, The"

"Intensity and Height" (Vallejo), 1229

"Interrupted Elegy" (Paz), 836

Invisible Threads (Yevtushenko), 1379

"Invitation, The" (Herbert), 474

Iron John (Bly), 105

"It Is Crying in My Heart" (Verlaine), 1253

"It may be good, like it who list" (Wyatt), 1335-1336

"It sifts from Leaden Sieves" (Dickinson), 289

"It was not Death, for I stood up" (Dickinson), 289

Jj

"Jailer, The" (Plath), 865

"Janet Waking" (Ransom), 933-935

Jerusalem (Blake), 94

"Jesu" (Herbert), 477

Jill (Larkin), 589

"Joseph" (Forché), 362

"Journey to the Harz, The" (Heine), 465

Journey to the Orient (Nerval), 797

Julian and Maddalo (Shelley), 1089

"June 1940" (Spender), 1139

Kk

"Kaddish" (Ginsberg), 392-393

"Kalaloch" (Forché), 361

Keats, John, 172, **559-577**, 991, 1101, 1164, 1167

Kerouac, Jack, 1121

"Kind pity chokes my spleen" (Donne), 305

King, Edward, 750

"Kingfishers, The" (Olson), 817

"Knight's Tale, The" (Chaucer), 203

Kostrowitzky, Guillaume Albert Wladimir Alexandre Apollinaire de. *See* Apollinaire, Guillaume

"Kral Majales" (Ginsberg), 394

"Kubla Khan" (Coleridge), 217

Ll

Labrunie, Gérard. *See* Nerval, Gérard de

Lady Chatterley's Lover (Lawrence), 591

"Lady Geraldine's Courtship" (Browning), 131

"Lady Lazarus" (Plath), 871
Lady of the Lake, The (Scott), 1058
La Fontaine, Jean de, 767
Laforgue, Jules, 319
"Lake Isle of Innisfree, The" (Yeats), 1351
"Lamarck Elaborated" (Wilbur), 1288
"Lamb, The" (Blake), 84
"Lament for Dark Peoples" (Hughes), 541
Lament for Ignacio Sánchez Mejías (García Lorca), 382
Lamia (Keats), 569-571
"Language of the Brag, The" (Olds), 805
"Lantern out of Doors, The" (Hopkins), 519
"Large Red Man Reading" (Stevens), 1166
Larkin, Philip, **578-590**
"Last Meeting" (Warren), 1265
Laura, 842
"Laura at the Piano" (Schiller), 1047-1048
Lawrence, D. H., **591-603**
Lay of the Last Minstrel, The (Scott), 1058
Leaflets (Rich), 945
Leaves of Grass (Whitman), 1271-1273
"Leda and the Swan" (Yeats), 1352-1355
Legend of Good Women, The (Chaucer), 198
"Legs, The" (Graves), 428
Less Deceived, The (Larkin), 582
"Let me not to the marriage of true minds" (Shakespeare), 1076
"Lethe" (H. D.), 440
Levertov, Denise, **604-616**
Li Po, **617-626**, 1200
"Lie, The" (Raleigh), 925
"Life and Death" (Yevtushenko), 1383
"Life at War" (Levertov), 611
Life Studies (Lowell), 653, 657
Light Around the Body, The (Bly), 99
"Lilacs" (Lowell), 646
"Limbo" (Heaney), 451
Lincoln, Abraham, 1280

"Lines Composed a Few Miles Above Tintern Abbey" (Wordsworth), 1317-1319
"Little Gidding" (Eliot), 330
"Little Girl, My String Bean, My Lovely Woman" (Sexton), 1068
Live or Die (Sexton), 1068
"Lives" (Rukeyser), 1003
"Logging" (Snyder), 1126
Longfellow, Henry Wadsworth, **627-638**
Lord Weary's Castle (Lowell), 654
Lost Son and Other Poems, The (Roethke), 993
"Lotos-Eaters, The" (Tennyson), 1178
"Love" (III) (Herbert), 474, 480
"Love Fossil" (Olds), 805
"Love is not all" (Millay), 728
"Love Lies Sleeping" (Bishop), 70
Love Poems (Sexton), 1069
"Love Song of J. Alfred Prufrock, The" (Eliot), 323-324
Loving a Woman in Two Worlds (Bly), 103
Lowell, Amy, **639-649**
Lowell, Robert, **650-669**
Lucilius, 524
"Luke Havergal" (Robinson), 980, 984
"Lullaby" (Auden), 37
Lupercal (Hughes), 549
"Lycidas" (Milton), 750
Lyrical Ballads (Wordsworth), 1313

Mm

Machado, Antonio, 377
"Madonna of the Evening Flowers" (Lowell), 647
Mallarmé, Stéphane, **670-678**, 1207
"Man Against the Sky, The" (Robinson), 980
"Man and Wife" (Lowell), 658
Man in the Black Coat Turns, The (Bly), 103
"Man-Moth, The" (Bishop), 69
Mandelstam, Nadezhda, 681
Mandelstam, Osip, 188, **679-691**
"Map, The" (Bishop), 72
Marmion (Scott), 1058

Marriage of Heaven and Hell, The (Blake), 79, 86-88
Marvell, Andrew, **692-704**
"Mary's Song" (Plath), 867
Maske Presented at Ludlow Castle, A (Milton), 750
"Mass" (Vallejo), 1230
Matsuo Bashō, **705-712**
Maud (Tennyson), 1184
Maud Martha (Brooks), 123
"Maudlin" (Plath), 869
Maximus Poems, The (Olson), 818
"Mayday on Holderness" (Hughes), 550
"Medallion" (Plath), 867
"Meditations of an Old Woman" (Roethke), 995
"Meeting-House Hill" (Lowell), 646
"Men of Careful Turns" (Brooks), 120
"Mending Wall" (Frost), 368, 373
"Menon's Laments for Diotima" (Hölderlin), 491
"Merlin" (Emerson), 341
Merrill, James, **713-723**
Metamorphoses (Ovid), 828-831
Metaphysical poets, 695
Metrical Letters (Petrarch), 850
"Michael" (Wordsworth), 1319-1322
Millay, Edna St. Vincent, **724-731**
"Miller's Tale, The" (Chaucer), 203
Mills of the Kavanaughs, The (Lowell), 653, 656
Miłosz, Czesław, **732-745**
Milton (Blake), 93
Milton, John, **746-759**
"Mind Breaths" (Ginsberg), 396
"Mind Is an Enchanting Thing, The" (Moore), 766
"Mind-Reader, The" (Wilbur), 1292
Mirabell (Merrill), 718
Mirrors and Windows (Nemerov), 774
"Miserie" (Herbert), 479
"Mock Confessional" (Ferlinghetti), 351
Modernist poets, 244, 1134
Modernistas, 1220
Mohn und Gedächtnis (Celan), 186
Monkey's Raincoat (Matsuo Bashō), 710
Monroe, Harriet, 1019

Mont Blanc (Shelley), 1094
"Moonlight" (Verlaine), 1252
"Moonlit Night" (Tu Fu), 1205
Moore, Marianne, **760-770**
Moortown (Hughes), 556
Morning Glory, The (Bly), 101
"Mortmain" (Warren), 1264
"Moss Gathering" (Roethke), 990
"Mother, The" (Brooks), 118
"Mother to Son" (Hughes), 541
Movement, The, 580
"Moving through the silent crowd" (Spender), 1137
"Mower, The" (Larkin), 588
"Much Madness is divinest Sense" (Dickinson), 294
Murder in the Cathedral (Eliot), 331
"Musèe des Beaux Arts" (Auden), 31
"My boddy in the walls captivated" (Raleigh), 923
"my father moved through dooms of love" (Cummings), 250
"My Father's Breasts" (Olds), 807
"My Italy" (Petrarch), 847
"My Last Duchess" (Browning), 142
"My lute awake" (Wyatt), 1337
"My Old Books Closed at the Name of Paphos" (Mallarmé), 673
"Myrtho" (Nerval), 799
"Myth" (Rukeyser), 1006
Myths and Texts (Snyder), 1125

Nn

"Naked and the Nude, The" (Graves), 425
"Narrow Fellow in the Grass, A" (Dickinson), 293
Narrow Road to the Deep North, The (Matsuo Bashō), 710
"Native Land" (Akhmatova), 6
"Nature that washt her hands in milke" (Raleigh), 920
Near the Ocean (Lowell), 661
Necessities of Life (Rich), 943
Nemerov, Howard, **771-779**
"Nenia" (Schiller), 1047
Neruda, Pablo, **780-792**
Nerval, Gérard de, **793-802**
Nettles (Lawrence), 599

New Criticism, 929
"New England" (Robinson), 980
New England Tragedies, The
   (Longfellow), 637
New Life, The (Dante), 258-261
New Poems (Heine), 465
"New Spring" (Heine), 466
"Nick and the Candlestick" (Plath),
   865, 870
Niemandsrose, Die (Celan), 188
Nietzsche, Friedrich, 524
"Night in Hell" (Rimbaud), 971
"Nightingale, The" (Coleridge), 219
Nights and Days (Merrill), 715
"Nine Monsters, The" (Vallejo), 1228
"No Worst, There Is None" (Hopkins),
   521
"Noble Spirit" (Petrarch), 847
"Nocturnal upon St. Lucy's Day,
   Being the Shortest Day, A"
   (Donne), 309
North (Heaney), 452
"North American Sequence"
   (Roethke), 992
"North American Time" (Rich), 950
"North Sea, The" (Heine), 465
North Ship, The (Larkin), 582
"Not palaces, an era's crown"
   (Spender), 1138
Notebook (Lowell), 664
Notebook 1967-68 (Lowell), 662
"Notes of a Scale" (Levertov), 613
Notes Toward a Supreme Fiction
   (Stevens), 1162
"Nun's Priest's Tale, The" (Chaucer),
   204

Oo

"Obit" (Lowell), 664
"Ode" (Emerson), 345
"Ode: Intimations of Immortality
   from Recollections of Early
   Childhood" (Wordsworth), 1322
"Ode on a Grecian Urn" (Keats),
   574-576
"Ode on Melancholy" (Keats), 573
"Ode to a Nightingale" (Keats),
   571-573

"Ode to Anacتوria" (Sappho),
   1034-1036
"Ode to Aphrodite" (Sappho), 1032
Ode to Charles Fourier (Breton), 109
"Ode to Psyche" (Keats), 563
"Ode to Stalingrad" (Neruda), 788
"Ode to the West Wind" (Shelley),
   1100
Odes (Horace), 531-534
Odes of Pindar, The (Pinder), 852
Odyssey (Homer), 494, 504-506, 1239
"Of De Witt Williams on His Way to
   Lincoln Cemetery" (Brooks), 117
"Of God we ask one favor"
   (Dickinson), 292
"Of Modern Poetry" (Stevens), 1164
"Of the Monastic Life" (Rilke), 958
Of Woman Born (Rich), 951
Olds, Sharon, **803-809**
"Olga poems" (Levertov), 612
Olson, Charles, **810-820**
Olympian Ode 1 (Pindar), 858
"On a Drop of Dew" (Marvell), 695
"On a withered branch" (Matsuo
   Bashō), 708
"On First Looking into Chapman's
   Homer" (Keats), 563
"On Looking at a Copy of Alice
   Meynell's Poems" (Lowell), 645
"On Neal's Ashes" (Ginsberg), 396
"On Sitting Down to Read King Lear
   Once Again" (Keats), 564
"On the Lake" (Goethe), 404
"On the Morning of Christ's Nativity"
   (Milton), 749
"One's-Self I Sing" (Whitman), 1272
"Only One, The" (Hölderlin), 492
Open House (Roethke), 992
"Operation, The" (Sexton), 1067
"Orchard" (H. D.), 440
"Ordinance of Wine" (Neruda), 787
"Oread" (H. D.), 436
Orghast (Hughes), 556
"Orion" (Rich), 945
"Otter, An" (Hughes), 549
Ouija board, 717
"Ourselves or Nothing" (Forché), 362
"Out of the Cradle Endlessly
   Rocking" (Whitman), 1278

"Over Sir John's Hill" (Thomas), 1196-1198

"Over 2000 Illustrations and a Complete Concordance" (Bishop), 70

Ovid, **821-831**

Oxford Movement, 509

Pp

"Pains of Sleep, The" (Coleridge), 222

"Pangolin, The" (Moore), 765

Pansies (Lawrence), 599

"Panther, The" (Rilke), 960

Paradise Lost (Milton), 751-755

Paradise Regained (Milton), 755

Paradiso (Dante), 262, 268, 276-282

"Paradox" (Warren), 1264

"Pardon, The" (Wilbur), 1292

"Pardoner's Tale, The" (Chaucer), 203

Paris Spleen (Baudelaire), 53

Parlement of Foules (Chaucer), 198

"Passage to India" (Whitman), 1281

Paterson (Williams), 1300-1306

"Patmos" (Hölderlin), 488, 492

Paz, Octavio, **832-840**

"Peninsula, The" (Heaney), 448

"Penseroso, Il" (Milton), 749

People, Yes, The (Sandburg), 1026

"Personals Ad" (Ginsberg), 397

Petrarca, Francesco. *See* Petrarch

Petrarch, **841-851**

Petrarch, Wyatt's translations of, 1330, 1333

"Philosopher, The" (Graves), 426

Phoenix and the Turtle, The (Shakespeare), 1075

"Piano Kissed by a Fragile Hand, The" (Verlaine), 1253

"Piazza Piece" (Ransom), 936

"Pied Beauty" (Hopkins), 518

Pier-Glass, The (Graves), 427

"Pike" (Hughes), 549

Pindar, **852-860**

Pisan Cantos, The (Pound), 912-913

"Place That Is Feared I Inhabit, The" (Forché), 360

"Plain Song" (Forché), 360

Plath, Sylvia, 547, **861-873**

Plumed Serpent, The (Lawrence), 593

"Plutonian Ode" (Ginsberg), 397

Pocahontas, 230

Poe, Edgar Allan, 234, **874-885**

"POEM, OR BEAUTY HURTS MR. VINAL" (Cummings), 252

Poem Without a Hero, A (Akhmatova), 7

"Poems of Our Climate" (Stevens), 1165

"Poet, The" (Emerson), 340, 346

Poet in New York (García Lorca), 382

"Poetry" (Moore), 763

"Poetry" (Paz), 835

Poetry magazine, 1019

"Poet's Works, The" (Paz), 836

"Point Reyes Poems" (Bly), 101

"(ponder,darling,these busted statues" (Cummings), 249-250

"Poor Christian Looks at the Ghetto, A" (Miłosz), 739

Pope, Alexander, 304, **886-902**

"Pope's Penis, The" (Olds), 808

"Porphyria's Lover" (Browning), 141

"Portrait of a Lady" (Eliot), 323

"Postcard from the Volcano, A" (Stevens), 1168

Pound, Ezra, 320, 326, 434, 617, 642, **903-917**

"Prairie" (Sandburg), 1025

"Praisd be Dianas faire and harmles light" (Raleigh), 922

"Praise" (Herbert), 477

"Prayer" (Akhmatova), 5

"Prayer, The" (Levertov), 609

"Prayer of Columbus" (Whitman), 1282

"Preface" (Poe), 879

Prelude, The (Wordsworth), 1323-1327

"Primero sueño." *See* "First Dream"

Princess, The (Tennyson), 1183

"Problem, The" (Emerson), 341

"Proem" (Hughes), 540

"Projective Verse" (Olson), 819, 1123

"Prometheus" (Goethe), 406

Prometheus Unbound (Shelley), 1095

"Prophet" (Lawrence), 597

Publius Ovidius Naso. *See* Ovid

Publius Vergilius Maro. *See* Vergil

"Punishment" (Heaney), 453

Purgatorio (Dante), 262, 267, 271-272, 276-277
"Pursuit" (Warren), 1261
Pythian Ode 8 (Pindar), 859
Pythian Ode 10 (Pindar), 857

Qq
"Quaker Graveyard in Nantucket, The" (Lowell), 654
Questions of Travel (Bishop), 70

Rr
Rainbow, The (Lawrence), 591
Raleigh, Sir Walter, **918-928**, 1108
Ransom, John Crowe, **929-939**, 1258
Rape of Lucrece, The (Shakespeare), 1074
Rape of the Lock, The (Pope), 893
"Rapture, to Laura" (Schiller), 1047
"Raven, The" (Poe), 877, 884
Red Crosse knight, 1156
"Red Wheelbarrow, The" (Williams), 1299
Regarding Wave (Snyder), 1128
Region of Unlikeness (Graham), 415
Remains of Elmet (Hughes), 555
"Remembrance" (Byron), 171
"Removing the Plate of the Pump on the Hydraulic System of the Backhoe" (Snyder), 1131
Report from Part One (Brooks), 123
Requiem (Akhmatova), 6
"Requiem for the Croppies" (Heaney), 448
Residence on Earth (Neruda), 786
"Resignation" (Schiller), 1048
"Return: An Elegy, The" (Warren), 1260
"Return of the Goddess" (Graves), 430
"Reunion" (Forché), 362
Reyes Basoalto, Neftalí Ricardo. *See* Neruda, Pablo
"Rhodora, The" (Emerson), 344
Rhymes (Petrarch), 846
Rich, Adrienne, **940-952**
"Richard Cory" (Robinson), 984
Rilke, Rainer Maria, **953-963**
Rimbaud, Arthur, **964-975**, 1249
Rime of the Ancient Mariner, The (Coleridge), 214-217

Ring and the Book, The (Browning), 148-150
Riprap (Snyder), 1124
"River, The" (Crane), 229
"River by Our Village, The" (Tu Fu), 1205
"Riverman, The" (Bishop), 71
"Road to Shu Is Hard, The" (Li Po), 624
Robinson, Edwin Arlington, **976-987**
Rock-Drill (Pound), 913
Rodin, Auguste, 955
Roethke, Theodore, **988-999**
Roman Elegies (Goethe), 405, 407
"Romance" (Poe), 879
Romances Without Words (Verlaine), 1253
Romantic poets, 462, 1053, 1085, 1088, 1162, 1310
Romantic primitivism, 1314
Romanzero (Heine), 466
"Roofwalker, The" (Rich), 944
"Root Cellar" (Roethke), 993
Rossetti, Dante Gabriel, 906
Rousseau, Jean-Jacques, 175, 1314
"Route of Evanescence, A" (Dickinson), 289
"r-p-o-p-h-e-s-s-a-g-r" (Cummings), 247
Rukeyser, Muriel, **1000-1008**
"Runes" (Nemerov), 774
"Running" (Wilbur), 1289
Russian Revolution, 2, 4, 679

Ss
Sacco and Vanzetti trial, 726
Sachs, Nelly, **1009-1016**
"Sacrifice, The" (Herbert), 478
"Sailing to Byzantium" (Yeats), 1364-1366
Salt Garden, The (Nemerov), 773
Samson Agonistes (Milton), 756
"San Sepolcro" (Graham), 416
Sandburg, Carl, **1017-1028**
"Sandpiper" (Bishop), 68
"Santorini: Stopping the Leak" (Merrill), 721
Sappho, **1029-1040**
Satan Says (Olds), 804
Satires (Horace), 530-531

"Scenario" (Levertov), 610

Schiller, Friedrich, 402, 483-484, 486, **1041-1052**

"Scholar-Gipsy, The" (Arnold), 25

Schubert, Franz, 459

Schumann, Robert, 459

Scott, Sir Walter, **1053-1062**

Scripts for the Pageant (Merrill), 719

"Sea-Drift" (Whitman), 1278

"Search, The" (Herbert), 475

Seaside and the Fireside, The (Longfellow), 633

Season in Hell, A (Rimbaud), 970

Season Songs (Hughes), 555-556

"Second Coming, The" (Yeats), 1355-1360

"Self Portrait" (Graham), 415

Sentences (Nemerov), 776

Sequence, Sometimes Metaphysical (Roethke), 996-998

"Seraph and the Poet, The" (Browning), 135

"Sermon on the Warpland" (Brooks), 120

"Seven Moments of Love" (Hughes), 541

77 Dream Songs (Berryman), 56

Sexton, Anne, **1063-1071**

Shaftesbury, Third Earl of, 1315

Shakespeare, William, **1072-1084**

"Shall I compare thee to a summer's day" (Shakespeare), 1076

"She Dances" (Sachs), 1015

Shelley, Mary, 1086

Shelley, Percy Bysshe, **1085-1104**, 1143

Shepheardes Calender, The (Spenser), 1146, 1151-1153

"Sheridan" (Lowell), 667

"Ship of Death, The" (Lawrence), 601

"Show Fare, Please" (Hughes), 542

"Shrine, The" (H. D.), 438

Sidney, Sir Philip, **1105-1118**

Silence in the Snowy Fields (Bly), 98

"Sinai" (Sachs), 1013

"since feeling is first" (Cummings), 250

"Sisters of Sexual Treasure, The" (Olds), 805

Six Gallery, 387, 1121

"Skunk Hour" (Lowell), 658

"Slate Ode" (Mandelstam), 687

Sleepers Joining Hands (Bly), 100

Smoke and Steel (Sandburg), 1025

"Smokey the Bear Sutra" (Snyder), 1129

"Snake" (Lawrence), 599

Snapshots of a Daughter-in-Law (Rich), 943

"Snow-Storm, The" (Emerson), 341

Snyder, Gary, **1119-1133**

"somewhere i have never travelled,gladly beyond" (Cummings), 250

"Somnambule Ballad" (García Lorca), 381

"Song Coming Toward Us" (Forché), 360

"Song of Autumn" (Verlaine), 1251

Song of Hiawatha, The (Longfellow), 635

Song of Los, The (Blake), 90

"Song of Myself" (Whitman), 1273-1275

"Song of the Horseman, The" (García Lorca), 380

Songs of Innocence and of Experience (Blake), 81-84

"Sonne, The" (Herbert), 477

Sonnet, Petrarchan or Italian, 131

"Sonnet 49" (Berryman), 60

"Sonnet—to Science" (Poe), 878

Sonnets (Shakespeare), 1075-1083

Sonnets from the Portuguese (Browning), 132

Sons and Lovers (Lawrence), 591

Sor Juana Inés de la, Cruz. *See* Cruz, Sor Juana Inés de la

Sorrows of Young Werther, The (Goethe), 399

"Sound of the Hunting Horn, The" (Verlaine), 1255

Southey, Robert, 179, 209

Spain (Auden), 34

Spain, Take This Cup from Me (Vallejo), 1228

Spanish Civil War, 377, 379, 782, 1138, 1223

Speech-Grille (Celan), 188

Speed of Darkness, The (Rukeyser), 1005

Spender, Stephen, **1134-1145**

Spenser, Edmund, **1146-1161**
"Sprig of Rosemary, A" (Lowell), 647
"Spring" (Hopkins), 518
Sprung rhythm, 513
"Stanza in Memory of the Author of 'Obermann' " (Arnold), 28
"Stanzas from the Grande Chartreuse" (Arnold), 27
"Stars and Cricket" (Paz), 836
Stations (Heaney), 451
"Steeple-Jack, The" (Moore), 764
Stevens, Wallace, **1162-1173**
Stevenson, Robert Louis, 1351
Stone (Mandelstam), 684
"Stopping by Woods on a Snowy Evening" (Frost), 367, 371
"Strange Fruit" (Heaney), 454
"Strange New Cottage in Berkeley, A" (Ginsberg), 391
"Straw Swan Under the Christmas Tree, A" (Levertov), 607
Street in Bronzeville, A (Brooks), 118
"Stretto" (Celan), 188
"Stumble Between Two Stars" (Vallejo), 1229
"Such hap as I am happed in" (Wyatt), 1337
"Sufficeth it to yow, my joyes interred" (Raleigh), 923
Sun Stone, The (Paz), 836
"Sunday Morning" (Stevens), 1167
"Supermarket in California, A" (Ginsberg), 391
Surrealism, 11, 106, 108
"Swan, The" (Baudelaire), 50-52
Sweeney Astray (Heaney), 455
"Sweet Shop Around the Corner, The" (Graves), 430
Symbolist poets, 9, 45, 326, 670
Symbolist poets, French, 226
Synge, John, 1345

Tt

"Taking Off My Clothes" (Forché), 361
"Tam O' Shanter" (Burns), 162
"Tannhäuser, Der" (Heine), 466
"Taste and See" (Levertov), 607
Tate, Allen, 930, 1258
"Taxi, The" (Lowell), 647

"Teeth Mother Naked at Last, The" (Bly), 100
"Television Was a Baby Crawling Toward That Deathchamber" (Ginsberg), 394
"Tell all the Truth but tell it slant" (Dickinson), 288
"Temper, The" (Herbert), 475
Temple, The (Herbert), 470, 472
Tennyson, Alfred, Lord, **1174-1187**
"Thanksgiving, The" (Herbert), 479
Theobald, Lewis, 900
Theocritus, 1235
"They flee from me that sometime did me seek" (Wyatt), 1335-1336
"13,000 People" (Lawrence), 600
"This afternoon, my love" (Cruz), 239
This Body Is Made of Camphor and Gopherwood (Bly), 101
"This Lime-Tree Bower My Prison" (Coleridge), 212
This Tree Will Be Here for a Thousand Years (Bly), 103
"This World is not Conclusion" (Dickinson), 292
Thomas, Dylan, **1188-1199**
"Those Who Want Out" (Levertov), 608
"Thought Fox, The" (Hughes), 549
"Thoughts During an Air Raid" (Spender), 1139
Thrones (Pound), 913
"Thyrsis" (Arnold), 26
"Tiger, The" (Blake), 84
"Tintern Abbey." *See* "Lines Composed a Few Miles Above Tintern Abbey"
Tiresias, 325
"To a Face in a Crowd" (Warren), 1260
"To a Friend" (Arnold), 23
"To a Mountain Daisy" (Burns), 159
"To a Mouse" (Burns), 159
"To a Poor Old Woman" (Williams), 1299
"To Autumn" (Keats), 573
To Bedlam and Part Way Back (Sexton), 1065
"To Brooklyn Bridge" (Crane), 228
"To Helen" (Poe), 879

"To His Coy Mistress" (Marvell), 250, 696

"To His Mistress Going to Bed" (Donne), 306

"To Juan at the Winter Solstice" (Graves), 428

"To Marguerite–Continued" (Arnold), 23

"To Robinson Jeffers" (Miłosz), 741

"To Speak of Woe That Is in Marriage" (Lowell), 658

"To the Muse" (Levertov), 608

"To the Reader" (Baudelaire), 47

Tocqueville, Alexis de, 335

"Todesfuge." *See* "Death Fugue"

Todorov, Tzvetan, 1208

"Tolland Man, The" (Heaney), 451

"Tomb of Edgar Poe, The" (Mallarmé), 672

"Tonight at Seven-Thirty" (Auden), 40

"Tower, The" (Yeats), 1349

"Transcendental Etude" (Rich), 948

Transformations (Sexton), 1069

"Travel" (Celan), 187

"Tree at My Window" (Frost), 368, 371

Trelawny, Edward John, 1087

Trilce (Vallejo), 1225-1228

Tristia (Mandelstam), 685

Triumphs (Petrarch), 847

Troilus and Criseyde (Chaucer), 199-201

Trojan War, 200, 494, 1238

Tu Fu, 617, **1200-1206**

Turning Wind, A (Rukeyser), 1003

Turtle Island (Snyder), 1130

Twenty Love Poems and a Song of Despair (Neruda), 784

"Two Look at Two" (Frost), 368

"Two Paintings by Gustav Klimt" (Graham), 417

"Two Tramps in Mud Time" (Frost), 368

"Two Voices in a Meadow" (Wilbur), 1290

"Tyrannus Nix?" (Ferlinghetti), 354

Uu

"Ulalume" (Poe), 879

"Ultima Ratio Regum" (Spender), 1138

"Ulysses" (Tennyson), 1178-1184

"Ulysses and Circe" (Lowell), 667

"Under Ben Bulben" (Yeats), 1368

"Underwear" (Ferlinghetti), 352

"Upon Appleton House" (Marvell), 700-703

Vv

"Valediction: Forbidding Mourning, A" (Donne), 308

Valéry, Paul, **1207-1219**

Vallejo, César, **1220-1232**

Van Winkle, Rip, 226

Vecher (Akhmatova), 2

"Vendémiaire" (Apollinaire), 16

Venetian Epigrams (Goethe), 405

Venus and Adonis (Shakespeare), 1074

"Venus Transiens" (Lowell), 647

"Verbal Alchemy" (Rimbaud), 971

Vergil, 264, 1149, **1233-1246**

Verlaine, Paul, 966, **1247-1256**

"Victory Celebration, The" (Schiller), 1046

Vietnam War, 97, 611, 652

"Virginia Britannia" (Moore), 766

Vision, A (Yeats), 1369

Vision of William, Concerning Piers the Plowman, The (Langland), 196

Visions of the Daughters of Albion (Blake), 91

"Visitant, The" (Roethke), 991

Vorticism, 642

"Vowels" (Rimbaud), 969

Ww

"Waking, The" (Roethke), 994-995

Waking, The (Roethke), 994

"Waking Early Sunday Morning" (Lowell), 661

"Waking in the Blue" (Lowell), 658

"Wales Visitation" (Ginsberg), 396

"Walking to Sleep" (Wilbur), 1292

Walls Do Not Fall, The (H. D.), 441

"Wanderer's Night Song" (Goethe), 404

"Wandering About Mount T'ai" (Li Po), 622

"Wanting to Die" (Sexton), 1068

War Stories (Nemerov), 777

Warren, Robert Penn, 930, **1257-1267**

"Was I never yet of your love grieved" (Wyatt), 1334

Waste Land, The (Eliot), 325-329

Water Street (Merrill), 715

"Waterlily Fire" (Rukeyser), 1004

Waverley novels (Scott), 1061

"We Real Cool" (Brooks), 117

"Weary Blues, The" (Hughes), 541

Weary Blues, The (Hughes), 540

"Weed, The" (Bishop), 69

"Welcome and Farewell" (Goethe), 406

"Well, I have lost you" (Millay), 728

West-Eastern Divan (Goethe), 405, 409

"West-Running Brook" (Frost), 368, 373

"What Are Years?" (Moore), 766

"What You Should Know to Be a Poet" (Snyder), 1129

"When Lilacs Last in the Dooryard Bloom'd" (Whitman), 1280

"Whip, The" (Robinson), 983-984

"White Goddess, The" (Graves), 429

White Goddess, The (Graves), 421

White Shroud (Ginsberg), 397

Whitman, Walt, 285, 336, 992, **1268-1283**

"Whitsun Weddings, The" (Larkin), 584

"Whoso list to hunt" (Wyatt), 1334

"Wife's Tale, The" (Heaney), 448

Wilbur, Richard, 287, **1284-1295**

Wild Patience Has Taken Me This Far, A (Rich), 947, 949

Will to Change, The (Rich), 946

William Tell (Schiller), 1051

Williams, William Carlos, 652, **1296-1309**

"Windhover, The" (Hopkins), 515-517

"Winding River, The" (Tu Fu), 1205

"Windows, The" (Mallarmé), 672

Windsor Forest (Pope), 893

Wintering Out (Heaney), 450

"Witchita Vortex Sutra" (Ginsberg), 395

Wodwo (Hughes), 551

"Woman Waits for Me, A" (Whitman), 1276

"Woodnotes" (Emerson), 345

Woolf, Virginia, 591

"Words" (Plath), 872

Words for the Wind (Roethke), 995

Wordsworth, Dorothy, 209, 1313

Wordsworth, William, 209, 990, 1164, **1310-1329**

"Work Without Hope" (Coleridge), 222

World War I, 246, 423

World War II, 538, 735, 737, 739, 766, 773, 1139, 1192; concentration camps, 186-187, 1012

"Wound Dresser, The" (Whitman), 1279

"Wreck of the *Deutschland*, The" (Hopkins), 511

Wyatt, Sir Thomas, **1330-1341**

Xx

Xanadu, 217

Yy

Yeats, William Butler, 1140, **1342-1373**

Yevtushenko, Yevgeny, **1374-1383**

You, Emperor, and Others (Warren), 1264

"you shall above all things be glad and young" (Cummings), 250

"You Who Have Wronged" (Miłosz), 742

Young Fate, The (Valéry), 1210

Zz

"Zima Junction" (Yevtushenko), 1379

"Zone" (Apollinaire), 9